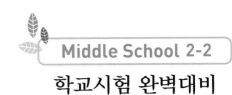

Middle School 2-2

학교시험 완벽대비

2학기 전과정

적중"100plus

영어 기출문제집

중**2**

천재 | 이재영

Best Collection

구성과 특징

교과서의 주요 학습 내용을 중심으로 학습 영역별 특성에 맞춰 단계별로 다양한 학습 기회를 제공하여
단원별 학습능력 평가는 물론 중간 및 기말고사 시험 등에 완벽하게 대비할 수 있도록 내용을 구성

Words & Expressions

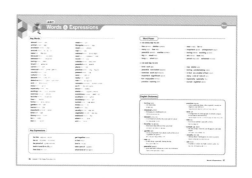

Step1
Key Words 단원별 핵심 단어 설명 및 풀이
Key Expression 단원별 핵심 숙어 및 관용어 설명
Word Power 반대 또는 비슷한 뜻 단어 배우기
English Dictionary 영어로 배우는 영어 단어

Step2 실력평가 단원별 수시평가 대비 주관식, 객관식 문제풀이

Step3 서술형 대비 학업성취도 및 수행능력평가 대비 서술형 문제풀이

Conversation

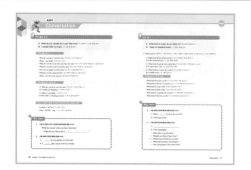

Step1
핵심 의사소통 소통에 필요한 주요 표현 방법 요약
핵심 Check 기본적인 표현 방법 및 활용능력 확인

Step2 대화문 익히기 교과서 대화문 심층 분석 및 확인

Step3 교과서 확인학습 빈칸 채우기를 통한 문장 완성 능력 확인

Step4 기본평가 시험대비 기초 학습 능력 평가

Step5 실력평가 단원별 수시평가 대비 주관식, 객관식 문제풀이

Step6 서술형 대비 학업성취도 및 수행능력평가 대비 서술형 문제풀이

Grammar

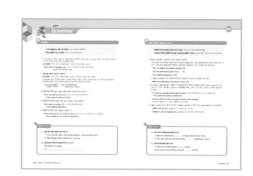

Step1
주요 문법 단원별 주요 문법 사항과 예문을 알기 쉽게 설명
핵심 Check 기본 문법사항에 대한 이해 여부 확인

Step2 기본평가 시험대비 기초 학습 능력 평가

Step3 실력평가 단원별 수시평가 대비 주관식, 객관식 문제풀이

Step4 서술형 대비 학업성취도 및 수행능력평가 대비 서술형 문제풀이

Reading

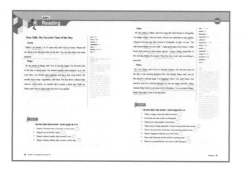

Step1
구문 분석 단원별로 제시된 문장에 대한 구문별 분석과 내용 설명
확인문제 문장에 대한 기본적인 이해와 인지능력 확인

Step2 확인학습A 빈칸 채우기를 통한 문장 완성 능력 확인

Step3 확인학습B 제시된 우리말을 영어로 완성하여 작문 능력 키우기

Step4 실력평가 단원별 수시평가 대비 주관식, 객관식 문제풀이

Step5 서술형 대비 학업성취도 및 수행능력평가 대비 서술형 문제풀이
교과서 구석구석 교과서에 나오는 기타 문장까지 완벽 학습

Composition

|영역별 핵심문제|

단어 및 어휘, 대화문, 문법, 독해 등 각 영역별 기출문제의 출제 유형을 분석하여 실전에 대비하고 연습할 수 있도록 문제를 배열

|단원별 예상문제|

기출문제를 분석한 후 새로운 시험 출제 경향을 더하여 새롭게 출제될 수 있는 문제를 포함하여 시험에 완벽하게 대비할 수 있도록 준비

|서술형 실전 및 창의사고력 문제|

학교 시험에서 점차 늘어나는 서술형 시험에 집중 대비하고 고득점을 취득하는데 만전을 기하기 위한 학습 코너

|단원별 모의고사|

영역별, 단계별 학습을 모두 마친 후 실전 연습을 위한 모의고사

교과서 파헤치기

- 단어Test1~3 영어 단어 우리말 쓰기, 우리말을 영어 단어로 쓰기, 영영풀이에 해당하는 단어와 우리말 쓰기
- 대화문Test1~2 대화문 빈칸 완성 및 전체 대화문 쓰기
- 본문Test1~5 빈칸 완성, 우리말 쓰기, 문장 배열연습, 영어 작문하기 복습 등 단계별 반복 학습을 통해 교과서 지문에 대한 완벽한 습득
- 구석구석지문Test1~2 지문 빈칸 완성 및 전문 영어로 쓰기

Lesson 5

Understanding Others

의사소통 기능

- 희망이나 바람 표현하기
  A: I have an important exam tomorrow.
  B: I hope you'll do well on the exam.

- 외모 묘사하기
  A: What does he look like?
  B: He has brown hair and brown eyes.

언어 형식

- want/ask/tell + 목적어 + to부정사
  Parents **want their children to be** honest.

- 접속사 before, after
  Before she has breakfast, Dora puts on her uniform.

Words & Expressions

Key Words

- **accuse** [əkjúːz] 동 고발하다, 비난하다
- **activity** [æktívəti] 명 활동
- **ago** [əgóu] 부 전에
- **allowance** [əláuəns] 명 용돈
- **annoucement** [ənáunsmənt] 명 발표, 공표
- **anytime** [énitàim] 부 언제든지, 언제나
- **appearance** [əpíərəns] 명 외모
- **arrest** [ərést] 동 체포하다
- **attack** [ətǽk] 동 공격하다
- **attitude** [ǽtitjùːd] 명 태도, 자세
- **avoid** [əvóid] 동 피하다
- **back** [bæk] 명 등, 뒤
- **beard** [biərd] 명 턱수염
- **behind** [biháind] 전 ~ 뒤에
- **bullying** [búliiŋ] 명 약자 괴롭히기
- **carry** [kǽri] 동 휴대하다, 지니다
- **character** [kǽriktər] 명 등장인물, 캐릭터
- **choice** [tʃɔis] 명 선택
- **choose** [tʃuːz] 동 선택하다, 고르다
- **confident** [kánfədənt] 형 자신감 있는
- **curly** [kə́ːrli] 형 곱슬곱슬한
- **difficulty** [dífikʌlti] 명 어려움
- **enter** [éntər] 동 들어가다, 참가[출전]하다
- **face** [feis] 동 직면하다, (힘든 상황에) 처하다
- **free** [friː] 동 석방하다
- **freedom** [fríːdəm] 명 자유
- **friendly** [fréndli] 형 다정한, 친절한
- **guilty** [gílti] 형 유죄의

- **hide(-hid-hidden)** [haid] 동 숨기다
- **judge** [dʒʌdʒ] 명 판사 동 판단하다
- **lucky** [lʌ́ki] 형 운이 좋은
- **mind** [maind] 동 신경 쓰다, 꺼리다
- **missing** [mísiŋ] 형 실종된, 행방불명된
- **Mongolia** [mɑŋgóuliə] 명 몽골
- **monthly** [mʌ́nθli] 형 매월의, 한 달에 한 번의
- **neighbor** [néibər] 명 이웃
- **ordinary** [ɔ́ːrdənèri] 형 평범한
- **pass** [pæs] 동 통과하다, 지나가다
- **ponytail** [póunitèil] 명 포니테일(말꼬리 모양으로 묶은 머리)
- **popular** [pápjulər] 형 인기 있는, 대중적인
- **president** [prézədənt] 명 회장
- **prison** [prízn] 명 감옥
- **promise** [prámis] 명 공약, 약속
- **protect** [prətékt] 동 보호하다
- **receive** [risíːv] 동 받다
- **right** [rait] 명 권리
- **score** [skɔːr] 동 득점하다
- **shout** [ʃaut] 동 소리치다, 외치다
- **shy** [ʃai] 형 부끄럼을 많이 타는, 수줍어하는
- **throw(-threw-thrown)** [θrou] 동 던지다
- **truth** [truːθ] 명 진실
- **victim** [víktim] 명 희생자
- **vote** [vout] 동 투표하다
- **whisper** [hwíspər] 동 속삭이다
- **worried** [wə́ːrid] 형 걱정하는

Key Expressions

- **accuse A of B** B 때문에 A를 고발하다
- **agree with+사람** ~에게 동의하다
- **a little** 약간, 조금
- **be afraid of ~** ~을 두려워하다
- **be for ~** ~을 지지하다, ~을 찬성하다
- **be good at ~** ~을 잘하다
- **bulletin board** 게시판
- **calm down** 진정하다
- **care for ~** ~을 돌보다
- **cut off ~** ~을 자르다

- **do well on ~** ~을 잘하다, 잘 보다
- **fight off ~** ~을 싸워 물리치다
- **go 동사원형+ing** ~하러 가다
- **look different from ~** ~와 다르게 보이다
- **look like ~** ~처럼 보이다
- **set 목적어 free** ~을 석방하다
- **so far** 지금까지
- **thanks to ~** ~ 덕분에
- **vote for ~** ~을 뽑다, ~에게 투표하다
- **would like to+동사원형** ~하고 싶다

Word Power

※ 여러 가지 품사로 쓰이는 단어

- □ **cause** (명) 원인 (동) 야기하다
- □ **fall** (명) 가을 (동) 떨어지다
- □ **change** (명) 잔돈, 변화 (동) 변하다
- □ **train** (명) 기차 (동) 훈련하다
- □ **kind** (명) 종류 (형) 친절한

- □ **face** (명) 얼굴 (동) 직면하다, 마주하다
- □ **judge** (명) 판사 (동) 판단하다
- □ **play** (명) 연극 (동) 놀다, 경기하다
- □ **mean** (동) 의미하다 (형) 못된, 비열한
- □ **like** (동) 좋아하다 (전) ~와 같은

※ 서로 반대되는 뜻을 가진 단어

- □ **ordinary** (평범한) ↔ **extraordinary** (비범한)
- □ **friendly** (친절한) ↔ **unfriendly** (불친절한)
- □ **guilty** (유죄의) ↔ **innocent** (무죄의)

- □ **difficulty** (어려움) ↔ **ease** (쉬움)
- □ **avoid** (피하다) ↔ **face** (직면하다)
- □ **popular** (인기 있는) ↔ **unpopular** (인기 없는)

※ 다양한 접미사를 붙여 동사가 명사로 바뀌는 단어

- □ **allow** (주다, 지급하다) – **allowance** (용돈)
- □ **assist** (도와주다) – **assistance** (도움, 원조)
- □ **free** (자유롭게 하다) – **freedom** (자유)

- □ **appear** (보이다) – **appearance** (외모)
- □ **judge** (판단하다) – **judgement** (판단)
- □ **act** (행동하다) – **action** (행동)

English Dictionary

- □ **allowance** 용돈
  → an amount of money that parents give to a child each week
  부모가 매주 아이에게 주는 돈
- □ **arrest** 체포하다
  → to take the person away to ask them about a crime that they might have committed
  저질렀을지도 모르는 범죄에 대해 심문하기 위해 사람을 데려가다
- □ **attack** 공격하다
  → to use violence to hurt or damage someone
  폭력을 사용하여 사람을 다치게 하거나 피해를 주다
- □ **attitude** 태도
  → how you think or feel about something
  어떤 것에 대해 생각하고 느끼는 방식
- □ **avoid** 피하다
  → to stay away from a person or place
  사람이나 장소로부터 멀리하다
- □ **bullying** 괴롭히기
  → an action to try to frighten someone who is smaller or weaker
  더 작거나 약한 사람을 겁주려고 하는 행위
- □ **cause** 야기하다
  → to make something happen
  어떤 일이 일어나도록 만들다

- □ **change** 잔돈
  → the money you get back when you pay more money than something costs
  어떤 것의 비용보다 더 많은 돈을 지불했을 때 돌려받는 돈
- □ **choose** 선택하다, 고르다
  → to decide which thing you want
  어느 것을 원하는지 결정하다
- □ **confidence** 자신감
  → the belief that you are able to do things well or be successful
  일을 잘하거나 성공할 수 있다는 믿음
- □ **neighbor** 이웃
  → someone who lives near you
  당신 근처에 사는 사람
- □ **protect** 보호하다
  → to keep someone or something safe from something dangerous or bad
  위험하거나 나쁜 것으로부터 어떤 사람이나 사물을 지키다
- □ **victim** 피해자, 희생자
  → someone who has been hurt or killed
  다치거나 살해된 사람
- □ **whisper** 속삭이다
  → to speak very quietly so that other people cannot hear
  다른 사람들이 들을 수 없도록 매우 조용히 말하다

서답형

01 다음 짝지어진 두 단어의 관계가 같도록 주어진 철자로 시작하는 단어를 쓰시오.

> friendly : unfriendly
> – extraordinary : o_____

서답형

02 다음 글의 빈칸에 영영 풀이에 맞는 알맞은 형태의 단어를 쓰시오.

> • We'll go out and look for him. Also, we'll make an _____ about a missing child.
> <영영 풀이> something that someone says officially, giving new information about something

➡ _____

03 다음 중 밑줄 친 단어의 우리말 뜻이 잘못된 것은?

① All my classmates are very <u>friendly</u>. 다정한
② I'll <u>vote for</u> Jang Jimin. ~에게 투표하다
③ <u>Bullying</u> is a big problem in many schools. 괴롭히기
④ When you <u>face</u> difficulties, just call me. 직면하다
⑤ They <u>whispered</u> behind his back, "What is he trying to hide?" 외쳤다

중요

[04~05] 다음 영영 풀이에 해당하는 단어를 고르시오.

04
> to keep someone or something safe from something dangerous or bad

① avoid   ② protect
③ choose   ④ change
⑤ cause

05
> an amount of money that parents give to a child each week

① victim   ② attitude
③ choice   ④ judge
⑤ allowance

서답형

06 다음 우리말에 맞게 주어진 철자로 시작하는 단어를 쓰시오.

> 그들은 그에게 턱수염을 그만 기르라고 말했다. Joseph은 신경 쓰지 않았다.
> ➡ They told him to stop growing a beard. Joseph did not m_____.

➡ _____

07 다음 빈칸에 들어갈 말로 알맞은 것은?

> People did not like a long beard very much. So they _____ the man with a beard.

① whispered   ② believed
③ avoided   ④ cared
⑤ freed

중요

08 다음 빈칸에 들어갈 단어가 알맞게 짝지어진 것은?

> Joseph was a big man, and he was able to fight them _____. But the men called the police and _____ him of attacking them. Poor Joseph was arrested.

① on – caused
② of – set
③ off – caused
④ off – accused
⑤ of – accused

01 다음 문장의 밑줄 친 단어를 알맞은 형태로 바꾸어 쓰시오.

(1) We should not judge people by their <u>appear</u>.

(2) He just wanted the <u>free</u> to have his beard.

➡ (1) _____ (2) _____

02 다음 영영 풀이에 해당하는 단어를 쓰시오.

(1) • to make something different
   • the money you get back when you pay more money than something costs

(2) • to teach a person or an animal how to do something
   • a number of cars connected together on a railway

➡ (1) _____ (2) _____

03 다음 문장에 공통으로 들어갈 단어를 쓰시오.

(1) • He said to the _____, "I'm the victim here."
   • We should not _____ people by the way they look.

(2) • You _____ the girl from Mongolia?
   • The police officer was not kind. He was _____ to her.

➡ (1) _____ (2) _____

04 다음 빈칸에 들어갈 말을 〈보기〉에서 찾아 쓰시오. (필요하면 변형하여 쓰시오.)

┌─── 보기
│ thanks to, care for, do well on, calm
│ down
└─

(1) I hope you'll _____ the exam.

(2) 42-year-old Joseph Palmer was an ordinary person. He had a job and _____ his family.

(3) He was freed _____ his son's letters.

05 다음 우리말과 같은 표현이 되도록 괄호 안의 지시대로 문장의 빈칸을 채우시오.

(1) 매사추세츠에 있는 작은 도시로 이사한 후에 그는 어려움에 직면하기 시작했다.
   ➡ After he moved to a small town in Massachusetts, he began to _____ _____. (복수형을 쓸 것.)

(2) Joseph은 다른 사람들과 달라 보였다.
   ➡ Joseph _____ _____ _____ other people. (look을 이용할 것.)

(3) 사람들은 Joseph이 단지 자신과 자신의 턱수염을 지키려다 감옥에 갇혔다는 것을 알게 되었다. (동명사를 이용할 것)
   ➡ People learned that Joseph was _____ _____ just for _____ himself and his beard.

Conversation

1 희망이나 바람 표현하기

A I have an important exam tomorrow. 나는 내일 중요한 시험이 있어.

B I hope you'll do well on the exam. 네가 시험을 잘 보길 바라.

■ 'I hope ~.'는 '나는 ~을 희망한다.'라는 뜻으로 자신의 소망을 나타낼 때 쓰는 표현이며 뒤에는 to부정사, 'that+주어+동사'가 온다. 경우에 따라 hope 대신 want 또는 wish를 사용할 수 있다.

희망이나 바람을 표현하기

- I hope to be a famous singer. 나는 유명한 가수가 되길 희망해.
  = I want to be a famous singer.
  = I'd like to be a famous singer.
- I hope to be a basketball player. 나는 농구선수가 되기를 희망한다.
- I want to be a famous writer. 나는 유명한 작가가 되고 싶다.

핵심 Check

1. 다음 대화의 빈칸에 알맞은 말을 고르시오.

   A: Are you going to watch a movie?

   B: Yes, _____

   ① I hope you'll find him soon.
   ② I hope to watch an action movie.
   ③ you will watch a movie tonight.
   ④ you go to the movies once a month.
   ⑤ I hope to be a famous actor.

2. 다음 대화의 밑줄 친 부분의 의도로 알맞은 것은?

   - I have an important exam tomorrow! <u>I hope I will pass it.</u>

   ① 바람 표현하기   ② 의도 묻기
   ③ 충고하기   ④ 안부 묻기
   ⑤ 칭찬하기

② 외모 묘사하기

A What does he look like? 그는 어떻게 생겼나요?

B He has brown hair and brown eyes. 그는 갈색 머리카락과 갈색 눈을 지녔어요.

- 인물의 외모나 모습을 묘사할 경우, 체형을 설명할 때는 주로 be동사를 사용하며, 이목구비나 머리 모양을 묘사할 때는 have동사를 사용한다. 또한 모자, 안경, 옷 등의 착용 상태를 묘사할 때는 '주어 + be동사+wearing ~.'으로 표현한다.

- 현재 진행 중인 동작을 생생하게 묘사할 때에는 'be동사의 현재형+동사원형-ing'의 현재진행형을 사용한다.

외모를 묘사하는 표현들

- **A:** What does he look like? 그는 어떻게 생겼니?

  B: He's tall and he has curly hair. 그는 키가 크고, 머리가 곱슬이야.

- **A:** Sujin, where is your sister, Somin? 수진아, 너의 여동생 소민이 어디에 있니?

  B: She's over there. She's wearing glasses. 그녀는 저기에 있어. 그녀는 안경을 쓰고 있어.

- **A:** What does he look like? 그는 어떻게 생겼나요?

  B: He has brown hair and brown eyes. 그는 갈색 머리이고 갈색 눈을 지녔어요.

  A: What is he wearing? 그는 무엇을 입고 있나요?

  B: He is wearing a green shirt. 그는 초록색 셔츠를 입고 있어요.

핵심 Check

3. 다음 대화의 빈칸에 들어갈 말로 알맞은 것을 <u>모두</u> 고르시오.

  A: What does she look like?

  B: _____

  ① She is playing the guitar.
  ② She always wears black pants.
  ③ She has brown hair and is wearing glasses.
  ④ She is boring.
  ⑤ She's tall and has long straight hair.

4. 다음 우리말에 맞도록 빈칸에 알맞은 것을 쓰시오.

  • 그녀의 개는 어떻게 생겼니?

  ➡ What does her dog _____ _____?

Communicate: Listen-Listen and Answer. Talk

G: Hi, I'm Gacha. I'm from Mongolia. ❶When I first came to Songji Middle School two months ago, I was so worried. I was a little shy, and ❷I wasn't good at Korean. However, I'm a lucky girl. All my classmates are nice and friendly. ❸I enjoy playing handball with them in P.E. class. I'm a good player. ❹They call me "Golden Hand." ❺There will be a sports day next week. ❻I hope my class will win in the handball event.

여: 안녕. 나는 Gacha라고 해. 나는 몽골에서 왔어. 두 달 전에 내가 처음 송지 중학교에 왔을 때, 나는 무척 걱정이 되었어. 나는 좀 수줍음을 탔고 한국어를 잘 못했어. 하지만 난 운이 좋은 아이야. 내 학급 친구들은 모두 멋지고 다정해. 나는 체육 시간에 친구들과 핸드볼 하는 것을 즐겨. 난 실력이 좋은 선수야. 친구들은 나를 '황금 손'이라고 불러. 다음 주에 운동회가 있을 거야. 난 우리 반이 핸드볼 대회에서 이기길 바라.

❶ When은 '~할 때'의 의미로 부사절을 이끄는 접속사이다. two months ago라는 과거 시점이 있어서 과거시제 came을 사용한다.
❷ be good at ~은 '~을 잘하다'라는 의미다.
❸ enjoy는 동명사를 목적어로 취하는 동사로 playing을 사용했다.
❹ 'call+목적어+목적보어'의 형태로 '~을 …라고 부르다'로 해석한다.
❺ next week이라는 미래 시점과 사용되어서 미래시제 will be를 사용했다.
❻ 'I hope (that)+주어+동사 ~'는 희망이나 바람을 나타내는 표현이다.

Check(√) True or False

(1) Gacha was worried and a little shy at first. T ☐ F ☐

(2) Though Gacha likes playing handball, she isn't good at playing handball. T ☐ F ☐

 Communicate: Listen-Listen and Answer. Dialog

B: Hi, Minsol. Is your class winning?

G: Of course. We have a great handball player.

B: ❶You mean the girl from Mongolia?

G: Yes, her name is Gacha.

B: I've heard a lot about her. But ❷what does she look like?

G: She's very tall and has a ponytail.

B: Oh, is she the girl ❸who scored the goal just now?

G: Yes, that's her seventh goal.

B: Wow, she's really great.

남: 안녕, 민솔아. 너희 반이 이기고 있니?
여: 물론이지. 우리는 훌륭한 핸드볼 선수가 있거든.
남: 몽골에서 온 여자아이 말하는 거니?
여: 응, 그녀의 이름은 Gacha야.
남: 그녀에 대해 많이 들었어. 그런데 그녀는 어떻게 생겼어?
여: 그녀는 키가 크고 말총머리를 하고 있어.
남: 아, 지금 막 골을 넣은 여자아이가 그녀니?
여: 맞아, 저건 그녀의 일곱 번째 골이야.
남: 와, 그녀는 정말 잘하는구나.

❶ 일반동사 의문문 'Do you mean ~?'에서 Do가 생략된 형태로 '~을 말하는 거니?'라는 의미다.
❷ 사람의 외모를 묻는 표현이다.
❸ 선행사(사람)를 수식할 때 관계대명사절을 이끄는 who를 사용한다.

Check(√) True or False

(3) Minsol's class is winning the handball game. T ☐ F ☐

(4) Gacha is very tall and has a ponytail. T ☐ F ☐

Communicate: Listen-Listen More

M: ❶What can I do for you?
G: I lost my younger brother.
M: Okay, ❷calm down. What's your brother's name?
G: His name is Wally Brown. He's five years old.
M: ❸What does he look like?
G: He has brown hair and brown eyes.
M: What is he wearing?
G: He is wearing a green shirt and black pants.
M: Can you tell me more?
G: Oh, he is carrying a red backpack.
M: All right. We'll go out and look for him. Also, we'll make an announcement about ❹a missing child.
G: Thank you so much. ❺I hope I'll find him soon.

❶ 상대방에게 도움을 주고자 할 때 사용하는 표현으로, '무엇을 도와줄까요?'라는 뜻이다.
❷ '진정해'라는 뜻이다.
❸ 사람의 외모를 묻는 표현이다.
❹ missing은 형용사로 '실종된, 행방불명된'의 뜻이다.
❺ 'I hope (that)+주어+동사 ~'는 희망이나 바람을 나타내는 표현이다.

 Communicate: Speak 2-Talk in pairs

A: I have an important exam tomorrow!
B: ❶I hope you'll do well on the exam.
A: ❷I hope so, too. Thanks.

❶ 희망이나 바람을 나타내는 표현으로, do well on은 '~을 잘하다'라는 뜻이다.
❷ '나도 그러길 바라'라는 의미다.

 Communicate: Speak 2-Talk in groups

A: What is your character's name?
B: His name is Buster.
A: ❶What does he look like?
B: ❷He has no hair.
A: Does he have big eyes?
B: Yes, he does.

❶ 사람의 외모를 묻는 표현이다.
❷ 사람의 이목구비나 머리 모양을 묘사할 때는 동사 have를 사용한다.

 Communicate: Speak-Rap Time

A: I hope you'll do your best in the final game.
B: Thanks. ❶I wish you the same.

A: ❷What does your sister look like, Claire?
B: She's tall and has long straight hair.

❶ '나도 네가 그러길 바라.'라는 뜻이다.
❷ 사람의 외모를 묻는 표현이다.

 My Speaking Portfolio

G: Look at the bulletin board. ❶There are posters for the next school president.
B: Yeah, I've already made my choice. ❷I'll vote for Jang Jimin.
G: You mean the boy with glasses? He looks smart, but I don't like his promises.
B: Then who will you choose?
G: Well, I am for number 1, Han Siwon. She wants to make our school a safe place.
B: She always has a ponytail, right?
G: Yes, and Hong Jiho seems okay.
B: ❸She looks friendly, but I don't like talent shows.

❶ 'There are+복수 명사' 형태로 '~가 있다'는 뜻이다.
❷ vote for ~는 '~에게 투표하다'라는 뜻이다.
❸ 'look+형용사' 형태로 '~처럼 보이다'라는 뜻이다.

 Wrap Up

1.
B: I hear there is a new student in your class.
G: Yes. She's from Jejudo. Oh, she's over there!
B: ❶ Which one? What does she look like?
G: ❷She has curly hair and is wearing glasses.

2.
G: You look sad. What's wrong, Jongmin?
B: My sister broke her arm this morning.
G: What happened?
B: She fell off her bike.
G: That's too bad. ❸I hope she'll get better soon.

❶ '어느 아이니?'의 뜻이다.
❷ 사람의 외모를 표현하는 말로 머리 모양을 묘사할 때는 동사 have를 사용한다.
❸ 희망이나 바람을 나타내는 표현이다.

• 다음 우리말과 일치하도록 빈칸에 알맞은 말을 쓰시오.

Communicate: Listen-Listen and Answer. Talk

G: Hi, I'm Gacha. I'm _____ Mongolia. When I first came to Songji Middle School two months _____, I was so _____. I was a little _____, and I wasn't _____ at Korean. However, I'm a _____ girl. All my classmates are nice and _____. I enjoy _____ handball with them in P.E. class. I'm a good player. They _____ me "Golden Hand." There will be a sports day next week. _____ _____ my class will win in the handball event.

Communicate: Listen-Listen and Answer. Dialog

B: Hi, Minsol. Is your class _____?
G: Of course. We have a _____ handball player.
B: You _____ the girl from Mongolia?
G: Yes, her name is Gacha.
B: I've heard a lot about her. But _____ does she _____ _____?
G: She's very tall and _____ a _____.
B: Oh, is she the girl _____ _____ the goal just now?
G: Yes, that's her _____ goal.
B: Wow, she's really great.

Communicate: Listen-Listen More

M: _____ can I do for you?
G: I _____ my younger brother.
M: Okay, _____ _____. What's your brother's name?
G: His name is Wally Brown. He's five years old.
M: _____ does he _____ _____?
G: He _____ brown hair and brown eyes.
M: What is he _____?
G: He is _____ a green shirt and black pants.
M: Can you tell me more?
G: Oh, he is _____ a red backpack.
M: All right. We'll go out and _____ _____ him. Also, we'll make an _____ about a _____ child.
G: Thank you so much. _____ _____ I'll find him soon.

Communicate: Speak 2-Talk in pairs

A: I _____ an _____ exam tomorrow!
B: I hope you'll _____ _____ _____ the exam.
A: I hope _____, too. Thanks.

해석

여: 안녕, 나는 Gacha라고 해. 나는 몽골에서 왔어. 두 달 전에 내가 처음 송지 중학교에 왔을 때, 나는 무척 걱정이 되었어. 나는 좀 수줍음을 탔고 한국어를 잘 못했어. 하지만 난 운이 좋은 아이야. 내 학급 친구들은 모두 멋지고 다정해. 나는 체육 시간에 친구들과 핸드볼 하는 것을 즐겨. 난 실력이 좋은 선수야. 친구들은 나를 '황금손'이라고 불러. 다음 주에 운동회가 있을 거야. 난 우리 반이 핸드볼 대회에서 이기길 바라.

남: 안녕, 민솔아. 너희 반이 이기고 있니?
여: 물론이지. 우리는 훌륭한 핸드볼 선수가 있거든.
남: 몽골에서 온 여자아이 말하니?
여: 응, 그녀의 이름은 Gacha야.
남: 그녀에 대해 많이 들었어. 그런데 그녀는 어떻게 생겼어?
여: 그녀는 키가 크고 말총머리를 하고 있어.
남: 아, 지금 막 골을 넣은 여자아이가 그녀니?
여: 맞아, 저건 그녀의 일곱 번째 골이야.
남: 와, 그녀는 정말 잘하는구나.

남: 무엇을 도와드릴까요?
여: 남동생을 잃어버렸어요.
남: 알겠어요, 진정하세요. 남동생 이름이 뭐죠?
여: 그의 이름은 Wally Brown이에요. 다섯 살이고요.
남: 어떻게 생겼나요?
여: 그는 갈색 머리이고 갈색 눈을 지녔어요.
남: 그는 무엇을 입고 있나요?
여: 그는 초록색 셔츠와 검은 바지를 입고 있어요.
남: 더 말해 줄 수 있나요?
여: 아, 그는 빨간 배낭을 메고 있어요.
남: 알겠어요. 우리가 나가서 그를 찾아볼게요. 또, 우리가 미아 방송을 할 겁니다.
여: 정말 감사합니다. 동생을 빨리 찾길 바라요.

A: 나는 내일 중요한 시험이 있어.
B: 네가 시험을 잘 보길 바라.
A: 나도 그러길 바라. 고마워.

Communicate: Speak 2-Talk in groups

A: _____ is your character's name?

B: His name is Buster.

A: _____ _____ he look _____?

B: He has _____ hair.

A: Does he _____ big eyes?

B: Yes, he does.

Communicate: Speak-Rap Time

(1) A: I lost my puppy this afternoon.

    B: _____ _____ you'll _____ him soon.

(2) A: I hope you'll _____ your _____ in the final game.

    B: Thanks. I wish you _____ _____.

(3) A: What does your sister _____ _____, Claire?

    B: She's tall and has long _____ hair.

(4) A: Is your father _____ a blue cap?

    B: Yeah. Now, he's _____ a map.

My Speaking Portfolio

G: Look at the _____ _____. There _____ posters for the next school president.

B: Yeah, I've already _____ my _____. I'll _____ _____ Jang Jimin.

G: You _____ the boy with glasses? He looks smart, but I don't like his _____.

B: Then who will you _____?

G: Well, I am for number 1, Han Siwon. She wants to make our school a safe place.

B: She always has a ponytail, right?

G: Yes, and Hong Jiho _____ _____.

B: She looks _____, but I don't like _____ _____.

Wrap Up

1. B: I hear there is a new student in your class.

    G: Yes. She's from Jejudo. Oh, she's _____ _____!

    B: _____ one? _____ _____ she _____ like?

    G: She has _____ hair and is _____ glasses.

2. G: You look _____. What's _____, Jongmin?

    B: My sister broke her arm this morning.

    G: What _____?

    B: She _____ _____ her bike.

    G: _____ _____ _____. _____ _____ she'll _____ _____ soon.

해석

A: 네 캐릭터의 이름은 뭐니?
B: 그의 이름은 Buster야.
A: 그는 어떻게 생겼니?
B: 그는 머리카락이 없어.
A: 그는 눈이 크니?
B: 응, 맞아.

(1) A: 나는 오늘 오후에 내 강아지를 잃어버렸어.
    B: 네가 그를 곧 찾기를 바랄게.
(2) A: 나는 네가 결선에서 최선을 다하길 바라.
    B: 고마워. 나도 네가 그러길 바라.
(3) A: 네 언니는 어떻게 생겼니, Claire?
    B: 그녀는 키가 크고 긴 생머리야.
(4) A: 네 아버지는 파란 모자를 쓰고 계시니?
    B: 응. 지금 지도를 보고 계셔.

여: 이 게시판을 봐. 다음 학생회장의 포스터가 있어.
남: 응, 나는 이미 결정을 내렸어. 나는 장지민에게 투표할 거야.
여: 안경을 쓴 남자아이 얘기하는 거야? 그는 똑똑해 보이지만 나는 그의 공약이 마음에 들지 않아.
남: 그럼 넌 누굴 선택할 거야?
여: 음, 나는 1 번 한시원을 지지해. 그녀는 우리 학교를 안전한 장소로 만들고 싶어 해.
남: 그녀는 항상 말총머리를 해, 그렇지?
여: 맞아, 그리고 홍지호도 괜찮아 보여.
남: 그녀는 친절해 보이지만, 나는 장기자랑이 싫어.

1. 남: 너희 반에 새로 온 학생이 있다고 들었어.
    여: 응. 그녀는 제주도에서 왔어. 어, 그녀가 저기에 있어!
    남: 어느 아이? 어떻게 생겼어?
    여: 그녀는 곱슬머리이고 안경을 끼고 있어
2. 여: 너 슬퍼 보여. 무슨 일이니, 종민아?
    남: 여동생이 오늘 아침에 팔이 부러졌어.
    여: 무슨 일이 있었는데?
    남: 자전거에서 떨어졌어.
    여: 안됐구나. 그녀가 곧 회복되기를 바라.

01 다음 우리말에 맞도록 빈칸에 알맞은 말을 쓰시오.

> A: 네 언니는 어떻게 생겼니, Claire?
> B: She's tall and has long straight hair.

➡ _____ does your sister _____ _____

02 다음 대화의 빈칸에 들어갈 말로 알맞은 것은?

> A: I lost my puppy this afternoon.
> B: _____

① She's tall and has long straight hair.
② I hope she'll get better soon.
③ I hope you'll find him soon.
④ He has brown hair and brown eyes.
⑤ He has no hair.

03 다음 대화의 빈칸에 들어갈 말로 가장 적절한 것은?

> A: I have an important exam tomorrow!
> B: I hope you'll _____ the exam.
> A: I hope so, too. Thanks.

① look like   ② do well on
③ care for   ④ look different from
⑤ get better

04 다음 대화의 밑줄 친 우리말에 맞게 주어진 단어를 알맞은 순서로 배열하시오.

> A: I hope you'll do your best in the final game.
> B: Thanks. <u>나도 네가 그러길 바라.</u>

(wish, you, I, the, same)

➡ _____

[01~03] 다음 대화를 읽고 물음에 답하시오.

Ben: Hi, Minsol. Is your class winning?

Minsol: Of course. We have a great handball player.

Ben: (A) the girl from Mongolia?

Minsol: Yes, her name is Gacha.

Ben: I've heard a lot about her. But what does she look like?

Minsol: She's very tall and has a ponytail.

Ben: Oh, is she the girl (B)지금 막 골을 넣은?

Minsol: Yes, that's her seventh goal.

Ben: Wow, she's really great.

01 위 대화의 빈칸 (A)에 들어갈 말로 알맞은 것은?

① I mean
② She is
③ You mean
④ You know
⑤ Guess what

서답형

02 위 대화의 밑줄 친 (B)의 우리말에 맞게 주어진 단어를 알맞은 순서로 배열하시오.

the, scored, who, goal, just, now

➡ _____

03 위 대화의 내용과 일치하지 <u>않는</u> 것은?

① Minsol and Ben are watching a handball game.
② Gacha is from Mongolia.
③ Minsol and Gacha are in the same class.
④ Gacha is very tall and has a ponytail.
⑤ Ben doesn't know about Gacha.

[04~05] 다음 대화를 읽고 물음에 답하시오.

G: Look at the bulletin board. There are posters for _____(A)_____.

B: Yeah, I've already made my choice. I'll vote for Jang Jimin.

G: You mean the boy with glasses? He looks smart, but I don't like his promises.

B: Then who will you choose?

G: Well, I am for number 1, Han Siwon. She wants to make our school a safe place.

B: (B)She always has a ponytail, right?

G: Yes, and Hong Jiho seems okay.

B: She looks friendly, but I don't like talent shows.

04 위 대화의 빈칸 (A)에 들어갈 말로 알맞은 것은?

① talent shows
② a safe school
③ the next school president
④ a beauty contest
⑤ class president election

중요

05 밑줄 친 (B)의 답을 얻을 수 있는 질문으로 알맞은 것은?

① What do you think of her?
② What does she look like?
③ How does she feel?
④ What is she looking for?
⑤ What does she like?

[06~07] 다음 대화를 읽고 물음에 답하시오.

B: My sister broke her arm this morning.

G: What happened?

B: She fell off her bike.

G: _____(A)_____. (B) 그녀가 곧 회복되기를 바라.

서답형

06 위 대화의 빈칸 (A)에 알맞은 말을 주어진 단어를 이용하여 쓰시오.

> that, bad

서답형 ➡ _____

07 위 대화의 밑줄 친 (B)의 우리말에 맞게 주어진 단어를 알맞은 순서로 배열하시오.

> she'll, hope, better, I, get, soon

➡ _____

[08~09] 다음 대화를 읽고 물음에 답하시오.

M: What can I do for you?
G: I lost my younger brother.
M: Okay, calm down. What's your brother's name?
G: His name is Wally Brown. He's five years old.
M: _____ (A) _____
G: He has brown hair and brown eyes.
M: What is he wearing?
G: He is wearing a green shirt and black pants.
M: _____ (B) _____
G: Oh, he is carrying a red backpack.
M: All right. We'll go out and look for him. Also, we'll make an announcement about a missing child.
G: Thank you so much. I hope I'll find him soon.

서답형

08 위 대화의 빈칸 (A), (B)에 들어갈 말을 〈보기〉에서 찾아 쓰시오.

┌─ 보기 ┤
• You mean the boy with glasses?
• What does he look like?
• Can you tell me more?
└──────

➡ (A) _____
  (B) _____

09 위 대화를 읽고 질문에 답할 수 없는 것을 고르시오.

① What's the girl's brother's name?
② How old is the girl's brother?
③ What does the girl's brother look like?
④ Where's the girl's brother?
⑤ What will the man do after the dialog?

10 다음 중 짝지어진 대화가 어색한 것을 고르시오.

① A: You look sad. What's wrong, Jongmin?
  B: My sister broke her arm this morning.
② A: I fell off my bike.
  B: I'm glad to hear that. I hope you'll get better soon.
③ A: Is your father wearing a blue cap?
  B: Yeah. Now, he's reading a map.
④ A: What does he look like?
  B: He has no hair.
⑤ A: What does she look like?
  B: She's very tall and has a ponytail.

서답형

11 다음 대화를 읽고, 주어진 문장을 완성하시오.

┌──────────────────────────
│ B: I hear there is a new student in your class.
│ G: Yes. She's from Jejudo. Oh, she's over there!
│ B: Which one? What does she look like?
│ G: She has curly hair and is wearing glasses.
└──────────────────────────

➡ The new student has _____ _____ and is wearing _____.

[01~02] 다음 대화를 읽고 물음에 답하시오.

B: Hi, Minsol. Is your class winning?

G: Of course. We have a great handball player.

B: You mean the girl from Mongolia?

G: Yes, her name is Gacha.

B: I've heard a lot about her. But ____(A)____?

G: She's very tall and has a ponytail.

B: Oh, is she the girl who scored the goal just now?

G: Yes, that's her seventh goal.

B: Wow, she's really great.

01 다음은 Minsol이 Gacha에 관해 언급한 글이다. 빈칸을 완성하시오.

➡ Gacha _____ _____ Mongolia. Gacha and I are in the _____ class. She has scored _____ goals so far.

02 위 대화의 빈칸 (A)에 알맞은 말을 쓰시오.

➡ _____

[03~04] 다음 대화를 읽고 물음에 답하시오.

G: Look at the bulletin board. There are posters for the next school president.

B: Yeah, I've already made my choice. I'll ____(A)____ Jang Jimin.

G: You mean the boy with ____(B)____? He looks smart, but I don't like his promises.

B: Then who will you choose?

G: Well, I am for number 1, Han Siwon. She wants to make our school a ____(C)____.

B: She always has a ____(D)____, right?

G: Yes, and Hong Jiho seems okay.

B: She looks friendly, but I don't like talent shows.

03 위 대화의 빈칸 (A)에 들어갈 표현을 주어진 영영 풀이를 참고하여 두 단어로 쓰시오.

> to choose someone in an election by making a mark on an official piece of paper

➡ _____

04 아래 그림을 참고하여 위 대화의 빈칸 (B)와 (D)에는 외모에 관한 단어를, (C)에는 공약에 관한 글을 쓰시오.

➡ (B) _____ (C) _____ (D) _____

05 다음 대화의 밑줄 친 우리말에 맞게 주어진 어휘를 알맞게 배열하시오.

M: What can I do for you?

G: I lost my younger brother.

M: Okay, calm down. What's your brother's name?

G: His name is Wally Brown. He's five years old.

M: What does he look like?

G: He has brown hair and brown eyes.

M: All right. We'll go out and look for him. Also, we'll 미아 방송을 할 겁니다. (about, announcement, make, missing, a, an, child)

G: Thank you so much. I hope I'll find him soon.

➡ _____

Grammar

① **want/ask/tell + 목적어 + to부정사**

- Parents **want** their children **to be** honest. 부모들은 그들의 아이들이 정직하기를 원한다.
- They **told** him **to stop** growing a beard. 그들은 그에게 턱수염을 그만 기르라고 말했다.

- 형태: want/ask/tell + 목적어 + to부정사

- 의미: ~가 …하기를 바라다, ~에게 …하기를 요청하다, ~에게 …하라고 말하다

- 동사 want, ask, tell 뒤에 목적어와 'to+동사원형'이 이어지면 '(목적어)가 ~하도록 원하다/요청하다/말하다'라는 의미를 나타낸다.

  - I **want** you **to finish** your homework first. 나는 네가 숙제를 먼저 끝내길 원한다.

  - Mom **told** me **to put** out the trash. 엄마는 나에게 쓰레기를 내놓으라고 말씀하셨다.

- to부정사를 목적격보어로 취하는 동사에는 want, ask, tell 외에도 advise, allow, beg, cause, enable, encourage, expect, force, get, help, need, order, persuade, require, teach, would like 등이 있다.

  - They **advised** him **to leave** the place as soon as possible.
    그들은 그에게 가능한 한 빨리 그 장소를 떠나라고 조언했다.

  - Will you please **help** him **to clear[clear]** the table? 그가 식탁 치우는 거 거들어 줄래?

- to부정사의 부정형은 'not[never]+to 동사원형'이다.

  - She **asked** me **not to say** anything. 그녀는 나에게 아무 말도 하지 말라고 요청했다.

  - The doctor **ordered** me **not to drink** alcohol. 의사는 나에게 술을 마시지 말라고 명령했다.

핵심 Check

1. 다음 우리말과 일치하도록 빈칸에 알맞은 말을 쓰시오. (철자가 주어진 것도 있음.)

(1) 우리는 그녀가 늦을 것이라고 예상했다.
➡ We _____ her _____ _____ late.

(2) 갑작스런 굉음 때문에 나는 펄쩍 뛰었다.
➡ A sudden noise c_____ me _____ j_____.

(3) 그들은 그에게 서류에 서명하도록 강요했다.
➡ They f_____ him _____ _____ the paper.

② 접속사 before, after

- **Before** she has breakfast, Dora puts on her uniform.
  아침을 먹기 전에 Dora는 교복을 입는다.

- **After** he was freed, Joseph traveled and told his story to lots of people.
  Joseph은 석방된 뒤에 순회를 하며 많은 사람들에게 자신의 이야기를 전했다.

■ 형태: Before/After + 주어 + 동사 ~, 주어 + 동사 …

주어 + 동사 … before/after + 주어 + 동사 ~.

■ 의미: before: ~하기 전에 / after: ~한 후에

■ before와 after는 두 개의 절을 연결해 주는 접속사로 어떤 일이 일어나기 전이나 후의 시간 관계를 나타낸다.

  • Please swing to the door **after** you entered. 들어오고 나서, 문 좀 닫아주세요.

  • Did she leave a message **before** she went? 그녀가 가기 전에 전갈을 남겼어요?

■ 시간이나 조건의 부사절에서는 현재시제를 사용하여 미래를 나타낸다.

  • It will be long **before** we meet again. 한참 지나야 다시 만나게 되겠군요.

  • I'll start **after** he comes. 그가 온 후에 출발하겠다.

  • **If** it is warm tomorrow, we will drive in the country. 내일 날씨가 포근하면 시골로 드라이브 가자.

핵심 Check

2. 다음 괄호 안에서 알맞은 말을 고르시오.

  (1) (Before / After) you leave the room, turn out the light.

  (2) After she (comes / will come), we will go on a picnic.

  (3) The road became wet (before / after) it rained.

  ➡ (1) _____ (2) _____ (3) _____

[01~02] 다음 문장의 빈칸에 들어갈 알맞은 말을 고르시오.

01

I asked him _____ off the TV.

① turn   ② turns   ③ turned

④ turning   ⑤ to turn

02

_____ Jacob went to bed, he washed his hands.

① Before   ② After   ③ While

④ During   ⑤ If

03 다음 중 가장 자연스러운 것은?

① Before I woke up, I ate a cup of coffee.

② Before I went to the library, I borrowed books at the library.

③ Do it after you forget.

④ Wendy understood the situation after she heard it from Sue.

⑤ After she went to bed, she took a shower.

04 다음 문장에서 어법상 <u>어색한</u> 것을 바르게 고쳐 다시 쓰시오.

(1) I want you clean the windows.

   ➡ _____

(2) Before I will have dinner, I will clean my room.

   ➡ _____

(3) He took my hand and asked me marrying him.

   ➡ _____

(4) Tell her buys a comfortable pair of shoes!

   ➡ _____

05 주어진 어휘를 이용하여 다음 우리말을 영작하시오.

Justin은 축구를 한 후에 과일을 먹었다. (had, soccer, some fruit)
(Justin으로 시작할 것)

   ➡ _____

01 다음 빈칸에 알맞은 것은?

> My parents want me _____ healthy food.

① eat　　　　　② eats
③ ate　　　　　④ eating
⑤ to eat

02 다음 빈칸에 들어갈 가장 알맞은 것은?

> • I turn off my phone. And then I pass the school gate.
> = _____ I pass the school gate, I turn off my phone.

① As　　　　② Before　　　③ After
④ But　　　　⑤ When

03 다음 중 어법상 바르지 않은 것은?

> My homeroom teacher ①told ②me ③be ④on time ⑤for class.

①　　　②　　　③　　　④　　　⑤

04 다음 우리말을 영어로 바르게 옮긴 것은?

> 진수는 아침을 먹기 전에 양치질을 한다.

① Jinsu brushes his teeth when he has breakfast.
② Jinsu brushes his teeth while he has breakfast.
③ Jinsu brushes his teeth after he has breakfast.
④ Jinsu brushes his teeth before he has breakfast.
⑤ Jinsu brushes his teeth if he has breakfast.

서답형

05 다음 괄호 안에서 알맞은 말을 고르시오.

(1) He told me (came / to come) home before 9 o'clock.
(2) Harry wanted me (doing / to do) it at once.
(3) My mom (expects / hopes) me to be a teacher.
(4) She allowed her daughter (go / to go) to the K-pop concert.
(5) The class started (after / before) the teacher arrived.
(6) I wash my hands (before / after) I go to bed.

➡ (1) _____ (2) _____ (3) _____
　 (4) _____ (5) _____ (6) _____

06 다음 빈칸에 적절하지 않은 것은?

> I _____ her to take part in the party.

① watched　　② wanted　　③ told
④ persuaded　　⑤ expected

07 다음 중 어법상 바르지 않은 것은?

① He knew the truth already before we told him about it.
② After she will come tomorrow, we will go camping.
③ He arrived at the station after the train left.
④ Before he meets her, he is already in love with her.
⑤ He will call Kelly after he arrives there.

08 다음 중 두 문장의 의미가 <u>다른</u> 것은?

① Sean expected that his son would exercise to be healthy.
➡ Sean expected his son to exercise to be healthy.

② I got up before the sun rises.
➡ After the sun rose, I got up.

③ Anna told me that I must wear a long sleeve shirt at the campsite.
➡ Anna told me to wear a long sleeve shirt at the campsite.

④ Take a bath before you go to bed.
➡ Take a bath before going to bed.

⑤ The restaurant was crowded, but we found a table.
➡ Though the restaurant was crowded, we found a table.

09 다음 두 문장이 뜻이 같도록 빈칸에 들어갈 알맞은 말은?

- Before you get into the swimming pool, do some exercises to warm up.
= _____ you do some exercises to warm up, get into the swimming pool.

① Before ② After ③ As
④ When ⑤ While

서답형

10 괄호 안의 동사를 어법에 맞게 고쳐 쓰시오.

(1) The police asked him (tell) them the truth.
(2) Her parents encouraged her (study) hard.
(3) Please help me (push) the boat.
➡ (1) _____ (2) _____ (3) _____

11 두 문장의 의미가 같도록 빈칸에 알맞은 말을 쓰시오.

Ms. Rose drank coffee after she finished cleaning the living room.
= Ms. Rose finished cleaning the living room _____ she drank coffee.

➡ _____

12 다음 중 어법상 <u>어색한</u> 부분을 찾아 바르게 고친 것은?

Yejun asked his mom play badminton with him that afternoon.

① asked → has asked
② his → him
③ play → to play
④ with → to
⑤ that → this

서답형

13 주어진 어휘를 바르게 배열하여 다음 우리말을 영어로 쓰시오.

(1) 그들은 테니스를 친 후에 쇼핑을 갔다. (they, they, went, played, shopping, tennis, after)
➡ _____

(2) 은지는 영화를 보기 전에 모자를 샀다. (Eunji, she, a hat, the movie, bought, watched, before)
➡ _____

(3) 선생님은 우리에게 체육관에 모이라고 말씀하셨다. (the teacher, the gym, us, gather, told, at, to)
➡ _____

(4) 지호는 도훈이에게 창문을 닦아 달라고 부탁했다. (Jiho, Dohun, the window, clean, asked, to)
➡ _____

14 다음 빈칸에 들어갈 동사 do의 형태가 <u>다른</u> 하나는?

① Jim wanted me _____ the dishes.
② She planned _____ some exercise regularly.
③ Our teacher asked us _____ our homework.
④ Did you expect him _____ his best?
⑤ Mom made us _____ it.

[15~16] 다음 중 어법상 옳은 것을 고르시오.

15 ① I read a book after I fell asleep last night.
② I brushed my teeth after I went to bed.
③ Before he eats food, he always washes his hands.
④ Before he bought the book, he read it.
⑤ Eric will go swimming when Sue will arrive.

16 ① The typhoon caused the old bridge to fall.
② They expect her participates in the ceremony.
③ Judy asked him make sandwiches.
④ Do you want me waking you up tomorrow morning?
⑤ The math teacher told us solving 10 problems every day.

17 다음 빈칸에 적절하지 <u>않은</u> 것은?

> _____ he visits my office, I will call you immediately.

① When   ② After   ③ If
④ Even if   ⑤ As soon as

18 다음 빈칸에 알맞은 말이 바르게 짝지어진 것은?

> When Yewon asked her dad _____ her bike, he told her _____ it.

① to fix – bringing
② to fix – to bring
③ fixing – to bring
④ fixing – bringing
⑤ fix – bring

19 다음 문장에서 어법상 어색한 부분을 바르게 고쳐 다시 쓰시오.

(1) She asked her brother helping her with her homework.
   ➡ _____

(2) Jim wanted her go shopping with him.
   ➡ _____

(3) They advised him left the place as soon as possible.
   ➡ _____

(4) After he rode his bike, Jason put on his helmet.
   ➡ _____

(5) She will be a good wife when she will get married.
   ➡ _____

01 다음 문장에서 어법상 어색한 부분을 바르게 고쳐 다시 쓰시오.

(1) Lucy's dad wants her is a police officer.

➡ _____

_____

(2) My mother asked me buy milk on my way home.

➡ _____

_____

(3) The teacher told the students bringing some water.

➡ _____

_____

(4) She got her two sons divided a cake exactly in half.

➡ _____

_____

(5) Her family environment forced her to not continue her studies.

➡ _____

_____

02 중요 주어진 단어를 바르게 배열하여 다음 우리말을 영어로 쓰시오.

(1) 내가 결정을 내리자마자 너에게 내 마음을 알릴 것이다. (I로 시작할 것)

(I, my, will, let, you, know, mind, I, make, a, decision, as soon as)

➡ _____

_____

(2) Nancy는 오빠가 자기에게 라면을 끓여 주기를 원했다.

(Nancy, brother, ramyeon, her, her, cook, wanted, for, to)

➡ _____

_____

03 중요 주어진 동사를 어법에 맞게 빈칸에 쓰시오.

(1) My best friend Jiho often asks me _____ him. (help)

(2) My dad doesn't allow me _____ out at night. (go)

(3) Marianne ordered him _____ with her. (stay)

(4) The manager warned him _____ any pictures there. (take, not)

(5) When Jenny _____, we will leave for Seoul. (come)

(6) The boys will go hiking after they _____ lunch. (have)

04 다음 우리말에 맞도록 빈칸에 알맞은 말을 쓰시오.

(1) Audrey는 숙제를 끝낸 후에 TV를 본다.

= Audrey _____ TV _____ she finishes her homework.

(2) 그는 수영하기 전에 준비 운동을 했다.

= _____ he swam, he _____ some warm-up exercises.

(3) 그가 돌아오면 저한테 전화해 달라고 부탁해 주시겠어요?

= Will you ask him _____ me when he _____ back?

(4) 그녀는 자기 딸에게 개에게 먹이를 주라고 말했다.

= She told her daughter _____ the dog.

05 적절한 접속사를 이용하여 〈보기〉에 주어진 문장과 연결하여 자연스러운 하나의 문장을 만드시오.

┌─ 보기 ─┐

- The students took a bus for one hour.
- They arrived at the museum.
- They went to the beach.

(1) They bought their swimming suit.

➡ _____

_____

(2) They arrived at their destination.

➡ _____

_____

(3) They appreciated the works in the museum.

➡ _____

_____

06 다음은 Angelina의 일요일 일정표이다. 빈칸에 알맞은 말을 시간의 전후 관계가 표현된 완전한 영어 문장으로 쓰시오.

time	what to do
10:00	go to church
13:00	have lunch with her family
15:00	study math in her room
18:00	go to the movie with James

(1) Angelina will have lunch with her family _____ .

(2) Angelina will study math in her room _____ .

(3) Angelina will go to the movie with James _____ .

07 다음 문장을 읽고 빈칸에 알맞은 말을 쓰시오.

┌─────────────────────────┐
Laura: I'm worried about my history grade.

Teacher: Study history a little harder. You can do it.
└─────────────────────────┘

➡ The teacher encourages _____ _____ a little harder.

08 다음 문장에서 어법상 어색한 부분을 바르게 고쳐 쓰시오.

(1) Before the sun sets, they can see many stars.

_____ ➡ _____

(2) Turn off the light after you leave the room.

_____ ➡ _____

(3) The migrating birds will come back when spring will come next year.

_____ ➡ _____

(4) I would like you meeting a friend of mine.

_____ ➡ _____

09 주어진 단어를 활용하여 다음 우리말을 영어로 쓰시오.

(1) 나의 부모님은 항상 내게 학교에서 최선을 다하라고 말씀하신다. (always, best, in school)

➡ _____

(2) 건강했기 때문에 그는 그 계획을 수행할 수 있었다. (good health, carry out, enable)

➡ _____

(3) Yuri는 내일 아침을 먹은 후에 교복을 입을 것이다. (put, her uniform) (Yuri로 시작할 것)

➡ _____

Reading

The Right To Be Different

In many ways, 42-year-old Joseph Palmer was an ordinary
<u>42-years-old(×)</u>

person. He had a job and cared for his family. But in 1830, after he
접속사 after 뒤에 오는 절이 먼저 일어난 일. 주절은 after가 이끄는 절보다 나중에 일어난 일

moved to a small town in Massachusetts, he began to face difficulties.
~으로 이사했다   = facing

Joseph looked different from other people: he had a long beard. People
감각동사 look+형용사 보어: ~하게 보이다

did not like it very much.
            a long beard

The town's people avoided the man with a beard. They did not want
피했다   = Joseph Palmer

to sit next to him. They even whispered behind his back, "What is he
want는 목적어로 to부정사를 취한다.   behind somebody's back: ~의 등 뒤에서

trying to hide?"
try+to부정사: ~을 하려고 노력하다

Some neighbors broke his windows. Others threw stones at him when
some .... others ...: 어떤 것[사람]들은 ..., 다른 것[사람]들은

he walked down the street. They told him to stop growing a beard.
                        tell+목적어+to부정사: (목적어)에게 ~하라고 말하다. stop은 동명사를 목적어로 취하는 동사

Joseph did not mind. He just wanted the freedom to have his beard.
                        the freedom을 꾸며 주는 형용사적 용법의 to부정사

right 권리
ordinary 평범한, 보통의
care for ~을 돌보다
face 직면하다, 대면하다
beard 수염, 턱수염
avoid 피하다
whisper 속삭이다, 속닥거리다
hide 숨기다
mind 신경 쓰다, 언짢아하다
freedom 자유

📎 확인문제

● 다음 문장이 본문의 내용과 일치하면 T, 일치하지 않으면 F를 쓰시오.

1 Joseph Palmer had a job and cared for his family. ☐

2 Before he moved to a small town in Massachusetts, Joseph began to face difficulties. ☐

3 Joseph looked different from other people. ☐

4 People liked Joseph's long beard very much. ☐

5 Some neighbors broke Joseph's windows. ☐

6 Joseph just wanted the freedom to live alone. ☐

28 Lesson 5. Understanding Others

One day, four men attacked Joseph and threw him on the ground.
V1   V2   = Joseph

"We're going to cut off your beard!" they shouted. Joseph was a big
자르다

man, and he was able to fight them off. But the men called the police
목적어가 인칭대명사이므로 fight off them이 아니라 fight them off가 적절하다.

and accused him of attacking them. Poor Joseph was arrested. He said
accuse A of B: A를 B 때문에 고발하다   수동태

to the judge, "I'm the victim here." Sadly, no one believed a man with
문장 전체를 수식하는 부사   ~을 가진

a beard, and he went to prison for over a year. 일 년이 넘는 기간 동안
감옥에 갔다. / the가 없는 경우에는 건물의 본래 목적을 나타낸다. go to school(학교에 다니다)과 비슷한 맥락으로 이해할 수 있다.

Joseph's son, Thomas, wanted people to know the truth. He sent
want+목적어+to부정사: (목적어)가 ~하기를 원하다

letters to newspapers across the country. People learned that Joseph
send는 to를 사용하여 3형식으로 고친다.   명사절을 이끄는 접속사

was in prison just for protecting himself and his beard. Many people
him(×)

became angry about this, so the judge finally decided to set Joseph
= Joseph was in prison just for protecting himself and his beard.   decide는 목적어로 to부정사를 취한다.

free.

After he was freed, Joseph traveled and told his story to lots of
석방되다   = many

people. Slowly, people's attitudes toward beards changed. Before
접속사 before는 '~ 전에'라는 뜻, 주절은 before가 이끄는 절에 앞서 일어난 일을 나타낸다.

Joseph died, a man with a beard became the President of the United
턱수염을 가진 남자

States. His name was Abraham Lincoln. He made beards popular, but
= Abraham Lincoln

Joseph Palmer fought for the right to have them.
the right를 수식하는 형용사적 용법의 to부정사   = beards

attack 공격하다
fight off ~을 싸워 물리치다
accuse 고발하다, 기소하다
arrest 체포하다
judge 판사
victim 희생자
prison 감옥
truth 진실
set free 석방하다
attitude 태도
toward ~을 향한
president 대통령

확인문제

● 다음 문장이 본문의 내용과 일치하면 T, 일치하지 않으면 F를 쓰시오.

1 Joseph said to the judge, "I'm the victim here." ☐

2 The judge believed Joseph and set him free. ☐

3 Joseph's son sent letters to newspapers across the country. ☐

4 People learned that Joseph was in prison just for protecting his family. ☐

5 After he was freed, Joseph traveled and told his story to lots of people. ☐

6 Joseph died before Abraham Lincoln became the President of America. ☐

● 우리말을 참고하여 빈칸에 알맞은 말을 쓰시오.

1 The Right To _____ _____

2 In many ways, 42-year-old Joseph Palmer was _____ _____
_____.

3 He had a job and _____ _____ his family.

4 But in 1830, after he moved to a small town in Massachusetts, he
began _____ _____ _____.

5 Joseph _____ _____ from other people: he had a long beard.

6 People _____ _____ _____ _____ very much.

7 The town's people avoided _____ _____ _____
_____.

8 They did not want to _____ _____ _____ _____.

9 They even whispered _____ _____ _____, "What is he
trying to hide?"

10 Some neighbors _____ _____ _____.

11 Others _____ _____ _____ him when he walked down
the street.

12 They told him to _____ _____ a beard.

13 Joseph did not _____.

14 He just wanted the freedom _____ _____ his beard.

15 One day, four men _____ Joseph and _____ him on the
ground.

---

1 다를 권리

2 여러 면에서 42살의 Joseph Palmer는 평범한 사람이었다.

3 그는 직업이 있었고 가족을 돌보았다.

4 하지만 1830년에 매사추세츠에 있는 작은 도시로 이사를 한 후에 그는 어려움에 직면하기 시작했다.

5 Joseph은 다른 사람들과 달라 보였다. 그는 기다란 턱수염을 기르고 있었다.

6 사람들은 그것을 별로 좋아하지 않았다.

7 마을 사람들은 턱수염을 가진 그 남자를 피했다.

8 그들은 그의 곁에 앉고 싶어 하지 않았다.

9 그들은 심지어 그의 등 뒤에서 "그가 무엇을 숨기려는 거지?" 라고 속삭였다.

10 어떤 이웃들은 그의 창문을 깼다.

11 다른 사람들은 그가 길을 걸어 내려갈 때 그에게 돌을 던졌다.

12 그들은 그에게 턱수염을 그만 기르라고 말했다.

13 Joseph은 신경 쓰지 않았다.

14 그는 그저 자신의 턱수염을 기를 자유를 원했다.

15 어느 날, 네 명의 남자가 Joseph을 공격했고 그를 바닥에 던졌다.

16 "We're going to _____ _____ your beard!" they shouted.

17 Joseph was a big man, and he was able to _____ _____ _____.

18 But the men called the police and _____ _____ _____ attacking them.

19 Poor Joseph _____ _____.

20 He said to the judge, "I'm _____ _____ here."

21 Sadly, no one believed _____ _____ _____ _____, and he _____ _____ _____ for over a year.

22 Joseph's son, Thomas, _____ people _____ _____ the truth.

23 He _____ letters _____ newspapers across the country.

24 People learned that Joseph _____ _____ _____ just for _____ _____ and his beard.

25 Many people _____ _____ about this, so the judge finally decided _____ _____ Joseph _____.

26 After he _____ _____, Joseph traveled and told his story to lots of people.

27 Slowly, people's _____ _____ changed.

28 Before Joseph died, a man _____ _____ _____ became the President of the United States.

29 _____ _____ was Abraham Lincoln.

30 He made beards _____, but Joseph Palmer _____ _____ the right to have them.

16 "우리가 당신의 턱수염을 잘라 버리겠어!"라고 그들은 소리쳤다.

17 Joseph은 덩치가 큰 사람이었고, 그는 그들을 싸워 물리칠 수 있었다.

18 하지만 그 남자들은 경찰을 불렀고, 자신들을 공격한 것으로 그를 고발했다.

19 불쌍한 Joseph은 체포되었다.

20 그는 "저는 여기서 희생자입니다."라고 판사에게 말했다.

21 슬프게도, 아무도 턱수염을 가진 남자를 믿지 않았고, 그는 일 년이 넘는 기간 동안 감옥에 갔다.

22 Joseph의 아들인 Thomas는 사람들이 진실을 알기를 원했다.

23 그는 전국에 있는 신문사에 편지를 보냈다.

24 사람들은 Joseph이 단지 자신과 자신의 턱수염을 지키려다 감옥에 갇혔다는 것을 알게 되었다.

25 많은 사람들은 이에 대해 분개했고, 그래서 판사는 결국 Joseph을 석방하기로 결정했다.

26 Joseph은 석방된 뒤에 순회를 하며 많은 사람들에게 자신의 이야기를 전했다.

27 사람들의 턱수염에 대한 태도는 서서히 변해갔다.

28 Joseph이 죽기 전에, 턱수염을 가진 남자가 미국의 대통령이 되었다.

29 그의 이름은 Abraham Lincoln (에이브러햄 링컨)이었다.

30 그는 턱수염을 대중적으로 만들었지만, Joseph Palmer는 그것을 기를 권리를 위하여 싸웠다.

● 우리말을 참고하여 본문을 영작하시오.

1 다를 권리

➡ _____

2 여러 면에서 42살의 Joseph Palmer는 평범한 사람이었다.

➡ _____

3 그는 직업이 있었고 가족을 돌보았다.

➡ _____

4 하지만 1830년에 매사추세츠에 있는 작은 도시로 이사를 한 후에 그는 어려움에 직면하기 시작했다.

➡ _____

5 Joseph은 다른 사람들과 달라 보였다. 그는 기다란 턱수염을 기르고 있었다.

➡ _____

6 사람들은 그것을 별로 좋아하지 않았다.

➡ _____

7 마을 사람들은 턱수염을 가진 그 남자를 피했다.

➡ _____

8 그들은 그의 곁에 앉고 싶어 하지 않았다.

➡ _____

9 그들은 심지어 그의 등 뒤에서 "그가 무엇을 숨기려는 거지?"라고 속삭였다.

➡ _____

10 어떤 이웃들은 그의 창문을 깼다.

➡ _____

11 다른 사람들은 그가 길을 걸어 내려갈 때 그에게 돌을 던졌다.

➡ _____

12 그들은 그에게 턱수염을 그만 기르라고 말했다.

➡ _____

13 Joseph은 신경 쓰지 않았다.

➡ _____

14 그는 그저 자신의 턱수염을 기를 자유를 원했다.

➡ _____

15 어느 날, 네 명의 남자가 Joseph을 공격했고 그를 바닥에 던졌다.

➡ _____

16 "우리가 당신의 턱수염을 잘라 버리겠어!"라고 그들은 소리쳤다.

➡ _____

17 Joseph은 덩치가 큰 사람이었고, 그는 그들을 싸워 물리칠 수 있었다.

➡ _____

18 하지만 그 남자들은 경찰을 불렀고, 자신들을 공격한 것으로 그를 고발했다.

➡ _____

19 불쌍한 Joseph은 체포되었다.

➡ _____

20 그는 "저는 여기서 희생자입니다."라고 판사에게 말했다.

➡ _____

21 슬프게도, 아무도 턱수염을 가진 남자를 믿지 않았고, 그는 일 년이 넘는 기간 동안 감옥에 갔다.

➡ _____

22 Joseph의 아들인 Thomas는 사람들이 진실을 알기를 원했다.

➡ _____

23 그는 전국에 있는 신문사에 편지를 보냈다.

➡ _____

24 사람들은 Joseph이 단지 자신과 자신의 턱수염을 지키려다 감옥에 갇혔다는 것을 알게 되었다.

➡ _____

25 많은 사람들은 이에 대해 분개했고, 그래서 판사는 결국 Joseph을 석방하기로 결정했다.

➡ _____

26 Joseph은 석방된 뒤에 순회를 하며 많은 사람들에게 자신의 이야기를 전했다.

➡ _____

27 사람들의 턱수염에 대한 태도는 서서히 변해갔다.

➡ _____

28 Joseph이 죽기 전에, 턱수염을 가진 남자가 미국의 대통령이 되었다.

➡ _____

29 그의 이름은 Abraham Lincoln(에이브러햄 링컨)이었다.

➡ _____

30 그는 턱수염을 대중적으로 만들었지만, Joseph Palmer는 그것을 기를 권리를 위하여 싸웠다.

➡ _____

[01~03] 다음 글을 읽고 물음에 답하시오.

In many ways, 42-year-old Joseph Palmer was an ordinary person. He had a job and ⓐ cared for his family. But in 1830, after he moved to a small town in Massachusetts, he began to face difficulties. Joseph looked different ___ⓑ___ other people: he had a long beard. People did not like it very much.

The town's people avoided the man ___ⓒ___ a beard. They did not want to sit next to him. They even whispered behind his back, "What is he trying to hide?"

01 위 글의 밑줄 친 ⓐcared for와 바꿔 쓸 수 있는 말을 모두 고르시오.

① cared about
② looked after
③ looked for
④ took off
⑤ took care of

02 위 글의 빈칸 ⓑ와 ⓒ에 들어갈 전치사가 바르게 짝지어진 것은?

① in – from
② from – on
③ from – with
④ for – on
⑤ for – with

03 Joseph Palmer에 대한 설명으로 옳지 않은 것을 고르시오.

① 그는 직업이 있었고 가족을 돌보았다.
② 매사추세츠주의 작은 도시로 이사를 한 후에 어려움에 직면하기 시작했다.
③ 그는 기다란 턱수염을 기르고 있었다.
④ 마을 사람들은 그를 피했고 그의 곁에 앉고 싶어 하지 않았다.
⑤ 그는 등 뒤에 무엇을 숨기고 있었다.

[04~06] 다음 글을 읽고 물음에 답하시오.

Some neighbors broke his windows. Others threw stones at him when he walked down the street. They told him ___ⓐ___ growing a beard. Joseph did not mind. He just wanted the freedom to have his beard.

One day, four men attacked Joseph and threw him on the ground. "We're going to cut off your beard!" they shouted. Joseph was a big man, and he was able to fight (A)[it / them] off. But the men called the police and accused him of attacking them. Poor Joseph was arrested. He said to the judge, ⓑ"I'm the victim here." (B)[Luckily / Sadly], no one believed a man with a beard, and he went to prison (C)[during / for] over a year.

서답형
04 위 글의 빈칸 ⓐ에 stop을 이용하여 알맞은 어구를 쓰시오.

➡ _____

서답형
05 위 글의 괄호 (A)~(C)에서 문맥이나 어법상 알맞은 낱말을 골라 쓰시오.

➡ (A) _____ (B) _____ (C) _____

06 밑줄 친 ⓑ를 통해 자신이 체포된 것에 대해 Joseph이 표현하고자 한 심경으로 가장 알맞은 것을 고르시오.

① bored
② scared
③ unfair
④ excited
⑤ ashamed

[07~10] 다음 글을 읽고 물음에 답하시오.

Joseph's son, Thomas, wanted people to know the truth. ⓐHe sent letters to newspapers across the country. People learned that Joseph was in prison just for protecting ⓑhimself and his beard. Many people became angry about this, so the judge Ⓐfinally decided to set Joseph free.

After he was freed, Joseph traveled and told ⓒhis story to lots of people. Slowly, people's attitudes toward beards changed. Before Joseph died, ⓓa man with a beard became the President of the United States. His name was Abraham Lincoln. ⓔHe made beards popular, but Joseph Palmer fought for the right Ⓑto have them.

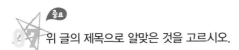

위 글의 제목으로 알맞은 것을 고르시오.

① Inform People of the Truth
② Hard-Won Right to Have a Beard
③ The Pressure of Public Opinion
④ Notice the Attitudes toward Beards
⑤ Abraham Lincoln vs Joseph Palmer

08 위 글의 밑줄 친 ⓐ~ⓔ 중 가리키는 대상이 같은 것끼리 짝 지어진 것은?

① ⓐ - ⓑ   ② ⓐ - ⓒ
③ ⓑ - ⓒ   ④ ⓒ - ⓓ
⑤ ⓒ - ⓔ

09 위 글의 밑줄 친 Ⓐfinally와 의미가 다른 말을 모두 고르시오.

① immediately   ② at last
③ after all   ④ exactly
⑤ in the end

10 위 글의 밑줄 친 Ⓑto have와 to부정사의 용법이 다른 것을 모두 고르시오.

① Are there any questions for me to answer?
② It is important to do your homework.
③ She was surprised to see the sight.
④ I want a book to read during my vacation.
⑤ It's time to leave for New York.

[11~13] 다음 독서 기록장을 읽고 물음에 답하시오.

The Right to Be Different

A Story About Joseph Palmer

I read the story about Joseph Palmer last week. I really enjoyed it. I learned from the story that we should not judge people by their _____ⓐ_____. Students who talk about other people's _____ⓐ_____ must read the story. However, I have a question about it. Why did Joseph Palmer want to have a beard?

서답형

11 위 독서 기록장의 빈칸 ⓐ에 appear를 알맞은 형태로 쓰시오.

➡ _____

서답형

12 다음 질문에 대한 알맞은 대답을 주어진 말로 시작하여 쓰시오. (7 단어)

Q: To whom does the writer want to recommend this story?

A: The writer wants to recommend this story to _____.

➡ _____

13 위 독서 기록장에서 알 수 없는 것을 고르시오.

① 제목   ② 주인공

③ 교훈   ④ 구입 장소

⑤ 궁금한 점

[14~16] 다음 글을 읽고 물음에 답하시오.

ⓐIn many ways, 42-year-old Joseph Palmer was an extraordinary person. He had a job and cared for his family. But in 1830, after he moved to a small town in Massachusetts, he began to face difficulties. Joseph looked different from other people: he had a long beard. People did not like it very much.

The town's people avoided the man with a beard. They did not want to sit next to him. They even whispered ⓑ그의 등 뒤에서, "What is he trying ⓒto hide?"

서답형

14 위 글의 밑줄 친 ⓐ에서 흐름상 어색한 부분을 찾아 고치시오.

➡ _____

서답형

15 위 글의 밑줄 친 ⓑ의 우리말에 맞게 3 단어로 영작하시오.

➡ _____

16 위 글의 밑줄 친 ⓒto hide와 to부정사의 용법이 다른 것을 모두 고르시오.

① Who is the best man to do the work?

② Her first mistake was to tell the information carelessly.

③ Tom decided to wash the dishes for his mom.

④ He got up early to go on a picnic.

⑤ It's not easy to lose weight in a short period of time.

[17~19] 다음 글을 읽고 물음에 답하시오.

_____ ⓐ _____ neighbors broke his windows. _____ ⓑ _____ threw stones at him when he walked down the street. They told him to stop growing a beard. Joseph did not mind. He just wanted the freedom to have his beard.

One day, four men attacked Joseph and threw him on the ground. "We're going to cut off your beard!" they shouted. Joseph was a big man, and he was able to fight them off. But the men called the police and accused him of attacking them. Poor Joseph was arrested. He said to the judge, "I'm the victim here." Sadly, no one believed a man with a beard, and he went to prison for over a year.

17 위 글의 빈칸 ⓐ와 ⓑ에 들어갈 알맞은 말을 고르시오.

① Some – The other

② Others – The others

③ Some – Others

④ Some – Another

⑤ Others – Some

18 위 글에서 Joseph에 대한 이웃들의 태도에 어울리는 속담을 고르시오.

① It never rains but it pours.

② Every dog has his day.

③ A stitch in time saves nine.

④ Don't count your chickens before they are hatched.

⑤ A tall tree catches much wind.

19 위 글의 내용과 일치하지 <u>않는</u> 것은?

① 어떤 이웃들은 Joseph의 집 창문을 깼다.

② Joseph은 그저 자신의 턱수염을 기를 자유를 원했다.

③ 어느 날, 네 명의 남자가 Joseph을 공격했고 그를 바닥에 던졌다.

④ Joseph은 덩치가 큰 사람이었지만 네 명의 남자들을 싸워 물리칠 수 없었다.

⑤ Joseph은 일 년이 넘는 기간 동안 감옥에 갔다.

[20~22] 다음 글을 읽고 물음에 답하시오.

A Story About Steve Jobs

I read a story about Steve Jobs. I really enjoyed ____ⓐ____ his story. I learned from the story that we should think (A)[different / differently]. Young people who study for the future must read the story. However, I have a question about the story. How was his middle school life? I still remember his saying, "Stay (B)[hungry / hungrily]. Stay (C)[foolish / foolishly]."

20 위 글의 빈칸 ⓐ에 read를 알맞은 형태로 쓰시오.

➡ _____

21 위 글의 괄호 (A)~(C)에서 어법상 알맞은 낱말을 골라 쓰시오.

➡ (A) _____ (B) _____ (C) _____

22 위 글의 종류로 알맞은 것을 고르시오.

① article　　　　② book report
③ diary　　　　④ essay
⑤ biography

[23~25] 다음 글을 읽고 물음에 답하시오.

Joseph's son, Thomas, wanted people to know the truth. (①) He sent letters to newspapers across the country. (②) Many people became angry about this, so the judge finally decided to set Joseph free. (③)

After he was freed, Joseph traveled and told his story to lots of people. (④) Slowly, people's attitudes toward beards changed. (⑤) Before Joseph died, a man with a beard became the President of the United States. His name was Abraham Lincoln. He made beards popular, but Joseph Palmer fought for the ⓐright to have them.

23 위 글의 흐름으로 보아, 주어진 문장이 들어가기에 가장 적절한 곳은?

People learned that Joseph was in prison just for protecting himself and his beard.

①　　　②　　　③　　　④　　　⑤

24 위 글에서 알 수 있는 Joseph Palmer의 성격으로 알맞은 것을 고르시오.

① funny　　　　② curious
③ generous　　　④ creative
⑤ strong-willed

25 위 글의 밑줄 친 ⓐright과 같은 의미로 쓰인 것을 고르시오.

① She had every <u>right</u> to be angry.
② Is this the <u>right</u> way to the beach?
③ Lee was standing <u>right</u> behind her.
④ Keep on the <u>right</u> side of the road.
⑤ Nothing goes <u>right</u> with me.

[01~03] 다음 글을 읽고 물음에 답하시오.

In many ways, (A)[42-year-old / 42-years-old] Joseph Palmer was an ordinary person. He had a job and cared for his family. But in 1830, after he moved to a small town in Massachusetts, he began to face difficulties. Joseph looked (B)[different / differently] from other people: he had a long beard. People did not like ⓐit very much.

The town's people avoided the man with a beard. They did not want (C)[sitting / to sit] next to him. They even whispered behind his back, "What is he trying to hide?"

중요
01 위 글의 괄호 (A)~(C)에서 어법상 알맞은 낱말을 골라 쓰시오.

➡ (A) _____ (B) _____ (C) _____

02 위 글의 밑줄 친 ⓐit이 가리키는 것을 본문에서 찾아 쓰시오.

➡ _____

고 난이도
03 Joseph Palmer가 매사추세츠주의 작은 도시로 이사를 한 후에 직면했던 어려움 네 가지를 우리말로 쓰시오.

➡ (1) _____
   (2) _____
   (3) _____
   (4) _____

[04~05] 다음 글을 읽고 물음에 답하시오.

Some neighbors broke his windows. Others threw stones at him when he walked down the street. They told him to stop growing a beard. Joseph did not mind. He just wanted the freedom to have his beard.

One day, four men attacked Joseph and threw him on the ground. "We're going to cut off your beard!" they shouted. Joseph was a big man, and he was able to fight them off. But the men called the police and accused him of attacking them. Poor Joseph was arrested. He said to the judge, "I'm the victim here." Sadly, no one believed a man with a beard, and he went to prison for over a year.

중요
04 다음 문장에서 위 글의 내용과 다른 부분을 고쳐 문장을 다시 쓰시오.

> Joseph called the police and accused the four men of attacking him.

➡ _____
  _____

05 have를 알맞은 형태로 변형하여, 다음 질문에 대한 대답을 쓰시오. (4 단어)

> Q: When Joseph said to the judge, "I'm the victim here," why did no one believe him?
> A: Because _____ .

➡ _____

[06~08] 다음 글을 읽고 물음에 답하시오.

ⓐJoseph의 아들인 Thomas는 사람들이 진실을 알기를 원했다. He sent letters to newspapers across the country. People learned that Joseph was ①in prison just ②for protecting himself and his beard. Many people became angry ③ about this, so the judge finally decided to set Joseph free.

After he was freed, Joseph traveled and told his story to lots of people. Slowly, people's attitudes ④toward beards changed. Before Joseph died, a man with a beard became the President of the United States. His name was Abraham Lincoln. ⓑHe made beards popular, but Joseph Palmer fought ⑤against the right to have them.

06 위 글의 밑줄 친 ⓐ의 우리말에 맞게 주어진 어휘를 이용하여 9 단어로 영작하시오.

> people, truth

➡

07 위 글의 밑줄 친 ①~⑤에서 전치사의 쓰임이 틀린 것을 찾아 고치시오.

_____번, ➡ _____

08 위 글의 밑줄 친 ⓑHe가 가리키는 것을 본문에서 찾아 쓰시오.

➡ _____

[09~13] 다음 글을 읽고 물음에 답하시오.

Some neighbors broke his windows. ⓐThe others threw stones at him when he walked down the street. They told him to stop ⓑgrow a beard. Joseph did not mind. He just wanted the freedom to have his beard.

One day, four men attacked Joseph and threw him on the ground. "We're going to cut off your beard!" they shouted. Joseph was a big man, and he was able to fight them off. But the men called the police and ⓒ자신들을 공격한 것으로 그를 고발했다. Poor Joseph was arrested. He said to the judge, "I'm the ___ⓓ___ here." Sadly, no one believed a man with a beard, and he went to prison for over a year.

09 위 글의 밑줄 친 ⓐ에서 어법상 틀린 것을 고치시오.

_____ ➡ _____

10 위 글의 밑줄 친 ⓑ를 알맞은 어형으로 고치시오.

➡ _____

11 위 글의 밑줄 친 ⓒ의 우리말에 맞게 한 단어를 보충하여, 주어진 어휘를 알맞게 배열하시오.

> attacking / them / him / accused

➡ _____

12 주어진 영영풀이를 참고하여 빈칸 ⓓ에 철자 v로 시작하는 단어를 쓰시오.

> someone who has been hurt or killed

➡ _____

13 다음 빈칸 (A)와 (B)에 알맞은 단어를 넣어 Joseph에 대한 소개를 완성하시오.

> Joseph just wanted the freedom to have his beard, but he went to prison for (A)_____ _____ _____ because of the prejudice of the neighbors about a man with (B)_____ _____.
>
> *prejudice: 편견

교과서

구석구석

My Speaking Portfolio

I will vote for Han Siwon. She looks confident and smart. She thinks school
　　　　　　　　　　　　　　 look+형용사 보어: ~하게 보이다

should be a safe place. I agree with her. I like her promises such as no more
~이어야 한다　　　　　　　　　　　　　　　　　　　　　　　　　　~와 같은

bullying. I hope Han Siwon becomes the next school president. I really want
　　　　 hope와 Han 사이에 접속사 that 생략　= will become

my school to be a safer place.
　 want의 목적격보어로 쓰인 to부정사

구문해설　• vote for: ~을 뽑다, ~에게 투표하다　• agree with: ~에 동의하다
　　　　　　　• bully: (약자를) 괴롭히다[왕따시키다], 협박하다

해석

나는 한시원을 뽑을 겁니다. 그녀는 자신감 있고 똑똑해 보입니다. 그녀는 학교가 안전한 장소가 되어야 한다고 생각합니다. 저는 그녀에게 동의합니다. 나는 집단 괴롭힘 없애기 같은 공약들이 좋습니다. 나는 한시원이 다음 학생회장이 되길 바랍니다. 나는 우리 학교가 더 안전한 장소가 되길 정말 바랍니다.

My Writing Portfolio: My Book Report

The Right to Be Different
　　　 형용사적 용법
A Story About Joseph Palmer

I read the story about Joseph Palmer last week. I really enjoyed it. I learned
　　　　　　　　　　　　　　　　　　　　　　　the story about Joseph Palmer

from the story that we should not judge people by their appearance. Students
　　　　　　 접속사　　　　　　　　　　　　　그들의 외모로

who talk about other people's appearance must read the story. However, I have
주격 관계대명사　　　　　　　　　　　　　~해야 한다　　　　그러나

a question about it. Why did Joseph Palmer want to have a beard?
　　　　　　　　　　　　　　　　　　want는 목적어로 to부정사를 취한다.

구문해설　• right 권리　• judge: (~로 미루어) 판단하다[여기다]　• appearance: 외모
　　　　　　　• however: 그러나　• beard: 턱수염

다른 권리

Joseph Palmer에 관한 이야기
나는 지난주에 Joseph Palmer에 관한 이야기를 읽었다. 나는 그게 정말 재미있었다. 나는 그 이야기로부터 우리는 사람들을 외모로 판단해서는 안 된다는 것을 배웠다. 다른 사람들의 외모에 관해 이야기하는 학생들은 이 이야기를 꼭 읽어야 한다. 하지만, 나는 그것에 관한 질문이 하나 있다. Joseph Palmer는 왜 턱수염을 기르고 싶었을까?

Words in Action

Welcome to the travel fair. Admission is free. What countries do you have in
　　　　　　　　　　　　　　　　　　　　　　　　　　　　~을 마음에 두다

mind? If you want to visit South America, you can look around the booths on
　　　 부사절을 이끄는 접속사로 '만약 ~ 한다면'의 의미　　　　　　　　　　형용사구

the left. If you get hungry, you can have drinks and a light snack.
　　　　　　　 get+형용사: ~해지다

구문해설　• fair 박람회　• admission 입장료　• free 무료의　• look around 둘러보다
　　　　　　　• light 가벼운

여행 박람회에 오신 것을 환영합니다. 입장료는 무료입니다. 여러분은 어떤 나라들을 마음에 두고 있나요? 여러분이 남아메리카를 방문하고 싶다면, 왼쪽에 있는 부스들을 살펴볼 수 있습니다. 배가 고파진다면, 음료와 간단한 간식을 드실 수 있습니다.

01 다음 주어진 두 단어의 관계가 같도록 빈칸에 알맞은 단어를 쓰시오.

act : action – appear : _____

02 다음 글의 빈칸 ⓐ와 ⓑ에 들어갈 단어가 바르게 짝지어진 것은?

One day, four men ____ⓐ____ ed Joseph and threw him on the ground. "We're going to ____ⓑ____ your beard!" they shouted.

① avoid – protect ② avoid – cut off
③ wait – protect ④ attack – fight off
⑤ attack – cut off

03 다음 밑줄 친 부분의 뜻이 **잘못된** 것은?

① After he <u>was freed</u>, Joseph traveled. 석방되었다
② Joseph Palmer fought for the <u>right</u> to have beards. 권리
③ Joseph Palmer was an <u>ordinary</u> person. 평범한
④ He said to the <u>judge</u>, "I'm the victim here." 판단하다
⑤ Joseph <u>looked different</u> from other people. 다르게 보였다

04 다음 영영 풀이에 해당하는 것을 고르시오.

• to make something happen
• the reason that something happens

① cut ② cause ③ fall
④ change ⑤ mean

05 다음 문장의 빈칸에 공통으로 들어갈 말을 쓰시오.

• I do well in subjects _____ social studies and history.
• He looks smart, but I don't _____ his promises.

06 빈칸에 주어진 단어를 알맞은 형태로 고쳐 쓰시오.

• The men called the police and accused him of attacking them. Poor Joseph _____ (arrest).

➡ _____

07 주어진 문장이 들어갈 위치로 알맞은 것은?

But what does she look like?

B: Hi, Minsol. Is your class winning?
G: Of course. We have a great handball player. (①)
B: You mean the girl from Mongolia?
G: Yes, her name is Gacha. (②)
B: I've heard a lot about her. (③)
G: She's very tall and has a ponytail. (④)
B: Oh, is she the girl who scored the goal just now?
G: Yes, that's her seventh goal. (⑤)
B: Wow, she's really great.

① ② ③ ④ ⑤

08 다음 질문에 대한 답으로 적절하지 <u>않은</u> 것은?

> A: What does he look like?

① He has long straight hair.
② He has a big head.
③ He is very tall.
④ He's reading a map.
⑤ He has blond hair.

[09~10] 다음 대화를 읽고 물음에 답하시오.

> M: What can I do for you?
> G: I lost my younger brother.
> M: Okay, calm down. What's your brother's name?
> G: His name is Wally Brown. He's five years old.
> M: What does he look like?
> G: He has brown hair and brown eyes.
> M: What is he wearing?
> G: He is wearing a green shirt and black pants.
> M: Can you tell me more?
> G: Oh, he is carrying a red backpack.
> M: All right. We'll go out and look for him. Also, we'll make an announcement about a missing child.
> G: Thank you so much. _____ (A)

09 위 대화의 빈칸 (A)에 들어갈 말로 적절한 것은?

① I hope you'll do well on the exam.
② I hope I'll find him soon.
③ I hope he'll enjoy an announcement about a missing child.
④ I hope so, too.
⑤ My cat is missing.

10 위 대화의 소녀의 남동생에 관한 정보로 일치하지 <u>않는</u> 것은?

① His name is Wally Brown.
② He's five years old.
③ He has brown hair and brown eyes.
④ He's wearing a green shirt and black pants.
⑤ He'll go out and look for a child.

11 다음 대화의 빈칸 (A)에 들어갈 말로 알맞은 것은?

> B: I hear there is a new student in your class.
> G: Yes. She's from Jejudo. Oh, she's over there!
> B: Which one? _____ (A)
> G: She has curly hair and is wearing glasses.

① What does she look like?
② What is she looking for?
③ Where is she?
④ How do you know her?
⑤ Where is she going?

12 주어진 말에 이어질 대화의 순서로 알맞은 것은?

> You look sad. What's wrong, Jongmin?

> (A) What happened?
> (B) She fell off her bike.
> (C) My sister broke her arm this morning.
> (D) That's too bad. I hope she'll get better soon.

① (A) – (B) – (C) – (D)
② (B) – (A) – (C) – (D)
③ (C) – (A) – (B) – (D)
④ (C) – (B) – (A) – (D)
⑤ (D) – (A) – (B) – (C)

Grammar

13 다음 빈칸에 들어갈 말로 어법상 적절한 것을 모두 고르시오.

> _____ John gets a haircut, he will wash his hair.

① Before ② Although ③ If
④ After ⑤ Because

14 지난 토요일에 Emily가 다음 그림 속의 1~3 순서대로 동물들을 보고 왔다. 내용에 맞게 빈칸을 알맞게 채우시오.

(1) Emily saw an elephant before _____ _____.

(2) Emily saw a giraffe _____ she saw a lion.

(3) Emily saw a lion _____.

15 다음 빈칸에 공통으로 들어갈 수 있는 것을 고르시오.

> • Wayne _____ her to take part in the party.
> • Harold _____ to know what was inside the box.

① asked ② wanted
③ invited ④ told
⑤ advised

16 다음 중 어법상 바르지 않은 것은?

① After they finished their homework, Miso and Mijin went out for dinner.
② He persuaded her coming to his party.
③ Before I get an allowance, I do a lot of house chores.
④ Did you make him paint the gate?
⑤ She forced him to give up smoking and drinking.

17 다음 문장을 주어진 단어로 시작하는 문장으로 바꾸어 쓰시오.

(1) Before we watched the movie, we ate ice cream.
➡ After _____
_____.

(2) After I pass the school gate, I untie my hair.
➡ Before _____
_____.

18 다음 문장에서 어법상 잘못된 부분을 바르게 고쳐 문장을 다시 쓰시오.

(1) I will take a photo of myself after I will get a haircut tomorrow.
➡ _____
_____

(2) Fiona wants Andrew doesn't come to the party.
➡ _____
_____

(3) The situation required me have strong belief.
➡ _____
_____

19 다음 빈칸에 들어갈 말로 알맞게 짝지어진 것은?

> • Vida warned her son _____ fast food.
> • Jerome asked me _____ the TV volume.

① not to eat – to turn down

② not eating – to turn down

③ not to eat – turning down

④ not eating – turning down

⑤ not eat – turn down

20 주어진 어휘를 이용하여 영작하시오. (8단어)

> 잠자리에 들기 전에 양치질을 해라. (brush, bed)

➡ _____

Reading

[21~22] 다음 글을 읽고 물음에 답하시오.

> In many ways, 42-year-old Joseph Palmer was an ordinary person. He had a job and cared for his family. But in 1830, after he moved to a small town in Massachusetts, he began to ⓐface difficulties. Joseph looked different from other people: he had a long ____ⓑ____. People did not like it very much.
>
> The town's people avoided the man with a ____ⓑ____. They did not want to sit next to him. They even whispered behind his back, "What is he trying to hide?"

21 위 글의 밑줄 친 ⓐface와 같은 의미로 쓰인 것을 고르시오.

① He buried his face in his hands.

② Look at the north face of the mountain.

③ He didn't face a financial crisis.

④ The face of the clock is covered with a simple glass cover.

⑤ Don't lose your face.

22 주어진 영영풀이를 참고하여 빈칸 ⓑ에 철자 b로 시작하는 단어를 쓰시오.

> the hair that grows on one's chin and cheeks

➡ _____

[23~25] 다음 글을 읽고 물음에 답하시오.

> Some neighbors broke his windows. Others threw stones at him when he walked down the street. They told him to stop growing a beard. Joseph did not mind. He just wanted the freedom ⓐto have his beard.
>
> One day, four men attacked Joseph and threw him on the ground. "We're going to cut off your beard!" they shouted. Joseph was a big man, and he was able to fight them off. But the men called the police and accused him of attacking them. Poor Joseph was arrested. He said to the judge, "I'm the victim here." Sadly, no one believed a man with a beard, and he went to prison for over a year.

23 위 글의 밑줄 친 ⓐto have와 to부정사의 용법이 같은 것을 모두 고르시오.

① Did you want to go there then?

② I have no house to live in.

③ She wants something cold to drink.

④ I'm happy to get the birthday present.

⑤ Jane had the kindness to help me.

24 위 글의 주제로 알맞은 것을 고르시오.

① various cases of bullying in our society

② the judge who sent the victim to prison

③ the importance of the good neighbors

④ unfair behavior towards a man with a beard

⑤ the way to grow a wonderful beard

25 위 글을 읽고 대답할 수 <u>없는</u> 질문은?

① When did some neighbors break Joseph's windows?

② Who told Joseph to stop growing a beard?

③ What did Joseph want?

④ What did Joseph say to the judge?

⑤ How long did Joseph go to prison?

[26~28] 다음 글을 읽고 물음에 답하시오.

Joseph's son, Thomas, wanted people to know the truth. He sent letters to newspapers across the country. People learned that Joseph was in prison just for protecting himself and his beard. Many people became angry about ⓐthis, so the judge finally decided to set Joseph free.

After he was freed, Joseph traveled and told his story to lots of people. Slowly, people's attitudes toward beards changed. Before Joseph died, a man with a beard became the President of the United States. His name was Abraham Lincoln. ⓑHe made beards popular, but Joseph Palmer fought for the right to have it.

26 위 글의 밑줄 친 ⓐthis가 가리키는 것을 본문에서 찾아 쓰시오.

➡ _____

_____

27 위 글의 밑줄 친 ⓑ에서 어법상 틀린 부분을 찾아 고치시오.

➡ _____

28 위 글의 내용과 일치하지 <u>않는</u> 것은?

① Joseph's son sent letters to newspapers across the country.

② Before Joseph traveled and told his story to lots of people, he was freed.

③ Joseph died after Abraham Lincoln became the President of the United States.

④ Joseph Palmer made beards popular.

⑤ Joseph fought for the right to have beards.

[29~30] 다음 독서 기록장을 읽고 물음에 답하시오.

A Story About Joseph Palmer

I read the story about Joseph Palmer last week. I really enjoyed it. I learned from the story that we should not judge people by their appearance. Students who talk about other people's appearance must read the story. ___ⓐ___, I have a question about it. Why did Joseph Palmer want to have a beard?

29 위 독서 기록장의 빈칸 ⓐ에 들어갈 알맞은 말을 고르시오.

① In addition   ② Therefore

③ However   ④ For example

⑤ Moreover

30 위 독서 기록장의 교훈으로 어울리는 속담을 고르시오.

① Too many cooks spoil the broth.

② Make hay while the sun shines.

③ Don't cry over spilt milk.

④ The grass is greener on the other side of the fence.

⑤ Don't judge a book by its cover.

출제율 90%

01 다음 짝지어진 단어의 관계가 같도록 빈칸에 알맞은 말을 쓰시오.

> guilty : innocent = friendly : _____

출제율 95%

02 〈보기〉에서 알맞은 단어를 선택하여 문장을 완성하시오.

┌─ 보기 ┌─
attack   attitude   avoid   whisper

• When a dog tried to (A)_____ me, my cat meowed loudly.
• I like your good (B)_____ : you always look on the bright side.

[03~04] 다음 대화를 읽고 물음에 답하시오.

M: What can I do for you?
G: I lost my younger brother.
M: Okay, ⓐcalm down. What's your brother's name?
G: His name is Wally Brown. He's five years old.
M: ⓑWhat does he look for?
G: He has brown hair and brown eyes.
M: What is he wearing?
G: ⓒHe is wearing a green shirt and black pants.
M: ⓓCan you tell me more?
G: Oh, he is carrying a red backpack.
M: All right. We'll go out and look for him. Also, we'll make an announcement about a missing child.
G: Thank you so much. ⓔI hope I'll find him soon.

출제율 85%

03 How does the girl feel and why? Complete the sentence.

➡ She is _____ because she _____ her younger brother.

출제율 95%

04 위 대화의 밑줄 친 어구의 쓰임이 적절하지 않은 것은?

① ⓐ   ② ⓑ   ③ ⓒ   ④ ⓓ   ⑤ ⓔ

출제율 100%

05 다음 중 짝지어진 대화가 어색한 것을 고르시오.

① A: I lost my puppy this afternoon.
   B: I hope you'll find him soon.
② A: What does your sister look like?
   B: She's a little fat and has long straight hair.
③ A: I plan to go fishing with my uncle on the weekend.
   B: I hope you'll find it soon.
④ A: I'll enter the school dance contest next week. I hope I won't make mistakes.
   B: Don't worry!
⑤ A: What does she look like?
   B: She has an oval face and big black eyes.

[06~07] 다음 대화를 읽고 물음에 답하시오.

Somin: Look at the bulletin board. There are posters for the next school president.
Dain: Yeah, I've already made my choice. I'll vote for Jang Jimin.
Somin: You mean the boy with glasses? He looks smart, but I don't like his promises.
Dain: Then who will you choose?
Somin: Well, I am for number 3, Hong Jiho. She wants to make our school fun and exciting.
Dain: She always has short hair, right?
Somin: Yes, and she looks friendly.

06 위 대화와 포스터를 참고하여 Somin이가 지지하는 후보자에 관한 글을 완성하시오.

3

Hong Jiho

I will _____ _____ Hong Jiho. She has _____ _____. She looks _____. She thinks school should be _____ _____ _____. I agree with her. I like her _____ such as monthly talent shows. I hope Hong Jiho becomes the next school president.

07 위 대화의 내용과 일치하지 <u>않는</u> 것은?

① There will be an election for the next school president.
② Dain supports Jang Jimin.
③ Jimin wears glasses.
④ Somin doesn't like Jimin's promises.
⑤ Hong Jiho is Somin's friend.

[08~09] 다음 글을 읽고 물음에 답하시오.

Hi, I'm Gacha. I'm from Mongolia. When I first came to Songji Middle School two months ago, I was so (A)[happy / worried]. I was a little shy, and I wasn't good at Korean. (B)[However / Moreover], I'm a lucky girl. All my classmates are nice and friendly. I enjoy playing handball with them in P.E. class. I'm a (C)[good / bad] player. They call me "Golden Hand." There will be a sports day next week. I hope my class will win in the handball event.

08 위 글을 읽고 다음 질문의 답을 완성하시오.

> What is Gacha's hope for the sports day?

➡ She _____ her _____ _____
_____ in the _____ event.

09 위 글의 괄호 (A)~(C)에서 알맞은 것을 고르시오.

	(A)	(B)	(C)
①	happy	However	bad
②	happy	Moreover	good
③	worried	Moreover	bad
④	worried	However	good
⑤	worried	However	bad

10 다음 대화의 빈칸 (A)와 (B)에 들어갈 말로 알맞은 것은?

A: What is your character's name?
B: Her name is Prettian.
C: _____ (A) _____
B: She's short and has a big head. She has an oval face and big black eyes.
D: _____ (B) _____
B: She's wearing a blue dress and big earrings.

① (A) What does she look like?
　(B) What is she wearing?
② (A) How does she look like?
　(B) What is she wearing?
③ (A) What does she look like?
　(B) Is she wearing sunglasses?
④ (A) How does she look like?
　(B) Can you tell me more?
⑤ (A) What is she looking at?
　(B) Where is she?

출제율 95%

11 다음 중 어법상 바르지 않은 것은? (2개)

> I am sure ①that he ②will beg me ③ buy ④him a toy when we ⑤will arrive at the shop.

출제율 100%

12 다음 중 어법상 어색한 문장의 개수는?

> ⓐ Sora dropped by her aunt's before she went to school.
> ⓑ Would you like me bringing any food to the party?
> ⓒ Her parents expected her won the contest.
> ⓓ After he had a long trip, he was very tired.
> ⓔ She told him was on time.

① 1개   ② 2개   ③ 3개   ④ 4개   ⑤ 5개

출제율 85%

13 주어진 어휘를 이용하여 다음 우리말을 영작하시오.

(1) 선생님은 내게 문을 닫아달라고 부탁하셨다.
(the teacher, ask, the door)

➡ _____

(2) Dr. Smith는 그녀에게 일찍 잠자리에 들라고 충고했다. (advise, early, go to bed)

➡ _____

(3) 축구 경기가 끝난 후에 선수들은 잔디 위에 누웠다. (the soccer match, the players, on the grass, lie, over)

➡ _____

_____

출제율 90%

14 다음 문장에서 어법상 어색한 부분을 바르게 고쳐 다시 쓰시오.

(1) Judy asked him made sandwiches.

➡ _____

(2) Tom expected Jane be thin.

➡ _____

(3) My advice caused him stop smoking.

➡ _____

[15~16] 다음 글을 읽고 물음에 답하시오.

> In many ways, 42-year-old Joseph Palmer was an ordinary person. He had a job and cared for his family. But in 1830, after he moved to a small town in Massachusetts, he began to face difficulties. ⓐJoseph looked like different from other people: he had a long beard. People did not like it very much.
>
> The town's people avoided ⓑthe man with a beard. They did not want to sit next to him. They even whispered behind his back, "What is he trying to hide?"

출제율 95%

15 위 글의 밑줄 친 ⓐ에서 어법상 틀린 부분을 고치시오.

_____ ➡ _____

출제율 90%

16 위 글의 밑줄 친 ⓑthe man with a beard가 가리키는 것을 본문에서 찾아 쓰시오.

➡ _____

[17~19] 다음 글을 읽고 물음에 답하시오.

> Some neighbors broke his windows. Others threw stones at him when he walked down the street. They told him to stop (A)[growing / to grow] a beard. Joseph did not ⓐmind. He just wanted the freedom (B)[having / to have] his beard.

One day, four men attacked Joseph and threw him on the ground. "We're going to cut off your beard!" they shouted. Joseph was a big man, and he was able to fight them off. But the men called the police and accused him of attacking them. Poor Joseph (C)[arrested / was arrested]. He said to the judge, "I'm the ⓑ_____ here." Sadly, no one believed a man with a beard, and he went to prison for over a year.

출제율 95%

17 위 글의 괄호 (A)~(C)에서 어법상 알맞은 낱말을 골라 쓰시오.

➡ (A) _____ (B) _____ (C) _____

출제율 90%

18 위 글의 밑줄 친 ⓐmind와 같은 의미로 쓰인 것을 고르시오.

① Out of sight, out of mind.
② Never mind! She didn't mean what she said.
③ Keep your mind on your work!
④ I want to meet the greatest mind of the time.
⑤ A sound mind in a sound body.

출제율 95%

19 위 글의 빈칸 ⓑ에 들어갈 알맞은 말을 고르시오.

① attacker ② lawyer ③ prisoner
④ bully ⑤ victim

[20~22] 다음 글을 읽고 물음에 답하시오.

Joseph's son, Thomas, wanted people to know the truth. He sent letters to newspapers across the country. People learned that Joseph was in prison just for protecting himself and his beard. Many people became angry about this, so the judge finally decided to set Joseph free.

After he was freed, Joseph traveled and told his story to lots of people. Slowly, people's attitudes toward beards changed. Before Joseph died, a man with a beard became the President of the United States. His name was Abraham Lincoln. He made beards popular, but Joseph Palmer fought for the right to have them.

출제율 85%

20 본문의 내용과 일치하도록 다음 빈칸 (A)와 (B)에 알맞은 단어를 쓰시오.

(A)_____ _____ finally decided to set Joseph free because many people became angry about the truth that Joseph was in prison just for protecting himself and (B)_____ _____.

출제율 100%

21 위 글의 내용에 이울리는 속담을 고르시오.

① No news is good news.
② The grass is greener on the other side of the fence.
③ Where there is a will, there is a way.
④ Look before you leap.
⑤ Practice makes perfect.

출제율 95%

22 위 글을 읽고 답할 수 없는 것을 고르시오.

① Why did Joseph's son send letters to newspapers across the country?
② What did people learn through the letters?
③ After Joseph was freed, what did he do?
④ How many people changed their attitudes toward beards?
⑤ Who made beards popular?

단원별 예상문제 **49**

01

다음 대화의 빈칸 (A)에 Gacha의 외모를 묻는 말을 쓰시오. (대명사를 이용할 것)

> B: Hi, Minsol. Is your class winning?
> G: Of course. We have a great handball player.
> B: You mean the girl from Mongolia?
> G: Yes, her name is Gacha.
> B: I've heard a lot about her. But ___(A)___
> G: She's very tall and has a ponytail.
> B: Oh, is she the girl who scored the goal just now?
> G: Yes, that's her seventh goal.
> B: Wow, she's really great.

➡ _____

02

다음 글은 학생회장 후보를 지지하는 글이다. 글을 보고 아래의 대화를 완성하시오.

> "I will vote for Han Siwon. She looks confident and smart. She thinks school should be a safe place. I agree with her. I like her promises such as no more bullying. I hope Han Siwon becomes the next school president. I really want my school to be a safer place."

⬇

> G: Look at the bulletin board. There are posters for the next _____ _____.
> B: Yeah, I've already made my choice. I'll _____ for Han Siwon.
> G: She always has a ponytail, right?
> B: Yes. She looks _____ and smart. And she wants to make _____ _____ _____ _____.

03

다음 대화의 밑줄 친 우리말에 맞게 주어진 어휘를 이용하여 문장을 완성하시오.

> A: I have an important exam tomorrow!
> B: (A)나는 네가 시험을 잘 보길 바라. (hope, will, do well)
> A: (B)나도 그러길 바라. (hope, so) Thanks.

➡ (A) _____
    (B) _____

04

다음 문장에서 어법상 어색한 부분을 바르게 고쳐 다시 쓰시오.

(1) My history teacher told us handed in the project by tomorrow.

➡ _____
_____

(2) The teacher warned the students be quiet in class.

➡ _____
_____

(3) Amy's best friend wants her listens to his songs.

➡ _____
_____

(4) Her manager always forces Melanie throwing away the trash.

➡ _____
_____

(5) The doctor encouraged Jack to not give up doing exercise.

➡ _____
_____

05 주어진 어휘를 이용하여 다음 우리말을 영작하시오.

(1) 엄마는 내게 그 개를 산책시키라고 말씀하셨다. (mom, walk the dog)

➡ _____

(2) Mark는 Maria가 복귀할 때까지 그녀의 고객들을 관리할 것이다. (control, customers, return)

➡ _____

06 다음 문장을 주어진 단어로 시작하는 문장으로 바꾸어 쓰시오.

> I set my alarm clock before I went to bed.

➡ After _____ .

[07~09] 다음 글을 읽고 물음에 답하시오.

Some neighbors broke his windows. Others threw stones at him when he walked down the street. They told him to stop growing a beard. Joseph did not mind. He just wanted the ⓐ to have his beard.

One day, four men attacked Joseph and threw him on the ground. "We're going to cut off your beard!" they shouted. ⓑJoseph은 덩치가 큰 사람이었고, 그는 그들을 싸워 물리칠 수 있었다. But the men called the police and accused him of attacking them. Poor Joseph was arrested. He said to the judge, "I'm the victim here." Sadly, no one believed a man with a beard, and he went to prison for over a year.

07 위 글의 빈칸 ⓐ에 free를 알맞은 형태로 쓰시오.

➡ _____

08 위 글의 밑줄 친 ⓑ의 우리말에 맞게 주어진 어휘를 이용하여 13 단어로 영작하시오.

> big, and, able, fight, off

➡ _____

_____

09 위 글의 내용과 일치하도록 다음 빈칸 (A)와 (B)에 알맞은 단어를 쓰시오.

> Though Joseph was a (A)_____ of bullying, he went to prison for over a year because no one believed a man with a (B)_____ .

[10~11] 다음 글을 읽고 물음에 답하시오.

Joseph's son, Thomas, wanted people to know the truth. He sent letters to newspapers across the country. People learned that Joseph was in prison just for (A)[preventing / protecting] himself and his beard. Many people became (B)[angry / angrily] about this, so the judge finally decided to set Joseph (C)[free / freely].

10 위 글의 괄호 (A)~(C)에서 문맥이나 어법상 알맞은 낱말을 골라 쓰시오.

➡ (A) _____ (B) _____ (C) _____

11 다음 질문에 대한 알맞은 대답을 주어진 단어로 시작하여 쓰시오. (10 단어)

> Q: How did people learn that Joseph was in prison just for protecting himself and his beard?
>
> A: They learned it because _____
>
> _____
>
> _____ .

01 (A)에 제시된 어구를 보고 사람의 외모를 묻는 질문과 그에 대한 대답을 쓰고, (B)는 주어진 상황에서 가질 수 있는 적절한 바람을 찾아 쓰시오.

> (A) Minsu – short hair, wearing jeans / Sumi – tall, a ponytail, wearing glasses
>
> (B) [상황] I lost my puppy this afternoon. / I have an important exam tomorrow!
> I'm going to my favorite singer's concert tonight.
>
> [바람] I hope you'll do well on the exam. / I hope you'll find it soon. /
> I hope you have a good time.

02 다음 〈보기〉의 동사와 to부정사를 이용하여 여러 가지 문장을 쓰시오.

> 보기
>
> want   ask   tell   allow   advise   force

(1) _____

(2) _____

(3) _____

(4) _____

(5) _____

(6) _____

03 다음 내용을 바탕으로 인물에 관한 책이나 이야기 중 감명 깊게 읽은 것을 정리하는 글을 쓰시오.

> • 주인공: Steve Jobs   • 교훈: We should think differently.
> • 추천 독자층: young people who study for the future
> • 궁금한 점: How was his middle school life?   • 기억에 남는 문구: Stay hungry. Stay foolish.

> A Story about Steve Jobs
>
> I read a story about Steve Jobs. I really enjoyed (A)_____ his story. I learned from the story that we should think (B)_____. Young people (C)_____ study for the future must read the story. However, I have a question about the story. (D)_____ was his middle school life? I still remember his saying, "(E)_____ Stay foolish."

단원별 모의고사

01 다음 단어에 대한 영어 설명이 <u>어색한</u> 것은?

① victim: someone who has been hurt or killed

② choose: to decide which thing you want

③ attack: an action to try to frighten someone who is smaller or weaker

④ attitude: how you think or feel about something

⑤ arrest: to take the person away to ask them about a crime that they might have committed

02 다음 짝지어진 단어의 관계가 같도록 빈칸에 알맞은 말을 쓰시오.

guilty : innocent = ease : _____

03 다음 영영풀이에 해당하는 단어를 고르시오.

v. drop down to the floor
n. the season between summer and winter

① fall ② continue ③ spring
④ autumn ⑤ face

04 대화의 빈칸에 들어갈 말로 <u>어색한</u> 것은?

A: What is your character's name?
B: His name is Buster.
A: What does he look like?
B: _____
A: Does he have big eyes?
B: Yes, he does.

① He has no hair.

② He's tall and has curly hair.

③ He has brown hair and is wearing glasses.

④ He is very kind and attractive.

⑤ He has a round face and short straight hair.

05 대화의 빈칸에 들어갈 알맞은 말은?

G: You look sad. What's wrong, Jongmin?
B: My sister broke her arm this morning.
G: What happened?
B: She ___(A)___ her bike.
G: That's too bad. I hope she'll ___(B)___ soon.

　　(A)　　　(B)
① broke – get better
② broke – fix it
③ felled – care for herself
④ got off – find him soon
⑤ fell off – get better

06 대화를 알맞은 순서로 배열한 것은?

(A) She has curly hair and is wearing glasses.

(B) I hear there is a new student in your class.

(C) Which one? What does she look like?

(D) Yes. She's from Jejudo. Oh, she's over there!

① (B) – (C) – (A) – (D)
② (B) – (D) – (C) – (A)
③ (C) – (A) – (B) – (D)
④ (C) – (B) – (D) – (A)
⑤ (D) – (C) – (B) – (A)

07 다음 대화의 빈칸에 들어갈 말로 가장 적절한 것은?

> A: I hope you'll do your best in the final game.
> B: Thanks. _____

① I'm a good player.
② I don't like your promises.
③ I wish you the same.
④ I don't like talent shows.
⑤ I hope you'll do well on the exam.

[08~10] 다음 대화를 읽고 물음에 답하시오.

> Man: What can I do for you?
> Girl: I lost my younger brother.
> Man: Okay, calm down. What's your brother's name? (①)
> Girl: His name is Wally Brown. He's five years old.
> Man: What does he look like? (②)
> Girl: He has brown hair and brown eyes.
> Man: What is he wearing? (③)
> Girl: He is wearing a green shirt and black pants.
> Man: _____(A)_____
> Girl: Oh, he is carrying a red backpack. (④)
> Man: All right. We'll go out and look for him. (⑤)
> Girl: Thank you so much. I hope I'll find him soon.

08 위 대화의 빈칸 (A)에 들어갈 말로 가장 자연스러운 것은?

① What does he like?
② Can you tell me more?
③ What does he look like?
④ Do you know where he is?
⑤ Is your brother wearing a blue cap?

09 위 대화의 (①)~(⑤) 중 주어진 문장이 들어갈 위치로 알맞은 것은?

> Also, we'll make an announcement about a missing child.

①   ②   ③   ④   ⑤

10 위 대화를 읽고 추론할 수 없거나 답을 할 수 없는 질문은?

① How does the girl feel?
② Where did the girl lose her brother?
③ Does the girl's brother have black hair?
④ What kind of color is her brother's backpack?
⑤ What will the man do after the dialog?

[11~12] 다음 대화를 읽고 물음에 답하시오.

> B: Hi, Minsol. Is your class winning?
> G: Of course. We have a great handball player.
> B: _____(A)_____
> G: Yes, her name is Gacha.
> B: I've heard a lot about her. But what does she look like?
> G: She's very tall and has a ponytail.
> B: Oh, (B)지금 막 골을 넣은 여자아이가 그녀니?
> G: Yes, that's her seventh goal.
> B: Wow, she's really great.

11 위 대화의 빈칸 (A)에 들어갈 말로 알맞은 것은?

① Who is she?
② What is her name?
③ Do you know where she is from?
④ What will you do for her?
⑤ You mean the girl from Mongolia?

12 위 대화의 밑줄 친 (B)의 우리말에 맞게 주어진 어구를 알맞게 배열하시오.

> she, is, who, the goal, the girl, scored, just now

➡ _____

13 다음 중 어법상 올바른 것은?

① Do you want me clean your house for you?
② He told Perry putting on a penguin shirt.
③ I would like you to explain the accident in more detail.
④ The doctor advised Kathy stopped smoking.
⑤ Ms. Green asked him carries the boxes.

14 다음 중 어법상 <u>이색한</u> 것은?

① I will go straight to the gym after I pass the school gate.
② I will wait for her until she will come back to me.
③ Before she passes the school gate, she ties her hair with a hairband.
④ After he did his homework, he watched TV.
⑤ She will buy a new coat as soon as she receives the money.

15 다음 빈칸에 들어갈 말로 알맞게 짝지어진 것은?

> • Do you expect me _____ up my dreams?
> • The students will ride bikes before they _____ lunch.

① to give – have   ② to give – will have
③ giving – have   ④ giving – will have
⑤ give – had

16 다음 상황에 알맞은 말을 어법에 맞게 빈칸에 쓰시오.

(1) The driver drove his car very fast. He said to the driver, "Don't drive so fast."
➡ He told the driver _____ _____ _____ _____.

(2) Paul is good at playing the guitar. So Bella said to Paul, "Will you play the piano for me?"
➡ Bella asked Paul _____ _____ _____ _____ _____.

17 그림을 참고하여 빈칸을 알맞게 채우시오.

18:00   20:00

➡ Bomi studied history _____.
➡ Bomi had dinner _____.

[18~19] 다음 글을 읽고 물음에 답하시오.

In many ways, 42-year-old Joseph Palmer was an ordinary person. He had a job and cared for his family. But in 1830, after he moved to a small town in Massachusetts, he began to face difficulties. Joseph looked different from other people: he had a long beard. People did not like it very much.

The town's people avoided the man with a beard. They did not want to sit next to him. They even whispered behind his ⓐ , "What is he trying to hide?"

18 다음 질문에 대한 알맞은 대답을 주어진 단어로 시작하여 쓰시오. (5 단어)

> **Q:** Why did Joseph Palmer look different from other people?
>
> **A:** Because _____ .

➡ _____

19 위 글의 빈칸 ⓐ에 들어갈 알맞은 말을 고르시오.

① legs　　② head　　③ hands
④ back　　⑤ shoulders

[20~22] 다음 글을 읽고 물음에 답하시오.

Some neighbors broke his windows. Others threw stones ___ⓐ___ him when he walked down the street. They told him to stop growing a beard. Joseph did not mind. He just wanted the freedom to have his beard.

One day, four men attacked Joseph and threw him on the ground. "We're going to cut off your beard!" they shouted. Joseph was a big man, and he was able to fight ⓑthem off. But the men called the police and accused him ___ⓒ___ attacking them. Poor Joseph was arrested. He said to the ⓓjudge, "I'm the victim here." Sadly, no one believed a man with a beard, and he went to prison for over a year.

20 위 글의 빈칸 ⓐ와 ⓒ에 들어갈 전치사가 바르게 짝지어진 것은?

① at – of　　② in – of　　③ in – from
④ to – in　　⑤ at – by

21 위 글의 밑줄 친 ⓑthem이 가리키는 것을 본문에서 찾아 쓰시오.

➡ _____

22 위 글의 밑줄 친 ⓓjudge와 같은 의미로 쓰인 것을 고르시오.

① Did the court judge him guilty?
② The judge sentenced him to five years in prison.
③ God will judge all men.
④ He is a good judge of wine.
⑤ You must not judge a man by his income.

[23~24] 다음 글을 읽고 물음에 답하시오.

Joseph's son, Thomas, wanted people to know the truth. He sent letters to newspapers across the country. ⓐ사람들은 Joseph이 단지 자신과 자신의 턱수염을 지키려다 감옥에 갇혔다는 것을 알게 되었다. Many people became angry about this, so the judge finally decided to set Joseph free.

After he was freed, Joseph traveled and told his story to lots of people. Slowly, people's attitudes toward beards changed. Before Joseph died, a man with a beard became the President of the United States. His name was Abraham Lincoln. He made beards popular, but Joseph Palmer fought for the right to have them.

23 위 글의 밑줄 친 ⓑ의 우리말에 맞게 한 단어를 보충하여, 주어진 어휘를 알맞게 배열하시오.

> that / people / his beard / Joseph / learned / himself / in prison / and / protecting / just / was

➡ _____
_____

24 Who made beards popular? Answer in English. (three words)

➡ _____

Lesson 6

Near and Dear

🎙 의사소통 기능

- 불만 나타내기
  A: I'm not happy with this restaurant.
  B: What's the problem?
  A: The food is too salty.

- 상기시키기
  A: I'm going to go hiking.
  B: Don't forget to take water.

🎙 언어 형식

- 사역동사
  I will **let** Robby **have** a pet.

- too+형용사/부사+to부정사
  The child is **too** short **to** ride the roller coaster.

Words & Expressions

Key Words

- **bowl** [boul] 명 사발, 그릇
- **catch** [kætʃ] 동 잡다
- **common** [kámən] 형 흔한, 보통의
- **customer service** 고객 지원 (센터)
- **discussion** [diskʌ́ʃən] 명 토론
- **either** [íːðər] (부정문에서) ~도 역시
- **exchange** [ikstʃéindʒ] 명 교환 동 교환하다
- **experience** [ikspíəriəns] 명 경험
- **feed** [fiːd] 동 먹이다
- **forget** [fərgét] 동 잊다, 망각하다
- **guest** [gest] 명 손님
- **hairdryer** [héərdràiər] 명 헤어드라이어
- **lie** [lai] 명 거짓말
- **listener** [lísnər] 명 청취자
- **message** [mésidʒ] 명 전갈, 메시지
- **parent** [péərənt] 명 어버이(아버지 또는 어머니)
- **pour** [pɔːr] 동 쏟다, 붓다
- **promise** [prámis] 동 약속하다
- **puppy** [pʌ́pi] 명 강아지
- **receipt** [risíːt] 명 영수증
- **refund** [rifʌ́nd] 명 환불, 환불금

- **repair** [ripέər] 동 고치다
- **sadness** [sǽdnis] 명 슬픔
- **salty** [sɔ́ːlti] 형 짠
- **scared** [skɛərd] 형 겁먹은
- **secret** [síːkrit] 명 비밀
- **share** [ʃɛər] 동 공유하다
- **stuff** [stʌf] 명 물건
- **suggestion** [səgdʒéstʃən] 명 제안, 의견
- **tear** [tiər] 동 찢다
- **teenage** [tíːneidʒ] 형 십 대의
- **text** [tekst] 동 문자 메시지를 보내다
- **traditional** [trədíʃənl] 형 전통적인
- **training** [tréiniŋ] 명 훈련, 훈육
- **trash** [træʃ] 명 쓰레기
- **truth** [truːθ] 명 진실, 사실
- **understand** [ʌndərstǽnd] 동 이해하다
- **upset** [ʌ́pset] 형 화난
- **wall** [wɔːl] 명 벽
- **without** [wiðáut] 전 ~ 없이
- **work** [wəːrk] 동 (기계가) 작동하다, 일하다
- **wrong** [rɔːŋ] 형 잘못된

Key Expressions

- **be in trouble** 곤경에 처하다
- **be sure to** ~ 반드시 ~하다
- **break down** 부수다
- **drop by** ~에 들르다
- **find out** 발견하다, 알아내다
- **give it a try** 한번 해 보다

- **near and dear** (관계가) 매우 친절한, 소중한
- **not ~ anymore** 더 이상 ~ 아니다
- **on one's own** 혼자 힘으로
- **start off with** ~으로 시작하다
- **take care of** ~을 돌보다, ~을 처리하다
- **tell a lie** 거짓말하다

Word Power

※ 서로 반대되는 뜻을 가진 어휘

- **speaker** (화자) ↔ **listener** (청취자)
- **happy** (행복한) ↔ **unhappy** (불행한)
- **true** (사실의) ↔ **false** (거짓의)
- **tell a lie** (거짓말하다) ↔ **tell the truth** (사실대로 말하다)
- **guest** (손님) ↔ **host** (주인)

- **kind** (친절한) ↔ **unkind** (불친절한)
- **forget** (잊다) ↔ **remember** (기억하다)
- **ancient** (고대의) ↔ **modern** (현대의)
- **wrong** (잘못된) ↔ **right** (올바른)
- **leave** (떠나다) ↔ **arrive** (도착하다)

English Dictionary

- **exchange** 교환하다
  → to give something to somebody and at the same time receive the same type of thing from them
  누군가에게 무언가를 주고 동시에 그들로부터 같은 유형의 것을 받다

- **feed** 먹이다
  to give food to a person or an animal
  사람이나 동물에게 음식을 주다

- **guest** 손님
  → a person that you have invited to your house or to a particular event that you are paying for
  당신의 집이나 당신이 지불하는 특정 행사에 초대된 사람

- **hairdryer** 헤어드라이어
  → a small machine used for drying your hair by blowing hot air over it
  뜨거운 공기를 머리 위로 불어서 당신의 머리를 건조시키기 위해 사용되는 작은 기계

- **listener** 청취자
  → a person who listens
  듣는 사람

- **promise** 약속하다
  → to tell somebody that you will definitely do or not do something, or that something will definitely happen
  누군가에게 당신이 반드시 무언가를 하거나 하지 않을 것이라고, 또는 무언가가 반드시 일어날 것이라고 이야기하다

- **puppy** 강아지
  → a young dog
  어린 개

- **receipt** 영수증
  → a piece of paper that shows that goods or services have been paid for
  상품이나 서비스가 지불되었다는 것을 보여주는 종이 조각

- **refund** 환불
  → a sum of money that is paid back to you, especially because you paid too much or because you returned goods to a shop/store
  당신이 너무 많이 지불했거나 또는 당신이 상품을 가게에 돌려주었기 때문에 당신에게 다시 지불되어야 하는 돈의 합계

- **repair** 고치다
  → to restore something that is broken, damaged or torn to good condition
  부서지거나, 손상되거나 또는 찢어진 무언가를 좋은 상태로 회복시키다

- **secret** 비밀
  → something that is known about by only a few people and not told to others
  오직 몇몇 사람에 의해서만 알려지거나 다른 사람들에게 말하지 않은 것

- **suggestion** 제안
  → an idea or a plan that you mention for somebody else to think about
  당신이 다른 누군가에게 생각해 보도록 언급하는 생각이나 계획

- **text** 문자 메시지를 보내다
  → to send somebody a written message using a mobile/cell phone
  휴대폰을 사용하여 쓴 메시지를 누군가에게 보내다

- **wall** 벽
  → a long vertical solid structure, made of stone, brick or concrete, that surrounds, divides or protects an area of land
  한 지역의 땅을 감싸거나, 나누거나 또는 보호하는 돌, 벽돌, 또는 콘크리트로 만들어진 길고 수직의 견고한 구조물

서답형

01 다음 짝지어진 단어의 관계가 같도록 빈칸에 알맞은 말을 쓰시오.

> wrong : right = speaker : _____

02 다음 영영풀이가 가리키는 것을 고르시오.

> a sum of money that is paid back to you, especially because you paid too much or because you returned goods to a shop/store

① repair ② refund
③ promise ④ share
⑤ tear

03 다음 중 밑줄 친 부분의 뜻풀이가 바르지 않은 것은?

① Don't <u>forget</u> to bring your helmet. 잊다
② Would you like my old TV in <u>exchange</u> for this camera? 환불
③ There were 20 <u>guests</u> at the party. 손님들
④ My <u>hairdryer</u> was broken, so I needed a new one. 헤어드라이어
⑤ The radio program has lots of young <u>listeners</u>. 청취자들

서답형

04 다음 문장의 빈칸에 들어갈 말을 〈보기〉에서 골라 쓰시오.

> ┤ 보기 ├
> take care of / drop by / break down / find out / start off with

(1) I will _____ your office tomorrow morning.

(2) Can you _____ those problems?
(3) Some day he will _____ the truth.
(4) You can _____ some movie clips.
(5) The fire fighters _____ the door to get into the house.

05 다음 주어진 문장의 밑줄 친 text와 같은 의미로 쓰인 것은?

> Text me when you get there.

① My job is to find out the errors on the <u>text</u>.
② I'll <u>text</u> you the final score.
③ The newspaper printed the full <u>text</u> of the President's speech.
④ Read the <u>text</u> carefully and answer the questions.
⑤ Have you ever read the medical <u>text</u>?

서답형

06 다음 문장의 빈칸에 들어갈 말을 〈보기〉에서 골라 쓰시오.

> ┤ 보기 ├
> suggestions / without / either / stuff / leave

(1) We cannot live _____ computers now.
(2) Can you remove all the _____ on your desk?
(3) Can I _____ a message for Mr. Winter?
(4) Yuri can't go to the party, and I can't _____.
(5) I have some _____ for you.

01 다음 짝지어진 단어의 관계가 같도록 빈칸에 알맞은 말을 쓰시오.

leave : arrive = forget : _____

02 다음 우리말에 맞게 빈칸에 알맞은 말을 쓰시오.

(1) 경찰들은 규칙적으로 훈련을 받아야 한다.
➡ Police officers should receive _____ regularly.

(2) 아이들을 먼저 먹이고 나중에 우리의 저녁을 먹자.
➡ Let's _____ the kids first and have our dinner later.

(3) 그 회사는 좋은 고객 지원 센터로 유명하다.
➡ The company is famous for its good _____.

03 다음 문장의 빈칸에 들어갈 말을 〈보기〉에서 골라 쓰시오.

┌─ 보기 ─┐
text / wall / secret / sharing / experience
└───────┘

(1) When I was young, I didn't like _____ a room with my sister.
(2) The war was a terrible _____ for everyone.
(3) There was a high _____ around the house.
(4) I won't tell anyone your _____.
(5) Can you _____ me the information now?

04 다음 우리말에 맞게 주어진 단어를 사용하여 영작하시오.

(1) 당신의 주문 영수증을 보여 주시겠어요? (order, can)
➡ _____

(2) 그들은 내가 구매한 물건 값을 전액 환불해 주었다. (full, purchase)
➡ _____

(3) Jessie는 그 소식을 비밀로 하겠다고 약속했다. (a secret, keep)
➡ _____

05 다음 우리말과 일치하도록 주어진 단어를 모두 배열하여 영작하시오.

(1) 당신은 새로운 언어를 공부하기 시작할 때, 약간의 어휘부터 시작해야 한다.
(should / when / with / you / you / a / language / off / new / start / some / study / vocabulary)
➡ _____

(2) 만약 네가 친구들에게 거짓말을 하면, 너는 그들을 잃을 수도 있다.
(friends / can / you / them / if / lose / a / lie / your / tell / to / you)
➡ _____

(3) 벽을 부수기 위해 내가 무엇을 해야 하나요?
(the / do / to / what / I / down / wall / should / break)
➡ _____

Conversation

교과서

① 불만 나타내기

> **A** I'm not happy with this restaurant. 나는 이 식당이 마음에 들지 않아.
>
> **B** What's the problem? 문제가 무엇이야?
>
> **A** The food is too salty. 음식이 너무 짜.

■ 불만을 나타낼 때 'I'm not happy with ~' 표현을 사용하여 나타낼 수 있다. 불만을 나타내는 말에 'What's the problem?', 'What's the matter?' 또는 'What's wrong with you?' 등을 사용하여 불만의 구체적인 이유를 물을 수 있다.

불만 나타내기

- I'm not happy with this computer. 나는 이 컴퓨터가 마음에 들지 않아.

- I want to complain about the noise from upstairs. 나는 윗층에서 나는 소음에 대해 불평하고 싶어요.

- I'm sorry to say this, but the waiters in this restaurant aren't very polite.
  이런 말해서 미안하지만, 이 식당의 웨이터들이 별로 공손하지 않네요.

- I've got a complaint about this restaurant. 이 식당에 대해 불만이 있어요.

핵심 Check

1. 다음 우리말과 일치하도록 빈칸에 알맞은 말을 쓰시오.

(1) **A:** I'm not _____ with this hair salon. (이 미용실이 마음에 들지 않네요.)

  B: What's _____ ? (문제가 무엇이에요?)

  A: I waited too long. (나는 너무 오래 기다렸어요.)

(2) **A:** I want to _____ about the plate in this restaurant.

  (나는 이 식당의 접시에 대해 불평하고 싶어요.)

  B: What's the _____ ? (문제가 무엇이죠?)

  A: The plate isn't clean. (접시가 깨끗하지 않아요.)

2 상기시키기

A I'm going to go hiking. 나는 하이킹을 갈 거야.

B Don't forget to take water. 물을 가져가는 것을 잊지 마.

■ 'Don't forget to ~'는 상대방에게 어떤 일을 해야 한다고 알려주거나 해야 할 일을 상기시켜 주기 위해 사용하는 표현으로 'Remember to + 동사원형' 또는 'Make sure that 주어 + 동사' 또는 'Be sure to + 동사원형' 등으로 바꾸어 쓸 수 있다.

상기시키기

• Don't forget to finish your report. 네 보고서를 끝마치는 것을 잊지 마.

• Remember to bring your homework tomorrow. 내일 네 숙제를 가져와야 하는 것을 기억해라.

• Be sure to drive slowly. 반드시 천천히 운전해야 해.

■ forget이나 remember 뒤에 -ing를 쓰면 '(과거에) ~했던 것을 잊다 또는 기억하다'라는 의미가 되고, 'to+동사원형'을 쓰면 '(미래에) ~해야 할 것을 잊다, 또는 기억하다'라는 의미를 나타낸다.

• forget + -ing: (과거에) ~했던 것을 잊다

• forget + to 동사원형: (미래에) ~해야 할 것을 잊다

• remember + -ing: (과거에) ~했던 것을 기억하다

• remember + to 동사원형: (미래에) ~해야 할 것을 기억하다

핵심 Check

2. 다음 우리말과 일치하도록 빈칸에 알맞은 말을 쓰시오.

(1) **A:** _____ _____ _____ take your umbrella. (너의 우산을 가져갈 것을 잊지 마라.)

B: Okay, I see. (응. 알겠어.)

(2) **A:** It looks like it's going to rain soon. _____ _____ close the windows.

(곧 비가 올 것 같아. 창문을 닫아야 한다는 것을 기억해라.)

B: Okay, I will. (응. 그럴게.)

(3) **A:** I'm going skating. (나는 스케이트를 타러 갈 거야.)

B: Be _____ _____ put gloves on. (반드시 장갑을 껴야 해.)

Communication Listen – Dialog 1

Minsol: ❶I'm not happy with Buster.

Dad: What's wrong?

Minsol: He ❷tore my homework into pieces again.

Dad: Puppies often do ❸that.

Minsol: This is not the first time. Sometimes I find my socks in the dog house.

Dad: Please be kind to ❹him. ❹He's just five months old.

Minsol: You're too nice to ❹him! ❹He needs some training.

Dad: Okay. Let's start ❺training in a few weeks.

Minsol: 저는 Buster가 마음에 들지 않아요.

Dad: 무엇이 문제니?

Minsol: Buster가 또다시 제 숙제를 찢어 놓았어요.

Dad: 강아지들은 종종 그런 일을 저지르지.

Minsol: 이번이 처음이 아니에요. 가끔 저는 제 양말을 개집에서 찾기도 해요.

Dad: Buster에게 잘해 주렴. 태어난 지 다섯 달 밖에 안 되었잖니.

Minsol: 아빠는 그를 너무 다정하게 대해 주세요! 그에게는 훈련이 좀 필요해요.

Dad: 좋아. 몇 주 뒤에 훈련을 시작해 보자꾸나.

❶ I'm not happy with ~: '나는 ~가 마음에 들지 않는다'라는 의미로 불만족을 나타내는 표현이다.
❷ tear 찢다 – tore (과거형) – torn (과거분사형)
❸ that은 숙제를 찢어 놓은 것을 가리킨다.
❹ him과 He 모두 Buster를 가리킨다.
❺ start는 동명사와 to부정사를 모두 목적어로 취할 수 있다.

Check(√) True or False

(1) Minsol feels bad because of Buster.   T ☐ F ☐

(2) Dad is angry because Buster tore his socks.   T ☐ F ☐

Communication: Listen – Listen More

(The phone rings.)

Mike: Customer Service. ❶How can I help you?

Sora: I bought a hairdryer at your store last week. I'm not happy with ❷it.

Mike: What is the problem?

Sora: It doesn't work well. I mean the air isn't hot enough.

Mike: I'm sorry. Do you want to ❸exchange it?

Sora: Well, can I get a ❹refund?

Mike: Sure. Will you please visit our store with the dryer?

Sora: Yes, I'll ❺drop by tomorrow afternoon.

Mike: Don't forget to bring the ❻receipt.

Sora: Okay. Thanks.

(전화벨이 울린다.)

Mike: 고객 센터입니다. 어떻게 도와드릴까요?

Sora: 제가 지난주에 가게에서 헤어드라이어를 샀는데요. 마음에 들지 않네요.

Mike: 무엇이 문제인가요?

Sora: 작동이 잘되지 않아요. 제 말은 충분히 뜨거운 바람이 나오질 않는다는 거예요.

Mike: 죄송합니다. 교환을 원하시나요?

Sora: 음. 환불받을 수 있을까요?

Mike: 물론이죠. 드라이어를 가지고 저희 가게를 방문해 주시겠어요?

Sora: 네. 내일 오후에 들를게요.

Mike: 영수증 가지고 오시는 걸 잊지 마세요.

Sora: 네. 고맙습니다.

❶ 도움을 제공할 때 쓰는 표현으로 'What can I do for you?' 등으로 바꾸어 쓸 수 있다.
❷ it은 지난주에 산 헤어드라이어를 가리킨다.
❸ exchange: 교환하다   ❹ refund: 환불
❺ drop by: ~에 들르다   ❻receipt: 영수증

Check(√) True or False

(3) Sora is not satisfied with the hairdryer that she bought last week.   T ☐ F ☐

(4) Sora doesn't need to bring the receipt to get a refund.   T ☐ F ☐

Communication: Listen – Dialog 2

Mom: Minsu, I'm ❶going out with your dad for a movie.

Minsu: When will you ❷be back, Mom?

Mom: ❸Around 8 o'clock. Don't forget to ❹feed Buster.

Minsu: Okay.

Mom: ❺Be sure to give him some water, too.

Minsu: No problem.

Mom: One more thing. Can you help Minsol with her science homework? Buster tore her homework into pieces.

Minsu: Hmm .... Okay. I'll do ❻that.

❶ go out: 외출하다, 나가다
❷ be back: 돌아오다
❸ around: 약, ~쯤
❹ feed: 먹이다
❺ be sure to: 반드시 ~하다
❻ that은 민솔이의 과학 숙제를 도와주는 것을 가리킨다.

❶ 같은 뜻의 표현으로 What's wrong?을 쓸 수 있다.
❷ for too long: 너무 오랫동안
❸ 상대방이 기분에 공감할 때 쓰는 표현으로 'I understand how you feel.'로 바꾸어 쓸 수 있다.
❹ get up과 병렬 구조를 나타낸다.
❺ give it a try: 한번 해 보다, 시도하다

Wrap Up – Listening ❺

G: You ❶look upset, Tommy.

B: I'm not happy with Sojin.

G: ❷What's wrong with her?

B: She isn't doing her ❸part of the group project.

G: ❹I think you should talk to her.

❶ look+형용사: ~처럼 보이다
❷ 문제가 무엇인지 묻는 질문으로 'What's the matter with her?' 또는 'What's the problem?' 등으로 바꾸어 쓸 수 있다.
❸ part: 역할
❹ 조언을 히는 표현으로 'In my opinion, you need to talk to her.' 또는 'I advise you to talk to her.' 등으로 바꾸어 쓸 수 있다.

My Speaking Portfolio – Step 3

A: I'm not very happy with my brother.

B: ❶What's the problem?

A: He uses the bathroom ❷for too long in the morning.

B: ❸I know how you feel.

A: What can I do?

B: Well, you can get up earlier and ❹use the bathroom first.

A: Okay, I'll ❺give it a try.

Wrap Up – Listening ❻

M: ❶Are you ready for your trip, Suji?

G: Yes, I am, Dad. ❷I'm ready to leave.

M: Do you have your ticket with you?

G: Yeah, I have ❸it on my phone.

M: Good. Don't forget to call me when you ❹ get to the train station.

G: Sure.

❶ be ready for: ~의 준비가 되다
❷ be ready to ~: ~할 준비가 되다
❸ it은 'the ticket'을 가리킨다.
❹ get to: ~에 도착하다

● 다음 우리말과 일치하도록 빈칸에 알맞은 말을 쓰시오.

Communication: Listen – Dialog 1

Minsol: I'm not _____ with Buster.

Dad: What's _____?

Minsol: He _____ my homework into _____ again.

Dad: Puppies often do _____.

Minsol: This is not the first time. Sometimes I find my _____ in the dog house.

Dad: Please be _____ to him. He's just _____ _____ old.

Minsol: You're _____ nice _____ him! He needs some _____.

Dad: Okay. Let's _____ _____ in a few weeks.

Communication: Listen – Dialog 2

Mom: Minsu, I'm _____ _____ with your dad for a movie.

Minsu: When will you be _____, Mom?

Mom: Around 8 o'clock. Don't forget _____ _____ Buster.

Minsu: Okay.

Mom: Be _____ to give him some water, too.

Minsu: No _____.

Mom: One _____ _____. Can you _____ Minsol _____ her science homework? Buster _____ her homework into pieces.

Minsu: Hmm .... Okay. I'll do that.

Communication: Listen – Listen More

(The phone rings.)

Mike: Customer Service. _____ can I _____ _____?

Sora: I bought a _____ at your _____ last week. I'm not _____ with it.

Mike: What is _____ _____?

Sora: It doesn't _____ well. I mean the air isn't hot _____.

Mike: I'm sorry. Do you want to _____ it?

Sora: Well, can I get a _____?

Mike: Sure. Will you please _____ our _____ with the dryer?

Sora: Yes, I'll _____ tomorrow afternoon.

Mike: Don't forget to bring the _____.

Sora: Okay. Thanks.

해석

Minsol: 저는 Buster가 마음에 들지 않아요.

Dad: 무엇이 문제니?

Minsol: Buster가 또 제 숙제를 찢어 놓았어요.

Dad: 강아지들은 종종 그런 일을 저지르지.

Minsol: 이번이 처음이 아니에요. 가끔 저는 제 양말을 개집에서 찾기도 해요.

Dad: Buster에게 잘해 주렴. 태어난 지 다섯 달 밖에 안 되었잖니.

Minsol: 아빠는 그를 너무 다정하게 대해 주세요! 그에게는 훈련이 좀 필요해요.

Dad: 좋아. 몇 주 뒤에 훈련을 시작해 보자꾸나.

Mom: 민수야, 엄마는 아빠랑 영화 보러 나간다.

Minsu: 언제 돌아오실 거예요, 엄마?

Mom: 8시쯤. Buster에게 밥 주는 것 잊지 말렴.

Minsu: 네.

Mom: 물도 꼭 주려무나.

Minsu: 그럴게요.

Mom: 한 가지 더. 민솔이 과학 숙제를 도와줄 수 있겠니? Buster가 민솔이의 숙제를 찢어 놓았거든.

Minsu: 음 …. 알겠어요. 그렇게 할게요.

(전화벨이 울린다.)

Mike: 고객 센터입니다. 어떻게 도와드릴까요?

Sora: 제가 지난주에 가게에서 헤어드라이어를 샀는데요. 마음에 들지 않네요.

Mike: 무엇이 문제인가요?

Sora: 작동이 잘되지 않아요. 제 말은 충분히 뜨거운 바람이 나오질 않는다는 거예요.

Mike: 죄송합니다. 교환을 원하시나요?

Sora: 음. 환불받을 수 있을까요?

Mike: 물론이죠. 드라이어를 가지고 저희 가게를 방문해 주시겠어요?

Sora: 네. 내일 오후에 들를게요.

Mike: 영수증 가지고 오시는 걸 잊지 마세요.

Sora: 네. 고맙습니다.

My Speaking Portfolio – Step 3

A: I'm _____ _____ _____ with my brother.

B: What's _____ _____ ?

A: He uses the _____ for too long in the morning.

B: I know _____ you _____.

A: What _____ I do?

B: Well, you can _____ _____ earlier and use the bathroom first.

A: Okay, I'll _____ it _____ _____.

해석

A: 나는 내 남동생이 별로 마음에 들지 않아.
B: 뭐가 문제니?
A: 그는 아침에 너무 오랫동안 욕실을 사용해.
B: 네 기분이 어떤지 알아.
A: 내가 무엇을 할 수 있을까?
B: 음, 너는 더 일찍 일어나서 욕실을 먼저 사용할 수 있어.
A: 알겠어, 내가 한번 해 볼게.

Wrap Up – Listening ❺

G: You look _____, Tommy.

B: I'm not _____ _____ Sojin.

G: What's _____ with her?

B: She isn't doing her _____ of the group project.

G: I think you _____ talk _____ her.

여: Tommy야, 기분이 안 좋아 보이는구나.
남: 나는 소진이 때문에 속상해.
여: 그 애에게 무슨 문제가 있니?
남: 그 애가 모둠 과제에서 맡은 일을 안 해.
여: 내 생각에 너는 그 애랑 이야기를 해 봐야 할 것 같아.

Wrap Up – Listening ❻

M: Are you ready for your _____, Suji?

G: Yes, I am, Dad. I'm _____ to leave.

M: Do you have your _____ with you?

G: Yeah, I have it _____ _____ _____.

M: Good. _____ _____ _____ _____ me when you _____ _____ the train station.

G: _____.

남: 여행 갈 준비 되었니, 수지야?
여: 네, 아빠. 저는 떠날 준비가 되었어요.
남: 표는 네가 가지고 있고?
여: 네, 제 전화기에 저장해 놓았어요.
남: 잘했구나. 기차역에 도착하면 내게 전화하는 걸 잊지 말렴.
여: 물론이죠.

[01~02] 다음 대화를 읽고 물음에 답하시오.

Mike: Customer Service. How can I help you?

Sora: I bought a hairdryer at your store last week. I'm not happy with it.

Mike: What is the problem? (A)

Sora: It doesn't work well. (B)

Mike: I'm sorry. Do you want to exchange it? (C)

Sora: Well, can I get a refund? (D)

Mike: Sure. Will you please visit our store with the dryer? (E)

Sora: Yes, I'll drop by tomorrow afternoon.

Mike: Don't forget to bring the receipt.

Sora: Okay. Thanks.

01 위 대화의 (A)~(E) 중 주어진 문장이 들어가기에 적절한 곳은?

> I mean the air isn't hot enough.

① (A)　　② (B)　　③ (C)　　④ (D)　　⑤ (E)

02 위 대화를 읽고 대답할 수 <u>없는</u> 것은?

① What did Sora buy at Mike's store last week?

② What was the matter with Sora's hairdryer?

③ What does Sora want Mike to do?

④ What should Sora bring to get a refund?

⑤ What is Sora going to exchange with her hairdryer?

03 다음 대화가 자연스럽게 이어지도록 순서대로 배열하시오.

> I'm not very happy with my brother.

(A) What can I do?

(B) What's the problem?

(C) I know how you feel.

(D) He uses the bathroom for too long in the morning.

(E) Well, you can get up earlier and use the bathroom first.

➡ _____

[01~03] 다음 대화를 읽고 물음에 답하시오.

Minsol: I'm not happy with Buster.

Dad: What's wrong?

Minsol: He tore my homework into pieces again.

Dad: Puppies often do that.

Minsol: This is not the first time. Sometimes I find my socks in the dog house.

Dad: Please be kind to him. He's just five months old.

Minsol: _____(A)_____ He needs some training.

Dad: Okay. Let's start training in a few weeks.

01 위 대화의 빈칸 (A)에 들어갈 말로 알맞은 것은?

① How kind you are!

② You're too nice to him!

③ He is too young to train a lot.

④ He is growing up so fast.

⑤ You need to keep your socks in your closet.

02 위 대화에서 나타난 Minsol의 기분으로 적절한 것은?

① excited   ② happy

③ nervous   ④ unpleased

⑤ satisfied

03 위 대화의 내용과 일치하지 <u>않는</u> 것은?

① Minsol은 Buster 때문에 기분이 좋지 않다.

② Buster는 Minsol의 숙제를 또 다시 찢어 놓았다.

③ Minsol은 가끔 양말을 개집에서 찾기도 한다.

④ Buster는 5살 되었다.

⑤ Minsol은 Buster가 훈련이 필요하다고 생각한다.

[04~06] 다음 대화를 읽고 물음에 답하시오.

Mom: Minsu, I'm going out with your dad for a movie.

Minsu: When will you be back, Mom?

Mom: Around 8 o'clock. Don't forget to feed Buster.

Minsu: Okay.

Mom: (a)Be sure to give him some water, too.

Minsu: No problem.

Mom: _____(A)_____ Can you help Minsol with her science homework? Buster tore her homework into pieces.

Minsu: Hmm .... Okay. I'll do that.

04 위 대화의 빈칸 (A)에 들어갈 말로 적절한 것은?

① One more thing   ② Conversely

③ However   ④ Therefore

⑤ On the other hand

05 위 대화의 밑줄 친 (a)와 바꾸어 쓸 수 있는 것을 <u>모두</u> 고르시오.

① Don't forget to give him some water, too.

② I'm doubtful if you can give him some water, too.

③ I'm curious if you can give him some water, too.

④ Remember to give him some water, too.

⑤ Do you want to give him some water, too?

서답형

06 위 대화에서 엄마가 부탁한 일의 목록을 완성하시오.

< To Do List>		
1	(A)_____ Buster	
2	Give (B)_____ to Buster	
3	Help Minsol with (C)_____	

[07~08] 다음 대화를 읽고 물음에 답하시오.

Amy: I'm not very happy with my brother.

Brian: What's the problem?

Amy: He uses the bathroom for too long in the morning.

Brian: I know ___(A)___ you feel.

Amy: What can I do?

Brian: Well, (B)you can get up earlier and use the bathroom first.

Amy: Okay, I'll give it a try.

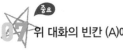

07 위 대화의 빈칸 (A)에 알맞은 말을 쓰시오.

➡ _____

08 위 대화의 밑줄 친 (B)와 바꾸어 쓸 수 없는 것은?

① how about getting up earlier and using the bathroom first?

② why don't you get up earlier and use the bathroom first?

③ I advise you to get up earlier and use the bathroom first.

④ I think you should get up earlier and use the bathroom first.

⑤ I'm wondering why you should get up earlier and use the bathroom first.

09 다음 대화가 자연스럽게 이어지도록 순서대로 배열하시오.

(A) What's wrong with her?

(B) I'm not happy with Sojin.

(C) I think you should talk to her.

(D) You look upset, Tommy.

(E) She isn't doing her part of the group project.

➡ _____

[10~11] 다음 대화를 읽고 물음에 답하시오.

Dad: Are you ready for your trip, Suji?

Suji: Yes, I am, Dad. (A) 저는 떠날 준비가 되었어요. (leave)

Dad: Do you have your ticket with you?

Suji: Yeah, I have it on my phone.

Dad: Good. Don't forget to call me when you get to the train station.

Suji: Sure.

서답형

10 위 대화의 밑줄 친 (A)의 우리말을 주어진 말을 써서 영작하시오.

➡ _____

11 위 대화의 내용과 일치하지 않는 것은?

① 수지는 떠날 준비가 되었다.

② 수지는 표를 전화기에 저장해 놓았다.

③ 수지는 기차를 탈 것이다.

④ 수지는 도착하면 아빠에게 전화를 할 것이다.

⑤ 수지는 기차역에서 표를 구매할 것이다.

12 다음 중 짝지어진 대화가 어색한 것은?

① A: I'm not happy with the science class. It's too boring.
   B: Same here. I hope it gets more exciting.

② A: I don't like this shirt. It's too small.
   B: Too small? You can exchange it at the mall.

③ A: Don't forget to finish your report.
   B: Okay. I won't forget.

④ A: It's raining heavily.
   B: Yes. Don't forget to drive slowly.

⑤ A: I'm going to walk my dog.
   B: Don't forget to bring your homework.

[01~02] 다음 대화를 읽고 물음에 답하시오.

Dad: Are you ready for your trip, Suji?

Suji: Yes, I am, Dad. I'm ready to leave.

Dad: Do you have your ticket with you?

Suji: Yeah, I have it on my phone.

Dad: Good. Don't forget to call me when you get to the train station.

Suji: Sure.

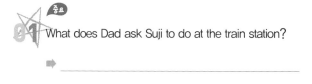

01 What does Dad ask Suji to do at the train station?

➡ _____

02 Where does Suji keep the ticket?

➡ _____

[03~05] 다음 대화를 읽고 물음에 답하시오.

Mom: Minsu, I'm going out with your dad for a movie.

Minsu: When will you be back, Mom?

Mom: Around 8 o'clock. Don't forget to feed Buster.

Minsu: Okay.

Mom: Be sure to give him some water, too.

Minsu: No problem.

Mom: One more thing. Can you help Minsol with her science homework? Buster tore her homework into pieces.

Minsu: Hmm .... Okay. I'll do that.

03 When will Minsu's mom come back?

➡ _____

04 What should Minsu do for Buster?

➡ _____

05 Why does Minsu's mom ask him to help Minsol with her homework?

➡ _____

06 다음 대화의 내용과 일치하도록 고객 상담 카드를 완성하시오.

Mike: Customer Service. How can I help you?

Sora: I bought a hairdryer at your store last week. I'm not happy with it.

Mike: What is the problem?

Sora: It doesn't work well. I mean the air isn't hot enough.

Mike: I'm sorry. Do you want to exchange it?

Sora: Well, can I get a refund?

Mike: Sure. Will you please visit our store with the dryer?

Sora: Yes, I'll drop by tomorrow afternoon.

Mike: Don't forget to bring the receipt.

Sora: Okay. Thanks.

<Customer Service>	
Customer Information	Name: Han Sora
Item	(A) _____
Problem	(B) _____
Request	(C) _____

07 다음 대화의 밑줄 친 우리말을 주어진 단어를 써서 영작하시오.

A: 나는 학교 점심 메뉴가 마음에 들지 않아요. (happy) I like the meat, but there isn't enough meat for me.

B: How about taking your own lunch box?

➡ _____

Grammar

① 사역동사

> • He **made** his sister **do** the dishes. 그는 여동생이 설거지를 하게 했다.
>
> • Alicia **had** me **find** her car key. Alicia는 내가 그녀의 자동차 열쇠를 찾게 했다.

■ 사역동사는 문장의 주어가 목적어에게 어떠한 행동을 하도록 시키는 동사로 make, have, let 등이 이에 속한다.

- Gloria **had** us **sing** together. Gloria는 우리가 함께 노래를 하게 했다.
- Paul **made** his wife **think** carefully. Paul은 그의 아내가 주의 깊게 생각하게 했다.
- I **let** him **use** my smartphone. 나는 그가 내 스마트폰을 사용하게 했다.

■ 사역동사는 5형식에 속하여 목적격 보어를 갖는데, 사역동사의 목적격 보어는 동사원형의 형태를 취하며, '~에게 …을 하게 하다'라고 해석한다.

- The teacher **made** us **help** each other. 선생님은 우리가 서로를 돕게 하셨다.
- Mom **made** me **cook** ramyeon for Dad. 엄마는 내가 아빠를 위해 라면을 끓이게 하셨다.
- Mr. Park **had** me **finish** the project by five. 박 선생님은 내가 그 프로젝트를 다섯 시까지 끝내게 하셨다.
- We **let** them **play** on the garden. 우리는 그들이 정원에서 놀게 했다.

■ 준사역동사인 help는 목적격 보어로 to부정사나 동사원형 형태를 취한다.

- David **helped** the woman **(to) cross** the road. David는 그 여성이 길을 건너는 것을 도와주었다.

■ 목적어와 목적격 보어의 관계가 수동인 경우 have와 get은 목적격 보어로 과거분사를 쓰며, let은 목적격 보어로 'be+p.p.' 형태를 쓴다.

- I **had** my car **fixed**. 나는 내 차가 수리되게 했다.
- **Let** it **be done** as they ask. 그들이 요청하는 대로 되게 하여라.

핵심 Check

1. 다음 우리말과 일치하도록 빈칸에 알맞은 말을 쓰시오.

(1) 그들은 우리가 최선을 다하게 만든다.

➡ They make us ＿＿＿＿ ＿＿＿＿ ＿＿＿＿.

(2) 그 남자는 우리가 그의 개를 찾게 했다.

➡ The man made ＿＿＿＿ ＿＿＿＿ ＿＿＿＿ ＿＿＿＿.

(3) 우리는 그 남자가 혼자 힘으로 설 수 있도록 도왔다.

➡ We ＿＿＿＿ the man ＿＿＿＿ on his own.

② too+형용사/부사+to부정사

- I am **too** tired **to** work more. 나는 너무 피곤해서 더 이상 일을 할 수 없다.
- This table is **too** heavy **to** move. 이 탁자는 옮기기에 너무 무겁다.

■ 'too ~ to V'는 '너무 ~해서 V할 수 없는'이라는 의미이다.
  - He is **too** young **to** ride the bike. 그는 너무 어려서 자전거를 탈 수 없어.

■ 'too ~ to V'는 'so ~ that 주어 can't 동사원형'으로 바꾸어 쓸 수 있다.
  - This soup is **too** salty **to** eat.
    = This soup is **so** salty **that** I can't eat it. 이 수프는 너무 짜서 먹을 수 없다.
  - Molly is **too** lazy **to** take the job.
    = Molly is **so** lazy **that** she can't take the job. Molly는 너무 게을러서 그 일자리를 잡을 수 없다.

■ 반면, '충분히 ~해서 …할 수 있다'는 의미를 나타낼 때에는 '형용사/부사+enough+to부정사'를 쓰고, 이는 'so+형용사/부사+that+주어+can+동사원형'과 같다.
  - The man is diligent **enough to** do the work.
    = The man is **so** diligent **that** he can do the work. 그 남자는 그 일을 할 만큼 충분히 부지런하다.
  - This house is warm **enough to** live in.
    = This house is **so** warm **that** we can live in it. 그 집은 살기에 충분히 따뜻해.
  - These roses are beautiful **enough to** attract many people.
    = These roses are **so** beautiful **that** they can attract many people.
    이 장미들은 많은 사람들을 끌어 모으기에 충분히 아름답다.

핵심 Check

2. 다음 우리말과 일치하도록 빈칸에 알맞은 말을 쓰시오.
  (1) 그는 너무 피곤해서 나와 대화할 수 없어.
    ➡ He is ＿＿＿＿ ＿＿＿＿ ＿＿＿＿ ＿＿＿＿ with me.
    ➡ He is ＿＿＿＿ ＿＿＿＿ ＿＿＿＿ ＿＿＿＿ ＿＿＿＿ with me.
  (2) 나는 너를 데리러 가기에 충분할 만큼 운전을 잘해.
    ➡ I drive ＿＿＿＿ ＿＿＿＿ ＿＿＿＿ ＿＿＿＿ you up.
    ➡ I drive ＿＿＿＿ ＿＿＿＿ ＿＿＿＿ ＿＿＿＿ ＿＿＿＿ you up.

01 다음 문장에서 어법상 <u>어색한</u> 부분을 바르게 고쳐 쓰시오.

(1) The sisters made me to buy the car.

_____ ➡ _____

(2) I had my sister fixed dinner.

_____ ➡ _____

(3) This chance is too good to missing.

_____ ➡ _____

(4) She is too sleepy that drive.

_____ ➡ _____

02 괄호 안에 주어진 단어를 어법에 맞게 바르게 배열하시오.

(1) Mom didn't let _____. (play / me / go out / and)

(2) Dad _____ my room every day. (clean / me / made)

(3) He didn't _____ home early. (go / me / let)

(4) Mr. Han is _____. (drive / tired / to / too)

(5) She was _____ she couldn't go to the party. (that / busy / so)

03 주어진 어구를 바르게 배열하여 다음 우리말을 영어로 쓰시오. 필요하다면 어형을 바꾸시오.   (1) instead of: ~ 대신에

(1) 그녀는 그녀를 대신하여 내가 그 일을 하도록 시킨다. (have / do / instead of / she / her / the job / me)

➡ _____

(2) Ms. Jones는 Mike가 그녀의 차를 운전하게 했다. (let / Ms. Jones / Mike / her / drive / car)

➡ _____

(3) 밖으로 나가기에는 너무 어둡다. (be / go / too / it / dark / to / outside)

➡ _____

(4) 그는 너무 아파서 학교에 갈 수 없었다. (to school / he / he / so sick / was / couldn't / that / go)

➡ _____

01 다음 빈칸에 들어갈 말로 가장 적절한 것은?

> Katherine had the man _____ the roof.

① fixed   ② to fixing   ③ fix
④ fixing   ⑤ to fix

중요
02 다음 중 빈칸에 들어갈 말로 가장 적절한 것은?

> A: Did you do well on the test?
> B: No. I was _____ on the test.

① so nervous to do well
② too nervous that I couldn't do well
③ so nervous that I can't do well
④ too nervous to do well
⑤ too nervous doing well

03 다음 중 빈칸에 들어갈 동사의 형태가 다른 하나는?

① Please let me _____ to his concert.
② Juliet had us _____ to school early in the morning.
③ Jack helped us _____ to the zoo by train.
④ Amelia made me _____ fishing with my brother.
⑤ They wanted me _____ there alone.

 서답형
04 주어진 단어를 활용하여 다음 우리말을 영어로 쓰시오.

> 너는 너무 어려서 자동차를 운전할 수 없어. (to / a car)

➡ _____

중요
05 다음 중 빈칸에 들어갈 수 <u>없는</u> 것은?

> She _____ her brother take care of the cat during the holidays.

① let   ② made
③ had   ④ helped
⑤ encouraged

06 다음 우리말을 영어로 바르게 옮긴 것을 <u>모두</u> 고르시오.

> Jimmy는 너무 약해서 그것을 들 수 없어.

① Jimmy is too weak to lifting it.
② Jimmy is so weak that he can't lift it.
③ Jimmy is weak enough to lift it.
④ Jimmy is too weak to lift it.
⑤ Jimmy is very weak that he couldn't lift it.

중요
07 다음 중 빈칸에 들어갈 말이 바르게 짝지어진 것은?

> • Jamie made me _____ out loud.
> • They slept _____ there in time.

① laughing – too much going
② laughing – so much that they could go
③ laugh – too much to go
④ laugh – much enough to going
⑤ to laugh – too much to go

서답형

08 to부정사를 이용하여 다음 문장과 같은 의미의 문장을 쓰시오.

> This coffee is so hot that I can't drink it.

➡ _____

중요

09 다음 중 어법상 어색한 것은?

① This bag is too heavy to carry.
② They walked so fast that I couldn't catch up with them.
③ Jessica made us doing the laundry.
④ Paul helped me to do my homework.
⑤ Did she let you play with your friends last night?

10 다음 중 주어진 문장과 같은 의미의 문장은?

> Brian was too busy to answer the phone.

① Brian was too busy that he can't answer the phone.
② Brian was very busy that he couldn't answer the phone.
③ Brian was busy enough to answer the phone.
④ Brian was so busy that he couldn't answer the phone.
⑤ Brian was so busy that he can't answer the phone.

중요

11 빈칸에 들어갈 알맞은 말을 고르시오.

> Mike had me _____ his bag while he was doing his job.

① to watch   ② watched
③ watch   ④ watching
⑤ to watching

서답형

12 to부정사를 이용하여 다음 두 문장을 하나의 문장으로 쓰시오.

> Ron got up so late. So, he couldn't catch the train.

➡ _____

중요

13 다음 중 어법상 어색한 것은?

> It was ①too late ②to go out alone. Did your parents ③let you ④going out ⑤ with your friends?

①   ②   ③   ④   ⑤

14 to부정사를 이용하여 다음 우리말을 영어로 옮길 때 여섯 번째로 오는 단어는?

> 나는 숙제를 끝마치기에는 너무 졸렸다.

① too   ② sleepy   ③ to
④ finish   ⑤ my

중요

15 다음 중 우리말을 영어로 바르게 옮기지 않은 것은?

① 그녀는 내가 그녀의 가방을 옮기게 했다.
→ She made me carry her bag.
② 나는 여동생이 내 방을 청소하게 했다.
→ I had my room clean by my sister.
③ Tom은 그의 여동생이 자신을 위해 파티를 열게 했다.
→ Tom had his sister throw a party for him.
④ Jenny는 너무 아파서 교회에 갈 수 없었다.
→ Jenny was too sick to go to church.
⑤ 그들은 내가 계속 무언가를 말하게 만들었다.
→ They made me keep talking something.

서답형

16 주어진 단어를 활용하여 다음 우리말을 that절을 이용하여 영어로 쓰시오.

> Judy는 너무 빨라서 결승선에서 멈출 수 없었다. (the finish line)

➡ _____

_____

17 다음 문장과 같은 의미의 문장은?

> I am too busy to spend much time with my family.

① My family is so busy that I can't spend time with them.

② I am so busy that I can spend much time with my family.

③ I am busy enough to spend much time with my family.

④ I am so busy that I can't spend much time with my family.

⑤ I can't spend much time with my family because they are too busy.

18 다음 빈칸에 들어갈 말로 가장 적절한 것은?

> Ms. Austin _____ her son eat the vegetables.

① wants   ② has   ③ forces

④ allows   ⑤ tells

19 다음 빈칸에 들어갈 말로 가장 적절한 것은?

> The traveler was _____ walk anymore. He needed something to drink.

① too thirsty to   ② to thirsty too

③ thirsty enough to   ④ to sleep too

⑤ too tired to

서답형

20 주어진 문장과 같은 의미의 문장을 쓰시오.

> The boy is so young that he can't solve the puzzle.

➡ _____

21 다음 빈칸에 들어갈 말로 적절한 것을 모두 고르시오.

> Amelia is _____ give us advice. Let's ask her.

① too wise to

② wise enough to

③ so wise that she couldn't

④ so wise that she can

⑤ so wise that she can't

22 다음 빈칸에 들어갈 말이 바르게 짝지어진 것은?

> • Please let me _____ the answer.
> • Miss White was too afraid _____ anything.

① seeing – to saying   ② see – say

③ see – to say   ④ to see – to say

⑤ to see – saying

23 다음 중 어법상 어색한 것은?

① Exercising regularly helps me to stay healthy.

② The teacher made us study hard.

③ Kelly was too shy to talk in front of many people.

④ Amelia let me take her umbrella.

⑤ Victor is so slow to walk with us.

01 다음 문장과 같은 의미의 문장을 지시에 맞게 쓰시오.

> Kevin is really tired. So, he can't go out.

(1) to부정사를 이용하여 한 문장으로

➡ _____

(2) that절을 이용하여 한 문장으로

➡ _____

02 다음 그림에 맞게 빈칸에 알맞은 말을 쓰시오.

> Today is Lion's birthday. Fox had Elephant _____. He also had the table _____. Hippo let Squirrel _____. Owl let Monkey _____ on the stage.

03 주어진 어구를 바르게 배열하여 다음 우리말을 영어로 쓰시오.

> 몇몇 학생들은 버스를 잡기에는 너무 늦었다.
> (the bus / some students / to / too / late / catch / were)

➡ _____

04 주어진 어구를 바르게 배열하여 다음 우리말을 영어로 쓰시오. 필요하다면 어형을 바꾸시오.

> 그 의사는 내가 여섯 시간마다 그 약을 먹게 했다. (every six hours / the doctor / take / have / the medicine / me)

➡ _____

_____

05 다음 대화의 빈칸에 들어갈 알맞은 말을 쓰시오.

> A: Mom, I want to live alone.
> B: Cindy, I can't let you _____.
>   You are too young _____.

06 다음 우리말을 지시에 맞게 영어로 쓰시오.

> Patrick은 충분히 키가 커서 농구를 잘할 수 있어.

(1) to부정사를 활용하여

➡ _____

_____

(2) that절을 활용하여

➡ _____

_____

07 다음 대화의 빈칸에 알맞은 말을 쓰시오.

> A: Why were you crying then?
> B: I saw a sad movie. It made me _____.

08 주어진 단어를 이용하여 다음 우리말을 영어로 쓰시오. 필요한 경우 단어 형태를 바꾸시오.

(1) 무엇이 네가 그렇게 생각하게 만들었니? (think / make)

➡ _____

(2) 어머니는 내가 자전거 사는 것을 허락하셨다. (let / buy)

➡ _____

(3) 너는 잠을 너무 많이 자서 그곳에 정시에 도착할 수 없었어. (sleep / to / get / on time)

➡ _____

09 다음 대화를 읽고 빈칸에 알맞은 말을 쓰시오.

> A: What's wrong, Papa Smurf? You look sad.
> B: I can't ride a roller coaster. I'm too old.
> A: Oh, that's too bad.

➡ Papa Smurf is too _____ a roller coaster, so he looks sad.

10 다음 주어진 문장과 같은 의미의 문장을 지시에 맞게 쓰시오.

> I was very shy, so I couldn't make friends easily.

(1) to부정사를 이용하여

➡ _____

(2) that절을 이용하여

➡ _____

11 다음 문장에서 어색한 부분을 찾아 바르게 고쳐 쓰시오.

(1) Frank usually lets his children to watch TV on weekends.

_____ ➡ _____

(2) My homeroom teacher had us left early today.

_____ ➡ _____

12 주어진 단어를 활용하여 다음 우리말을 영어로 쓰시오.

> 나의 삼촌은 내가 케이크 한 조각을 먹게 허락하셨다. (let / have)

➡ _____

13 주어진 단어를 활용하여 다음 대화를 영어로 쓰시오.

> A: 그가 너에게 이 문제를 풀게 했니? (make)
> B: 응. 하지만 이 문제는 너무 어려워서 풀 수 없어. (difficult / to)

➡ A: _____
   B: _____

14 to부정사를 이용하여 다음 문장과 같은 의미의 문장을 쓰시오.

> She is so kind that she can accept your apology.

➡ _____

Reading

Do You Hear Me?

Breeze: Good evening, listeners. This is your DJ, Breeze. Today
       _{동격}
we have a special guest, Andy Kim. He's a hip-hop artist.
       동격
Welcome, Andy.

Andy: Nice to meet you and thank you for having me.
      thank A for B: B에 관하여 A에게 감사하다

Breeze: Okay. What do our listeners want to tell their family? This
     직접목적어   수여동사   간접목적어
evening we will find out by reading some letters from them.
       by Ving: V함으로써
Andy, will you start off with the letter from a teenage girl?
          ~로부터

Andy: Sure.

Andy: Hello. I'm a 15-year-old girl from Wonju. I want to tell you
    15-year-old가 뒤의 명사 girl을 수식. year를 단수로 씀.
about my mom. My mom tries to do everything for me. She
cleans my room without asking me, so it's sometimes hard to
       동명사   가주어 it   진주어 to V
find my stuff. She also buys books and makes me study them.
          사역동사+목적어+동사원형
I want to say to my mom, "I know you love me, but I'm not a
baby anymore. Please let me take care of things myself."
      사역동사+목적어+동사원형   재귀대명사 강조 용법

guest: 손님
find out: 알아내다
start off with: ~으로 시작하다
teenage: 십 대의
without: ~ 없이
stuff: 물건
not ~ anymore: 더 이상 ~가 아니다
take care of: ~을 처리하다, 돌보다

확인문제

- 다음 문장이 본문의 내용과 일치하면 T, 일치하지 <u>않으면</u> F를 쓰시오.

1 Breeze is a radio show host. ☐

2 Andy wants to tell something to his family. ☐

3 The girl wants to thank her mom for organizing her things instead of her. ☐

4 The girl doesn't want to be treated like a baby. ☐

5 The girl wants her mom to allow her to take care of things herself. ☐

Breeze: I felt <u>the same way</u> when I was in middle school.
똑같이

Andy: Many moms think their kids are <u>too young to do</u> things <u>on their</u>
너무 ~해서 V할 수 없는   by themselves: 스스로

<u>own</u>. I hope the girl's mom will get the message.

Breeze: <u>So do I</u>. Andy, will you please read the next letter?
I hope so, too.

Andy: Hi. I'm a father of two children. One is a high school girl, and

the other is a middle school boy. <u>They're too busy to talk with</u>
나머지 다른 하나를 가리키는 대명사   They are so busy that they can't talk with me

<u>me</u>. When I get home from work, they <u>just</u> <u>say hi</u> and go back
단지   인사를 하다

to their rooms. Sometimes I ask them about their school life,

but they only give short answers. We don't talk much <u>at the</u>
식탁에서

<u>table</u>, <u>either</u>. I want to say to my kids, "I love you so much, and
부정에 대한 동의 (~도 역시)

I want to spend more time with you."

Breeze: Andy, did you talk with your parents often <u>when</u> you were
부사절 접속사

younger?

Andy: Not really. I loved them very much, but I thought <u>they were too</u>
they were so old that they couldn't understand me.

<u>old to understand me</u>.

Breeze: I see. Does anyone have suggestions for the "sad" dad? Text
understand

<u>your idea to us</u>.
=us your idea

---

on one's own: 혼자 힘으로

message: 전갈, 메시지

either: (부정문에서) ~도 역시

suggestion: 제안, 의견

text: 문자 메시지를 보내다

확인문제

● 다음 문장이 본문의 내용과 일치하면 T, 일치하지 <u>않으면</u> F를 쓰시오.

1 A number of moms think that their kids are old enough to do things by
   themselves. ☐

2 Breeze wants the girl's mom to get the message. ☐

3 Breeze doesn't understand the girl's feelings well. ☐

4 The father wants their children to study harder. ☐

5 Andy had a lot of conversation with his parents when he was younger. ☐

6 Listeners can text their suggestions for the sad father to the radio program. ☐

● 우리말을 참고하여 빈칸에 알맞은 말을 쓰시오.

1 Breeze: _____ _____, listeners. _____ _____ your DJ, Breeze.

2 Today we have _____ _____ _____, Andy Kim.

3 He's a hip-hop artist. _____, Andy.

4 Andy: Nice _____ _____ _____ and thank you _____ _____ _____.

5 Breeze: Okay. What do our listeners _____ _____ their family?

6 This evening we will find out _____ _____ _____ from them.

7 Andy, will you _____ _____ _____ the letter _____ a teenage girl?

8 Andy: _____.

9 Andy: Hello. I'm a 15-year-old girl _____ Wonju.

10 I want _____ _____ _____ about my mom.

11 My mom _____ _____ _____ everything for me.

12 She cleans my room _____ _____ me, so it's sometimes _____ _____ _____ my stuff.

13 She also _____ books and makes _____ _____ _____.

14 I want _____ _____ to my mom, "I know you love me, but I'm not a baby _____. Please _____ _____ _____ _____ _____ things myself."

1 Breeze: 안녕하세요, 청취자 여러분. 저는 여러분의 디제이, Breeze입니다.

2 오늘은 특별한 손님, Andy Kim 씨를 모셨습니다.

3 그는 힙합 아티스트이시죠. 환영합니다, Andy.

4 Andy: 반갑습니다, 그리고 초대해 주셔서 고맙습니다.

5 Breeze: 네. 우리 청취자분들은 가족에게 무슨 말을 하고 싶어 하실까요?

6 오늘 저녁에 우리는 청취자분들로부터 온 몇몇 편지들을 읽으며 알아보려 합니다.

7 Andy, 십 대 소녀에게서 온 편지로 시작해 주시겠어요?

8 Andy: 알겠습니다.

9 Andy: 안녕하세요. 저는 원주에 사는 15세 소녀입니다.

10 저는 저의 엄마에 관해 이야기하고 싶습니다.

11 엄마는 저를 위해 모든 것을 해 주려고 하십니다.

12 엄마는 제게 물어보지도 않고 방을 청소해 주시고, 그래서 가끔은 제 물건을 찾기가 힘들 때도 있습니다.

13 또 엄마는 책을 사 와서는 저에게 그것들을 공부하라고 시키세요.

14 저는 엄마께 "엄마가 저를 사랑하는 것은 알지만 전 더 이상 아기가 아니에요. 제 일을 스스로 할 수 있게 해 주세요."라고 말씀드리고 싶습니다.

15 Breeze: I felt _____ _____ _____ when I was in middle school.

16 Andy: Many moms think their kids are _____ _____ _____ _____ things on their own.

17 I hope the girl's mom will _____ _____ _____.

18 Breeze: So _____ _____. Andy, will you please read the next letter?

19 Andy: Hi. I'm a father _____ _____ _____.

20 _____ is a high school girl, and _____ is a middle school boy.

21 They're _____ _____ _____ _____ with me.

22 When I _____ home from work, they just say hi and _____ _____ _____ their rooms.

23 Sometimes I ask _____ about their school life, but they only _____ _____ _____.

24 We _____ _____ _____ at the table, _____.

25 I want to say to my kids, "I love you so much, and I want _____ _____ _____ _____ with you."

26 Breeze: Andy, did you talk with your parents _____ when you were _____?

27 Andy: Not really. I loved _____ very much, but I thought they were _____ _____ _____ _____ me.

28 Breeze: I see. Does anyone have _____ for the "sad" dad? _____ _____ _____ to us.

---

15 Breeze: 저도 중학교 때 똑같은 기분을 느꼈습니다.

16 Andy: 많은 어머님들이 자녀들이 혼자 힘으로 무언가를 하기에는 너무 어리다고 생각합니다.

17 소녀의 어머님께서 메시지를 들으시길 바랍니다.

18 Breeze: 동감입니다. Andy, 다음 편지를 읽어 주시겠어요?

19 Andy: 안녕하세요. 저는 두 아이의 아버지입니다.

20 한 명은 고등학생인 여자아이이고, 나머지 한 명은 중학생인 남자아이입니다.

21 아이들은 저와 대화를 하기에는 너무 바쁩니다.

22 제가 일을 하고 집에 돌아오면, 아이들은 그저 인사만 하고 자신의 방으로 돌아갑니다.

23 가끔씩 저는 아이들에게 학교생활에 관해 묻기도 하지만, 아이들은 그냥 짤막한 대답만 합니다.

24 우리는 식사 자리에서조차 대화를 많이 하지 않습니다.

25 저는 아이들에게 "너희들을 무척 사랑한단다. 그리고 너희들과 더 많은 시간을 보내고 싶단다."라고 말하고 싶습니다.

26 Breeze: Andy, 어렸을 때 부모님과 자주 대화를 했나요?

27 Andy: 사실 그렇지는 않습니다. 저는 부모님을 무척 사랑하지만, 부모님이 저를 이해해 주시기에는 너무 나이가 들었다고 생각했습니다.

28 Breeze: 그렇군요. '슬픈' 아빠에게 해 드릴 제안이 있으신 분 계신가요? 여러분의 생각을 저희에게 문자로 보내 주세요.

● 우리말을 참고하여 본문을 영작하시오.

1 Breeze: 안녕하세요, 청취자 여러분. 저는 여러분의 디제이, Breeze입니다.

➡ _____

2 오늘은 특별한 손님, Andy Kim 씨를 모셨습니다.

➡ _____

3 그는 힙합 아티스트이시죠. 환영합니다, Andy.

➡ _____

4 Andy: 반갑습니다, 그리고 초대해 주셔서 고맙습니다.

➡ _____

5 Breeze: 네. 우리 청취자분들은 가족에게 무슨 말을 하고 싶어 하실까요?

➡ _____

6 오늘 저녁에 우리는 청취자분들로부터 온 몇몇 편지들을 읽으며 알아보려 합니다.

➡ _____

7 Andy, 십 대 소녀에게서 온 편지로 시작해 주시겠어요?

➡ _____

8 Andy: 알겠습니다.

➡ _____

9 Andy: 안녕하세요. 저는 원주에 사는 15세 소녀입니다.

➡ _____

10 저는 저의 엄마에 관해 이야기하고 싶습니다.

➡ _____

11 엄마는 저를 위해 모든 것을 해 주려고 하십니다.

➡ _____

12 엄마는 제게 물어보지도 않고 방을 청소해 주시고, 그래서 가끔은 제 물건을 찾기가 힘들 때도 있습니다.

➡ _____

13 또 엄마는 책을 사 와서는 저에게 그것들을 공부하라고 시키세요.

➡ _____

14 저는 엄마께 "엄마가 저를 사랑하는 것은 알지만 전 더 이상 아기가 아니에요. 제 일을 스스로 할 수 있게 해 주세요."라고 말씀드리고 싶습니다.

➡ _____

_____

15 Breeze: 저도 중학교 때 똑같은 기분을 느꼈습니다.

➡ _____

16 Andy: 많은 어머님들이 자녀들이 혼자 힘으로 무언가를 하기에는 너무 어리다고 생각합니다.

➡ _____

17 소녀의 어머님께서 메시지를 들으시길 바랍니다.

➡ _____

18 Breeze: 동감입니다. Andy, 다음 편지를 읽어 주시겠어요?

➡ _____

19 Andy: 안녕하세요. 저는 두 아이의 아버지입니다.

➡ _____

20 한 명은 고등학생인 여자아이이고, 나머지 한 명은 중학생인 남자아이입니다.

➡ _____

21 아이들은 저와 대화를 하기에는 너무 바쁩니다.

➡ _____

22 제가 일을 하고 집에 돌아오면, 아이들은 그저 인사만 하고 자신의 방으로 돌아갑니다.

➡ _____

23 가끔씩 저는 아이들에게 학교생활에 관해 묻기도 하지만, 아이들은 그냥 쌀쌀한 대답만 합니다.

➡ _____

24 우리는 식사 자리에서조차 대화를 많이 하지 않습니다.

➡ _____

25 저는 아이들에게 "너희들을 무척 사랑한단다, 그리고 너희들과 더 많은 시간을 보내고 싶단다."
라고 말하고 싶습니다.

➡ _____

26 Breeze: Andy, 어렸을 때 부모님과 자주 대화를 했나요?

➡ _____

27 Andy: 사실 그렇지는 않습니다. 저는 부모님을 무척 사랑하지만, 부모님이 저를 이해해
주시기에는 너무 나이가 들었다고 생각했습니다.

➡ _____

28 Breeze: 그렇군요. '슬픈' 아빠에게 해 드릴 제안이 있으신 분 계신가요? 여러분의 생각을
저희에게 문자로 보내 주세요.

➡ _____

[01~03] 다음 글을 읽고 물음에 답하시오.

Breeze: Good evening, listeners. This is your DJ, Breeze. Today we have a special guest, Andy Kim. He's a hip-hop artist. Welcome, Andy.

Andy: Nice to meet you and thank you for having me.

Breeze: Okay. What do our listeners want to tell their family? This evening we will find out by reading some letters from them. Andy, will you start off with the letter from a teenage girl?

Andy: Sure.

01 다음 중 위 글의 내용과 일치하지 <u>않는</u> 것은?

① 이 방송은 저녁 방송이다.
② 청취자들과 함께하는 방송이다.
③ Andy는 특별 손님이다.
④ DJ가 직접 사연을 읽어 준다.
⑤ 청취자들은 이 프로그램을 통해 가족에게 하고 싶은 말을 한다.

02 다음 중 위 글에 이어질 내용으로 가장 적절한 것은?

① Talking about family problems with Breeze
② Reading a letter from a listener
③ Singing one of his songs
④ Calling one of the listeners
⑤ Writing a letter to their listeners to make them happy

서답형
03 다음과 같이 풀이되는 말을 위 글에서 찾아 쓰시오.

someone who is invited to an event

➡ _____

[04~07] 다음 글을 읽고 물음에 답하시오.

Andy: Hello. ⓐI'm a 15-year-old girl from Wonju. I want to tell you about my mom. My mom tries to do everything for me. She cleans my room without asking me, so it's sometimes hard to find my stuff. She also buys books and makes me study them. I want to say to my mom, "I know you love me, but I'm not a baby anymore. Please let me take care of things myself."

Breeze: I felt ⓑthe same way when I was in middle school.

Andy: Many moms think their kids are too young to do things ⓒon their own. I hope the girl's mom will get the message.

04 다음 중 밑줄 친 ⓐ에 관하여 답할 수 <u>없는</u> 것은?

① Where does she live?
② Who does the girl want to talk about?
③ How often does her mother clean her room?
④ Why is it hard for her to find her stuff?
⑤ What does her mom buy for her?

05 밑줄 친 ⓑ의 의미로 가장 적절한 것은?

① 엄마에 대한 사랑
② 엄마가 방 청소를 해 주는 것
③ 엄마와 사이가 좋지 않은 것
④ 엄마가 자신을 아기 취급을 하는 것
⑤ 엄마와 대화가 없는 것

서답형

06 What does the girl's mom try to do for her? Answer in English with a full sentence.

➡ _____

07 다음 중 밑줄 친 ⓒ를 대신하여 쓸 수 있는 것은?

① on their minds   ② by themselves
③ with some help   ④ at their surprise
⑤ in that way

[08~12] 다음 글을 읽고 물음에 답하시오.

Breeze: So do I. Andy, will you please read the next letter?

Andy: Hi. I'm a father of two children. One is a high school girl, and ___(A)___ is a middle school boy. They're too busy to talk with me. When I get home ___(B)___ work, they just say hi and go back to their rooms. Sometimes I ask them about their school life, but they only give short answers. We don't talk much at the table, either. I want to say to my kids, "I love you so much, and I want to spend more time with you."

Breeze: Andy, did you talk with your parents often when you were younger?

Andy: Not really. I loved them very much, but I thought they were too old to understand me.

Breeze: I (C)see. Does anyone have suggestions for the "sad" dad? Text your idea to us.

08 다음 중 빈칸 (A)에 들어갈 말로 가장 적절한 것은?

① the others   ② another
③ other   ④ the other
⑤ others

중요

09 다음 중 빈칸 (B)에 들어갈 말과 같은 말이 들어가는 것은?

① Who took care _____ your plants while you were away?
② My father graduated _____ Harvard University.
③ I want to get out _____ this room.
④ The box was full _____ interesting things.
⑤ We are really looking forward _____ meeting you again.

서답형

10 Why don't the children talk with their father much? Answer in English with a full sentence. Use the word 'Because.'

➡ _____

11 다음 중 밑줄 친 (C)를 대신하여 쓸 수 있는 것은?

① am sorry   ② don't know
③ understand   ④ watch
⑤ imagine

중요

12 다음 중 위 글의 내용과 일치하지 않는 것은?

① Andy reads the next letter.
② Listeners can text their ideas about the sad dad.
③ Andy used to talk with his parents a lot.
④ The man who wrote the letter has two children.
⑤ The father wants to spend more time with his children.

[13~18] 다음 글을 읽고 물음에 답하시오.

Breeze: Good evening, listeners. This is your DJ, Breeze. Today we have a special guest, Andy Kim. He's a hip-hop artist. Welcome, Andy.

Andy: Nice to meet you and thank you _____(A)_____.

Breeze: Okay. What do our listeners want to tell their family? This evening we will find out by reading some letters from (B)them. Andy, will you start off with the letter from a teenage girl?

Andy: Sure.

Andy: Hello. I'm a 15-year-old girl from Wonju. I want to tell you about my mom. My mom tries to do everything for me. She cleans my room without asking me, so it's sometimes hard to find my stuff. She also buys books and makes me study them. I want to say to my mom, "I know you love me, but I'm not a baby anymore. Please let me take care of things (C)myself."

13 문맥상 빈칸 (A)에 들어갈 말로 가장 적절한 것은?

① to let me read this letter
② to seeing me coming here
③ for having me
④ for watching me read it
⑤ for reading it to me

서답형

14 밑줄 친 (B)가 가리키는 것을 위 글에서 찾아 쓰시오.

➡ _____

서답형

15 What does the girl try to talk about in the letter? Answer in English with a full sentence.

➡ _____

16 다음 중 위 글을 읽고 알 수 <u>없는</u> 것은?

① the name of the radio DJ
② the subject of the broadcast
③ what the guest does for a living
④ the name of the guest
⑤ the name of the person who sent a letter

17 다음 중 밑줄 친 (C)와 쓰임이 같은 것은?

① I couldn't make <u>myself</u> understood.
② Did you enjoy <u>yourself</u>?
③ Stella looked at <u>herself</u> through the mirror.
④ Did you really make the cookies <u>yourself</u>?
⑤ Tom kept talking about <u>himself</u>.

18 다음 중 위 글의 내용과 일치하는 것은?

① The radio host is Andy.
② There are a couple of guests.
③ Andy wants the DJ to read a letter.
④ Listeners send letters to the program.
⑤ The girl says in the letter that she doesn't want to study.

[19~23] 다음 글을 읽고 물음에 답하시오.

Breeze: I felt the same way when I was in middle school.

Andy: Many moms think their kids are too young to do things ①on their own. I hope the girl's mom will get the message.

Breeze: (A)So do I. Andy, will you please read the next letter?

Andy: Hi. I'm a father of two children. One is a high school girl, and the other is a middle school boy. They're ②<u>too busy</u> to talk with me. When I get home from work, they just say hi and go back to their rooms. Sometimes I ③<u>ask</u> them about their school life, but they only give short answers. We ④<u>talk</u> much at the table, either. I want to say to my kids, "I love you so much, and I want to spend more time with you."

Breeze: Andy, did you talk with your parents often when you were younger?

Andy: ⑤<u>Not really</u>. I loved them very much, but I thought they were too old to understand me.

Breeze: I see. Does anyone have suggestions for the "sad" dad? Text your idea to us.

19 밑줄 친 (A)의 의미로 가장 적절한 것은?

① I want you to understand that, too.
② I hope to get the message, too.
③ I am too young to do anything alone, either.
④ I felt the same way when I was young, too.
⑤ I hope that she gets the message, too.

서답형
20 How many children does the father have? Answer in English with a full sentence.

➡ _____

중요
21 다음 중 사연 신청자가 집에서 느끼는 감정으로 가장 적절한 것은?

① happy   ② satisfied
③ lonely   ④ excited
⑤ nervous

22 다음 중 위 글을 읽고 답할 수 있는 것은?

① Who sent the first letter?
② How many family members does the father have?
③ Why are the father's children busy?
④ What does the father want to say to their children?
⑤ How many listeners will text their idea?

23 ①~⑤ 중 글의 흐름상 <u>어색한</u> 것은?

①   ②   ③   ④   ⑤

[24~25] 다음 글을 읽고 물음에 답하시오.

This is a letter from a father who wants to share his experience with the "sad" father.

My kids and I did not talk much. There was a wall between us. I wanted to break it ___(A)___. I tried to spend more time with my children on weekends. We played computer games, rode bikes, and went shopping together. In this way, I had more chances to talk with them. I came to know more about them.

24 다음 중 빈칸 (A)에 들어갈 말로 가장 적절한 것은?

① into   ② down   ③ up
④ away   ⑤ off

서답형
25 What did the father do to have more chances to talk with his children? Answer in English and use the words below.

(and / with / on weekends)

➡ _____

_____

[01~03] 다음 글을 읽고 물음에 답하시오.

Breeze: Good evening, listeners. This is your DJ, Breeze. Today we have a special guest, Andy Kim. He's a hip-hop artist. Welcome, Andy.

Andy: Nice to meet you and thank you for having me.

Breeze: Okay. What do our listeners want to tell their family? This evening we will find out by reading some letters from them. Andy, will you start off with the letter from a teenage girl?

Andy: Sure.

중요

01 What does Andy Kim do? Answer in English with a full sentence.

➡ _____

02 How will Breeze find out what listeners want to tell their family? Answer in English with a full sentence.

➡ _____

_____

03 위 글의 내용에 맞게 빈칸에 알맞은 말을 쓰시오.

On the radio show, Breeze introduces a
_____ _____, _____ _____.
She wants him _____ _____ a
letter from one of the listeners. He will
_____ _____ with the letter sent by
a _____ _____.

[04~06] 다음 글을 읽고 물음에 답하시오.

Andy: Hello. I'm a 15-year-old girl from Wonju. I want to tell you about my mom. My mom tries to do everything for me. She cleans my room without asking me, so it's sometimes hard to find my stuff. She also buys books and makes me study them. I want to say to my mom, "I know you love me, but I'm not a baby anymore. (A)제 일을 스스로 할 수 있게 해 주세요."

Breeze: I felt the same way when I was in middle school.

04 주어진 단어를 바르게 배열하여 밑줄 친 우리말 (A)를 영어로 쓰시오. (please로 시작할 것)

(things / me / myself / let / of / take / please / care)

➡ _____

중요

05 What problem does the girl have when her mother cleans her room? Answer in English with a full sentence.

➡ _____

06 According to the letter, what does the girl's mom try to do? Answer in English with a full sentence. Use the word 'daughter.'

➡ _____

[07~10] 다음 글을 읽고 물음에 답하시오.

Andy: Many moms think their kids are too young to do things on their own. I hope the girl's mom will get the message.

Breeze: So do I. Andy, will you please read the next letter?

Andy: Hi. I'm a father of two children. One is a high school girl, and the other is a middle school boy. (A)They're too busy to talk with me. When I get home from work, they just say hi and go back to their rooms. Sometimes I ask them about their school life, but they only give short answers. We don't talk much at the table, either. I want to say to my kids, "I love you so much, and I want to spend more time with you."

Breeze: Andy, did you talk with your parents often when you were younger?

Andy: Not really. I loved them very much, but I thought they were too old to understand me.

Breeze: I see. Does anyone have suggestions for the "sad" dad? Text your idea to us.

07 주어진 단어를 이용하여 밑줄 친 (A)를 대신하여 쓸 수 있는 문장을 쓰시오.

(that)

➡ _____

08 위 글의 내용에 맞게 빈칸에 알맞은 말을 쓰시오.

The person who wrote the letter is a dad of _____ _____. The problem he has is that his kids don't have time to _____ _____ _____. He wishes to _____ _____ _____ with his kids.

09 According to the conversation, what do many moms think about their kids? Use the phrase below.

(many of them)

➡ _____

_____

10 Write the reason why Andy didn't talk with his parents often when he was young. Use the phrase 'It's because.'

➡ _____

_____

[11~12] 다음 글을 읽고 물음에 답하시오.

This is a letter from a father who wants to share his experience with the "sad" father.

My kids and I did not talk much. There was a wall between us. I wanted to break (A)it down. I tried to spend more time with my children on weekends. We played computer games, rode bikes, and went shopping together. In this way, (B)저는 아이들과 이야기할 기회를 더 많이 가졌습니다. I came to know more about them.

11 밑줄 친 (A)가 가리키는 것을 위 글에서 찾아 쓰시오.

➡ _____

12 주어진 단어를 활용하여 밑줄 친 우리말 (B)를 8 단어로 이루어진 한 문장의 영어로 쓰시오.

(chance)

➡ _____

교과서

구석구석

My Writing Portfolio

Hello, I am a 15-year-old girl from Busan. I want to say to my brother Jaeho,
_{to부정사를 목적어로 취하는 동사}

"Sorry." I told Mom his secret last Friday. Mom got so angry, so he was in
_{4형식 동사(tell+간접목적어+직접목적어)}   _{= became}

trouble. I was too scared to say sorry to him at that time. I promise I will never
_{I was so scared that I couldn't say sorry to him at that time.}

tell his secrets again.

구문해설 • be in trouble: 곤경에 처하다 • scared: 무서운 • promise: ～을 약속하다

Have Fun Together

• I have nothing to do. I have no friends.
_{to부정사의 형용사적 용법}

• Everything is too small. I don't like this place very much.

• Heungbu is richer than me now. I'm not happy with it.
_{비교급+than}   _{～이 마음에 들지 않는다}

• Mom made us leave home. We're not happy with it.
_{사역동사+목적어+동사원형: (목적어)가 ～하게 하다}

• This soup smells good, but I can't eat it.
_{감각동사+형용사}

구문해설 • place: 곳, 장소 • leave: 떠나다 • smell: 냄새가 나다

Wrap Up – Reading Read and answer 3

This is a letter from a father who wants to share his experience with the "sad"
_{주격 관계대명사}

father.

My kids and I did not talk much. There was a wall between us. I wanted to

break it down. I tried to spend more time with my children on weekends. We
_{= the wall}   _{= ～하려고 노력했다}

played computer games, rode bikes, and went shopping together. In this way, I

had more chances to talk with them. I came to know more about them.
_{= opportunities}   _{= my children}   _{come to+동사원형: ～하게 되다}   _{= my children}

구문해설 • wall: 벽 • share: 공유하다, 나누다 • break down: 허물다, 부수다

해석

안녕하세요. 저는 부산에 살고 있는 15살 소녀예요. 저는 저의 오빠 재호에게 "미안해."라고 말하고 싶어요. 저는 지난주에 오빠의 비밀을 엄마께 말씀드렸어요. 엄마는 정말 화가 나셨고, 오빠는 곤경에 처했죠. 그 당시에 저는 오빠에게 미안하다고 말하기엔 너무 무서웠어요. 오빠의 비밀을 다시는 이야기하지 않겠다고 약속할게요.

• 나는 할 일이 없어. 나는 친구가 없어.

• 모든 것이 너무 작아. 나는 이곳이 별로 마음에 안 들어.

• 이제 흥부가 나보다 더 부자야. 나는 그것이 마음에 안 들어.

• 엄마는 우리가 집을 떠나게 하셨어. 우리는 그것이 마음이 안 들어.

• 이 수프는 냄새가 좋은데, 나는 그것을 먹을 수 없어.

이것은 '슬픈' 아버지와 경험을 공유하고 싶은 한 아버지로부터 온 편지입니다.

제 아이들과 저는 대화를 많이 하지 않았습니다. 우리 사이에는 벽이 있었어요. 저는 그것을 허물고 싶었습니다. 저는 주말마다 아이들과 더 많은 시간을 보내려고 노력했어요. 우리는 함께 컴퓨터 게임을 했고, 자전거를 탔고, 쇼핑을 갔습니다. 이 방법으로 저는 아이들과 이야기할 기회를 더 많이 가졌습니다. 저는 그들을 더 잘 알게 되었죠.

---

01 다음 짝지어진 단어의 관계가 같도록 빈칸에 알맞은 말을 쓰시오.

> happy : unhappy = true : _____

02 다음 중 밑줄 친 부분의 뜻풀이가 바르지 <u>않은</u> 것은?

① I'm <u>scared</u> of spiders. 무서워하는
② Do you have any <u>suggestions</u>? 제안들
③ My sister was so upset because the dog <u>tore</u> up her new shoes. 찢었다
④ This magazine is for <u>teenage</u> boys and girls. 십대의
⑤ I think I can't live <u>without</u> a car. ~와 함께

03 다음 우리말에 맞게 빈칸에 알맞은 말을 쓰시오.

(1) 네 도시락을 반드시 가져와라.
　➡ Be _____ to bring your lunch box.
(2) 상점은 내게 다른 가방으로 교환해 주었다.
　➡ The store gave me an _____ for another bag.
(3) 영수증을 안전한 장소에 보관해라.
　➡ Keep the _____ in a safe place.
(4) Emma는 내게 매우 소중하다.
　➡ Emma is _____ _____ to me.
(5) 당신의 정답 중 세 개가 잘못되었다.
　➡ Three of your answers were _____.
(6) 그의 옷은 낡고 찢기었다.
　➡ His clothes were old and _____.

04 다음 영영풀이가 가리키는 것을 고르시오.

> to give something to somebody and at the same time receive the same type of thing from them

① catch
② tear
③ vote
④ promise
⑤ exchange

05 다음 문장에 공통으로 들어갈 말을 고르시오.

> • Jane suffered from her family _____s.
> • When I was in _____, I usually talk to my parents.
> • I have _____ sleeping at night.

① wall
② bowl
③ trouble
④ stuff
⑤ training

06 다음 우리말을 주어진 단어를 이용하여 영작하시오.

(1) 그녀는 절대 거짓말을 하지 않는다. (tell)
　➡ _____
(2) Tom은 규칙을 위반했기 때문에 곤경에 처했다. (trouble, because)
　➡ _____
(3) Jimmy는 더 이상 그 팀의 일원이 아니었다. (anymore)
　➡ _____

Conversation

[07~09] 다음 대화를 읽고 물음에 답하시오.

Minsol: I'm not happy ⓐwith Buster.

Dad: _____(A)_____

Minsol: He ⓑteared my homework into pieces again.

Dad: Puppies often ⓒdo that.

Minsol: This is not the first time. Sometimes I find my socks in the dog house.

Dad: Please be kind to him. He's just five months ⓓold.

Minsol: You're too nice to him! He needs some training.

Dad: Okay. Let's start ⓔtraining in a few weeks.

07 위 대화의 빈칸 (A)에 들어갈 말로 어색한 것은?

① What's the matter?

② What's wrong?

③ What's the problem?

④ Is anything wrong?

⑤ What do you do?

08 위 대화에서 밑줄 친 ⓐ~ⓔ 중 어법상 어색한 것을 찾아 바르게 고치시오.

➡ _____

09 위 대화를 읽고 대답할 수 없는 것은?

① How does Minsol feel about Buster?

② Why isn't Minsol happy with Buster?

③ How many times has Buster torn Minsol's homework?

④ What are Dad and Minsol going to do with Buster?

⑤ Who brought Minsol's socks to the dog house?

10 다음 대화가 자연스럽게 이어지도록 순서대로 배열하시오.

Mike: Customer Service. How can I help you?

Sora: I bought a hairdryer at your store last week. I'm not happy with it.

Mike: What is the problem?

(A) Well, can I get a refund?

(B) Yes, I'll drop by tomorrow afternoon.

(C) I'm sorry. Do you want to exchange it?

(D) Sure. Will you please visit our store with the dryer?

(E) It doesn't work well. I mean the air isn't hot enough.

➡ _____

[11~13] 다음 대화를 읽고 물음에 답하시오.

Mom: Minsu, I'm ⓐgoing out with your dad for a movie.

Minsu: When will you be back, Mom?

Mom: ⓑAround 8 o'clock. Don't forget ⓒfeeding Buster.

Minsu: Okay.

Mom: Be sure ⓓto give him some water, too.

Minsu: No problem.

Mom: One more thing. Can you help Minsol with her science homework? Buster tore her homework ⓔinto pieces.

Minsu: Hmm .... Okay. I'll do that.

11 위 대화의 밑줄 친 ⓐ~ⓔ 중 어색한 것을 찾아 바르게 고치시오.

_____ ➡ _____

12 위 대화에서 다음 영영풀이가 가리키는 말을 찾아 쓰시오.

to give food to a person or an animal

➡ _____

13 위 대화의 내용과 일치하지 <u>않는</u> 것은?

① 엄마와 아빠는 영화 보러 나갈 것이다.

② 엄마와 아빠는 8시에 영화를 볼 것이다.

③ 엄마는 민수에게 Buster에게 밥을 줄 것을 부탁하였다.

④ 엄마는 민수에게 민솔의 과학 숙제를 도와줄 것을 요청하였다.

⑤ Buster가 민솔의 과학 숙제를 찢었다.

[14~15] 다음 대화를 읽고 물음에 답하시오.

Amy: I'm not very happy with my brother.

Brian: What's the problem?

Amy: He uses the bathroom for too long in the morning.

Brian: I know how you feel.

Amy: What can I do?

Brian: Well, you can get up earlier and use the bathroom first.

Amy: Okay, I'll give it a try.

14 What's the matter with Amy?

➡ _____

_____

15 What is Brian's suggestion?

➡ _____

_____

Grammar

16 다음 중 어법상 <u>어색한</u> 것은?

① They felt so happy that they could help everyone.

② Does he let you play with your friends?

③ Mrs. James has us read a book carefully.

④ We are too hungry to waiting in line.

⑤ Don't make me sing in front of many people.

17 다음 중 빈칸에 들어갈 말로 가장 적절한 것은?

My uncle made me _____ the dog.

① walking   ② to walk   ③ walk

④ to walking   ⑤ walked

18 다음 주어진 문장과 같은 의미의 문장은?

I allowed my younger sister to use my computer.

① I wanted my younger sister to use my computer.

② I told my younger sister to use my computer.

③ I made my younger sister to use my computer.

④ I let my younger sister use my computer.

⑤ I didn't know my younger sister used my computer.

19 다음 빈칸에 들어갈 말로 가장 적절한 것은?

• You always make me _____ good.
• I am too busy _____ care of plants.

① to feel – taking   ② to feel – to take

③ feel – take   ④ feel – to take

⑤ feeling – to take

20 다음 우리말을 영어로 바르게 옮긴 것은?

그 선생님은 우리가 일기를 쓰게 하셨다.

① The teacher wanted us keep a diary.

② The teacher promised us to keep a diary.

③ The teacher had us keep a diary.

④ The teacher thought we kept a diary.

⑤ The teacher told us to keep a diary.

21 that절을 이용하여 다음 우리말을 영어로 옮길 때 네 번째와 일곱 번째로 오는 단어는?

그 개는 공원까지 달려가기에는 너무 약했다.

① dog – weak   ② so – that
③ so – he   ④ weak – couldn't
⑤ weak – run

22 다음 중 빈칸에 들어갈 말로 적절하지 <u>않은</u> 것은?

The woman _____ Kathy to wear a dress.

① wanted   ② told   ③ helped
④ asked   ⑤ made

23 다음 중 어법상 바르지 <u>않은</u> 것은?

Mr. Kim ①had me ②answer the question. But I was ③too upset ④that I ⑤couldn't answer the question.

①   ②   ③   ④   ⑤

24 다음 그림에 맞게 빈칸에 알맞은 말을 쓰시오.

Gargamel tells Azrael to catch the smurfs, but Azrael is _____ _____ _____ them.

25 주어진 어구를 바르게 배열하여 다음 우리말을 영어로 쓰시오. 필요하다면 단어의 형태를 바꾸시오.

그 버스 운전사는 내가 버스에서 내리게 하였다.
(make / the bus driver / me / the bus / get off)

➡ _____

26 주어진 어구를 바르게 배열하여 다음 우리말을 영어로 쓰시오.

보건 선생님은 내가 양호실에서 쉬도록 허락하셨다.
(the nurse's office / the nurse teacher / in / me / rest / let)

➡ _____

Reading

[27~29] 다음 글을 읽고 물음에 답하시오.

Breeze: Good evening, listeners. This is your DJ, Breeze. Today we have a special guest, Andy Kim. He's a hip-hop artist. Welcome, Andy.
Andy: Nice to meet you and thank you for (A) <u>having me</u>.
Breeze: Okay. What do our listeners want to tell their family? This evening we will find out ____ⓐ____ reading some letters from them. Andy, will you start off with the letter from a teenage girl?
Andy: Sure.

27 다음 중 빈칸 ⓐ에 들어갈 말로 가장 적절한 것은?

① on   ② in   ③ by   ④ at   ⑤ to

28 다음 중 밑줄 친 (A)를 대신할 수 있는 말로 가장 적절한 것은?

① eating lunch with me
② inviting me
③ having a good time with me
④ bringing some letters to me
⑤ talking about me

29 다음 중 위 글의 내용과 일치하는 것은?

① Andy Kim is the program host.
② You can hear the show in the morning.
③ Andy Kim is an artist who draws paintings.
④ Andy wrote some letters for the show.
⑤ There are two people at the show.

[30~33] 다음 글을 읽고 물음에 답하시오.

Andy: Hello. I'm a 15 year-old girl from Wonju. I want to tell you about my mom. My mom tries to do ①everything for me. She cleans my room ②with asking me, so it's sometimes hard (A)to find my stuff. She also buys books and makes me ___ⓐ___ them. I want to say to my mom, "I know you ③love me, but I'm not a baby anymore. Please let ④me take care of things ⑤myself."

Breeze: I felt the same way when I was in middle school.

Andy: Many moms think their kids are too young to do things on their own. I hope the girl's mom will get the message.

30 빈칸 ⓐ에 study를 어법에 맞게 쓰시오.

➡ _____

31 ①~⑤ 중 글의 흐름상 어색한 것은?

①   ②   ③   ④   ⑤

32 다음 중 밑줄 친 (A)와 그 쓰임이 같은 것은?

① To achieve the goal, I really tried hard.
② I went to the market to buy some fruit.
③ She has something to tell you.
④ It was not easy to forgive you.
⑤ I was happy to meet them again.

33 다음 빈칸에 들어갈 말이 위 글의 내용에 맞게 바르게 짝지어진 것은?

> The girl is _____ with her mother who treats her like a _____.

① satisfied – grown-up
② happy – teenager
③ sad – stranger
④ unhappy – baby
⑤ thankful – lady

34 자연스러운 글이 되도록 [A]~[C]를 바르게 배열하시오.

> My kids and I did not talk much. There was a wall between us.
> [A] We played computer games, rode bikes, and went shopping together.
> [B] I wanted to break it down. I tried to spend more time with my children on weekends.
> [C] In this way, I had more chances to talk with them. I came to know more about them.

➡ _____

01 다음 영영풀이가 가리키는 것을 고르시오.

> a small machine used for drying your hair by blowing hot air over it

① trash   ② wall

③ receipt   ④ hairdryer

⑤ secret

02 다음 대화가 자연스럽게 이어지도록 순서대로 배열하시오.

> Minsol: I'm not happy with Buster.
>
> Dad: What's wrong?
>
> Minsol: He tore my homework into pieces again.

> (A) This is not the first time. Sometimes I find my socks in the dog house.
>
> (B) Okay. Let's start training in a few weeks.
>
> (C) Puppies often do that.
>
> (D) You're too nice to him! He needs some training.
>
> (E) Please be kind to him. He's just five months old.

➡ _____

[03~04] 다음 대화를 읽고 물음에 답하시오.

> Mom: Minsu, I'm going out with your dad for a movie.
>
> Minsu: When will you be back, Mom?
>
> Mom: Around 8 o'clock. Don't (A)[remember / forget] to feed Buster.
>
> Minsu: Okay.
>
> Mom: Be (B)[sure / unsure] to give him some water, too.

> Minsu: No problem.
>
> Mom: One more thing. Can you help Minsol with her science homework? Buster tore her homework into (C)[pieces / peace].
>
> Minsu: Hmm .... Okay. I'll do that.

03 위 대화의 괄호 (A)~(C)에 들어갈 말로 바르게 짝지어진 것은?

	(A)	(B)	(C)
①	remember	sure	pieces
②	remember	unsure	peace
③	forget	unsure	pieces
④	forget	unsure	peace
⑤	forget	sure	pieces

04 위 대화의 내용과 일치하지 <u>않는</u> 것은?

① Minsu's mom asks him to feed Buster.

② Minsu is going to give water to Buster.

③ Minsu is going to help Minsol with her science homework.

④ Minsol's homework was torn by Buster.

⑤ Minsu is going to be back home around 8 o'clock.

[05~07] 다음 대화를 읽고 물음에 답하시오.

> Mike: Customer Service. How can I help you?
>
> Sora: I bought a hairdryer at your store last week. I'm not happy with it.
>
> Mike: What is the problem?
>
> Sora: It doesn't work well. I mean the air isn't hot enough.
>
> Mike: I'm sorry. Do you want to exchange it?
>
> Sora: Well, can I get a refund?

Mike: Sure. Will you please visit our store with the dryer?

Sora: Yes, I'll drop by tomorrow afternoon.

Mike: Don't forget to bring the receipt.

Sora: Okay. Thanks.

출제율 90%

5 What's the problem of Sora's hairdryer?

➡ _____

출제율 95%

6 What should Sora bring to the store to get a refund?

➡ _____

출제율 85%

7 When is Sora going to visit the store with the dryer?

➡ _____

[08~09] 다음 대화를 읽고 물음에 답하시오.

Emma: You look upset, Tommy.

Tommy: I'm not happy with Sojin.

Emma: What's wrong with her?

Tommy: She isn't doing her part of the group project.

Emma: _____(A)

출제율 95%

8 위 대화의 빈칸 (A)에 들어갈 말을 <보기>에 주어진 단어들을 모두 배열하여 완성하시오.

┌─── 보기 ───┐
think / talk / her / I / you / to / should
└─────────────┘

➡ _____

출제율 100%

9 위 대화에서 나타난 Tommy의 기분으로 적절한 것은?

① annoyed   ② lonely

③ excited   ④ satisfied

⑤ nervous

출제율 90%

10 다음 우리말을 주어진 단어를 이용하여 영작하시오.

(1) Kelly는 이번 주말 삼촌 댁에 들를 것이다. (drop)

➡ _____
  _____

(2) 그녀는 혼자 힘으로 그 수학 문제를 풀었다. (own)

➡ _____
  _____

(3) Mike는 Steve가 거둔 성공의 비밀을 알아내고 싶어 했다. (out)

➡ _____
  _____

출제율 90%

11 다음 우리말을 영어로 바르게 옮긴 것을 모두 고르시오.

┌─────────────────────────────┐
나는 너무 실망해서 잠을 잘 수 없었어.
└─────────────────────────────┘

① I was very disappointed because I couldn't fall asleep.

② I was too disappointed to fall asleep.

③ I fell asleep because I was very disappointed.

④ I was disappointed enough to fall asleep.

⑤ I was so disappointed that I couldn't fall asleep.

12 출제율 90%

다음 중 빈칸에 들어갈 수 없는 것은?

> My parents _____ me visit my grandparents more often.

① made   ② had
③ let   ④ helped
⑤ advised

13 출제율 95%

빈칸에 들어갈 말이 바르게 짝지어진 것은?

> • He didn't let my brother _____ with his robot.
> • You are _____ to work for a living.

① to play – too young
② to play – so young
③ play – so young
④ play – too young
⑤ play – very young

14 출제율 95%

다음 중 어법상 바르지 않은 것은?

① Did you make her go home alone?
② Everyone is too busy to play with me.
③ Mr. Park had me finished my job by five.
④ Let me go to my favorite singer's concert.
⑤ The truck is too tall to go through the tunnel.

15 출제율 85%

다음 대화의 빈칸에 알맞은 말을 쓰시오.

> A: Jason, why didn't you play soccer yesterday?
> B: I was so sick _____.

➡ _____

16 출제율 95%

주어진 단어를 활용하여 다음 우리말을 영어로 쓰시오.

> 그 화가는 너무 화가 나서 그의 그림에 집중할 수 없었다. (painter / angry / too / focus on)

➡ _____

17 출제율 90%

적절한 사역동사를 사용하여 다음 빈칸에 알맞은 말을 쓰시오.

> A: Who allowed you to use the science room?
> B: Mr. White _____.

➡ _____

[18~22] 다음 글을 읽고 물음에 답하시오.

Breeze: ①So do I. Andy, will you please read the next letter?

Andy: Hi. I'm a father of two children. One is a high school girl, and the other is a middle school boy. They're too busy ②to talk with me. When I get home ____ⓐ____ work, they just say hi and go back ____ⓑ____ their rooms. Sometimes I ask ③them about their school life, but they only give short answers. We don't talk much at the table, ④too. I want to say to my kids, "I love you so ⑤much, and I want to spend more time with you."

Breeze: Andy, did you talk with your parents often when you were younger?

Andy: Not really. I loved them very much, but I thought (A)they were too old to understand me.

Breeze: I see. Does anyone have suggestions for the "sad" dad? Text your idea to us.

18 출제율 90%

빈칸 ⓐ와 ⓑ에 들어갈 말이 바르게 짝지어진 것은?

① to – into
② to – to
③ from – from
④ from – to
⑤ into – from

19 출제율 95%

①~⑤ 중 어법상 바르지 <u>않은</u> 것은?

①　②　③　④　⑤

20 출제율 90%

다음 중 위 글의 내용과 일치하지 <u>않는</u> 것은?

① Andy is reading a letter from a father of two children.
② The father's daughter is a high school student.
③ He has more conversation with his children at the table.
④ The father wants to have more time with his kids.
⑤ The father wants to tell his kids that he loves them.

21 출제율 90%

빈칸에 알맞은 말을 써서 밑줄 친 (A)를 대신할 수 있는 문장을 완성하시오.

they were ＿＿＿＿ ＿＿＿＿ ＿＿＿＿
＿＿＿＿ ＿＿＿＿ understand me.

22 출제율 90%

What do the children do when their father asks them about their school life? Answer in English with six words.

➡ ＿＿＿＿＿＿＿＿＿＿＿＿＿＿＿＿

[23~25] 다음 글을 읽고 물음에 답하시오.

Breeze: Do you want to say ＿＿(A)＿＿ to your family or a friend? Please leave your story. We will share your story with our listeners.

Jiwon: Hello, I am a 15-year-old girl from Busan. I want to say to my brother Jaeho, "Sorry." I told Mom his secret last Friday. Mom got so angry, so he was in trouble. I was too scared to say sorry to him at that time. I promise I will never tell his secrets again.

23 출제율 95%

글의 흐름상 빈칸 (A)에 들어갈 말로 가장 적절한 것은?

① your secret
② thanks
③ sorry
④ everything
⑤ how lovely they are

24 출제율 100%

다음 중 위 글을 읽고 답할 수 <u>없는</u> 것은?

① How old is Jiwon?
② Where does Jiwon live?
③ When did Jiwon tell his brother's secret to her mom?
④ What was her brother's secret?
⑤ Why didn't Jiwon say sorry to her brother at that time?

25 출제율 90%

What does Jiwon promise? Answer in English with a full sentence.

➡ ＿＿＿＿＿＿＿＿＿＿＿＿＿＿＿＿
＿＿＿＿＿＿＿＿＿＿＿＿＿＿＿＿

[01~03] 다음 대화를 읽고 물음에 답하시오.

Minsol: (A)저는 Buster가 마음에 들지 않아요.
(happy)

Dad: What's wrong?

Minsol: He tore my homework into pieces again.

Dad: Puppies often do that.

Minsol: This is not the first time. Sometimes I find my socks in the dog house.

Dad: Please be kind to him. He's just five months old.

Minsol: You're too nice to him! He needs some training.

Dad: Okay. Let's start training in a few weeks.

01 위 대화의 밑줄 친 (A)의 우리말을 주어진 단어를 사용하여 영작하시오.

➡ _____

02 How old is Buster?

➡ _____

03 What does Minsol suggest to her father?

➡ _____

04 to부정사를 활용하여 다음 주어진 문장과 같은 의미의 문장을 쓰시오.

Yesterday they were very busy, so they couldn't start their meeting on time.

➡ _____
_____

05 다음 그림을 보고 빈칸에 알맞은 말을 쓰시오.

Greedy is picking a lot of apples. However, Lazy is too _____ them.

06 주어진 문장과 같은 의미의 문장을 쓰시오.

My dog is too big to go into the dog house.

➡ _____

07 주어진 단어를 활용하여 다음 우리말을 영어로 쓰시오.

그 남자는 내가 그의 차를 밀게 했다.
(make / push)

➡ _____

08 다음 대화의 빈칸에 알맞은 말을 쓰시오. 한 칸에 하나의 단어만 쓰시오.

A: The hall looks very small. I think it can't hold all the students.
B: I agree. The hall is _____ _____ _____ _____ all the students.

9 주어진 단어를 활용하여 다음 우리말을 영어로 쓰시오.

(1) 그녀는 내가 그녀의 피아노를 연주하게 했다. (have)

➡ _____

(2) 나는 그들이 산책을 하게 허락했다. (let, take)

➡ _____

(3) 그는 네가 그 산을 오르게 했니? (make)

➡ _____

[10~12] 다음 글을 읽고 물음에 답하시오.

Breeze: Good evening, listeners. This is your DJ, Breeze. Today we have a special guest, Andy Kim. He's a hip-hop artist. Welcome, Andy.

Andy: Nice to meet you and thank you for having me.

Breeze: Okay. What do our listeners want to tell their family? This evening we will find out by reading some letters from them. Andy, will you start off with the letter from a teenage girl?

Andy: Sure.

Andy: Hello. I'm a 15-year-old girl from Wonju. I want to tell you about my mom. My mom tries to do everything for me. She cleans my room without asking me, so it's sometimes hard to find my stuff. She also buys books and makes me study them. I want to say to my mom, "I know you love me, but I'm not a baby anymore. Please let me take care of things myself."

10 Whose letter will Andy read first? Answer in English with a full sentence.

➡ _____

11 Write the reason why the girl sometimes has hard time finding her stuff. Use the phrase 'It's because.'

➡ _____
_____

12 위 글의 내용에 맞게 빈칸에 알맞은 말을 쓰시오.

The girl's mom treats her like a baby. She cleans her room and even makes her _____ _____ that she buys for her.

[13~14] 다음 글을 읽고 물음에 답하시오.

This is a letter from a father who wants to share his experience with the "sad" father.

My kids and I did not ①talk much. There was a wall between us. I wanted to ②break it down. I tried to spend more time with my children on weekends. We played computer games, rode bikes, and went shopping ③together. In this way, I had ④less chances to ⑤talk with them. I came to know more about them.

13 ①~⑤ 중 글의 흐름상 어색한 것을 찾아 바르게 고쳐 쓰시오.

_____ ➡ _____

14 By sending a letter, what does the father want to do? Answer in English with a full sentence.

➡ _____
_____

01 다음 대화의 내용과 일치하도록 Sora의 일기를 완성하시오.

> Mike: Customer Service. How can I help you?
>
> Sora: I bought a hairdryer at your store last week. I'm not happy with it.
>
> Mike: What is the problem?
>
> Sora: It doesn't work well. I mean the air isn't hot enough.
>
> Mike: I'm sorry. Do you want to exchange it?
>
> Sora: Well, can I get a refund?
>
> Mike: Sure. Will you please visit our store with the dryer?
>
> Sora: Yes, I'll drop by tomorrow afternoon.
>
> Mike: Don't forget to bring the receipt.
>
> Sora: Okay. Thanks.

> Mon, Sep 23th, 2019
>
> I bought a new hairdryer at the store last week but I was not satisfied with it. It had a problem that (A)_____. I called the customer service and explained this problem. I wanted to (B)_____ rather than exchanging the hairdryer. To get the refund, I need to visit the store (C)_____. So, I'll drop by the store tomorrow afternoon.

02 다음 라디오 신청자의 사연을 완성하시오.

> • 사과하고 싶은 사람: my mother
>
> • 내가 한 일: I talked back to her in a very rude way.
>
> • 한 일의 결과: We haven't talked to each other for several days.
>
> • 하고 싶은 말: I will never talk back to you in such a rude way again.

> Hello. I'm a 15-year-old boy from Seoul. I want to say sorry to _____. The other day, I had an argument with my mother. She complained about my tight school uniform, and _____. Since then, _____.
>
> "Mom, I promise _____. Please accept my apology."

단원별 모의고사

01 다음 주어진 문장의 밑줄 친 work와 같은 의미로 쓰인 것은?

> The switch doesn't <u>work</u>, so I need to call the repair man.

① Doctors often <u>work</u> very long hours.
② This machine <u>works</u> by electricity.
③ Tony <u>works</u> for an engineering company.
④ My daughter is <u>working</u> as a police officer.
⑤ Jane <u>works</u> too hard.

02 다음 문장에 공통으로 들어갈 말을 고르시오.

> • I believe my son won't tell a _____.
> • Please _____ on the bed.
> • Why did you _____ to me?

① lie   ② understand
③ feed   ④ pour
⑤ exchange

03 다음 우리말과 일치하도록 주어진 단어를 모두 배열하여 영작하시오.

(1) 모든 학생들을 먹일 충분한 음식이 없다.
(is / all / food / to / there / not / students / enough / feed)

➡ _____

(2) 우유를 이 그릇에 부어주시겠어요?
(you / this / would / milk / bowl / pour / into)

➡ _____

(3) 짠 음식은 네 건강에 좋지 않다.
(not / food / your / is / health / for / salty / good)

➡ _____

[04~05] 다음 대화를 읽고 물음에 답하시오.

Emma: You look upset, Tommy.
Tommy: _____ (A)
Emma: What's wrong with her?
Tommy: She isn't doing her part of the group project.
Emma: I think you should talk to her.

04 위 대화의 빈칸 (A)에 들어갈 말로 적절한 것을 <u>모두</u> 고르시오.

① I was fascinated with Sojin.
② I'm not happy with Sojin.
③ I'm satisfied with Sojin.
④ I don't feel good with Sojin.
⑤ I really appreciate Sojin.

05 Why is Tommy upset?

➡ _____
_____

[06~07] 다음 대화를 읽고 물음에 답하시오.

Amy: I'm not very happy with my brother.
Brian: What's the problem?
Amy: He uses the bathroom for too long in the morning.
Brian: I know how you feel.
Amy: What can I do?
Brian: Well, (A)너는 더 일찍 일어나서 욕실을 먼저 사용할 수 있을 거야.
Amy: Okay, I'll give it a try.

06 위 대화의 밑줄 친 (A)의 우리말을 <보기>에 주어진 어구를 모두 배열하여 영작하시오.

> ┤ 보기 ├
> get up / and / earlier / you / the bathroom / first / use / can

➡ _____

07 위 대화의 내용과 일치하지 않는 것은?

① Amy는 남동생 때문에 기분이 좋지 않다.

② Amy의 남동생은 아침에 너무 오랫동안 욕실을 사용한다.

③ Brian은 Amy의 기분에 공감하였다.

④ Brian은 아침에 일찍 일어나 욕실을 먼저 사용할 것을 조언하였다.

⑤ Amy는 남동생과 욕실 사용 문제에 대해 이야기할 것이다.

[08~10] 다음 대화를 읽고 물음에 답하시오.

Mike: Customer Service. How can I help you?

Sora: I bought a hairdryer at your store last week. _____ (A)

Mike: What is the problem?

Sora: It doesn't work well. I mean the air isn't hot enough.

Mike: I'm sorry. Do you want to exchange it?

Sora: Well, can I get a refund?

Mike: Sure. Will you please visit our store with the dryer?

Sora: Yes, I'll drop by tomorrow afternoon.

Mike: Don't forget to bring the receipt.

Sora: Okay. Thanks.

08 위 대화의 빈칸 (A)에 들어갈 말로 어색한 것은?

① I'm sorry to say this, but I don't like it.

② I'm not happy with it.

③ I want to complain about it.

④ I'm not satisfied with it.

⑤ I'm so glad to have it.

09 위 대화에서 다음의 영영풀이가 나타내는 말을 찾아 쓰시오.

a piece of paper that shows that goods or services have been paid for

➡ _____

10 위 대화의 내용과 일치하지 않는 것은?

① 소라는 지난주에 헤어드라이어를 샀다.

② 헤어드라이어가 잘 작동하지 않는다.

③ 헤어드라이어가 충분히 뜨거운 바람이 나오지 않는다.

④ 소라는 헤어드라이어를 교환하기를 원한다.

⑤ 소라는 영수증을 갖고 내일 오후에 가게에 들릴 것이다.

[11~12] 다음 대화를 읽고 물음에 답하시오.

Minsol: I'm not (A)[sad / happy] with Buster.

Dad: What's wrong?

Minsol: _____ ⓐ _____

Dad: Puppies often do that.

Minsol: This is not the first time. Sometimes I find my socks in the dog house.

Dad: Please be kind to him. He's just five months old.

Minsol: You're too (B)[strict / nice] to him! He needs some training.

Dad: Okay. Let's start training in (C)[a few / few] weeks.

11 빈칸 ⓐ에 들어갈 말을 <보기>에 주어진 단어들을 모두 배열하여 영작하시오.

┌─ 보기 ┤
tore / again / he / into / my / pieces / homework
└──────

➡ _____

12 위 대화의 (A)~(C)에 들어갈 말로 바르게 짝지어진 것은?

	(A)	(B)	(C)
①	sad	strict	a few
②	sad	nice	few
③	happy	nice	a few
④	happy	nice	few
⑤	happy	strict	a few

13 다음 중 빈칸에 들어갈 말로 적절하지 <u>않은</u> 것은?

> Mom _____ us clean the windows.

① made
② helped
③ had
④ taught
⑤ let

14 다음 중 어법상 바르지 <u>않은</u> 것을 <u>모두</u> 고르면?

① Sora let us use her smartphone anytime we wanted.
② Julia is brave enough to say what she wants.
③ Wendy woke up so late to hear the news.
④ What made you call me at night?
⑤ Do you have her goes to school on foot?

15 다음 중 주어진 문장과 같은 의미의 문장은?

> My room is too dirty to invite my friends.

① My room is dirty enough to invite my friends.
② My room is so dirty that I can't invite my friends.
③ My room is so dirty that I can invite my friends.
④ My room is very dirty because I invite my friends.
⑤ My room is so dirty that I couldn't invite my friends.

16 주어진 단어를 활용하여 다음 우리말을 영어로 쓰시오.

> 나는 Jamie가 창문을 열게 했다. (make)

➡ _____

17 빈칸에 알맞은 말을 써서 다음 문장과 같은 의미의 문장을 완성하시오.

> I couldn't hear what you were saying because I was too far away from you.

➡ I was too _____
 what you were saying.

[18~22] 다음 글을 읽고 물음에 답하시오.

Breeze: Good evening, listeners. This is your DJ, Breeze. Today we have a special guest, Andy Kim. He's a hip-hop artist. Welcome, Andy.

Andy: Nice to meet you and thank you for having me.

Breeze: Okay. What do our listeners want to tell their family? This evening we will find out by reading some letters from them. Andy, will you start off with the letter from a teenage girl?

Andy: Sure.

Andy: Hello. I'm a 15-year-old girl from Wonju. I want to tell you about my mom. My mom tries to do everything for me. She cleans my room without asking me, so it's sometimes hard to find my stuff. She also buys books and makes me study them. I want to say to my mom, "I know you love me, but I'm not a baby anymore. Please let me take care of things myself."

Breeze: I felt the same way when I was in middle school.

Andy: Many moms think their kids are too young to do things __(A)__ their own. I hope the girl's mom will get the message.

18 다음 중 빈칸 (A)에 들어갈 말로 가장 적절한 것은?

① by   ② at   ③ on   ④ for   ⑤ in

19 다음 물음에 대한 대답을 글의 내용에 맞게 완성하시오.

Q: How did Breeze feel about her mother when she was in middle school?

A: She felt that _____ _____ _____ _____ _____ _____.

20 다음 중 위 글의 사연을 잘못 이해한 사람은?

① Sally: Breeze understands the girl's feelings.

② David: She is satisfied with her mom because she cleans her room instead of her.

③ Peter: The girl doesn't want her mom to do everything for her.

④ Julia: I hope that someday I can be a special guest of a show like Andy.

⑤ Kathy: If I have something to tell my family, I will send a letter to the show.

21 What does the girl want her mother to do?

➡ _____

_____

22 다음 빈칸에 들어갈 말로 가장 적절한 것은?

Andy thinks the girl's problem is very _____.

① unique   ② special

③ boring   ④ common

⑤ difficult

[23~24] 다음 글을 읽고 물음에 답하시오.

Andy: Hi. I'm a father of two children. One is a high school girl, and the other is a middle school boy. They're too busy to talk with me. When I get home from work, they just say hi and go back to their rooms. Sometimes I ask them about their school life, but they only give short answers. We don't talk much at the table, either. I want to say to my kids, "I love you so much, and I want to spend more time with you."

Breeze: Andy, did you talk with your parents often when you were younger?

Andy: Not really. I loved them very much, but I thought they were too old to understand me.

Breeze: I see. Does anyone have suggestions for the "sad" dad? Text your idea to us.

23 다음 중 위 글의 내용과 일치하지 않는 것은?

① The father has a son who is a middle school student.

② The father thinks there is not enough talking in his house.

③ Andy hardly talked with his parents when he was younger.

④ The kids are so busy that they can't talk with his father.

⑤ Andy didn't talk with his parents because he didn't love them.

24 What does Breeze ask the listeners to do? Use the words below.

(by texting them)

➡ _____

_____

Lesson

Special

Reading for Fun 3
Diary

A Diary from Athens

교과서
Words & Expressions

Key Words

- **about**[əbáut] 부 약, 대략
- **Agora**[ǽgərə] 명 아고라 (고대 그리스) 시민의 정치 집회, 집회장, 시장, 광장
- **almost**[ɔ́:lmoust] 부 거의
- **assembly**[əsémbli] 명 집회, 국회, 민회
- **Athenian**[əθí:niən] 명 아테네 사람
- **Athens**[ǽθinz] 명 아테네
- **character**[kǽriktər] 명 등장인물
- **citizen**[sítəzən] 명 시민
- **count**[kaunt] 동 수를 세다
- **develop**[divéləp] 동 개발하다, 발달시키다
- **diary**[dáiəri] 명 일기
- **discussion**[diskʌ́ʃən] 명 토론
- **final**[fáinl] 형 마지막의, 최종의
- **hold**[hould] 동 담다, 수용하다

- **gather**[gǽðər] 동 모으다, 모이다, 집결하다
- **impossible**[impásəbl] 형 불가능한
- **male**[meil] 형 남자의, 수컷의
- **matter**[mǽtər] 명 일, 문제, 안건
- **meaning**[mí:niŋ] 명 의미
- **outdoor**[áutdɔr] 형 야외의, 실외의
- **person**[pə́:rsn] 명 사람, 인간, 인물
- **question**[kwéstʃən] 동 질문하다
- **sadness**[sǽdnis] 명 슬픔
- **state**[steit] 명 국가
- **stay**[stei] 명 체류, 방문
- **talent**[tǽlənt] 명 재능
- **traditional**[trədíʃənl] 형 전통적인
- **vote**[vout] 동 투표하다
- **way**[wei] 명 방식

Key Expressions

- **a lot of** 많은
- **be busy -ing** ~하느라 바쁘다
- **between A and B** A와 B 사이에
- **by -ing** ~함으로써
- **gathering place** 모이는 장소
- **in addition to** ~에 더하여, ~일뿐 아니라

- **over the age of 20** 20살 이상의
- **so far** 지금까지
- **take part in** ~에 참여하다
- **thousands of** 수천의
- **too ~ to ...** 너무 ~해서 …하다

Word Power

※ 서로 반대되는 뜻을 가진 어휘

□ **final** (마지막의, 최종의) ↔ **initial** (처음의, 최초의)
□ **male** (남자의, 수컷의) ↔ **female** (여자의, 암컷의)
□ **ask** (질문하다) ↔ **answer** (답하다)

□ **possible** (가능한) ↔ **impossible** (불가능한)
□ **outdoor** (실외의) ↔ **indoor** (실내의)
□ **sad** (슬픈) ↔ **glad** (기쁜)

※ 서로 비슷한 뜻을 가진 어휘

□ **almost** (거의) : **nearly** (거의)
□ **gather** (모으다, 모이다, 집결하다) : **assemble** (모으다, 모이다)
□ **talent** (재능) : **gift** (재능)
□ **vote** (투표하다) : **elect, choose** (선거하다, 뽑다)

□ **develop** (개발하다) : **cultivate** (계발[연마]하다)
□ **stay** (체류, 방문) : **visit** (방문)
□ **traditional** (전통적인) : **conventional** (전통적인)
□ **way** (방식) : **method** (방법, 방식)

English Dictionary

□ **assembly** 집회, 국회, 민회
→ a meeting of a large group of people, especially one that happens regularly for a particular purpose
특히 특정한 목적을 위해 정기적으로 일어나는 많은 사람들의 모임

□ **citizen** 시민
→ someone who lives in a particular town or city
특정한 마을이나 도시에 사는 사람

□ **count** 수를 세다
→ to say numbers
수를 말하다

□ **hold** 담다, 수용하다
→ to contain something
무언가를 포함하다

□ **impossible** 불가능한
→ not able to happen
일어날 수 없는

□ **male** 남자의, 수컷의
→ typical of or relating to men or boys
남자들이나 소년들에게 전형적인 또는 관련된

□ **outdoor** 야외의, 실외의
→ happening or used outside; not in a building
밖에서 일어나거나 사용되는; 건물 안에서가 아닌

□ **question** 질문하다
→ to ask someone questions
누군가에게 질문을 묻다

□ **state** 국가
→ the government of a country
한 국가의 정부

□ **stay** 체류, 방문
→ a period of time that you spend in a place
한 장소에서 보내는 기간

□ **talent** 재능
→ a natural ability to do something
어떤 것을 하는 타고난 능력

□ **vote** 투표하다
→ to choose someone in an election
투표에서 누군가를 선택하다

Reading

A Diary from Athens

1st Day _ I am visiting my aunt and uncle in Athens. Today I went to the Agora in the center of the city. It is a gathering place for Athenians.
형용사구   = The Agora   아테네 사람들

There were a lot of stores, and people were busy talking and shopping.
There were+복수 명사 = many   be busy -ing: ~하느라 바쁘다. talking과 shopping은 병렬 관계

2nd Day _ My uncle went to the Assembly. Any male citizens over
민회, 집회   주어

the age of 20 can take part in the Assembly and vote on important
형용사구   ~에 참여하다   take와 병렬 관계 ~에 관한

matters. After they each speak freely about the matters, they vote
시간 부사절 접속사 '~한 후에'   부사로 동사 'speak'수식

by showing their hands. My uncle said, "Counting thousands of hands
by -ing: ~함으로써   동명사 주어   수천 의

is almost impossible."
단수 동사   거의(부사)

3rd Day _ I went to the Agora again. I heard a very interesting discussion between a teacher named Socrates and his students. Socrates
between A and B: A와 B 사이의   과거분사로 a teacher 수식

questioned his students on the meaning of life. I was too young to
질문했다   ~에 관해   too young to

understand it, but I liked their way of discussing matters.
too 형용사 to부정사: 너무 ~해서 ~할 수 없다   discuss는 타동사이므로 전치사 'about'을 사용하지 않는다.
(= so young that I couldn't understand it)

 확인문제

● 다음 문장이 본문의 내용과 일치하면 T, 일치하지 않으면 F를 쓰시오.

1 Agora is a place where Athenians gather. ☐

2 Agora had many stores in the past. ☐

3 All the male citizens had to participate in the Assembly. ☐

4 Socrates and his students discussed the meaning of life. ☐

---

assembly 집회, 국회, 민회

male 남자의, 수컷의

citizen 시민

take part in ~에 참여하다

vote 투표하다

count 수를 세다

impossible 불가능한

question 질문하다

meaning 의미

discuss ~에 관해 토론하다

4th Day _ Today was the best day so far. I went to the Theater of
지금까지

Dionysus. At the outdoor theater which can hold about 17,000 people,
선행사   주격 관계대명사   대략(부사)

we watched *Antigone*, a play by Sophocles. In addition to traditional
'Antigone'을 설명하는 동격구   ～에 더하여

songs and dances, the play had an interesting story. I sat far from the
연극(= *Antigone*)   ～로부터 멀리

stage, but I could feel the characters' sadness.

5th Day _ Today is the final day of my stay in Athens. My aunt and

uncle said to me, "You must develop your talent. You can help make
간접화법: My aunt and uncle told me to develop my talent.   help+동사원형/to부정사

Athens a great state." Now I want to go to school and become a better
want는 to부정사를 목적어로 취한다.   go와 병렬 관계. to go and (to) become

person.

so far 지금까지

outdoor 야외의, 실외의

hold 담다, 수용하다

traditional 전통적인

stay 체류, 방문

talent 재능

state 국가

character 등장인물

sadness 슬픔

확인문제

● 다음 문장이 본문의 내용과 일치하면 T, 일치하지 않으면 F를 쓰시오.

1 The writer thought today was the best day because he went to the Theater of
Dionysus. ☐

2 *Antigone* was the play which had an interesting story as well as traditional songs
and dances. ☐

3 The writer watched *Antigone*, a play by Sophocles, at the indoor theater. ☐

4 The writer stayed in Athens for five days. ☐

5 The writer wants to go to school and to learn from Socrates. ☐

● 우리말을 참고하여 빈칸에 알맞은 말을 쓰시오.

1 A _____ from _____

2 **1st Day** _ I am _____ my _____ and _____ in _____.

3 Today I went to the Agora in the _____ of the city.

4 It is a _____ place for Athenians.

5 There _____ _____ _____ _____ stores, and people were _____ _____ and _____.

6 **2nd Day** _ My uncle went to the _____.

7 _____ _____ _____ over the age of 20 can _____ _____ _____ the Assembly and _____ on important _____.

8 After they _____ speak _____ about the _____, they _____ _____ _____ their hands.

9 My uncle said, "_____ _____ _____ hands is _____ impossible."

10 **3rd Day** _ I went to the Agora _____.

11 I _____ a very _____ _____ _____ a teacher _____ Socrates _____ his students.

1	아테네에서 쓴 일기
2	첫째 날: 나는 아테네에 있는 숙부와 숙모 댁을 방문 중이다.
3	오늘은 도시 중심에 있는 아고라에 갔다.
4	아고라는 아테네 사람들이 모이는 장소이다.
5	많은 상점들이 있었고, 사람들은 이야기하고 쇼핑하느라 분주했다.
6	둘째 날: 숙부는 민회로 가셨다.
7	20살 이상의 모든 남자 시민은 민회에 참여하여 중요한 안건에 관해 투표할 수 있다.
8	그들은 각자 안건에 관해 자유롭게 의견을 말한 후, 손을 들어 투표한다.
9	숙부는 "수천 명의 손을 세는 것은 거의 불가능해."라고 말씀하셨다.
10	셋째 날: 나는 또 아고라에 갔다.
11	소크라테스라고 불리는 선생님과 그의 제자들이 나누고 있는 매우 재미있는 토론을 경청했다.

12 Socrates _____ his students _____ the _____ of life.

13 I was _____ young _____ understand it, but I liked their _____ of _____ matters.

14 **4th Day** _ Today was the _____ day _____ _____.

15 I _____ to the Theater of Dionysus.

16 At the _____ theater _____ can _____ _____ 17,000 people, we _____ *Antigone*, a _____ by Sophocles.

17 _____ _____ _____ _____ songs and dances, the _____ had an _____ story.

18 I sat _____ from the _____, but I could feel the _____ _____.

19 **5th Day** _ Today is the _____ day of my _____ in Athens.

20 My aunt and uncle said to me, "You _____ _____ your _____. You can _____ _____ Athens a great _____."

21 Now I _____ _____ _____ to school and become _____ _____ person.

12	소크라테스는 제자들에게 인생의 의미에 관해 질문하였다.
13	나는 그것을 이해하기에 너무 어렸지만, 나는 그들의 토론 방식이 마음에 들었다.
14	넷째 날: 오늘은 지금까지의 날 중 최고의 날이었다.
15	나는 디오니소스 극장에 갔다.
16	약 17,000명을 수용할 수 있는 야외 극장에서 소포클레스의 연극 '안티고네'를 관람하였다.
17	전통적으로 있던 노래와 춤에 더하여, '안티고네'에는 흥미로운 이야기가 있었다.
18	나는 무대에서 먼 곳에 앉아 있었지만, 등장인물들의 슬픔을 느낄 수 있었다.
19	다섯째 날: 오늘은 아테네에서 머무는 마지막 날이다.
20	숙부와 숙모는 "네 재능을 개발해야 된다. 너는 아테네를 위대한 국가로 만드는 데에 기여할 수 있어."라고 말씀하셨다.
21	이제 나는 학교에 다니며 더 나은 사람이 되고 싶다.

● 우리말을 참고하여 본문을 영작하시오.

1 아테네에서 쓴 일기

➡ _____

2 첫째 날: 나는 아테네에 있는 숙부와 숙모 댁을 방문 중이다.

➡ _____

3 오늘은 도시 중심에 있는 아고라에 갔다.

➡ _____

4 아고라는 아테네 사람들이 모이는 장소이다.

➡ _____

5 많은 상점들이 있었고, 사람들은 이야기하고 쇼핑하느라 분주했다.

➡ _____

6 둘째 날: 숙부는 민회로 가셨다.

➡ _____

7 20살 이상의 모든 남자 시민은 민회에 참여하여 중요한 안건에 관해 투표할 수 있다.

➡ _____

8 그들은 각자 안건에 관해 자유롭게 의견을 말한 후, 손을 들어 투표한다.

➡ _____

9 숙부는 "수천 명의 손을 세는 것은 거의 불가능해."라고 말씀하셨다.

➡ _____

10 셋째 날: 나는 또 아고라에 갔다.

➡ _____

11 소크라테스라고 불리는 선생님과 그의 제자들이 나누고 있는 매우 재미있는 토론을 경청했다.

➡ _____

12 소크라테스는 제자들에게 인생의 의미에 관해 질문하였다.

➡ _____

13 나는 그것을 이해하기에 너무 어렸지만, 나는 그들의 토론 방식이 마음에 들었다.

➡ _____

14 넷째 날: 오늘은 지금까지의 날 중 최고의 날이었다.

➡ _____

15 나는 디오니소스 극장에 갔다.

➡ _____

16 약 17,000명을 수용할 수 있는 야외 극장에서 소포클레스의 연극 '안티고네'를 관람하였다.

➡ _____

17 전통적으로 있던 노래와 춤에 더하여, '안티고네'에는 흥미로운 이야기가 있었다.

➡ _____

18 나는 무대에서 먼 곳에 앉아 있었지만, 등장인물들의 슬픔을 느낄 수 있었다.

➡ _____

19 다섯째 날: 오늘은 아테네에서 머무는 마지막 날이다.

➡ _____

20 숙부와 숙모는 "네 재능을 개발해야 된다. 너는 아테네를 위대한 국가로 만드는 데에 기여할 수 있어."

라고 말씀하셨다.

➡ _____

_____

21 이제 나는 학교에 다니며 더 나은 사람이 되고 싶다.

➡ _____

01 다음 빈칸에 알맞은 말을 〈보기〉에서 골라 쓰시오.

┌─ 보기 ─┐
assembly, hold, so far, discussion, take part in, talent, question

(1) He didn't _____ the weekly meeting.

(2) She showed an early _____ for drawing.

(3) Our school has _____ on Fridays.

(4) _____ everything about their plan went well.

(5) The elevator _____s about 10 people.

(6) The English teacher will _____ her students about grammar.

(7) We had a _____ about solving the problem.

02 다음 영영풀이에 해당하는 단어를 〈보기〉에서 찾아 쓰시오.

┌─ 보기 ─┐
vote, stay, citizen, hold, impossible

(1) someone who lives in a particular town or city

➡ _____

(2) to contain something

➡ _____

(3) a period of time that you spend in a place

➡ _____

(4) to choose someone in an election

➡ _____

(5) not able to happen

➡ _____

03 주어진 우리말에 맞게 빈칸에 알맞은 말을 쓰시오.

(1) 현대적인 도시 이외에도 멕시코에는 많은 고대 유적들이 있다.
• _____ _____ _____ modern cities, Mexico has many ancient ruins.

(2) Kathy는 한국 무용 대회에 참가했었어.
• Kathy _____ _____ _____ the Korean dance contest.

(3) 내 친구들이랑 겨울 스포츠를 즐기느라 바빴어.
• I _____ _____ _____ winter sports with my friends.

(4) 이 선수들은 나이가 23세가 넘을 수 있다.
• These players can be _____ _____ _____ 23.

(5) 그렇게 해서 그는 부자가 되었다.
• He became rich _____ _____ that.

(6) 남녀 간에 다를 게 없잖아요.
• There's no difference _____ men _____ women.

04 다음 문장을 어법에 맞게 고쳐 쓰시오.

(1) They were busy to prepare for class.
➡ _____

(2) A lot of preparation were needed.
➡ _____

(3) I liked their way of discussion matters.
➡ _____

05 다음 문장을 같은 뜻을 갖는 문장으로 바꿔 쓰시오.

(1) Charlotte is too sick to go to school today.
➡ _____
_____

(2) The box is too heavy for me to carry.

➡ _____

_____

(3) The math problems were easy enough for us to solve.

➡ _____

_____

(4) The ribbon was too short to tie with.

➡ _____

_____

06 다음 우리말을 괄호 안에 주어진 어휘를 이용하여 영작하시오.

(1) 그가 너무 빨리 말해서 나는 이해할 수가 없었다. (speak, to, fast, 8 단어)

➡ _____

(2) 그는 너무 어려서 운전할 수 없다. (young, that, drive a car, 10 단어)

➡ _____

(3) 사람들을 기억하는 것은 중요하다. (remember, important, 4 단어)

➡ _____

[07~09] 다음 글을 읽고 물음에 답하시오.

1st Day _ I am visiting my aunt and uncle in Athens. Today I went to the Agora in the center of the city. It is a gathering place for Athenians. There were a lot of stores, and (A) 사람들은 이야기하고 쇼핑하느라 분주했다.

2nd Day _ My uncle went to the Assembly. Any male citizens over the age of 20 can take part in the Assembly and vote on important matters. After they each speak freely about the matters, they vote by showing their hands. My uncle said, "Counting thousands of hands is almost impossible."

07 위 글의 밑줄 친 (A)의 우리말 해석에 맞게 주어진 단어를 활용하여 영어로 쓰시오.

be / busy

➡ _____

08 위 글에서 다음 영영풀이에 해당하는 단어를 찾아 쓰시오.

a meeting of a large group of people, especially one that happens regularly for a particular purpose

➡ _____

09 What did male citizens do in the Assembly? (Fill in the blanks.)

➡ They _____ on _____ _____ _____ _____ their hands.

[10~12] 다음 글을 읽고 물음에 답하시오.

3rd Day _ I went to the Agora again. I heard a very interesting discussion between a teacher named Socrates and his students. Socrates questioned his students on the meaning of life. (A)I was too young to understand it, but I liked their way of discussing matters.

4th Day _ Today was the best day so far. I went to the Theater of Dionysus. (B) 약 17,000명을 수용할 수 있는 야외 극장에서, we watched *Antigone*, a play by Sophocles. In addition to traditional songs and dances, the play had an interesting story. I sat far from the stage, but I could feel the characters' sadness.

10 위 글의 밑줄 친 (A)와 같은 의미가 되도록 'so'를 이용하여 쓰시오.

➡ _____

11 위 글 (B)의 우리말 해석에 맞게 주어진 단어를 알맞은 순서로 배열하시오.

the / which / can / at / about / outdoor / theater / hold / 17,000 people

➡ _____

_____

12 Where did the writer go on the fourth day of the stay?

➡ _____

[13~14] 다음 글을 읽고 물음에 답하시오.

5th Day _ Today is the final day of my stay in Athens. (A)My aunt and uncle said to me, "You must develop your talent. You can help make Athens a great state." Now I want to go to school and become a better person.

13 위 글의 밑줄 친 (A)를 같은 표현으로 바꿀 때, 'tell'과 'to부정사'를 이용하여 쓰시오.

➡ _____

14 위 글은 아테네 방문 5일차의 일기다. 일기의 내용에 어울리는 제목을 주어진 철자로 시작하는 단어로 완성하시오.

A New G_____ for My Life

15 다음 글을 읽고, 글의 내용과 일치하지 <u>않는</u> 문장을 찾아 바르게 고쳐 쓰시오. (본문에 있는 문장을 적을 것)

2nd Day _ My uncle went to the Assembly. Any male citizens over the age of 20 can take part in the Assembly and vote on important matters. After they each speak freely about the matters, they vote by showing their hands. My uncle said, "Counting thousands of hands is almost impossible."

3rd Day _ I went to the Agora again. I heard a very interesting discussion between a teacher named Socrates and his students. Socrates questioned his students on the meaning of life. I was too young to understand the meaning of life, but I liked their way of discussing matters.

① On the second day, the writer learned about the Assembly.

② Every citizen can take part in the Assembly to vote on important matters.

③ The writer heard Socrates and his students discussing the meaning of life.

④ Socrates' students were too young to understand the meaning of life.

➡ 틀린 문장 번호: _____

➡ 바르게 고친 문장:

(1) _____

_____

(2) _____

_____

출제율 90%

01 다음 중 짝지어진 단어의 관계가 나머지와 다른 하나는?

① wide : narrow
② male : female
③ sad : glad
④ stay : visit
⑤ impossible : possible

출제율 90%

02 다음 영영풀이에 해당하는 단어로 알맞은 것은?

> happening or used outside; not in a building

① assembly
② question
③ nearly
④ almost
⑤ outdoor

출제율 100%

03 다음 빈칸에 공통으로 들어갈 말을 고르시오.

> • He speaks Japanese well in addition _____ English.
> • The soup is too hot _____ eat.

① at
② to
③ for
④ of
⑤ from

출제율 90%

04 다음 빈칸에 알맞은 말이 바르게 짝지어진 것은?

> • How many countries have you been to so _____?
> • Most people think he is an adult _____ the age of 18.

① far – over
② far – under
③ now – over
④ now – under
⑤ near – below

출제율 90%

05 다음 영영풀이에 해당하는 단어를 주어진 철자로 시작하여 쓰시오.

> typical of or relating to men or boys

① count
② final
③ male
④ meaning
⑤ traditional

출제율 95%

06 다음 우리말에 맞게 빈칸에 알맞은 말을 쓰시오.

(1) 그는 종종 바보 같은 질문을 해서 나를 놀린다.
   • He often makes fun of me _____ asking silly questions.
(2) 나는 '지구 살리기' 캠페인에 참가해야만 해.
   • I must _____ _____ in the 'Save the Earth' campaign.
(3) 지금까지 전 이 옷에 만족해요.
   • So _____, I am satisfied with this dress.
(4) Boston과 New York 사이의 거리는 400킬로미터이다.
   • The distance _____ Boston and New York is 400 km.

출제율 100%

07 다음 중 어법상 어색한 것은?

① She is too weak to go there.
② There is a lot of guys selling things.
③ They were busy reading many fun books.
④ Having good friends is very important.
⑤ The writer of the diary stayed in Athens for five days.

08 다음 중 어법상 적절한 것은? *출제율 95%*

① She is tired enough to walk.

② My aunt said me that I must develop my talent.

③ They vote by showing their hands.

④ The writer decided going to school.

⑤ I heard a very interesting discussion between a teacher naming Socrates and his students.

09 다음 문장을 같은 뜻을 갖는 문장으로 바꿔 쓰시오. *출제율 100%*

(1) The soup is too hot for us to eat.

➡ _____

(2) I was too tired to visit you.

➡ _____

(3) Anne is wise enough to lead them.

➡ _____

10 다음 문장을 어법에 맞게 고쳐 쓰시오. *출제율 90%*

(1) I saw something calling a walking bus.

➡ _____
_____

(2) I was busy to take notes and to listen to the teacher.

➡ _____
_____

(3) Consumers are smart enough knowing that.

➡ _____
_____

(4) His family was very poor to educate him further.

➡ _____
_____

(5) The bag was big enough that it could hold almost 1,000 presents.

➡ _____
_____

(6) But he became too heavy that he couldn't move at all.

➡ _____
_____

(7) This problem is so hard that I can't solve.

➡ _____
_____

(8) This computer is small enough to me to carry.

➡ _____
_____

[11~13] 다음 글을 읽고 물음에 답하시오.

1st Day _ I ⓐam visiting my aunt and uncle in Athens. Today I went to the Agora in the center of the city. It is a gathering place for Athenians. There ⓑwere a lot of stores, and people were busy talking and shopping.

2nd Day _ My uncle went to the Assembly. Any male citizens over the age of 20 can take part in the Assembly and ⓒvote on important matters. After they each speak ⓓfreely about the matters, _____(A)_____. My uncle said, "Counting thousands of hands ⓔare almost impossible."

✏출제율 95%

11 위 글의 밑줄 친 ⓐ~ⓔ 중 어법상 어색한 것은?

① ⓐ ② ⓑ ③ ⓒ ④ ⓓ ⑤ ⓔ

✏출제율 90%

12 위 글의 빈칸 (A)에 알맞은 말을 다음 주어진 단어를 이용하여 쓰시오. (한 단어를 추가하고 필요하면 어형을 바꿀 것.)

| show / by / their / they / hands |

➡ _____

✏출제율 100%

13 위 글의 내용과 일치하지 <u>않는</u> 것은?

① The writer is visiting his aunt and uncle in Athens.
② On the first day, the writer visited the Agora.
③ The Assembly seems to function as a place for democracy.
④ The writer took part in the Assembly and voted on the important matters.
⑤ We can guess that thousands of people voted on the important matters in the Assembly.

[14~15] 다음 글을 읽고 물음에 답하시오.

Today is the final day of my stay in Athens. My aunt and uncle said to me, "You must develop your talent. <u>너는 아테네를 위대한 국가로 만드는 데에 기여할 수 있어.</u>" Now I want to go to school and become a better person.

✏출제율 100%

14 위 글의 마지막 부분에서 필자가 느끼는 심경으로 가장 알맞은 것을 고르시오.

① embarrassed ② excited
③ ashamed ④ bored
⑤ determined

✏출제율 90%

15 위 글의 밑줄 친 우리말에 맞게 주어진 어구를 이용하여 영어로 쓰시오.

| help / Athens / a great state |

➡ _____

[16~18] 다음 글을 읽고 물음에 답하시오.

I went to the Agora again. I heard a very ___(A)___ (interest) discussion between a teacher ___(B)___ (name) Socrates and his students. Socrates ___(C)___ (question) his students on the meaning of life. I was too young to understand ⓐit, but <u>나는 그들의 토론 방식이 마음에 들었다.</u>

✏출제율 95%

16 위 글의 빈칸 (A)~(C)에 괄호 안에 주어진 단어를 알맞은 형태로 변형해서 쓰시오.

➡ (A) _____ (B) _____ (C) _____

✏출제율 85%

17 위 글의 밑줄 친 우리말에 맞게 주어진 단어를 활용하여 영어로 쓰시오.

| like / way / of / discuss / matters |

➡ _____

✏출제율 90%

18 위 글의 밑줄 친 ⓐ가 가리키는 내용을 본문에서 찾아 쓰시오.

➡ _____

[19~20] 다음 글을 읽고 물음에 답하시오.

4th Day _ Today was the best day so _____ⓐ_____. I went to the Theater of Dionysus. At the outdoor theater which can hold about 17,000 people, we watched *Antigone*, a play by Sophocles. _____(A)_____ traditional songs and dances, the play had an interesting story. I sat ⓑ from the stage, but I could feel the characters' sadness.

19 위 글의 빈칸 (A)에 들어갈 알맞은 말을 고르시오.

① Because of ② In spite of
③ Thanks to ④ In addition to
⑤ According to

20 위 글의 ⓐ와 ⓑ에 공통으로 들어갈 말로 알맞은 것은?

① on ② far ③ away
④ near ⑤ under

[21~23] 다음 글을 읽고 물음에 답하시오.

1st Day _ I am visiting my aunt and uncle in Athens. Today I went to the Agora in the center of the city. It is a gathering place for Athenians. There were a lot of stores, and people were busy talking and shopping.

2nd Day _ My uncle went to the Assembly. Any male citizens over the age of 20 can take part in the Assembly and vote on important matters. After they each speak freely about the matters, they vote by showing their hands. My uncle said, "(A)수천 명의 손을 세는 것은 거의 불가능해."

3rd Day _ I went to the Agora again. I heard a very interesting discussion between a teacher named Socrates and his students. Socrates questioned his students on the meaning of life. I was too young to understand it, but I liked their way of discussing matters.

4th Day _ Today was the best day so far. I went to the Theater of Dionysus. At the outdoor theater which can hold about 17,000 people, we watched *Antigone*, a play by Sophocles. In addition to traditional songs and dances, the play had an interesting story. I sat far from the stage, but I could feel the characters' sadness.

5th Day _ Today is the final day of my stay in Athens. My aunt and uncle said to me, "You must develop your talent. You can help make Athens a great state." Now I want to go to school and become a better person.

21 위 글의 제목으로 알맞은 것을 고르시오.

① Athens: A New City
② Socrates and His Way of Discussion
③ History Travels to Athens
④ A Diary from Athens
⑤ What a Wonderful Play!

22 다음은 위 글에서 언급된 'Agora'의 기능을 요약한 글이다. 첫째 날과 셋째 날을 참고하여 빈칸에 알맞은 말을 쓰시오.

➡ Agora is the place for gathering, _____, _____ and _____.

23 위 글의 밑줄 친 (A)의 우리말 해석에 맞게 주어진 단어를 활용하여 영어로 쓰시오. (동명사 주어로 시작할 것)

thousand / almost / impossible

➡ _____

Lesson 7

A Life Full of Fun

🎤 의사소통 기능

- 경험 묻고 답하기
  A: Have you ever touched a snake?
  B: No, I haven't.

- 절차 묻고 답하기
  A: Do you know how to make fried rice?
  B: Sure. It's easy. First, cut the vegetables into small pieces. Next, ...

🎤 언어 형식

- 현재완료
  Ms. Green **has studied** Spanish for three years.
- 명사를 수식하는 현재분사와 과거분사
  Look at the **falling** leaves.

Words & Expressions

Key Words

- **alive** [əláiv] 혱 살아 있는
- **among** [əmʌ́ŋ] 젼 ~ 중에
- **amusing** [əmjúːziŋ] 혱 재미있는, 즐거운
- **animated movie** 만화영화
- **appear** [əpíər] 동 나타나다, 등장하다
- **boil** [bɔil] 동 끓이다, 끓다
- **box office** 극장 매표소
- **caricature** [kǽrikətʃər] 몡 캐리커쳐, (풍자) 만화
- **cartoon** [kɑːrtúːn] 몡 만화
- **cartoonist** [kɑːrtúːnist] 몡 만화가
- **chef** [ʃef] 몡 요리사
- **choose** [tʃuːz] 동 고르다, 선택하다
- **comic strip** 신문 연재만화
- **common** [kámən] 혱 공통의
- **creative** [kriéitiv] 혱 창의적인, 독창적인
- **develop** [divéləp] 동 개발하다, 만들다
- **dirty** [də́ːrti] 혱 더러운
- **drawing** [drɔ́ːiŋ] 몡 그림
- **education** [èdʒukéiʃən] 몡 교육
- **fascinating** [fǽsənèitiŋ] 혱 매력적인
- **fry** [frai] 동 볶다, 튀기다
- **lastly** [lǽstli] 부 마지막으로
- **machine** [məʃíːn] 몡 기계
- **movement** [múːvmənt] 몡 움직임
- **pepper** [pépər] 몡 고추
- **plate** [pleit] 몡 접시
- **pollute** [pəlúːt] 동 오염시키다
- **pour** [pɔːr] 동 붓다
- **probably** [prábəbli] 부 아마도
- **publish** [pʌ́bliʃ] 동 출판하다
- **recipe** [résəpi] 몡 조리법, 비법
- **remain** [riméin] 동 계속 ~이다
- **sauce** [sɔːs] 몡 소스
- **select** [silékt] 동 선택하다, 고르다
- **showtime** [ʃóutaim] 몡 상영 시간
- **silly** [síli] 혱 어리석은
- **simple** [símpl] 혱 간단한, 단순한
- **sneaker** [sníkər] 몡 운동화
- **spread** [spred] 동 펴 바르다
- **sunscreen** [sʌ́nskrìːn] 몡 자외선 차단제
- **taste** [teist] 동 맛보다, 먹다
- **translate** [trænsléit] 동 번역하다
- **type** [taip] 몡 형태
- **usual** [júːʒuəl] 혱 평소의, 보통의
- **washing powder** (세탁용) 세제, 가루비누
- **well-known** 혱 유명한, 잘 알려진

Key Expressions

- **be made into** ~로 만들어지다
- **can't wait to** ~가 기대되다
- **catch one's interest** ~의 관심을 끌다
- **come together** 합쳐지다
- **cut A into pieces** A를 조각으로 자르다
- **jump out at** ~에게 금방 눈에 띄다, ~에게 분명히 보이다
- **make fun of** ~을 놀리다
- **of all ages** 모든 연령의
- **pay for** ~에 대한 돈을 내다
- **play a role** 역할을 하다
- **take a look** 살펴보다
- **ups and downs** 기복
- **watch out** 조심하다

Word Power

※ 서로 반대되는 뜻을 가진 어휘

- appear (나타나다) ↔ disappear (사라지다)
- dirty (더러운) ↔ clean (깨끗한)
- silly (어리석은) ↔ clever, bright (영리한)
- kind (친절한) ↔ unkind (불친절한)

- alive (살아 있는) ↔ dead (죽은)
- usual (평소의, 보통의) ↔ unusual (특이한)
- first (처음(으로), 맨 먼저) ↔ lastly (마지막으로)
- high (높은) ↔ low (낮은)

※ 요리와 관련된 어휘

- cut (자르다)
- boil (끓이다)
- put (놓다)
- fry (볶다, 튀기다)
- pour (붓다)
- spread (바르다)
- add (더하다)
- bake (굽다)

English Dictionary

- **amusing** 재미있는, 즐거운
  → causing laughter
  웃음을 유발하는

- **appear** 나타나다
  → to start to be seen
  보이기 시작하다

- **caricature** 풍자만화
  → a funny drawing of somebody that exaggerates some of their features
  누군가의 어떤 특징들을 과장하는 재미있는 그림

- **develop** 개발하다, 만들다
  → to invent something new
  새로운 무언가를 고안하다

- **education** 교육
  → a process of teaching and learning
  가르치고 배우는 과정

- **fascinating** 매력적인
  → extremely interesting
  매우 흥미로운

- **fry** 볶다, 튀기다
  → to cook something in hot fat or oil
  뜨거운 지방 또는 기름으로 무언가를 요리하다

- **movement** 움직임
  → the act of moving
  움직이는 행동

- **publish** 출판하다
  → to make information available to people in a book, magazine, or newspaper
  책, 잡지, 또는 신문으로 사람들에게 이용 가능한 정보를 만들다

- **remain** 계속 ~하다
  → to stay in the same place or in the same condition
  같은 장소 또는 같은 상태에 머무르다

- **silly** 어리석은
  → showing little thought; foolish
  생각이 거의 없음을 보여주는; 바보 같은

- **sunscreen** 자외선 차단제
  → a type of lotion that you put on your skin to protect it from being damaged by the sun
  태양에 의해 손상되는 것으로부터 피부를 보호하기 위해 피부에 바르는 로션의 한 유형

- **translate** 번역하다
  → to be changed from one language to another
  하나의 언어에서 다른 언어로 바뀌다

- **usual** 평소의, 보통의
  → normal; happening most often
  보통의; 가장 자주 일어나는

01 다음 단어들 중 요리와 관련이 없는 것은?

① pour   ② bake
③ fry   ④ cook
⑤ publish

02 다음 중 단어의 명사형이 틀린 것은?

① educate – education
② pollute – pollution
③ suggest – suggestion
④ translate – translation
⑤ agree – agreetion

03 다음 영영풀이가 가리키는 것을 고르시오.

| to be changed from one language to another |

① translate   ② publish
③ remain   ④ pour
⑤ taste

04 다음 중 밑줄 친 부분의 뜻풀이가 바르지 않은 것은?

① Cindy is a creative storybook writer. 창의적인
② Korean people think education for children is important for the future. 교육
③ Do you know how to use this washing machine? 기계
④ It's fascinating to see how babies grow into children. 당황스러운
⑤ Cartoonists often work with writers who create ideas. 만화가

05 다음 우리말에 맞게 빈칸에 알맞은 말을 쓰시오.

(1) 마지막으로, 뜨거운 물을 붓고 기다리세요.
  ➡ _____, pour hot water and wait.
(2) 나는 빵에 버터와 잼을 발랐다.
  ➡ I _____ butter and jam on the bread.
(3) 접시 위에 어떤 음식도 남기지 마라.
  ➡ Don't leave any food on your _____.
(4) 콩으로 간장을 담근다.
  ➡ Soybean _____ _____ _____ soy sauce.
(5) 이 그림은 나의 관심을 끌었다.
  ➡ This picture _____ _____ _____.
(6) 지도 좀 함께 보자.
  ➡ Let's _____ _____ _____ at the map together.

06 다음 주어진 문장의 밑줄 친 spread와 같은 의미로 쓰인 것은?

| I need a knife to spread butter on bread. |

① I'll spread strawberry jam on the toast for you.
② I saw the bird spread its wings.
③ Before the party, we need to spread a cloth on the table.
④ Virus spread rapidly during the holidays.
⑤ The fire spread to the building before the fire fighters arrived.

01 다음 짝지어진 단어의 관계가 같도록 빈칸에 알맞은 말을 쓰시오.

> clean : dirty = _____ : alive

02 다음 문장의 빈칸에 들어갈 말을 〈보기〉에서 골라 쓰시오.

┤ 보기 ├
> usual / well-known / creative / silly / cartoonist

(1) She came up with a _____ solution to the problem.
(2) The _____ is good at drawing cute animals.
(3) I hope I didn't make any _____ mistakes.
(4) There was more rainfall than _____ this summer.
(5) Stephen Hawking is one of the most _____ scientists.

03 다음 우리말에 맞게 빈칸에 알맞은 말을 쓰시오.

(1) 극장의 극장 매표소 옆에 매점이 있다.
  ⇒ There is a snack bar next to the _____ _____ in the theater.
(2) 다른 상영 시간을 골라줄 수 있나요?
  ⇒ Can you pick another _____?
(3) 책에 얼마의 돈을 냈나요?
  ⇒ How much did you _____ _____ the book?

04 다음 우리말과 일치하도록 주어진 어구를 모두 배열하여 완성하시오.

(1) 너는 네 친구들을 놀려서는 안 된다.
  (make / friends / your / you / should / of / fun / not)
  ⇒ _____
(2) Lucy는 삶의 기복에서 항상 침착하다.
  (Lucy / downs / life's / calm / always / is / through / and / ups)
  ⇒ _____
(3) 나는 매일 그날의 웹툰을 살펴본다.
  (take / at / a look / the webtoons / I / the day / of)
  ⇒ _____

05 다음 〈보기〉에 주어진 단어를 사용하여 빈칸을 완성하시오.

┤ 보기 ├
> agreement / suggestion / amusement / education / pollution

> <The Best Animated Movie for Children's _____>
> Animals welcome to the city's plan to build an _____ park in the forest. However, they soon suffer from serious _____. An old elephant makes a _____. The animals and the city reach an _____ to create a better world for everyone.

Conversation

1 경험 묻고 답하기

> **A** Have you ever touched a snake? 뱀을 만져 본 적 있니?
>
> **B** No, I haven't. 아니, 없어.

■ 'Have you ever + 과거분사 ~?'는 경험을 묻는 표현으로 'Have you ever been to ~?'는 '~에 가 본 적이 있니?'라는 의미이다. 이에 대한 대답으로 긍정일 때는 'Yes, I have.', 부정일 때는 'No, I haven't.'로 대답한다. Have you?는 상대방에게서 받은 질문을 다시 상대방에게 묻는 표현으로 반복된 부분은 생략한다.

■ **경험 묻고 답하기**

• 현재까지의 경험을 물을 때 현재완료 시제를 사용하므로 'Have you ever + 과거분사 ~?' 형태에 유의한다.

• 경험하지 못한 것으로 '전혀 ~해 본 적이 없다.'라고 강조하기 위해 'No, I've never ~'로 대답할 수 있다.

• 과거의 경험은 과거 시제를 이용한다.

ex) Did you touch the snake? – 과거에 뱀을 만졌는지 묻는 표현

Have you ever touched the snake? – 과거부터 현재까지 뱀을 만져 본 적이 있는지 묻는 표현

핵심 Check

1. 다음 우리말과 일치하도록 빈칸에 알맞은 말을 쓰시오.

(1) **A:** Have you ever _____ a sport star? (스포츠 스타를 만나 본 적 있어?)

　B: No, I _____. _____ you? (아니, 없어. 너는?)

　A: Yes, I _____. (나는 만나 본 적이 있어.)

(2) **A:** _____ _____ _____ _____ to Dokdo? (독도에 가 본 적 있니?)

　B: Yes, I _____ _____ there. (응, 거기에 가 보았어.)

　A: Wow, when _____ you go there? (와, 언제 그곳에 갔었니?)

② **절차 묻고 답하기**

A Do you know how to make fried rice? 어떻게 볶음밥을 만드는지 아니?

B Sure. It's easy. First, cut the vegetables into small pieces. Next, ...
물론이죠. 쉬워요. 첫째, 채소를 작은 조각으로 자르세요. 다음 ....

■ 서수를 사용하여 어떤 절차의 순서를 열거할 수 있다. 이때, 'Second, Third' 대신에 'Next, Then'을 쓸 수 있다.

 • first / first of all: 먼저, 우선

 • then / next: 다음에는

 • lastly / finally: 마지막으로

■ **절차 묻고 답하기**

 • How can I buy a subway ticket from a machine? 기계로부터 지하철 표를 어떻게 살 수 있나요?

 1. First, select "Language." 첫째, 언어를 선택하세요.

 2. Second, choose where to go. 둘째, 어디로 갈지 선택하세요.

 3. Lastly, pay the fare, and get the ticket. 마지막으로, 요금을 지불하고, 표를 받으세요.

핵심 Check

2. 다음 우리말과 일치하도록 빈칸에 알맞은 말을 쓰시오.

 (1) **A:** Do you know _____ _____ make *ramyeon*? (어떻게 라면을 만드는지 아니?)

   B: Sure. It's easy to make. _____, boil water in a pot. _____, put noodles in the pot. (물론이지. 만들기 쉬워. 첫째, 냄비에 물을 끓여. 둘째, 면을 냄비에 넣어.)

   A: Okay. What should I do _____? (알겠어. 그 다음에는 무엇을 해야 하니?)

   B: _____ them for 3-4 minutes. (그것을 3~4분 동안 끓여.)

 (2) **A:** Do you know how to _____ _____ _____?

   (너는 어떻게 쉽게 잠이 드는지 알고 있니?)

   B: _____ _____ _____, take a warm bath and drink a glass of milk. _____, stretch and relax your body. _____, read a boring book. (우선, 따뜻한 목욕을 하고 우유 한 잔을 마셔. 다음, 몸을 스트레칭하고 휴식을 취해. 마지막으로, 지루한 책을 읽어.)

   A: I see. Thank you for your advice. (알겠어. 조언해 주어 고마워.)

A. Communication: Listen –Dialog 1

Jane: Kevin, you look ❶down.

Kevin: Nothing ❷serious. Sometimes my feelings change a lot.

Jane: I understand. Many teens have ❸ups and downs in their feelings.

Kevin: Oh, really?

Jane: ❹Have you watched the ❺animated movie "Shining Days"?

Kevin: ❻No, I haven't. Why do you ask?

Jane: ❼It is about a teenager's feelings. ❼It will help you ❽understand your feelings better.

Kevin: That sounds good! I'll watch ❼it.

Jane: Kevin, 너 기분이 안 좋아 보이는구나.

Kevin: 별거 아니에요. 때때로 제 감정이 많이 바뀌어요.

Jane: 이해한단다. 많은 십 대가 감정의 기복이 있지.

Kevin: 아, 정말요?

Jane: 'Shining Days'라는 만화 영화를 본 적이 있니?

Kevin: 아니요, 본 적이 없어요. 왜 물으세요?

Jane: 그건 십 대의 감정에 관한 거야. 그건 네가 네 감정을 더 잘 이해하도록 도와줄 거야.

Kevin: 괜찮은 거 같네요! 그걸 볼게요.

❶ down: 우울한 = depressed = blue　　　　❷ serious: 심각한

❸ ups and downs: 기복

❹ Have you ever p.p. ~?: '~해 본 적이 있니?'라고 경험을 묻는 표현이다.

❺ animated movie: 만화영화

❻ 경험 유무를 묻는 질문에 'Yes, I have.' 또는 'No, I haven't.'로 대답한다.

❼ It은 모두 "Shining Days"를 가리킨다.

❽ help의 목적격 보어로 원형부정사 understand가 쓰였다.

Check(√) True or False

(1) Kevin looks down because of serious problems.　　　　T ☐　F ☐

(2) Kevin hasn't watched the animated movie "Shining Days".　　　　T ☐　F ☐

 B. Wrap Up – Listening ❺

Judy: ❶Have you ever been to Sokcho?

Minsu: Yes, I have. ❷Actually my uncle lives ❸there, so I visit ❹him every year.

Judy: Really? Then, you've climbed Mt. Seorak, ❺haven't you?

Minsu: Yes, I've climbed to the top of the mountain ❻twice.

Judy: 너는 속초에 가 본 적이 있니?

Minsu: 응, 가 본 적이 있어. 사실은 내 삼촌이 거기 살아서, 나는 매년 그를 방문해.

Judy: 정말? 그러면, 너는 설악산을 올라 본 적이 있지, 그렇지 않니?

Minsu: 응, 그 산의 정상에 올라간 적이 두 번 있어.

❶ Have you ever been to ~?: ~에 가 본 적이 있니?　　　　❷ actually: 사실은, 실제로

❸ there는 Sokcho를 가리킨다.　　　　❹ him은 Minsu's uncle을 가리킨다.

❺ 부가의문으로 '그렇지 않니?'라며 다시 한 번 확인하는 표현이다.

❻ twice: 두 번

Check(√) True or False

(3) Minsu's uncle lives in Sokcho.　　　　T ☐　F ☐

(4) Minsu climbs to the top of Mt. Seorak every year.　　　　T ☐　F ☐

Communication: Listen – Dialog 2

Emily: Oh, look at the long line at the ❶box office.

Tony: Yeah, there's a ticket machine over there. Let's buy the tickets from the machine.

Emily: All right. Do you know how to use the machine?

Tony: Sure. It's easy. ❷First, select a movie and a showtime.

Emily: Okay. We can watch the seven o'clock show. Then what?

Tony: Well, ❸select ❹the number of tickets and choose our seats.

Emily: Okay. Two tickets, and I want to sit in the back.

Tony: No problem. ❺Lastly, ❻pay for the tickets.

Emily: It's very simple.

❶ box office: 극장 매표소
❷ 절차를 답하는 표현으로 first(첫째), second(둘째), next(다음) 등을 사용한다.
❸ 명령문이므로 동사원형으로 시작한다.
❹ the number of: ~의 수, cf. a number of: 많은
❺ lastly: 마지막으로
❻ pay for: ~에 대한 돈을 내다

Communication – Listen more

Suji: Good morning, ❶Chef Garcia!

Garcia: Hello, Suji. ❷Have you ever made nacho pizza?

Suji: Nacho pizza? ❸No, I haven't.

Garcia: Kids will love ❹it, and I'll tell you how to make ❹it.

Suji: Sounds good!

Garcia: It's easy to make. First, ❺put nacho chips on a plate and ❻spread pizza sauce on ❼them.

Suji: Okay. Let me help you with the pizza sauce.

Garcia: Thanks. Next, put some ham, onions, and ❽peppers on top.

Suji: Okay. Then?

Garcia: Add cheese and bake for about 12 minutes in the oven.

Suji: I ❾can't wait to taste it!

❶ chef: 요리사
❷ Have you ever ~?: '~해 본 적이 있니?'라며 경험을 묻는 질문이다.
❸ 경험이 없을 때는 No, I haven't., 경험이 있을 때는 'Yes, I have.'라고 대답한다.
❹ it은 모두 'nacho pizza'를 가리킨다.
❺ put A on B: A를 B 위에 놓다
❻ spread: 바르다
❼ them은 nacho chips를 가리킨다.
❽ pepper: 고추
❾ can't wait to ~: ~가 기대되다

Communicate: Speak

Anna: Do you know how to make ❶fried rice?

Jinsu: Sure. It's easy. First, ❷cut the vegetables into small ❸pieces.

Anna: Okay. What do you do next?

Jinsu: Put some oil in the pan. ❹Then, fry the vegetables with rice.

Anna: Wow, it's really simple.

❶ fried rice: 볶음밥
❷ cut A into B: A를 B로 자르다
❸ piece: 조각
❹ Next 또는 After that 등으로 바꾸어 쓸 수 있다.

Wrap Up – Listen ❻

Mike: Today, I'll tell you how to ❶draw a bear's face. First, draw a big circle for the face. ❷Next, make two circles on top of the face. ❸After that, draw two circles for its eyes and ❹color ❺them black. Then, draw a small circle for the nose. Lastly, make a mouth.

❶ draw: 그리다
❷ Next는 Second로 바꾸어 쓸 수 있다.
❸ After that은 Third 또는 Next로 바꾸어 쓸 수 있다.
❹ color는 동사로 '색칠하다'를 뜻한다.
❺ them은 two circles를 가리킨다.

● 다음 우리말과 일치하도록 빈칸에 알맞은 말을 쓰시오.

Communication: Listen – Dialog 1

Jane: Kevin, you look _____.

Kevin: Nothing _____. Sometimes my feelings change _____ _____.

Jane: I understand. Many teens have _____ _____ _____ in their feelings.

Kevin: Oh, really?

Jane: _____ _____ _____ the animated movie "Shining Days"?

Kevin: No, _____ _____. _____ do you ask?

Jane: It is about a teenager's _____. It will help you _____ your feelings _____.

Kevin: That _____ good! I'll _____ it.

Jane: Kevin, 너 기분이 안 좋아 보이는 구나.
Kevin: 별거 아니에요. 때때로 제 감정이 많이 바뀌어요.
Jane: 이해한단다. 많은 십 대가 감정의 기복이 있지.
Kevin: 아, 정말요?
Jane: 'Shining Days'라는 만화영화를 본 적이 있니?
Kevin: 아니요, 본 적이 없어요. 왜 물으세요?
Jane: 그건 십 대의 감정에 관한 거야. 그건 네가 네 감정을 더 잘 이해하도록 도와줄 거야.
Kevin: 괜찮은 거 같네요! 그걸 볼게요.

Communication: Listen – Dialog 2

Emily: Oh, look at the long _____ at the box office.

Tony: Yeah, there's a _____ _____ over there. Let's buy the tickets _____ the _____.

Emily: All right. Do you know _____ _____ _____ _____ _____?

Tony: Sure. It's easy. First, _____ a movie and a showtime.

Emily: Okay. We can _____ the seven o'clock show. Then _____?

Tony: Well, _____ the number of tickets and choose our _____.

Emily: Okay. Two tickets, and I want to sit in the _____.

Tony: No problem. _____, _____ _____ the tickets.

Emily: It's very _____.

Emily: 아, 극장 매표소에 길게 늘어선 줄을 좀 봐.
Tony: 네, 저쪽에 발매기가 하나 있어요. 저 기계에서 표를 사요.
Emily: 좋아. 그 기계를 어떻게 쓰는지 아니?
Tony: 그럼요. 쉬워요. 먼저, 영화와 상영 시간을 골라요.
Emily: 알았어. 우리는 7시 영화를 볼 수 있겠네. 그리고 뭘 하니?
Tony: 음, 표 매수를 선택하고 우리의 좌석을 골라요.
Emily: 좋아. 표 두 장, 그리고 나는 뒤에 앉고 싶어.
Tony: 좋아요. 마지막으로 표 값을 내요.
Emily: 정말 간단하구나.

Communication: Listen More

Suji: Good morning, Chef Garcia!

Garcia: Hello, Suji. _____ _____ _____ _____ nacho pizza?

Suji: Nacho pizza? _____, _____ _____.

Garcia: Kids will love it, and I'll tell you _____ _____ _____ it.

Suji: Sounds good!

Garcia: It's easy to make. _____, _____ nacho chips _____ a plate and _____ pizza sauce on them.

Suji: Okay. Let me _____ you _____ the pizza sauce.

Garcia: Thanks. _____, put some ham, onions, and _____ on top.

Suji: Okay. Then?

Garcia: _____ cheese and _____ for about 12 minutes in the _____.

Suji: I can't _____ to _____ it!

Communicate: Speak

Anna: Do you know how to make _____ _____?

Jinsu: Sure. It's easy. First, _____ the vegetables _____ small pieces.

Anna: Okay. What do you do _____?

Jinsu: _____ some oil in the pan. Then, _____ the vegetables with rice.

Anna: Wow, it's really _____.

Wrap Up – Listening ⑤

Judy: _____ you ever _____ to Sokcho?

Minsu: Yes, I _____. _____ my uncle lives there, so I visit him every year.

Judy: Really? Then, _____ _____ Mt. Seorak, _____ _____?

Minsu: Yes, I've climbed to the top of the mountain _____.

Wrap Up – Listening ⑥

Mike: Today, I'll tell you _____ _____ _____ a bear's face. _____, draw a big _____ for the face. _____, make two circles on top of the face. After that, _____ two circles for its eyes and _____ them black. Then, draw a small _____ for the nose. _____, make a mouth.

[01~02] 다음 설명을 읽고 물음에 답하시오.

> Mike: Today, I'll tell you how to draw a bear's face. First, draw a big circle for the face. Next, make two circles on top of the face. After that, draw two circles for its eyes and color them black. Then, draw a small circle for the nose. Lastly, make a mouth.

01 How many circles do Mike need to draw a bear's face?

➡ _____

02 위 설명의 내용과 일치하지 <u>않는</u> 것은?

① Mike는 곰의 얼굴을 그리는 법을 설명하고 있다.
② 첫 번째로, 얼굴에 해당하는 큰 원을 그린다.
③ 두 번째로, 얼굴 위에 두 개의 원을 그린다.
④ 세 번째로, 눈에 해당하는 두 개의 원을 그리고 검게 색칠한다.
⑤ 마지막으로, 코에 해당하는 작은 원을 그린다.

[03~04] 다음 대화를 읽고 물음에 답하시오.

> Anna: <u>너는 볶음밥을 만드는 법을 아니?</u> (fried, how)
> Jinsu: Sure. It's easy. First, cut the vegetables into small pieces.
> Anna: Okay. What do you do next?
> Jinsu: Put some oil in the pan. Then, fry the vegetables with rice.
> Anna: Wow, it's really simple.

03 위 대화의 밑줄 친 우리말을 주어진 단어를 사용하여 영작하시오.

➡ _____

04 위 대화에서 언급한 볶음밥을 만드는 법을 간략히 우리말로 설명하시오.

➡ _____

05 다음 우리말을 주어진 단어를 모두 배열하여 영작하시오.

(1) 나는 전에 Baltimore에 가 본 적이 없다. (been / I've / before / Baltimore / never / to)
   ➡ _____
(2) 너는 중국에 가 보았니? (ever / China / you / to / have / been)
   ➡ _____

[01~03] 다음 대화를 읽고 물음에 답하시오.

Jane: Kevin, you look (A)down.
Kevin: Nothing serious. Sometimes my feelings change a lot.
Jane: I understand. Many teens have ups and downs in their feelings.
Kevin: Oh, really?
Jane: (B)"Shining Days"라는 만화영화를 본 적이 있니?
Kevin: ____(a)____ Why do you ask?
Jane: It is about a teenager's feelings. It will help you understand your feelings better.
Kevin: That sounds good! I'll watch it.

위 대화의 빈칸 (a)에 들어갈 말로 적절한 것은?

① No, I'm not. ② No, I haven't.
③ No, I don't. ④ No, I have.
⑤ No, I didn't.

02 위 대화의 밑줄 친 (A)와 바꾸어 쓸 수 있는 것은?

① depressed ② happy
③ satisfied ④ excited
⑤ pleased

서답형
03 위 대화의 밑줄 친 (B)의 우리말을 다음 〈보기〉의 주어진 어구를 모두 배열하여 영작하시오.

보기
watched / the / have / animated / you / movie "Shining Days"

➡ _____

_____

[04~05] 다음 대화를 읽고 물음에 답하시오.

Emily: Oh, look at the long line at the box office.
Tony: Yeah, there's a ticket machine over there. Let's buy the tickets from the machine.
Emily: All right. Do you know (A)[how / what] to use the machine?
Tony: Sure. It's easy. First, select a movie and a showtime.
Emily: Okay. We can watch the seven o'clock show. Then what?
Tony: Well, select the number of tickets and (B)[to choose / choose] our seats.
Emily: Okay. Two tickets, and I want to sit in the back.
Tony: No problem. (C)[Lately / Lastly], pay for the tickets.
Emily: It's very simple.

04 위 대화의 빈칸 (A)~(C)에 들어갈 말로 적절한 것끼리 짝지어진 것은?

	(A)	(B)	(C)
①	how	to choose	Lately
②	how	choose	Lately
③	how	choose	Lastly
④	what	choose	Lastly
⑤	what	to choose	Lately

위 대화의 내용과 일치하지 않는 것은?

① 극장 매표소에 줄이 길게 늘어서 있다.
② Emily와 Tony는 발매기에서 표를 샀다.
③ 발매기에서 표를 사기 위해 먼저 영화와 상영 시간을 골라야 한다.
④ 표 값을 지불 한 후 표 매수와 좌석을 고를 수 있다.
⑤ Emily는 뒷좌석에 앉고 싶어 한다.

[06~07] 다음 대화를 읽고 물음에 답하시오.

Suji: Good morning, Chef Garcia!
Garcia: Hello, Suji. Have you ever made nacho pizza?
Suji: Nacho pizza? No, I haven't.
Garcia: Kids will love it, and I'll tell you how to make it.
Suji: Sounds good!
Garcia: It's easy to make. First, ____ⓐ____ nacho chips on a plate and spread pizza sauce on them.
Suji: Okay. Let me ____ⓑ____ you with the pizza sauce.
Garcia: Thanks. Next, put some ham, onions, and peppers on top.
Suji: Okay. Then?
Garcia: Add cheese and ____ⓒ____ for about 12 minutes in the oven.
Suji: I can't ____ⓓ____ to taste it!

서답형

06 다음 〈보기〉에 주어진 단어를 위 대화의 빈칸에 알맞게 쓰시오.

┌─ 보기 ┐
put / bake / wait / help
└───────────────────┘

➡ ⓐ _____ ⓑ _____
　 ⓒ _____ ⓓ _____

중요

07 위 대화를 읽고 대답할 수 <u>없는</u> 것은?

① What is Garcia talking about?
② What do Garcia and Suji need to make the nacho pizza?
③ How long should Garcia and Suji bake the pizza in the oven?
④ What should Garcia and Suji do after spreading pizza source on the nacho chips?
⑤ What ingredient should Garcia and Suji prepare to make pizza source?

서답형

08 다음 대화가 자연스럽게 이어지도록 순서대로 배열하시오.

(A) Okay. What do you do next?
(B) Wow, it's really simple.
(C) Sure. It's easy. First, cut the vegetables into small pieces.
(D) Put some oil in the pan. Then, fry the vegetables with rice.
(E) Do you know how to make fried rice?

➡ _____

서답형

[09~10] 다음 대화를 읽고 물음에 답하시오.

Judy: (a)속초에 가 본 적이 있니?
Minsu: Yes, I have. Actually my uncle lives there, so I visit him every year.
Judy: Really? Then, you've climbed Mt. Seorak, ____(A)____?
Minsu: Yes, I've climbed to the top of the mountain twice.

09 위 대화의 빈칸 (A)에 들어갈 부가의문문을 완성하시오.

➡ _____

10 밑줄 친 (a)의 우리말을 영작하시오.

➡ _____

서답형

11 다음 주어진 우리말과 일치하도록 주어진 단어를 모두 배열하여 완성하시오.

(1) 독도에 가 본 적이 있니?
(ever / to / you / have / Dokdo / been)
➡ _____

(2) 나는 해리포터 시리즈를 읽어 본 적이 있다.
(have / the / I / read / series / Harry Potter)
➡ _____

[01~04] 다음 대화를 읽고 물음에 답하시오.

Suji: Good morning, Chef Garcia!

Garcia: Hello, Suji. Have you ever made nacho pizza?

Suji: Nacho pizza? No, I haven't.

Garcia: Kids will love it, and I'll tell you how to make it.

Suji: Sounds good!

Garcia: It's easy to make. First, put nacho chips on a plate and spread pizza sauce on them.

Suji: Okay. Let me help you with the pizza sauce.

Garcia: Thanks. Next, put some ham, onions, and peppers on top.

Suji: Okay. Then?

Garcia: Add cheese and bake for about 12 minutes in the oven.

Suji: I can't wait to taste it!

01 대화에 맞게 조리 순서를 빈칸에 쓰시오.

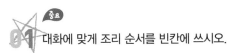

➡ _____

02 What will the cook make?

➡ _____

03 What did the cook do first to make the dish?

➡ _____

04 What ingredients did the cook put on the chips?

➡ _____

05 다음 대화에서 (A)~(E)가 자연스럽게 이어지도록 순서대로 배열하시오.

Emily: Oh, look at the long line at the box office.

Tony: Yeah, there's a ticket machine over there. Let's buy the tickets from the machine.

Emily: All right. Do you know how to use the machine?

(A) Okay. Two tickets, and I want to sit in the back.

(B) No problem. Lastly, pay for the tickets.

(C) Second, select the number of tickets and choose our seats.

(D) Sure. It's easy. First, select a movie and a showtime.

(E) Okay. We can watch the seven o'clock show. Then what?

➡ _____

[06~07] 다음 대화를 읽고 물음에 답하시오.

Judy: Have you ever been to Sokcho?

Minsu: Yes, I have. Actually my uncle lives there, so I visit him every year.

Judy: Really? Then, you've climbed Mt. Seorak, haven't you?

Minsu: Yes, I've climbed to the top of the mountain twice.

06 Has Minsu climbed Mt. Seorak?

➡ _____

07 Why does Minsu visit Sokcho every year?

➡ _____

Grammar

1 현재완료

> • They **have known** each other for five years. 그들은 5년째 서로를 알고 있다.
> • **Have** you **been** to Japan? 일본에 가 본 적이 있니?

■ 현재완료는 과거의 사건이 현재까지 영향을 미칠 때 사용한다. 'have[has]+p.p.'의 형태로, 부정형은 'have[has] not+p.p.'이며, 의문형은 'Have[Has]+주어+p.p. ~?'로 나타낸다.

   • She **has talked** with him for an hour. 그녀는 그와 한 시간 동안 대화를 나누었어.
   • I **have seen** the play once. 나는 그 연극을 한 번 본 적이 있어.

■ 현재완료는 '완료, 경험, 계속, 결과'의 네 가지 용법으로 쓰인다. 완료 용법은 'just, already, yet'과 같은 부사와 주로 함께 쓰이며, 경험은 'ever, never, once, before' 등과 같은 부사와 함께 쓰인다. 'How long ~?'으로 묻는 질문이나 'for+기간', 'since+특정 시점'은 현재완료의 계속 용법에 속한다. 결과 용법은 특별한 부사와 어울리지 않고 과거에 발생한 사건으로 인하여 현재까지 영향을 미치고 있는 상태를 나타내는 용법이다.

   • Diana **has finished** her laundry. Diana는 그녀의 빨래를 끝냈다. 〈완료〉
   • Paul **has made** bread since 2 o'clock. Paul은 두 시부터 빵을 만들어 왔다. 〈계속〉
   • They **have** never **been to** China. 그들은 중국에 가 본 적이 없어. 〈경험〉
   • The boys **have gone to** their home. 그 소년들은 집에 가고 없어. 〈결과〉

* have been to와 have gone to의 사용에 유의한다. '~에 가 본 적이 있다'는 경험은 have been to로 표현하고, '~에 가고 없다'는 결과는 have gone to로 표현한다.

■ 현재완료는 과거의 일이 현재까지 영향을 미칠 때 쓰는 시제이므로 과거를 나타내는 어구인 yesterday, last year, ~ ago 등과 함께 쓸 수 없다.

   • When have you eaten the food? (×)
   • When **did** you **eat** the food?   (○)

핵심 Check

1. 다음 우리말과 일치하도록 빈칸에 알맞은 말을 쓰시오.

(1) Jason은 세 시간 동안 깨어 있다.

➡ Jason _____ _____ awake for three hours.

(2) 그 기차는 막 떠났다.

➡ The train _____ just _____.

(3) 나는 지금까지 너에게 여러 번 전화했어.

➡ I _____ _____ you so many times until now.

2 명사를 수식하는 현재분사와 과거분사

- Be quiet. There is a **sleeping** baby. 조용히 해. 자고 있는 아기가 있어.
- Pick up a **fallen** leaf. 떨어진 잎 하나를 주워라.

■ 분사는 Ving 형태를 취하는 현재분사와, p.p. 형태를 취하는 과거분사로 나뉘며, 모두 명사를 수식하거나 설명하는 형용사 역할을 한다. 현재분사는 '~하는'이라는 의미로 주로 해석되어 능동이나 진행의 의미를 나타내고, 과거분사는 '~된'이라는 의미로 주로 해석되어 수동이나 완료의 의미를 나타낸다.

- I saw **singing** girls. 나는 노래하는 소녀들을 봤어.
- The **disappointing** behavior made my mom upset. 그 실망스러운 행동은 우리 엄마를 화나게 했다.

■ 분사가 단독으로 명사를 수식할 때에는 일반적으로 명사 앞에서 수식하지만, 분사가 다른 어구와 함께 명사를 수식할 때에는 명사 뒤에서 수식한다.

- Do you see the boys **playing** basketball? 농구하는 소녀들이 보이나요?
- Kevin found a vase **broken** by Sally. Kevin은 Sally에 의해 깨진 꽃병을 발견했다.
- People **living** in the town felt happy. 그 마을에 사는 사람들은 행복했다.

■ '사역동사(have, make)+목적어+과거분사', '지각동사+목적어+과거분사', 'get+목적어+과거분사'는 목적어와 목적보어의 관계가 수동인 경우 쓰인다.

- Jason **had** the woman **ask** some questions. Jason은 그 여자가 몇 가지 질문을 하게 했다.
  = Jason **had** some questions **asked** by the woman.

■ 'Ving'로 형태가 같은 현재분사와 동명사의 차이를 구별해야 한다. 현재분사는 '~하는', '~하는 중인'이라고 해석되고, 동명사는 '~하는 것'이라고 해석되거나 'V를 용도로 하는 명사'로 해석된다.

- There is a woman **waiting** for someone. 누군가를 기다리는 여자가 있습니다. – **현재분사**
- I can't find the **waiting** room. 나는 대기실을 찾을 수 없어요. – **동명사 (기다리는 용도로 쓰이는 방 – 대기실)**

핵심 Check

2. 다음 주어진 동사를 어법에 맞게 빈칸에 쓰시오.

(1) 무언가를 타이핑하는 그 소녀를 아니?
  ➡ Do you know the girl _____ something? (type)

(2) Adam은 우리에게 지루한 이야기를 해줬어.
  ➡ Adam told us a _____ story. (bore)

(3) 그것은 BTS에 의해 불려진 노래야.
  ➡ It is a song _____ by BTS. (sing)

Grammar 시험대비 기본평가

01 다음 문장에서 어법상 <u>어색한</u> 부분을 바르게 고쳐 쓰시오.

(1) My father hasn't gone to the museum until now.

_____ ➡ _____

(2) We saw the program several times until now.

_____ ➡ _____

(3) I did nothing since yesterday.

_____ ➡ _____

(4) We have work for this company for five years.

_____ ➡ _____

02 다음 주어진 단어를 어법에 맞게 빈칸에 쓰시오.

(1) People _____ in the town felt happy. (live)

(2) Do you know a baby _____ over there? (cry)

(3) I read the book _____ by a famous author. (write)

(4) Nick was holding a spoon _____ of gold. (make)

(5) Watch out for the _____ dog. (bark)

03 주어진 단어를 바르게 배열하여 다음 우리말을 영어로 쓰시오. 필요하다면 어형을 바꾸시오.

(1) 여섯 살 이후로 나는 책을 500권 읽었다. (read / since / was / I / have / 500 books / six / I)

➡ _____

(2) 그 소년은 벌써 우유를 마셨어. (the milk / the boy / drink / has / already)

➡ _____

(3) 이것은 구워진 감자인가요? (this / is / bake / a / potato)

➡ _____

(4) 너의 침낭을 찾았니? (bag / sleep / find / did / you / your)

➡ _____

(4) sleeping bag: 침낭

01 다음 빈칸에 들어갈 말로 가장 적절한 것은?

> The man has worked for the company
> _____ 2010.

① at ② in ③ for
④ since ⑤ during

02 다음 빈칸에 들어갈 말로 적절하지 <u>않은</u> 것은?

> Have you ever _____ Jenny before?

① called ② met
③ saw ④ played with
⑤ talked with

03 다음 빈칸에 들어갈 말이 바르게 짝지어진 것은?

> • I saw something _____ in the kitchen.
> • A girl _____ Jessica came to see you.

① burned – name
② burned – named
③ burning – named
④ burning – naming
⑤ burning – to name

04 다음 중 어법상 바르지 <u>않은</u> 것은?

① Have you ever taken first prize before?
② What time did he go out last night?
③ People have stoped buying our products recently.
④ They made her go there alone.
⑤ We have never seen the boys and girls before.

05 다음 중 밑줄 친 부분과 쓰임이 같은 것은?

> I <u>have been</u> to Mexico several times.

① Colin <u>has gone</u> to the theater without an umbrella.
② We <u>have</u> just <u>made</u> some cookies.
③ Terry <u>hasn't called</u> her friends yet.
④ He <u>has played</u> the guitar since he was an elementary school student.
⑤ They <u>have visited</u> the museum four times.

06 다음 빈칸에 들어갈 말로 가장 적절한 것은?

> He _____ her for three years until now.

① met ② is meeting
③ meets ④ has met
⑤ is met

07 다음 중 빈칸에 들어갈 말로 적절하지 <u>않은</u> 것은? (2개)

> My parents _____ the fence fixed.

① had ② saw
③ got ④ helped
⑤ seemed

08 적절한 시제를 활용하여 다음 두 문장을 하나의 문장으로 표현하시오.

> Eunji started to live in Busan when she was five years old. She still lives in Busan.

➡ _____

_____

09 다음 문장의 밑줄 친 부분과 쓰임이 같은 것은?

> The boring movie made students fall asleep.

① Writing a letter is easy.
② Did you enjoy baking bread?
③ I am not interested in playing computer games.
④ She kept yelling at me.
⑤ Who is the girl raising her hand?

10 다음 중 어법상 틀린 것은?

> A: ①Has your brother ②climbed Mt. Seorak?
> B: Yes, he ③does. He ④has climbed Mt. Seorak two times ⑤before.

①　　　　②　　　　③　　　　④　　　　⑤

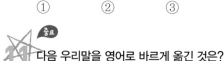

11 다음 우리말을 영어로 바르게 옮긴 것은?

① 웃고 있는 저 소녀를 아니?
　➡ Do you know that smile girl?
② 그 부상당한 남자는 어디에 있니?
　➡ Where is the injuring man?
③ 언제 그녀를 처음 만났니?
　➡ When have you met her first?
④ 그 책을 몇 번이나 읽었니?
　➡ How many times have you read the book?
⑤ 나는 이곳에서 3년 동안 살고 있어요.
　➡ I have lived here since three years.

서답형
12 현재완료 시제와 주어진 단어를 활용하여 다음 우리말을 영어로 쓰시오.

> 나는 지금 막 냉동피자 한 조각을 먹었어.
> (freeze / just / have / piece)

➡ _____

13 (A)~(C)에 들어갈 말이 바르게 짝지어진 것은?

> • The (A)[exciting / excited] game made us pleased.
> • I (B)[played / have played] the guitar since I was five years old.
> • (C)[Have you found / Did you find] your wallet yesterday?

① excited – have played – Have you found
② excited – played – Did you find
③ exciting – have played – Have you found
④ exciting – played – Have you found
⑤ exciting – have played – Did you find

14 다음 대화의 빈칸에 들어갈 말로 가장 적절한 것은?

> A: _____ this movie?
> B: Yes. I have seen it once.

① Have you made
② Have you heard about
③ Have you seen
④ Did you see
⑤ Did you want to see

15 빈칸에 들어갈 말을 바르게 짝지은 것은?

> Tom is Paul's English teacher. Tom _____ Paul since he was ten years old. Tom _____ Paul very well.

① teaches – has known
② will teach – knew
③ is teaching – is knowing
④ has taught – knows
⑤ has taught – has known

서답형

16 주어진 단어를 활용하여 다음 우리말을 영어로 쓰시오.

> 나는 중고차 한 대를 샀어.

➡ _____

중요

17 다음 중 빈칸에 들어갈 말이 다른 하나는?

① I haven't seen her _____ yesterday.

② Jina has danced ballet _____ she was very young.

③ He has talked with someone _____ an hour.

④ Julie has knitted a hat _____ last month.

⑤ My sisters have ridden their bikes _____ this morning.

18 다음 밑줄 친 두 문장을 하나의 문장으로 바르게 바꾼 것은?

> A. Where is your brother?
> B: He went to a mall. He is not here.

① He used to be in a mall.

② He has been here.

③ He wanted to go to a mall.

④ He has been in a mall.

⑤ He has gone to a mall.

중요

19 빈칸에 들어갈 말이 바르게 짝지어진 것은?

> He _____ all day under the _____ sun since this morning. He is very tired.

① is working – burned

② works – burning

③ worked – burned

④ has worked – burning

⑤ has worked – burned

중요

20 다음 중 어법상 바르지 않은 것은?

> A: How long ①have you played the drums?
> B: I ②have played the drums ③for 5 years.
> A: Do you like playing them?
> B: Yes. Playing the drums ④makes me ⑤ amusing.

①   ②   ③   ④   ⑤

서답형

21 주어진 단어를 활용하여 다음 우리말을 영어로 쓰시오.

> 그 놀라운 소식은 사실이 아니야.
> (surprise / true)

➡ _____

22 다음 우리말을 영어로 옮길 때 세 번째와 일곱 번째 오는 단어를 바르게 짝지은 것은?

> 나는 전에 내 남동생과 싸운 적이 있어요.

① have – with   ② have – brother

③ with – before   ④ fought – brother

⑤ fought – before

서답형

23 주어진 단어를 바르게 배열하여 다음 우리말을 영어로 쓰시오. 두 개의 단어는 어법에 맞게 변형하시오.

> 부서진 창문을 통해 집 안으로 찬바람이 불어 왔다. (the / house / the / break / into / through / window / cold / blow / winds)

➡ _____

_____

서답형

24 excite를 어법에 맞게 빈칸에 쓰시오.

> A: The concert was _____!
> B: I agree. The _____ fans rushed into the stadium.

01 다음 우리말 의미에 맞게 주어진 단어를 빈칸에 쓰시오.

bake / slice / sleep / cheer / rise / dance

(1) 우리는 아침 일찍 해변에서 일출을 봤습니다.
➡ Early in the morning, we saw the _____ sun at the beach.

(2) 잠자는 고양이 앞에 있는 구운 감자가 보이니?
➡ Do you see the _____ potatoes in front of the _____ cat?

(3) 나의 친구들은 무대에서 춤추는 소녀들이야.
➡ My friends are the girls _____ on the stage.

(4) 나는 환호하는 군중들 중 한 명이었어.
➡ I was one of the _____ crowds.

(5) 이 자른 치즈를 어디에 두어야 하나요?
➡ Where should I put this _____ cheese?

02 적절한 시제를 활용하여 다음 두 문장을 하나의 문장으로 표현하시오.

• Jenny made friends with Christina in 2010.
• They are still friends.

➡ _____

03 주어진 단어를 활용하여 다음 대화를 영어로 쓰시오.

A: 볶음밥을 요리해 본 적이 있니?
(cook / ever / fry)
B: 응, 나는 그것을 여러 번 요리해 봤어.
(many times)

➡ A: _____
  B: _____

04 주어진 단어를 활용하여 다음 우리말을 영어로 쓰시오.

전에 다른 나라에 가 본 적이 있니?
(before / other)

➡ _____

05 주어진 동사를 내용과 어법에 맞게 빈칸에 쓰시오.

be / rain / lose / drive / read

(1) My uncle _____ the car in 2009.
(2) The weather _____ warm recently. It's still warm.
(3) It _____ since last night.
(4) Clara _____ her key the other day.
(5) Zach _____ the book several times until now.

06 주어진 어구를 바르게 배열하여 다음 우리말을 영어로 쓰시오. 필요하다면 어형을 바꾸시오.

빨간 모자를 쓰고 있는 소녀를 보아라.
(a red cap / the boy / at / wear / look)

➡ _____

07 주어진 단어를 활용하여 다음 우리말을 영어로 쓰시오.

나의 남동생은 어젯밤부터 아파요. (sick)

➡ _____

08 다음 밑줄 친 부분이 현재분사인지 동명사인지 구별하고, 그렇게 구별한 이유를 서술하시오.

> (1) Look! There is a <u>swimming</u> baby.
> (2) Where can we find a <u>swimming</u> pool?

➡ (1) _____ 이유: _____

_____

(2) _____ 이유: _____

_____

09 주어진 어구를 활용하여 다음 우리말을 영어로 쓰시오.

(1) 나는 지금까지 제주도에 두 번 가봤어요.
(Jejudo / twice / until now)
➡ _____

(2) 나는 어제 그 유리창을 깼어요. (break)
➡ _____

(3) 우리는 아직 그 영화를 보지 못했습니다.
(have)
➡ _____

10 다음 상황을 읽고 빈칸에 알맞은 말을 쓰시오.

> Jason was born in Canada in 2001. He moved to Seoul in 2011. He started to learn *taekwondo* as soon as he arrived in Seoul. He is eighteen years old now. He still learns *taekwondo*. He likes *taekwondo*.

> Jason _____(live) in Seoul since _____. He took his first *taekwondo* lesson in _____. He _____(learn) *taekwondo* _____ eight years.

11 다음 상황을 설명하는 문장을 한 문장으로 바꿔 쓰시오.

> My grandmother broke her right arm last month. She can't use it now.

➡ _____

12 주어진 단어를 바르게 배열하여 다음 우리말을 영어로 쓰시오. 필요하다면 어형을 변형하시오.

> 그녀는 내게 삶은 달걀 하나와 다진 당근을 가져오게 하였다.
> (carrot / she / make / boil / chop / a / and / egg / bring / me)

➡ _____

13 다음 대화의 빈칸에 알맞은 말을 쓰시오.

> A: Does James work for this company?
> B: Yes, he does. Actually he _____ for this company for five years.

➡ _____

14 다음 문장에서 어법상 어색한 부분을 찾아 바르게 고쳐 쓰시오.

(1) I am boring with his lecture.
_____ ➡ _____

(2) This is a bag making in China.
_____ ➡ _____

(3) It is an excited adventure movie.
_____ ➡ _____

(4) He approached the barked dog.
_____ ➡ _____

Reading

The World of Cartoons

Boat! Land!

Did you laugh when you saw the cartoon above? If so, the cartoonist
= If you laughed when you saw the cartoon above
was successful. Cartoonists are the people who make cartoons. They
                                              주격 관계대명사
want to catch your interest, and usually, make you laugh with simple
                                            사역동사+목적어+동사원형   ~으로(도구, 수단)
language and creative drawings.

People have made cartoons for hundreds of years. There are many
        현재완료-계속   수백의
types of cartoons, and they play different roles. One form of cartoon is
a picture with a few words. It is sometimes called a "gag cartoon." The
        ~이 있는   ~라고 불린다
cartoonist makes a funny character, and the character makes you laugh
                                                        사역동사
by doing or saying silly things.
전치사 by의 목적어로 doing과 saying
Another type of cartoon is called a caricature. In a caricature, some
남아 있는 것 중 또 다른 하나를 가리킬 때
parts of a character are different or bigger than usual. Look at the
                                    big의 비교급
picture on the right. Which parts of the man's face jump out at you?
                              S   V
Artists have used this type of cartoon to make fun of well-known
        현재완료 - 계속   ~하기 위해서(to부정사의 부사적 용법 중 목적)
people.

cartoonist: 만화가

successful: 성공한, 성공적인

catch one's interest: ~의 관심을
끌다

creative: 창의적인, 독창적인

type: 형태

play a role: 역할을 하다

silly: 어리석은

caricature: 캐리커처

usual: 평소의, 보통의

jump out at: ~에게 금방 눈에 띄다,
~에게 분명히 보이다

make fun of: ~을 놀리다

well-known: 잘 알려진, 유명한

📎 **확인문제**

● 다음 문장이 본문의 내용과 일치하면 T, 일치하지 않으면 F를 쓰시오.

1 We can say that a cartoonist was successful when he made us think about something seriously. ☐

2 A few words are used in a gag cartoon. ☐

3 A funny character in a gag cartoon makes you laugh by doing or saying silly things. ☐

4 A gag cartoon is used to make fun of famous people. ☐

5 A caricature describes people as they are. ☐

When several cartoon pictures come together and tell a story, we have a comic strip. Comic strips have been in newspapers for many years. They are often just amusing stories. People have also used comic strips for education. Comics can make information clearer and easier to learn. You have probably seen comic history or science books.

You have surely seen many cartoon movies, or animated movies, too. These are very popular among people of all ages. Movement and sounds are added to pictures, so they come alive. Artists and writers can develop fascinating characters and tell interesting stories through animation.

In the 1990s, a new type of cartoon was developed. It is called a webtoon. Webtoons are published online, so you can read them anytime, anywhere on your phone or computer. They are very popular, and some of them are even made into TV dramas or movies.

New forms of cartoons may appear in the future. They could be different and even more exciting than now, but one thing will remain the same: they will help us laugh, relax, and learn.

---

come together: 합쳐지다

comic strip: 신문의 연재만화

amusing: 재미있는, 즐거운

education: 교육

probably: 아마도

surely: 분명히, 확실히

among: ~ 중에

of all ages: 모든 연령의

movement: 움직임

develop: 개발하다, 만들다

fascinating: 매력적인

animation: 만화영화 제작

publish: 출판하다

be made into: ~로 만들어지다

appear: 나타나다, 등장하다

remain: 계속 ~이다

확인문제

● 다음 문장이 본문의 내용과 일치하면 T, 일치하지 <u>않으면</u> F를 쓰시오.

1 A comic strip doesn't tell a story. ☐

2 We can't see comic strips in newspapers. ☐

3 Newspapers can make information clearer. ☐

4 There are comic history books. ☐

5 Webtoons were developed in the 1990s. ☐

6 All of the webtoons were made into TV dramas or movies. ☐

● 우리말을 참고하여 빈칸에 알맞은 말을 쓰시오.

1 Boat! _____ !

2 Did you _____ when you _____ the cartoon _____ ?

3 If _____ , the cartoonist was _____ .

4 Cartoonists are the people _____ _____ _____ .

5 They want _____ _____ your interest, and usually, _____ _____ _____ with simple language and _____ _____ .

6 People _____ _____ cartoons _____ hundreds of years.

7 There are _____ _____ _____ _____ , and they play different roles.

8 One form of cartoon _____ a picture with _____ _____ _____ .

9 It _____ sometimes _____ a "gag cartoon."

10 The cartoonist _____ _____ _____ _____ , and the character makes you _____ by _____ or _____ silly things.

11 _____ type of cartoon _____ _____ a caricature.

12 In a caricature, _____ _____ of a character _____ _____ or _____ _____ _____ .

13 Look at the picture _____ the right.

14 _____ _____ of the man's face _____ out at you?

15 Artists _____ _____ this type of cartoon _____ _____ _____ _____ well-known people.

16 When _____ cartoon pictures _____ _____ and tell a story, we have _____ _____ _____ .

1 배다! 육지다!

2 위의 만화를 보고 웃었는가?

3 그랬다면 그 만화가는 성공했다.

4 만화가들은 만화를 만드는 사람들이다.

5 그들은 여러분의 관심을 끌고, 대개는 간단한 말과 독창적인 그림으로 여러분을 웃게 하고 싶어 한다.

6 사람들은 수백 년 동안 만화를 만들어 왔다.

7 만화에는 많은 종류가 있으며, 그것들은 다양한 역할을 한다.

8 만화의 한 형태로 몇 마디 말을 쓴 그림이 있다.

9 간혹 그것은 '개그 만화'라고 불린다.

10 만화가는 웃긴 캐릭터를 만들고, 그 캐릭터는 우스꽝스러운 행동이나 말을 함으로써 여러분을 웃게 만든다.

11 다른 종류의 만화는 캐리커처라고 불린다.

12 캐리커처에서 캐릭터의 어떤 부분은 평소와 다르거나 더 크다.

13 오른쪽의 그림을 보아라.

14 남자 얼굴의 어떤 부분이 여러분에게 분명히 보이는가?

15 미술가들은 유명한 사람들을 풍자하기 위해 이런 종류의 만화를 그려 왔다.

16 몇 가지 만화 그림이 모여서 이야기를 들려주게 되면, 그것이 연재만화가 된다.

150 Lesson 7. A Life Full of Fun

17 Comic strips _____ _____ in newspapers _____ many years.

18 They are often _____ _____ _____.

19 People _____ _____ _____ comic strips _____ _____.

20 Comics can _____ information _____ and _____ _____ _____.

21 You _____ _____ _____ comic history or science books.

22 You _____ _____ _____ many cartoon movies, or _____ _____, too.

23 These are very _____ _____ _____ _____ _____.

24 Movement and sounds _____ _____ _____ pictures, so they _____ _____.

25 Artists and writers can _____ _____ characters and tell _____ stories _____ animation.

26 In the 1990s, a new type of cartoon _____ _____.

27 It _____ _____ a webtoon.

28 Webtoons _____ _____ online, so you can _____ _____ anytime, anywhere _____ your phone or computer.

29 They are very _____, and some of _____ _____ even made _____ TV dramas or movies.

30 New forms of cartoons _____ _____ in the future.

31 They could be _____ and even more _____ now, but one thing will _____ the same: they will help us _____, _____, and _____.

17 연재만화는 여러 해 동안 신문에 실려 왔다.

18 그것들은 종종 그저 재미있는 이야기이다.

19 사람들은 연재만화를 교육용으로 사용해 오기도 했다.

20 만화는 정보를 더 명료하고 더 배우기 쉽게 만들 수 있다.

21 여러분은 아마 만화 역사책이나 과학책을 본 적이 있을 것이다.

22 여러분은 많은 만화영화도 당연히 봤을 것이다.

23 이것들은 모든 연령대의 사람들에게 매우 인기가 많다.

24 동작이나 소리가 그림에 더해져서 그림들이 생생하게 살아난다.

25 미술가들과 작가들은 매력적인 캐릭터를 개발하고 만화영화 제작을 통해 생생있는 이야기를 들려준다.

26 1990년대에 새로운 형식의 만화가 개발되었다.

27 그건 웹툰이라고 불린다.

28 웹툰은 온라인으로 출판되기 때문에 여러분이 휴대 전화나 컴퓨터로 언제 어디서나 볼 수 있다.

29 그것은 매우 인기가 있고, 그들 가운데 일부는 심지어 텔레비전 드라마나 영화로 만들어지기도 한다.

30 미래에는 새로운 형태의 만화가 나타날지도 모른다.

31 그것은 지금과는 다르고 한층 더 재미있겠지만, 한 가지는 같을 것이다. 그것은 우리가 웃고, 쉬고, 배우도록 도와줄 것이다.

● 우리말을 참고하여 본문을 영작하시오.

1 배다! 육지다!

➡ _____

2 위의 만화를 보고 웃었는가?

➡ _____

3 그랬다면 그 만화가는 성공했다.

➡ _____

4 만화가들은 만화를 만드는 사람들이다.

➡ _____

5 그들은 여러분의 관심을 끌고, 대개는 간단한 말과 독창적인 그림으로 여러분을 웃게 하고 싶어 한다.

➡ _____

6 사람들은 수백 년 동안 만화를 만들어 왔다.

➡ _____

7 만화에는 많은 종류가 있으며, 그것들은 다양한 역할을 한다.

➡ _____

8 만화의 한 형태로 몇 마디 말을 쓴 그림이 있다.

➡ _____

9 간혹 그것은 '개그 만화'라고 불린다.

➡ _____

10 만화가는 웃긴 캐릭터를 만들고, 그 캐릭터는 우스꽝스러운 행동이나 말을 함으로써 여러분을 웃게 만든다.

➡ _____

11 다른 종류의 만화는 캐리커처라고 불린다.

➡ _____

12 캐리커처에서 캐릭터의 어떤 부분은 평소와 다르거나 더 크다.

➡ _____

13 오른쪽의 그림을 보아라.

➡ _____

14 남자 얼굴의 어떤 부분이 여러분에게 분명히 보이는가?

➡ _____

15 미술가들은 유명한 사람들을 풍자하기 위해 이런 종류의 만화를 그려 왔다.

➡ _____

16 몇 가지 만화 그림이 모여서 이야기를 들려주게 되면, 그것이 연재만화가 된다.

➡ _____

17 연재만화는 여러 해 동안 신문에 실려 왔다.

➡ _____

18 그것들은 종종 그저 재미있는 이야기이다.

➡ _____

19 사람들은 연재만화를 교육용으로 사용해 오기도 했다.

➡ _____

20 만화는 정보를 더 명료하고 더 배우기 쉽게 만들 수 있다.

➡ _____

21 여러분은 아마 만화 역사책이나 과학책을 본 적이 있을 것이다.

➡ _____

22 여러분은 많은 만화영화도 당연히 봤을 것이다.

➡ _____

23 이것들은 모든 연령대의 사람들에게 매우 인기가 많다.

➡ _____

24 동작이나 소리가 그림에 더해져서 그림들이 생생하게 살아난다.

➡ _____

25 미술가들과 작가들은 매력적인 캐릭터를 개발하고 만화영화 제작을 통해 재미있는 이야기를 들려준다.

➡ _____

26 1990년대에 새로운 형식의 만화가 개발되었다.

➡ _____

27 그건 웹툰이라고 불린다.

➡ _____

28 웹툰은 온라인으로 출판되기 때문에 여러분이 휴대 전화나 컴퓨터로 언제 어디서나 볼 수 있다.

➡ _____

29 그것은 매우 인기가 있고, 그들 가운데 일부는 심지어 텔레비전 드라마나 영화로 만들어지기도 한다.

➡ _____

30 미래에는 새로운 형태의 만화가 나타날지도 모른다.

➡ _____

31 그것은 지금과는 다르고 한층 더 재미있겠지만, 한 가지는 같을 것이다. 그것은 우리가 웃고, 쉬고, 배우도록 도와줄 것이다.

➡ _____

_____

[01~07] 다음 글을 읽고 물음에 답하시오.

Boat!

Land!

Did you ①laugh when you saw the cartoon above? If so, the cartoonist was ②successful. Cartoonists are the people who make cartoons. They want to catch your interest, and usually, make you laugh with simple language and creative drawings.

People have made cartoons for hundreds of years. There are many types of cartoons, and they play ③the same roles. One form of cartoon is a picture with a few words. It is sometimes called a "gag cartoon." The cartoonist makes a funny character, and the character makes you laugh ___(A)___ doing or saying ④silly things.

Another type of cartoon is called a caricature. In a caricature, some parts of a character are different or bigger than ⑤usual. Look at the picture on the right. Which parts of the man's face jump out at you? Artists have used this type of cartoon to make fun of well-known people.

01 ①~⑤ 중 글의 흐름상 어색한 것은?

① ② ③ ④ ⑤

02 다음 중 빈칸 (A)에 들어갈 말과 같은 말이 들어가는 것은?

① Are you interested _____ the movie?

② Don't give _____ your dream.

③ Please turn _____ the light when you go out.

④ I feel very proud _____ you.

⑤ Let's check them one _____ one.

03 What is the second type of cartoon called? Answer in five words.

➡ _____

04 What does a cartoonist make in a gag cartoon? Answer in English with a full sentence.

➡ _____

05 Which is TRUE about a caricature?

① There are many types of caricatures.

② It makes fun of famous people.

③ Cartoonists don't have an interest in it.

④ It doesn't make people laugh.

⑤ It describes people as they are.

06 다음 중 위 글을 읽고 답할 수 <u>없는</u> 것은?

① What do cartoonists want to do?

② What do cartoonists use to make people laugh?

③ How long have people made cartoons?

④ What is the third type of cartoon?

⑤ What is a gag cartoon?

07 What do cartoonists do? Answer in English with a full sentence.

➡ _____

[08~10] 다음 글을 읽고 물음에 답하시오.

When several cartoon pictures come together and tell a story, we have a comic strip. Comic strips have been in newspapers ___(A)___ many years.

[A] You have probably seen comic history or science books. You have surely seen many cartoon movies, or animated movies, too.

[B] They are often just amusing stories. People have also used comic strips for education. Comics can make information clearer and easier to learn.

[C] These are very popular among people of all ages. Movement and sounds are added to pictures, so they come alive.

Artists and writers can develop fascinating characters and tell interesting stories through animation.

08 다음 중 빈칸 (A)에 들어갈 말과 다른 말이 들어가는 것은?

① I haven't seen her _____ a while.
② Carrie has met him _____ a long time.
③ They have lived here _____ last year.
④ She has known him _____ ten years.
⑤ Jina has danced _____ an hour.

09 자연스러운 글이 되도록 [A]~[C]를 바르게 배열한 것은?

① [A] – [C] – [B]
② [B] – [A] – [C]
③ [B] – [C] – [A]
④ [C] – [B] – [A]
⑤ [C] – [A] – [B]

10 Which is NOT true about comic strips?

① It has a story.
② It is also used as an educational purpose.
③ It has one picture.
④ We can see it in newspapers.
⑤ Its stories are amusing.

[11~13] 다음 글을 읽고 물음에 답하시오.

In the 1990s, a new type of cartoon was developed. It is (A)[calling / called] a webtoon. Webtoons are published online, so you can read (B)[it / them] anytime, anywhere on your phone or computer. They are very popular, and some of them are even made into TV dramas or movies.

New forms of cartoons may (C)[appear / be appeared] in the future. They could be different and even more exciting than now, but one thing will remain the same: they will help us laugh, relax, and learn.

11 (A)~(C)에서 어법상 옳은 것을 바르게 짝지은 것은?

① calling – it – appear
② calling – it – be appeared
③ calling – them – be appeared
④ called – them – appear
⑤ called – it – appear

서답형

12 Write the reason why we can read webtoons anytime, anywhere on our phone or computer. Use the phrase 'It's because'.

➡ _____

13 다음 중 위 글을 읽고 답할 수 <u>없는</u> 것은?

① When was a new type of cartoon developed?

② Where are webtoons published?

③ What do we call a new type of cartoon?

④ Who usually sees webtoons?

⑤ What do cartoons help us to do?

[14~16] 다음 글을 읽고 물음에 답하시오.

Boat!

Land!

Did you laugh when you saw the cartoon above? If so, the cartoonist was successful. Cartoonists are the people ____(A)____ make cartoons. They want to catch your interest, and usually, make you laugh with simple language and creative drawings.

People have made cartoons for hundreds of years. There are many types of cartoons, and they play different roles.

14 빈칸 (A)에 들어갈 말로 적절한 것을 <u>모두</u> 고르시오.

① which   ② that   ③ whom
④ who   ⑤ what

15 다음 중 위 글에 이어질 내용으로 가장 적절한 것은?

① the reason why people see cartoons

② the number of cartoonists

③ various types of cartoons

④ how cartoons have survived for hundreds of years

⑤ what cartoonists want to draw

서답형

16 다음과 같이 풀이되는 말을 위 글에서 찾아 쓰시오.

achieving results you wanted or hoped for

➡ _____

[17~20] 다음 글을 읽고 물음에 답하시오.

One form of cartoon is a picture with a few words. It is sometimes called a "gag cartoon." The cartoonist makes a funny character, and the character makes you laugh by doing or saying silly things.

Another type of cartoon is called a caricature. In a caricature, some parts of a character are different or bigger than usual. Look at the picture on the right. Which parts of the man's face jump out at you? Artists have used this type of cartoon to make fun of well-known people.

서답형

17 How do the characters in a gag cartoon make people laugh? Answer in English with a full sentence.

➡ _____
_____

18 다음 중 위 글을 바르게 이해한 사람은?

① 은지: Cartoonists don't want to draw gag cartoons.

② 준석: There are more than two types of cartoons.

③ 지민: It is unnatural to laugh when we see a character in a gag cartoon.

④ 태형: Cartoonists who draw caricatures aren't interested in famous people.

⑤ 정국: Artists draw a caricature to make someone feel good.

19 다음 중 개그 만화에서 볼 수 있는 것은?

① A man's eyes jumping out at readers

② Two characters talking too much

③ A picture with no words

④ A character saying stupid things

⑤ A character's arms bigger than usual

20 What do we call a picture with a few words? Answer in English with six words.

➡ _____

[21~26] 다음 글을 읽고 물음에 답하시오.

When several cartoon pictures come together and tell a story, we have a comic strip. Comic strips have been in newspapers for many years. They are often just (A)[amusing / amused] stories. People have also used comic strips for education. Comics can make information clearer and easier to learn. You have probably seen comic history or science books.

You have surely seen many cartoon movies, or animated movies, (B)[too / either]. These are very popular among people of all ages. Movement and sounds are added to pictures, so they come (C)[live / alive]. Artists and writers can develop fascinating characters and tell interesting stories through animation.

① In the 1990s, a new type of cartoon was developed. ② Webtoons are published online, so you can read them anytime, anywhere on your phone or computer. ③ They are very popular, and some of them are even made into TV dramas or movies. ④

New forms of cartoons may appear in the future. ⑤ They could be different and even more exciting than now, but (D)one thing will remain the same: they will help us laugh, relax, and learn.

21 다음 중 주어진 문장이 들어가기에 가장 적절한 곳은?

> It is called a webtoon.

①   ②   ③   ④   ⑤

22 (A)~(C)에서 어법상 옳은 것을 바르게 짝지은 것은?

① amused – either – alive
② amused – too – live
③ amusing – too – alive
④ amusing – too – live
⑤ amusing – either – alive

23 다음 물음에 완전한 문장의 영어로 답하시오.

> Q: What is a comic strip made of and what does it tell?

➡ _____

_____

24 Write the reason why people have used comic strips for education. Use the phrase 'It's because'.

➡ _____

_____

25 다음 중 위 글을 읽고 답할 수 있는 것은?

① How many cartoon pictures do we need to make a comic strip?
② Who makes the animated movies?
③ Where can we read webtoons?
④ How many webtoons were made into TV dramas or movies?
⑤ How do cartoons make people laugh?

26 밑줄 친 (D)가 의미하는 것을 위 글에서 찾아 우리말로 쓰시오.

➡ _____

[01~07] 다음 글을 읽고 물음에 답하시오.

Boat!

Land!

Did you laugh when you saw the cartoon above? (A)If so, the cartoonist was successful. Cartoonists are the people who make cartoons. They want to catch your interest, and usually, make you laugh with simple language and creative drawings.

_____(a)_____

There are many types of cartoons, and (B) they play different roles. One form of cartoon is a picture with a few words. It is sometimes called a "gag cartoon." The cartoonist makes a funny character, and the character makes you laugh by doing or saying silly things.

Another type of cartoon is called a caricature. In a caricature, some parts of a character are different or bigger than usual. Look at the picture on the right. Which parts of the man's face jump out at you? Artists have used this type of cartoon to make fun of well-known people.

01 다음 두 문장을 하나의 문장으로 빈칸 (a)에 쓰시오. 주어진 단어를 활용하시오.

> People started to make cartoons hundreds of years ago. They still make cartoons now. (for)

➡ _____

02 What do cartoonists use to make people laugh? Answer in English with a full sentence.

➡ _____

03 밑줄 친 (A)가 의미하는 것을 구체적으로 쓰시오.

➡ _____

04 밑줄 친 (B)가 가리키는 것을 위 글에서 찾아 쓰시오.

➡ _____

05 According to the passage, what does a gag cartoon make us do? Answer in English with a full sentence.

➡ _____

06 Which type of cartoon is this picture? Answer in English with a full sentence.

Take a look. We are famous.

➡ _____

07 다음 중 위 글의 내용과 일치하지 않는 것을 두 군데 찾아 바르게 고치시오.

> Cartoonists make cartoons. They make you laugh with simple language and creative drawings. There are various types of cartoons. One form of cartoon is a picture with many words. There is a funny character which makes you laugh by doing wise things. Caricature is another type of cartoon. In a caricature, some parts of a character are bigger than usual.

_____ ➡ _____

_____ ➡ _____

[08~13] 다음 글을 읽고 물음에 답하시오.

When several cartoon pictures come together and tell a story, we have a comic strip. Comic strips have been in newspapers for many years. They are often just amusing stories. People have also used comic strips for education. Comics can make information clearer and easier to learn. You have probably seen comic history or science books.

You have surely seen many cartoon movies, or animated movies, too. These are very popular among people of all ages. Movement and sounds are added to pictures, so they come alive. Artists and writers can develop fascinating characters and tell interesting stories through animation.

In the 1990s, a new type of cartoon was developed. It is called a webtoon. Webtoons are published online, so you can read them anytime, anywhere on your phone or computer. They are very popular, and some of them are even made into TV dramas or movies.

New forms of cartoons may appear in the future. They could be different and even more exciting than now, but one thing will remain the same: they will help us laugh, relax, and learn.

08 If you want to deliver information more clearly, what type of cartoon can you use?

➡ _____

중요

09 위 글의 내용에 맞게 빈칸에 알맞은 말을 쓰시오.

> In the way that _____,
> pictures come alive.

➡ _____

10 What can artists and writers do through animation? Answer in English with eleven words.

➡ _____
_____

11 When were webtoons developed? Answer in English with a full sentence.

➡ _____

고난이도

12 위 글의 내용에 맞게 대화의 빈칸을 채우시오.

> A: Look! There are some cartoon pictures and they tell a story. What is it?
> B: It is called _____.
> A: How is the story?
> B: It is usually _____. It is also used for _____.

13 위 글의 내용에 맞게 빈칸에 알맞은 말을 쓰시오.

> Although new forms of cartoons may appear in the future, they _____ just like now.

➡ _____

구석구석

해석

My Speaking Portfolio – Step 3

Here is a useful tip for you. I've washed my sneakers this way many times.

= 현재완료 (경험)

First, put the sneakers, warm water, and washing powder in a plastic bag.

동명사

Then close the bag and leave it for seven minutes. Lastly, take the sneakers

= Next. And that

out of the bag and wash them. They'll look like new sneakers.

= the sneakers   look like+명사: ~처럼 보이다

구문해설 • useful: 유용한 • sneakers: 운동화 • washing powder: 세제 • plastic bag: 비닐봉지

여기 당신을 위한 유용한 조언이 있어요. 나는 내 운동화를 여러 번 이런 방식으로 세탁했어요. 첫째, 운동화, 온수, 그리고 세제를 비닐봉지에 넣으세요. 그리고 비닐봉지를 묶어 7분 동안 두세요. 마지막으로 운동화를 비닐봉지에서 꺼내 씻으세요. 그들은 새 운동화처럼 보일 거예요.

My Writing Portfolio

Giyeong, My Favorite Cartoon Character

My favorite cartoon character is Giyeong of *Black Rubber Shoes*. He is an

elementary school student. He is humorous and kind. However, he is not very

그러나

smart and sometimes causes trouble. I like him because he looks on the bright

주어 he에 수의 일치   이유를 이끄는 접속사

side of everything and always tries to help others.

다른 사람들

구문해설 • favorite: 가장 좋아하는 • elementary school: 초등학교 • cause: 유발하다

• look on: ~을 바라보다

기영, 내가 가장 좋아하는 만화 캐릭터

내가 가장 좋아하는 만화 캐릭터는 〈검정 고무신〉의 기영이다. 그는 초등학교 학생이다. 그는 재미있고 친절하다. 하지만, 그는 별로 똑똑하지 않고, 때때로 말썽을 피운다. 그는 모든 것의 긍정적인 면을 보고 항상 다른 이들을 도우려 하기 때문에 나는 그를 좋아한다.

Words in Action B

The Best Animated Movie for Children's Education

Animals welcome the city's plan to build an amusement park in the forest.

to부정사의 형용사적 용법(the city's plan 수식)

However, they soon suffer from serious pollution. An old elephant makes a

곧

suggestion. The animals and the city reach an agreement to create a better

world for everyone.

구문해설 • amusement park: 놀이공원 • suffer from: ~으로 고통 받다 • suggestion: 제안

• reach an agreement: 합의점에 도달하다

아이들의 교육을 위한 최고의 만화영화

동물들은 숲속에 놀이공원을 지으려는 도시의 계획을 환영한다. 하지만, 그들은 곧 심각한 오염에 시달린다. 나이 든 코끼리가 한 가지 제안을 한다. 동물들과 도시는 모든 이들을 위한 더 좋은 세상을 만들기 위한 합의에 이른다.

01 다음 영영풀이가 가리키는 것을 고르시오.

> a type of lotion that you put on your skin to protect it from being damaged by the sun

① sunscreen   ② raincoat
③ sauce   ④ sneaker
⑤ plate

02 다음 중 밑줄 친 부분의 뜻풀이가 바르지 않은 것은?

① He made a silly mistake. 어리석은
② Why don't you boil water first? 끓이다
③ Spread butter on the bread with the knife. 번지다
④ Cartoons are often fun for people of all ages. 만화
⑤ It's hard to choose just one flavor of ice cream. 고르다

03 다음 우리말을 주어진 단어를 이용하여 영작하시오.

(1) Emma는 오렌지 주스를 유리잔에 부어 그것을 마셨다. (glass, drank)

➡ _____

(2) 우리는 설거지해야 할 많은 접시가 있다. (wash, of)

➡ _____

(3) 나는 달걀과 많은 채소를 볶는 것을 좋아한다. (eggs, lots)

➡ _____

04 다음 문장의 빈칸에 들어갈 말을 〈보기〉에서 골라 쓰시오. (필요한 경우 형태를 바꿀 것.)

> ┤ 보기 ├
> of all ages / watch out / comic strip / jump out at me / come together

(1) When technology and imagination _____, amazing inventions can be created.
(2) His first _____ was published in 1972.
(3) _____ for cars when you ride a bike.
(4) The singer is loved by people _____.
(5) The red balloon really _____.

05 다음 주어진 문장의 밑줄 친 down과 같은 의미로 쓰인 것은?

> You look down. What's wrong with you?

① He bent down to pick up the paper.
② She jumped down off the table.
③ Today, I feel a little down.
④ The stone rolled down the hill.
⑤ Listening to the music, tears ran down on my face.

06 다음 대화가 자연스럽게 이어지도록 순서대로 배열하시오.

> (A) Yes, I've climbed to the top of the mountain twice.
> (B) Have you ever been to Sokcho?
> (C) Really? Then, you've climbed Mt. Seorak, haven't you?
> (D) Yes, I have. Actually my uncle lives there, so I visit him every year.

➡ _____

[07~08] 다음 대화를 읽고 물음에 답하시오.

Emily: Oh, look at the long line at the box office.
Tony: Yeah, there's a ticket machine over there.
_____ (A) _____
Emily: All right. Do you know how to use the machine?
Tony: Sure. It's easy. First, select a movie and a showtime.
Emily: Okay. We can watch the seven o'clock show. Then what?
Tony: Well, select the number of tickets and choose our seats.
Emily: Okay. Two tickets, and I want to sit in the back.
Tony: No problem. Lastly, pay for the tickets.
Emily: It's very simple.

07 위 대화의 빈칸 (A)에 들어갈 말로 <u>어색한</u> 것은?

① Let's buy the tickets from the machine.
② How about buying the tickets from the machine?
③ Why don't we buy the tickets from the machine?
④ I think we can buy the tickets from the machine.
⑤ Have you bought the tickets from the machine?

08 위 대화의 내용과 일치하도록 표를 완성하시오.

<How to Use a Ticket Machine>

Step	What to do
1	select (A)_____ and (B)_____
2	select the number of tickets and (C)_____
3	(D)_____

[09~11] 다음 대화를 읽고 물음에 답하시오.

Suji: Good morning, Chef Garcia!
Garcia: Hello, Suji. (A)<u>나초 피자를 만들어 본 적 있나요?</u>
Suji: Nacho pizza? No, I haven't.
Garcia: Kids will love it, and I'll tell you how to make ⓐ<u>it</u>.
Suji: Sounds good!
Garcia: It's easy to make. First, put nacho chips on a plate and spread pizza sauce on ⓑ <u>them</u>.
Suji: Okay. Let me help you with the pizza sauce.
Garcia: Thanks. Next, put some ham, onions, and peppers on top.
Suji: Okay. Then?
Garcia: Add cheese and bake for about 12 minutes in the oven.
Suji: I can't wait to taste it!

09 위 대화의 밑줄 친 (A)의 우리말을 6단어로 영작하시오.

➡ _____

10 위 대화의 밑줄 친 ⓐ와 ⓑ가 가리키는 것을 각각 찾아 쓰시오.

➡ ⓐ _____ ⓑ _____

11 위 대화의 내용과 일치하지 <u>않는</u> 것은?

① 수지는 나초 피자를 만들어 본 적이 없다.
② 나초 피자를 만들기는 쉽다.
③ 나초 피자를 만들기 위해 접시 위에 나초 칩을 올려놓고 그 위에 피자 소스를 바른다.
④ 햄, 양파, 피망으로 피자 소스를 만든다.
⑤ 치즈를 올리고 약 12분 동안 오븐에서 굽는다.

12 다음 대화의 내용과 일치하지 <u>않는</u> 것은?

> Anna: Do you know how to make fried rice?
>
> Jinsu: Sure. It's easy. First, cut the vegetables into small pieces.
>
> Anna: Okay. What do you do next?
>
> Jinsu: Put some oil in the pan. Then, fry the vegetables with rice.
>
> Anna: Wow, it's really simple.

① Jinsu knows how to make fried rice.

② To make fried rice, Anna and Jinsu need vegetables, oil, and rice.

③ Before putting some oil in the pan, Anna needs to cut the vegetables into small pieces.

④ Anna needs to fry the small pieces of vegetables with rice after putting some oil in the pan.

⑤ Anna helps Jinsu cut the vegetables into small pieces.

13 다음 대화의 빈칸 (A)~(C)에 들어갈 알맞은 말을 고르시오

> Jane: Kevin, you look (A)[up / down].
>
> Kevin: Nothing (B)[seriously / serious]. Sometimes my feelings change a lot.
>
> Jane: I understand. Many teens have ups and downs in their feelings.
>
> Kevin: Oh, really?
>
> Jane: Have you watched the animated movie "Shining Days"?
>
> Kevin: No, I haven't. Why do you ask?
>
> Jane: It is about a teenager's feelings. It will help you (C)[understand / understanding] your feelings better.
>
> Kevin: That sounds good! I'll watch it.

➡ (A) _____ (B) _____ (C) _____

14 다음 중 동사의 과거분사형으로 바르지 <u>않은</u> 것은?

① put – put ② read – read

③ do – done ④ cut – cut

⑤ drive – droven

15 다음 우리말을 영어로 바르게 옮긴 것은?

> 나의 아버지는 전에 미국에 가 본 적이 없다.

① My father didn't go to America.

② My father doesn't have been to America before.

③ My father has gone to America now.

④ My father has not visited America once.

⑤ My father hasn't been to America before.

16 다음 빈칸에 들어갈 말이 바르게 짝지어진 것은?

> • Kevin has been in U.K. _____.
>
> • Kevin has been in U.K. _____ this Monday.
>
> • Kevin has been in U.K. _____ a week.

① for – since – yet

② once – since – for

③ yet – for – since

④ yet – since – for

⑤ ago – for – since

17 주어진 어구를 바르게 배열하여 다음 우리말을 영어로 쓰시오. 필요하다면 어형을 바꾸시오.

> 무대 위에서 뛰고 있는 소년을 아니?
> (know / jump / you / on / the boy / the stage / do)

➡ _____

18 다음 중 어법상 올바른 문장은?

① When have you seen the singer?
② I have called him two hours ago.
③ I didn't have talked with her for a while.
④ Ryan has been to Spain with his family.
⑤ She has lived in New York when she was young.

19 다음 두 문장을 하나의 문장으로 바르게 쓴 것은?

> I forgot her address. I still can't remember it.

① I have remembered her address.
② I want to remember her address.
③ I forgot her address.
④ I have forgotten her address.
⑤ I haven't forgotten her address.

20 다음 중 빈칸에 들어갈 동사 bake의 형태가 다른 하나는?

① I know the girl _____ some bread.
② They ate _____ potatoes for lunch.
③ What is she _____?
④ We saw her _____ many cookies.
⑤ She needed _____ soda.

21 주어진 단어를 활용하여 다음 우리말을 영어로 쓰시오.

> 나는 작년부터 이 문제를 가지고 있었어.
> (have / problem)

➡ _____

22 주어진 문장의 밑줄 친 부분과 쓰임이 같은 것은?

> I have never seen an elephant.

① Paul has lost his laptop computer.
② Julian has gone to his home.
③ They have been married for 15 years.
④ How long have you stayed here?
⑤ She has used the chair once.

23 다음 중 밑줄 친 부분을 바르게 고치지 않은 것은?

> ⓐ Korea has been in a war in 1952.
> ⓑ Cynthia played tennis since 2011.
> ⓒ I saw my favorite singer once until now.
> ⓓ My cousin has lost his cellphone a week ago.
> ⓔ Who has put this paper on the table the other day?

① ⓐ: was   ② ⓑ: has played
③ ⓒ: have seen   ④ ⓓ: lost
⑤ ⓔ: putted

24 다음 빈칸에 알맞은 말을 쓰시오.

> 그 도난당한 차는 옆 블록에서 발견되었어.
> The _____ car was _____ on the next block.

25 다음 두 문장을 하나의 문장으로 표현하시오.

> They went to the library at noon. They are still in the library.

➡ _____

Reading

[26~28] 다음 글을 읽고 물음에 답하시오.

Boat!

Land!

Did you laugh when you saw the cartoon above? ① If so, the cartoonist was successful. ② They want to catch your interest, and usually, make you laugh with simple language and creative drawings. ③ People (A)have made cartoons for hundreds of years. ④ There are many types of cartoons, and they play different roles. ⑤ One form of cartoon is a picture with a few words. It is sometimes called a "gag cartoon." The cartoonist makes a funny character, and the character makes you laugh by doing or saying silly things.

26 다음 중 주어진 문장이 들어가기에 가장 적절한 곳은?

> Cartoonists are the people who make cartoons.

①   ②   ③   ④   ⑤

27 다음 중 밑줄 친 (A)와 쓰임이 같은 것은?

① I have been to Paris twice.

② They have gone out.

③ He has read the book for an hour.

④ We haven't met each other before.

⑤ She has lost her key.

28 다음 중 위 글의 내용과 일치하는 것은?

① A cartoonist is successful when he or she makes us sad.

② Cartoonists use language which is not simple.

③ Cartoons were made recently.

④ Cartoonists make us laugh with creative drawings.

⑤ We can find lots of words in a gag cartoon.

[29~30] 다음 글을 읽고 물음에 답하시오.

Another type of cartoon is called a caricature. In a caricature, some parts of a character are different or bigger than ___(A)___ . Look at the picture on the right. Which parts of the man's face jump out at you? Artists have used this type of cartoon to make fun of well-known people.

When several cartoon pictures come together and tell a story, we have a comic strip. Comic strips have been in newspapers for many years. They are often just amusing stories. People have also used comic strips for education. Comics can make information clearer and easier to learn. You have probably seen comic history or science books.

29 다음과 같이 풀이되는 말을 빈칸 (A)에 쓰시오.

> normal; happening most often

➡ _____

30 다음 중 위 글의 앞에 나올 내용으로 가장 적절한 것은?

① lives of many cartoonists

② a type of cartoon made into movies

③ types of cartoon

④ how to make cartoons

⑤ reasons why cartoons are popular

[01~02] 다음 대화를 읽고 물음에 답하시오.

Jane: Kevin, you look down.

Kevin: Nothing ⓐserious. Sometimes my feelings change a lot.

Jane: I understand. Many teens have ⓑups and downs in their feelings.

Kevin: Oh, really?

Jane: Have you ⓒwatching the animated movie "Shining Days"?

Kevin: No, I ⓓhaven't. Why do you ask?

Jane: It is about a teenager's feelings. It will help you ⓔunderstand your feelings better.

Kevin: That sounds good! I'll watch it.

🖊 출제율 90%

01 위 대화의 밑줄 친 ⓐ~ⓔ 중 어법상 어색한 것을 찾아 바르게 고치시오.

_____ ➡ _____

🖊 출제율 100%

02 위 대화를 읽고 대답할 수 없는 것은?

① What does Kevin look like?

② According to Jane, what do teenagers have in their feelings?

③ What does Jane suggest to Kevin?

④ What kind of movie is "Shining Days"?

⑤ How can watching "Shining Days" help Kevin?

[03~05] 다음 대화를 읽고 물음에 답하시오.

Emily: Oh, look at the long line at the box office.

Tony: Yeah, there's a ticket machine over there. Let's buy the tickets from the machine.

Emily: All right. Do you know how to use the machine?

Tony: Sure. It's easy. First, select a movie and a showtime.

Emily: Okay. We can watch the seven o'clock show. Then what?

Tony: Well, select the number of tickets and choose our seats.

Emily: Okay. Two tickets, and I want to sit in the back.

Tony: No problem. Lastly, pay for the tickets.

Emily: It's very simple.

🖊 출제율 90%

03 From what do Tony and Emily want to buy the tickets?

➡ _____

🖊 출제율 95%

04 What time will Tony and Emily watch the movie?

➡ _____

🖊 출제율 85%

05 Where does Emily want to sit?

➡ _____

🖊 출제율 95%

06 다음 대화에서 (A)~(E)가 자연스럽게 이어지도록 순서대로 배열하시오.

Suji: Good morning, Chef Garcia!

Garcia: Hello, Suji. Have you ever made nacho pizza?

Suji: Nacho pizza? No, I haven't.

Garcia: Kids will love it, and I'll tell you how to make it.

Suji: Sounds good!

(A) Okay. Let me help you with the pizza sauce.

(B) Lastly, add cheese and bake for about 12 minutes in the oven.

(C) It's easy to make. First, put nacho chips on a plate and spread pizza sauce on them.

(D) Okay. Then?

(E) Thanks. Next, put some ham, onions, and peppers on top.

➡ _____

[07~09] 다음 대화를 읽고 물음에 답하시오.

Anna: Do you know how to make fried rice?

Jinsu: Sure. It's easy. First, (A)[cut / put] the vegetables into small pieces.

Anna: Okay. What do you do next?

Jinsu: (B)[Bake / Put] some oil in the pan. Then, (C)[fry / spread] the vegetables with rice.

Anna: Wow, it's really simple.

07 위 대화의 빈칸 (A)~(C)에 들어갈 말로 바르게 짝지어진 것은?

	(A)	(B)	(C)
①	cut	Bake	fry
②	cut	Put	spread
③	cut	Put	fry
④	put	Put	spread
⑤	put	Bake	fry

08 What should Anna and Jinsu do after putting some oil in the pan?

➡ _____

09 What ingredients should Anna and Jinsu prepare to make fried rice?

➡ _____

10 다음 짝지어진 대화가 <u>어색한</u> 것은?

① A: Have you ever cooked fried rice?
   B: Yes, I have cooked it many times.

② A: I have never been to Beijing. How about you?
   B: I went there last summer.

③ A: Have you ever touched a snake?
   B: Yes, I did. I was so scared.

④ A: You have been to Canada. Haven't you?
   B: No, I haven't.

⑤ A: Have you been to Busan?
   B: Busan? No, I've never been there.

11 다음 문장에서 쓰인 현재완료의 용법이 나머지와 <u>다른</u> 하나는?

① We have just eaten dinner.

② Has the concert already started?

③ They haven't met each other yet.

④ I have had a headache for an hour.

⑤ She has just found the ticket.

12 다음 중 어법상 올바른 것은?

① The man has made a big mistake at work yesterday.

② Mr. Jones is practicing the flute for three years.

③ I don't want to eat freezing food.

④ The walking boy with his friends is my brother.

⑤ Cindy has been interested in painting for many years.

출제율 95%

13 다음 빈칸에 들어갈 말이 바르게 짝지어진 것은?

> • The _____ chicken will be served.
> • Do you know the _____ boy?

① cook – shout
② cooking – shouted
③ cooking – shouting
④ cooked – shouted
⑤ cooked – shouting

출제율 100%

14 다음 빈칸에 들어갈 시제가 다른 하나는?

① Kelly _____ her laptop computer yesterday. She was relieved.
② Tom _____ the book ten times until now. He really likes reading it.
③ Brad wants to know when Angela _____ home last night.
④ Molly _____ some pictures of Zach when they traveled together.
⑤ When I was young, I _____ a lamb.

출제율 95%

15 주어진 동사를 어법에 맞게 빈칸에 쓰시오.

(1) I met a boy _____ Chris last week. (name)
(2) When are you going to fix the _____ refrigerator? (break)
(3) The _____ news made her say nothing. (surprise)

출제율 90%

16 주어진 단어를 활용하여 다음 우리말을 영어로 쓰시오. 필요하다면 어형을 바꾸시오.

> 나는 추천된 책을 살 거야.
> (the / I / book / will / recommend / buy)

➡ _____

출제율 95%

17 현재완료 시제를 이용하여 다음 우리말을 영어로 쓰시오.

> Smith씨는 작년부터 내게 영어를 가르쳐 주고 있다.

➡ _____

[18~24] 다음 글을 읽고 물음에 답하시오.

When several cartoon pictures come together and tell a story, we have a comic strip. Comic strips have been in newspapers for many years. They are often just amusing stories. People have also used comic strips for education. Comics can make information clearer and easier ⓐto learn. You have probably seen comic history or science books.

You have surely seen many cartoon movies, or animated movies, too. These are very popular among people of all ages. Movement and sounds are added to pictures, so they come alive. Artists and writers can develop fascinating characters and tell __(A)__ stories through animation.

In the 1990s, a new type of cartoon was developed. It is called a webtoon. Webtoons are published online, so you can read them anytime, anywhere on your phone or computer. They are very popular, and some of them are even made into TV dramas or movies.

New forms of cartoons may appear in the future. (B)They could be different and even more exciting than now, but one thing will remain the same: they will help us laugh, relax, and learn.

출제율 90%

18 주어진 단어를 어법에 맞게 빈칸 (A)에 쓰시오.

> interest

➡ _____

19 밑줄 친 (B)가 가리키는 것을 위 글에서 찾아 쓰시오.

➡ _____

20 다음 중 밑줄 친 ⓐ와 쓰임이 같은 것은?

① We want you to visit your uncle.

② It is difficult to learn a foreign language.

③ He went to the market to buy milk.

④ The problem is easy to solve.

⑤ You need something warm to wear.

21 Choose one that is NOT true about a comic strip.

① There are history books using it.

② It has been used for education.

③ The stories are amusing.

④ It is published online.

⑤ It is made of several cartoon pictures.

22 According to the passage, what makes pictures come alive? Answer in English with a full sentence.

➡ _____

_____

23 다음 중 위 글의 내용을 잘못 이해한 사람은?

① Sam: In order to make a comic strip, I need some cartoon pictures and a story.

② Tom: I will look into newspapers to find a comic strip.

③ Jim: There are many science books using comic strips.

④ June: Only children like animated movies.

⑤ Paul: Sometimes comics are used to teach history easily.

24 다음 중 위 글을 읽고 답할 수 없는 것은?

① What does a comic strip have?

② How do pictures come alive?

③ What do writers tell through animation?

④ How long does it take to make a comic strip?

⑤ What is very popular among people of all ages?

[25~26] 다음 글을 읽고 물음에 답하시오.

My favorite cartoon character is Giyeong of *Black Rubber Shoes*. He is an elementary school student. He is humorous and kind. ___(A)___ , he is not very smart and sometimes causes trouble. I like him because he looks on the bright side of everything and always tries to help others.

25 다음 중 빈칸 (A)에 들어갈 말로 가장 적절한 것은?

① In addition ② However

③ For example ④ Moreover

⑤ Fortunately

26 Write the reason why the writer likes the cartoon character. Answer in English with a full sentence.

➡ _____

_____

[01~03] 다음 대화를 읽고 물음에 답하시오.

Jane: Kevin, you look down.
Kevin: Nothing serious. Sometimes my feelings change a lot.
Jane: I understand. Many teens have ups and downs in their feelings.
Kevin: Oh, really?
Jane: Have you watched the animated movie "Shining Days"?
Kevin: No, I haven't. Why do you ask?
Jane: It is about a teenager's feelings. It will help you understand your feelings better.
Kevin: That sounds good! I'll watch it.

01 Has Kevin seen "Shining Days"?

➡ _____

02 What kind of Movie is "Shining Days"?

➡ _____

03 How can watching "Shining Days" help Kevin?

➡ _____

04 다음 두 문장의 차이를 서술하시오.

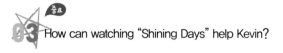

(1) Amelia has been to Canada.
(2) Amelia has gone to Canada.

➡ _____
_____
_____

05 다음 두 문장을 하나의 문장으로 쓰시오.

I lost my favorite book. I don't have it now.

➡ _____

06 주어진 단어를 활용하여 다음 우리말을 영어로 쓰시오.

그 울고 있는 소년은 삶은 달걀을 다섯 개 먹었어요. (cry / boil)

➡ _____

07 다음은 한국을 방문한 Steve의 일기 중 일부이다. Steve의 경험을 말하는 문장을 완성하시오.

I _____ a lot of Korean food, but _____ *sannakji* yet. I want to eat it someday.

08 다음 빈칸에 알맞은 말을 쓰시오.

그녀는 떨리는 목소리로 "부끄러운 줄 아세요." 라고 그에게 말했다.
She told in _____, "Shame on you."

[09~10] 다음 글을 읽고 물음에 답하시오.

My favorite cartoon character is Giyeong of *Black Rubber Shoes*. He is an elementary school student. He is humorous and kind.

However, he is not very smart and sometimes causes trouble. I like him because he looks on the bright side of everything and always tries to help others.

09 What cartoon is the writer's favorite character from? Answer in English with a full sentence.

➡ _____

10 What's the character like? Answer in English with a full sentence.

➡ _____

_____

[11~13] 다음 글을 읽고 물음에 답하시오.

People have made cartoons for hundreds of years. There are many types of cartoons, and they play different roles. One form of cartoon is a picture with a few words. It is sometimes called a "gag cartoon." The cartoonist makes a funny character, and the character makes you laugh by doing or saying silly things.

Another type of cartoon is called a caricature. In a caricature, some parts of a character are different or bigger than usual. Look at the picture on the right. Which parts of the man's face jump out at you?

_____(A)_____

When several cartoon pictures come together and tell a story, we have a comic strip. Comic strips have been in newspapers for many years. They are often just amusing stories. People have also used comic strips for education.

11 주어진 글을 하나의 문장으로 빈칸 (A)에 쓰시오.

Artists used this type of cartoon to make fun of well-known people. They still use it.

➡ _____

_____

12 주어진 단어를 바르게 배열하여 위 글의 제목을 쓰시오.

(roles / types / their / various / of / and / cartoons)

➡ _____

13 위 글의 내용에 맞게 빈칸에 알맞은 말을 쓰시오.

There are three types of cartoons in the passage. One is _____. A funny character in the cartoon _____ by doing and saying silly things. Another is _____. It is used to make fun of famous people. The other is _____. They have _____ stories.

14 Read the following paragraph and write the reason why artists have drawn a caricature. Answer in English with a full sentence.

Another type of cartoon is called a caricature. In a caricature, some parts of a character are different or bigger than usual. Look at the picture on the right. Which parts of the man's face jump out at you? Artists have used this type of cartoon to make fun of well-known people.

➡ _____

_____

01 다음 대화의 내용과 일치하도록 Kevin의 일기를 완성하시오.

> Jane: Kevin, you look down.
>
> Kevin: Nothing serious. Sometimes my feelings change a lot.
>
> Jane: I understand. Many teens have ups and downs in their feelings.
>
> Kevin: Oh, really?
>
> Jane: Have you watched the animated movie "Shining Days"?
>
> Kevin: No, I haven't. Why do you ask?
>
> Jane: It is about a teenager's feelings. It will help you understand your feelings better.
>
> Kevin: That sounds good! I'll watch it.

> Mon, Nov 4th, 2019
>
> Today, I was (A)_____ with nothing serious. These days, my feelings changed a lot. At that time, Jane came to me and understood my feeling, saying that many teens have (B)_____ in their feelings. To understand my feelings better, she suggested (C)_____. She explained that it is about (D)_____. It sounded good, so I decided to see this movie soon.

02 다음 만화 캐릭터에 관한 정보를 보며 글을 완성하시오.

• 캐릭터: Iron Man 　　　 - from Tales of Suspense 　　　 - a genius scientist • 특징: - owns a weapon company 　　　 - invented a suit of armor to save his life	• 좋아하는 이유: 　 - is very rich 　 - is the leader of the superhero team, the Avengers

> My favorite cartoon character is _____ of _____. He is _____.
> He _____ and _____. I like _____
> because _____.

단원별 모의고사

1 다음 영영풀이가 가리키는 것을 고르시오.

> a process of teaching and learning

① teacher　　② learner
③ classroom　④ education
⑤ educator

2 다음 우리말에 맞게 주어진 어휘를 사용하여 영작하시오.

(1) Jake는 연극에서 산타 클로스 역할을 했다. (Santa Clause, role)

　➡ _____

(2) 사람들이 나를 놀릴 때 화가 난다. (fun, angry)

　➡ _____

(3) 채소를 작은 조각으로 자르세요. (cut, pieces)

　➡ _____

3 다음 우리말을 주어진 단어를 이용하여 영작하시오.

(1) 축구 팀원들은 공통의 목표를 갖고 있다. (goal)

　➡ _____

(2) 만화영화로 영어를 배우는 것은 재미있다. (it, animated)

　➡ _____

(3) 삶에는 기복이 있다. (there, ups)

　➡ _____

4 다음 문장의 빈칸에 들어갈 말을 〈보기〉에서 골라 쓰시오.

> ┌─ 보기 ─┐
> movement / amusing / publish / probably

(1) I like to listen to _____ stories on the radio.

(2) The old lady _____ knows more about the building than anyone.

(3) The cat made a sudden _____ and caught a mouse.

(4) They agreed to _____ the new novel next year.

[05~07] 다음 대화를 읽고 물음에 답하시오.

Suji: Good morning, Chef Garcia!

Garcia: Hello, Suji. Have you ever made nacho pizza?

Suji: Nacho pizza? No, I haven't.

Garcia: Kids will love it, and I'll tell you how to make it.

Suji: Sounds good!

Garcia: It's easy to make. First, put nacho chips on a plate and spread pizza sauce on them.

Suji: Okay. (A)Let me help you with the pizza sauce.

Garcia: Thanks. Next, put some ham, onions, and peppers on top.

Suji: Okay. Then?

Garcia: Add cheese and bake for about 12 minutes in the oven.

Suji: (B)I can't wait to taste it!

5 위 대화의 밑줄 친 (A)와 바꾸어 쓸 수 있는 것은?

① I'll give you a hand with the pizza sauce.

② I want you to help me with the pizza sauce.

③ Would you help me with the pizza sauce?

④ I need your help with the pizza sauce.

⑤ Can you give me your hand with the pizza sauce?

06 위 대화의 밑줄 친 (B)와 바꾸어 쓸 수 있는 것은?

① I don't want to wait to taste it.
② I don't like to taste it.
③ I'm not good at tasting it.
④ I'm looking forward to tasting it.
⑤ I haven't tasted it.

07 위 대화의 내용과 일치하도록 빈칸을 완성하시오.

<How to make nacho pizza>

Step	Procedure
1	put _____ on a plate
2	_____ pizza sauce on the nacho chips
3	put _____ on top
4	add _____ and bake for _____ in the oven

[08~10] 다음 대화를 읽고 물음에 답하시오.

Jane: Kevin, you look down.
Kevin: Nothing serious. Sometimes my feelings change a lot.
Jane: ⓐ I understand. Many teens have _____(A)_____ in their feelings.
Kevin: ⓑ Oh, really?
Jane: ⓒ Have you watched the animated movie "Shining Days"?
Kevin: ⓓ No, I haven't. Why do you ask?
Jane: ⓔ It will help you understand your feelings better.
Kevin: That sounds good! I'll watch it.

08 위 대화의 빈칸 (A)에 '기복'을 나타내는 표현을 3단어로 완성하시오.

➡ _____

09 위 대화의 ⓐ~ⓔ 중 주어진 문장이 들어가기에 적절한 곳은?

It is about a teenager's feelings.

① ⓐ ② ⓑ ③ ⓒ ④ ⓓ ⑤ ⓔ

10 위 대화의 내용과 일치하지 <u>않는</u> 것은?

① Kevin은 기분이 안 좋아 보인다.
② Kevin은 때때로 감정이 많이 바뀌는 심각한 문제를 갖고 있다.
③ 많은 십대들이 감정의 기복이 있다.
④ Shining Days라는 만화영화는 십 대의 감정에 관한 것이다.
⑤ Jane은 Shining Days라는 영화가 Kevin의 감정을 더 잘 이해하도록 도와줄 것이라고 생각한다.

[11~12] 다음 대화를 읽고 물음에 답하시오.

Emily: Oh, look at the long line at the box office.
Tony: Yeah, there's a ticket machine over there. Let's buy the tickets from the machine.
Emily: All right. (A)그 기계를 어떻게 쓰는지 아니?
Tony: Sure. It's easy. First, select a movie and a showtime.
Emily: Okay. We can watch the seven o'clock show. Then what?
Tony: Well, select the number of tickets and choose our seats.
Emily: Okay. Two tickets, and I want to sit in the back.
Tony: No problem. Lastly, pay for the tickets.
Emily: It's very simple.

11 위 대화의 밑줄 친 (A)의 우리말을 <보기>에 주어진 단어를 모두 사용하여 영작하시오.

┌─ 보기 ─┐
know / to / you / machine / the / do / how / use

➡ _____

12 위 대화의 내용과 일치하는 것은?

① Emily and Tony are going to buy their tickets at the ticket counter.

② Emily and Tony are going to sit in the middle.

③ Emily and Tony have to choose seats before they select the showtime.

④ Emily already knows how to buy tickets using the ticket machine.

⑤ Emily and Tony have to pay for the tickets after choosing their seats.

13 다음 빈칸에 들어갈 말로 가장 적절한 것은?

Linda hasn't found her car key _____.

① just   ② already   ③ ago
④ yet   ⑤ before

14 다음 중 주어진 문장의 밑줄 친 부분과 쓰임이 같은 것은?

Where can I find a recycling bin?

① Can you see the crying baby?

② I heard someone calling my name.

③ Who shot the flying bird?

④ There are boys flying kites.

⑤ Diana couldn't find her sleeping bag.

15 다음 중 어법상 바르지 않은 것은?

① Look at the man playing the violin.

② Patrick has just finished the project.

③ Someone called you when you went out.

④ There was an unexpecting danger around us.

⑤ Susan has used this coffee machine for ten years.

16 주어진 단어를 활용하여 다음 우리말을 여덟 단어로 이루어진 한 문장으로 쓰시오.

이러한 표현들은 종종 구어체 영어에서 사용된다. (expression / use / speak)

➡ _____

[17~20] 다음 글을 읽고 물음에 답하시오.

Boat! Land!

Did you laugh when you saw the cartoon above? If so, the cartoonist was successful. Cartoonists are the people who make cartoons. They want to catch ①your interest, and usually, make you (A)[laugh / to laugh] with simple language and creative drawings.

People have made cartoons for hundreds of years. There are ②many types of cartoons, and they play different roles. One form of cartoon is a picture with a few words. It is sometimes called a "gag cartoon." The cartoonist makes a funny character, and the character makes you laugh by doing or (B)[say / saying] silly things.

Another type of cartoon is called a caricature. In a caricature, some parts of a character (C)[is / are] different or bigger than usual. Look at the picture on the right. Which parts of the man's face jump out at you? Artists have used this type of cartoon to make fun of well-known people.

When several cartoon pictures ③come together and tell a story, we have a comic strip. Comic strips have been in newspapers for many years. They are often just amusing stories. People ④have also used comic strips for education. Comics can make information clearer and ⑤more difficult to learn. You have probably seen comic history or science books.

17 ①~⑤ 중 글의 흐름상 어색한 것은?

①   ②   ③   ④   ⑤

18 (A)~(C)에서 어법상 알맞은 것을 쓰시오.

➡ (A) _____ (B) _____ (C) _____

19 How long have people made cartoons? Answer in English with a full sentence.

➡ _____

20 다음 중 위 글의 내용과 일치하는 것은?

① Cartoonists aren't interested in drawing creative things.
② People who draw a gag cartoon use as many words as possible.
③ There is only one picture in a comic strip.
④ We can't find a comic strip in newspapers now.
⑤ Comics help us understand history or science clearly.

In the 1990s, a new type of cartoon was developed. It is called a webtoon. Webtoons are published online, so you can read them anytime, anywhere on your phone or computer. They are very popular, and some of them are even made into TV dramas or movies.

New forms of cartoons may appear in the future. They could be different and even more exciting than now, but one thing will remain the same: they will help us laugh, relax, and learn.

21 위 글의 내용과 일치하지 않는 것은?

① Many cartoon movies are loved by people of all ages.
② Artists develop fascinating characters through animation.
③ Webtoons are read online.
④ Some TV dramas are based on webtoons.
⑤ The writer doesn't think a new type of cartoon will appear.

[21~22] 다음 글을 읽고 물음에 답하시오.

You have surely seen many cartoon movies, or animated movies, too. These are very popular among people of all ages. Movement and sounds are added to pictures, so they come alive. Artists and writers can develop fascinating characters and tell interesting stories through animation.

22 웹툰의 강점으로 가장 적절한 것은?

① They have funny characters.
② They are easy to read whenever you want.
③ They have the latest information.
④ They are loved by people of all ages.
⑤ They have sounds and movement.

Lesson 8

Viva, South America!

🎙 의사소통 기능

- 어떤 사실을 알고 있는지 묻고 답하기

  A: Do you know what the capital of Peru is?

  B: Yes. It's Lima.

- 놀람 표현하기

  A: You know what? Dogs can smile.

  B: Really? That's surprising.

🎙 언어 형식

- 최상급

  Suji is **the tallest** student in our school.

- 간접의문문

  Do you know **how old the building is**?

Words & Expressions

Key Words

- **across**[əkrɔ́ːs] 부 건너서, 가로질러
- **area**[ɛ́əriə] 명 지역
- **benefit**[bénəfit] 명 이익, 혜택
- **bridge**[bridʒ] 명 다리
- **capital**[kǽpətl] 명 수도
- **contain**[kəntéin] 동 포함하다
- **continent**[kántənənt] 명 대륙
- **desert**[dézərt] 명 사막
- **especially**[ispéʃəli] 부 특히
- **fantastic**[fæntǽstik] 형 환상적인, 엄청난
- **flow**[flou] 동 흐르다
- **Mars**[maːrz] 명 화성
- **mountain range** 산맥
- **natural**[nǽtʃərəl] 형 자연의, 천연의
- **ocean**[óuʃən] 명 대양
- **origin**[ɔ́ːrədʒin] 명 기원, 원산
- **outer space** 우주, 외계
- **patience**[péiʃəns] 명 인내심
- **pepper**[pépər] 명 고추
- **per**[pəːr] 전 ~당, ~마다
- **pilot**[páilət] 명 조종사
- **prepare**[pripɛ́ər] 동 준비하다

- **probably**[prábəbli] 부 아마도
- **rainforest**[réinfɔ̀ːrist] 명 열대 우림
- **ride**[raid] 동 타다
- **roller coaster** 롤러코스터
- **salt flat** 솔트 플랫 (바닷물이 증발하고 남은 염분으로 이루어진 평원)
- **scared**[skɛərd] 형 겁먹은, 무서워하는
- **sea level** 해수면
- **shy**[ʃai] 형 수줍은, 부끄럼 타는
- **similar**[símələr] 형 비슷한, 유사한
- **social studies** 사회(과목)
- **soil**[sɔil] 명 흙, 토양
- **sunrise**[sʌ́nraiz] 명 해돋이, 일출
- **sunscreen**[sʌ́nskriːn] 명 자외선 차단제
- **through**[θruː] 전 ~을 통하여
- **tourist**[túərist] 명 관광객
- **unique**[juːníːk] 형 독특한
- **view**[vjuː] 명 전망
- **waterfall**[wɔ́ːtərfɔ̀l] 명 폭포
- **wide**[waid] 형 넓은
- **wonder**[wʌ́ndər] 명 경이, 놀라움
- **work of art** 예술품, 미술품

Key Expressions

- **all year round** 일 년 내내, 연중
- **at first** 처음에는
- **be full of** ~으로 가득하다
- **be similar to** ~와 비슷하다
- **by oneself** 혼자서, 홀로

- **by the way** 그건 그렇고
- **go away** 없어지다
- **name after** ~을 따라 이름 짓다
- **throw a party** 파티를 열다
- **to be honest** 솔직히 말하면

Word Power

※ 서로 반대되는 뜻을 가진 어휘

☐ **wide** (넓은) ↔ **narrow** (좁은)

☐ **similar** (비슷한, 유사한) ↔ **different** (다른)

☐ **benefit** (이익) ↔ **loss** (손실, 손해)

☐ **sunrise** (해돋이, 일출) ↔ **sunset** (일몰)

☐ **natural** (자연의) ↔ **artificial** (인공적인)

☐ **unique** (독특한) ↔ **usual** (평범한)

☐ **patient** (인내심 있는) ↔ **impatient** (성급한, 조급한)

☐ **dry** (마른) ↔ **wet** (젖은)

※ 복합어

rain	snow	back	hand
rainbow (무지개)	**snowball** (눈뭉치)	**backache** (요통)	**handbag** (핸드백)
raincoat (우비)	**snowboard** (스노보드)	**background** (배경)	**handball** (핸드볼)
raindrop (빗방울)	**snowman** (눈사람)	**backpack** (배낭)	**handbook** (안내서)
rainfall (강우)	**snow storm** (눈보라)	**backseat** (뒷자리)	**handcart** (손수레)

English Dictionary

☐ **across** 건너서, 가로질러
→ from one side of something to the other
어떤 것의 한쪽에서 다른 쪽으로

☐ **benefit** 이익
→ an advantage that something gives you
무언가가 당신에게 주는 이점

☐ **continent** 대륙
→ a large mass of land surrounded by sea
바다에 의해 둘러싸인 거대한 땅

☐ **natural** 천연의, 자연의
→ existing in nature; not made or caused by humans
자연에 존재하는; 인간에 의해 만들어지거나 야기되지 않은

☐ **origin** 기원
→ the point from which something starts; the cause of something
무언가가 시작되는 기점; 무언가의 원인

☐ **patience** 인내심
→ the ability to stay calm without becoming angry
화내지 않고 침착함을 유지하는 능력

☐ **pilot** 조종사
→ a person who operates the controls of an aircraft, especially as a job
특히 직업으로 항공기 조종장치를 작동하는 사람

☐ **prepare** 준비하다
→ to make a plan for something that will happen
일어날 무언가에 대한 계획을 세우다

☐ **rainforest** 열대 우림
→ a forest in a tropical area that receives a lot of rain
많은 비가 오는 열대 지역의 숲

☐ **soil** 토양, 흙
→ the top layer of the earth in which plants and trees grow
식물들과 나무들이 자라는 땅의 표층

☐ **waterfall** 폭포
→ a place where a stream or river falls from a high place, for example over a cliff or rock
예를 들어 절벽이나 바위와 같은 높은 장소로부터 냇물 또는 강이 떨어지는 장소

☐ **wide** 넓은
→ measuring a large distance from one side to the other
한쪽에서 다른 쪽까지 멀리 떨어진 거리를 나타내는

☐ **wonder** 경이, 놀라움
→ a thing that causes a feeling of great surprise or admiration
엄청난 놀라움 또는 예찬의 감정을 야기하는 것

서답형

01 다음 짝지어진 단어의 관계가 같도록 빈칸에 알맞은 말을 쓰시오.

similar : different = _____ : narrow

중요

02 다음 중 밑줄 친 부분의 뜻풀이가 바르지 <u>않은</u> 것은?

① Asia is the largest <u>continent</u> in the world. 대륙
② My father usually <u>prepares</u> my dinner for me. 준비한다
③ He and his mother have very <u>similar</u> interests. 비슷한
④ The waterfall is a natural <u>wonder</u> which attracts lots of tourists. 호기심을 갖다
⑤ The planet gets a lot of oxygen from the <u>rainforest</u>. 열대 우림

서답형

03 다음 우리말에 맞게 빈칸에 알맞은 말을 쓰시오.

(1) 우리는 폭포를 볼 때까지 강 옆을 걸었다.
 ➡ We walked next to the river until we could see the _____.
(2) 이 지역의 사람들은 마실 물을 충분히 갖고 있지 않다.
 ➡ People in this _____ do not have enough water to drink.
(3) 내 동생은 강아지들에게 참을성이 없다.
 ➡ My sister has no _____ with the puppies.

04 다음 영영풀이가 가리키는 것을 고르시오.

the ability to stay calm without becoming angry

① patience ② view
③ wonder ④ desert
⑤ capital

서답형

05 다음 문장의 빈칸에 들어갈 말을 〈보기〉에서 골라 쓰시오.

┌── 보기 ├──
similar / unique / probably / wide / across

(1) I will _____ be home by midnight.
(2) The river is so wide that we cannot swim _____.
(3) You can imagine how _____ the ocean is.
(4) Spanish is _____ to Portuguese in many ways.
(5) Jack has a _____ hair color, so anyone can easily find him.

중요

06 다음 문장에 공통으로 들어갈 말을 고르시오.

• Coffee, tea and soft drinks usually _____ caffeine.
• Each pack _____s twenty apple pies.
• Actually, the gold medal _____s only 1.34 percent of gold.

① contain ② flow
③ spend ④ prepare
⑤ view

01 다음 짝지어진 단어의 관계가 같도록 빈칸에 알맞은 말을 쓰시오.

> teach : teacher = tour : _____

02 다음 우리말에 맞게 빈칸에 알맞은 말을 쓰시오.

(1) 그들은 우주 공간에 어떤 생명체들이 있다고 믿는다.
　➡ They believe there are some creatures in _____ _____.

(2) 나는 폭포의 크기에 놀랐다.
　➡ I was surprised at the size of the _____.

(3) 고추는 많은 비타민 C를 함유하고 있다.
　➡ Peppers _____ a lot of vitamin C.

03 다음 문장의 빈칸에 들어갈 말을 〈보기〉에서 골라 알맞은 형태로 쓰시오.

> ┤ 보기 ├
> go away / all year round / be full of / by oneself / social studies / throw a party

(1) A lot of tourists visit Europe _____.
(2) I felt like all my stress _____.
(3) I don't want to stay here _____.
(4) At first, I didn't have any interest in _____.
(5) The park _____ children and their parents.
(6) Kathy decided to _____ this weekend.

04 다음 우리말에 맞게 주어진 단어를 사용하여 영작하시오.

(1) 감자 가격은 100 그램당 250원이다. (per)
　➡ _____
　_____

(2) 사하라 사막의 기후는 매우 뜨겁고 건조하다.
　➡ _____

(3) 당신은 이 대륙에서 코알라들과 캥거루들을 찾을 수 있다. (find, on)
　➡ _____
　_____

05 다음 우리말과 일치하도록 주어진 단어를 모두 배열하여 영작하시오.

(1) 이 지역은 일 년 내내 습하다.
(is / year / this / humid / all / region / round)
　➡ _____
　_____

(2) 한국의 동쪽에 큰 산맥이 있다.
(side / Korea / there / of / is / on / the / eastern / a / mountain / big / range)
　➡ _____
　_____

(3) 경기장은 흥분한 축구팬들로 가득했다.
(was / full / the / of / fans / soccer / stadium / excited)
　➡ _____
　_____

(4) 그건 그렇고 누가 이 영화를 감독했는지 알고 있니?
(know / by / do / way / who / the / directed / movie / the / you)
　➡ _____
　_____

Conversation

1 어떤 사실을 알고 있는지 묻고 답하기

A Do you know what the capital of Peru is? 페루의 수도가 무엇인지 알고 있니?

B Yes. It's Lima. 응. 리마야.

■ 어떤 것에 관해 알고 있는지 물을 때는 'Do you know ~?'를 이용해 표현한다. 특정 인물에 관해 알고 있는지 물을 때는 'Do you know who ~ is?'로 표현하고, 사물에 관해 알고 있는지 물을 때는 'Do you know what ~ is?'로 표현한다.

알고 있는지 묻기

- Do you know who wrote the book? 누가 그 책을 썼는지 알고 있니?
- Do you know where Fred put the bread? Fred가 어디에 빵을 두었는지 알고 있니?
- Guess who she is. 그녀가 누군지 맞혀 봐.
- Can you guess what it is? 이게 무엇인지 추측할 수 있겠니?

핵심 Check

1. 다음 우리말과 일치하도록 빈칸에 알맞은 말을 쓰시오.

(1) **A:** _____ _____ _____ that December 10 is Ray's birthday?

(너는 12월 10일이 Ray의 생일인 거 알고 있니?)

B: Yes. I'm going to _____ a surprise party for him.

(응. 나는 그를 위해 깜짝 파티를 열어 주려고 해.)

(2) **A:** Do you know _____ _____ _____ _____ is?

(너는 이 건물이 얼마나 오래되었는지 아니?)

B: No, I have no idea. (아니. 나는 몰라.)

182 Lesson 8. Viva, South America!

② 놀람 표현하기

A You know what? Dogs can smile. 그거 알아? 개들이 웃을 수 있대.

B Really? That's surprising. 정말? 놀랍구나.

■ 상대방이 놀라운 사실이나 잘 몰랐던 사실을 설명할 때 That's surprising.(정말 놀랍구나.), 'What a surprise!' 또는 'I can't believe it.'을 통해 놀라움을 표현할 수 있다.

놀람 표현하기

- What a surprise! 정말 놀랍다!
- That's incredible. 굉장하다.
- I can't believe it. 믿을 수가 없어.
- You're kidding. 농담이겠죠.
- You're joking. 농담이겠죠.
- (It's) Unbelievable. 믿을 수 없어.
- That's amazing. 굉장하다.

✎ 핵심 Check

2. 다음 우리말과 일치하도록 빈칸에 알맞은 말을 쓰시오.

(1) **A:** _____ _____ _____? Koalas only spend 15 minutes a day on social activity.

   (그거 알아? 코알라들은 하루에 15분만 사회활동에 쓴데.)

   B: Really? That's _____. (정말? 놀랍구나.)

(2) **A:** I _____ that elephants use sand as sunscreen.

   (나는 코끼리들이 모래를 자외선 차단제로 사용한다고 들었어.)

   B: I _____ believe it. (정말 놀랍구나.)

Communication: Listen –Dialog 1

Sujin: Dad, I like this tomato soup.

Dad: I'm happy you like ❶it.

Sujin: ❷By the way, do you know ❸where the tomato was first grown?

Dad: Italy or somewhere in Europe?

Sujin: No, the tomato came from South America.

Dad: Really? How did you know ❹that?

Sujin: I learned it from Ms. Song, my ❺social studies teacher.

Dad: That's good.

Sujin: 아빠, 저는 이 토마토 수프가 마음에 들어요.

Dad: 네가 좋아하니 기쁘구나.

Sujin: 그런데 아빠는 토마토가 처음에 어디에서 재배되었는지 아세요?

Dad: 이탈리아나 유럽 어딘가가 아닐까?

Sujin: 아니에요. 토마토는 남아메리카에서 왔어요.

Dad: 정말? 너는 그걸 어떻게 알았니?

Sujin: 저는 그걸 사회 선생님이신 송 선생님께 배웠어요.

Dad: 훌륭하구나.

---

❶ it은 tomato soup을 가리킨다.
❷ By the way: 그런데
❸ 간접의문문 형태로 '의문사+주어+동사' 어순으로 이어진다.
❹ that은 토마토가 남아메리카에서 왔다는 것을 가리킨다.
❺ social studies: 사회(과목)

Check(√) True or False

(1) Sujin's teacher doesn't know where the tomato came from.　　　　T ☐ F ☐

(2) The tomato was first grown in South America.　　　　T ☐ F ☐

Wrap Up – Listening ❻

Mike: Do you know Sumin ❶won first prize at the speech contest?

Sue: ❷I can't believe it. She was very quiet and ❸shy last year.

Mike: Yeah. She ❹joined the drama club this year, and she has changed a lot.

Sue: I see. I want to join the club, too.

Mike: 너는 수민이가 말하기 대회에서 우승한 걸 알고 있니?

Sue: 그것 참 놀랍다. 작년에 그 애는 정말 조용하고 수줍음이 많았는데.

Mike: 맞아. 그 애가 올해 연극 동아리에 가입했는데, 많이 바뀌었다.

Sue: 그렇구나. 나도 그 동아리에 가입하고 싶다.

---

❶ win (the) first prize: 일등상을 타다, 일등으로 입상하다
❷ 놀라움을 표현하며 'What a surprise!' 또는 'That's amazing.'으로 바꾸어 쓸 수 있다.
❸ shy: 수줍음이 많은
❹ join: 가입하다

Check(√) True or False

(3) It was Sumin who won first prize at the speech contest.　　　　T ☐ F ☐

(4) Sumin changed a lot before joining the drama club.　　　　T ☐ F ☐

Communication: Listen – Dialog 2

Jenny: Did you see the pictures ❶Ms. Song took?

Brian: What pictures?

Jenny: She traveled around South America ❷by herself last summer.

Brian: Really? ❸What a surprise!

Jenny: She showed us pictures of beautiful places. I ❹especially liked the pictures of pyramids.

Brian: Are there pyramids in South America?

Jenny: Yes. She said some pyramids are about 3,800 meters above ❺sea level.

Brian: I can't believe it.

❶ the pictures (that/which) Ms. Song took. 목적격 관계대명사가 생략되었다.
❷ by oneself: 혼자서
❸ 놀라움을 표현하며 'That's surprising!' 또는 'I can't believe it.' 등으로 바꾸어 표현할 수 있다.
❹ especially: 특히
❺ sea level: 해수면

Communication – Listen More

Hana: How was the roller coaster ride, Jongha?

Jongha: It was ❶fantastic. I really enjoyed ❷it.

Hana: Ha ha. You closed your eyes ❸while riding.

Jongha: Did you see? ❹To be honest, I was really scared at first.

Hana: Do you know ❺how fast this roller coaster is?

Jongha: I have no idea.

Hana: It goes ❻as fast as 140 km per hour.

Jongha: Wow! That's surprising!

Hana: Let's ride ❼it one more time!

Jongha: Look at the sign. We can't ride ❼it after 8 p.m.

Hana: Oh, maybe next time.

❶ fantastic: 환상적인
❷ it은 the roller coaster ride를 가리킨다.
❸ while ~ing: ~하는 동안
❹ To be honest: 솔직히 말하면
❺ 간접의문문으로 '의문사+주어+동사' 어순으로 이어진다.
❻ 'as 원급 as' 형태로 원급 비교를 나타낸다.
❼ it은 the roller coaster를 가리킨다.

Communicate: Speak

Amy: Do you know what the ❶capital of Peru is?

Jinsu: I have no idea. What is ❷it?

Amy: It's Lima.

Jinsu: I didn't know that.

❶ capital: 수도
❷ it은 페루의 수도를 가리킨다.

Wrap Up – Listening ❺

Jack: Do you know Junha got a puppy?

Minji: No. Where did he get it? From a ❶pet shop?

Jack: No. ❷I heard he got the puppy from his uncle.

Minji: I want ❸one, too.

❶ pet shop: 애완 동물 가게
❷ I heard (that) ~ = I was told (that) ~
❸ one은 a puppy를 가리킨다.

● 다음 우리말과 일치하도록 빈칸에 알맞은 말을 쓰시오.

Communication: Listen – Dialog 1

Sujin: Dad, I like this _____ _____.

Dad: I'm _____ you like it.

Sujin: _____ _____ _____, do you know _____ the tomato was first _____?

Dad: Italy or _____ in Europe?

Sujin: No, the tomato came from _____ _____.

Dad: Really? _____ did you know that?

Sujin: I learned it from Ms. Song, my _____ _____ teacher.

Dad: That's good.

해석

Sujin: 아빠, 저는 이 토마토 수프가 마음에 들어요.
Dad: 네가 좋아하니 기쁘구나.
Sujin: 그런데 아빠는 토마토가 처음에 어디에서 재배되었는지 아세요?
Dad: 이탈리아나 유럽 어딘가가 아닐까?
Sujin: 아니에요, 토마토는 남아메리카에서 왔어요.
Dad: 정말? 너는 그걸 어떻게 알았니?
Sujin: 저는 그걸 사회 선생님이신 송 선생님께 배웠어요.
Dad: 훌륭하구나.

Communication: Listen – Dialog 2

Jenny: Did you see the pictures Ms. Song _____?

Brian: What pictures?

Jenny: She _____ around South America _____ _____ last summer.

Brian: Really? What a _____!

Jenny: She showed us pictures of beautiful places. I _____ liked the pictures of _____.

Brian: _____ _____ pyramids in South America?

Jenny: Yes. She said some pyramids are about 3,800 meters _____ _____ _____.

Brian: I _____ _____ _____.

Jenny: 너 송 선생님께서 찍은 사진들을 봤니?
Brian: 무슨 사진?
Jenny: 선생님께서는 지난여름에 혼자 남아메리카로 여행을 다녀오셨대.
Brian: 정말? 그것 참 놀랍다!
Jenny: 선생님께서 우리들에게 아름다운 장소들의 사진을 보여 주셨어. 나는 특히 피라미드 사진이 마음에 들더라.
Brian: 남아메리카에 피라미드가 있어?
Jenny: 응. 선생님께서 몇몇 피라미드는 해발 3,800미터 정도에 위치하고 있다고 하셨어.
Brian: 정말 놀랍다.

Communication: Listen More

Hana: _____ _____ the roller coaster ride, Jongha?

Jongha: It was _____. I really enjoyed it.

Hana: Ha ha. You _____ your eyes while _____.

Jongha: Did you see? _____ _____ _____, I was really _____ at first.

Hana: Do you know _____ _____ this roller coaster _____?

Jongha: I have _____ _____.

Hana: It goes _____ _____ _____ 140 km per hour.

Jongha: Wow! That's _____!

Hana: Let's _____ it one more time!

Jongha: Look at the _____. We can't ride it _____ 8 p.m.

Hana: Oh, _____ next time.

Communicate: Speak

Amy: Do you know _____ _____ _____ _____ _____?

Jinsu: I have _____ _____. What is it?

Amy: It's Lima.

Jinsu: I didn't _____ that.

Wrap Up – Listening ❺

Jack: Do you know Junha got a _____?

Minji: No. _____ did he get it? From a pet shop?

Jack: No. I _____ he got the puppy from his _____.

Minji: I want one, too.

Wrap Up – Listening ❻

Mike: Do you know Sumin _____ _____ _____ at the speech contest?

Sue: I can't believe it. She was very _____ and _____ last year.

Mike: Yeah. She _____ the drama club this year, and she _____ _____ a lot.

Sue: I see. I want to _____ the club, _____.

해석

Hana: 롤러코스터 어땠어, 종하야?
Jongha: 신나더라. 난 정말 재미있었어.
Hana: 하하. 너는 타는 동안에 눈을 감고 있던걸.
Jongha: 봤어? 솔직히 말하면 처음에는 정말 무서웠어.
Hana: 너 이 롤러코스터가 얼마나 빠른지 알고 있니?
Jongha: 모르겠어.
Hana: 이건 시속 140km로 달린대.
Jongha: 와! 정말 놀랍다!
Hana: 우리 한 번 더 타자!
Jongha: 표지판을 봐. 저녁 8시 이후에는 그것을 탈 수 없어.
Hana: 아, 다음에 타지 뭐.

Amy: 너는 페루의 수도가 어디인지 알고 있니?
Jinsu: 아니 모르겠어. 어디야?
Amy: 리마야.
Jinsu: 그건 몰랐네

Jack: 너는 준하에게 강아지가 생긴 걸 알고 있니?
Minji: 아니. 어디에서 났대? 애완동물 가게에서?
Jack: 아니. 나는 그가 강아지를 삼촌댁에서 얻었다고 들었어.
Minji: 나도 강아지를 키우고 싶다.

Mike: 너는 수민이가 말하기 대회에서 우승한 걸 알고 있니?
Sue: 그것 참 놀랍다. 작년에 그 애는 정말 조용하고 수줍음이 많았는데.
Mike: 맞아. 그 애가 올해 연극 동아리에 가입했는데, 많이 바뀌었대.
Sue: 그렇구나. 나도 그 동아리에 가입하고 싶다.

[01~02] 다음 대화를 읽고 물음에 답하시오.

> Jack: (A)Do you know Junha got a puppy?
> Minji: No. Where did he get it? From a pet shop?
> Jack: No. (B)I heard he got the puppy from his uncle. (that, told)
> Minji: I want one, too.

01 위 대화의 밑줄 친 (A)와 의도가 같은 것을 모두 고르시오.

① Do you wonder if Junha got a puppy?
② Have you heard Junha got a puppy?
③ Is Junha likely to get a puppy?
④ You know Junha got a puppy, don't you?
⑤ Is it possible for Junha to get a puppy?

02 위 대화의 밑줄 친 (B)와 의미가 같도록 주어진 단어를 사용하여 다시 쓰시오.

➡ _____

[03~04] 다음 대화를 읽고 물음에 답하시오.

> Mike: Do you know Sumin won first prize at the speech contest?
> Sue: (A)정말 놀랍구나. (can't) She was very quiet and shy last year.
> Mike: Yeah. She joined the drama club this year, and she has changed a lot.
> Sue: I see. I want to join the club, too.

03 위 대화의 밑줄 친 (A)의 우리말을 주어진 단어를 사용하여 영작하시오.

➡ _____

04 위 대화의 내용과 일치하지 않는 것은?

① 말하기 대회에서 수민이가 우승하였다.
② 수민이는 작년에 정말 조용하고 수줍음이 많았다.
③ 수민이는 올해 연극 동아리에 가입했다.
④ Sue도 연극 동아리에 가입하고 싶어 한다.
⑤ 연극 동아리는 작년과 올해 많이 바뀌었다.

[01~03] 다음 대화를 읽고 물음에 답하시오.

Sujin: Dad, I like this tomato soup.

Dad: I'm happy you like it.

Sujin: By the way, (A)토마토가 처음에 어디에서 재배되었는지 아세요?

Dad: Italy or somewhere in Europe?

Sujin: No, the tomato came from South America.

Dad: Really? _____(B)_____

Sujin: I learned it from Ms. Song, my social studies teacher.

Dad: That's good.

서답형

01 위 대화의 밑줄 친 (A)의 우리말을 〈보기〉에 주어진 단어를 모두 배열하여 완성하시오.

┌─── 보기 ───┐
where / grown / first / was / know / you / do / tomato / the
└───────────┘

➡ _____

02 위 대화의 빈칸 (B)에 들어갈 말로 적절한 것을 모두 고르시오.

① How do you like it?

② How did you know that?

③ What did you know about that?

④ Where did you learn?

⑤ What did you learn about that?

03 위 대화를 읽고 대답할 수 없는 것은?

① Does Sujin like the tomato soup?

② Where is the origin of the tomato?

③ What did Sujin learn from Ms. Song?

④ What subject does Ms. Song teach?

⑤ What was first grown in Italy?

[04~05] 다음 대화를 읽고 물음에 답하시오.

Jenny: Did you see the pictures Ms. Song took?

Brian: What pictures?

Jenny: She traveled around South America by herself last summer.

Brian: Really? (A)What a surprise!

Jenny: She showed us pictures of beautiful places. I especially liked the pictures of pyramids.

Brian: Are there pyramids in South America?

Jenny: Yes. She said some pyramids are about 3,800 meters above sea level.

Brian: I can't believe it.

04 위 대화의 밑줄 친 (A)와 바꾸어 쓰기 어색한 것은?

① Unbelievable!

② That's amazing!

③ That's surprising!

④ I can't believe it.

⑤ What a relief!

05 위 대화의 내용과 일치하지 않는 것은?

① Ms. Song took a trip to South America by herself last summer.

② Jenny saw Ms. Song's pictures of beautiful places in South America.

③ Ms. Song took some pictures of pyramids in South America.

④ Jenny heard that some pyramids were about 3,800 meters above sea level.

⑤ Brian didn't believe that there were some pyramids about 3,800 meters above sea level.

[06~07] 다음 대화를 읽고 물음에 답하시오.

> Hana: How was the roller coaster ride, Jongha?
>
> Jongha: It was fantastic. I really enjoyed it.
>
> Hana: Ha ha. You closed your eyes while (A)[ridden / riding].
>
> Jongha: Did you see? To be honest, I was really (B)[scared / scaring] at first.
>
> Hana: (D)Do you know how fast is this roller coaster?
>
> Jongha: I have no idea.
>
> Hana: It goes as fast as 140 km per hour.
>
> Jongha: Wow! That's (C)[surprised / surprising]!
>
> Hana: Let's ride it one more time!
>
> Jongha: Look at the sign. We can't ride it after 8 p.m.
>
> Hana: Oh, maybe next time.

06 위 대화의 (A)~(C)에 들어갈 말로 바르게 짝지어진 것은?

	(A)	(B)	(C)
①	ridden	scared	surprised
②	ridden	scaring	surprising
③	riding	scared	surprising
④	riding	scaring	surprising
⑤	riding	scared	surprised

서답형

07 위 대화의 밑줄 친 (D)를 어법상 바르게 고치시오.

➡ _____

08 다음 짝지어진 대화가 어색한 것은?

① A: You know what? Tom and Junho are cousins.
   B: That's surprising.

② A: Did you hear Jason won first prize?
   B: At the national contest? What a surprise!

③ A: Look. A seven-year-old boy's cartoon is a big hit.
   B: The drawings are great. I can't believe it.

④ A: Do you know what the capital of Peru is?
   B: Yes, I have. Can you tell me what it is?

⑤ A: Do you know who wrote this book?
   B: I have no idea.

09 다음 대화에서 (A)~(E)가 자연스럽게 이어지도록 순서대로 배열하시오.

> Jenny: Did you see the pictures Ms. Song took?
>
> Brian: What pictures?
>
> Jenny: She traveled around South America by herself last summer.
>
> Brian: Really? What a surprise!
>
> (A) I can't believe it.
>
> (B) Are there pyramids in South America?
>
> (C) Yes. She said some pyramids are about 3,800 meters above sea level.
>
> (D) She showed us pictures of beautiful places. I especially liked the pictures of pyramids.

➡ _____

Conversation 서술형 시험대비

[01~02] 다음 대화를 읽고 물음에 답하시오.

Jenny: Did you see the pictures Ms. Song took?

Brian: What pictures?

Jenny: She traveled around South America by ___(A)___ last summer.

Brian: Really? What a surprise!

Jenny: She showed us pictures of beautiful places. I especially liked the pictures of pyramids.

Brian: Are there pyramids in South America?

Jenny: Yes. She said some pyramids are about 3,800 meters above sea level.

Brian: I can't believe it.

01 위 대화의 빈칸 (A)에 '혼자서, 홀로'의 의미가 되도록 빈칸을 완성하시오.

➡ _____

02 What are Jenny and Brian talking about?

➡ _____
_____

[03~04] 다음 대화를 읽고 물음에 답하시오.

Jack: Do you know Junha got a puppy?

Minji: No. Where did he get it? From a pet shop?

Jack: No. I heard he got the puppy from his uncle.

Minji: I want one, too.

03 What did Junha get from his uncle?

➡ _____

04 What does Minji want to get?

➡ _____

05 다음 대화의 내용과 일치하도록 빈칸을 완성하시오.

Mike: Do you know Sumin won first prize at the speech contest?

Sue: I can't believe it. She was very quiet and shy last year.

Mike: Yeah. She joined the drama club this year, and she has changed a lot.

Sue: I see. I want to join the club, too.

⬇

Today, I heard the winner of the speech contest was (A)_____. I was surprised a lot. She is not what she used to be last year. Last year, she was very (B)_____. But she has changed a lot after (C)_____ this year. I want to be a more active and confident person like Sumin.

06 다음 대화에서 (A)~(E)가 자연스럽게 이어지도록 배열하시오.

Sujin: Dad, I like this tomato soup.

Dad: I'm happy you like it.

(A) Really? How did you know that?

(B) Italy or somewhere in Europe?

(C) By the way, do you know where the tomato was first grown?

(D) No, the tomato came from South America.

(E) I learned it from Ms. Song, my social studies teacher.

➡ _____

Grammar 교과서

1 최상급

> • He is **the tallest** boy of them. 그는 그들 중에서 가장 키가 큰 소년이다.
> • You are **the kindest** person that I have ever known. 너는 내가 아는 사람 중 가장 친절해.

■ 셋 이상을 비교하여 정도가 가장 높은 것을 나타낼 때 최상급을 사용한다. 형용사의 최상급은 정관사 the를 사용하지만, 부사의 최상급에서는 정관사 the를 생략하는 것이 일반적이다.

구분	최상급	예
대부분의 형용사/부사	+-(e)st	tallest, shortest
'자음+y'로 끝나는 경우	-y → -iest	happiest, earliest
'단모음+단자음'으로 끝나는 경우	마지막 자음 추가 + -est	biggest, hottest
-ous, -ful 등으로 끝나는 2음절어 / 3음절 이상인 경우	most +	most famous most exciting
불규칙 변화	best, worst, most, least	

> • Today is **the hottest** day of the year. 오늘은 연중 가장 더운 날이다.
> • The rose is **the most beautiful** flower in my garden. 장미는 내 정원에서 가장 아름다운 꽃이야.
> • This is **the brightest** color of all. 이것은 모든 색 중에서 가장 밝은 색이야.

■ 비교급과 원급을 이용하여 최상급의 의미를 표현할 수 있다.

> • Julia is **the prettiest** in her class. Julia는 그녀의 반에서 가장 예쁘다.
> = Julia is **prettier than any other** girl in her class. (비교급+than any other+단수 명사)
> Julia는 반에 있는 다른 어떤 소녀보다 더 예쁘다.
> = Julia is **prettier than all the other** girls in her class. (비교급+than all the other+복수 명사)
> Julia는 반에 있는 다른 모든 소녀들보다 더 예쁘다.
> = **No other** girl in her class is **as pretty as** Julia. (부정 주어+so[as] 원급 as)
> 그녀의 반에 있는 다른 어떤 소녀도 Julia만큼 예쁘지 않다.
> = **No other** girl in her class is **prettier than** Julia. (부정 주어+비교급+than)
> 그녀의 반에 있는 다른 어떤 소녀도 Julia보다 더 예쁘지 않다.

핵심 Check

1. 다음 우리말과 일치하도록 주어진 단어를 이용하여 빈칸에 알맞은 말을 쓰시오.

(1) Alex는 셋 중에서 가장 재미있는 소년이야. (funny)

➡ Alex is ＿＿＿＿ ＿＿＿＿ ＿＿＿＿ of the three.

(2) 에베레스트산은 세계에서 가장 높은 산이다. (high)

➡ Mt. Everest is ＿＿＿＿ ＿＿＿＿ ＿＿＿＿ in the world.

2 간접의문문

- I wonder **why** she is upset. 나는 그녀가 왜 화가 났는지 궁금해.
- Do you want to know **when** you should go? 언제 가야 하는지 알고 싶니?

■ 간접의문문은 명사절을 이끌며 주어, 목적어, 보어 역할을 한다. 의문사가 있는 간접의문문은 '의문사+주어+동사' 어순으로 쓰인다. 직접의문문인 '의문사+동사+주어 ~?'의 어순과 혼동하지 않도록 유의한다.

- **Who** are you going to meet? 〈직접의문문〉 누구를 만날 예정이니?

  Can you tell me **who** you are going to meet? 〈간접의문문〉 네가 누구를 만날 건지 말해 줄래?

- I wonder **when** he bought the car. 나는 언제 그가 그 차를 샀는지 궁금해.

- I forgot **where** I put my key. 나는 열쇠를 어디에 뒀는지 잊어버렸어.

■ 다음과 같이 의문사가 주어 역할을 하는 경우가 있다. 이때에는 '의문사+동사'의 어순이 된다.

- He asked me **who** called him. 그는 누가 그에게 전화했는지 내게 물었다.

■ 의문사가 없는 경우 간접의문문의 어순은 'if/whether+주어+동사'로 쓴다.

- Can you tell me? + Do you like her?
  → Can you tell me **if[whether]** you like her? 그녀를 좋아하는지 말해 줄래?

- Let me know **if[whether]** the letter arrived safely. 그 편지가 안전하게 도착했는지 내게 알려줘.

- I wonder **if[whether]** the girl came alone. 그 소녀가 혼자 왔는지 궁금해.

■ 주절에 think, believe, imagine 등과 같은 동사가 있을 경우 간접의문문을 만들 때에는 의문사를 문두로 배치한다.

- **How old** do you think she is? 그녀가 몇 살이라고 생각해?

- **Who** do you believe stole the money? 누가 그 돈을 훔쳤다고 믿는 거야?

핵심 Check

2. 다음 우리말과 일치하도록 빈칸에 알맞은 말을 쓰시오.
   (1) 나는 그들이 제때에 그 파티에 왔는지 궁금해.
      ➡ I wonder _____ they came to the party in time.
   (2) 그가 언제 떠났는지 말해 줘.
      ➡ Tell me _____ _____ _____.
   (3) 그가 얼마나 키가 큰지 아니?
      ➡ Do you know _____ _____ _____ _____?

01 다음 문장에서 어법상 어색한 부분을 바르게 고쳐 쓰시오.

(1) I don't know what is she doing.

_____ ➡ _____

(2) Ted didn't know how did she break in his house.

_____ ➡ _____

(3) He is the famousest movie star of the five.

_____ ➡ _____

(4) James is busiest man in the company.

_____ ➡ _____

02 주어진 형용사의 최상급을 빈칸에 쓰시오.

(1) This is _____ pen of all. (cheap)

(2) This is _____ book of the seven. (interesting)

(3) It is _____ museum in the world. (big)

(4) It is _____ problem. (difficult)

(5) It is _____ snowfall in ten years. (heavy)

03 주어진 어구를 바르게 배열하여 다음 우리말을 영어로 쓰시오.

(3) go out: 나가다

(1) 그가 왜 늦게 왔는지 말해 줘. (late / tell / came / why / me / he)

➡ _____

(2) 그녀가 어디로 가고 있는지 말해 줄래? (going / tell / you / she / can / me / where / is)

➡ _____

(3) 그 소년이 언제 나갔는지 기억하니? (out / do / the boy / you / when / remember / went)

➡ _____

(4) June은 누가 그 집을 지었는지 모른다. (the house / doesn't / June / who / know / built)

➡ _____

(5) 누가 들어왔는지 아니? (in / know / came / who / do / you)

➡ _____

01 다음 중 최상급의 형태가 <u>다른</u> 하나는?

① popular   ② interesting

③ likely   ④ simple

⑤ amazing

02 다음 빈칸에 들어갈 말로 가장 적절한 것은?

> Do you remember _____?

① who the ball kicked

② when was she going home

③ what did happen last night

④ when my birthday is

⑤ how can you get here

03 다음 중 주어진 문장과 같은 의미의 문장은?

> Jessica is the smartest girl of all.

① Jessica is as smart as all the other girls.

② Jessica is not smarter than all.

③ No other girl is as smart as Jessica.

④ Anyone is smarter than Jessica.

⑤ Jessica is not as smart as all.

서답형
04 주어진 단어를 활용하여 다음 우리말을 영어로 쓰시오.

> Branda는 그들이 그녀의 도움을 필요로 하는지 추측하려고 애썼다.
> (try to guess)

➡ _____

05 다음 우리말을 영어로 바르게 옮긴 것은?

> 그 시계가 얼마인지 아니?

① Do you know how the watch is much?

② Do you know how much is the watch?

③ Do you know how long you have to watch it?

④ Do you know how much the watch is?

⑤ Do you know how expensive the watch is?

서답형
06 주어진 단어를 활용하여 다음 우리말을 영어로 쓰시오.

> 그것은 세상에서 가장 쉬운 일이 아니다.
> (that / job)

➡ _____

07 다음 빈칸에 들어갈 말로 적절하지 <u>않은</u> 것은?

> I want to know _____ she will throw a party for him. Can I ask her?

① why   ② when

③ if   ④ whether

⑤ that

서답형
08 다음 빈칸에 알맞은 말을 각각 쓰시오.

> No other animal in the world is bigger than this whale.
> = This whale is _____ than any other animal in the world.
> = No other animal is as _____ as this whale.
> = This whale is _____ animal in the world.

09 다음 중 주어진 문장의 밑줄 친 부분과 쓰임이 같은 것은?

> We don't know if he will help us.

① If you want to take part in the race, let us know.
② You can go to the party if you want to.
③ I will call you back if I find your book.
④ Can you give her this message if you see her?
⑤ Can you tell me if you bought the bag?

10 다음 중 문장의 전환이 바르지 않은 것은?

① I wonder. Are you a student?
　→ I wonder whether you are a student.
② Can you tell me? When is your birthday?
　→ Can you tell me when your birthday is?
③ I want to know. How did he finish his homework?
　→ I want to know how he finished his homework.
④ I am not certain. Is she clever?
　→ I am not certain if she is clever.
⑤ Do you believe? Who made the cookies yesterday?
　→ Do you believe who made the cookies yesterday?

11 8 단어로 이루어진 문장으로 다음 우리말을 영어로 쓸 때 세 번째와 다섯 번째 오는 단어를 바르게 짝지은 것은?

> 그 영화에서 가장 재미있는 캐릭터는 누구니?

① the – in
② funniest – in
③ the – character
④ funniest – the
⑤ is – character

12 다음 중 의미가 다른 하나는?

① Her voice is the most beautiful in our class.
② Her voice is more beautiful than any other voice in our class.
③ No other voice in our class is more beautiful than her voice.
④ Her voice is as beautiful as all the other voices in our class.
⑤ No other voice in our class is as beautiful as her voice.

[서답형]

13 빈칸에 알맞은 말을 쓰시오.

> 영국 사람들은 건강이 가장 중요한 것이라고 생각한다.

➡ The British think ＿＿＿＿＿＿＿＿＿
＿＿＿＿＿＿＿＿＿＿.

[서답형]

14 같은 의미가 되도록 빈칸에 알맞은 말을 쓰시오.

> Tom is the most diligent man in the office.
> = No other man in the office is ＿＿＿＿
> ＿＿＿＿ than Tom.

15 다음 중 빈칸에 들어갈 말이 바르게 짝지어진 것은?

> • Do you know ＿＿＿＿＿＿＿?
> • It is ＿＿＿＿＿＿＿ hotel that I've ever visited.

① what time it is – more comfortable
② how he is old – more comfortable
③ who did the laundry – the most comfortable
④ what time is it – the most comfortable
⑤ who broke it – more comfortable

16 주어진 단어를 어법에 맞게 활용하여 다음 우리말을 영어로 쓰시오.

> David는 우리 학교에서 최고의 학생이다.
> (good)

➡ _____

17 다음 중 어법상 바르지 <u>않은</u> 것은?

① Do you know what he is eating?
② Can you tell me who the leader is?
③ Which one is the prettyest dress?
④ I want the cutest doll in this store.
⑤ I remember when she gave me the card.

18 다음 중 주어진 문장과 같은 의미의 문장은?

> This train is the fastest train in the world.

① This train is not as fast as all the other trains in the world.
② No other train in the world is faster than this train.
③ This train is as fast as the other train in the world.
④ This train is faster than the other train.
⑤ This train is not faster than any other train in the world.

19 다음 빈칸에 알맞은 말을 쓰시오.

> 나무늘보는 지구상에서 가장 게으른 동물이다.
> Sloths are _____ on earth.

20 다음 대화의 빈칸에 알맞은 말을 세 단어로 쓰시오.

> A: I want to know _____.
> B: He works at a bank.

➡ _____

21 다음 빈칸에 들어갈 말로 가장 적절한 것은?

> I would like to know. Are you safe?
> = I would like to know _____ you are safe.

① that   ② when
③ how   ④ when
⑤ if

22 다음 우리말을 영어로 <u>잘못</u> 옮긴 것은?

① 이것은 세상에서 가장 위험한 직업입니다.
→ This is the most dangerous job in the world.
② 그녀가 언제 나갈 건지 알려줘.
→ Let me know when she will go out.
③ 바이칼 호수는 지구상에서 가장 깊은 호수로 알려져 있습니다.
→ Lake Baikal is known as the deepest lake on the earth.
④ 누가 이 꽃병을 깨트렸는지는 중요하지 않아.
→ Who broke this vase doesn't matter.
⑤ 이 물은 내가 본 것 중 가장 깨끗한 물이야.
→ This water is the most clean water that I've ever seen.

23 주어진 단어를 활용하여 다음 우리말을 영어로 쓰시오.

> 누가 그 결정을 내렸는지 궁금해요.
> (wonder / make)

➡ _____

24 다음 두 문장을 하나의 문장으로 쓰시오.

> Do you think? How can we get to the park?

➡ _____

01 단어 long을 활용하여 다음 빈칸에 알맞은 말을 어법에 맞게 쓰시오.

> The Amazon River is _____ river in the world. It is _____ than any other river in the world.

02 다음 두 문장을 하나의 문장으로 쓰시오.

(1) Can I ask? Are you mad at me?

➡ _____

(2) Do you know? Where does Tom live?

➡ _____

(3) Can you tell me? Who is she?

➡ _____

(4) I wonder. What happened to you?

➡ _____

(5) Please tell me. Why did he break the promise?

➡ _____

(6) Do you think? When will the book be published?

➡ _____

(7) Let me know. Is she going to tell him the truth?

➡ _____
_____

03 다음 빈칸에 알맞은 말을 쓰시오.

> No other boy in our gym is as brave as John.
> = John is _____ in our gym.

04 다음은 네 개 식당의 평점이다. good과 bad를 활용하여 빈칸에 알맞은 말을 쓰시오.

> Restaurant A: ★★★
> Restaurant B: ★★★★☆
> Restaurant C: ★☆
> Restaurant D: ★★☆

(1) Restaurant C is _____ restaurant of the four.

(2) Restaurant B is _____ restaurant of the four.

(3) No other restaurant of the four is _____ than restaurant C.

05 다음 대화의 빈칸에 알맞은 말을 쓰시오.

> A: Where is he going?
> B: I don't know _____, but I think he will tell us later.

06 주어진 단어를 활용하여 다음 우리말을 영어로 쓰시오.

> 2월은 1년 중 가장 짧은 달이다.
> (of the year)

➡ _____

07 다음 빈칸에 알맞은 말을 쓰시오.

> Jason은 우리 반에서 가장 인기 있는 소년이야.
> Jason is _____ boy in our class.

08 주어진 단어를 바르게 배열하여 다음 우리말을 영어로 쓰시오. 필요하다면 단어를 추가하시오.

> 한국에서 가장 유명한 장소들을 소개할게.
> (in / me / introduce / let / famous / places / Korea)

➡ _____

09 주어진 단어를 바르게 배열하여 대화를 완성하시오.

> A: I wonder (thinks / who / a thief / him)
> B: Mary and Jocelyn.

➡ _____

10 다음 우리말과 일치하도록 주어진 단어를 이용하여 빈칸에 알맞은 말을 쓰시오.

> 그는 내가 아는 사람 중 가장 창의적인 사람이야.
> (creative)
> He is _____ that I've ever known.

11 다음 대화의 빈칸에 알맞은 말을 쓰시오.

> A: Do you know _____?
> B: He is seventeen years old.

12 주어진 단어를 활용하여 다음 우리말을 영어로 쓰시오.

> 지구상에서 가장 추운 도시는 어디야?
> (on earth)

➡ _____

13 다음 문장과 같은 뜻의 문장을 완성하시오.

> Education is the most important thing in the world.

➡ No other thing in the world _____
_____.

➡ No other thing in the world _____
_____.

➡ Education is _____
_____ in the world.

➡ Education is _____
_____ in the world.

14 주어진 단어를 활용하여 다음 우리말을 영어로 쓰시오.

> 그녀가 누구라고 생각해? (think / who)

➡ _____

15 다음 대화를 읽고 빈칸에 알맞은 말을 쓰시오.

> Alex: Where are you going?
> Emily: I am going to a theater.
> Alex: Are you going there to see a movie?
> Emily: No. I do a part-time job there.

➡ Alex wants to know _____.
So Emily tells him that she is going to a theater. Alex wonders _____
_____. Emily says that she is going there to do a part-time job.

Reading

Home of Natural Wonders

Do you know <u>where the driest desert on Earth is?</u> <u>How about the</u>
　　　　　　　간접의문문 (의문사+주어+동사)　　　　　　　　　　　～은 어때?
highest waterfall? Yes, they are both in South America. This continent
<u>is full of</u> natural <u>wonders that will surprise you.</u>
= is filled with　　　　　　　　　　주격 관계대명사

Atacama Desert

The Atacama is the driest desert on Earth. In some parts, it gets
almost no rain <u>at all</u> — only 1–3 millimeters <u>per year</u>! The ground
　　　　　　　　(부정문에서) 전혀　　　　　　　　　　　　　= a year
in some areas is <u>so dry that</u> no plants can grow. Do you know <u>what</u>
　　　　　　　　　so 원인 that 결과　　　　　　　　　　　　간접의문문 (의문사+주어+동사)
<u>scientists do in such a dry place?</u> <u>The soil in this desert is very similar</u>
the Atacama Desert를 의미('such+a+형용사+명사'의 어순에 주의)
to the soil on Mars, so they prepare for <u>trips to outer space.</u> The
　　　　　　　　　　　　　　　　　　　　　　　우주로의 여행
Atacama is also <u>one of the</u> best places on Earth <u>to</u> watch stars.
　　　　　　　　one of the 최상급+복수 명사: ~ 중 가장 …한　　to부정사의 형용사적 용법

Angel Falls

<u>If</u> you go to Venezuela, you can see the world's highest waterfall. It
조건절을 이끄는 부사절 접속사(~라면)
is 979 meters high. Clouds often cover the top, so you need patience
and a little luck <u>to get</u> a good view.
　　　　　　　　부사적 용법(목적)

natural: 자연의, 천연의
wonder: 경이, 놀라움
desert: 사막
waterfall: 폭포
continent: 대륙
be full of: ~으로 가득하다
both: 둘 다
area: 지역
soil: 토양, 흙
similar: 비슷한
prepare for: ~을 준비하다
outer space: 우주 공간
patience: 인내심
luck: 운

 확인문제

● 다음 문장이 본문의 내용과 일치하면 T, 일치하지 <u>않으면</u> F를 쓰시오.

1　The world's highest waterfall is in South America. ☐

2　It is impossible to see a drop of rain in the Atacama Desert. ☐

3　In the Atacama, plants can't grow because of hot weather. ☐

4　Angel Falls is more than a thousand meters high. ☐

5　Getting a good view of Angel Falls is easy. ☐

Actually, the waterfall is named after Jimmie Angel, a pilot from the
United States who first flew over the waterfall in 1933. You can still
get to the top of the beautiful waterfall only by plane.

The Amazon

The Amazon runs across the continent through seven countries. It
travels from Peru in the west and flows into the Atlantic Ocean. The
Amazon River is interesting in many ways. For the most part, it has
no bridges. That is because it usually runs through rainforests and wet
areas, not cities or towns. Also, in many places the river is very wide,
so you cannot see the other side! You probably do not want to swim in
this river. It is home to some very big snakes and fish that eat meat.

The Andes

The Andes are the world's longest mountain range. Do you know
how long the mountain range is? It is about 7,000 kilometers long! It
also contains the highest mountains outside of Asia. About a third of
the people in South America live in the Andes. Many unique animals
also live there.

name after: ~을 따라 이름 짓다
across: ~을 건너서, ~을 가로질러
rainforest: (열대) 우림
wide: 넓은
probably: 아마도
mountain range: 산맥
contain: 들어 있다, 포함하다
unique: 독특한

확인문제

● 다음 문장이 본문의 내용과 일치하면 T, 일치하지 <u>않으면</u> F를 쓰시오.

1 You need to get on a plane if you want to get to the top of Angel Falls. ☐
2 The Amazon River has many bridges. ☐
3 The Amazon River is narrow enough to see the other side. ☐
4 It is not a good idea to swim in the Amazon River. ☐
5 No other mountain range is longer than the Andes. ☐
6 Many ordinary animals can be found in the Andes. ☐

● 우리말을 참고하여 빈칸에 알맞은 말을 쓰시오.

1 Do you know _____ _____ _____ _____ on Earth is?

2 How about _____ _____ waterfall?

3 Yes, _____ _____ _____ in South America.

4 This continent _____ _____ _____ natural wonders _____ will surprise you.

5 The Atacama is _____ _____ _____ on Earth.

6 In some parts, _____ _____ almost no rain _____ _____ — only 1–3 millimeters per year!

7 The ground in some areas _____ _____ _____ _____ no plants can grow.

8 Do you know _____ _____ _____ in such a dry place?

9 The soil in this desert is very _____ _____ the soil on Mars, so _____ _____ _____ _____ to outer space.

10 The Atacama is also _____ _____ _____ _____ on Earth to watch stars.

11 If you go to Venezuela, you can _____ _____ _____ waterfall.

12 _____ is 979 meters _____ .

13 Clouds often _____ the top, so you need _____ and a little _____ to get a good view.

14 Actually, the waterfall is _____ _____ Jimmie Angel, a pilot from the United States _____ first _____ over the waterfall in 1933.

1 여러분은 지구에서 가장 건조한 사막이 어디인지 알고 있나요?

2 가장 높은 폭포는 어떠한가요?

3 그렇습니다. 그것들은 둘 다 남아메리카에 있습니다.

4 이 대륙은 여러분을 놀라게 할 자연 경관으로 가득하답니다.

5 아타카마 사막은 지구에서 가장 건조한 사막입니다.

6 몇몇 지역은 비가 전혀 오지 않아서, 연간 강수량이 1~3mm에 그칩니다!

7 어떤 지역의 토양은 너무 건조해서 어떤 식물도 자랄 수가 없습니다.

8 이처럼 건조한 곳에서 과학자들이 무슨 일을 하는지 알고 있나요?

9 이 사막의 토양은 화성의 토양과 아주 비슷해서, 그들은 우주로의 여행을 준비합니다.

10 또한 아타카마 사막은 지구에서 별을 관측하기에 가장 좋은 장소 가운데 하나이기도 합니다.

11 여러분이 베네수엘라에 간다면, 세계에서 가장 높은 폭포를 볼 수 있을 것입니다.

12 그것은 높이가 979m입니다.

13 구름이 꼭대기 부분을 자주 에워싸기 때문에, 멋진 경치를 보려면 인내심과 약간의 운이 필요합니다.

14 사실 그 폭포는 1933년에 처음으로 폭포 너머 비행을 한 미국의 비행사 Jimmie Angel에게서 이름을 따왔습니다.

15 You can _____ _____ _____ the top of the beautiful waterfall only _____ plane.

16 The Amazon _____ _____ the continent _____ seven countries.

17 It _____ _____ Peru in the west and _____ _____ the Atlantic Ocean.

18 The Amazon River _____ _____ in many ways.

19 For the most part, it has _____ _____.

20 That is _____ _____ _____ _____ _____ rainforests and wet areas, not cities or towns.

21 Also, in many places the river is very wide, so you cannot _____ _____ _____ _____!

22 You probably do not want to _____ _____ this river.

23 It is _____ to some very big snakes and fish _____ eat meat.

24 The Andes are _____ _____ _____ mountain _____.

25 Do you know _____ _____ _____ _____ is?

26 It is _____ 7,000 kilometers _____!

27 It also _____ the highest _____ outside of Asia.

28 About _____ _____ _____ _____ _____ in South America live in the Andes.

29 Many _____ _____ also live there.

15 여전히 비행기로만 그 아름다운 폭포의 꼭대기에 갈 수 있습니다.

16 아마존강은 일곱 개의 나라를 거쳐 대륙을 가로질러 흐릅니다.

17 그것은 서쪽의 페루에서 시작하여 대서양으로 흘러갑니다.

18 아마존강은 많은 점에서 흥미롭습니다.

19 강의 대부분에는 다리가 없습니다.

20 그것은 강이 대개 도시나 마을이 아닌, 열대 우림과 습지를 지나 흐르기 때문입니다.

21 또한 많은 곳에서 강이 너무 넓어서 그 건너편을 볼 수조차 없습니다!

22 여러분은 아마도 이 강에서 헤엄치고 싶지 않을 것입니다.

23 이곳은 몇몇 아주 큰 뱀과 고기를 먹는 물고기들의 서식지입니다.

24 안데스 산맥은 세계에서 가장 긴 산맥입니다.

25 여러분은 그 산맥의 길이가 얼마인지 아시나요?

26 그것은 약 7,000km입니다.

27 또한 그곳에는 아시아 외의 지역에서 가장 높은 산이 있습니다.

28 남아메리카 인구의 3분의 1 정도가 안데스 산맥에 살고 있습니다.

29 그리고 독특한 동물들이 많이 서식하고 있기도 합니다.

● 우리말을 참고하여 본문을 영작하시오.

1 여러분은 지구에서 가장 건조한 사막이 어디인지 알고 있나요?

➡ _____

2 가장 높은 폭포는 어떠한가요?

➡ _____

3 그렇습니다, 그것들은 둘 다 남아메리카에 있습니다.

➡ _____

4 이 대륙은 여러분을 놀라게 할 자연 경관으로 가득하답니다.

➡ _____

5 아타카마 사막은 지구에서 가장 건조한 사막입니다.

➡ _____

6 몇몇 지역은 비가 전혀 오지 않아서, 연간 강수량이 1~3mm에 그칩니다!

➡ _____

7 어떤 지역의 토양은 너무 건조해서 어떤 식물도 자랄 수가 없습니다.

➡ _____

8 이처럼 건조한 곳에서 과학자들이 무슨 일을 하는지 알고 있나요?

➡ _____

9 이 사막의 토양은 화성의 토양과 아주 비슷해서, 그들은 우주로의 여행을 준비합니다.

➡ _____

10 또한 아타카마 사막은 지구에서 별을 관측하기에 가장 좋은 장소 가운데 하나이기도 합니다.

➡ _____

11 여러분이 베네수엘라에 간다면, 세계에서 가장 높은 폭포를 볼 수 있을 것입니다.

➡ _____

12 그것은 높이가 979m입니다.

➡ _____

13 구름이 꼭대기 부분을 자주 에워싸기 때문에, 멋진 경치를 보려면 인내심과 약간의 운이 필요합니다.

➡ _____

14 사실 그 폭포는 1933년에 처음으로 폭포 너머 비행을 한 미국의 비행사 Jimmie Angel에게서 이름을 따왔습니다.

➡ _____

_____

15▶ 여전히 비행기로만 그 아름다운 폭포의 꼭대기에 갈 수 있습니다.

➡ _____

16▶ 아마존강은 일곱 개의 나라를 거쳐 대륙을 가로질러 흐릅니다.

➡ _____

17▶ 그것은 서쪽의 페루에서 시작하여 대서양으로 흘러갑니다.

➡ _____

18▶ 아마존강은 많은 점에서 흥미롭습니다.

➡ _____

19▶ 강의 대부분에는 다리가 없습니다.

➡ _____

20▶ 그것은 강이 대개 도시나 마을이 아닌, 열대 우림과 습지를 지나 흐르기 때문입니다.

➡ _____

21▶ 또한 많은 곳에서 강이 너무 넓어서 그 건너편을 볼 수조차 없습니다!

➡ _____

22▶ 여러분은 아마도 이 강에서 헤엄치고 싶지 않을 것입니다.

➡ _____

23▶ 이곳은 몇몇 아주 큰 뱀과 고기를 먹는 물고기들의 서식지입니다.

➡ _____

24▶ 안데스 산맥은 세계에서 가장 긴 산맥입니다.

➡ _____

25▶ 여러분은 그 산맥의 길이가 얼마인지 아시나요?

➡ _____

26▶ 그것은 약 7,000km입니다.

➡ _____

27▶ 또한 그곳에는 아시아 외의 지역에서 가장 높은 산이 있습니다.

➡ _____

28▶ 남아메리카 인구의 3분의 1 정도가 안데스 산맥에 살고 있습니다.

➡ _____

29▶ 그리고 독특한 동물들이 많이 서식하고 있기도 합니다.

➡ _____

[01~05] 다음 글을 읽고 물음에 답하시오.

Do you know ①where the driest desert on Earth is? How about ②the highest waterfall? Yes, they are both in South America. This continent ③is full of natural wonders that will surprise you.

Atacama Desert

The Atacama is the driest desert on Earth. In some parts, it gets almost no rain at all — only 1–3 millimeters per year! The ground in some areas is so dry ____(A)____ no plants can grow. Do you know what scientists do in such a dry place? The soil in this desert is very ④similar to the soil on Mars, so they prepare for trips to outer space. The Atacama is also one of the best ⑤place on Earth to watch stars.

01 빈칸 (A)에 들어갈 말로 가장 적절한 것은?

① who   ② when   ③ what
④ that   ⑤ which

서답형
02 다음과 같이 풀이되는 말을 위 글에서 찾아 쓰시오.

a large mass of land surrounded by sea

➡ _____

중요
03 다음 중 위 글의 내용과 일치하는 것은?

① The Atacama has the highest waterfall in the world.
② The ground of the Atacama is always wet.
③ Scientists aren't interested in the Atacama.
④ It is hard to see stars in the Atacama.
⑤ Thanks to the Atacama, scientists can prepare for trips to outer space.

04 ①~⑤ 중 어법상 바르지 않은 것은?

①   ②   ③   ④   ⑤

서답형
05 According to the passage, where is the Atacama? Answer in English with a full sentence.

➡ _____

[06~08] 다음 글을 읽고 물음에 답하시오.

Angel Falls

If you go to Venezuela, you can see the world's highest waterfall. It is 979 meters high. Clouds often cover the top, so you need patience and a little luck to get a good view. Actually, the waterfall is named ____(A)____ Jimmie Angel, a pilot from the United States who first flew over the waterfall in 1933. You can still get to the top of the beautiful waterfall only by plane.

중요
06 다음 중 빈칸 (A)에 들어갈 말과 같은 말이 들어가는 것은?

① Did you turn _____ the light when you went out of the room?
② My dad is always busy _____ playing golf.
③ The glass is full _____ orange juice.
④ My sister is good _____ speaking English and Chinese.
⑤ Jamie has looked _____ the injured dog since yesterday.

서답형
07 When did Jimmie Angel first fly over Angel Falls? Answer in English with a full sentence.

➡ _____

08 다음 중 위 글을 읽고 답할 수 있는 것은?

① Where is Venezuela?

② How wide is Angel Falls?

③ When did Jimmie Angel start his flying?

④ Why do you need a little luck to get a good view of Angel Falls?

⑤ Why is it impossible to get to the top of Angel Falls?

[09~13] 다음 글을 읽고 물음에 답하시오.

The Amazon

The Amazon runs across the continent through seven countries. It travels from Peru in the west and flows into the Atlantic Ocean. The Amazon River is ___(A)___ in many ways. For the most part, it has no bridges. That is because it usually runs through rainforests and wet areas, not cities or towns. Also, in many places the river is very wide, so you cannot see the other side! You probably do not want to swim in this river. It is home to some very big snakes and fish that eat meat.

The Andes

The Andes are the world's longest mountain range. Do you know how long the mountain range is? It is about 7,000 kilometers long! It also contains the highest mountains outside of Asia. About a third of the people in South America live in the Andes. Many (B)unique animals also live there.

서답형

09 단어 interest를 어법에 맞게 빈칸 (A)에 쓰시오.

➡ _____

10 밑줄 친 (B)를 대신하여 쓰일 수 있는 것은?

① common   ② ordinary

③ unusual   ④ regular

⑤ familiar

중요
11 다음 중 위 글의 내용을 바르게 이해한 학생은?

① 주하: 아마존강이 남미 대륙 전체를 거쳐 흐른다니, 정말 대단해.

② 경수: 아마존강은 결국 태평양으로 흘러가는 거군.

③ 예지: 강이 너무 넓어서 건너편을 볼 수 없을 정도라니, 대단히 넓은 강임에 분명해.

④ 성재: 아마존강이 세계에서 가장 긴 강이라는 것은 몰랐어.

⑤ 진하: 아마존강에서 수영하는 것이 내 소망이야.

서답형

12 Where does the Amazon River start from? Answer in English with a full sentence.

➡ _____

중요
13 다음 중 위 글을 읽고 안데스 산맥에 관하여 알 수 있는 정보는?

① the length of the Andes

② the lives of people who live in the Andes

③ the kinds of the animals

④ the height of the Andes

⑤ the number of people who live in South America

[14~17] 다음 글을 읽고 물음에 답하시오.

Do you know where the driest desert on Earth is? How about the highest waterfall? Yes, they are both in South America. This continent is full of natural wonders ___(A)___ will surprise you.

Atacama Desert

The Atacama is the driest desert on Earth. ① In some parts, it gets almost no rain at all — only 1–3 millimeters per year! ② The ground in some areas is so dry that no plants can grow. ③ The soil in this desert is very similar to the soil on Mars, so they prepare for trips to outer space. ④ The Atacama is also one of the best places on Earth to watch stars. ⑤

14 빈칸 (A)에 들어갈 말로 가장 적절한 것은?

① which ② what ③ who
④ when ⑤ why

15 ①~⑤ 중 주어진 문장이 들어가기에 가장 적절한 곳은?

Do you know what scientists do in such a dry place?

① ② ③ ④ ⑤

다음 중 위 글을 읽고 답할 수 없는 것은?

① Where is the Atacama located?
② Where is the highest waterfall?
③ How much does it rain in some parts of the Atacama?
④ What continent is full of natural wonders?
⑤ How many stars can be watched in the Atacama?

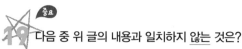

17 Write the reason why it is impossible that plants can grow in some parts of the Atacama. Use the phrase 'It's because.'

➡ _____

[18~20] 다음 글을 읽고 물음에 답하시오.

Angel Falls

If you go to Venezuela, you can see the world's highest waterfall. It is 979 meters high. Clouds often cover the top, so you need patience and a little luck to get a good (A) view. Actually, the waterfall is named after Jimmie Angel, a pilot from the United States who first flew over the waterfall in 1933. You can still get to the top of the beautiful waterfall only by plane.

18 다음 중 밑줄 친 (A)와 같은 의미로 사용된 것은?

① Jason and I have different views.
② His views on the subject were well known.
③ The view from the hotel room was fantastic.
④ He has a positive view on the issue.
⑤ What is needed is exchanging views.

다음 중 위 글의 내용과 일치하지 않는 것은?

① Angel Falls lies in Venezuela.
② No other waterfall in the world is as high as Angel Falls.
③ You can see a clear view of the waterfall anytime you want.
④ The waterfall is named after a pilot from the United States.
⑤ You can't get to the top of Angel Falls without a plane.

서답형

20 Who was Jimmie Angel? Answer in English with a full sentence.

➡ _____

_____

[21~22] 다음 글을 읽고 물음에 답하시오.

The Amazon

The Amazon runs (A)[into / across] the continent through seven countries. It travels from Peru in the west and flows into the Atlantic Ocean. The Amazon River is interesting in many ways. For the most part, it has no bridges. (B)[That is because / That is why] it usually runs through rainforests and wet areas, not cities or towns. Also, in many places the river is very wide, so you cannot see (C)[another / the other] side! You probably do not want to swim in this river. It is home to some very big snakes and fish that eat meat.

중요

21 (A)~(C) 중 어법상 옳은 것끼리 바르게 짝지은 것은?

① into – That is because – another

② into – That is why – the other

③ into – That is because – the other

④ across – That is because – the other

⑤ across – That is why – another

서답형

22 Write the reason why it is dangerous to swim in the Amazon River. Use the word below.

| (because) |

➡ _____

_____

[23~24] 다음 글을 읽고 물음에 답하시오.

The Andes

The Andes are the world's longest mountain range. (A)Do you know how the mountain range is long? It is about 7,000 kilometers long! It also contains the highest mountains outside of Asia. (B)About a third of the people in South America live in the Andes. Many unique animals also live there.

서답형

23 위 글의 밑줄 친 (A)를 어법에 맞게 고쳐 쓰시오.

➡ _____

24 다음 중 밑줄 친 (B)를 대신하여 쓰일 수 있는 것은?

① Roughly   ② Closely

③ Fairly   ④ Almost

⑤ Mostly

중요

25 다음 글을 읽고 알 수 없는 것은?

I went to Kaieteur Falls with my family. The waterfall sits in the Amazon Rainforest in Guyana, and it is 226 meters high. I was surprised at the size of the waterfall. I could see the brown rocks and green trees there. My trip to Kaieteur Falls made me feel good. I felt like all my stress went away.

① where the waterfall is

② how high the waterfall is

③ how the writer felt when he first saw the waterfall

④ what the writer saw there

⑤ how the writer got to the waterfall

[01~05] 다음 글을 읽고 물음에 답하시오.

Do you know where the driest desert on Earth is? How about the highest waterfall? Yes, they are both in South America. This continent is full of natural wonders that will surprise you.

Atacama Desert

(a)The Atacama is the driest desert on Earth. In some parts, it gets almost no rain at all — only 1–3 millimeters per year! The ground in some areas is so ___(A)___ that no plants can grow. Do you know what scientists do in such a dry place? The soil in this desert is very similar to the soil on Mars, so they prepare for trips to outer space. The Atacama is also one of the best places on Earth to watch stars.

01 빈칸 (A)에 들어갈 알맞은 말을 위 글에서 찾아 어법에 맞게 쓰시오.

➡ _____

02 Write the reason why the Atacama is the driest desert on Earth. Use the phrase 'Because.'

➡ _____
_____

03 다음 빈칸에 알맞은 말을 써서 밑줄 친 (a)를 대신하여 쓸 수 있는 문장을 완성하시오.

No other desert on earth _____
_____ _____ the Atacama.

04 위 글의 내용에 맞게 빈칸에 알맞은 말을 쓰시오.

Atacama Desert is _____ desert on Earth. Its soil is very _____ the soil on _____. It is one of the best places _____.

05 What can you see in South America? Answer in English with a full sentence.

➡ _____
_____

[06~09] 다음 글을 읽고 물음에 답하시오.

Angel Falls

If you go to Venezuela, you can see the world's highest waterfall. It is 979 meters high. Clouds often cover the top, so you need patience and a little luck to get a good view. Actually, the waterfall is named after Jimmie Angel, a pilot from the United States who first flew over the waterfall in 1933. You can still get to the top of the beautiful waterfall only by plane.

06 How did the world's highest waterfall get its name?

➡ _____
_____
_____

07 Write the reason why you need patience and a little luck to get a good view when you want to see Angel Falls. Use the phrase 'It's because.'

➡ _____

08 다음은 위 글의 내용을 요약한 것이다. 글의 내용에 맞게 빈 칸에 알맞은 말을 쓰시오.

> Angel Falls is the _____ waterfall on Earth. It is named after an American _____. You can reach the top only by _____.

09 According to the passage, how high is the waterfall? Answer in English with a full sentence.

➡ _____

[10~14] 다음 글을 읽고 물음에 답하시오.

The Amazon

The Amazon runs across the continent through seven countries.

[A] That is because it usually runs through rainforests and wet areas, not cities or towns.
[B] The Amazon River is interesting in many ways. For the most part, it has no bridges.
[C] It travels from Peru in the west and flows into the Atlantic Ocean.

Also, in many places the river is very wide, so you cannot see the other side! You probably do not want to swim in this river. It is home to some very big snakes and fish that eat meat.

The Andes

The Andes are the world's longest mountain range. (D)여러분은 그 산맥의 길이가 얼마인지 아시나요? It is about 7,000 kilometers long! It also contains the highest mountains outside of Asia. About a third of the people in South America live in the Andes. Many unique animals also live there.

10 자연스러운 글이 되도록 [A]~[C]를 바르게 나열하시오.

➡ _____

11 위 글의 내용에 맞게 다음 빈칸에 알맞은 말을 쓰시오.

> A: Do you know _____ _____ _____ _____ _____ in the world is?
> B: Yes, I do. They are the Andes. The Andes are _____ _____ any other mountain range in the world.

12 밑줄 친 우리말 (D)를 영어로 쓰시오.

➡ _____

13 아마존강에 대한 두 사람의 대화를 완성하시오.

> A: I wonder _____ _____ _____ _____ _____ _____.
> B: In many places, it is too _____ to _____ the other side.

14 According to the passage, where does the Amazon River flow into? Answer in English with a full sentence.

➡ _____

해석

My Speaking Portfolio

A: Which country do you want to visit?

B: Brazil. Do you know where Brazil is?
_{의문사+주어+동사}

A: Yes, I do. It's in South America. Do you know that Brazil is the biggest
_{= the+최상급}
country in South America?

B: What a surprise! I didn't know that. So, what's the first thing you want to
_{what으로 시작하는 감탄문} _{= thing that(= which) you}
see in Brazil?

A: I want to see Iguazu Falls from the sky.

구문해설 • country: 나라, 국가 • sky: 하늘

A: 너는 어느 나라를 가 보고 싶니?

B: 브라질. 너는 브라질이 어디에 있는지 알고 있니?

A: 응, 알아. 그건 남아메리카에 있어. 너는 남아메리카에서 브라질이 가장 큰 나라라는 거 알고 있니?

B: 정말 놀랍다! 그건 몰랐네. 그러면 너는 브라질에서 가장 처음으로 보고 싶은 게 뭐야?

A: 나는 하늘에서 이구아수 폭포를 보고 싶어.

My Writing Portfolio

A Day in Nature

I went to Kaieteur Falls with my family. The waterfall sits in the Amazon
_{(어떤 곳에) 있다}
Rainforest in Guyana, and it is 226 meters high. I was surprised at the size
_{= Kaieteur Falls} _{~에 놀랐다}
of the waterfall. I could see the brown rocks and green trees there. My trip to
Kaieteur Falls made me feel good. I felt like all my stress went away.
_{사역동사+목적어+동사원형} _{~한 느낌이 들었다}

구문해설 • sit in: ~에 위치해 있다 • surprised: 놀란

자연에서의 하루

나는 가족과 함께 카이에투 폭포에 갔다. 그 폭포는 가이아나에 있는 아마존 열대 우림에 위치하고 있고, 높이는 226m이다. 나는 폭포의 크기에 놀랐다. 나는 그곳에서 갈색 바위와 초록색 나무를 볼 수 있었다. 카이에투 폭포로의 여행은 나를 기분 좋게 만들어 주었다. 내 모든 스트레스가 사라진 것 같았다.

Wrap Up – Reading

Salar de Uyuni in Bolivia is the world's largest salt flat. Thousands of years
_{세계에서 가장 큰} _{수천의}
ago, there was water, but it all dried up. Now, a large salt desert is left about
_{뒤의 명사에 수의 일치} _{수동태}
3,656 meters above sea level. Salar de Uyuni is one of the most visited natural
_{one of the 최상급+복수 명사}
wonders of South America, too. All year round a lot of people visit this place
_{= many}
to take pictures of its unique natural beauty. In fact, the salt flat makes any
_{to부정사의 부사적 용법 중 목적 (~하기 위해서)} _{사실}
tourist a great photographer. Every picture you take in Salar de Uyuni will be
_{앞에 관계대명사 that 생략}
a beautiful work of art!

구문해설 • dry up: 마르다 • above sea level: 해발 • all year round: 일 년 내내
• unique: 독특한 • flat: 평원

볼리비아에 있는 살라르 데 우유니는 세계에서 가장 큰 솔트 플랫(소금 평원)이다. 수천 년 전에는 그곳에 물이 있었지만, 모두 말라버렸다. 지금은 해발 약 3,656미터에 큰 소금 사막이 남겨져 있다. 살라르 데 우유니는 또한 방문객이 가장 많은 남아메리카의 자연 경관 중의 하나이다. 일 년 내내 많은 사람들이 독특한 자연의 아름다움을 사진으로 찍기 위해 이 장소를 방문한다. 사실, 그 솔트 플랫은 어떤 방문객도 훌륭한 사진작가로 만든다. 살라르 데 우유니에서 당신이 찍은 모든 사진은 아름다운 예술 작품이 될 것이다!

영역별 핵심문제

1 다음 짝지어진 단어의 관계가 같도록 빈칸에 알맞은 말을 쓰시오.

possible : impossible = patient : _____

2 다음 영영풀이가 가리키는 것을 고르시오.

a person who operates the controls of an aircraft, especially as a job

① tourist   ② pilot
③ guide   ④ steward
⑤ crew

3 다음 중 밑줄 친 부분의 뜻풀이가 바르지 <u>않은</u> 것은?

① I want to know the <u>origin</u> of the civilization. 기원
② My favorite subject is <u>social studies</u>. 사회
③ The band is <u>especially</u> popular in Japan. 특히
④ Josh has always been <u>scared</u> of dogs. 수줍음 많은
⑤ The casting for the movie was <u>fantastic</u>. 엄청난, 환상적인

4 다음 주어진 문장의 밑줄 친 flow와 다른 의미로 쓰인 것은?

As I was listening to the music, tears began to <u>flow</u> from my eyes.

① The river <u>flows</u> northward to the sea.
② Rivers <u>flow</u> to the ocean.
③ I can't find where the water is <u>flowing</u> out.
④ The spring has a <u>flow</u> of 300 gallons a minute.
⑤ The Han River <u>flows</u> through Seoul from east to west.

5 다음 문장에 공통으로 들어갈 말을 고르시오.

• Are you able to _____ a horse?
• My children _____ the bus to school every day.
• Jimmy and I went out to _____ a bike.

① view   ② ride
③ fly   ④ contain
⑤ wonder

6 다음 우리말에 맞게 빈칸에 알맞은 말을 쓰시오.

(1) 그 마을은 Monsanto 산을 따라 이름 지어졌다.
➡ The village is _____ the mountain, Monsanto.

(2) 우리는 선생님을 위해 깜짝 파티를 열 계획 중이다.
➡ We are planning to _____ a surprise _____ for my teacher.

(3) 솔직히 말하면, 나는 연극 동아리에 가입하고 싶지 않아.
➡ _____, I don't want to join the drama club.

Conversation

[07~09] 다음 대화를 읽고 물음에 답하시오.

Sujin: Dad, I like this tomato soup.
Dad: I'm happy you like (A)it.
Sujin: By the way, (B)do you know where was the tomato first grown?
Dad: Italy or somewhere in Europe?
Sujin: No, the tomato came from South America.
Dad: Really? How did you know that?
Sujin: I learned (C)it from Ms. Song, my social studies teacher.
Dad: That's good.

07 위 대화의 (A)와 (C)의 it이 각각 가리키는 것을 찾아 쓰시오.

➡ (A) _____
(C) _____

08 위 대화의 밑줄 친 (B)를 어법상 바르게 고치시오.

➡ _____

09 위 대화의 내용과 일치하지 <u>않는</u> 것은?

① 수진은 토마토 수프가 마음에 든다.
② 아빠는 수진이가 토마토 수프를 좋아해서 기분이 좋다.
③ 토마토는 남아메리카에서 왔다.
④ 수진은 송 선생님에게서 사회를 배운다.
⑤ 토마토 수프는 이탈리아에서 전해졌다.

[10~12] 다음 대화를 읽고 물음에 답하시오.

Hana: How was the roller coaster ride, Jongha?
Jongha: It was fantastic. I really enjoyed it.
Hana: Ha ha. You closed your eyes while riding.

Jongha: Did you see? To be honest, I was really scared at first.
Hana: Do you know how fast this roller coaster is?
Jongha: I have no idea.
Hana: _____(A)_____
Jongha: Wow! That's surprising!
Hana: Let's ride it one more time!
Jongha: Look at the sign. We can't ride it after 8 p.m.
Hana: Oh, maybe next time.

10 위 대화의 빈칸 (A)에 들어갈 말을 〈보기〉에 주어진 어구를 모두 사용하여 영작하시오.

┌─── 보기 ├───
fast / as / per / it / as / goes / 140 km / hour
└──────────────

➡ _____

11 위 대화의 내용과 일치하도록 롤러코스터 안내문을 완성하시오.

<Enjoy the roller coaster!>
1) Must be at least 120 cm tall to ride.
2) Runs as fast as (A)_____.
3) Can enjoy from 10 a.m to (B)_____.

12 위 대화에서 롤러코스터를 타는 동안 종하의 기분 변화로 적절한 것은?

① joyful → nervous
② fantastic → worried
③ worried → disappointed
④ scared → pleased
⑤ fantastic → fearful

[13~14] 다음 대화를 읽고 물음에 답하시오.

Jenny: Did you see the pictures Ms. Song took?

Brian: What pictures?

Jenny: She traveled around South America (A)[by / of] herself last summer.

Brian: Really? (B)[How / What] a surprise!

Jenny: She showed us pictures of beautiful places. I especially liked the pictures of pyramids.

Brian: Are there pyramids in South America?

Jenny: Yes. She said some pyramids are about 3,800 meters above sea level.

Brian: I (C)[can / can't] believe it.

13 위 대화의 괄호 (A)~(C)에 들어갈 알맞은 말을 고르시오.

➡ (A) _____ (B) _____ (C) _____

14 위 대화의 내용과 일치하도록 Jenny의 일기를 완성하시오.

I was impressed that Ms. Song traveled around South America by herself last summer. I thought she was really brave. She showed me (A)_____
_____. Among them, I love (B)_____. She explained that (C)_____
_____. It sounded very interesting, so I decided to visit there someday.

15 11단어를 이용하여 다음 문장을 영어로 쓸 때, 다섯 번째로 오는 단어는?

그는 내가 만나 본 사람 중 가장 지루한 사람이야.

① the   ② most   ③ boring
④ person   ⑤ that

16 다음 중 주어진 문장의 밑줄 친 부분과 쓰임이 같은 것은?

Tell me who broke into your house.

① That is the man who told me how to get to the post office.
② Where is the boy who was wearing a cap?
③ I don't remember who you were talking about.
④ The boy who Jessica likes is my cousin.
⑤ Did you find the man who bought you coffee?

17 다음 중 주어진 문장과 같은 의미의 문장을 모두 고르시오.

Nothing is more valuable than honesty.

① Honesty is not as valuable as everything.
② No other thing is less valuable than honesty.
③ Honesty is not as valuable as nothing.
④ Honesty is the most valuable thing.
⑤ Honesty is more valuable than anything else.

영역별 핵심문제 **215**

18 다음 우리말을 영어로 바르게 옮긴 것은?

> 누가 너를 파티에 초대했는지 말해 줄래?

① Can you tell me who you invited to the party?
② Can you tell me who you want to invite to the party?
③ Can you tell me who was invited to the party?
④ Can you tell me who wanted to invite you to the party?
⑤ Can you tell me who invited you to the party?

19 주어진 어구를 활용하여 다음 우리말을 영어로 쓰시오.

> 너는 네 삶에서 가장 행복한 순간을 기억하고 있니? (remember, of your life)

➡ _____

20 다음 중 어법상 바르지 <u>않은</u> 것은?

① I want to know when you bought this lamp.
② I am fastest runner on our team.
③ Do you know who wrote this book?
④ What is the tallest building in this city?
⑤ Tell me where you are going to meet Jackson tomorrow.

21 다음 빈칸에 들어갈 말로 가장 적절한 것은?

> No other planet in our solar system is as bright as Venus.
> = Venus is _____ in our solar system.

① not as bright as the other planet
② the least bright planet
③ brighter than all the other planet
④ the brightest planet
⑤ less bright than other planet

22 다음 중 어법상 바르지 <u>않은</u> 것은?

> A: I ①<u>wonder</u> how ②<u>you think</u> about the cake.
> B: ③<u>It</u> was very good. Actually it was ④<u>the deliciousest</u> cake that ⑤<u>I've ever</u> eaten.

23 다음 빈칸에 알맞은 말을 일곱 단어로 쓰시오.

> A: Who is the wisest man in the town?
> B: No other man _____ Patrick.

24 다음 대화를 읽고 빈칸에 알맞은 말을 쓰시오.

> Jack: Are you free?
> Paul: Not really.

➡ Jack wants to know _____.

25 다음 두 문장을 하나의 문장으로 쓰시오.

> I wonder. Did you find what you were looking for?

➡ _____
_____

26 최상급과 주어진 단어를 활용하여 다음 우리말을 영어로 쓰시오.

> 내게 목요일은 그 주 중 최악의 날이었어. (bad, for)

➡ _____

Reading

[27~29] 다음 글을 읽고 물음에 답하시오.

(A)Do you know where is the driest desert on Earth? How about the highest waterfall? Yes, they are ①both in South America. This continent is full of natural wonders that will ②surprise you.

Atacama Desert

The Atacama is the driest desert on Earth. In some parts, it gets almost ③no rain at all — only 1–3 millimeters per year! The ground in some areas is so dry that no plants can grow. Do you know what scientists do in such a ④dry place? The soil in this desert is very ⑤different from the soil on Mars, so they prepare for trips to outer space. The Atacama is also one of the best places on Earth to watch stars.

27 밑줄 친 (A)에서 어법상 틀린 것을 찾아 바르게 고쳐 쓰시오.

➡ _____

28 ①~⑤ 중 글의 흐름상 어색한 것은?

①   ②   ③   ④   ⑤

29 다음 중 위 글의 내용과 일치하는 것은?

① We find natural wonders in South America.

② The Atacama is not as dry as all the other deserts in the world.

③ Scientists want to explore the Atacama Desert to study the desert.

④ It is impossible to watch stars in the Atacama because of sand.

⑤ Some areas of the Atacama aren't very dry.

[30~33] 다음 글을 읽고 물음에 답하시오.

Salar de Uyuni in Bolivia is the world's largest salt flat. Thousands of years ago, there was water, but it all dried up. Now, a large salt desert is left about 3,656 meters above sea level. Salar de Uyuni is one of the most visited natural wonders of South America, too. (A) All year round a lot of people visit this place (B)to take pictures of its unique natural beauty. In fact, the salt flat makes any tourist a great ⓐ_____. Every picture you take in Salar de Uyuni will be a beautiful work of art!

30 빈칸 ⓐ에 들어갈 말로 가장 적절한 것은?

① scientist   ② painter

③ dentist   ④ photographer

⑤ pianist

31 밑줄 친 (A)의 의미로 가장 적절한 것은?

① Round and round

② Throughout the year

③ All your efforts

④ Over and over

⑤ Time after time

32 다음 중 밑줄 친 (B)와 쓰임이 같은 것은?

① They decided to break the promise.

② It is my job to protect you.

③ Is there anything to wear?

④ He went out to buy some fruit.

⑤ Polly felt sad to see the bird die.

33 Where is the world's largest salt flat? Answer in English with a full sentence.

➡ _____

[01~02] 다음 대화를 읽고 물음에 답하시오.

Jenny: Did you see the pictures Ms. Song took?

Brian: What pictures?

Jenny: She traveled around South America by herself last summer.

Brian: (A) Really? What a surprise!

Jenny: (B) I especially liked the pictures of pyramids.

Brian: (C) Are there pyramids in South America?

Jenny: (D) Yes. She said some pyramids are about 3,800 meters above sea level.

Brian: (E) I can't believe it.

01 위 대화의 (A)~(E) 중 주어진 문장이 들어가기에 적절한 곳은?

> She showed us pictures of beautiful places.

① (A) ② (B) ③ (C) ④ (D) ⑤ (E)

02 위 대화를 읽고 대답할 수 없는 것은?

① Where did Ms. Song travel last summer?
② With whom did Ms. Song take a trip around South America?
③ What did Ms. Song show Jenny?
④ What pictures did Jenny especially like?
⑤ How long did Ms. Song stay in South America?

[03~05] 다음 대화를 읽고 물음에 답하시오.

Hana: How was the roller coaster ride, Jongha?

Jongha: It was fantastic. I really enjoyed it.

Hana: Ha ha. You closed your eyes while riding.

Jongha: Did you see? _____(A)_____, I was really scared at first.

Hana: Do you know how fast this roller coaster is?

Jongha: I have no idea.

Hana: It goes as fast as 140 km per hour.

Jongha: Wow! _____(B)_____

Hana: Let's ride it one more time!

Jongha: Look at the sign. We can't ride it after 8 p.m.

Hana: Oh, maybe next time.

03 위 대화의 빈칸 (A)에 '솔직히 말하자면'을 뜻하는 표현을 주어진 단어를 사용하여 쓰시오. (be)

➡ _____

04 위 대화의 빈칸 (B)에 들어가기에 알맞은 것은?

① I'm sorry for that.
② I can't believe it.
③ Thank you for your help.
④ I'm curious about it.
⑤ I'm not happy with it.

05 위 대화의 내용과 일치하지 않는 것은?

① 종하는 롤러코스터가 정말 재미있었다.
② 종하는 롤러코스터를 타는 동안 눈을 감고 있었다.
③ 롤러코스터는 시속 140 km로 달린다.
④ 롤러코스터는 저녁 8시 이후에는 탈 수 없다.
⑤ 종하는 무서워서 롤러코스터를 한 번 더 타지 않았다.

[06~08] 다음 대화를 읽고 물음에 답하시오.

Sujin: Dad, I like this tomato soup.

Dad: I'm happy you like it.

Sujin: _____(A)_____, do you know where the tomato was first grown?

Dad: Italy or somewhere in Europe?

Sujin: No, the tomato came from South America.

Dad: Really? How did you know that?

Sujin: I learned it from Ms. Song, my social studies teacher.

Dad: That's good.

06 위 대화의 빈칸 (A)에 '그건 그렇고'를 뜻하는 말을 3 단어로 쓰시오.

➡ _____

07 Where did the tomato come from?

➡ _____

08 Who taught the origin of the tomato to Sujin?

➡ _____

[09~10] 다음 대화를 읽고 물음에 답하시오.

Jane: _____(A)_____

Brian: Brazil. Do you know where Brazil is?

Jane: Yes, I do. It's in South America. Do you know that Brazil is the biggest country in South America?

Brian: What a surprise! I didn't know that. So, what's the first thing you want to see in Brazil?

Jane: I want to see Iguazu Falls from the sky.

09 위 대화의 빈칸에 들어갈 질문을 〈보기〉에 있는 단어를 모두 배열하여 영작하시오.

┌─ 보기 ─┐

you / country / visit / to / do / want / which

➡ _____

10 위 대화의 내용과 일치하지 않는 것은?

① Brian은 브라질을 방문하고 싶어 한다.

② 브라질은 남아메리카에 위치해 있다.

③ 브라질은 남아메리카에서 가장 큰 국가이다.

④ Jane은 브라질에 가면 이구아수 폭포를 보고 싶어 한다.

⑤ Brian은 브라질이 남아메리카에 위치해 있다는 것에 놀랐다.

11 다음 중 최상급의 형태가 다른 하나는?

① dark   ② thick

③ long   ④ helpful

⑤ fast

12 다음 중 빈칸에 들어갈 말로 가장 적절한 것은?

I'd like to know. Did she push you first?
= I'd like to know _____ you first.

① why she pushed

② whether did she push

③ when she pushed

④ if she pushed

⑤ how did she pushed

출제율 95%

13 다음 중 의미가 <u>다른</u> 하나는?

① Your advice is the most helpful advice.

② Your advice is more helpful than any other advice.

③ No other advice is as good as your advice.

④ No other advice is more helpful than your advice.

⑤ Your advice is not more helpful than any other advice.

출제율 90%

14 주어진 단어를 활용하여 다음 우리말을 영어로 쓰시오.

> 그녀가 무엇을 하고 있다고 생각해?
> (think / do)

➡ _____

출제율 100%

15 다음 중 어법상 바르지 <u>않은</u> 것은?

① Jack is one of the most thoughtful student in the class.

② I forgot where I put my umbrella.

③ No other car is as fast as my car.

④ How we talk to people is important.

⑤ The dress is more beautiful than any other dress in this room.

출제율 95%

16 다음 두 문장을 하나의 문장으로 쓰시오.

> Please tell me. Did she tell you her number?

➡ _____

출제율 90%

17 다음 빈칸에 들어갈 말로 가장 적절한 것은?

> No other clock in this store is as cheap as this clock.
> = This clock is _____ in this store.

① cheaper than other clocks

② not as cheap as that clock

③ the most cheap clock

④ cheaper than any other clock

⑤ not the cheapest clock

[18~21] 다음 글을 읽고 물음에 답하시오.

Do you know where the driest desert on Earth is? How about the highest waterfall? Yes, they are both in South America. This continent is full of natural wonders that will surprise you.

Atacama Desert

The Atacama is the driest desert on Earth. In some parts, it gets almost no rain at all — only 1–3 millimeters per year! The ground in some areas is so dry that no plants can grow. Do you know what scientists do in (A)<u>such a dry place</u>? The soil in this desert is very similar to the soil on Mars, so they prepare for trips to outer space. The Atacama is also one of the best places on Earth (B)<u>to watch</u> stars.

출제율 90%

18 밑줄 친 (A)가 의미하는 것을 위 글에서 찾아 쓰시오.

➡ _____

출제율 95%

19 다음 중 밑줄 친 (B)와 쓰임이 같은 것은?

① I hope <u>to see</u> you again.

② It is good <u>to have</u> dinner with her.

③ He went out <u>to find</u> his watch.

④ She felt sad <u>to hear</u> the news.

⑤ I need something <u>to write</u> about.

20 다음 중 위 글의 내용과 일치하지 <u>않는</u> 것은?

① The highest waterfall is in South America.
② Natural wonders of South America will surprise you.
③ Scientists enjoy their trip to the Atacama.
④ Only 1–3mm of rain falls per year in some parts of the Atacama.
⑤ Scientists prepare for trips to outer space in the Atacama.

21 다음은 위 글을 요약한 것이다. 빈칸에 알맞은 말을 쓰시오.

> The Atacama is _____ _____ _____ in the world. It is a good place to _____ _____ _____ and _____ _____.

[22~25] 다음 글을 읽고 물음에 답하시오.

Angel Falls

If you go to Venezuela, you can see the world's highest waterfall. It is 979 meters high. Clouds often cover the top, so you need patience and a little luck to get a good view. Actually, the waterfall is named after Jimmie Angel, a pilot from the United States who first flew over the waterfall in 1933. You can still get to the top of the beautiful waterfall only by plane.

The Amazon

The Amazon runs across the continent through seven countries. It travels from Peru in the west and flows into the Atlantic Ocean. The Amazon River is interesting in many ways. For the most part, it has no bridges. That

is because it usually runs through rainforests and wet areas, not cities or towns. Also, in many places the river is very wide, ___(A)___ you cannot see the other side! You probably do not want to swim in this river. It is home to some very big snakes and fish that eat meat.

22 다음 중 (A)에 들어갈 말로 가장 적절한 것은?

① although ② so ③ when
④ because ⑤ however

23 다음과 같이 풀이되는 말을 위 글에서 찾아 쓰시오.

> the ability to stay calm without becoming angry

➡ _____

24 다음 중 위 글의 내용과 일치하는 것은?

① The world's highest waterfall is in Peru.
② You can climb to the top of the waterfall.
③ You cannot easily see the top of the waterfall because of clouds.
④ It is safe to swim in the Amazon River.
⑤ Fish that live in the Amazon only eat meat.

25 According to the passage, how many countries does the Amazon run through? Answer in English with a full sentence.

➡ _____

단원별 예상문제 **221**

[01~03] 다음 대화를 읽고 물음에 답하시오.

> Mike: Do you know Sumin won first prize at the speech contest?
>
> Sue: I can't believe it. She was very quiet and shy last year.
>
> Mike: Yeah. She joined the drama club this year, and she has changed a lot.
>
> Sue: I see. I want to join the club, too.

01 Who won the speech contest?

➡ _____

 What was Sumin's characteristic last year?

➡ _____

03 What club did Sumin join this year?

➡ _____

04 주어진 단어를 활용하여 다음 대화의 빈칸에 알맞은 말을 쓰시오.

> A: You drink a lot. I wonder _____ (how / water) a day.
> B: I drink ten cups of water a day.

➡ _____

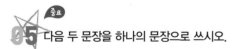 다음 두 문장을 하나의 문장으로 쓰시오.

(1) I'd like to know. Are you comfortable?

➡ _____

(2) I wonder. When did you come home?

➡ _____

06 다음 그림을 보고 빈칸에 알맞은 말을 쓰시오.

(1) Stuart is _____ student in the class. (smart)

(2) Carl is _____ student in the class. (noisy)

07 다음 우리말을 조건에 맞게 문장을 완성하시오.

> 내게는 다른 어떤 스포츠도 테니스를 치는 것만큼 신나지 않아.

(1) 최상급을 이용하여

➡ _____

to me.

(2) 부정 주어와 원급을 이용하여

➡ _____

to me.

[08~09] 다음 글을 읽고 물음에 답하시오.

> Do you know where the driest desert on Earth is? How about the highest waterfall? Yes, (A)they are both in South America. This continent is full of natural wonders that will surprise you.
>
> Atacama Desert
>
> The Atacama is the driest desert on Earth. In some parts, it gets almost no rain at all — only 1–3 millimeters per year! The ground in some areas is so dry that no plants can grow.

Do you know what scientists do in such a dry place? The soil in this desert is very similar to the soil on Mars, so they prepare for trips to outer space. The Atacama is also one of the best places on Earth to watch stars.

08 밑줄 친 (A)가 가리키는 것을 위 글에서 찾아 쓰시오.

➡ _____

09 위 글의 내용에 맞게 빈칸에 알맞은 말을 쓰시오.

> A: I wonder what scientists do in the Atacama.
> B: _____ (A) _____
> A: Why do they do that in the desert?
> B: It's because _____ (B) _____ .

➡ (A) _____
   (B) _____

[10~12] 다음 글을 읽고 물음에 답하시오.

Salar de Uyuni in Bolivia is the world's largest salt flat. Thousands of years ago, there was water, but it all dried up. Now, a large salt desert is left about 3,656 meters above sea level. Salar de Uyuni is one of the most visited natural wonders of South America, too. All year round a lot of people visit this place to take pictures of its unique natural beauty. In fact, the salt flat makes any tourist a great photographer. (A)Every picture you take in Salar de Uyuni will be a beautiful work of art!

10 According to the passage, how was Salar de Uyuni made? Answer in Korean.

➡ _____

11 Write the reason why the writer says like the underlined (A). Use the phrase 'It's because.'

➡ _____
   _____

12 다음 문장에서 위 글의 내용과 일치하지 않는 부분을 바르게 고쳐 쓰시오.

> (1) Salar de Uyuni is located about 3,656 meters under sea level.
> (2) People visit Salar de Uyuni during a certain period.
> (3) Salar de Uyuni is the most visited natural wonder of South America.

➡ (1) _____
     ➡ _____
   (2) _____
     ➡ _____
   (3) _____
     ➡ _____

01 다음 대화의 내용과 일치하도록 Sujin의 일기를 완성하시오.

> Sujin: Dad, I like this tomato soup.
>
> Dad: I'm happy you like it.
>
> Sujin: By the way, do you know where the tomato was first grown?
>
> Dad: Italy or somewhere in Europe?
>
> Sujin: No, the tomato came from South America.
>
> Dad: Really? How did you know that?
>
> Sujin: I learned it from Ms. Song, my social studies teacher.
>
> Dad: That's good.

> Mon, Dec 2th, 2019
>
> I was happy when I tasted my father's tomato soup. It was so delicious. When I tasted the soup, I remembered what I learned from Ms. Song, my (A)_____ teacher. She let me know (B)_____ the tomato was first grown. I asked my father if he knew about it or not. At first, he guessed the tomato was from (C)_____. I told him that (D)_____. I was proud of myself when I shared what I learned from the teacher with my father.

02 다음 질문과 답변을 읽고 Jason이 가 본 장소에 관한 글을 완성하시오.

> Q: Where did you go? A: I went to Gwanak Mountain.
>
> Q: Who were you with? A: I was with my family.
>
> Q: What did you learn about the place? A: It is 632 meters high and is in the south of Seoul.
>
> Q: What did you see? A: I saw the bridges over the Han River.
>
> Q: How did you feel? A: I felt like all my stress went away.

> I went to _____ with _____. The mountain is _____.
> It is in _____. I saw _____. My trip to Gwanak Mountain made me feel good. I felt like _____.

단원별 모의고사

01 다음 영영풀이가 가리키는 것을 고르시오.

> a place where a stream or river falls from a high place, for example over a cliff or rock

① rainforest ② waterfall
③ snowstorm ④ rainfall
⑤ ocean

02 다음 문장의 빈칸에 들어갈 말을 〈보기〉에서 골라 쓰시오.

┌─ 보기 ─┐
wonders / sunrise / scared / Mars / view

(1) Have you ever watched _____?
(2) I would like a room with a nice _____.
(3) NASA found the new evidence about water on _____.
(4) My sister looked _____ when she saw the bear.
(5) The Grand Canyon is one of the natural _____ of the world.

03 다음 주어진 문장의 밑줄 친 wonder와 같은 의미로 쓰인 것은?

> There is no one who can find out all the wonders of the sea.

① I think AI is one of the wonders of modern science.
② I wonder if I can ask you a favor.
③ I wonder what happened to you.
④ I always wondered why he didn't want to marry.
⑤ I wonder whether my brother is at home or not.

04 다음 우리말과 일치하도록 주어진 단어를 모두 배열하여 영작하시오.

(1) 수많은 예술품들이 도난당했다.
(art / a / of / works / stolen / were / number / of)
➡ _____

(2) 암스테르담은 해수면보다 4미터 아래에 있다.
(sea / is / 4 meters / Amsterdam / level / below)
➡ _____

05 다음 대화가 자연스럽게 이어지도록 순서대로 배열하시오.

> (A) I want one, too.
> (B) No. Where did he get it? From a pet shop?
> (C) Do you know Junha got a puppy?
> (D) No. I heard he got the puppy from his uncle.

➡ _____

[06~08] 다음 대화를 읽고 물음에 답하시오.

Hana: How was the roller coaster ride, Jongha?
Jongha: It was fantastic. I really enjoyed it.
Hana: Ha ha. You closed your eyes while riding.
Jongha: Did you see? (A)To be honest, I was really scared at first.
Hana: Do you know how fast this roller coaster is?
Jongha: I have no idea.
ⓐ Wow! That's surprising!
ⓑ Oh, maybe next time.
ⓒ Let's ride it one more time!
ⓓ It goes as fast as 140 km per hour.
ⓔ Look at the sign. We can't ride it after 8 p.m.

06 위 대화에서 ⓐ~ⓔ가 자연스럽게 이어지도록 순서대로 배열하시오.

➡ _____

07 위 대화에서 밑줄 친 (A)와 바꾸어 쓸 수 있는 것은?

① Generally speaking
② Frankly speaking
③ Strictly speaking
④ Broadly speaking
⑤ Personally speaking

08 위 대화의 내용과 일치하는 것은?

① Hana was scared when she rode the roller coaster.
② While riding the roller coaster, Jongha felt fantastic first but he was scared later.
③ Jongha couldn't open his eyes because of strong winds.
④ The roller coaster is much faster than 140 km per hour.
⑤ The roller coaster runs until 8 p.m.

[09~10] 다음 대화를 읽고 물음에 답하시오.

> Sujin: Dad, I like this tomato soup.
> Dad: I'm happy you like it.
> Sujin: (A)[By / On] the way, do you know where the tomato was first grown?
> Dad: Italy or somewhere in Europe?
> Sujin: No, the tomato came from South America.
> Dad: Really? (B)[What / How] did you know that?
> Sujin: I (C)[taught / learned] it from Ms. Song, my social studies teacher.
> Dad: That's good.

09 위 대화의 빈칸 (A)~(C)에 들어갈 말로 알맞은 것을 고르시오.

➡ (A) _____ (B) _____ (C) _____

10 위 대화의 내용과 일치하는 것은?

① Dad liked his tomato soup so much.
② The tomato came from Italy in Europe.
③ Sujin learns social studies from Ms. Song.
④ Ms. Song has been to South America.
⑤ Sujin knows when the tomato came from South America.

11 다음 우리말을 주어진 단어를 이용하여 영작하시오.

(1) 그 산맥은 많은 독특한 식물과 동물의 서식지이다. (range, unique, home)

➡ _____
_____

(2) 나는 처음에는 그를 전혀 이해할 수 없었다. (at, couldn't, all)

➡ _____
_____

(3) 솔직히 말하면, 나는 집에 머물며 TV를 보고 싶어. (honest)

➡ _____
_____

12 우리말과 일치하도록 빈칸을 채우시오.

(1) 고래는 바다에서 가장 큰 동물들이다.
➡ _____ are the largest animals in the ocean.

(2) 이 천연 돌다리는 이 마을의 상징이다.
➡ This _____ stone bridge is the symbol of this town.

(3) 이 음료에는 어떤 알코올도 포함되어 있지 않다.
➡ This drink does not _____ any alcohol.

13 다음 중 밑줄 친 부분의 쓰임이 나머지와 다른 하나는?

① Can you tell me if she will come?
② I wonder if he wants to see me.
③ I'm not sure if the news is true.
④ I will go if they invite me.
⑤ I don't know if she locked the door.

14 다음 중 빈칸에 들어갈 말로 적절한 것을 모두 고르시오.

No other waterfall in the world is as wide as Iguazu Falls.
= Iguazu Falls is _____ in the world.

① as wide as all the other waterfalls
② more wider than any other waterfall
③ the widest waterfall
④ wider than all the other waterfalls
⑤ the most widest waterfall

15 다음 중 어법상 바르지 않은 것은?

① That was the most wonderful trip.
② Can you tell me why you didn't help her?
③ Bob thinks he is the most handsome student in his school.
④ I need to know when they booked the restaurant.
⑤ Tell me who your book found.

16 주어진 단어를 활용하여 다음 우리말을 영어로 옮기시오. 필요하다면 어형을 바꿀 것.

싱가포르는 내가 방문해 본 도시 중 가장 흥미로운 곳 중 하나야. (Singapore / interesting / place / ever / visit)

➡ _____
_____

17 다음 두 문장을 하나의 문장으로 쓰시오.

(1) Do you know? Why is she upset?
➡ _____
(2) I wonder. Does he sing well?
➡ _____

[18~19] 다음 글을 읽고 물음에 답하시오.

Atacama Desert
ⓐThe Atacama is the driest desert on Earth.

[A] The ground in some areas is so dry that no plants can grow. Do you know what scientists do in such a dry place?
[B] In some parts, it gets almost no rain at all — only 1–3 millimeters per year!
[C] The soil in this desert is very similar to the soil on Mars, so they prepare for trips to outer space.

The Atacama is also one of the best places on Earth to watch stars.

18 다음 중 밑줄 친 ⓐ를 대신하여 쓸 수 있는 문장은?

① The Atacama is not drier than all the other deserts on Earth.
② The Atacama is not as dry as all the other deserts on Earth.
③ No other desert on Earth is drier than the Atacama.
④ No deserts on Earth are not as dry as the Atacama.
⑤ The Atacama is as dry as all the other deserts on Earth.

19 자연스러운 내용이 되도록 [A]~[C]를 바르게 나열하시오.

➡ _____

[20~22] 다음 글을 읽고 물음에 답하시오.

Angel Falls

If you go to Venezuela, you can see the world's highest waterfall. It is 979 meters high. Clouds often cover the top, so you need patience and a little luck to get a good view. Actually, the waterfall is named after Jimmie Angel, a pilot from the United States who first flew over the waterfall in 1933. You can still get to the top of the beautiful waterfall only by plane.

20 다음 중 Angel Falls에 관하여 언급된 것을 <u>모두</u> 고르시오.

① its height
② its width
③ the number of visitors
④ the origin of its name
⑤ its depth

21 How can you get to the top of Angel Falls? Answer in English with a full sentence. Use the word 'there.'

➡ _____

22 다음 중 위 글을 읽고 답할 수 <u>없는</u> 것은?

① Where is Angel Falls?
② What is the highest waterfall in the world?
③ Who first flew over the waterfall?
④ When did Jimmie Angel first fly over Angel Falls?
⑤ How old was Jimmie Angel when he first flew over the waterfall?

23 ①~⑤ 중 주어진 문장이 들어가기에 가장 적합한 곳은?

In fact, the salt flat makes any tourist a great photographer.

Salar de Uyuni in Bolivia is the world's largest salt flat. ① Thousands of years ago, there was water, but it all dried up. ② Now, a large salt desert is left about 3,656 meters above sea level. ③ Salar de Uyuni is one of the most visited natural wonders of South America, too. ④ All year round a lot of people visit this place to take pictures of its unique natural beauty. ⑤ Every picture you take in Salar de Uyuni will be a beautiful work of art!

①   ②   ③   ④   ⑤

[24~25] 다음 글을 읽고 물음에 답하시오.

The Amazon runs across the continent through seven countries. It travels from Peru in the west and flows into the Atlantic Ocean. The Amazon River is interesting in many ways. For the most part, it has no bridges. That is because it usually runs through rainforests and wet areas, not cities or towns. Also, in many places the river is very wide, so you cannot see the other side! You probably do not want to swim in this river. It is home to some very big snakes and fish that eat meat.

24 Write the reason why for the most part, the Amazon doesn't have bridges. Answer in English starting with 'Because'.

➡ _____
_____

25 위 글의 내용에 맞게 빈칸에 알맞은 말을 쓰시오.

The Amazon runs across _____ _____ in South America. For the most part, there are no _____ over the river. Some very big _____ and meat-eating _____ live in the river.

Reading for Fun 4

Play

The Two Stones

Words & Expressions

Key Words

□ **allow** [əláu] 동 허락하다, 허가하다

□ **anymore** [ènimɔ́ːr] 부 (부정문 · 의문문에서) 지금은, 이제는 (더 이상) (= **any longer**)

□ **borrow** [bárou] 동 빌리다

□ **carefully** [kέərfəli] 부 주의 깊게

□ **celebrate** [séləbrèit] 동 축하하다

□ **character** [kǽriktər] 명 등장인물

□ **drop** [drɑp] 동 떨어뜨리다

□ **either** [íːðər] 부 (부정문에서) 역시, 또한

□ **happen** [hǽpən] 동 일어나다, 생기다, 발생하다

□ **instead** [instéd] 부 대신에

□ **loudly** [láudli] 부 큰소리로

□ **mean** [miːn] 형 비열한, 못된

□ **million** [míljən] 명 백만

□ **narrator** [nǽreitər] 명 (연극 · 영화 · TV 등의) 해설자, 내레이터

□ **peso** [péisou] 명 페소《필리핀 · 멕시코 및 중남미 여러 나라의 화폐 단위》

□ **pick** [pik] 동 고르다

□ **poor** [puər] 형 가난한

□ **prison** [prízn] 명 감옥

□ **save** [seiv] 동 (목숨을) 구하다

□ **servant** [sə́ːrvənt] 명 하인

□ **terrible** [térəbl] 형 끔찍한

□ **trick** [trik] 명 속임수

Key Expressions

□ **don't[doesn't] have to** ~할 필요가 없다

□ **money lender** 대부업자

□ **pay back** (돈을) 갚다

□ **right away** 즉시, 바로

□ **say to oneself** 중얼거리다

□ **to oneself** 혼자

Word Power

※ 희곡 용어

☐ 해설 (**narration**): 희곡의 첫머리에 등장하여 인물, 배경 등을 설명하고, 관객에게 이야기의 내용을 설명하는 말로 해설자(**narrator**)가 직접 관객에게 말을 함

☐ 대화 (**dialog**): 등장인물끼리 주고받는 말

☐ 독백 (**monolog**): 등장인물이 상대역 없이 혼자 하는 말

☐ 방백 (**aside**): 관객에게는 들리나 상대역에게는 들리지 않는 것으로 약속하고 하는 말

☐ 지시문 (**direction**): 등장인물들의 대사와 대사 사이에서 무대 장치, 분위기, 등장인물의 행동, 표정, 퇴장 시기, 말투 등을 지시하는 말

※ 연극의 배역과 관련된 표현 (Roles for Actors)

☐ **lead role** 주연

☐ **supporting role** 조연

☐ **bit part** 단역

☐ **extra** 엑스트라

☐ **cameo** 카메오, 유명인이 잠시 출연하는 역할

☐ **villain** 악역

English Dictionary

☐ **borrow** 빌리다
→ to take something and promise to return it
어떤 것을 가져가고 그것을 돌려주기로 약속하다

☐ **celebrate**: 축하하다
→ to do something enjoyable because of a special occasion or to mark someone's success
특별한 행사나 누군가의 성공을 기념하기 위해 즐거운 것을 하다

☐ **character**: 등장인물
→ a person who appears in a story, book, play, movie, or television show
이야기, 책, 연극, 영화, 텔레비전 프로에 나오는 인물

☐ **happen**: 발생하다, 일어나다
→ to take place, especially without being planned
특히 계획 없이 일어나다

☐ **instead** 대신에
→ in place of
~을 대신해서, ~ 대신에

☐ **mean** 비열한, 못된
→ not kind to people
사람들에게 친절하지 않은

☐ **narrator**: 해설자, 내레이터
→ a person who tells a story, especially in a book, play, or movie
특히 책이나 연극이나 영화에서 이야기를 하는 사람

☐ **pick** 고르다
→ to choose from a group
한 무리로부터 선택하다

☐ **prison**: 감옥
→ a building where people are kept as a punishment for a crime they have committed
사람들이 저지른 범죄에 대한 처벌로 갇혀 있는 건물

☐ **save** (목숨을) 구하다
→ to help someone get away from danger or harm
누군가를 위험이나 해로부터 빠져나가도록 돕다

☐ **servant** 하인
→ a person whose job is to do another person's housework, often living in the home
직업이 다른 사람의 집안일을 하는 것이고, 종종 그 집에서 사는 사람

☐ **trick** 속임수
→ a plan to deceive someone
누군가를 속이려는 계획

Reading

The Two Stones

Characters: Father, Daughter, Money Lender, Friends, Narrator
　　　　　　등장인물　　　　　　　　　　　　대부업자

Narrator: A long time ago, in a small village in South America, there
　　　　　　　오래 전에　　　　　　　　부사구　　　　　형용사구
lived a farmer and his daughter. The farmer was poor, and had to
'~가 살았다'. there는 부사로 의미가 없다.　　　　　　　　　must(= have to)의 과거형 '~해야 했다'
borrow three million pesos from a money lender. But the money
　　　　　　　　millions(×)
lender was not kind, and when the farmer asked for one month
　　　　　　　　　　　부사절 접속사 '~할 때'　　　　~을 요구했다
to pay back the money, she didn't allow him anymore time.
부사적 용법(목적): '~하기 위해'　　　　　　　　　　allow+간접목적어+직접목적어

Money Lender: You have no money? That's okay. Your daughter will
　　　　　　　　Do you have no money?에서 Do가 생략된 형태
become my servant instead.

Father and Daughter: Oh, no!

Daughter: I don't want to be your servant.
　　　　　　　　want는 to부정사를 목적어로 취하는 동사다
Father: I don't want that, either! *(to Money Lender)* No, thank you.
　　　　　　　　　　부정문에서 '또한'
Money Lender: Do you want to go to prison? Then, let's play a game. I
　　　　　　　　　　　　　　　　　　　　let's+동사원형: ~하자
will put two stones in a bag. One is white, and the other is black.
　　　　　　　　　　　　　가리키는 대상이 두 개일 때, 하나는 one. 다른 하나는 the other 로 지칭한다.
Your daughter will pick one.
　　　　　　　　　= a stone
Daughter: What happens if I pick the white one?
　　　　　　　　　　조건 부사절로 '~한다면'　　= stone을 가리키는 부정대명사
Money Lender: Then you will be my servant.

Friends: Oh, no! She's mean. How terrible!
　　　　　　　'How+형용사+주어+동사' 어순의 감탄문으로 뒤에 'it is'가 생략되어 있다.
Daughter: What happens if I pick the black one?

---

character 등장인물
money lender 대부업자
narrator 해설자
borrow 빌리다
million 백만
pay back (돈을) 갚다
allow 허락하다
servant 하인
instead 대신에
pick 고르다
mean 야비한, 못된
terrible 끔찍한

확인문제

● 다음 문장이 본문의 내용과 일치하면 T, 일치하지 않으면 F를 쓰시오.

1 The farmer and his daughter had to borrow money. ☐

2 The money lender was mean. ☐

3 The money lender suggested playing a game with the farmer. ☐

4 If the daughter picks the white stone, she will be the money lender's servant. ☐

Money Lender: Then you will be free, and your father doesn't have to
~할 필요가 없다
pay back my money.
갚다

Father: What happens if she doesn't play this game with you?

Money Lender: *(loudly)* Then you will go to prison!

Father, Daughter, and Friends: Oh, no! Prison!

(Money Lender picks up two stones. Daughter looks carefully at her.)
동사 'look at'을 수식하는 부사가 되어야 한다.

Daughter: *(to herself)* Oh! She has picked up two white stones! She
혼잣말로   현재완료
will make me become her servant. What should I do?
사역동사+목적어+동사원형

Narrator: Stop and think. What should she do? She cannot pick a
black one.
= stone

(Daughter picks a stone from the bag. She drops it right away.)

Daughter: Oh, no! I'm sorry, I've dropped it. *(to Money Lender)* But
it's okay. Show us the stone in the bag. Then we will know
딸이 돌을 떨어뜨린 것   = Show the stone in the bag to us.
which one I picked.
간접의문문으로 의문사(which one)+주어(I)+동사(picked)

Money Lender: *(to herself)* I cannot tell them about my trick! Oh, no!

(Money Lender shows everyone the white stone. Friends and Father
= Money Lender shows the white stone to everyone
start celebrating.)
start+동명사/to부정사

Friends: She picked the black one! They are free!

Narrator: Good thinking has saved Father and Daughter!

---

don't[doesn't] have to ~할 필요가
없다
loudly 큰소리로
prison 감옥
carefully 주의 깊게
to oneself 혼자서
drop 떨어뜨리다
right away 즉시, 바로
trick 속임수
save 구하다

📎 **확인문제**

● 다음 문장이 본문의 내용과 일치하면 T, 일치하지 <u>않으면</u> F를 쓰시오.

1 If the farmer's daughter doesn't play the game with the money lender, she will go to prison. ☐

2 The daughter found out the money lender's trick. ☐

3 The daughter dropped the stone to win the game. ☐

4 The money lender told the farmer and his daughter about her trick. ☐

● 우리말을 참고하여 빈칸에 알맞은 말을 쓰시오.

1 The _____ _____

2 _____ : Father, Daughter, _____ _____, Friends, _____

3 Narrator: A long time _____, in a small _____ in South America, _____ _____ a farmer and his daughter.

4 The farmer was poor, and _____ _____ _____ three _____ pesos _____ a money lender.

5 But _____ _____ _____ was not kind, and when the farmer _____ _____ one month _____ _____ _____ the money, she didn't _____ him _____ time.

6 Money Lender: You have _____ money? That's okay.

7 Your daughter will become my _____ _____.

8 Father and Daughter: Oh, no!

9 Daughter: I don't want _____ _____ your _____.

10 Father: I don't want that, _____! *(to Money Lender)* No, _____ _____.

11 Money Lender: Do you want to go to _____?

12 Then, _____ _____ a game. I will _____ two stones in a bag.

13 _____ is white, and _____ _____ is black. Your daughter will _____ one.

14 Daughter: What _____ _____ I pick the white one?

15 Money Lender: _____ you will be my _____.

16 Friends: Oh, no! She's _____. _____ _____!

17 Daughter: What happens _____ I _____ the black one?

1	두 개의 돌
2	등장인물: 아버지, 딸, 대부업자, 친구들, 해설자
3	해설자: 오래 전 남아메리카의 작은 마을에 농부와 그의 딸이 살았습니다.
4	농부는 가난했고, 대부업자로부터 3백만 페소를 빌려야 했습니다.
5	하지만 대부업자는 친절하지 않았고, 농부가 돈을 갚을 때까지 한 달을 기다려 달라고 하자, 더 이상의 시간을 허락해 주지 않았습니다.
6	대부업자: 돈이 없다는 거죠? 좋아요
7	대신 당신 딸이 내 하녀가 돼야겠네요.
8	아버지와 딸: 오, 안 돼!
9	딸: 저는 당신의 하녀가 되고 싶지 않아요.
10	아버지: 나도 그것을 원하지 않아! *(대부업자에게)* 사양하겠습니다.
11	대부업자: 감옥에 가고 싶은가요?
12	그렇다면, 게임을 하나 합시다. 내가 가방에 돌 두 개를 넣겠어요.
13	하나는 흰색이고, 다른 하나는 검은색이죠. 당신 딸이 하나를 집을 거예요.
14	딸: 제가 흰 돌을 집으면 어떻게 되죠?
15	대부업자: 그러면 넌 내 하녀가 될 거야.
16	친구들: 오, 안 돼! 그녀는 야비해. 정말 끔찍해!
17	딸: 제가 검은 돌을 집으면 어떻게 되죠?

18 Money Lender: Then you will be _____, and your father _____ _____ _____ pay back my money.

19 Father: What happens if she _____ _____ this game _____ you?

20 Money Lender: (_____) _____ you will go to _____!

21 Father, Daughter, and Friends: Oh, no! _____!

22 *(Money Lender _____ _____ two stones. Daughter _____ _____ _____ her.)*

23 Daughter: (_____ _____) Oh! She has _____ _____ two white stones!

24 She will _____ me _____ her servant. What _____ I do?

25 Narrator: _____ _____ _____. What should she do?

26 She _____ _____ a black one.

27 *(Daughter picks a stone from the bag. She _____ it _____ _____.)*

28 Daughter Oh, no! I'm sorry, I've _____ it.

29 *(to Money Lender)* But it's _____.

30 _____ _____ _____ _____ in the bag.

31 Then we will know _____ _____ I picked.

32 Money Lender: (_____ _____) I _____ _____ them about my _____! Oh, no!

33 *(Money Lender _____ _____ _____ _____ _____ _____.*

34 *Friends and Father start _____.)*

35 Friends: She _____ the black one! They are _____!

36 Narrator: _____ _____ has _____ Father and Daughter!

---

18 대부업자: 그러면 넌 자유로워 질 것이고, 네 아버지는 내 돈을 갚을 필요가 없어.

19 아버지: 내 딸이 당신과 이 게임 을 하지 않으면 어떻게 되죠?

20 대부업자: *(큰소리로)* 그러면 당 신은 감옥에 가게 되겠죠!

21 아버지, 딸, 친구들. 오, 안 돼! 감옥이라니!

22 *(대부업자는 두 개의 돌을 집는 다. 딸은 주의 깊게 그녀를 본 다.)*

23 딸: *(혼잣말로)* 오! 그녀는 두 개 의 흰 돌을 집었어!

24 그녀는 나를 자신의 하녀로 만 들 거야. 어떻게 하면 좋지?

25 해설자: 가만히 생각해 보세요. 그녀는 어떻게 하면 좋을까요?

26 그녀는 검은 돌을 집을 수 없어 요.

27 *(딸은 가방에서 돌을 하나 집는 다. 그녀는 그것을 바로 떨어뜨 린다.)*

28 딸: 오, 안 돼! 미안해요, 제가 돌을 떨어뜨렸어요.

29 *(대부업자에게)* 하지만 괜찮아 요.

30 가방에 있는 돌을 우리에게 보 여주세요.

31 그러면 제가 무엇을 집었는지 우리가 알게 될 테니까요.

32 대부업자: *(혼잣말로)* 그들에게 내 속임수를 말할 수 없어! 오, 안 돼!

33 *(대부업자는 모두에게 흰 돌을 보여 준다.*

34 *친구들과 아버지는 축하하기 시 작한다.)*

35 친구들: 그녀는 검은 돌을 집었 어! 그들은 자유야!

36 해설자: 현명한 생각이 아버지 와 딸을 구했습니다!

● 우리말을 참고하여 본문을 영작하시오.

1 두 개의 돌

➡ _____

2 등장인물: 아버지, 딸, 대부업자, 친구들, 해설자

➡ _____

3 해설자: 오래 전 남아메리카의 작은 마을에 농부와 그의 딸이 살았습니다.

➡ _____

4 농부는 가난했고, 대부업자로부터 3백만 페소를 빌려야 했습니다.

➡ _____

5 하지만 대부업자는 친절하지 않았고, 농부가 돈을 갚을 때까지 한 달을 기다려 달라고 하자, 더 이상의 시간을 허락해 주지 않았습니다.

➡ _____

➡ _____

6 대부업자: 돈이 없다는 거죠? 좋아요

➡ _____

7 대신 당신 딸이 내 하녀가 돼야겠네요.

➡ _____

8 아버지와 딸: 오, 안 돼!

➡ _____

9 딸: 저는 당신의 하녀가 되고 싶지 않아요.

➡ _____

10 아버지: 나도 그것을 원하지 않아! *(대부업자에게)* 사양하겠습니다.

➡ _____

11 대부업자: 감옥에 가고 싶은가요?

➡ _____

12 그렇다면, 게임을 하나 합시다. 내가 가방에 돌 두 개를 넣겠어요.

➡ _____

13 하나는 흰색이고, 다른 하나는 검은색이죠. 당신 딸이 하나를 집을 거예요.

➡ _____

14 딸: 제가 흰 돌을 집으면 어떻게 되죠?

➡ _____

15 대부업자: 그러면 넌 내 하녀가 될 거야.

➡ _____

16 친구들: 오, 안 돼! 그녀는 야비해. 정말 끔찍해!

➡ _____

17 딸: 제가 검은 돌을 집으면 어떻게 되죠?

➡ _____

18 대부업자: 그러면 넌 자유로워질 것이고, 네 아버지는 내 돈을 갚을 필요가 없어.

➡ _____

19 아버지: 내 딸이 당신과 이 게임을 하지 않으면 어떻게 되죠?

➡ _____

20 대부업자: *(큰소리로)* 그러면 당신은 감옥에 가게 되겠죠!

➡ _____

21 아버지, 딸, 친구들: 오, 안 돼! 감옥이라니!

➡ _____

22 *(대부업자는 두 개의 돌을 집는다. 딸은 주의 깊게 그녀를 본다.)*

➡ _____

23 딸: *(혼잣말로)* 오! 그녀는 두 개의 흰 돌을 집었어!

➡ _____

24 그녀는 나를 자신의 하녀로 만들 거야. 어떻게 하면 좋지?

➡ _____

25 해설자: 가만히 생각해 보세요. 그녀는 어떻게 하면 좋을까요?

➡ _____

26 그녀는 검은 돌을 집을 수 없어요.

➡ _____

27 *(딸은 가방에서 돌을 하나 집는다. 그녀는 그것을 바로 떨어뜨린다.)*

➡ _____

28 딸: 오, 안 돼! 미안해요, 제가 돌을 떨어뜨렸어요. *(대부업자에게)* 하지만 괜찮아요.

➡ _____

29 가방에 있는 돌을 우리에게 보여주세요.

➡ _____

30 그러면 제가 무엇을 집었는지 우리가 알게 될 테니까요.

➡ _____

31 대부업자: *(혼잣말로)* 그들에게 내 속임수를 말할 수 없어! 오, 안 돼!

➡ _____

32 *(대부업자는 모두에게 흰 돌을 보여 준다. 친구들과 아버지는 축하하기 시작한다.)*

➡ _____

33 친구들: 그녀는 검은 돌을 집었어! 그들은 자유야!

➡ _____

34 해설자: 현명한 생각이 아버지와 딸을 구했습니다!

➡ _____

서술형 실전문제

01 다음 빈칸에 알맞은 말을 〈보기〉에서 골라 쓰시오.

보기

instead, borrow, right away, mean, servant, pick, pay back

(1) The old man had _____ to do all the cleaning and cooking for him.

(2) I'll _____ the money with interest.

(3) She has to _____ the right answer.

(4) Would you be able to start working _____ ?

(5) I don't care for the mountains, so let's go to the beach _____ .

(6) May I _____ your camera for a few days?

(7) It was _____ of you not to invite him to the party.

02 다음 영영풀이에 해당하는 단어를 〈보기〉에서 찾아 쓰시오.

보기

save, borrow, mean, trick

(1) a plan to deceive someone

➡ _____

(2) not kind to people

➡ _____

(3) to help someone get away from danger or harm

➡ _____

(4) to take something and promise to return it

➡ _____

03 주어진 우리말에 맞게 빈칸에 알맞은 말을 쓰시오.

(1) 하나는 고속도로이고 다른 하나는 샛길입니다.

• _____ is the expressway and _____ _____ is a side road.

(2) 제가 흰 것을 집으면 어떻게 되죠?

• What happens if I pick the white _____ ?

(3) 당신이 할 수 없는 일을 나한테 시키지 마세요!

• Don't make _____ _____ what you can't do!

(4) 어느 것을 갖고 싶은지 말해 줘.

• Tell me _____ _____ you want to have.

(5) 지금까지 그녀는 200마리의 길 잃은 개들을 구했다.

• So far, she _____ _____ 200 lost dogs.

04 다음 문장을 어법에 맞게 고쳐 쓰시오.

(1) He has served this school since twenty years.

➡ _____

(2) He has two balls. One is white and another is red.

➡ _____

05 다음 두 문장을 한 문장으로 바꿔 쓰시오.

(1) I don't know. What did Sarah want me to do?

➡ _____
_____

(2) Will you tell me? Do you want to go shopping with me?

➡ _____

_____

(3) Do you think? What does he want?

➡ _____

_____

(4) Let me know. Will you go there?

➡ _____

_____

[06~08] 다음 글을 읽고 물음에 답하시오.

Characters: Father, Daughter, Money Lender, Friends, Narrator

Narrator: A long time ago, in a small village in South America, (A)농부와 그의 딸이 살았습니다. The farmer was poor, and had to borrow three million pesos from a money lender. But the money lender was not kind, and when the farmer asked for one month to pay back the money, she didn't allow him anymore time.

Money Lender: You have no money? That's okay. Your daughter will become my servant instead.

Father and Daughter: Oh, no!

Daughter: I don't want to be your servant.

Father: I don't want that, either!

(to Money Lender) No, thank you.

06 위 글의 밑줄 친 (A)의 우리말에 맞게 주어진 단어를 이용하여 영어로 쓰시오.

there

➡ _____

07 위 글에서 다음 영영풀이에 해당하는 단어를 찾아 쓰시오.

a person whose job is to do another person's housework, often living in the home

➡ _____

08 Where is the setting of the story?

➡ It _____.

[09~12] 다음 글을 읽고 물음에 답하시오.

Money Lender: You have no money? That's okay. Your daughter will become my servant instead.

Father and Daughter: Oh, no!

Daughter: I don't want to be your servant.

Father: (A)I don't want that, either!

(to Money Lender) No, thank you.

Money Lender: Do you want to go to prison? Then, let's play a game. I will put two stones in a bag. (B)One is white, and another is black. Your daughter will pick one.

Daughter: What happens if I pick the white one?

Money Lender: Then you will be my servant.

Friends: Oh, no! She's mean. (C)정말 끔찍해!

Daughter: What happens if I pick the black one?

Money Lender: Then you will be free, and (D)네 아버지는 내 돈을 갚을 필요가 없어.

09 위 글의 밑줄 친 (A)와 같은 의미의 문장으로 바꾸어 쓸 때 빈칸에 알맞은 말을 쓰시오.

➡ I don't _____ my daughter _____ _____ _____ _____, either!

10 위 글의 밑줄 친 (B)에서 어법상 어색한 것을 찾아 바르게 고쳐 문장을 쓰시오.

➡ _____

11 위 글의 밑줄 친 (C)의 우리말에 맞게 주어진 단어를 사용하여 '주어+동사'가 있는 완전한 문장으로 감탄문을 완성하시오.

terrible

➡ _____

12 위 글의 밑줄 친 (D)의 우리말에 맞게 주어진 단어를 활용하여 영어로 쓰시오.

have to / pay back

➡ _____

[13~15] 다음 글을 읽고 물음에 답하시오.

> **Father:** What happens if she doesn't play this game with you?
>
> **Money Lender:** *(loudly)* Then you will go to prison!
>
> **Father, Daughter, and Friends:** Oh, no! Prison!
>
> *(Money Lender picks up two stones. Daughter looks carefully at her.)*
>
> **Daughter:** *(to herself)* Oh! She has picked up two white stones! (A)그녀는 나를 자신의 하녀로 만들 거야. What should I do?
>
> **Narrator:** Stop and think. What should she do? She cannot pick a black one.
>
> *(Daughter picks a stone from the bag. She drops it right away.)*
>
> **Daughter:** Oh, no! I'm sorry, I've dropped it. *(to Money Lender)* But it's okay. (B) Show us the stone in the bag. Then we will know which one I picked.

Money Lender: *(to herself)* I cannot tell them about my trick! Oh, no!

(Money Lender shows everyone the white stone. Friends and Father start celebrating.)

Friends: She picked the black one! They are free!

Narrator: Good thinking has saved Father and Daughter!

13 위 글의 밑줄 친 (A)의 우리말에 맞게 주어진 단어를 이용하여 영작하시오. (7 words)

make / become

➡ _____

14 위 글의 밑줄 친 (B)를 같은 의미의 문장으로 바꾸어 쓰시오.

➡ _____

15 위 글을 읽고, 글의 내용과 일치하지 않는 문장을 찾아 바르게 고쳐 쓰시오.

① If the farmer doesn't play the game with money lender, his daughter will go to prison.
② Money lender picked up two white stones.
③ The farmer's daughter picked a stone and dropped it right away.
④ Actually the farmer's daughter picked a black stone.

➡ 틀린 문장 번호: _____

➡ 바르게 고친 문장:

(1) _____

_____

(2) _____

_____

01 다음 단어들 중 성격이 <u>다른</u> 하나를 고르시오.

① lead role ② villain
③ cameo ④ character
⑤ bit part

02 다음 영영풀이의 빈칸에 해당하는 단어로 알맞은 것은?

> If someone is _____ed to do something, it is all right for them to do it and they will not get into trouble

① borrow ② trick ③ lend
④ mean ⑤ allow

03 다음 빈칸에 알맞은 말을 고르시오.

> • I did not need the brush _____, so I threw it out.

① also ② anymore
③ too ④ away
⑤ either

04 다음 우리말에 맞게 빈칸에 알맞은 말을 쓰시오.

(1) 길을 건너기 전에 양쪽을 주의 깊게 살펴라.
  • Look both ways _____ before crossing the street.
(2) 내가 네 책을 빌려도 될까?
  • Can I _____ your book?

05 다음 영영풀이에 해당하는 단어를 주어진 철자로 시작하여 쓰시오.

> to do something enjoyable because of a special occasion or to mark someone's success

➡ c_____

06 다음 중 밑줄 친 부분의 뜻풀이가 바르지 <u>않은</u> 것은?

① I don't like Jack, <u>either</u>. (역시)
② I can't hear you if you don't speak <u>loudly</u>. (큰소리로)
③ It's just a <u>trick</u> of hers. (재능)
④ The police sent him to <u>prison</u>. (감옥)
⑤ The man is <u>mean</u> and careless, and stupid. (사악한, 못된)

07 다음 중 어법상 어색한 것은?

① I don't like to say things twice, too.
② Do you know who she is?
③ I need a pen. Can you lend me one?
④ How happy she was!
⑤ We will know which one she liked.

08 다음 중 어법상 적절한 것은?

① She picked black one.
② Do you think why she left the party so early?
③ Friends and Father start to celebrate.
④ I have two sisters. One is older than me and another is younger than me.
⑤ What nice the old lady is!

출제율 90%

09 다음 문장을 어법에 맞게 고쳐 쓰시오.

(1) You can choose one or another of the two rooms.

➡ _____

(2) I'm not sure that he will come or not.

➡ _____

[10~12] 다음 희곡을 읽고 물음에 답하시오.

> _____(A)_____ : Father, Daughter, Money Lender, Friends, Narrator
>
> Narrator: A long time ago, in a small village in South America, there ⓐlived a farmer and his daughter. The farmer was poor, and ⓑhad to borrowing three million pesos from a money lender. But the money lender was not kind, and ⓒwhen the farmer asked for one month to pay back the money, she didn't allow him ⓓanymore time.
>
> Money Lender: You have no money? That's okay. Your daughter will become my servant instead.
>
> Father and Daughter: Oh, no!
>
> Daughter: I don't want to be your servant.
>
> Father: I don't want that, ⓔeither!
> (to Money Lender) No, thank you.

출제율 90%

10 아래의 영영풀이를 보고, 빈칸 (A)에 들어갈 말을 쓰시오. (복수형으로 쓸 것)

> <영영풀이> a person represented in a film, play, or story

➡ _____

출제율 90%

11 위 글의 밑줄 친 ⓐ~ⓔ 중 어법상 어색한 것은?

① ⓐ ② ⓑ ③ ⓒ ④ ⓓ ⑤ ⓔ

출제율 100%

12 위 글의 내용과 일치하지 않는 것은?

① A farmer and his daughter lived in a small village in South America.

② The farmer had to lend three million pesos to a money lender.

③ The money lender was mean.

④ The farmer asked for one month to pay back the money.

⑤ Unless the farmer pays back the money, his daughter will be the money lender's servant.

[13~16] 다음 글을 읽고 물음에 답하시오.

> Money Lender: You have no money? That's okay. (①) Your daughter will become my servant instead.
>
> Father and Daughter: Oh, no! (②)
>
> Daughter: I don't want to be your servant.
>
> Father: I don't want that, either!
> (to Money Lender) No, thank you.
>
> Money Lender: (③) Do you want to go to prison? Then, let's play a game. (④) One is white, and the other is black. Your daughter will pick one. (⑤)
>
> Daughter: What happens if I pick the white one?
>
> Money Lender: Then you will be my servant.
>
> Friends: Oh, no! She's ____ⓐ____. How terrible!
>
> Daughter: What happens if I pick the black one?
>
> Money Lender: Then you will be free, and your father doesn't have to pay back my money.

✏️ 출제율 95%

13 위 글의 빈칸 ⓐ에 들어갈 'the money lender'의 성격으로 알맞은 것은?

① kind ② smart

③ stupid ④ thoughtful

⑤ mean

✏️ 출제율 95%

14 위 글에서 주어진 문장이 들어갈 위치로 알맞은 것은?

> I will put two stones in a bag.

① ② ③ ④ ⑤

✏️ 출제율 95%

15 위 글은 희곡의 일부분이다. 이야기의 전개 구조상 해당되는 부분은?

① Setting ② Characters

③ Conflict ④ Climax

⑤ Solution

✏️ 출제율 95%

16 위 글을 읽고 다음 물음에 영어로 답하시오. (should를 사용할 것)

Q: Which color stone should the daughter pick if she doesn't want to be the money lender's servant?

➡ _____

[17~21] 다음 글을 읽고 물음에 답하시오.

Father: What happens if she doesn't play this game with you?

Money Lender: (____ⓐ____) Then you will go to prison! (①)

Father, Daughter, and Friends: Oh, no! Prison! (②)

Daughter: (____ⓑ____) Oh! She has picked up two white stones! (③) She will make me become her servant. What should I do? (④)

Narrator: Stop and think. What should she do? She cannot pick a black one.

(Daughter picks a stone from the bag. She ____ⓒ____ *.)*

Daughter: Oh, no! I'm sorry, I've dropped it. (____ⓓ____) But it's okay. Show us the stone in the bag. Then we will know which one I picked. (⑤)

Money Lender: (____ⓔ____) I cannot tell them about my trick! Oh, no!

(Money Lender shows everyone the white stone. Friends and Father start celebrating.)

Friends: She picked the ____ⓕ____ one! They are free!

Narrator: Good thinking has saved Father and Daughter!

✏️ 출제율 95%

17 주어진 문장은 희곡의 '지시문'에 해당한다. (①)~(⑤) 중 들어갈 위치로 알맞은 것은?

> *(Money Lender picks up two stones. Daughter looks carefully at her.)*

① ② ③ ④ ⑤

✏️ 출제율 95%

18 위 글의 빈칸 ⓐ~ⓔ에 들어갈 말로 어색한 것은?

① loudly

② to herself

③ drops it right away

④ to her father

⑤ to herself

✏️ 출제율 100%

19 위 글의 흐름상 빈칸 ⓕ에 들어갈 단어를 본문에서 찾아 쓰시오.

➡ _____

20 위 글을 읽고 다음 질문에 대한 답의 빈칸을 채우시오.

> Q: What did the daughter do when she knew the two stones in the money lender's bag were both white?
>
> ➡ She _____ the stone that she _____ from the bag _____.

21 위 글은 희곡의 전개 방식에서 어디에 해당되는 부분인가?

① Conflict → Climax
② Development → Conflict
③ Conflict → Development
④ Development → Climax
⑤ Climax → Solution

[22~24] 다음 글을 읽고 물음에 답하시오.

Characters: Father, Daughter, Money Lender, Friends, Narrator

Narrator: A long time ago, in a small village in South America, there lived a farmer and his daughter. The farmer was poor, and had to borrow three million pesos from a money lender. But the money lender was not kind, and when the farmer asked for one month to pay back the money, she didn't allow him anymore time.

_____ⓐ : You have no money? That's okay. Your daughter will become my servant __(A)__ .

Father and Daughter: Oh, no!

Daughter: I don't want to be your servant.

_____ⓑ : I don't want that, either! *(to Money Lender)* No, thank you.

Money Lender: Do you want to go to prison? Then, let's play a game. I will put two stones in a bag. One is white, and the other is black. Your daughter will pick one.

_____ⓒ : What happens if I pick the white one?

Money Lender: Then you will be my servant.

_____ⓓ : Oh, no! (B)She's mean. How terrible!

Daughter: What happens if I pick the black one?

Money Lender: Then you will be free, and your father doesn't have to pay back my money.

22 위 글의 등장인물을 참고하여, 빈칸 ⓐ~ⓓ는 각각 누구의 대사인지 쓰시오.

> ➡ ⓐ _____ ⓑ _____
> ⓒ _____ ⓓ _____

23 위 글의 빈칸 (A)에 들어갈 말로 알맞은 것은?

① however   ② though
③ instead   ④ unless
⑤ otherwise

24 위 글의 밑줄 친 (B)의 정보를 바탕으로 'the money lender'가 다음에 취하는 행동으로 알맞은 것은?

① The money lender praises the farmer's daughter.
② The money lender puts one black stone and one white stone in a bag.
③ The money lender puts two black stones in a bag.
④ The money lender puts two white stones in a bag.
⑤ The money lender frees the farmer from his debt.

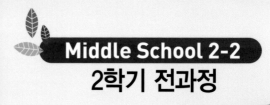

Middle School 2-2
2학기 전과정

중간 + 기말
적중100 plus
영어 기출문제집

영어 중 2
천재 | 이재영

Best Collection

내용문의 중등영어발전소 적중100 편집부 TEL 070-7707-0457

INSIGHT
on the textbook

교과서 파헤치기

영어 기출 문제집

적중 100 plus
2학기 전과정

영어 중 2

천재 | 이재영

INSIGHT
on the textbook
교과서 파헤치기

※ 다음 영어를 우리말로 쓰시오.

01 attitude

02 accuse

03 throw

04 behind

05 promise

06 protect

07 avoid

08 bullying

09 difficulty

10 free

11 appearance

12 character

13 guilty

14 worried

15 judge

16 shy

17 prison

18 beard

19 missing

20 attack

21 neighbor

22 freedom

23 confident

24 president

25 receive

26 right

27 allowance

28 truth

29 arrest

30 victim

31 ordinary

32 friendly

33 whisper

34 popular

35 care for ~

36 be afraid of ~

37 calm down

38 set+목적어+free

39 accuse A of B

40 thanks to ~

41 be for ~

42 fight off ~

43 vote for ~

※ 다음 우리말을 영어로 쓰시오.

01	등		22	인기 있는, 대중적인	
02	통과하다, 지나가다		23	언제든지, 언제나	
03	활동		24	공약, 약속	
04	휴대하다, 지니다		25	매월의, 한 달에 한 번의	
05	소리치다, 외치다		26	득점하다	
06	희생자		27	자유	
07	투표하다		28	보호하다	
08	선택		29	자신감 있는	
09	들어가다, 참가[출전]하다		30	용돈	
10	숨기다		31	이웃	
11	속삭이다		32	고발하다, 비난하다	
12	다정한, 친절한		33	실종된, 행방불명된	
13	외모		34	감옥	
14	체포하다		35	지금까지	
15	운이 좋은		36	~을 두려워하다	
16	직면하다, (힘든 상황에) 처하다		37	B 때문에 A를 고발하다	
17	신경 쓰다, 꺼리다		38	~을 자르다	
18	유죄의		39	~을 잘하다	
19	선택하다, 고르다		40	~ 덕분에	
20	곱슬곱슬한		41	~을 뽑다, ~에게 투표하다	
21	평범한		42	~에게 동의하다	
			43	~을 돌보다	

※ 다음 영영풀이에 알맞은 단어를 <보기>에서 골라 쓴 후, 우리말 뜻을 쓰시오.

1 _____ : to make something happen: _____

2 _____ : someone who lives near you: _____

3 _____ : to stay away from a person or place: _____

4 _____ : to get points, goals, runs, etc., in a game or contest: _____

5 _____ : how you think or feel about something: _____

6 _____ : the belief that you are able to do things well or be successful: _____

7 _____ : a person who appears in a story, book, play, movie, or television show: _____

8 _____ : to speak very quietly so that other people cannot hear: _____

9 _____ : to use violence to hurt or damage someone: _____

10 _____ : an action to try to frighten someone who is smaller or weaker: _____

11 _____ : to decide which thing you want: _____

12 _____ : to keep someone or something safe from something dangerous or bad: _____

13 _____ : the money you get back when you pay more money than something costs: _____

14 _____ : someone who has been hurt or killed: _____

15 _____ : an amount of money that parents give to a child each week: _____

16 _____ : to take the person away to ask them about a crime that they might have committed: _____

보기			
attack	allowance	cause	score
neighbor	victim	bullying	attitude
choose	avoid	protect	confidence
whisper	change	character	arrest

※ 다음 우리말과 일치하도록 빈칸에 알맞은 말을 쓰시오.

Communicate: Listen - Listen and Answer. Talk

G: Hi, I'm Gacha. I'm _____ Mongolia. When I first came to Songji Middle School two months _____, I was so _____. I was a little _____, and I wasn't _____ at Korean. However, I'm a _____ girl. All my classmates are nice and _____. I enjoy _____ handball with them in P.E. class. I'm a good player. They _____ me "Golden Hand." There _____ _____ a sports day next week. _____ _____ my class _____ _____ in the handball event.

여: 안녕, 나는 Gacha라고 해. 나는 몽골에서 왔어. 두 달 전에 내가 처음 송지 중학교에 왔을 때, 나는 무척 걱정이 되었어. 나는 좀 수줍음을 탔고 한국어를 잘 못했어. 하지만 난 운이 좋은 아이야. 내 학급 친구들은 모두 멋지고 다정해. 나는 체육 시간에 친구들과 핸드볼 하는 것을 즐겨. 난 실력이 좋은 선수야. 친구들은 나를 '황금손'이라고 불러. 다음 주에 운동회가 있을 거야. 난 우리 반이 핸드볼 대회에서 이기길 바라.

Communicate: Listen - Listen and Answer. Dialog

B: Hi, Minsol. _____ your class _____?
G: Of _____. We have a _____ _____ _____.
B: You _____ _____ _____ _____ Mongolia?
G: Yes, _____ _____ is Gacha.
B: I've heard a lot about her. But _____ does she _____ _____?
G: She's _____ _____ and _____ a _____.
B: Oh, is she the girl _____ _____ the goal _____ _____?
G: Yes, that's _____ _____ _____.
B: Wow, she's _____ _____.

남: 안녕, 민솔아. 너희 반이 이기고 있니?
여: 물론이지. 우리는 훌륭한 핸드볼 선수가 있거든.
남: 몽골에서 온 여자아이 말하니?
여: 응, 그녀의 이름은 Gacha야.
남: 그녀에 대해 많이 들었어. 그런데 그녀는 어떻게 생겼어?
여: 그녀는 키가 크고 말총머리를 하고 있어.
남: 아, 지금 막 골을 넣은 여자아이가 그녀니?
여: 맞아, 저건 그녀의 일곱 번째 골이야.
남: 와, 그녀는 정말 잘하는구나.

Communicate: Listen - Listen More

M: _____ _____ _____ _____ for you?
G: I _____ my _____ _____.
M: Okay, _____ _____. What's your _____ name?
G: His name is Wally Brown. He's _____ _____ _____.
M: _____ does he _____ _____?
G: He _____ brown hair and brown eyes.
M: What _____ he _____?
G: He is _____ a _____ and black pants.
M: Can you _____ _____ _____?
G: Oh, he is _____ _____ _____.
M: All right. We'll go out and _____ _____ him. Also, we'll _____ _____ about a _____ child.
G: Thank you so much. _____ _____ I'll _____ him soon.

남: 무엇을 도와드릴까요?
여: 남동생을 잃어버렸어요.
남: 알겠어요, 진정하세요. 남동생 이름이 뭐죠?
여: 그의 이름은 Wally Brown이에요. 다섯 살이고요.
남: 어떻게 생겼나요?
여: 그는 갈색 머리이고 갈색 눈을 지녔어요.
남: 그는 무엇을 입고 있나요?
여: 그는 초록색 셔츠와 검은 바지를 입고 있어요.
남: 더 말해 줄 수 있나요?
여: 아, 그는 빨간 배낭을 메고 있어요.
남: 알겠어요. 우리가 나가서 그를 찾아볼게요. 또, 우리가 미아 방송을 할 겁니다.
여: 정말 감사합니다. 동생을 빨리 찾길 바라요.

Communicate: Speak 2 - Talk in pairs

A: I _____ _____ _____ _____ _____ tomorrow!
B: _____ _____ you'll _____ _____ _____ the exam.
A: I _____ _____, _____. Thanks.

A: 나는 내일 중요한 시험이 있어!
B: 네가 시험을 잘 보길 바라.
A: 나도 그러길 바라. 고마워.

Communicate: Speak 2 - Talk in groups

A: _____ is _____ _____ _____?
B: _____ _____ is Buster.
A: _____ _____ he _____ _____?
B: He _____ _____ _____.
A: Does he _____ _____ _____?
B: Yes, he _____.

Communicate: Speak - Rap Time

(1) A: I _____ my puppy _____ _____.
   B: _____ _____ you'll _____ him soon.
(2) A: I hope you'll _____ _____ _____ in the final game.
   B: Thanks. _____ _____ you _____ _____.
(3) A: _____ _____ your sister _____ _____, Claire?
   B: She's tall and _____ _____ _____ _____.
(4) A: _____ your father _____ a blue cap?
   B: Yeah. Now, he's _____ _____ _____.

My Speaking Portfolio

G: _____ _____ the _____ _____. There _____ posters
   for the next _____ _____.
B: Yeah, I've _____ _____ my _____. I'll _____ _____
   Jang Jimin.
G: You _____ the boy _____ _____? He _____,
   but I don't like his _____.
B: Then _____ _____ you _____?
G: Well, I am for number 1, Han Siwon. She _____ _____
   _____ our school _____ _____ _____.
B: She _____ _____ a ponytail, _____?
G: Yes, and Hong Jiho _____ _____.
B: She _____, but I don't like _____ _____.

Wrap Up

1. B: I hear _____ _____ a new student in your class.
   G: Yes. She's _____ Jejudo. Oh, she's _____ _____!
   B: _____ one? _____ _____ she _____ like?
   G: She has _____ hair and is _____ _____.
2. G: You _____ _____. What's _____, Jongmin?
   B: My sister _____ _____ _____ this morning.
   G: What _____?
   B: She _____ _____ her bike.
   G: _____ _____ _____. _____ _____ she'll _____
      _____ soon.

A: 네 캐릭터의 이름은 뭐니?
B: 그의 이름은 Buster야.
A: 그는 어떻게 생겼니?
B: 그는 머리카락이 없어.
A: 그는 눈이 크니?
B: 응, 맞아.

(1) A: 나는 오늘 오후에 내 강아지를 잃어버렸어.
   B: 네가 그를 곧 찾기를 바랄게.
(2) A: 나는 네가 결선에서 최선을 다하길 바라.
   B: 고마워. 나도 네가 그러길 바라.
(3) A: 네 언니는 어떻게 생겼니, Claire?
   B: 그녀는 키가 크고 긴 생머리야.
(4) A: 네 아버지는 파란 모자를 쓰고 계시니?
   B: 응. 지금 지도를 보고 계셔.

여: 이 게시판을 봐. 다음 학생회장의 포스터가 있어.
남: 응, 나는 이미 결정을 내렸어. 나는 장지민에게 투표할 거야.
여: 안경을 쓴 남자아이 얘기하는 거야? 그는 똑똑해 보이지만 나는 그의 공약이 마음에 들지 않아.
남: 그럼 넌 누굴 선택할 거야?
여: 음, 나는 1번 한시원을 지지해. 그녀는 우리 학교를 안전한 장소로 만들고 싶어 해.
남: 그녀는 항상 말총머리를 해, 그렇지?
여: 맞아, 그리고 홍지호도 괜찮아 보여.
남: 그녀는 친절해 보이지만, 나는 장기자랑이 싫어.

1. 남: 너희 반에 새로 온 학생이 있다고 들었어.
   여: 응. 그녀는 제주도에서 왔어. 어, 그녀가 저기에 있어!
   남: 어느 아이? 어떻게 생겼어?
   여: 그녀는 곱슬머리이고 안경을 끼고 있어.
2. 여: 너 슬퍼 보여. 무슨 일이니, 종민아?
   남: 여동생이 오늘 아침에 팔이 부러졌어.
   여: 무슨 일이 있었는데?
   남: 자전거에서 떨어졌어.
   여: 안됐구나. 그녀가 곧 회복되기를 바라.

Step2

※ 다음 우리말에 맞도록 대화를 영어로 쓰시오.

Communicate: Listen - Listen and Answer. Talk

G: _____
_____
_____
_____
_____
_____

여: 안녕, 나는 Gacha라고 해. 나는 몽골에서 왔어. 두 달 전에 내가 처음 송지 중학교에 왔을 때, 나는 무척 걱정이 되었어. 나는 좀 수줍음을 탔고 한국어를 잘 못했어. 하지만 난 운이 좋은 아이야. 내 학급 친구들은 모두 멋지고 다정해. 나는 체육 시간에 친구들과 핸드볼 하는 것을 즐겨. 난 실력이 좋은 선수야. 친구들은 나를 '황금손'이라고 불러. 다음 주에 운동회가 있을 거야. 난 우리 반이 핸드볼 대회에서 이기길 바라.

Communicate: Listen - Listen and Answer. Dialog

B: _____
G: _____
B: _____
G: _____
B: _____
G: _____
B: _____
G: _____
B: _____

남: 안녕, 민솔아. 너희 반이 이기고 있니?
여: 물론이지. 우리는 훌륭한 핸드볼 선수가 있거든.
남: 몽골에서 온 여자아이 말하니?
여: 응, 그녀의 이름은 Gacha야.
남: 그녀에 대해 많이 들었어. 그런데 그녀는 어떻게 생겼어?
여: 그녀는 키가 크고 말총머리를 하고 있어.
남: 아, 지금 막 골을 넣은 여자아이가 그녀니?
여: 맞아, 저건 그녀의 일곱 번째 골이야.
남: 와, 그녀는 정말 잘하는구나.

Communicate: Listen - Listen More

M: _____
G: _____
M: _____
G: _____
M: _____
G: _____
M: _____
G: _____
M: _____
G: _____
M: _____
_____
G: _____

남: 무엇을 도와드릴까요?
여: 남동생을 잃어버렸어요.
남: 알겠어요, 진정하세요. 남동생 이름이 뭐죠?
여: 그의 이름은 Wally Brown이에요. 다섯 살이고요.
남: 어떻게 생겼나요?
여: 그는 갈색 머리이고 갈색 눈을 지녔어요.
남: 그는 무엇을 입고 있나요?
여: 그는 초록색 셔츠와 검은 바지를 입고 있어요.
남: 더 말해 줄 수 있나요?
여: 아, 그는 빨간 배낭을 메고 있어요.
남: 알겠어요. 우리가 나가서 그를 찾아볼게요. 또, 우리가 미아 방송을 할 겁니다.
여: 정말 감사합니다. 동생을 빨리 찾길 바라요.

Communicate: Speak 2 - Talk in pairs

A: _____
B: _____
A: _____

A: 나는 내일 중요한 시험이 있어!
B: 네가 시험을 잘 보길 바라.
A: 나도 그러길 바라. 고마워.

Communicate: Speak 2 - Talk in groups

A: _____

B: _____

A: _____

B: _____

A: _____

B: _____

A: 네 캐릭터의 이름은 뭐니?
B: 그의 이름은 Buster야.
A: 그는 어떻게 생겼니?
B: 그는 머리카락이 없어.
A: 그는 눈이 크니?
B: 응, 맞아.

Communicate: Speak - Rap Time

(1) A: _____

    B: _____

(2) A: _____

    B: _____

(3) A: _____

    B: _____

(4) A: _____

    B: _____

(1) A: 나는 오늘 오후에 내 강아지를 잃어버렸어.
   B: 네가 그를 곧 찾기를 바랄게.
(2) A: 나는 네가 결선에서 최선을 다하길 바라.
   B: 고마워. 나도 네가 그러길 바라.
(3) A: 네 언니는 어떻게 생겼니, Claire?
   B: 그녀는 키가 크고 긴 생머리야.
(4) A: 네 아버지는 파란 모자를 쓰고 계시니?
   B: 응. 지금 지도를 보고 계셔.

My Speaking Portfolio

G: _____

B: _____

G: _____

B: _____

G: _____

B: _____

G: _____

B: _____

여: 이 게시판을 봐. 다음 학생회장의 포스터가 있어.
남: 응, 나는 이미 결정을 내렸어. 나는 장지민에게 투표할 거야.
여: 안경을 쓴 남자아이 얘기하는 거야? 그는 똑똑해 보이지만 나는 그의 공약이 마음에 들지 않아.
남: 그럼 넌 누굴 선택할 거야?
여: 음, 나는 1번 한시원을 지지해. 그녀는 우리 학교를 안전한 장소로 만들고 싶어 해.
남: 그녀는 항상 말총머리를 해, 그렇지?
여: 맞아, 그리고 홍지호도 괜찮아 보여.
남: 그녀는 친절해 보이지만, 나는 장기 자랑이 싫어.

Wrap Up

1. B: _____

   G: _____

   B: _____

   G: _____

2. G: _____

   B: _____

   G: _____

   B: _____

   G: _____

1. 남: 너희 반에 새로 온 학생이 있다고 들었어.
   여: 응. 그녀는 제주도에서 왔어. 어, 그녀가 저기에 있어!
   남: 어느 아이? 어떻게 생겼어?
   여: 그녀는 곱슬머리이고 안경을 끼고 있어.
2. 여: 너 슬퍼 보여. 무슨 일이니, 종민아?
   남: 여동생이 오늘 아침에 팔이 부러졌어.
   여: 무슨 일이 있었는데?
   남: 자전거에서 떨어졌어.
   여: 안됐구나. 그녀가 곧 회복되기를 바라.

※ 다음 우리말과 일치하도록 빈칸에 알맞은 것을 골라 쓰시오.

1 The _____ To Bc _____
A. Different   B. Right

2 In many _____, 42-year-old Joseph Palmer was an _____
_____.
A. ordinary   B. ways   C. person

3 He _____ a job and _____ _____ his family.
A. for   B. cared   C. had

4 But in 1830, _____ he _____ to a small town in
Massachusetts, he began to _____ _____.
A. face   B. moved   C. difficulties   D. after

5 Joseph _____ _____ from _____ people: he had a long
beard.
A. different   B. other   C. looked

6 People _____ not _____ it very much.
A. like   B. did

7 The town's people _____ the man _____ a _____.
A. with   B. avoided   C. beard

8 They _____ not want to _____ next _____ him.
A. to   B. did   C. sit

9 They even _____ _____ his back, "What is he _____ to
hide?"
A. behind   B. trying   C. whispered

10 _____ neighbors _____ his windows.
A. broke   B. some

11 Others _____ stones _____ him when he walked _____
the street.
A. threw   B. down   C. at

12 They _____ him to _____ _____ a beard.
A. stop   B. told   C. growing

13 Joseph _____ not _____.
A. mind   B. did

14 He _____ wanted the freedom _____ _____ his beard.
A. have   B. just   C. to

15 _____ day, four men _____ Joseph and _____ him on
the ground.
A. attacked   B. one   C. threw

1 다를 권리

2 여러 면에서 42살의 Joseph Palmer는 평범한 사람이었다.

3 그는 직업이 있었고 가족을 돌보았다.

4 하지만 1830년에 매사추세츠에 있는 작은 도시로 이사를 한 후에 그는 어려움에 직면하기 시작했다.

5 Joseph은 다른 사람들과 달라 보였다. 그는 기다란 턱수염을 기르고 있었다.

6 사람들은 그것을 별로 좋아하지 않았다.

7 마을 사람들은 턱수염을 가진 그 남자를 피했다.

8 그들은 그의 곁에 앉고 싶어 하지 않았다.

9 그들은 심지어 그의 등 뒤에서 "그가 무엇을 숨기려는 거지?" 라고 속삭였다.

10 어떤 이웃들은 그의 창문을 깼다.

11 다른 사람들은 그가 길을 걸어 내려갈 때 그에게 돌을 던졌다.

12 그들은 그에게 턱수염을 그만 기르라고 말했다.

13 Joseph은 신경 쓰지 않았다.

14 그는 그저 자신의 턱수염을 기를 자유를 원했다.

15 어느 날, 네 명의 남자가 Joseph을 공격했고 그를 바닥에 던졌다.

16 "We're going to _____ _____ your beard!" they _____.

    A. cut   B. shouted   C. off

17 Joseph was a big man, and he was _____ to _____ them _____.

    A. fight   B. able   C. off

18 But the men _____ the police and _____ him _____ attacking them.

    A. accused   B. called   C. of

19 Poor Joseph _____ _____.

    A. arrested   B. was

20 He said to the _____, "I'm the _____ here."

    A. victim   B. judge

21 Sadly, no one _____ a man _____ a beard, and he went to _____ for _____ a year.

    A. with   B. over   C. believed   D. prison

22 Joseph's son, Thomas, _____ people to _____ the _____.

    A. know   B. wanted   C. truth

23 He _____ letters _____ newspapers _____ the country.

    A. sent   B. across   C. to

24 People learned that Joseph was _____ _____ just for _____ _____ and his beard.

    A. prison   B. himself   C. protecting   D. in

25 Many people _____ _____ about this, so the judge finally decided to _____ Joseph _____.

    A. angry   B. free   C. set   D. became

26 After he was _____, Joseph _____ and told his story to _____ of people.

    A. freed   B. lots   C. traveled

27 Slowly, people's _____ _____ beards _____.

    A. toward   B. changed   C. attitudes

28 _____ Joseph _____, a man with a _____ became the President of the United States.

    A. died   B. before   C. beard

29 _____ _____ was Abraham Lincoln.

    A. name   B. his

30 He _____ beards _____, but Joseph Palmer _____ for the _____ to have them.

    A. fought   B. right   C. popular   D. made

16 "우리가 당신의 턱수염을 잘라 버리겠어!"라고 그들은 소리쳤다.

17 Joseph은 덩치가 큰 사람이었고, 그는 그들을 싸워 물리칠 수 있었다.

18 하지만 그 남자들은 경찰을 불렀고, 자신들을 공격한 것으로 그를 고발했다.

19 불쌍한 Joseph은 체포되었다.

20 그는 "저는 여기서 희생자입니다."라고 판사에게 말했다.

21 슬프게도, 아무도 턱수염을 가진 남자를 믿지 않았고, 그는 일 년이 넘는 기간 동안 감옥에 갔다.

22 Joseph의 아들인 Thomas는 사람들이 진실을 알기를 원했다.

23 그는 전국에 있는 신문사에 편지를 보냈다.

24 사람들은 Joseph이 단지 자신과 자신의 턱수염을 지키려다 감옥에 갇혔다는 것을 알게 되었다.

25 많은 사람들은 이에 대해 분개했고, 그래서 판사는 결국 Joseph을 석방하기로 결정했다.

26 Joseph은 석방된 뒤에 순회를 하며 많은 사람들에게 자신의 이야기를 전했다.

27 사람들의 턱수염에 대한 태도는 서서히 변해갔다.

28 Joseph이 죽기 전에, 턱수염을 가진 남자가 미국의 대통령이 되었다.

29 그의 이름은 Abraham Lincoln(에이브러햄 링컨)이었다.

30 그는 턱수염을 대중적으로 만들었지만, Joseph Palmer는 그것을 기를 권리를 위하여 싸웠다.

Step2

※ 다음 우리말과 일치하도록 빈칸에 알맞은 말을 쓰시오.

1   The _____ _____

2   _____ _____ _____, 42-year-old Joseph Palmer was _____ _____.

3   He _____ _____ _____ and _____ _____ his family.

4   But in 1830, _____ he _____ _____ a small town in Massachusetts, he began _____ _____ _____.

5   Joseph _____ _____ _____ other people: he had a long beard.

6   People _____ _____ _____ _____ very much.

7   The town's people _____ _____ _____ _____ _____.

8   They did not want _____ _____ _____ _____.

9   They even whispered _____ _____ _____, "What is he _____ _____ _____?"

10   _____ neighbors _____ _____ _____.

11   _____ _____ _____ _____ him when he _____ _____ the street.

12   They _____ him _____ _____ _____ a beard.

13   Joseph _____ _____ _____.

14   He just wanted the _____ _____ _____ his beard.

15   One day, four men _____ Joseph and _____ _____ _____ _____ _____.

1   다를 권리

2   여러 면에서 42살의 Joseph Palmer는 평범한 사람이었다.

3   그는 직업이 있었고 가족을 돌보았다.

4   하지만 1830년에 매사추세츠에 있는 작은 도시로 이사를 한 후에 그는 어려움에 직면하기 시작했다.

5   Joseph은 다른 사람들과 달라 보였다. 그는 기다란 턱수염을 기르고 있었다.

6   사람들은 그것을 별로 좋아하지 않았다.

7   마을 사람들은 턱수염을 가진 그 남자를 피했다.

8   그들은 그의 곁에 앉고 싶어 하지 않았다.

9   그들은 심지어 그의 등 뒤에서 "그가 무엇을 숨기려는 거지?"라고 속삭였다.

10   어떤 이웃들은 그의 창문을 깼다.

11   다른 사람들은 그가 길을 걸어 내려갈 때 그에게 돌을 던졌다.

12   그들은 그에게 턱수염을 그만 기르라고 말했다.

13   Joseph은 신경 쓰지 않았다.

14   그는 그저 자신의 턱수염을 기를 자유를 원했다.

15   어느 날, 네 명의 남자가 Joseph을 공격했고 그를 바닥에 던졌다.

16 "We're going to _____ _____ your beard!" they _____.

17 Joseph was a big man, and he _____ _____ _____ _____ _____ _____.

18 But the men called the police and _____ _____ _____ them.

19 Poor Joseph _____ _____.

20 He said to _____ _____, "I'm _____ _____ here."

21 Sadly, no one believed _____ _____ _____ _____ _____, and he _____ _____ _____ _____ for over a year.

22 Joseph's son, Thomas, _____ people _____ _____ the truth.

23 He _____ letters _____ newspapers _____ _____ _____.

24 People learned that Joseph _____ _____ _____ just for _____ _____ and his beard.

25 Many people _____ _____ about this, so the judge finally _____ _____ _____ _____ Joseph _____.

26 After he _____ _____, Joseph traveled and told his story to _____ _____ people.

27 Slowly, people's _____ _____ _____ _____ _____.

28 _____ Joseph _____, a man _____ _____ _____ became the President of the United States.

29 _____ _____ was Abraham Lincoln.

30 He _____ _____ _____, but Joseph Palmer _____ the _____ _____ _____ them.

16 "우리가 당신의 턱수염을 잘라 버리겠어!"라고 그들은 소리쳤다.

17 Joseph은 덩치가 큰 사람이었고, 그는 그들을 싸워 물리칠 수 있었다.

18 하지만 그 남자들은 경찰을 불렀고, 자신들을 공격한 것으로 그를 고발했다.

19 불쌍한 Joseph은 체포되었다.

20 그는 "저는 여기서 희생자입니다."라고 판사에게 말했다.

21 슬프게도, 아무도 턱수염을 가진 남자를 믿지 않았고, 그는 일 년이 넘는 기간 동안 감옥에 갔다.

22 Joseph의 아들인 Thomas는 사람들이 진실을 알기를 원했다.

23 그는 전국에 있는 신문사에 편지를 보냈다.

24 사람들은 Joseph이 단지 자신과 자신의 턱수염을 지키려다 감옥에 갇혔다는 것을 알게 되었다.

25 많은 사람들은 이에 대해 분개했고, 그래서 판사는 결국 Joseph을 석방하기로 결정했다.

26 Joseph은 석방된 뒤에 순회를 하며 많은 사람들에게 자신의 이야기를 전했다.

27 사람들의 턱수염에 대한 태도는 서서히 변해갔다.

28 Joseph이 죽기 전에, 턱수염을 가진 남자가 미국의 대통령이 되었다.

29 그의 이름은 Abraham Lincoln (에이브러햄 링컨)이었다.

30 그는 턱수염을 대중적으로 만들었지만, Joseph Palmer는 그것을 기를 권리를 위하여 싸웠다.

Step3

※ 다음 문장을 우리말로 쓰시오.

1 The Right To Be Different

➡ _____

2 In many ways, 42-year-old Joseph Palmer was an ordinary person.

➡ _____

3 He had a job and cared for his family.

➡ _____

4 But in 1830, after he moved to a small town in Massachusetts, he began to face difficulties.

➡ _____

5 Joseph looked different from other people: he had a long beard.

➡ _____

6 People did not like it very much.

➡ _____

7 The town's people avoided the man with a beard.

➡ _____

8 They did not want to sit next to him.

➡ _____

9 They even whispered behind his back, "What is he trying to hide?"

➡ _____

10 Some neighbors broke his windows.

➡ _____

11 Others threw stones at him when he walked down the street.

➡ _____

12 They told him to stop growing a beard.

➡ _____

13 Joseph did not mind.

➡ _____

14 He just wanted the freedom to have his beard.

➡ _____

15 One day, four men attacked Joseph and threw him on the ground.

➡ _____

16 "We're going to cut off your beard!" they shouted.

➡ _____

17 Joseph was a big man, and he was able to fight them off.

➡ _____

18 But the men called the police and accused him of attacking them.

➡ _____

19 Poor Joseph was arrested.

➡ _____

20 He said to the judge, "I'm the victim here."

➡ _____

21 Sadly, no one believed a man with a beard, and he went to prison for over a year.

➡ _____

22 Joseph's son, Thomas, wanted people to know the truth.

➡ _____

23 He sent letters to newspapers across the country.

➡ _____

24 People learned that Joseph was in prison just for protecting himself and his beard.

➡ _____

25 Many people became angry about this, so the judge finally decided to set Joseph free.

➡ _____

26 After he was freed, Joseph traveled and told his story to lots of people.

➡ _____

27 Slowly, people's attitudes toward beards changed.

➡ _____

28 Before Joseph died, a man with a beard became the President of the United States.

➡ _____

29 His name was Abraham Lincoln.

➡ _____

30 He made beards popular, but Joseph Palmer fought for the right to have them.

➡ _____

※ 다음 괄호 안의 단어들을 우리말에 맞도록 바르게 배열하시오.

1 (Right / The / Different / Be / To)

➡ _____

2 (many / in / ways, / Joseph / 42-year-old / Palmer / an / was / person. / ordinary)

➡ _____

3 (had / he / job / a / and / for / cared / family. / his)

➡ _____

4 (in / but / 1830, / he / after / to / moved / small / a / town / Massachusetts, / in / began / he / difficulties. / face / to)

➡ _____

5 (looked / Joseph / from / different / people: / other / had / he / beard. / long / a)

➡ _____

6 (did / people / like / not / much. / it / very)

➡ _____

7 (town's / the / people / avoided / man / the / beard. / a / with)

➡ _____

8 (did / they / want / not / sit / to / him. / to / next)

➡ _____

9 (even / they / behind / whispered / back, / his / "what / he / is / hide?" / to / trying)

➡ _____

10 (neighbors / some / windows. / his / broke)

➡ _____

11 (threw / others / at / stones / him / when / walked / he / street. / the / down)

➡ _____

12 (told / they / to / him / growing / stop / beard. / a)

➡ _____

13 (did / Joseph / mind. / not)

➡ _____

14 (just / he / wanted / freedom / the / have / to / beard. / his)

➡ _____

15 (day, / one / men / four / Joseph / attacked / and / him / threw / ground. / the / on)

➡ _____

1 다를 권리

2 여러 면에서 42살의 Joseph Palmer는 평범한 사람이었다.

3 그는 직업이 있었고 가족을 돌보았다.

4 하지만 1830년에 매사추세츠에 있는 작은 도시로 이사를 한 후에 그는 어려움에 직면하기 시작했다.

5 Joseph은 다른 사람들과 달라 보였다. 그는 기다란 턱수염을 기르고 있었다.

6 사람들은 그것을 별로 좋아하지 않았다.

7 마을 사람들은 턱수염을 가진 그 남자를 피했다.

8 그들은 그의 곁에 앉고 싶어 하지 않았다.

9 그들은 심지어 그의 등 뒤에서 "그가 무엇을 숨기려는 거지?"라고 속삭였다.

10 어떤 이웃들은 그의 창문을 깼다.

11 다른 사람들은 그가 길을 걸어 내려갈 때 그에게 돌을 던졌다.

12 그들은 그에게 턱수염을 그만 기르라고 말했다.

13 Joseph은 신경 쓰지 않았다.

14 그는 그저 자신의 턱수염을 기를 자유를 원했다.

15 어느 날, 네 명의 남자가 Joseph을 공격했고 그를 바닥에 던졌다.

16 (going / "we're / cut / to / your / off / beard!" / shouted. / they)
➡ _____

17 (was / Joseph / big / a / man, / and / was / he / to / able / off. / them / fight)
➡ _____

18 (the / but / called / men / police / the / and / him / accused / of / them / attacking)
➡ _____

19 (Joseph / poor / arrested. / was)
➡ _____

20 (said / he / the / to / judge, / "I'm / the / here." / victim)
➡ _____

21 (no / sadly, / one / a / believed / man / with / beard, / a / and / went / he / prison / to / for / year. / a / over)
➡ _____

22 (son, / Joseph's / Thomas, / people / wanted / know / to / truth. / the)
➡ _____

23 (sent / he / letters / newspapers / to / country. / the / across)
➡ _____

24 (learned / people / Joseph / that / in / was / prison / just / protecting / for / himself / beard. / his / and)
➡ _____

25 (people / many / angry / became / this, / about / so / judge / the / decided / finally / set / to / free. / Joseph)
➡ _____

26 (he / after / freed, / was / Joseph / and / traveled / told / story / his / people. / of / lots / to)
➡ _____

27 (people's / slowly, / attitudes / beards / changed. / toward)
➡ _____

28 (Joseph / before / died, / man / a / with / beard / a / became / President / the / of / States. / United / the)
➡ _____

29 (name / his / Lincoln. / Abraham)
➡ _____

30 (made / he / popular, / beards / but / Palmer / Joseph / for / fought / right / the / them. / have / to)
➡ _____

16 "우리가 당신의 턱수염을 잘라 버리겠어!"라고 그들은 소리쳤다.

17 Joseph은 덩치가 큰 사람이었고, 그는 그들을 싸워 물리칠 수 있었다.

18 하지만 그 남자들은 경찰을 불렀고, 자신들을 공격한 것으로 그를 고발했다.

19 불쌍한 Joseph은 체포되었다.

20 그는 "저는 여기서 희생자입니다."라고 판사에게 말했다.

21 슬프게도, 아무도 턱수염을 가진 남자를 믿지 않았고, 그는 일 년이 넘는 기간 동안 감옥에 갔다.

22 Joseph의 아들인 Thomas는 사람들이 진실을 알기를 원했다.

23 그는 전국에 있는 신문사에 편지를 보냈다.

24 사람들은 Joseph이 단지 자신과 자신의 턱수염을 지키려다 감옥에 갇혔다는 것을 알게 되었다.

25 많은 사람들은 이에 대해 분개했고, 그래서 판사는 결국 Joseph을 석방하기로 결정했다.

26 Joseph은 석방된 뒤에 순회를 하며 많은 사람들에게 자신의 이야기를 전했다.

27 사람들의 턱수염에 대한 태도는 서서히 변해갔다.

28 Joseph이 죽기 전에, 턱수염을 가진 남자가 미국의 대통령이 되었다.

29 그의 이름은 Abraham Lincoln (에이브러햄 링컨)이었다.

30 그는 턱수염을 대중적으로 만들었지만, Joseph Palmer는 그것을 기를 권리를 위하여 싸웠다.

※ 다음 우리말을 영어로 쓰시오.

1 다를 권리

➡ _____

2 여러 면에서 42살의 Joseph Palmer는 평범한 사람이었다.

➡ _____

3 그는 직업이 있었고 가족을 돌보았다.

➡ _____

4 하지만 1830년에 매사추세츠에 있는 작은 도시로 이사를 한 후에 그는 어려움에 직면하기 시작했다.

➡ _____

5 Joseph은 다른 사람들과 달라 보였다. 그는 기다란 턱수염을 기르고 있었다.

➡ _____

6 사람들은 그것을 별로 좋아하지 않았다.

➡ _____

7 마을 사람들은 턱수염을 가진 그 남자를 피했다.

➡ _____

8 그들은 그의 곁에 앉고 싶어 하지 않았다.

➡ _____

9 그들은 심지어 그의 등 뒤에서 "그가 무엇을 숨기려는 거지?"라고 속삭였다.

➡ _____

10 어떤 이웃들은 그의 창문을 깼다.

➡ _____

11 다른 사람들은 그가 길을 걸어 내려갈 때 그에게 돌을 던졌다.

➡ _____

12 그들은 그에게 턱수염을 그만 기르라고 말했다.

➡ _____

13 Joseph은 신경 쓰지 않았다.

➡ _____

14 그는 그저 자신의 턱수염을 기를 자유를 원했다.

➡ _____

15 어느 날, 네 명의 남자가 Joseph을 공격했고 그를 바닥에 던졌다.

➡ _____

16 "우리가 당신의 턱수염을 잘라 버리겠어!"라고 그들은 소리쳤다.

➡ _____

17 Joseph은 덩치가 큰 사람이었고, 그는 그들을 싸워 물리칠 수 있었다.

➡ _____

18 하지만 그 남자들은 경찰을 불렀고, 자신들을 공격한 것으로 그를 고발했다.

➡ _____

19 불쌍한 Joseph은 체포되었다.

➡ _____

20 그는 "저는 여기서 희생자입니다."라고 판사에게 말했다.

➡ _____

21 슬프게도, 아무도 턱수염을 가진 남자를 믿지 않았고, 그는 일 년이 넘는 기간 동안 감옥에 갔다.

➡ _____

22 Joseph의 아들인 Thomas는 사람들이 진실을 알기를 원했다.

➡ _____

23 그는 전국에 있는 신문사에 편지를 보냈다.

➡ _____

24 사람들은 Joseph이 단지 자신과 자신의 턱수염을 지키려다 감옥에 갇혔다는 것을 알게 되었다.

➡ _____

25 많은 사람들은 이에 대해 분개했고, 그래서 판사는 결국 Joseph을 석방하기로 결정했다.

➡ _____

26 Joseph은 석방된 뒤에 순회를 하며 많은 사람들에게 자신의 이야기를 전했다.

➡ _____

27 사람들의 턱수염에 대한 태도는 서서히 변해갔다.

➡ _____

28 Joseph이 죽기 전에, 턱수염을 가진 남자가 미국의 대통령이 되었다.

➡ _____

29 그의 이름은 Abraham Lincoln(에이브러햄 링컨)이었다.

➡ _____

30 그는 턱수염을 대중적으로 만들었지만, Joseph Palmer는 그것을 기를 권리를 위하여 싸웠다.

➡ _____

※ 다음 우리말과 일치하도록 빈칸에 알맞은 말을 쓰시오.

My Speaking Portfolio

1. I _____ _____ for Han Siwon.

2. She _____ _____ and _____ .

3. She _____ school _____ _____ a safe place.

4. I _____ _____ her.

5. I like her promises _____ _____ no more _____ .

6. I _____ Han Siwon _____ the next school president.

7. I really want my school _____ _____ _____ _____

    _____ .

1. 나는 한시원을 뽑을 겁니다.
2. 그녀는 자신감 있고 똑똑해 보입니다.
3. 그녀는 학교가 안전한 장소가 되어야 한다고 생각합니다.
4. 저는 그녀에게 동의합니다.
5. 나는 집단 괴롭힘 없애기 같은 공약들이 좋습니다.
6. 나는 한시원이 다음 학생회장이 되길 바랍니다.
7. 나는 우리 학교가 더 안전한 장소가 되길 정말 바랍니다.

My Writing Portfolio: My Book Report

1. The _____ _____ _____ Different

2. A Story _____ Joseph Palmer

3. I read the story _____ Joseph Palmer _____ _____ .

4. I _____ _____ it.

5. I _____ _____ the story _____ we should not judge people

    by their _____ .

6. Students _____ _____ about other people's appearance

    _____ read the story.

7. _____, I _____ _____ _____ about it.

8. _____ did Joseph Palmer want _____ _____ _____

    _____ ?

1. 다른 권리
2. Joseph Palmer에 관한 이야기
3. 나는 지난주에 Joseph Palmer에 관한 이야기를 읽었다.
4. 나는 그게 정말 재미있었다.
5. 나는 그 이야기로부터 우리는 사람들을 외모로 판단해서는 안 된다는 것을 배웠다.
6. 다른 사람들의 외모에 관해 이야기하는 학생들은 이 이야기를 꼭 읽어야 한다.
7. 하지만, 나는 그것에 관한 질문이 하나 있다.
8. Joseph Palmer는 왜 턱수염을 기르고 싶었을까?

Words in Action

1. _____ _____ the travel fair. _____ is _____ .

2. What countries do you _____ _____ _____ ?

3. _____ you want _____ _____ South America, you can

    _____ _____ the booths on the left.

4. If you _____ _____ , you can have drinks and _____

    _____ _____ .

1. 여행 박람회에 오신 것을 환영합니다. 입장료는 무료입니다.
2. 여러분은 어떤 나라들을 마음에 두고 있나요?
3. 여러분이 남아메리카를 방문하고 싶다면, 왼쪽에 있는 부스들을 살펴볼 수 있습니다.
4. 배가 고파진다면, 음료와 간단한 간식을 드실 수 있습니다.

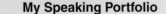

※ 다음 우리말을 영어로 쓰시오.

My Speaking Portfolio

1. 나는 한시원을 뽑을 겁니다.
   ➡ _____

2. 그녀는 자신감 있고 똑똑해 보입니다.
   ➡ _____

3. 그녀는 학교가 안전한 장소가 되어야 한다고 생각합니다.
   ➡ _____

4. 저는 그녀에게 동의합니다.
   ➡ _____

5. 나는 집단 괴롭힘 없애기 같은 공약들이 좋습니다.
   ➡ _____

6. 나는 한시원이 다음 학생회장이 되길 바랍니다.
   ➡ _____

7. 나는 우리 학교가 더 안전한 장소가 되길 정말 바랍니다.
   ➡ _____

My Writing Portfolio: My Book Report

1. 다를 권리
   ➡ _____

2. Joseph Palmer에 관한 이야기
   ➡ _____

3. 나는 지난주에 Joseph Palmer에 관한 이야기를 읽었다.
   ➡ _____

4. 나는 그게 정말 재미있었다.
   ➡ _____

5. 나는 그 이야기로부터 우리는 사람들을 외모로 판단해서는 안 된다는 것을 배웠다.
   ➡ _____

6. 다른 사람들의 외모에 관해 이야기하는 학생들은 이 이야기를 꼭 읽어야 한다.
   ➡ _____

7. 하지만, 나는 그것에 관한 질문이 하나 있다.
   ➡ _____

8. Joseph Palmer는 왜 턱수염을 기르고 싶었을까?
   ➡ _____

Words in Action

1. 여행 박람회에 오신 것을 환영합니다. 입장료는 무료입니다.
   ➡ _____

2. 여러분은 어떤 나라들을 마음에 두고 있나요?
   ➡ _____

3. 여러분이 남아메리카를 방문하고 싶다면, 왼쪽에 있는 부스들을 살펴볼 수 있습니다.
   ➡ _____

4. 배가 고파진다면, 음료와 간단한 간식을 드실 수 있습니다.
   ➡ _____

※ 다음 영어를 우리말로 쓰시오.

01	trash		23	repair	
02	common		24	suggestion	
03	pour		25	receipt	
04	traditional		26	sadness	
05	discussion		27	tear	
06	share		28	understand	
07	experience		29	secret	
08	feed		30	bowl	
09	truth		31	promise	
10	wrong		32	listener	
11	guest		33	text	
12	scared		34	either	
13	refund		35	take care of	
14	training		36	tell a lie	
15	salty		37	drop by	
16	exchange		38	be in trouble	
17	stuff		39	give it a try	
18	upset		40	break down	
19	work		41	on one's own	
20	without		42	not ~ anymore	
21	message		43	be sure to	
22	teenage		44	find out	

※ 다음 우리말을 영어로 쓰시오.

01 강아지	_____
02 제안, 의견	_____
03 훈련, 훈육	_____
04 약속하다	_____
05 잘못된	_____
06 비밀	_____
07 쓰레기	_____
08 교환; 교환하다	_____
09 사발, 그릇	_____
10 물건	_____
11 ~ 없이	_____
12 전통적인	_____
13 경험	_____
14 고치다	_____
15 겁먹은	_____
16 흔한	_____
17 먹이다	_____
18 손님	_____
19 영수증	_____
20 화난	_____
21 진실, 사실	_____
22 (기계가) 작동하다	_____

23 쏟다, 붓다	_____
24 짠	_____
25 거짓말	_____
26 토론	_____
27 (부정문에서) ~도 역시	_____
28 십 대의	_____
29 공유하다	_____
30 청취자	_____
31 환불, 환불금	_____
32 전갈, 메시지	_____
33 슬픔	_____
34 찢다	_____
35 더 이상 ~ 아니다	_____
36 부수다	_____
37 ~에 들르다	_____
38 ~으로 시작하다	_____
39 반드시 ~하다	_____
40 혼자 힘으로	_____
41 곤경에 처하다	_____
42 ~을 돌보다, ~을 처리하다	_____
43 거짓말하다	_____
44 발견하다, 알아내다	_____

※ 다음 영영풀이에 알맞은 단어를 <보기>에서 골라 쓴 후, 우리말 뜻을 쓰시오.

1 _____ : between 13 and 19 years old: _____

2 _____ : a person who listens: _____

3 _____ : a young dog: _____

4 _____ : to send somebody a written message using a mobile/cell phone:
_____

5 _____ : an idea or a plan that you mention for somebody else to think about:
_____

6 _____ : to restore something that is broken, damaged or torn to good condition:
_____

7 _____ : something that is known about by only a few people and not told to
others: _____

8 _____ : a small machine used for drying your hair by blowing hot air over it:
_____

9 _____ : a piece of paper that shows that goods or services have been paid for:
_____

10 _____ : to give food to a person or an animal: _____

11 _____ : a sum of money that is paid back to you, especially because you paid too
much or because you returned goods to a shop/store: _____

12 _____ : a long vertical solid structure, made of stone, brick or concrete, that
surrounds, divides or protects an area of land: _____

13 _____ : the knowledge and skill that you have gained through doing something for
a period of time: _____

14 _____ : to give something to somebody and at the same time receive the same
type of thing from them: _____

15 _____ : a person that you have invited to your house or to a particular event that
you are paying for: _____

16 _____ : to tell somebody that you will definitely do or not do something, or that
something will definitely happen: _____

보기			
wall	suggestion	refund	exchange
repair	listener	hairdryer	feed
promise	text	secret	teenage
puppy	guest	receipt	experience

※ 다음 우리말과 일치하도록 빈칸에 알맞은 말을 쓰시오.

Communication: Listen – Dialog 1

Minsol: I'm not _____ _____ Buster.

Dad: What's _____?

Minsol: He _____ my homework _____ _____ again.

Dad: Puppies _____ do _____.

Minsol: This is not the first time. _____ I find my _____ in the dog house.

Dad: Please be _____ to him. He's just _____ _____ old.

Minsol: You're _____ nice _____ him! He needs some _____.

Dad: Okay. Let's _____ _____ in _____ _____ weeks.

Communication: Listen – Dialog 2

Mom: Minsu, I'm _____ _____ _____ your dad for a movie.

Minsu: When will you _____ _____, Mom?

Mom: _____ 8 o'clock. Don't forget _____ _____ Buster.

Minsu: Okay.

Mom: _____ _____ to give him some water, _____.

Minsu: No _____.

Mom: One _____ _____. Can you _____ Minsol _____ her science homework? Buster _____ her homework into pieces.

Minsu: Hmm .... Okay. I'll do that.

Communication: Listen – Listen More

(The phone rings.)

Mike: Customer Service. _____ can I _____ _____?

Sora: I _____ a _____ at your _____ last week. I'm not _____ _____ it.

Mike: What is _____ _____?

Sora: It doesn't _____ well. I mean the air isn't hot _____.

Mike: I'm sorry. Do you _____ _____ _____ it?

Sora: Well, can I _____ _____ _____ _____?

Mike: Sure. Will you please _____ our _____ with the dryer?

Sora: Yes, I'll _____ _____ tomorrow afternoon.

Mike: _____ _____ to bring the _____.

Sora: Okay. Thanks.

Minsol: 저는 Buster가 마음에 들지 않아요.

Dad: 무엇이 문제니?

Minsol: Buster가 또 제 숙제를 찢어 놓았어요.

Dad: 강아지들은 종종 그런 일을 저지르지.

Minsol: 이번이 처음이 아니에요. 가끔 저는 제 양말을 개집에서 찾기도 해요.

Dad: Buster에게 잘해 주렴. 태어난 지 다섯 달 밖에 안 되었잖니.

Minsol: 아빠는 그를 너무 다정하게 대해 주세요! 그에게는 훈련이 좀 필요해요.

Dad: 좋아. 몇 주 뒤에 훈련을 시작해 보자꾸나.

Mom: 민수야, 엄마는 아빠랑 영화 보러 나간다.

Minsu: 언제 돌아오실 거예요, 엄마?

Mom: 8시쯤. Buster에게 밥 주는 것 잊지 말렴.

Minsu: 네.

Mom: 물도 꼭 주려무나.

Minsu: 그럴게요.

Mom: 한 가지 더. 민솔이 과학 숙제를 도와줄 수 있겠니? Buster가 민솔이의 숙제를 찢어 놓았거든.

Minsu: 음 …. 알겠어요. 그렇게 할게요.

(전화벨이 울린다.)

Mike: 고객 센터입니다. 어떻게 도와 드릴까요?

Sora: 제가 지난주에 가게에서 헤어드라이어를 샀는데요. 마음에 들지 않네요.

Mike: 무엇이 문제인가요?

Sora: 작동이 잘되지 않아요. 제 말은 충분히 뜨거운 바람이 나오질 않는다는 거예요.

Mike: 죄송합니다. 교환을 원하시나요?

Sora: 음. 환불받을 수 있을까요?

Mike: 물론이죠. 드라이어를 가지고 저희 가게를 방문해 주시겠어요?

Sora: 네. 내일 오후에 들를게요.

Mike: 영수증 가지고 오시는 걸 잊지 마세요.

Sora: 네. 고맙습니다.

My Speaking Portfolio – Step 3

A: I'm _____ _____ _____ _____ my brother.

B: What's _____ _____?

A: He uses the _____ _____ _____ _____ in the morning.

B: I know _____ you _____.

A: What _____ I do?

B: Well, you can _____ _____ _____ and _____ the bathroom first.

A: Okay, I'll _____ it _____ _____.

Wrap Up – Listening ❺

G: You _____ _____, Tommy.

B: I'm _____ _____ _____ Sojin.

G: What's _____ _____ her?

B: She isn't _____ _____ _____ of the group project.

G: I _____ you _____ _____ _____ her.

Wrap Up – Listening ❻

M: _____ you _____ _____ your _____, Suji?

G: Yes, I am, Dad. I'm _____ _____ _____.

M: Do you have _____ _____ _____ you?

G: Yeah, I have it _____ _____ _____.

M: Good. _____ _____ _____ _____ _____ me when you _____ _____ the train station.

G: _____.

A: 나는 내 남동생이 별로 마음에 들지 않아.

B: 뭐가 문제니?

A: 그는 아침에 너무 오랫동안 욕실을 사용해.

B: 네 기분이 어떤지 알아.

A: 내가 무엇을 할 수 있을까?

B: 음, 너는 더 일찍 일어나서 욕실을 먼저 사용할 수 있어.

A: 알겠어, 내가 한번 해 볼게.

여: Tommy야, 기분이 안 좋아 보이는 구나.

남: 나는 소진이 때문에 속상해.

여: 그 애에게 무슨 문제가 있니?

남: 그 애가 모둠 과제에서 맡은 일을 안 해.

여: 내 생각에 너는 그 애랑 이야기를 해 봐야 할 것 같아.

남: 여행 갈 준비 되었니, 수지야?

여: 네, 아빠. 저는 떠날 준비가 되었어요.

남: 표는 네가 가지고 있고?

여: 네, 제 전화기에 저장해 놓았어요.

남: 잘했구나. 기차역에 도착하면 내게 전화하는 걸 잊지 말렴.

여: 물론이죠.

※ 다음 우리말에 맞도록 대화를 영어로 쓰시오.

Communication: Listen – Dialog 1

Minsol: _____

Dad: _____

Minsol: _____

Dad: _____

Minsol: _____

Dad: _____

Minsol: _____

Dad: _____

Minsol: 저는 Buster가 마음에 들지 않아요.

Dad: 무엇이 문제니?

Minsol: Buster가 또 제 숙제를 찢어 놓았어요.

Dad: 강아지들은 종종 그런 일을 저지르지.

Minsol: 이번이 처음이 아니에요. 가끔 저는 제 양말을 개집에서 찾기도 해요.

Dad: Buster에게 잘해 주렴. 태어난 지 다섯 달 밖에 안 되었잖니.

Minsol: 아빠는 그를 너무 다정하게 대해 주세요! 그에게는 훈련이 좀 필요해요.

Dad: 좋아. 몇 주 뒤에 훈련을 시작해 보자꾸나.

Communication: Listen – Dialog 2

Mom: _____

Minsu: _____

Mom: _____

Minsu: _____

Mom: _____

Minsu: _____

Mom: _____

Minsu: _____

Mom: 민수야, 엄마는 아빠랑 영화 보러 나간다.

Minsu: 언제 돌아오실 거예요, 엄마?

Mom: 8시쯤. Buster에게 밥 주는 것 잊지 말렴.

Minsu: 네.

Mom: 물도 꼭 주려무나.

Minsu: 그럴게요.

Mom: 한 가지 더. 민솔이 과학 숙제를 도와줄 수 있겠니? Buster가 민솔이의 숙제를 찢어 놓았거든.

Minsu: 음 …. 알겠어요. 그렇게 할게요.

Communication: Listen – Listen More

(The phone rings.)

Mike: _____

Sora: _____

Mike: _____

Sora: _____

Mike: _____

Sora: _____

Mike: _____

Sora: _____

Mike: _____

Sora: _____

(전화벨이 울린다.)

Mike: 고객 센터입니다. 어떻게 도와드릴까요?

Sora: 제가 지난주에 가게에서 헤어드라이어를 샀는데요. 마음에 들지 않네요.

Mike: 무엇이 문제인가요?

Sora: 작동이 잘되지 않아요. 제 말은 충분히 뜨거운 바람이 나오질 않는다는 거예요.

Mike: 죄송합니다. 교환을 원하시나요?

Sora: 음. 환불받을 수 있을까요?

Mike: 물론이죠. 드라이어를 가지고 저희 가게를 방문해 주시겠어요?

Sora: 네. 내일 오후에 들를게요.

Mike: 영수증 가지고 오시는 걸 잊지 마세요.

Sora: 네. 고맙습니다.

My Speaking Portfolio – Step 3

A: _____

B: _____

A: _____

B: _____

A: _____

B: _____

A: _____

A: 나는 내 남동생이 별로 마음에 들지 않아.
B: 뭐가 문제니?
A: 그는 아침에 너무 오랫동안 욕실을 사용해.
B: 네 기분이 어떤지 알아.
A: 내가 무엇을 할 수 있을까?
B: 음, 너는 더 일찍 일어나서 욕실을 먼저 사용할 수 있어.
A: 알겠어, 내가 한번 해 볼게.

Wrap Up – Listening ❺

G: _____

B: _____

G: _____

B: _____

G: _____

여: Tommy야. 기분이 안 좋아 보이는구나.
남: 나는 소지이 때문에 속상해.
여: 그 애에게 무슨 문제가 있니?
남: 그 애가 모둠 과제에서 맡은 일을 안 해.
여: 내 생각에 너는 그 애랑 이야기를 해 봐야 할 것 같아.

Wrap Up – Listening ❻

M: _____

G: _____

M: _____

G: _____

M: _____

G: _____

남: 여행 갈 준비 되었니, 수지야?
여: 네, 아빠. 저는 떠날 준비가 되었어요.
남: 표는 네가 가지고 있고?
여: 네, 제 전화기에 저장해 놓았어요.
남: 잘했구나. 기차역에 도착하면 내게 전화하는 걸 잊지 말렴.
여: 물론이죠.

※ 다음 우리말과 일치하도록 빈칸에 알맞은 것을 골라 쓰시오.

1 Breeze: Good evening, _____. _____ is _____ DJ, Breeze.

　　A. your　　　　　　B. this　　　　　　C. listeners

2 Today we have _____ _____ _____, Andy Kim.

　　A. special　　　　　B. guest　　　　　C. a

3 He's a _____ _____. _____, Andy.

　　A. welcome　　　　B. artist　　　　　C. hip-hop

4 Andy: Nice _____ meet you and thank you _____ _____ me.

　　A. having　　　　　B. to　　　　　　C. for

5 Breeze: Okay. What do our _____ want to _____ their _____?

　　A. tell　　　　　　B. listeners　　　　C. family

6 This evening we will find _____ _____ _____ some _____ from them.

　　A. out　　　　　　B. letters　　　　　C. reading　　　　D. by

7 Andy, will you _____ _____ _____ the letter _____ a teenage girl?

　　A. with　　　　　　B. start　　　　　C. from　　　　　D. off

8 _____: _____.

　　A. sure　　　　　　B. Andy

9 Andy: Hello. I'm _____ 15-year-old _____ _____ Wonju.

　　A. from　　　　　　B. a　　　　　　C. girl

10 I want _____ _____ you _____ my mom.

　　A. about　　　　　B. tell　　　　　C. to

11 My mom _____ _____ _____ everything for me.

　　A. tries　　　　　　B. do　　　　　　C. to

12 She cleans my room _____ _____ me, so it's sometimes _____ _____ find my stuff.

　　A. asking　　　　　B. to　　　　　C. without　　　　D. hard

13 She also _____ books and makes _____ _____ _____.

　　A. study　　　　　　B. buys　　　　　C. them　　　　　D. me

14 I want to _____ to my mom, "I know you love me, but I'm not a baby _____. Please _____ me _____ care of things myself."

　　A. take　　　　　　B. let　　　　　C. anymore　　　　D. say

15 Breeze: I _____ the _____ _____ when I was in middle school.

A. way   B. felt   C. same

16 Andy: Many moms think their kids are _____ young _____ do _____ on their _____.

A. to   B. too   C. own   D. things

17 I _____ the girl's mom will _____ the _____.

A. get   B. hope   C. message

18 Breeze: _____ _____ I. Andy, will you please _____ the next letter?

A. do   B. read   C. so

19 Andy: Hi. I'm a _____ _____ two _____.

A. of   B. father   C. children

20 _____ is a high school girl, and _____ _____ is a middle school boy.

A. other   B. one   C. the

21 They're _____ _____ _____ _____ with me.

A. busy   B. talk   C. to   D. too

22 When I _____ home from _____, they just say hi and _____ _____ to their rooms.

A. back   B. get   C. go   D. work

23 Sometimes I _____ them about their school _____, but they only _____ short _____.

A. answers   B. life   C. give   D. ask

24 We _____ _____ _____ at the table, _____.

A. either   B. much   C. don't   D. talk

25 I want to _____ to my kids, "I love you so much, and I want to _____ _____ _____ with you."

A. time   B. spend   C. say   D. more

26 Breeze: Andy, did you talk _____ your parents _____ when you were _____?

A. with   B. often   C. younger

27 Andy: Not really. I loved them very much, but I thought they were _____ _____ _____ _____ me.

A. to   B. old   C. too   D. understand

28 Breeze: I see. Does anyone have _____ for the "sad" dad? _____ your _____ to us.

A. suggestions   B. idea   C. text

15 Breeze: 저도 중학교 때 똑같은 기분을 느꼈습니다.

16 Andy: 많은 어머님들이 자녀들이 혼자 힘으로 무언가를 하기에는 너무 어리다고 생각합니다.

17 소녀의 어머님께서 메시지를 들으시길 바랍니다.

18 Breeze: 동감입니다. Andy, 다음 편지를 읽어 주시겠어요?

19 Andy: 안녕하세요. 저는 두 아이의 아버지입니다.

20 한 명은 고등학생인 여자아이이고, 나머지 한 명은 중학생인 남자아이입니다.

21 아이들은 저와 대화를 하기 에는 너무 바쁩니다.

22 제가 일을 하고 집에 돌아오면, 아이들은 그저 인사만 하고 자신의 방으로 돌아갑니다

23 가끔씩 저는 아이들에게 학교생활에 관해 묻기도 하지만, 아이들은 그냥 짤막한 대답만 합니다.

24 우리는 식사 자리에서조차 대화를 많이 하지 않습니다.

25 저는 아이들에게 "너희들을 무척 사랑한단다, 그리고 너희들과 더 많은 시간을 보내고 싶단다."라고 말하고 싶습니다.

26 Breeze: Andy, 어렸을 때 부모님과 자주 대화를 했나요?

27 Andy: 사실 그렇지는 않습니다. 저는 부모님을 무척 사랑하지만, 부모님이 저를 이해해 주시기에는 너무 나이가 들었다고 생각했습니 다.

28 Breeze: 그렇군요. '슬픈' 아빠에게 해 드릴 제안이 있으신 분계신가요? 여러분의 생각을 저희에게 문자로 보내 주세요.

※ 다음 우리말과 일치하도록 빈칸에 알맞은 말을 쓰시오.

1 Breeze: _____ _____, listeners. _____ _____ your DJ, Breeze.

2 Today we have _____ _____ _____, Andy Kim.

3 He's a _____ _____. _____, Andy.

4 Andy: Nice _____ _____ _____ and _____ _____ _____ _____ _____.

5 Breeze: Okay. What do our listeners _____ _____ their family?

6 This evening we will _____ _____ _____ _____ _____ _____ from them.

7 Andy, will you _____ _____ _____ the letter _____ a _____ _____?

8 Andy: _____.

9 Andy: Hello. I'm a _____ girl _____ Wonju.

10 I want _____ _____ _____ about my mom.

11 My mom _____ _____ _____ everything for me.

12 She cleans my room _____ _____ me, so it's sometimes _____ _____ _____ _____ _____ _____.

13 She also _____ books and makes _____ _____ _____ _____.

14 I want _____ _____ to my mom, "I know you love me, but I'm not a baby _____. Please _____ _____ _____ _____ _____ things _____."

1 Breeze: 안녕하세요. 청취자 여러분. 저는 여러분의 디제이, Breeze입니다.

2 오늘은 특별한 손님, Andy Kim 씨를 모셨습니다.

3 그는 힙합 아티스트이시죠. 환영합니다, Andy.

4 Andy: 반갑습니다. 그리고 초대해 주셔서 고맙습니다.

5 Breeze: 네. 우리 청취자분들은 가족에게 무슨 말을 하고 싶어 하실까요?

6 오늘 저녁에 우리는 청취자분들로부터 온 몇몇 편지들을 읽으며 알아보려 합니다.

7 Andy, 십 대 소녀에게서 온 편지로 시작해 주시겠어요?

8 Andy: 알겠습니다.

9 Andy: 안녕하세요. 저는 원주에 사는 15세 소녀입니다.

10 저는 저의 엄마에 관해 이야기하고 싶습니다.

11 엄마는 저를 위해 모든 것을 해 주려고 하십니다.

12 엄마는 제게 물어보지도 않고 방을 청소해 주시고, 그래서 가끔은 제 물건을 찾기가 힘들 때도 있습니다.

13 또 엄마는 책을 사 와서는 저에게 그것들을 공부하라고 시키세요.

14 저는 엄마께 "엄마가 저를 사랑하는 것은 알지만 전 더 이상 아기가 아니에요. 제 일을 스스로 할 수 있게 해 주세요."라고 말씀드리고 싶습니다.

15 Breeze: I felt _____ _____ _____ _____ I was in middle school.

16 Andy: Many moms think their kids are _____ _____ _____ _____ things _____ _____ _____.

17 I hope the girl's mom will _____ _____ _____.

18 Breeze: So _____ _____. Andy, will you please read the next letter?

19 Andy: Hi. I'm a father _____ _____ _____.

20 _____ is a high school girl, and _____ _____ is a middle school boy.

21 They're _____ _____ _____ _____ _____ with me.

22 When I _____ home _____ _____, they just say hi and _____ _____ _____ their rooms.

23 Sometimes I ask _____ about their _____ _____, but they only _____ _____ _____.

24 We _____ _____ _____ at the table, _____.

25 I want to say to my kids, "I love you so much, and I want _____ _____ _____ _____ _____ with you."

26 Breeze: Andy, did you talk with your parents _____ _____ _____ _____ _____?

27 Andy: Not really. I loved _____ very much, but I _____ they were _____ _____ _____ _____ _____ me.

28 Breeze: I see. Does anyone have _____ for the "sad" dad? _____ _____ _____ _____ to us.

15 Breeze: 저도 중학교 때 똑같은 기분을 느꼈습니다.

16 Andy: 많은 어머님들이 자녀들이 혼자 힘으로 무언가를 하기에는 너무 어리다고 생각합니다.

17 소녀의 어머님께서 메시지를 들으시길 바랍니다.

18 Breeze: 동감입니다. Andy, 다음 편지를 읽어 주시겠어요?

19 Andy: 안녕하세요. 저는 두 아이의 아버지입니다.

20 한 명은 고등학생인 여자아이이고, 나머지 한 명은 중학생인 남자아이입니다.

21 아이들은 저와 대화를 하기에는 너무 바쁩니다.

22 제가 일을 하고 집에 돌아오면, 아이들은 그저 인사만 하고 자신의 방으로 돌아갑니다.

23 가끔씩 저는 아이들에게 학교생활에 관해 묻기도 하지만, 아이들은 그냥 짤막한 대답만 합니다.

24 우리는 식사 자리에서조차 대화를 많이 하지 않습니다.

25 저는 아이들에게 "너희들을 무척 사랑한단다, 그리고 너희들과 더 많은 시간을 보내고 싶단다."라고 말하고 싶습니다.

26 Breeze: Andy, 어렸을 때 부모님과 자주 대화를 했나요?

27 Andy: 사실 그렇지는 않습니다. 저는 부모님을 무척 사랑하지만, 부모님이 저를 이해해 주시기에는 너무 나이가 들었다고 생각했습니다.

28 Breeze: 그렇군요. '슬픈' 아빠에게 해 드릴 제안이 있으신 분 계신가요? 여러분의 생각을 저희에게 문자로 보내 주세요.

※ 다음 문장을 우리말로 쓰시오.

1 Breeze: Good evening, listeners. This is your DJ, Breeze.

➡ _____

2 Today we have a special guest, Andy Kim.

➡ _____

3 He's a hip-hop artist. Welcome, Andy.

➡ _____

4 Andy: Nice to meet you and thank you for having me.

➡ _____

5 Breeze: Okay. What do our listeners want to tell their family?

➡ _____

6 This evening we will find out by reading some letters from them.

➡ _____

7 Andy, will you start off with the letter from a teenage girl?

➡ _____

8 Andy: Sure.

➡ _____

9 Andy: Hello. I'm a 15-year-old girl from Wonju.

➡ _____

10 I want to tell you about my mom.

➡ _____

11 My mom tries to do everything for me.

➡ _____

12 She cleans my room without asking me, so it's sometimes hard to find my stuff.

➡ _____

13 She also buys books and makes me study them.

➡ _____

14 I want to say to my mom, "I know you love me, but I'm not a baby anymore. Please let me take care of things myself."

➡ _____

_____

15▷ Breeze: I felt the same way when I was in middle school.

➡ _____

16▷ Andy: Many moms think their kids are too young to do things on their own.

➡ _____

17▷ I hope the girl's mom will get the message.

➡ _____

18▷ Breeze: So do I. Andy, will you please read the next letter?

➡ _____

19▷ Andy: Hi. I'm a father of two children.

➡ _____

20▷ One is a high school girl, and the other is a middle school boy.

➡ _____

21▷ They're too busy to talk with me.

➡ _____

22▷ When I get home from work, they just say hi and go back to their rooms.

➡ _____

23▷ Sometimes I ask them about their school life, but they only give short answers.

➡ _____

24▷ We don't talk much at the table, either.

➡ _____

25▷ I want to say to my kids, "I love you so much, and I want to spend more time with you."

➡ _____

26▷ Breeze: Andy, did you talk with your parents often when you were younger?

➡ _____

27▷ Andy: Not really. I loved them very much, but I thought they were too old to understand me.

➡ _____
_____

28▷ Breeze: I see. Does anyone have suggestions for the "sad" dad? Text your idea to us.

➡ _____

※ 다음 괄호 안의 단어들을 우리말에 맞도록 바르게 배열하시오.

1 (Breeze: / evening, / good / listeners. // is / this / DJ, / your / Breeze.)
➡ _____

2 (we / today / have / a / guest, / special / Kim. / Andy)
➡ _____

3 (a / he's / artist. / hip-hop // Andy. / welcome)
➡ _____

4 (Andy: / to / nice / you / meet / and / you / thank / for / me. / having)
➡ _____

5 (Breeze: / okay. // do / what / listeners / our / to / want / tell / family? / their)
➡ _____

6 (evening / this / will / we / find / by / out / some / reading / from / them. / letters)
➡ _____

7 (Andy, / you / will / off / start / with / letter / the / a / from / girl? / teenage)
➡ _____

8 (Andy: / sure.)
➡ _____

9 (Andy: / hello. // I'm / a / girl / 15-year-old / Wonju. / from)
➡ _____

10 (want / I / tell / to / you / about / mom. / my)
➡ _____

11 (mom / my / to / tries / do / for / me. / everything)
➡ _____

12 (she / my / cleans / room / asking / without / me, / it's / so / sometimes / to / hard / my / stuff. / find)
➡ _____
_____

13 (also / she / books / buys / and / me / makes / them. / study)
➡ _____

14 (I / say / to / want / to / mom, / my / "I / love / you / know / me, / but / not / I'm / anymore. // a / baby // let / please / me / care / of / take / myself." / things)
➡ _____

1 Breeze: 안녕하세요, 청취자 여러분. 저는 여러분의 디제이, Breeze입니다.

2 오늘은 특별한 손님, Andy Kim 씨를 모셨습니다.

3 그는 힙합 아티스트이시죠. 환영합니다, Andy.

4 Andy: 반갑습니다, 그리고 초대해 주셔서 고맙습니다.

5 Breeze: 네. 우리 청취자분들은 가족에게 무슨 말을 하고 싶어하실까요?

6 오늘 저녁에 우리는 청취자분들로부터 온 몇몇 편지들을 읽으며 알아보려 합니다.

7 Andy, 십 대 소녀에게서 온 편지로 시작해 주시겠어요?

8 Andy: 알겠습니다.

9 Andy: 안녕하세요. 저는 원주에 사는 15세 소녀입니다.

10 저는 저의 엄마에 관해 이야기하고 싶습니다.

11 엄마는 저를 위해 모든 것을 해 주려고 하십니다.

12 엄마는 제게 물어보지도 않고 방을 청소해 주시고, 그래서 가끔은 제 물건을 찾기가 힘들 때도 있습니다.

13 또 엄마는 책을 사 와서는 저에게 그것들을 공부하라고 시키세요.

14 저는 엄마께 "엄마가 저를 사랑하는 것은 알지만 전 더 이상 아기가 아니에요. 제 일을 스스로 할 수 있게 해 주세요."라고 말씀드리고 싶습니다.

15 (Breeze: / felt / I / the / way / same / I / when / was / in / school. / middle)

➡ _____

16 (Andy: / moms / many / their / think / kids / too / are / young / do / to / on / things / own. / their)

➡ _____

17 (hope / I / girl's / the / mom / will / the / get / message.)

➡ _____

18 (Breeze: / do / I. / so // Andy, / you / will / read / please / the / letter? / next)

➡ _____

19 (Andy: / hi. // I'm / father / a / two / of / children.)

➡ _____

20 (is / one / high / a / girl, / school / and / other / the / is / school / middle / a / boy.)

➡ _____

21 (too / they're / busy / talk / to / me. / with)

➡ _____

22 (when / get / I / home / work, / from / just / they / hi / say / go / and / to / back / rooms. / their)

➡ _____

23 (I / sometimes / them / ask / their / about / life, / school / they / but / give / only / answers. / short)

➡ _____
_____

24 (don't / we / much / talk / the / at / either. / table,)

➡ _____

25 (want / I / say / to / my / to / kids, / "I / you / love / much, / so / and / want / I / spend / to / time / more / you." / with)

➡ _____
_____

26 (Breeze: / did / Andy, / talk / you / your / with / parents / when / often / were / you / younger?)

➡ _____

27 (Andy: / really. / not // loved / I / very / them / much, / I / but / they / thought / too / were / old / understand / to / me.)

➡ _____

28 (Breeze: / see. / I // anyone / does / suggestions / have / the / for / day? / "sad" // your / text / to / idea / us.)

➡ _____
_____

---

15 Breeze: 저도 중학교 때 똑같은 기분을 느꼈습니다.

16 Andy: 많은 어머님들이 자녀들이 혼자 힘으로 무언가를 하기에는 너무 어리다고 생각합니다.

17 소녀의 어머님께서 메시지를 들으시길 바랍니다.

18 Breeze: 동감입니다. Andy, 다음 편지를 읽어 주시겠어요?

19 Andy: 안녕하세요. 저는 두 아이의 아버지입니다.

20 한 명은 고등학생인 여자아이이고, 나머지 한 명은 중학생인 남자아이입니다.

21 아이들은 저와 대화를 하기에는 너무 바쁩니다.

22 제가 일을 하고 집에 돌아오면, 아이들은 그저 인사만 하고 자신의 방으로 돌아갑니다.

23 가끔씩 저는 아이들에게 학교생활에 관해 묻기도 하지만, 아이들은 그냥 짧막한 대답만 합니다.

24 우리는 식사 자리에서조차 대화를 많이 하지 않습니다.

25 저는 아이들에게 "너희들을 무척 사랑한단다, 그리고 너희들과 더 많은 시간을 보내고 싶단다."라고 말하고 싶습니다.

26 Breeze: Andy, 어렸을 때 부모님과 자주 대화를 했나요?

27 Andy: 사실 그렇지는 않습니다. 저는 부모님을 무척 사랑하지만, 부모님이 저를 이해해 주시기에는 너무 나이가 들었다고 생각했습니다.

28 Breeze: 그렇군요. '슬픈' 아빠에게 해 드릴 제안이 있으신 분 계신가요? 여러분의 생각을 저희에게 문자로 보내 주세요.

※ 다음 우리말을 영어로 쓰시오.

1 Breeze: 안녕하세요, 청취자 여러분. 저는 여러분의 디제이, Breeze입니다.

➡ _____

2 오늘은 특별한 손님, Andy Kim 씨를 모셨습니다.

➡ _____

3 그는 힙합 아티스트이시죠. 환영합니다, Andy.

➡ _____

4 Andy: 반갑습니다, 그리고 초대해 주셔서 고맙습니다.

➡ _____

5 Breeze: 네. 우리 청취자분들은 가족에게 무슨 말을 하고 싶어 하실까요?

➡ _____

6 오늘 저녁에 우리는 청취자분들로부터 온 몇몇 편지들을 읽으며 알아보려 합니다.

➡ _____

7 Andy, 십 대 소녀에게서 온 편지로 시작해 주시겠어요?

➡ _____

8 Andy: 알겠습니다.

➡ _____

9 Andy: 안녕하세요. 저는 원주에 사는 15세 소녀입니다.

➡ _____

10 저는 저의 엄마에 관해 이야기하고 싶습니다.

➡ _____

11 엄마는 저를 위해 모든 것을 해 주려고 하십니다.

➡ _____

12 엄마는 제게 물어보지도 않고 방을 청소해 주시고, 그래서 가끔은 제 물건을 찾기가 힘들 때도 있습니다.

➡ _____

13 또 엄마는 책을 사 와서는 저에게 그것들을 공부하라고 시키세요.

➡ _____

14 저는 엄마께 "엄마가 저를 사랑하는 것은 알지만 전 더 이상 아기가 아니에요. 제 일을 스스로 할 수 있게 해 주세요."라고 말씀드리고 싶습니다.

➡ _____

_____

15 Breeze: 저도 중학교 때 똑같은 기분을 느꼈습니다.

➡ _____

16 Andy: 많은 어머님들이 자녀들이 혼자 힘으로 무언가를 하기에는 너무 어리다고 생각합니다.

➡ _____

17 소녀의 어머님께서 메시지를 들으시길 바랍니다.

➡ _____

18 Breeze: 동감입니다. Andy, 다음 편지를 읽어 주시겠어요?

➡ _____

19 Andy: 안녕하세요. 저는 두 아이의 아버지입니다.

➡ _____

20 한 명은 고등학생인 여자아이이고, 나머지 한 명은 중학생인 남자아이입니다.

➡ _____

21 아이들은 저와 대화를 하기에는 너무 바쁩니다.

➡ _____

22 제가 일을 하고 집에 돌아오면, 아이들은 그저 인사만 하고 자신의 방으로 돌아갑니다.

➡ _____

23 가끔씩 저는 아이들에게 학교생활에 관해 묻기도 하지만, 아이들은 그냥 짤막한 대답만 합니다.

➡ _____

24 우리는 식사 자리에서조차 대화를 많이 하지 않습니다.

➡ _____

25 저는 아이들에게 "너희들을 무척 사랑한단다, 그리고 너희들과 더 많은 시간을 보내고 싶단다."
라고 말하고 싶습니다.

➡ _____

26 Breeze: Andy, 어렸을 때 부모님과 자주 대화를 했나요?

➡ _____

27 Andy: 사실 그렇지는 않습니다. 저는 부모님을 무척 사랑하지만, 부모님이 저를 이해해
주시기에는 너무 나이가 들었다고 생각했습니다.

➡ _____

28 Breeze: 그렇군요. '슬픈' 아빠에게 해 드릴 제안이 있으신 분 계신가요? 여러분의 생각을
저희에게 문자로 보내 주세요.

➡ _____

※ 다음 우리말과 일치하도록 빈칸에 알맞은 말을 쓰시오.

My Writing Portfolio

1. Hello, I am a _____ _____ _____ Busan.

2. I _____ _____ _____ to my brother Jaeho, "Sorry."

3. I _____ Mom _____ _____ last Friday.

4. Mom _____ so _____, so he _____ _____ _____.

5. I was _____ scared _____ say sorry to him _____ _____ _____.

6. I _____ I will _____ _____ his _____ again.

1. 안녕하세요. 저는 부산에 살고 있는 15 살 소녀예요.
2. 저는 저의 오빠 재호에게 "미안해."라 고 말하고 싶어요.
3. 저는 지난주에 오빠의 비밀을 엄마께 말씀드렸어요.
4. 엄마는 정말 화가 나셨고, 오빠는 곧 곤 경에 처했죠.
5. 그 당시에 저는 오빠에게 미안하다고 말하기엔 너무 무서웠어요.
6. 오빠의 비밀을 다시는 이야기하지 않 겠다고 약속할게요.

Have Fun Together

1. I have _____ _____ _____. I have no friends.

2. Everything _____ too small. I don't like this _____ very much.

3. Heungbu is _____ _____ me now. I'm _____ _____ _____ it.

4. Mom _____ _____ _____ home. We're not happy with it.

5. This soup _____ _____, but I can't eat it.

1. 나는 할 일이 없어. 나는 친구가 없어.
2. 모든 것이 너무 작아. 나는 이곳이 별 로 마음에 안 들어.
3. 이제 흥부가 나보다 더 부자야. 나는 그것이 마음에 안 들어.
4. 엄마는 우리가 집을 떠나게 하셨어. 우리는 그것이 마음이 안 들어.
5. 이 수프는 냄새가 좋은데, 나는 그것 을 먹을 수 없어.

Wrap Up – Reading Read and answer 3

1. This is a letter _____ a father _____ wants _____ _____ his experience _____ the "sad" father.

2. My kids and I _____ _____ _____ much.

3. There was a wall _____ us. I wanted to _____ it _____.

4. I _____ _____ _____ more time with my children _____ _____.

5. We played computer games, _____ _____, and _____ _____ together.

6. In this way, I had more _____ _____ _____ _____ them.

7. I _____ _____ _____ more about them.

1. 이것은 '슬픈' 아버지와 경험을 공유하고 싶은 한 아버지로부터 온 편지입니다.
2. 제 아이들과 저는 대화를 많이 하지 않았습니다.
3. 우리 사이에는 벽이 있었어요. 저는 그것을 허물고 싶었습니다.
4. 저는 주말마다 아이들과 더 많은 시간 을 보내려고 노력했어요.
5. 우리는 함께 컴퓨터 게임을 했고, 자 전거를 탔고, 쇼핑을 갔습니다.
6. 이 방법으로 저는 아이들과 이야기할 기회를 더 많이 가졌습니다.
7. 저는 그들을 더 잘 알게 되었죠.

※ 다음 우리말을 영어로 쓰시오.

My Writing Portfolio

1. 안녕하세요. 저는 부산에 살고 있는 15살 소녀예요.
   ➡ _____

2. 저는 저의 오빠 재호에게 "미안해."라고 말하고 싶어요.
   ➡ _____

3. 저는 지난주에 오빠의 비밀을 엄마께 말씀드렸어요.
   ➡ _____

4. 엄마는 정말 화가 나셨고, 오빠는 곤경에 처했죠.
   ➡ _____

5. 그 당시에 저는 오빠에게 미안하다고 말하기엔 너무 무서웠어요.
   ➡ _____

6. 오빠의 비밀을 다시는 이야기하지 않겠다고 약속할게요..
   ➡ _____

Have Fun Together

1. 나는 할 일이 없어. 나는 친구가 없어.
   ➡ _____

2. 모든 것이 너무 작아. 나는 이곳이 별로 마음에 안 들어.
   ➡ _____

3. 이제 흥부가 나보다 더 부자야. 나는 그것이 마음에 안 들어.
   ➡ _____

4. 엄마는 우리가 집을 떠나게 하셨어. 우리는 그것이 마음이 안 들어.
   ➡ _____

5. 이 수프는 냄새가 좋은데, 나는 그것을 먹을 수 없어.
   ➡ _____

Wrap Up – Reading Read and answer 3

1. 이것은 '슬픈' 아버지와 경험을 공유하고 싶은 한 아버지로부터 온 편지입니다.
   ➡ _____

2. 제 아이들과 저는 대화를 많이 하지 않았습니다.
   ➡ _____

3. 우리 사이에는 벽이 있었어요. 저는 그것을 허물고 싶었습니다.
   ➡ _____

4. 저는 주말마다 아이들과 더 많은 시간을 보내려고 노력했어요.
   ➡ _____

5. 우리는 함께 컴퓨터 게임을 했고, 자전거를 탔고, 쇼핑을 갔습니다.
   ➡ _____

6. 이 방법으로 저는 아이들과 이야기할 기회를 더 많이 가졌습니다.
   ➡ _____

7. 저는 그들을 더 잘 알게 되었죠.
   ➡ _____

※ 다음 영어를 우리말로 쓰시오.

01 diary _____

02 matter _____

03 state _____

04 assembly _____

05 way _____

06 traditional _____

07 vote _____

08 Athens _____

09 character _____

10 male _____

11 outdoor _____

12 person _____

13 develop _____

14 final _____

15 hold _____

16 count _____

17 gather _____

18 impossible _____

19 discussion _____

20 meaning _____

21 stay _____

22 about _____

23 almost _____

24 citizen _____

25 Athenian _____

26 question _____

27 sadness _____

28 talent _____

29 gathering place _____

30 take part in _____

31 thousands of _____

32 a lot of _____

33 be busy -ing _____

34 by -ing _____

35 so far _____

36 between A and B _____

37 too ~ to … _____

38 over the age of 20 _____

39 in addition to _____

※ 다음 우리말을 영어로 쓰시오.

01 의미

02 아테네

03 전통적인

04 수를 세다

05 남자의, 수컷의

06 모이다, 집결하다

07 체류, 방문

08 재능

09 토론

10 일기

11 일, 문제, 안건

12 마지막의, 최종의

13 담다, 수용하다

14 집회, 국회, 민회

15 불가능한

16 거의

17 질문하다

18 시민

19 야외의, 실외의

20 약, 대략

21 사람, 인간, 인물

22 투표하다

23 방식

24 개발하다, 발달시키다

25 슬픔

26 아테네 사람

27 등장인물

28 국가

29 모이는 장소

30 지금까지

31 많은

32 수천의

33 ~함으로써

34 ~에 참여하다

35 ~하느라 바쁘다

36 A와 B 사이에

37 20살 이상의

38 너무 ~해서 …하다

39 ~에 더하여, ~일뿐 아니라

※ 다음 영영풀이에 알맞은 단어를 <보기>에서 골라 쓴 후, 우리말 뜻을 쓰시오.

1 _____ : to say numbers: _____

2 _____ : not able to happen: _____

3 _____ : the government of a country: _____

4 _____ : to contain something: _____

5 _____ : a natural ability to do something: _____

6 _____ : to ask someone questions: _____

7 _____ : a period of time that you spend in a place: _____

8 _____ : to choose someone in an election: _____

9 _____ : happening or used outside; not in a building: _____

10 _____ : someone who lives in a particular town or city: _____

11 _____ : typical of or relating to men or boys: _____

12 _____ : a meeting of a large group of people, especially one that happens
              regularly for a particular purpose: _____

보기			
state	outdoor	stay	vote
assembly	impossible	hold	count
male	citizen	question	talent

※ 다음 우리말과 일치하도록 빈칸에 알맞은 것을 골라 쓰시오.

1 A _____ from _____
   A. Athens   B. Diary

2 **1st Day** _ I am _____ my _____ and _____ in _____.
   A. uncle   B. visiting   C. Athens   D. aunt

3 Today I _____ to the Agora in the _____ of the _____.
   A. center   B. went   C. city

4 It is a _____ _____ for _____.
   A. Athenians   B. place   C. gathering

5 There were a _____ of stores, and people were _____ _____ and _____.
   A. talking   B. lot   C. shopping   D. busy

6 **2nd Day** _ My uncle _____ _____ the _____.
   A. Assembly   B. to   C. went

7 Any _____ citizens over the age of 20 can take _____ in the Assembly and _____ on important _____.
   A. vote   B. matters   C. part   D. male

8 After they _____ speak _____ about the _____, they vote by _____ their hands.
   A. matters   B. each   C. showing   D. freely

9 My uncle said, "_____ _____ of hands is _____ impossible."
   A. almost   B. thousands   C. counting

10 **3rd Day** _ I _____ to the Agora _____.
   A. again   B. went

11 I _____ a very interesting discussion _____ a teacher _____ Socrates _____ his students.
   A. named   B. and   C. heard   D. between

---

1 아테네에서 쓴 일기

2 첫째 날: 나는 아테네에 있는 숙부와 숙모 댁을 방문 중이다.

3 오늘은 도시 중심에 있는 아고라에 갔다.

4 아고라는 아테네 사람들이 모이는 장소이다.

5 많은 상점들이 있었고, 사람들은 이야기하고 쇼핑하느라 분주했다.

6 둘째 날: 숙부는 민회로 가셨다.

7 20살 이상의 모든 남자 시민은 민회에 참여하여 중요한 안건에 관해 투표할 수 있다.

8 그들은 각자 안건에 관해 자유롭게 의견을 말한 후, 손을 들어 투표한다.

9 숙부는 "수천 명의 손을 세는 것은 거의 불가능해."라고 말씀하셨다.

10 셋째 날: 나는 또 아고라에 갔다.

11 소크라테스라고 불리는 선생님과 그의 제자들이 나누고 있는 매우 재미있는 토론을 경청했다.

12 Socrates _____ his students _____ the _____ of life.

A. on   B. questioned   C. meaning

13 I was _____ young _____ understand it, but I liked their _____ of _____ matters.

A. way   B. to   C. discussing   D. too

14 **4th Day** _ Today was the _____ day _____ _____.

A. far   B. best   C. so

15 I _____ _____ the Theater _____ Dionysus.

A. to   B. went   C. of

16 At the _____ theater which can _____ about 17,000 people, we _____ *Antigone*, a _____ by Sophocles.

A. watched   B. play   C. outdoor   D. hold

17 In _____ to _____ songs and dances, the _____ had an _____ story.

A. interesting   B. traditional   C. play   D. addition

18 I sat _____ from the _____, but I could feel the _____ _____.

A. characters'   B. stage   C. sadness   D. far

19 **5th Day** _ Today is the _____ day of my _____ Athens.

A. stay   B. final   C. in

20 My aunt and uncle said to me, "You must _____ your _____. You can help _____ Athens a great _____."

A. make   B. develop   C. state   D. talent

21 Now I _____ to _____ to school and _____ a _____ person.

A. better   B. go   C. want   D. become

---

12 소크라테스는 제자들에게 인생의 의미에 관해 질문하였다.

13 나는 그것을 이해하기에 너무 어려웠지만, 나는 그들의 토론 방식이 마음에 들었다.

14 넷째 날: 오늘은 지금까지의 날 중 최고의 날이었다.

15 나는 디오니소스 극장에 갔다.

16 약 17,000 명을 수용할 수 있는 야외 극장에서 소포클레스의 연극 '안티고네'를 관람하였다.

17 전통적으로 있던 노래와 춤에 더하여, '안티고네'에는 흥미로운 이야기가 있었다.

18 나는 무대에서 먼 곳에 앉아 있었지만, 등장인물들의 슬픔을 느낄 수 있었다.

19 다섯째 날: 오늘은 아테네에서 머무는 마지막 날이다.

20 숙부와 숙모는 "네 재능을 개발해야 된다. 너는 아테네를 위대한 국가로 만드는 데에 기여할 수 있어."라고 말씀하셨다.

21 이제 나는 학교에 다니며 더 나은 사람이 되고 싶다.

본문 Test

Step2

※ 다음 우리말과 일치하도록 빈칸에 알맞은 말을 쓰시오.

1 A _____ from _____

2 **1st Day** _ I am _____ my _____ and _____ in _____ .

3 Today I _____ _____ the Agora in the _____ of the city.

4 It is a _____ _____ for Athenians.

5 There _____ _____ _____ _____ stores, and people were _____ _____ and _____ .

6 **2nd Day** _ My uncle _____ _____ the _____ .

7 _____ _____ _____ over the age of 20 can _____ _____ _____ the Assembly and _____ on important _____ .

8 After they _____ speak _____ about the _____ , they _____ _____ _____ their hands.

9 My uncle said, " _____ _____ _____ hands is _____ _____ ."

10 **3rd Day** _ I _____ _____ the Agora _____ .

11 I _____ a very _____ _____ _____ a teacher _____ Socrates _____ his students.

1 아테네에서 쓴 일기

2 첫째 날: 나는 아테네에 있는 숙부와 숙모 댁을 방문 중이다.

3 오늘은 도시 중심에 있는 아고라에 갔다.

4 아고라는 아테네 사람들이 모이는 장소이다.

5 많은 상점들이 있었고. 사람들은 이야기하고 쇼핑하느라 분주했다.

6 둘째 날: 숙부는 민회로 가셨다.

7 20살 이상의 모든 남자 시민은 민회에 참여하여 중요한 안건에 관해 투표할 수 있다.

8 그들은 각자 안건에 관해 자유롭게 의견을 말한 후, 손을 들어 투표한다.

9 숙부는 "수천 명의 손을 세는 것은 거의 불가능해."라고 말씀하셨다.

10 셋째 날: 나는 또 아고라에 갔다.

11 소크라테스라고 불리는 선생님과 그의 제자들이 나누고 있는 매우 재미있는 토론을 경청했다.

12 Socrates _____ his students _____ the _____ _____
_____.

13 I was _____ young _____ understand it, but I liked their
_____ _____ _____ _____.

14 **4th Day** _ Today was the _____ day _____ _____.

15 I _____ _____ the Theater of Dionysus.

16 At the _____ theater _____ can _____ _____ 17,000
people, we _____ *Antigone*, a _____ by Sophocles.

17 _____ _____ _____ _____ songs and dances, the
_____ had an _____ story.

18 I _____ _____ from the _____, but I _____ _____
the _____ _____.

19 **5th Day** _ Today is the _____ _____ of my _____ _____
Athens.

20 My aunt and uncle said to me, "You _____ _____ your
_____. You can _____ _____ Athens a great _____."

21 Now I _____ _____ _____ to school and _____
_____ _____ person.

12 소크라테스는 제자들에게 인생
의 의미에 관해 질문하였다.

13 나는 그것을 이해하기에 너무
어렸지만, 나는 그들의 토론 방
식이 마음에 들었다.

14 넷째 날: 오늘은 지금까지의 날
중 최고의 날이었다.

15 나는 디오니소스 극장에 갔다.

16 약 17,000 명을 수용할 수 있는
야외 극장에서 소포클레스의 연
극 '안티고네'를 관람하였다.

17 전통적으로 있던 노래와 춤에
더하여, '안티고네'에는 흥미로
운 이야기가 있었다.

18 나는 무대에서 먼 곳에 앉아 있
었지만, 등장인물들의 슬픔을
느낄 수 있었다.

19 다섯째 날: 오늘은 아테네에서
머무는 마지막 날이다.

20 숙부와 숙모는 "네 재능을 개발
해야 된다. 너는 아테네를 위대
한 국가로 만드는 데에 기여할
수 있어."라고 말씀하셨다.

21 이제 나는 학교에 다니며 더 나
은 사람이 되고 싶다.

※ 다음 문장을 우리말로 쓰시오.

1 ▷ A Diary from Athens

➡ _____

2 ▷ **1st Day** _ I am visiting my aunt and uncle in Athens.

➡ _____

3 ▷ Today I went to the Agora in the center of the city

➡ _____

4 ▷ It is a gathering place for Athenians.

➡ _____

5 ▷ There were a lot of stores, and people were busy talking and shopping.

➡ _____

6 ▷ **2nd Day** _ My uncle went to the Assembly.

➡ _____

7 ▷ Any male citizens over the age of 20 can take part in the Assembly and vote on important matters.

➡ _____

8 ▷ After they each speak freely about the matters, they vote by showing their hands.

➡ _____

9 ▷ My uncle said, "Counting thousands of hands is almost impossible."

➡ _____

10 ▷ **3rd Day** _ I went to the Agora again.

➡ _____

11 ▷ I heard a very interesting discussion between a teacher named Socrates and his students.

➡ _____

12 ▸ Socrates questioned his students on the meaning of life.

➡ _____

13 ▸ I was too young to understand it, but I liked their way of discussing matters.

➡ _____

14 ▸ **4st Day** _ Today was the best day so far.

➡ _____

15 ▸ I went to the Theater of Dionysus.

➡ _____

16 ▸ At the outdoor theater which can hold about 17,000 people, we watched *Antigone*, a play by Sophocles.

➡ _____

17 ▸ In addition to traditional songs and dances, the play had an interesting story.

➡ _____

18 ▸ I sat far from the stage, but I could feel the characters' sadness.

➡ _____

19 ▸ **5th Day** _ Today is the final day of my stay in Athens.

➡ _____

20 ▸ My aunt and uncle said to me, "You must develop your talent. You can help make Athens a great state."

➡ _____

➡ _____

21 ▸ Now I want to go to school and become a better person.

➡ _____

※ 다음 괄호 안의 단어들을 우리말에 맞도록 바르게 배열하시오.

1 (Diary / A / Athens / from)

➡ _____

2 (Day / 1st / _ / I / visiting / am / aunt / my / and / in / uncle / Athens.)

➡ _____

3 (I / today / to / went / Agora / the / the / in / of / center / city. / the)

➡ _____

4 (is / it / gathering / a / place / Athenians. / for)

➡ _____

5 (were / there / lot / a / of / stores, / and / were / people / talking / busy / shopping. / and)

➡ _____

6 (Day / 2nd / _ / uncle / my / to / went / Assembly. / the)

➡ _____

7 (male / any / over / citizens / the / of / age / can / 20 / part / take / in / Assembly / the / and / on / vote / matters. / important)

➡ _____

_____

8 (they / after / speak / each / about / freely / matters, / the / vote / they / showing / by / hands. / their)

➡ _____

_____

9 (uncle / my / said, / thousands / "counting / hands / of / is / impossible." / almost)

➡ _____

10 (Day / 3rd / _ / went / I / to / again. / Agora / the)

➡ _____

11 (heard / I / very / a / discussion / interesting / a / between / teacher / named / and / Socrates / his / students.)

➡ _____

_____

---

1 아테네에서 쓴 일기

2 첫째 날: 나는 아테네에 있는 숙부와 숙모 댁을 방문 중이다.

3 오늘은 도시 중심에 있는 아고라에 갔다.

4 아고라는 아테네 사람들이 모이는 장소이다.

5 많은 상점들이 있었고, 사람들은 이야기하고 쇼핑하느라 분주했다.

6 둘째 날: 숙부는 민회로 가셨다.

7 20살 이상의 모든 남자 시민은 민회에 참여하여 중요한 안건에 관해 투표할 수 있다.

8 그들은 각자 안건에 관해 자유롭게 의견을 말한 후, 손을 들어 투표한다.

9 숙부는 "수천 명의 손을 세는 것은 거의 불가능해."라고 말씀하셨다.

10 셋째 날: 나는 또 아고라에 갔다.

11 소크라테스라고 불리는 선생님과 그의 제자들이 나누고 있는 매우 재미있는 토론을 경청했다.

12 (questioned / Socrates / students / his / the / on / of / life. / meaning)

  ➡ _____

13 (was / I / to / young / too / understand / it, / I / but / liked / way / their / discussing / of / matters.)

  ➡ _____

    _____

14 (Day / 4th / _ / was / today / best / the / day / far. / so)

  ➡ _____

15 (went / I / the / to / Dionysus. / of / Theater)

  ➡ _____

16 (the / at / theater / outdoor / can / which / about / hold / people, / 17,000 / watched / we *Antigone*, / play / a / Sophocles. / by)

  ➡ _____

    _____

17 (addition / in / traditional / to / dances, / and / songs / play / the / an / had / story. / interesting)

  ➡ _____

    _____

18 (I / far / sat / the / from / stage, / I / but / could / the / feel / sadness. / characters')

  ➡ _____

19 (Day / 5th / _ / is / today / final / the / of / day / stay / my / Athens. / in)

  ➡ _____

20 (aunt / my / and / said / uncle / me, / to / "you / develop / must / talent. / your // can / you / make / help / a / Athens / state." / great)

  ➡ _____

    _____

21 (I / now / to / want / to / go / school / and / become / better / a / person.)

  ➡ _____

---

12 소크라테스는 제자들에게 인생의 의미에 관해 질문하였다.

13 나는 그것을 이해하기에 너무 어렸지만, 나는 그들의 토론 방식이 마음에 들었다.

14 넷째 날: 오늘은 지금까지의 날 중 최고의 날이었다.

15 나는 디오니소스 극장에 갔다.

16 약 17,000 명을 수용할 수 있는 야외 극장에서 소포클레스의 연극 '안티고네'를 관람하였다.

17 전통적으로 있던 노래와 춤에 더하여, '안티고네'에는 흥미로운 이야기가 있었다.

18 나는 무대에서 먼 곳에 앉아 있었지만, 등장인물들의 슬픔을 느낄 수 있었다.

19 다섯째 날: 오늘은 아테네에서 머무는 마지막 날이다.

20 숙부와 숙모는 "네 재능을 개발해야 된다. 너는 아테네를 위대한 국가로 만드는 데에 기여할 수 있어."라고 말씀하셨다.

21 이제 나는 학교에 다니며 더 나은 사람이 되고 싶다.

※ 다음 우리말을 영어로 쓰시오.

1 아테네에서 쓴 일기

➡ _____

2 첫째 날: 나는 아테네에 있는 숙부와 숙모 댁을 방문 중이다.

➡ _____

3 오늘은 도시 중심에 있는 아고라에 갔다.

➡ _____

4 아고라는 아테네 사람들이 모이는 장소이다.

➡ _____

5 많은 상점들이 있었고, 사람들은 이야기하고 쇼핑하느라 분주했다.

➡ _____

6 둘째 날: 숙부는 민회로 가셨다

➡ _____

7 20살 이상의 모든 남자 시민은 민회에 참여하여 중요한 안건에 관해 투표할 수 있다.

➡ _____

8 그들은 각자 안건에 관해 자유롭게 의견을 말한 후, 손을 들어 투표한다.

➡ _____

9 숙부는 "수천 명의 손을 세는 것은 거의 불가능해."라고 말씀하셨다.

➡ _____

10 셋째 날: 나는 또 아고라에 갔다.

➡ _____

11 소크라테스라고 불리는 선생님과 그의 제자들이 나누고 있는 매우 재미있는 토론을 경청했다.

➡ _____

12 소크라테스는 제자들에게 인생의 의미에 관해 질문하였다.

➡ _____

13 나는 그것을 이해하기에 너무 어렸지만, 나는 그들의 토론 방식이 마음에 들었다.

➡ _____

14 넷째 날: 오늘은 지금까지의 날 중 최고의 날이었다.

➡ _____

15 나는 디오니소스 극장에 갔다.

➡ _____

16 약 17,000명을 수용할 수 있는 야외 극장에서 소포클레스의 연극 '안티고네'를 관람하였다.

➡ _____

17 전통적으로 있던 노래와 춤에 더하여, '안티고네'에는 흥미로운 이야기가 있었다.

➡ _____

18 나는 무대에서 먼 곳에 앉아 있었지만, 등장인물들의 슬픔을 느낄 수 있었다.

➡ _____

19 다섯째 날: 오늘은 아테네에서 머무는 마지막 날이다.

➡ _____

20 숙부와 숙모는 "네 재능을 개발해야 된다. 너는 아테네를 위대한 국가로 만드는 데에 기여할 수 있어." 라고 말씀하셨다.

➡ _____

➡ _____

21 이제 나는 학교에 다니며 더 나은 사람이 되고 싶다.

➡ _____

※ 다음 영어를 우리말로 쓰시오.

01 chef

02 pollute

03 boil

04 showtime

05 probably

06 fascinating

07 appear

08 machine

09 education

10 pour

11 select

12 lastly

13 creative

14 movement

15 common

16 alive

17 amusing

18 plate

19 taste

20 develop

21 simple

22 publish

23 usual

24 recipe

25 among

26 remain

27 silly

28 well-known

29 sunscreen

30 translate

31 choose

32 caricature

33 animated movie

34 cartoonist

35 pay for

36 jump out at

37 make fun of

38 can't wait to

39 ups and downs

40 watch out

41 cut A into pieces

42 play a role

43 come together

※ 다음 우리말을 영어로 쓰시오.

01 나타나다, 등장하다
_____

02 요리사
_____

03 오염시키다
_____

04 번역하다
_____

05 창의적인, 독창적인
_____

06 개발하다, 만들다
_____

07 만화가
_____

08 더러운
_____

09 살아 있는
_____

10 교육
_____

11 출판하다
_____

12 볶다, 튀기다
_____

13 마지막으로
_____

14 평소의, 보통의
_____

15 붓다
_____

16 ~ 중에
_____

17 자외선 차단제
_____

18 기계
_____

19 상영 시간
_____

20 어리석은
_____

21 끓이다
_____

22 간단한, 단순한
_____

23 극장 매표소
_____

24 공통의
_____

25 만화영화
_____

26 선택하다
_____

27 조리법, 비법
_____

28 고추
_____

29 접시
_____

30 맛보다, 먹다
_____

31 유명한, 잘 알려진
_____

32 아마도
_____

33 매력적인
_____

34 움직임
_____

35 조심하다
_____

36 역할을 하다
_____

37 ~로 만들어지다
_____

38 살펴보다
_____

39 ~가 기대되다
_____

40 기복
_____

41 ~을 놀리다
_____

42 ~에 대한 돈을 내다
_____

43 모든 연령의
_____

※ 다음 영영풀이에 알맞은 단어를 <보기>에서 골라 쓴 후, 우리말 뜻을 쓰시오.

1 _____ : the act of moving: _____

2 _____ : normal, happening most often: _____

3 _____ : the time when a play, movie, etc., begins: _____

4 _____ : causing laughter: _____

5 _____ : a process of teaching and learning: _____

6 _____ : to start to be seen: _____

7 _____ : showing little thought; foolish: _____

8 _____ : to invent something new: _____

9 _____ : extremely interesting: _____

10 _____ : to be changed from one language to another: _____

11 _____ : to cook something in hot fat or oil: _____

12 _____ : to stay in the same place or in the same condition: _____

13 _____ : a funny drawing of somebody that exaggerates some of their features:

_____

14 _____ : to make information available to people in a book, magazine, or newspaper:

_____

15 _____ : a type of lotion that you put on your skin to protect it from being damaged

by the sun: _____

16 _____ : a professional cook who usually is in charge of a kitchen in a restaurant:

_____

보기			
remain	silly	education	caricature
fascinating	appear	publish	amusing
movement	chef	translate	usual
fry	develop	sunscreen	showtime

※ 다음 우리말과 일치하도록 빈칸에 알맞은 말을 쓰시오.

Communication: Listen – Dialog 1

Jane: Kevin, you _____ _____.

Kevin: Nothing _____. _____ my feelings change _____

_____.

Jane: I understand. Many _____ have _____ _____ _____

in their feelings.

Kevin: Oh, _____?

Jane: _____ _____ _____ the _____ _____ "Shining

Days"?

Kevin: No, _____ _____. _____ do you _____?

Jane: It is about a _____ _____. It _____ _____ you _____

your feelings _____.

Kevin: That _____ good! I'll _____ it.

Communication: Listen – Dialog 2

Emily: Oh, _____ _____ the long _____ at the box office.

Tony: Yeah, there's a _____ _____ over there. _____ _____

the tickets _____ the _____.

Emily: All right. Do you know _____ _____ _____ _____

_____?

Tony: Sure. It's easy. First, _____ a movie and a _____.

Emily: Okay. We can _____ the seven o'clock show. Then _____?

Tony: Well, _____ the number of tickets and _____ our _____.

Emily: Okay. Two tickets, and I want to _____ _____ _____

_____.

Tony: No _____. _____, _____ _____ the tickets.

Emily: It's very _____.

Communication: Listen More

Suji: Good morning, Chef Garcia!

Garcia: Hello, Suji. _____ _____ _____ _____ nacho pizza?

Suji: Nacho pizza? _____, _____ _____.

Garcia: Kids will love it, and I'll tell you _____ _____ _____ it.

Suji: _____ good!

Garcia: It's easy to make. _____, _____ nacho chips _____ a _____ and _____ pizza sauce on them.

Suji: Okay. Let me _____ you _____ the pizza sauce.

Garcia: Thanks. _____, put some ham, onions, and _____ on top.

Suji: Okay. Then?

Garcia: _____ cheese and _____ _____ _____ 12 minutes in the _____.

Suji: I _____ _____ _____ _____ it!

Communicate: Speak

Anna: Do you know _____ _____ make _____ _____?

Jinsu: Sure. It's easy. First, _____ the vegetables _____ small pieces.

Anna: Okay. What do you do _____?

Jinsu: _____ some oil in the pan. Then, _____ the vegetables _____ _____.

Anna: Wow, it's really _____.

Wrap Up – Listening ❺

Judy: _____ you ever _____ _____ Sokcho?

Minsu: Yes, I _____. _____ my uncle lives there, so I visit him _____ _____.

Judy: Really? Then, _____ _____ Mt. Seorak, _____ _____?

Minsu: Yes, I've climbed to the top of the mountain _____.

Wrap Up – Listening ❻

Mike: Today, I'll tell you _____ _____ _____ a bear's face. _____, draw a big _____ for the face. _____, make two circles on top of the face. After that, _____ two circles for its eyes and _____ them black. Then, _____ a small _____ for the nose. _____, _____ a mouth.

Suji: 안녕하세요, Garcia 셰프님!
Garcia: 안녕하세요, 수지 씨. 나초 피자를 만들어 본 적 있나요?
Suji: 나초 피자요? 아뇨, 만들어 본 적 없어요.
Garcia: 아이들이 그걸 매우 좋아할 거예요. 그럼 제가 어떻게 만드는지 알려 드리죠.
Suji: 좋아요!
Garcia: 만들기 쉬워요. 첫째로 접시 위에 나초 칩을 올려놓고 그것들 위에 피자 소스를 바르세요.
Suji: 네, 피자 소스를 제가 도와드릴게요.
Garcia: 고맙습니다. 다음으로 햄, 양파, 피망을 위에 올리세요.
Suji: 네. 그다음에는요?
Garcia: 치즈를 올리고 오븐에서 약 12분 동안 구우세요.
Suji: 빨리 맛보고 싶군요!

Anna: 너는 볶음밥을 만드는 법을 아니?
Jinsu: 물론이야. 그건 쉬워. 먼저 채소를 작은 조각으로 잘라.
Anna: 알았어. 다음엔 뭘 하니?
Jinsu: 팬에 기름을 둘러. 그러고는 채소를 밥과 함께 볶아.
Anna: 와, 정말 간단하구나.

Judy: 너는 속초에 가 본 적이 있니?
Minsu: 응, 가 본 적이 있어. 사실은 내 삼촌이 거기 살아서, 나는 매년 그를 방문해.
Judy: 정말? 그러면, 너는 설악산을 올라 본 적이 있지, 그렇지 않니?
Judy: 응, 그 산의 정상에 올라간 적이 두 번 있어.

Mike: 오늘 나는 곰의 얼굴을 그리는 방법을 네게 말해 줄게. 첫 번째로, 얼굴에 해당하는 큰 원을 그려. 다음에, 얼굴 위에 두 개의 원을 그려. 그 후에 눈에 해당하는 두 개의 원을 그리고 그것들을 검게 색칠해. 그리고 코에 해당하는 작은 원을 그려. 마지막으로 입을 만들어.

대화문 Test

※ 다음 우리말에 맞도록 대화를 영어로 쓰시오.

Communication: Listen – Dialog 1

Jane: _____

Kevin: _____

Jane: _____

Kevin: _____

Jane: _____

Kevin: _____

Jane: _____

_____

Kevin: _____

Jane: Kevin, 너 기분이 안 좋아 보이는 구나.

Kevin: 별거 아니에요. 때때로 제 감정이 많이 바뀌어요.

Jane: 이해한단다. 많은 십 대가 감정의 기복이 있지.

Kevin: 아, 정말요?

Jane: 'Shining Days'라는 만화영화를 본 적이 있니?

Kevin: 아니요, 본 적이 없어요. 왜 물으세요?

Jane: 그건 십 대의 감정에 관한 거야. 그건 네가 네 감정을 더 잘 이해하도록 도와줄 거야.

Kevin: 괜찮은 거 같네요! 그걸 볼게요.

Communication: Listen – Dialog 2

Emily: _____

Tony: _____

_____

Emily: _____

Tony: _____

Emily: _____

Tony: _____

Emily: _____

Tony: _____

Emily: _____

Emily: 아, 극장 매표소에 길게 늘어선 줄을 좀 봐.

Tony: 네, 저쪽에 발매기가 하나 있어요. 저 기계에서 표를 사요.

Emily: 좋아. 그 기계를 어떻게 쓰는지 아니?

Tony: 그럼요. 쉬워요. 먼저, 영화와 상영 시간을 골라요.

Emily: 알았어. 우리는 7시 영화를 볼 수 있겠네. 그리고 뭘 하니?

Tony: 음, 표 매수를 선택하고 우리의 좌석을 골라요.

Emily: 좋아. 표 두 장, 그리고 나는 뒤에 앉고 싶어.

Tony: 좋아요. 마지막으로 표 값을 내요.

Emily: 정말 간단하구나.

Communication: Listen More

Suji: _____

Garcia: _____

Suji: _____

Garcia: _____

Suji: _____

Garcia: _____

Suji: _____

Garcia: _____

Suji: _____

Garcia: _____

Suji: _____

Communicate: Speak

Anna: _____

Jinsu: _____

Anna: _____

Jinsu: _____

Anna: _____

Wrap Up – Listening ❺

Judy: _____

Minsu: _____

Judy: _____

Minsu: _____

Wrap Up – Listening ❻

Mike: _____

_____

_____

Suji: 안녕하세요, Garcia 셰프님!

Garcia: 안녕하세요, 수지 씨. 나초 피자를 만들어 본 석 있나요?

Suji: 나초 피자요? 아뇨, 만들어 본 적 없어요.

Garcia: 아이들이 그걸 매우 좋아할 거예요. 그럼 제가 어떻게 만드는지 알려 드리죠.

Suji: 좋아요!

Garcia: 만들기 쉬워요. 첫째로 접시 위에 나초 칩을 올려놓고 그것들 위에 피자 소스를 바르세요.

Suji: 네, 피자 소스를 제가 도와드릴게요.

Garcia: 고맙습니다. 다음으로 햄, 양파, 피망을 위에 올리세요.

Suji: 네. 그다음에는요?

Garcia: 치즈를 올리고 오븐에서 약 12분 동안 구우세요.

Suji: 빨리 맛보고 싶군요!

Anna: 너는 볶음밥을 만드는 법을 아니?

Jinsu: 물론이야. 그건 쉬워. 먼저 채소를 작은 조각으로 칠라.

Anna: 알았어. 다음엔 뭘 하니?

Jinsu: 팬에 기름을 둘러. 그러고는 채소를 밥과 함께 볶아.

Anna: 와, 정말 간단하구나.

Judy: 너는 속초에 가 본 적이 있니?

Minsu: 응, 가 본 적이 있어. 사실은 내 삼촌이 거기 살아서, 나는 매년 그를 방문해.

Judy: 정말? 그러면, 너는 설악산을 올라 본 적이 있지, 그렇지 않니?

Judy: 응, 그 산의 정상에 올라간 적이 두 번 있어.

Mike: 오늘 나는 곰의 얼굴을 그리는 방법을 네게 밀해 줄게. 첫 번째로, 얼굴에 해당하는 큰 원을 그려. 다음에, 얼굴 위에 두 개의 원을 그려. 그 후에 눈에 해당하는 두 개의 원을 그리고 그것들을 검게 색칠해. 그리고 코에 해당하는 작은 원을 그려. 마지막으로 입을 만들어.

※ 다음 우리말과 일치하도록 빈칸에 알맞은 것을 골라 쓰시오.

1 _____! _____!
A. Land   B. Boat

2 Did you _____ when you _____ the cartoon _____?
A. above   B. saw   C. laugh

3 If _____, the cartoonist was _____.
A. successful   B. so

4 Cartoonists are the people _____ _____ _____.
A. cartoons   B. make   C. who

5 They want to _____ your interest, and usually, _____ you _____ with simple language and _____ drawings.
A. catch   B. laugh   C. creative   D. make

6 People _____ _____ cartoons _____ _____ of years.
A. hundreds   B. made   C. have   D. for

7 There are many _____ of _____, and they play _____ _____.
A. roles   B. types   C. different   D. cartoons

8 _____ form of cartoon _____ a picture with _____ _____ words.
A. few   B. one   C. is   D. a

9 It _____ sometimes _____ a "gag cartoon."
A. called   B. is

10 The cartoonist _____ a funny _____, and the character makes you _____ by doing or _____ silly things.
A. laugh   B. saying   C. character   D. makes

11 _____ type of cartoon _____ a caricature.
A. is   B. another   C. called

12 In a caricature, some _____ of a character are _____ or _____ than _____.
A. bigger   B. parts   C. different   D. usual

13 Look _____ the picture _____ the _____.
A. on   B. at   C. right

14 _____ _____ of the man's face _____ _____ at you?
A. out   B. parts   C. which   D. jump

15 Artists _____ _____ this type of cartoon to _____ _____ of well-known people.
A. used   B. fun   C. have   D. make

16 When _____ cartoon pictures _____ _____ and tell a story, we have a comic _____.
A. together   B. come   C. strip   D. several

1 배다! 육지다!

2 위의 만화를 보고 웃었는가?

3 그랬다면 그 만화가는 성공했다.

4 만화가들은 만화를 만드는 사람들이다.

5 그들은 여러분의 관심을 끌고, 대개는 간단한 말과 독창적인 그림으로 여러분을 웃게 하고 싶어 한다.

6 사람들은 수백 년 동안 만화를 만들어 왔다.

7 만화에는 많은 종류가 있으며, 그것들은 다양한 역할을 한다.

8 만화의 한 형태로 몇 마디 말을 쓴 그림이 있다.

9 간혹 그것은 '개그 만화'라고 불린다.

10 만화가는 웃긴 캐릭터를 만들고, 그 캐릭터는 우스꽝스러운 행동이나 말을 함으로써 여러분을 웃게 만든다.

11 다른 종류의 만화는 캐리커처라고 불린다.

12 캐리커처에서 캐릭터의 어떤 부분은 평소와 다르거나 더 크다.

13 오른쪽의 그림을 보아라.

14 남자 얼굴의 어떤 부분이 여러분에게 분명히 보이는가?

15 미술가들은 유명한 사람들을 풍자하기 위해 이런 종류의 만화를 그려 왔다.

16 몇 가지 만화 그림이 모여서 이야기를 들려주게 되면, 그것이 연재만화가 된다.

17 Comic strips _____ _____ in newspapers _____ many _____.

   A. for   B. been   C. years   D. have

18 They are often _____ _____ _____.

   A. just   B. stories   C. amusing

19 People _____ _____ _____ comic strips for _____.

   A. education   B. have   C. used   D. also

20 Comics can _____ information _____ and _____ to _____.

   A. learn   B. easier   C. make   D. clearer

21 You _____ _____ _____ comic history or science books.

   A. seen   B. probably   C. have

22 You _____ _____ _____ many cartoon movies, or _____ movies, too.

   A. animated   B. surely   C. seen   D. have

23 These are very _____ _____ people of _____ _____.

   A. among   B. ages   C. popular   D. all

24 Movement and sounds are _____ _____ pictures, so they _____ _____.

   A. come   B. added   C. to   D. alive

25 Artists and writers can _____ _____ characters and tell _____ stories _____ animation.

   A. interesting   B. develop   C. through   D. fascinating

26 In the 1990s, a new _____ of cartoon _____ _____.

   A. was   B. type   C. developed

27 It _____ _____ a webtoon.

   A. called   B. is

28 Webtoons _____ _____ online, so you can _____ them anytime, anywhere _____ your phone or computer.

   A. read   B. on   C. published   D. are

29 They are very _____, and some of _____ are _____ made _____ TV dramas or movies.

   A. them   B. into   C. popular   D. even

30 New _____ of cartoons _____ _____ in the future.

   A. appear   B. forms   C. may

31 They could be _____ and even more _____ than now, but one thing will _____ the same: they will help us laugh, _____, and learn.

   A. relax   B. different   C. remain   D. exciting

17 연재만화는 여러 해 동안 신문에 실려 왔다.

18 그것들은 종종 그저 재미있는 이야기이다.

19 사람들은 연재만화를 교육용으로 사용해 오기도 했다.

20 만화는 정보를 더 명료하고 더 배우기 쉽게 만들 수 있다.

21 여러분은 아마 만화 역사책이나 과학책을 본 적이 있을 것이다.

22 여러분은 많은 만화영화도 당연히 봤을 것이다.

23 이것들은 모든 연령대의 사람들에게 매우 인기가 많다.

24 동작이나 소리가 그림에 더해져서 그림들이 생생하게 살아난다.

25 미술가들과 작가들은 매력적인 캐릭터를 개발하고 만화영화 제작을 통해 재미있는 이야기를 들려준다.

26 1990년대에 새로운 형식의 만화가 개발되었다.

27 그건 웹툰이라고 불린다.

28 웹툰은 온라인으로 출판되기 때문에 여러분이 휴대 전화나 컴퓨터로 언제 어디서나 볼 수 있다.

29 그것은 매우 인기가 있고, 그들 가운데 일부는 심지어 텔레비전 드라마나 영화로 만들어지기도 한다.

30 미래에는 새로운 형태의 만화가 나타날지도 모른다.

31 그것은 지금과는 다르고 한층 더 재미있겠지만, 한 가지는 같을 것이다. 그것은 우리가 웃고, 쉬고, 배우도록 도와줄 것이다.

※ 다음 우리말과 일치하도록 빈칸에 알맞은 말을 쓰시오.

1 Boat! _____!

2 Did you _____ _____ you _____ the cartoon _____?

3 If _____, the _____ was _____.

4 Cartoonists are the people _____ _____ _____.

5 They want _____ _____ your interest, and usually, _____ _____ _____ with simple language and _____ _____.

6 People _____ _____ cartoons _____ _____ _____ _____.

7 There are _____ _____ _____ _____, and they play _____ _____.

8 _____ _____ of cartoon _____ a picture with _____ _____ _____.

9 It _____ _____ _____ a "gag cartoon."

10 The cartoonist _____ _____ _____ _____, and the character _____ you _____ by _____ or _____ silly things.

11 _____ type of cartoon _____ _____ a caricature.

12 In a caricature, _____ _____ of a character _____ _____ or _____ _____ _____.

13 _____ _____ the picture _____ the right.

14 _____ _____ of the man's face _____ _____ at you?

15 Artists _____ _____ this type of cartoon _____ _____ _____ _____ _____ _____.

16 When _____ cartoon pictures _____ _____ and tell a story, we have _____ _____ _____.

1 배다! 육지다!

2 위의 만화를 보고 웃었는가?

3 그랬다면 그 만화가는 성공했다.

4 만화가들은 만화를 만드는 사람들이다.

5 그들은 여러분의 관심을 끌고, 대개는 간단한 말과 독창적인 그림으로 여러분을 웃게 하고 싶어 한다.

6 사람들은 수백 년 동안 만화를 만들어 왔다.

7 만화에는 많은 종류가 있으며, 그것들은 다양한 역할을 한다.

8 만화의 한 형태로 몇 마디 말을 쓴 그림이 있다.

9 간혹 그것은 '개그 만화'라고 불린다.

10 만화가는 웃긴 캐릭터를 만들고. 그 캐릭터는 우스꽝스러운 행동이나 말을 함으로써 여러분을 웃게 만든다.

11 다른 종류의 만화는 캐리커처라고 불린다.

12 캐리커처에서 캐릭터의 어떤 부분은 평소와 다르거나 더 크다.

13 오른쪽의 그림을 보아라.

14 남자 얼굴의 어떤 부분이 여러분에게 분명히 보이는가?

15 미술가들은 유명한 사람들을 풍자하기 위해 이런 종류의 만화를 그려 왔다.

16 몇 가지 만화 그림이 모여서 이야기를 들려주게 되면, 그것이 연재만화가 된다.

17 Comic strips _____ _____ in newspapers _____ _____ _____.

18 They are often _____ _____ _____.

19 People _____ _____ _____ comic strips _____ _____.

20 Comics can _____ information _____ and _____ _____ _____.

21 You _____ _____ _____ comic history or science books.

22 You _____ _____ _____ many cartoon movies, or _____ _____, _____.

23 These are very _____ _____.

24 _____ and sounds _____ _____ _____ pictures, so they _____ _____.

25 Artists and writers can _____ _____ _____ and tell _____ stories _____ animation.

26 In the 1990s, a new _____ cartoon _____ _____.

27 It _____ _____ a webtoon.

28 Webtoons _____ _____ online, so you can _____ _____ anytime, anywhere _____ your phone or computer.

29 They are very _____, and some of _____ _____ even _____ _____ TV dramas or movies.

30 New _____ of cartoons _____ _____ in the future.

31 They could be _____ and even more _____ _____ now, but one thing will _____ the same: they will help us _____, _____, and _____.

17 연재만화는 여러 해 동안 신문에 실려 왔다.

18 그것들은 종종 그저 재미있는 이야기이다.

19 사람들은 연재만화를 교육용으로 사용해 오기도 했다.

20 만화는 정보를 더 명료하고 더 배우기 쉽게 만들 수 있다.

21 여러분은 아마 만화 역사책이나 과학책을 본 적이 있을 것이다.

22 여러분은 많은 만화영화도 당연히 봤을 것이다.

23 이것들은 모든 연령대의 사람들에게 매우 인기가 많다.

24 동작이나 소리가 그림에 더해져서 그림들이 생생하게 살아난다.

25 미술가들과 작가들은 매력적인 캐릭터를 개발하고 만화영화 제작을 통해 재미있는 이야기를 들려준다.

26 1990년대에 새로운 형식의 만화가 개발되었다.

27 그건 웹툰이라고 불린다.

28 웹툰은 온라인으로 출판되기 때문에 여러분이 휴대 전화나 컴퓨터로 언제 어디서나 볼 수 있다.

29 그것은 매우 인기가 있고, 그들 가운데 일부는 심지어 텔레비전 드라마나 영화로 만들어지기도 한다.

30 미래에는 새로운 형태의 만화가 나타날지도 모른다.

31 그것은 지금과는 다르고 한층 더 재미있겠지만, 한 가지는 같을 것이다. 그것은 우리가 웃고, 쉬고, 배우도록 도와줄 것이다.

※ 다음 문장을 우리말로 쓰시오.

1   Boat! Land!

➡ _____

2   Did you laugh when you saw the cartoon above?

➡ _____

3   If so, the cartoonist was successful.

➡ _____

4   Cartoonists are the people who make cartoons.

➡ _____

5   They want to catch your interest, and usually, make you laugh with simple language and creative drawings.

➡ _____

6   People have made cartoons for hundreds of years.

➡ _____

7   There are many types of cartoons, and they play different roles.

➡ _____

8   One form of cartoon is a picture with a few words.

➡ _____

9   It is sometimes called a "gag cartoon."

➡ _____

10   The cartoonist makes a funny character, and the character makes you laugh by doing or saying silly things.

➡ _____

11   Another type of cartoon is called a caricature.

➡ _____

12   In a caricature, some parts of a character are different or bigger than usual.

➡ _____

13   Look at the picture on the right.

➡ _____

14   Which parts of the man's face jump out at you?

➡ _____

15   Artists have used this type of cartoon to make fun of well-known people.

➡ _____

16 When several cartoon pictures come together and tell a story, we have a comic strip.

➡ _____

17 Comic strips have been in newspapers for many years.

➡ _____

18 They are often just amusing stories.

➡ _____

19 People have also used comic strips for education.

➡ _____

20 Comics can make information clearer and easier to learn.

➡ _____

21 You have probably seen comic history or science books.

➡ _____

22 You have surely seen many cartoon movies, or animated movies, too.

➡ _____

23 These are very popular among people of all ages.

➡ _____

24 Movement and sounds are added to pictures, so they come alive.

➡ _____

25 Artists and writers can develop fascinating characters and tell interesting stories through animation.

➡ _____

26 In the 1990s, a new type of cartoon was developed.

➡ _____

27 It is called a webtoon.

➡ _____

28 Webtoons are published online, so you can read them anytime, anywhere on your phone or computer.

➡ _____

29 They are very popular, and some of them are even made into TV dramas or movies.

➡ _____

30 New forms of cartoons may appear in the future.

➡ _____

31 They could be different and even more exciting than now, but one thing will remain the same: they will help us laugh, relax, and learn.

➡ _____

_____

※ 다음 괄호 안의 단어들을 우리말에 맞도록 바르게 배열하시오.

1 (land! / boat!)
➡ _____

2 (you / did / when / laugh / saw / you / cartoon / above? / the)
➡ _____

3 (so, / if / cartoonist / the / successful. / was)
➡ _____

4 (are / cartoonists / people / the / make / who / cartoons.)
➡ _____

5 (want / they / catch / to / interest, / your / usually, / and / you / make / laugh / simple / with / language / and / drawings. / creative)
➡ _____

6 (have / people / cartoons / made / hundreds / for / years. / of)
➡ _____

7 (are / there / many / of / types / cartoons, / and / play / they / roles. / different)
➡ _____

8 (form / one / cartoon / of / is / picture / a / with / words. / few / a)
➡ _____

9 (is / it / sometimes / a / called / cartoon." / "gag)
➡ _____

10 (cartoonist / the / a / makes / character, / funny / and / character / the / you / makes / laugh / doing / by / or / silly / things. / saying)
➡ _____
_____

11 (type / another / cartoon / of / called / is / caricature. / a)
➡ _____

12 (a / in / caricature, / parts / some / a / of / character / different / are / than / or / bigger / usual.)
➡ _____

13 (at / look / picture / the / the / right. / on)
➡ _____

14 (parts / which / the / of / face / man's / out / jump / you? / at)
➡ _____

15 (have / artists / used / type / this / of / cartoon / make / to / fun / make / of / people. / well-known)
➡ _____

16 (several / when / pictures / cartoon / together / come / and / a / tell / story, / have / we / comic / a / strip.)
➡ _____
_____

1 배다! 육지다!

2 위의 만화를 보고 웃었는가?

3 그랬다면 그 만화는 성공했다.

4 만화가들은 만화를 만드는 사람들이다.

5 그들은 여러분의 관심을 끌고, 대개는 간단한 말과 독창적인 그림으로 여러분을 웃게 하고 싶어 한다.

6 사람들은 수백 년 동안 만화를 만들어 왔다.

7 만화에는 많은 종류가 있으며, 그것들은 다양한 역할을 한다.

8 만화의 한 형태로 몇 마디 말을 쓴 그림이 있다.

9 간혹 그것은 '개그 만화'라고 불린다.

10 만화가는 웃긴 캐릭터를 만들고, 그 캐릭터는 우스꽝스러운 행동이나 말을 함으로써 여러분을 웃게 만든다.

11 다른 종류의 만화는 캐리커처라고 불린다.

12 캐리커처에서 캐릭터의 어떤 부분은 평소와 다르거나 더 크다.

13 오른쪽의 그림을 보아라.

14 남자 얼굴의 어떤 부분이 여러분에게 분명히 보이는가?

15 미술가들은 유명한 사람들을 풍자하기 위해 이런 종류의 만화를 그려 왔다.

16 몇 가지 만화 그림이 모여서 이야기를 들려주게 되면, 그것이 연재만화가 된다.

17 (strips / comic / been / have / newspapers / in / for / years. / many)
➡ _____

18 (are / they / just / often / stories. / amusing)
➡ _____

19 (have / people / also / comic / used / for / strips / education.)
➡ _____

20 (can / comics / make / clearer / information / and / to / learn. / easier)
➡ _____

21 (have / you / seen / probably / history / comic / or / books. / science)
➡ _____

22 (have / you / seen / surely / cartoon / many / movies, / or / movies, / too. / animated)
➡ _____

23 (are / these / popular / very / people / among / all / of / ages.)
➡ _____

24 (sounds / and / movement / added / are / pictures, / to / they / so / alive. / come)
➡ _____

25 (writers / and / artists / develop / can / characters / fascinating / and / interesting / tell / stories / animation. / through)
➡ _____

26 (the / in /. 1990s, / new / a / of / type / was / cartoon / developed.)
➡ _____

27 (is / it / called / webtoon. / a)
➡ _____

28 (are / webtoons / published / online, / you / so / read / can / anytime. / them / anywhere / your / on / computer. / or / phone)
➡ _____

29 (are / they / popular, / very / some / and / them / of / even / are / into / made / dramas / TV / movies. / or)
➡ _____

30 (forms / new / cartoons / of / appear / may / future. / the / in)
➡ _____

31 (could / they / different / be / even / and / exciting / more / now, / than / one / but / will / thing / remain / same: / the / will / they / us / help / laugh, / and / relax, / learn.)
➡ _____

---

17 연재만화는 여러 해 동안 신문에 실려 왔다.

18 그것들은 종종 그저 재미있는 이야기이다.

19 사람들은 연재만화를 교육용으로 사용해 오기도 했다.

20 만화는 정보를 더 명료하고 더 배우기 쉽게 만들 수 있다.

21 여러분은 아마 만화 역사책이나 과학책을 본 적이 있을 것이다.

22 여러분은 많은 만화영화도 당연히 봤을 것이다.

23 이것들은 모든 연령대의 사람들에게 매우 인기가 많다.

24 동작이나 소리가 그림에 더해져서 그림들이 생생하게 살아난다.

25 미술가들과 작가들은 매력적인 캐릭터를 개발하고 만화영화 제작을 통해 재미있는 이야기를 들려준다.

26 1990년대에 새로운 형식의 만화가 개발되었다.

27 그건 웹툰이라고 불린다.

28 웹툰은 온라인으로 출판되기 때문에 여러분이 휴대 전화나 컴퓨터로 언제 어디서나 볼 수 있다.

29 그것은 매우 인기가 있고, 그들 가운데 일부는 심지어 텔레비전 드라마나 영화로 만들어지기도 한다.

30 미래에는 새로운 형태의 만화가 나타날지도 모른다.

31 그것은 지금과는 다르고 한층 더 재미있겠지만, 한 가지는 같을 것이다. 그것은 우리가 웃고, 쉬고, 배우도록 도와줄 것이다.

※ 다음 우리말을 영어로 쓰시오.

1 배다! 육지다!

➡ _____

2 위의 만화를 보고 웃었는가?

➡ _____

3 그랬다면 그 만화가는 성공했다.

➡ _____

4 만화가들은 만화를 만드는 사람들이다.

➡ _____

5 그들은 여러분의 관심을 끌고, 대개는 간단한 말과 독창적인 그림으로 여러분을 웃게 하고 싶어 한다.

➡ _____

6 사람들은 수백 년 동안 만화를 만들어 왔다.

➡ _____

7 만화에는 많은 종류가 있으며, 그것들은 다양한 역할을 한다.

➡ _____

8 만화의 한 형태로 몇 마디 말을 쓴 그림이 있다.

➡ _____

9 간혹 그것은 '개그 만화'라고 불린다.

➡ _____

10 만화가는 웃긴 캐릭터를 만들고, 그 캐릭터는 우스꽝스러운 행동이나 말을 함으로써 여러분을 웃게 만든다.

➡ _____

11 다른 종류의 만화는 캐리커처라고 불린다.

➡ _____

12 캐리커처에서 캐릭터의 어떤 부분은 평소와 다르거나 더 크다.

➡ _____

13 오른쪽의 그림을 보아라.

➡ _____

14 남자 얼굴의 어떤 부분이 여러분에게 분명히 보이는가?

➡ _____

15 미술가들은 유명한 사람들을 풍자하기 위해 이런 종류의 만화를 그려 왔다.

➡ _____

16 몇 가지 만화 그림이 모여서 이야기를 들려주게 되면, 그것이 연재만화가 된다.

➡ _____

17 연재만화는 여러 해 동안 신문에 실려 왔다.

➡ _____

18 그것들은 종종 그저 재미있는 이야기이다.

➡ _____

19 사람들은 연재만화를 교육용으로 사용해 오기도 했다.

➡ _____

20 만화는 정보를 더 명료하고 더 배우기 쉽게 만들 수 있다.

➡ _____

21 여러분은 아마 만화 역사책이나 과학책을 본 적이 있을 것이다.

➡ _____

22 여러분은 많은 만화영화도 당연히 봤을 것이다.

➡ _____

23 이것들은 모든 연령대의 사람들에게 매우 인기가 많다.

➡ _____

24 동작이나 소리가 그림에 더해져서 그림들이 생생하게 살아난다.

➡ _____

25 미술가들과 작가들은 매력적인 캐릭터를 개발하고 만화영화 제작을 통해 재미있는 이야기를 들려준다.

➡ _____

26 1990년대에 새로운 형식의 만화가 개발되었다.

➡ _____

27 그건 웹툰이라고 불린다.

➡ _____

28 웹툰은 온라인으로 출판되기 때문에 여러분이 휴대 전화나 컴퓨터로 언제 어디서나 볼 수 있다.

➡ _____

29 그것은 매우 인기가 있고, 그들 가운데 일부는 심지어 텔레비전 드라마나 영화로 만들어지기도 한다.

➡ _____

30 미래에는 새로운 형태의 만화가 나타날지도 모른다.

➡ _____

31 그것은 지금과는 다르고 한층 더 재미있겠지만, 한 가지는 같을 것이다. 그것은 우리가 웃고, 쉬고, 배우도록 도와줄 것이다.

➡ _____

_____

※ 다음 우리말과 일치하도록 빈칸에 알맞은 말을 쓰시오.

My Speaking Portfolio – Step 3

1. _____ is a _____ _____ for you.

2. I've _____ my sneakers this way _____ _____.

3. First, put the sneakers, _____ water, and _____ _____ in a plastic bag.

4. _____ close the bag and _____ it _____ _____ _____.

5. _____, take the sneakers _____ _____ the bag and wash _____.

6. They'll _____ _____ new sneakers.

1. 여기 당신을 위한 유용한 조언이 있어요.
2. 나는 내 운동화를 여러 번 이런 방식으로 세탁했어요.
3. 첫째, 운동화, 온수, 그리고 세제를 비닐봉지에 넣으세요.
4. 그리고 비닐봉지를 묶어 7분 동안 두세요.
5. 마지막으로 운동화를 비닐봉지에서 꺼내 씻으세요.
6. 그들은 새 운동화처럼 보일 거예요.

My Writing Portfolio

1. Giyeong, My Favorite _____ _____

2. My _____ _____ _____ is Giyeong of *Black Rubber Shoes*.

3. He is an _____ _____ student. He is _____ and _____.

4. _____, he is not very smart and sometimes _____ _____.

5. I like him _____ he looks on the _____ _____ of everything and always _____ _____ help _____.

1. 기영, 내가 가장 좋아하는 만화 캐릭터
2. 내가 가장 좋아하는 만화 캐릭터는 〈검정 고무신〉의 기영이다.
3. 그는 초등학교 학생이다. 그는 재미있고 친절하다.
4. 하지만, 그는 그렇게 똑똑하진 않고, 때때로 말썽을 피운다.
5. 그는 모든 것의 긍정적인 면을 보고 항상 다른 이들을 도우려 하기 때문에 나는 그를 좋아한다.

Words in Action B

1. The Best _____ _____ for Children's Education

2. Animals welcome the city's plan _____ _____ an amusement park _____ _____ _____.

3. However, they _____ _____ _____ serious _____.

4. An old elephant _____ _____ _____.

5. The animals and the city _____ _____ _____ _____ a better world for everyone.

1. 아이들의 교육을 위한 최고의 만화영화
2. 동물들은 숲속에 놀이공원을 지으려는 도시의 계획을 환영한다.
3. 하지만, 그들은 곧 심각한 오염에 시달린다.
4. 나이 든 코끼리가 한 가지 제안을 한다.
5. 동물들과 도시는 모든 이들을 위한 더 좋은 세상을 만들기 위한 합의에 이른다.

※ 다음 우리말을 영어로 쓰시오.

My Speaking Portfolio – Step 3

1. 여기 당신을 위한 유용한 조언이 있어요.
   ➡ _____

2. 나는 내 운동화를 여러 번 이런 방식으로 세탁했어요.
   ➡ _____

3. 첫째, 운동화, 온수, 그리고 세제를 비닐봉지에 넣으세요.
   ➡ _____

4. 그리고 비닐봉지를 묶어 7분 동안 두세요.
   ➡ _____

5. 마지막으로 운동화를 비닐봉지에서 꺼내 씻으세요.
   ➡ _____

6. 그들은 새 운동화처럼 보일 거예요.
   ➡ _____

My Writing Portfolio

1. 기영, 내가 가장 좋아하는 만화 캐릭터
   ➡ _____

2. 내가 가장 좋아하는 만화 캐릭터는 〈검정 고무신〉의 기영이다.
   ➡ _____

3. 그는 초등학교 학생이다. 그는 재미있고 친절하다.
   ➡ _____

4. 하지만, 그는 그렇게 똑똑진 않고, 때때로 말썽을 피운다.
   ➡ _____

5. 그는 모든 것의 긍정적인 면을 보고 항상 다른 이들을 도우려 하기 때문에 나는 그를 좋아한다.
   ➡ _____

Words in Action B

1. 아이들의 교육을 위한 최고의 만화영화
   ➡ _____

2. 동물들은 숲속에 놀이공원을 지으려는 도시의 계획을 환영한다.
   ➡ _____

3. 하지만, 그들은 곧 심각한 오염에 시달린다.
   ➡ _____

4. 나이 든 코끼리가 한 가지 제안을 한다.
   ➡ _____

5. 동물들과 도시는 모든 이들을 위한 더 좋은 세상을 만들기 위한 합의에 이른다.
   ➡ _____

※ 다음 영어를 우리말로 쓰시오.

01 pilot _____

02 sunrise _____

03 benefit _____

04 prepare _____

05 bridge _____

06 area _____

07 per _____

08 natural _____

09 probably _____

10 capital _____

11 view _____

12 continent _____

13 scared _____

14 similar _____

15 fantastic _____

16 flow _____

17 shy _____

18 sunscreen _____

19 mountain range _____

20 unique _____

21 waterfall _____

22 soil _____

23 ocean _____

24 wonder _____

25 patience _____

26 work of art _____

27 outer space _____

28 especially _____

29 origin _____

30 rainforest _____

31 contain _____

32 sea level _____

33 through _____

34 wide _____

35 go away _____

36 be similar to _____

37 to be honest _____

38 all year round _____

39 be full of _____

40 name after _____

41 by oneself _____

42 throw a party _____

43 by the way _____

※ 다음 우리말을 영어로 쓰시오.

01 준비하다

02 이익, 혜택

03 전망

04 넓은

05 수도

06 경이, 놀라움

07 다리

08 기원, 원산

09 인내심

10 폭포

11 특히

12 해돋이, 일출

13 관광객

14 자외선 차단제

15 환상적인, 엄청난

16 독특한

17 흐르다

18 화성

19 수줍은, 부끄럼 타는

20 산맥

21 비슷한, 유사한

22 ~을 통하여

23 흙, 토양

24 대륙

25 ~당, ~마다

26 지역

27 해수면

28 겁먹은, 무서워하는

29 자연의, 천연의

30 포함하다

31 아마도

32 열대 우림

33 대양

34 건너서, 가로질러

35 ~을 따라 이름 짓다

36 그건 그렇고

37 없어지다

38 일 년 내내, 연중

39 ~으로 가득하다

40 ~와 비슷하다

41 솔직히 말하면

42 파티를 열다

43 혼자서, 홀로

※ 다음 영영풀이에 알맞은 단어를 <보기>에서 골라 쓴 후, 우리말 뜻을 쓰시오.

1 _____ : to make a plan for something that will happen: _____

2 _____ : an advantage that something gives you: _____

3 _____ : a part of country, town: _____

4 _____ : a forest in a tropical area that receives a lot of rain: _____

5 _____ : a large mass of land surrounded by sea: _____

6 _____ : from one side of something to the other: _____

7 _____ : a thing that causes a feeling of great surprise or admiration: _____

8 _____ : the ability to stay calm without becoming angry: _____

9 _____ : the top layer of the earth in which plants and trees grow: _____

10 _____ : existing in nature; not made or caused by humans: _____

11 _____ : a large area of land that has very little water and very few plants growing
on it: _____

12 _____ : measuring a large distance from one side to the other: _____

13 _____ : the point from which something starts; the cause of something:
_____

14 _____ : a person who operates the controls of an aircraft, especially as a job:
_____

15 _____ : a place where a stream or river falls from a high place, for example over
a cliff or rock: _____

16 _____ : a structure built over something such as a river so that people or vehicles
can get across: _____

※ 다음 우리말과 일치하도록 빈칸에 알맞은 말을 쓰시오.

Communication: Listen – Dialog 1

Sujin: Dad, I like this _____ _____.

Dad: I'm _____ you _____ it.

Sujin: _____ _____ _____, do you know _____ the tomato _____ _____ _____?

Dad: Italy or _____ _____ _____?

Sujin: No, the tomato _____ _____ _____ _____.

Dad: Really? _____ did you know that?

Sujin: I learned it from Ms. Song, my _____ _____ teacher.

Dad: That's good.

Sujin: 아빠, 저는 이 토마토 수프가 마음에 들어요.
Dad: 네가 좋아하니 기쁘구나.
Sujin: 그런데 아빠는 토마토가 처음에 어디에서 재배되었는지 아세요?
Dad: 이탈리아나 유럽 어딘가가 아닐까?
Sujin: 아니에요. 토마토는 남아메리카에서 왔어요.
Dad: 정말? 너는 그걸 어떻게 알았니?
Sujin: 저는 그걸 사회 선생님이신 송 선생님께 배웠어요.
Dad: 훌륭하구나.

Communication: Listen – Dialog 2

Jenny: _____ you _____ the pictures Ms. Song _____?

Brian: _____ pictures?

Jenny: She _____ _____ South America _____ _____ last summer.

Brian: Really? What a _____!

Jenny: She _____ _____ _____ of beautiful places. I _____ liked the pictures of _____.

Brian: _____ _____ pyramids in _____ _____?

Jenny: Yes. She said some pyramids are _____ 3,800 meters _____ _____ _____.

Brian: I _____ _____ _____.

Jenny: 너 송 선생님께서 찍은 사진들을 봤니?
Brian: 무슨 사진?
Jenny: 선생님께서는 지난여름에 혼자 남아메리카로 여행을 다녀오셨대.
Brian: 정말? 그것 참 놀랍다!
Jenny: 선생님께서 우리들에게 아름다운 장소들의 사진을 보여 주셨어. 나는 특히 피라미드 사진이 마음에 들더라.
Brian: 남아메리카에 피라미드가 있어?
Jenny: 응. 선생님께서 몇몇 피라미드는 해발 3,800미터 정도에 위치하고 있다고 하셨어.
Brian: 정말 놀랍다.

Communication: Listen More

Hana: _____ _____ the roller coaster ride, Jongha?

Jongha: It was _____ . I _____ _____ it.

Hana: Ha ha. You _____ your eyes _____ _____ .

Jongha: Did you see? _____ _____ _____ , I was really _____

_____ _____ .

Hana: Do you know _____ _____ this roller coaster _____ ?

Jongha: I have _____ _____ .

Hana: It goes _____ _____ _____ 140 km per hour.

Jongha: Wow! That's _____ !

Hana: _____ _____ it one more time!

Jongha: Look at the _____ . We can't ride it _____ 8 p.m.

Hana: Oh, _____ _____ _____ .

Communicate: Speak

Amy: Do you know _____ _____ _____ _____ _____

_____ ?

Jinsu: I have _____ _____ . What is it?

Amy: It's Lima.

Jinsu: I _____ _____ that.

Wrap Up – Listening ❺

Jack: Do you know Junha _____ _____ _____ ?

Minji: No. _____ did he get it? From a _____ _____ ?

Jack: No. I _____ he got the puppy from his _____ .

Minji: I _____ one, _____ .

Wrap Up – Listening ❻

Mike: Do you know Sumin _____ _____ _____ at the speech

contest?

Sue: I can't believe it. She was very _____ and _____ last year.

Mike: Yeah. She _____ the drama club this year, and she _____

_____ _____ _____ .

Sue: I see. I _____ _____ _____ the club, _____ .

Hana: 롤러코스터 어땠어, 종하야?
Jongha: 신나더라. 난 정말 재미있었어.
Hana: 하하. 너는 타는 동안에 눈을 감고 있던걸.
Jongha: 봤어? 솔직히 말하면 처음에는 정말 무서웠어.
Hana: 너 이 롤러코스터가 얼마나 빠른지 알고 있니?
Jongha: 모르겠어.
Hana: 이건 시속 140km로 달린대.
Jongha: 와! 정말 놀랍다!
Hana: 우리 한 번 더 타자!
Jongha: 표지판을 봐. 저녁 8시 이후에는 그것을 탈 수 없어.
Hana: 아, 다음에 타지 뭐.

Amy: 너는 페루의 수도가 어디인지 알고 있니?
Jinsu: 아니 모르겠어. 어디야?
Amy: 리마야.
Jinsu: 그건 몰랐네.

Jack: 너는 준하에게 강아지가 생긴 걸 알고 있니?
Minji: 아니. 어디에서 났대? 애완동물 가게에서?
Jack: 아니. 나는 그가 강아지를 삼촌 댁에서 얻었다고 들었어.
Minji: 나도 강아지를 키우고 싶다.

Mike: 너는 수민이가 말하기 대회에서 우승한 걸 알고 있니?
Sue: 그것 참 놀랍다. 작년에 그 애는 정말 조용하고 수줍음이 많았는데.
Mike: 맞아. 그 애가 올해 연극 동아리에 가입했는데, 많이 바뀌었대.
Sue: 그렇구나. 나도 그 동아리에 가입하고 싶다.

※ 다음 우리말에 맞도록 대화를 영어로 쓰시오.

Communication: Listen – Dialog 1

Sujin: _____

Dad: _____

Sujin: _____

Dad: _____

Sujin: _____

Dad: _____

Sujin: _____

Dad: _____

Sujin: 아빠, 저는 이 토마토 수프가 마음에 들어요.
Dad: 네가 좋아하니 기쁘구나.
Sujin: 그런데 아빠는 토마토가 처음에 어디에서 재배되었는지 아세요?
Dad: 이탈리아나 유럽 어딘가가 아닐까?
Sujin: 아니에요, 토마토는 남아메리카에서 왔어요.
Dad: 정말? 너는 그걸 어떻게 알았니?
Sujin: 저는 그걸 사회 선생님이신 송 선생님께 배웠어요.
Dad: 훌륭하구나.

Communication: Listen – Dialog 2

Jenny: _____

Brian: _____

Jenny: _____

Brian: _____

Jenny: _____
_____

Brian: _____

Jenny: _____

Brian: _____

Jenny: 너 송 선생님께서 찍은 사진들을 봤니?
Brian: 무슨 사진?
Jenny: 선생님께서는 지난여름에 혼자 남아메리카로 여행을 다녀오셨대.
Brian: 정말? 그것 참 놀랍다!
Jenny: 선생님께서 우리들에게 아름다운 장소들의 사진을 보여 주셨어. 나는 특히 피라미드 사진이 마음에 들더라.
Brian: 남아메리카에 피라미드가 있어?
Jenny: 응. 선생님께서 몇몇 피라미드는 해발 3,800미터 정도에 위치하고 있다고 하셨어.
Brian: 정말 놀랍다.

Communication: Listen More

Hana: _____
Jongha: _____
Hana: _____
Jongha: _____
Hana: _____
Jongha: _____
Hana: _____
Jongha: _____
Hana: _____
Jongha: _____
Hana: _____

Hana: 롤러코스터 어땠어, 좋하야?
Jongha: 신나더라. 난 정말 재미있었어.
Hana: 하하. 너는 타는 동안에 눈을 감고 있던걸.
Jongha: 봤어? 솔직히 말하면 처음에는 정말 무서웠어.
Hana: 너 이 롤러코스터가 얼마나 빠른지 알고 있니?
Jongha: 모르겠어.
Hana: 이건 시속 140km로 달린대.
Jongha: 와! 정말 놀랍다!
Hana: 우리 한 번 더 타자!
Jongha: 표지판을 봐. 저녁 8시 이후에는 그것을 탈 수 없어.
Hana: 아, 다음에 타지 뭐.

Communicate: Speak

Amy: _____
Jinsu: _____
Amy: _____
Jinsu: _____

Amy: 너는 페루의 수도가 어디인지 알고 있니?
Jinsu: 아니 모르겠어. 어디야?
Amy: 리마야.
Jinsu: 그건 몰랐네.

Wrap Up – Listening ❺

Jack: _____
Minji: _____
Jack: _____
Minji: _____

Jack: 너는 준하에게 강아지가 생긴 걸 알고 있니?
Minji: 아니. 어디에서 났대? 애완동물 가게에서?
Jack: 아니. 나는 그가 강아지를 삼촌 댁에서 얻었다고 들었어.
Minji: 나도 강아지를 키우고 싶다.

Wrap Up – Listening ❻

Mike: _____
Sue: _____
Mike: _____
Sue: _____

Mike: 너는 수민이가 말하기 대회에서 우승한 걸 알고 있니?
Sue: 그것 참 놀랍다. 작년에 그 애는 정말 조용하고 수줍음이 많았는데.
Mike: 맞아. 그 애가 올해 연극 동아리에 가입했는데, 많이 바뀌었대.
Sue: 그렇구나. 나도 그 동아리에 가입하고 싶다.

Step1

※ 다음 우리말과 일치하도록 빈칸에 알맞은 것을 골라 쓰시오.

1 Do you know _____ the _____ _____ on Earth is?

A. driest   B. where   C. desert

2 How _____ _____ _____ waterfall?

A. highest   B. about   C. the

3 Yes, _____ are _____ in _____ America.

A. both   B. they   C. South

4 This continent is _____ of natural _____ _____ will _____ you.

A. wonders   B. full   C. surprise   D. that

5 The Atacama is _____ _____ _____ on Earth.

A. desert   B. driest   C. the

6 In some _____, it _____ almost no rain at _____ — only 1–3 millimeters _____ year!

A. all   B. per   C. gets   D. parts

7 The ground in some _____ is _____ dry _____ no plants can _____.

A. that   B. so   C. grow   D. areas

8 Do you know _____ do in a _____ place?

A. dry   B. such   C. what   D. scientists

9 The soil in this desert is very _____ to the soil on Mars, _____ they _____ for tips to _____ space.

A. prepare   B. similar   C. outer   D. so

10 The Atacama is also _____ of the _____ _____ on Earth to _____ stars.

A. places   B. one   C. best   D. watch

11 _____ you go _____ Venezuela, you can see the _____ _____ waterfall.

A. highest   B. world's   C. to   D. if

12 It is 979 _____ _____.

A. high   B. meters

13 Clouds often _____ the top, so you need _____ and a little _____ to get a good _____.

A. view   B. patience   C. luck   D. cover

14 Actually, the waterfall is _____ _____ Jimmie Angel, a pilot from the United States who first _____ _____ the waterfall in 1933.

A. after   B. flew   C. named   D. over

1 여러분은 지구에서 가장 건조한 사막이 어디인지 알고 있나요?

2 가장 높은 폭포는 어떠한가요?

3 그렇습니다, 그것들은 둘 다 남아메리카에 있습니다.

4 이 대륙은 여러분을 놀라게 할 자연 경관으로 가득하답니다.

5 아타카마 사막은 지구에서 가장 건조한 사막입니다.

6 몇몇 지역은 비가 전혀 오지 않아서, 연간 강수량이 1~3mm에 그칩니다!

7 어떤 지역의 토양은 너무 건조해서 어떤 식물도 자랄 수가 없습니다.

8 이처럼 건조한 곳에서 과학자들이 무슨 일을 하는지 알고 있나요?

9 이 사막의 토양은 화성의 토양과 아주 비슷해서, 그들은 우주로의 여행을 준비합니다.

10 또한 아타카마 사막은 지구에서 별을 관측하기에 가장 좋은 장소 가운데 하나이기도 합니다.

11 여러분이 베네수엘라에 간다면, 세계에서 가장 높은 폭포를 볼 수 있을 것입니다.

12 그것은 높이가 979m입니다.

13 구름이 꼭대기 부분을 자주 에워싸기 때문에, 멋진 경치를 보려면 인내심과 약간의 운이 필요합니다.

14 사실 그 폭포는 1933년에 처음으로 폭포 너머 비행을 한 미국의 비행사 Jimmie Angel에게서 이름을 따왔습니다.

15 You can still _____ _____ the _____ of the beautiful waterfall only _____ plane.

    A. by   B. get   C. top   D. to

16 The Amazon _____ _____ the continent _____ seven countries.

    A. across   B. through   C. runs

17 It _____ _____ Peru in the west and _____ _____ the Atlantic Ocean.

    A. flows   B. travels   C. into   D. from

18 The Amazon River is _____ _____ many _____.

    A. ways   B. interesting   C. in

19 For the _____ part, it has _____ _____.

    A. no   B. most   C. bridges

20 That is _____ it usually _____ _____ rainforests and _____ areas, not cities or towns.

    A. through   B. because   C. runs   D. wet

21 Also, in many _____ the river is very _____, so you cannot see the _____ _____!

    A. wide   B. other   C. places   D. side

22 You _____ do not want to _____ _____ this river.

    A. swim   B. probably   C. in

23 It is _____ to some very big snakes and fish _____ eat _____.

    A. that   B. home   C. meat

24 The Andes are _____ _____ _____ mountain _____.

    A. longest   B. range   C. world's   D. the

25 Do you know _____ _____ the _____ _____ is?

    A. range   B. long   C. how   D. mountain

26 It is _____ 7,000 kilometers _____!

    A. long   B. about

27 It also _____ the highest _____ _____ of Asia.

    A. mountains   B. contains   C. outside

28 _____ a _____ of the _____ in South America live in the Andes.

    A. third   B. about   C. people

29 Many _____ animals _____ _____ there.

    A. live   B. unique   C. also

---

15 여전히 비행기로만 그 아름다운 폭포의 꼭대기에 갈 수 있습니다.

16 아마존강은 일곱 개의 나라를 거쳐 대륙을 가로질러 흐릅니다.

17 그것은 서쪽의 페루에서 시작하여 대서양으로 흘러갑니다.

18 아마존강은 많은 점에서 흥미롭습니다.

19 강의 대부분에는 다리가 없습니다.

20 그것은 강이 대개 도시나 마을이 아닌, 열대 우림과 습지를 지나 흐르기 때문입니다.

21 또한 많은 곳에서 강이 너무 넓어서 그 건너편을 볼 수조차 없습니다!

22 여러분은 아마도 이 강에서 헤엄치고 싶지 않을 것입니다.

23 이곳은 몇몇 아주 큰 뱀과 고기를 먹는 물고기들의 서식지입니다.

24 안데스 산맥은 세계에서 가장 긴 산맥입니다.

25 여러분은 그 산맥의 길이가 얼마인지 아시나요?

26 그것은 약 7,000km입니다.

27 또한 그곳에는 아시아 외의 지역에서 가장 높은 산이 있습니다.

28 남아메리카 인구의 3분의 1 정도가 안데스 산맥에 살고 있습니다.

29 그리고 독특한 동물들이 많이 서식하고 있기도 합니다.

Step2

※ 다음 우리말과 일치하도록 빈칸에 알맞은 말을 쓰시오.

1 Do you know _____ _____ _____ _____ on Earth is?

2 How _____ _____ _____ _____?

3 Yes, _____ _____ _____ in South America.

4 This continent _____ _____ _____ natural wonders _____ _____ _____ you.

5 The Atacama is _____ _____ _____ on Earth.

6 In some parts, _____ _____ almost no rain _____ _____ — only 1–3 millimeters _____ _____!

7 The ground in some areas _____ _____ _____ _____ no plants _____ _____.

8 Do you know _____ _____ _____ in _____ _____ _____ _____?

9 The soil in this desert is very _____ _____ the soil on Mars, so _____ _____ _____ _____ to _____ _____.

10 The Atacama is also _____ _____ on Earth _____ _____ _____.

11 If you go to Venezuela, you can _____ _____ _____ _____ _____.

12 _____ is 979 _____ _____.

13 Clouds often _____ the top, so you need _____ and a little _____ to get a _____ _____.

14 Actually, the waterfall is _____ _____ Jimmie Angel, a pilot from the United States _____ first _____ over the waterfall in 1933.

1 여러분은 지구에서 가장 건조한 사막이 어디인지 알고 있나요?

2 가장 높은 폭포는 어떠한가요?

3 그렇습니다. 그것들은 둘 다 남 아메리카에 있습니다.

4 이 대륙은 여러분을 놀라게 할 자연 경관으로 가득하답니다.

5 아타카마 사막은 지구에서 가장 건조한 사막입니다.

6 몇몇 지역은 비가 전혀 오지 않 아서, 연간 강수량이 1~3mm에 그칩니다!

7 어떤 지역의 토양은 너무 건조 해서 어떤 식물도 자랄 수가 없 습니다.

8 이처럼 건조한 곳에서 과학자들 이 무슨 일을 하는지 알고 있나 요?

9 이 사막의 토양은 화성의 토양 과 아주 비슷해서, 그들은 우주 로의 여행을 준비합니다.

10 또한 아타카마 사막은 지구에서 별을 관측하기에 가장 좋은 장 소 가운데 하나이기도 합니다.

11 여러분이 베네수엘라에 간다면, 세계에서 가장 높은 폭포를 볼 수 있을 것입니다.

12 그것은 높이가 979m입니다.

13 구름이 꼭대기 부분을 자주 에 워싸기 때문에, 멋진 경치를 보 려면 인내심과 약간의 운이 필 요합니다.

14 사실 그 폭포는 1933년에 처음 으로 폭포 너머 비행을 한 미국 의 비행사 Jimmie Angel에게서 이름을 따왔습니다.

15 You can _____ _____ _____ the top of the beautiful waterfall _____ _____ _____.

16 The Amazon _____ _____ the continent _____ seven countries.

17 It _____ _____ Peru in the west and _____ _____ the _____ _____.

18 The Amazon River _____ _____ in _____ _____.

19 For the most part, it has _____ _____.

20 That is _____ _____ _____ _____ _____ rainforests and _____ _____, not cities or towns.

21 Also, in many places the river is very wide, so you cannot _____ _____ _____ _____!

22 You _____ do not want to _____ _____ this river.

23 It is _____ to some very big snakes and fish _____ eat meat.

24 The Andes are _____ _____ _____ _____ _____.

25 Do you know _____ _____ is?

26 It is _____ 7,000 kilometers _____!

27 It also _____ the highest _____ _____ of Asia.

28 About _____ _____ _____ _____ _____ in South America _____ _____ the Andes.

29 Many _____ _____ also _____ _____.

15 여전히 비행기로만 그 아름다운 폭포의 꼭대기에 갈 수 있습니다.

16 아마존강은 일곱 개의 나라를 거쳐 대륙을 가로질러 흐릅니다.

17 그것은 서쪽의 페루에서 시작하여 대서양으로 흘러갑니다.

18 아마존강은 많은 점에서 흥미롭습니다.

19 강의 대부분에는 다리가 없습니다.

20 그것은 강이 대개 도시나 마을이 아닌, 열대 우림과 습지를 지나 흐르기 때문입니다.

21 또한 많은 곳에서 강이 너무 넓어서 그 건너편을 볼 수조차 없습니다!

22 여러분은 아마도 이 강에서 헤엄치고 싶지 않을 것입니다.

23 이곳은 몇몇 아주 큰 뱀과 고기를 먹는 물고기들의 서식지입니다.

24 안데스 산맥은 세계에서 가장 긴 산맥입니다.

25 여러분은 그 산맥의 길이가 얼마인지 아시나요?

26 그것은 약 7,000km입니다.

27 또한 그곳에는 아시아 외의 지역에서 가장 높은 산이 있습니다.

28 남아메리카 인구의 3분의 1 정도가 안데스 산맥에 살고 있습니다.

29 그리고 독특한 동물들이 많이 서식하고 있기도 합니다.

※ 다음 문장을 우리말로 쓰시오.

1 Do you know where the driest desert on Earth is?

➡ _____

2 How about the highest waterfall?

➡ _____

3 Yes, they are both in South America.

➡ _____

4 This continent is full of natural wonders that will surprise you.

➡ _____

5 The Atacama is the driest desert on Earth.

➡ _____

6 In some parts, it gets almost no rain at all — only 1–3 millimeters per year!

➡ _____

7 The ground in some areas is so dry that no plants can grow.

➡ _____

8 Do you know what scientists do in such a dry place?

➡ _____

9 The soil in this desert is very similar to the soil on Mars, so they prepare for trips to outer space.

➡ _____

10 The Atacama is also one of the best places on Earth to watch stars.

➡ _____

11 If you go to Venezuela, you can see the world's highest waterfall.

➡ _____

12 It is 979 meters high.

➡ _____

13 Clouds often cover the top, so you need patience and a little luck to get a good view.

➡ _____

14 Actually, the waterfall is named after Jimmie Angel, a pilot from the United States who first flew over the waterfall in 1933.

➡ _____

15 ▸ You can still get to the top of the beautiful waterfall only by plane.

➡ _____

16 ▸ The Amazon runs across the continent through seven countries.

➡ _____

17 ▸ It travels from Peru in the west and flows into the Atlantic Ocean.

➡ _____

18 ▸ The Amazon River is interesting in many ways.

➡ _____

19 ▸ For the most part, it has no bridges.

➡ _____

20 ▸ That is because it usually runs through rainforests and wet areas, not cities or towns.

➡ _____

21 ▸ Also, in many places the river is very wide, so you cannot see the other side!

➡ _____

22 ▸ You probably do not want to swim in this river.

➡ _____

23 ▸ It is home to some very big snakes and fish that eat meat.

➡ _____

24 ▸ The Andes are the world's longest mountain range.

➡ _____

25 ▸ Do you know how long the mountain range is?

➡ _____

26 ▸ It is about 7,000 kilometers long!

➡ _____

27 ▸ It also contains the highest mountains outside of Asia.

➡ _____

28 ▸ About a third of the people in South America live in the Andes.

➡ _____

29 ▸ Many unique animals also live there.

➡ _____

※ 다음 괄호 안의 단어들을 우리말에 맞도록 바르게 배열하시오.

1 (you / do / know / where / the / desert / driest / on / is? / Earth)
➡ _____

2 (about / how / the / waterfall? / highest)
➡ _____

3 (yes, / are / they / borth / South / in / America.)
➡ _____

4 (continent / this / is / of / full / wonders / natural / will / that / you. / surpeise)
➡ _____

5 (Atacama / the / is / the / desert / driest / Earth. / on)
➡ _____

6 (some / in / parts, / gets / it / no / almost / rain / all / at / — / 1-3 / only / per / millimeters / year!)
➡ _____

7 (ground / the / some / in / areas / is / dry / so / no / that / plants / grow. / can)
➡ _____

8 (you / do / what / know / do / scientists / in / do / such / place? / dry / a)
➡ _____

9 (soil / the / this / in / desert / very / is / to / similar / soil / the / Mars, / on / so / prepare / they / trips / for / outer / to / space.)
➡ _____

10 (Atacama / the / also / is / of / one / best / the / places / Earth / on / stars. / watch / to)
➡ _____

11 (you / if / to / go / Venezuela, / you / see / can / world's / the / waterfall. / highest)
➡ _____

12 (is / it / meters / 979 / high.)
➡ _____

13 (often / clouds / the / cover / top, / you / so / patience / need / and / little / a / to / luck / get / view. / good / a)
➡ _____

14 (actually, / waterfall / the / named / is / after / Angel, / Jimmie / pilot / a / from / United / the / States / first / who / over / flew / waterfall / the / 1933. / in)
➡ _____

1 여러분은 지구에서 가장 건조한 사막이 어디인지 알고 있나요?

2 가장 높은 폭포는 어떠한가요?

3 그렇습니다. 그것들은 둘 다 남 아메리카에 있습니다.

4 이 대륙은 여러분을 놀라게 할 자연 경관으로 가득하답니다.

5 아타카마 사막은 지구에서 가장 건조한 사막입니다.

6 몇몇 지역은 비가 전혀 오지 않아서, 연간 강수량이 1~3mm에 그칩니다!

7 어떤 지역의 토양은 너무 건조해서 어떤 식물도 자랄 수가 없습니다.

8 이처럼 건조한 곳에서 과학자들이 무슨 일을 하는지 알고 있나요?

9 이 사막의 토양은 화성의 토양과 아주 비슷해서, 그들은 우주로의 여행을 준비합니다.

10 또한 아타카마 사막은 지구에서 별을 관측하기에 가장 좋은 장소 가운데 하나이기도 합니다.

11 여러분이 베네수엘라에 간다면, 세계에서 가장 높은 폭포를 볼 수 있을 것입니다.

12 그것은 높이가 979m입니다.

13 구름이 꼭대기 부분을 자주 에워싸기 때문에, 멋진 경치를 보려면 인내심과 약간의 운이 필요합니다.

14 시실 그 폭포는 1933년에 처음으로 폭포 너머 비행을 한 미국의 비행사 Jimmie Angel에게서 이름을 따왔습니다.

15 (can / you / get / still / to / top / the / of / beautiful / the / waterfall / by / plane. / only)

➡ _____

16 (Amazon / the / across / runs / the / through / continent / countries. / seven)

➡ _____

17 (travels / it / Peru / from / the / in / west / and / into / flows / Atlantic / the / Ocean.)

➡ _____

18 (Amazon / the / River / is / interesting / many / ways. / in)

➡ _____

19 (the / for / part, / most / has / it / bridges. / no)

➡ _____

20 (is / that / because / usually / it / through / runs / rainforests / wet / and / areas, / cities / not / towns. / or)

➡ _____
_____

21 (also, / many / in / places / river / the / is / wide, / very / you / so / see / cannot / the / side! / other)

➡ _____
_____

22 (probably / you / not / do / want / swim / to / in / river. / this)

➡ _____

23 (is / it / to / home / some / big / very / snakes / and / that / fish / meat. / eat)

➡ _____

24 (Andes / the / are / world's / the / mountain / longest / range.)

➡ _____

25 (you / do / how / know / the / long / range / mountain / is?)

➡ _____

26 (is / it / about / kilometers / 7,000 / long!)

➡ _____

27 (also / it / contains / highest / the / mountains / of / Asia. / outside)

➡ _____

28 (a / about / third / of / people / the / South / in / live / America / the / in / Andes.)

➡ _____

29 (unique / many / also / animals / there. / live)

➡ _____

15 여전히 비행기로만 그 아름다운 폭포의 꼭대기에 갈 수 있습니다.

16 아마존강은 일곱 개의 나라를 거쳐 대륙을 가로질러 흐릅니다.

17 그것은 서쪽의 페루에서 시작하여 대서양으로 흘러갑니다.

18 아마존강은 많은 점에서 흥미롭습니다.

19 강의 대부분에는 다리가 없습니다.

20 그것은 강이 대개 도시나 마을이 아닌, 열대 우림과 습지를 지나 흐르기 때문입니다.

21 또한 많은 곳에서 강이 너무 넓어서 그 건너편을 볼 수조차 없습니다!

22 여러분은 아마도 이 강에서 헤엄치고 싶지 않을 것입니다.

23 이곳은 몇몇 아주 큰 뱀과 고기를 먹는 물고기들의 서식지입니다.

24 안데스 산맥은 세계에서 가장 긴 산맥입니다.

25 여러분은 그 산맥의 길이가 얼마인지 아시나요?

26 그것은 약 7,000km입니다.

27 또한 그곳에는 아시아 외의 지역에서 가장 높은 산이 있습니다.

28 남아메리카 인구의 3분의 1 정도가 안데스 산맥에 살고 있습니다.

29 그리고 독특한 동물들이 많이 서식하고 있기도 합니다.

※ 다음 우리말을 영어로 쓰시오.

1 여러분은 지구에서 가장 건조한 사막이 어디인지 알고 있나요?

➡ _____

2 가장 높은 폭포는 어떠한가요?

➡ _____

3 그렇습니다, 그것들은 둘 다 남아메리카에 있습니다.

➡ _____

4 이 대륙은 여러분을 놀라게 할 자연 경관으로 가득하답니다.

➡ _____

5 아타카마 사막은 지구에서 가장 건조한 사막입니다.

➡ _____

6 몇몇 지역은 비가 전혀 오지 않아서, 연간 강수량이 1~3mm에 그칩니다!

➡ _____

7 어떤 지역의 토양은 너무 건조해서 어떤 식물도 자랄 수가 없습니다.

➡ _____

8 이처럼 건조한 곳에서 과학자들이 무슨 일을 하는지 알고 있나요?

➡ _____

9 이 사막의 토양은 화성의 토양과 아주 비슷해서, 그들은 우주로의 여행을 준비합니다.

➡ _____

10 또한 아타카마 사막은 지구에서 별을 관측하기에 가장 좋은 장소 가운데 하나이기도 합니다.

➡ _____

11 여러분이 베네수엘라에 간다면, 세계에서 가장 높은 폭포를 볼 수 있을 것입니다.

➡ _____

12 그것은 높이가 979m입니다.

➡ _____

13 구름이 꼭대기 부분을 자주 에워싸기 때문에, 멋진 경치를 보려면 인내심과 약간의 운이 필요합니다.

➡ _____

14 사실 그 폭포는 1933년에 처음으로 폭포 너머 비행을 한 미국의 비행사 Jimmie Angel에게서 이름을 따왔습니다.

➡ _____
_____

15 여전히 비행기로만 그 아름다운 폭포의 꼭대기에 갈 수 있습니다.

➡ _____

16 아마존강은 일곱 개의 나라를 거쳐 대륙을 가로질러 흐릅니다.

➡ _____

17 그것은 서쪽의 페루에서 시작하여 대서양으로 흘러갑니다.

➡ _____

18 아마존강은 많은 점에서 흥미롭습니다.

➡ _____

19 강의 대부분에는 다리가 없습니다.

➡ _____

20 그것은 강이 대개 도시나 마을이 아닌, 열대 우림과 습지를 지나 흐르기 때문입니다.

➡ _____

21 또한 많은 곳에서 강이 너무 넓어서 그 건너편을 볼 수조차 없습니다!

➡ _____

22 여러분은 아마도 이 강에서 헤엄치고 싶지 않을 것입니다.

➡ _____

23 이곳은 몇몇 아주 큰 뱀과 고기를 먹는 물고기들의 서식지입니다.

➡ _____

24 안데스 산맥은 세계에서 가장 긴 산맥입니다.

➡ _____

25 여러분은 그 산맥의 길이가 얼마인지 아시나요?

➡ _____

26 그것은 약 7,000km입니다.

➡ _____

27 또한 그곳에는 아시아 외의 지역에서 가장 높은 산이 있습니다.

➡ _____

28 남아메리카 인구의 3분의 1 정도가 안데스 산맥에 살고 있습니다.

➡ _____

29 그리고 독특한 동물들이 많이 서식하고 있기도 합니다.

➡ _____

※ 다음 우리말과 일치하도록 빈칸에 알맞은 말을 쓰시오.

My Speaking Portfolio

1. A: _____ _____ do you want _____ _____?

2. B: Brazil. Do you know _____ _____ _____?

3. A: Yes, I do. It's _____ _____ _____. Do you know that Brazil is _____ _____ _____ in South America?

4. B: _____ _____ _____! I didn't know that. So, what's _____ _____ _____ you want to see in Brazil?

5. A: I want _____ _____ Iguazu Falls _____ the sky.

My Writing Portfolio

1. A _____ in _____

2. I _____ _____ Kaieteur Falls _____ my family.

3. The waterfall _____ _____ the Amazon Rainforest in Guyana, and it is 226 _____ _____.

4. I _____ _____ the size of the waterfall.

5. I could see the _____ _____ and _____ _____ there.

6. _____ _____ _____ Kaieteur Falls _____ _____ _____ good.

7. I _____ _____ all my stress _____ _____.

Wrap Up - Reading

1. Salar de Uyuni in Bolivia is _____ _____ _____ salt flat.

2. _____ _____ _____ ago, there was water, but it _____ _____ _____.

3. Now, a large salt desert _____ _____ _____ 3,656 meters _____ _____ _____.

4. Salar de Uyuni is _____ _____ _____ _____ _____ _____ of South America, too.

5. _____ _____ _____ a lot of people visit this place to take pictures of its _____ _____ _____.

6. _____ _____, the salt flat _____ any _____ a great photographer.

7. _____ _____ you _____ in Salar de Uyuni will be a _____ _____ _____!

1. A: 너는 어느 나라를 가 보고 싶니?
2. B: 브라질. 너는 브라질이 어디에 있는지 알고 있니?
3. A: 응, 알아. 그건 남아메리카에 있어. 너는 남아메리카에서 브라질이 가장 큰 나라라는 거 알고 있니?
4. B: 정말 놀랍다! 그건 몰랐네. 그러면 너는 브라질에서 가장 처음으로 보고 싶은 게 뭐야?
5. A: 나는 하늘에서 이구아수폭포를 보고 싶어.

1. 자연에서의 하루
2. 나는 가족과 함께 카이에투 폭포에 갔다.
3. 그 폭포는 가이아나에 있는 아마존 열대우림에 위치하고 있고, 높이는 226m이다.
4. 나는 폭포의 크기에 놀랐다.
5. 나는 그곳에서 갈색 바위와 초록색 나무를 볼 수 있었다.
6. 카이에투 폭포로의 여행은 나를 기분 좋게 만들어 주었다.
7. 내 모든 스트레스가 사라진 것 같았다.

1. 볼리비아에 있는 살라르 데 우유니는 세계에서 가장 큰 솔트 플랫(소금 평원)이다.
2. 수천 년 전에는 그곳에 물이 있었지만, 모두 말라버렸다.
3. 지금은 해발 약 3,656미터에 큰 소금 사막이 남겨져 있다.
4. 살라르 데 우유니는 또한 방문객이 가장 많은 남아메리카의 자연 경관 중의 하나이다.
5. 일 년 내내 많은 사람들이 독특한 자연의 아름다움을 사진으로 찍기 위해 이 장소를 방문한다.
6. 사실, 그 솔트 플랫은 어떤 방문객도 훌륭한 사진작가로 만든다.
7. 살라르 데 우유니에서 당신이 찍은 모든 사진은 아름다운 예술 작품이 될 것이다!

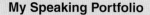

※ 다음 우리말을 영어로 쓰시오.

My Speaking Portfolio

1. A: 너는 어느 나라를 가 보고 싶니?
➡ _____

2. B: 브라질. 너는 브라질이 어디에 있는지 알고 있니?
➡ _____

3. A: 응, 알아. 그건 남아메리카에 있어. 너는 남아메리카에서 브라질이 가장 큰 나라라는 거 알고 있니?
➡ _____

4. B: 정말 놀랍다! 그건 몰랐네. 그러면 너는 브라질에서 가장 처음으로 보고 싶은 게 뭐야?
➡ _____

5. A: 나는 하늘에서 이구아수폭포를 보고 싶어.
➡ _____

My Writing Portfolio

1. 자연에서의 하루
➡ _____

2. 나는 가족과 함께 카이에투 폭포에 갔다.
➡ _____

3. 그 폭포는 가이아나에 있는 아마존 열대우림에 위치하고 있고, 높이는 226m이다.
➡ _____

4. 나는 폭포의 크기에 놀랐다.
➡ _____

5. 나는 그곳에서 갈색 바위와 초록색 나무를 볼 수 있었다.
➡ _____

6. 카이에투 폭포로의 여행은 나를 기분 좋게 만들어 주었다.
➡ _____

7. 내 모든 스트레스가 사라진 것 같았다.
➡ _____

Wrap Up - Reading

1. 볼리비아에 있는 살라르 데 우유니는 세계에서 가장 큰 솔트 플랫(소금 평원)이다.
➡ _____

2. 수천 년 전에는 그곳에 물이 있었지만, 모두 말라버렸다.
➡ _____

3. 지금은 해발 약 3,656미터에 큰 소금 사막이 남겨져 있다.
➡ _____

4. 살라르 데 우유니는 또한 방문객이 가장 많은 남아메리카의 자연 경관 중의 하나이다.
➡ _____

5. 일 년 내내 많은 사람들이 독특한 자연의 아름다움을 사진으로 찍기 위해 이 장소를 방문한다.
➡ _____

6. 사실, 그 솔트 플랫은 어떤 방문객도 훌륭한 사진작가로 만든다.
➡ _____

7. 살라르 데 우유니에서 당신이 찍은 모든 사진은 아름다운 예술 작품이 될 것이다!
➡ _____

※ 다음 영어를 우리말로 쓰시오.

01 pick _____

02 celebrate _____

03 either _____

04 happen _____

05 trick _____

06 mean _____

07 borrow _____

08 carefully _____

09 million _____

10 anymore _____

11 servant _____

12 narrator _____

13 poor _____

14 instead _____

15 loudly _____

16 prison _____

17 save _____

18 allow _____

19 terrible _____

20 character _____

21 drop _____

22 don't[doesn't] have to _____

23 money lender _____

24 pay back _____

25 right away _____

26 say to oneself _____

27 to oneself _____

※ 다음 우리말을 영어로 쓰시오.

01	가난한	
02	빌리다	
03	떨어뜨리다	
04	백만	
05	주의 깊게	
06	(목숨을) 구하다	
07	속임수	
08	해설자, 내레이터	
09	끔찍한	
10	일어나다, 생기다	
11	허락하다, 허가하다	
12	대신에	
13	고르다	

14	큰소리로	
15	등장인물	
16	비열한, 못된	
17	지금은, 이제는 (더 이상)	
18	감옥	
19	하인	
20	(부정문에서) 역시, 또한	
21	축하하다	
22	즉시, 바로	
23	중얼거리다	
24	대부업자	
25	(돈을) 갚다	
26	혼잣말로	
27	~할 필요가 없다	

※ 다음 영영풀이에 알맞은 단어를 <보기>에서 골라 쓴 후, 우리말 뜻을 쓰시오.

1 _____ : in place of: _____

2 _____ : a plan to deceive someone: _____

3 _____ : to choose from a group: _____

4 _____ : not kind to people: _____

5 _____ : to take something and promise to return it: _____

6 _____ : a person who appears in a story, book, play, movie, or television show:
_____

7 _____ : to take place, especially without being planned: _____

8 _____ : a person who tells a story, especially in a book, play, or movie:
_____

9 _____ : a building where people are kept as a punishment for a crime they have
committed: _____

10 _____ : to help someone get away from danger or harm: _____

11 _____ : to do something enjoyable because of a special occasion or to mark
someone's success: _____

12 _____ : a person whose job is to do another person's housework, often living in
the home: _____

보기

save	celebrate	pick	mean
instead	servant	character	borrow
prison	trick	happen	narrator

※ 다음 우리말과 일치하도록 빈칸에 알맞은 것을 골라 쓰시오.

1 The _____ _____
A. Stones   B. Two

2 _____ : Father, Daughter, _____ _____ , Friends, _____
A. Lender   B. Characters   C. Narrator   D. Money

3 Narrator: A long time _____ , in a small _____ in South America, _____ _____ a farmer and his daughter.
A. there   B. ago   C. lived   D. village

4 The farmer was poor, and _____ to _____ three _____ pesos _____ a money lender.
A. borrow   B. from   C. million   D. had

5 But the money lender was not kind, and when the farmer asked _____ one month to _____ back the money, she didn't _____ him _____ time.
A. allow   B. for   C. anymore   D. pay

6 Money Lender: You _____ _____ money? That's okay.
A. no   B. have

7 Your daughter will _____ my _____ _____ .
A. servant   B. become   C. instead

8 Father and _____ : Oh, _____ !
A. no   B. Daughter

9 Daughter: I don't want _____ _____ your _____ .
A. be   B. servant   C. to

10 Father: I don't _____ that, _____ ! (to Money Lender) No, _____ you.
A. either   B. thank   C. want

11 Money Lender: Do you want _____ _____ to _____ ?
A. to   B. go   C. prison

12 Then, _____ _____ a game. I will _____ two stones in a bag.
A. play   B. put   C. let's

13 _____ is white, and _____ _____ is black. Your daughter will _____ one.
A. the   B. pick   C. one   D. other

14 Daughter: What _____ I pick the white _____ ?
A. one   B. if   C. happens

15 Money Lender: _____ you will _____ my _____ .
A. be   B. then   C. servant

16 Friends: Oh, no! She's _____ . _____ _____ !
A. how   B. mean   C. terrible

17 Daughter: _____ happens _____ I _____ the black one?
A. if   B. pick   C. what

---

1 두 개의 돌

2 등장인물: 아버지, 딸, 대부업자, 친구들, 해설자

3 해설자: 오래 전 남아메리카의 작은 마을에 농부와 그의 딸이 살았습니다.

4 농부는 가난했고, 대부업자로부터 3백만 페소를 빌려야 했습니다.

5 하지만 대부업자는 친절하지 않았고, 농부가 돈을 갚을 때까지 한 달을 기다려 달라고 하자, 더 이상의 시간을 허락해 주지 않았습니다.

6 대부업자: 돈이 없다는 거죠? 좋아요

7 대신 당신 딸이 내 하녀가 돼야 겠네요.

8 아버지와 딸: 오, 안 돼!

9 딸: 저는 당신의 하녀가 되고 싶지 않아요.

10 아버지: 나도 그것을 원하지 않아! (대부업자에게) 사양하겠습니다.

11 대부업자: 감옥에 가고 싶은가요?

12 그렇다면, 게임을 하나 합시다. 내가 가방에 돌 두 개를 넣겠어요.

13 하나는 흰색이고, 다른 하나는 검은색이죠. 당신 딸이 하나를 집을 거예요.

14 딸: 제가 흰 돌을 집으면 어떻게 되죠?

15 대부업자: 그러면 넌 내 하녀가 될 거야.

16 친구들: 오, 안 돼! 그녀는 야비해. 정말 끔찍해!

17 딸: 제가 검은 돌을 집으면 어떻게 되죠?

18 Money Lender: Then you will be _____, and your father doesn't _____ to _____ _____ my money.
A. have   B. back   C. free   D. pay

19 Father: What _____ if she _____ play this game _____ you?
A. with   B. doesn't   C. happens

20 Money Lender: (_____) _____ you will go to _____!
A. then   B. loudly   C. prison

21 Father, _____, and _____: Oh, no! _____!
A. Prison   B. Friends   C. Daughter

22 (Money Lender _____ _____ two stones. Daughter looks _____ _____ her.)
A. carefully   B. picks   C. at   D. up

23 Daughter: (_____ _____) Oh! She has _____ _____ two white stones!
A. picked   B. herself   C. up   D. to

24 She will _____ me _____ her servant. What _____ I do?
A. should   B. become   C. make

25 Narrator: _____ and _____. What _____ she do?
A. should   B. think   C. stop

26 She _____ _____ a black _____.
A. pick   B. one   C. cannot

27 (Daughter picks a stone _____ the bag. She _____ it _____ _____.)
A. drops   B. away   C. right   D. from

28 Daughter Oh, no! I'm _____, I've _____ it.
A. dropped   B. sorry

29 (to Money Lender) _____ it's _____.
A. okay   B. but

30 _____ _____ the _____ in the bag.
A. us   B. show   C. stone

31 Then we will know _____ _____ I _____.
A. one   B. which   C. picked

32 Money Lender: (_____ _____) I _____ tell them about my _____! Oh, no!
A. herself   B. trick   C. to   D. cannot

33 (Money Lender _____ _____ the white _____.
A. everyone   B. shows   C. stone

34 Friends and Father _____ _____.)
A. celebrating   B. start

35 Friends: She _____ the black _____! They are _____!
A. free   B. picked   C. one

36 Narrator: _____ _____ has _____ Father and Daughter!
A. thinking   B. saved   C. good

18 대부업자: 그러면 넌 자유로워질 것이고, 네 아버지는 내 돈을 갚을 필요가 없어.

19 아버지: 내 딸이 당신과 이 게임을 하지 않으면 어떻게 되죠?

20 대부업자: (큰소리로) 그러면 당신은 감옥에 가게 되겠죠!

21 아버지, 딸, 친구들: 오, 안 돼! 감옥이라니!

22 (대부업자는 두 개의 돌을 집는다. 딸은 주의 깊게 그녀를 본다.)

23 딸: (혼잣말로) 오! 그녀는 두 개의 흰 돌을 집었어!

24 그녀는 나를 자신의 하녀로 만들 거야. 어떻게 하면 좋지?

25 해설자: 가만히 생각해 보세요. 그녀는 어떻게 하면 좋을까요?

26 그녀는 검은 돌을 집을 수 없어요.

27 (딸은 가방에서 돌을 하나 집는다. 그녀는 그것을 바로 떨어뜨린다.)

28 딸: 오, 안 돼! 미안해요, 제가 돌을 떨어뜨렸어요.

29 (대부업자에게) 하지만 괜찮아요.

30 가방에 있는 돌을 우리에게 보여주세요.

31 그러면 제가 무엇을 집었는지 우리가 알게 될 테니까요.

32 대부업자: (혼잣말로) 그들에게 내 속임수를 말할 수 없어! 오, 안 돼!

33 (대부업자는 모두에게 흰 돌을 보여 준다.

34 친구들과 아버지는 축하하기 시작한다.)

35 친구들: 그녀는 검은 돌을 집었어! 그들은 자유야!

36 해설자: 현명한 생각이 아버지와 딸을 구했습니다!

※ 다음 우리말과 일치하도록 빈칸에 알맞은 말을 쓰시오.

1 The _____ _____

2 _____ : Father, Daughter, _____ _____, Friends, _____

3 Narrator: A _____ _____ _____, in a small _____ in South America, _____ _____ a farmer and his daughter.

4 The farmer was poor, and _____ _____ _____ three _____ pesos _____ a _____ _____.

5 But _____ _____ _____ was not kind, and when the farmer _____ _____ one month _____ _____ _____ the money, she didn't _____ him _____ time.

6 Money Lender: You _____ _____ money? That's okay.

7 Your daughter _____ _____ my _____ _____.

8 Father and Daughter: Oh, _____!

9 Daughter: I don't want _____ _____ your _____.

10 Father: I don't want that, _____! *(to Money Lender)* No, _____ _____.

11 Money Lender: Do you want to _____ _____ _____?

12 Then, _____ _____ a game. I will _____ two stones in a bag.

13 _____ is white, and _____ _____ is black. Your daughter will _____ _____.

14 Daughter: What _____ _____ I _____ the white one?

15 Money Lender: _____ you _____ _____ my _____.

16 Friends: Oh, no! She's _____. _____ _____!

17 Daughter: What happens _____ I _____ the black one?

1	두 개의 돌
2	등장인물: 아버지, 딸, 대부업자, 친구들, 해설자
3	해설자: 오래 전 남아메리카의 작은 마을에 농부와 그의 딸이 살았습니다.
4	농부는 가난했고, 대부업자로부터 3백만 페소를 빌려야 했습니다.
5	하지만 대부업자는 친절하지 않았고, 농부가 돈을 갚을 때까지 한 달을 기다려 달라고 하자, 더 이상의 시간을 허락해 주지 않았습니다.
6	대부업자: 돈이 없다는 거죠? 좋아요
7	대신 당신 딸이 내 하녀가 돼야겠네요.
8	아버지와 딸: 오, 안 돼!
9	딸: 저는 당신의 하녀가 되고 싶지 않아요.
10	아버지: 나도 그것을 원하지 않아! *(대부업자에게)* 사양하겠습니다.
11	대부업자: 감옥에 가고 싶은가요?
12	그렇다면, 게임을 하나 합시다. 내가 가방에 돌 두 개를 넣겠어요.
13	하나는 흰색이고, 다른 하나는 검은색이죠. 당신 딸이 하나를 집을 거예요.
14	딸: 제가 흰 돌을 집으면 어떻게 되죠?
15	대부업자: 그러면 넌 내 하녀가 될 거야.
16	친구들: 오, 안 돼! 그녀는 야비해. 정말 끔찍해!
17	딸: 제가 검은 돌을 집으면 어떻게 되죠?

18 Money Lender: Then you will be _____, and your father _____ _____ _____ _____ _____ my money.

19 Father: What _____ if she _____ _____ this game _____ you?

20 Money Lender: (_____) _____ you will go to _____!

21 Father, Daughter, and Friends: Oh, no! _____!

22 (Money Lender _____ _____ two stones. Daughter _____ _____ _____ her.)

23 Daughter: (_____ _____) Oh! She has _____ _____ two _____ _____!

24 She will _____ me _____ her servant. _____ _____ I do?

25 Narrator: _____ _____ _____. What should she do?

26 She _____ _____ a black one.

27 (Daughter picks a stone from the bag. She _____ it _____ _____.)

28 Daughter Oh, no! I'm sorry, I've _____ it.

29 (to Money Lender) But it's _____.

30 _____ _____ _____ _____ in the bag.

31 Then we will know _____ _____ _____ _____ _____.

32 Money Lender: (_____ _____) I _____ _____ them about my _____! Oh, no!

33 (Money Lender _____ _____ _____ _____ _____.

34 Friends and Father _____ _____.)

35 Friends: She _____ the black one! They are _____!

36 Narrator: _____ _____ has _____ Father and Daughter!

---

18 대부업자: 그러면 넌 자유로워 질 것이고, 네 아버지는 내 돈을 갚을 필요가 없어.

19 아버지: 내 딸이 당신과 이 게임 을 하지 않으면 어떻게 되죠?

20 대부업자: (큰소리로) 그러면 당 신은 감옥에 가게 되겠죠!

21 아버지, 딸, 친구들: 오, 안 돼! 감옥이라니!

22 (대부업자는 두 개의 돌을 집는 다. 딸은 주의 깊게 그녀를 본다.)

23 딸: (혼잣말로) 오! 그녀는 두 개 의 흰 돌을 집었어!

24 그녀는 나를 자신의 하녀로 만 들 거야. 어떻게 하면 좋지?

25 해설자: 가만히 생각해 보세요. 그녀는 어떻게 하면 좋을까요?

26 그녀는 검은 돌을 집을 수 없어요.

27 (딸은 가방에서 돌을 하나 집는 다. 그녀는 그것을 바로 떨어뜨 린다.)

28 딸: 오, 안 돼! 미안해요, 제가 돌을 떨어뜨렸어요.

29 (대부업자에게) 하지만 괜찮아요.

30 가방에 있는 돌을 우리에게 보 여주세요.

31 그러면 제가 무엇을 집었는지 우리가 알게 될 테니까요.

32 대부업자: (혼잣말로) 그들에게 내 속임수를 말할 수 없어! 오, 안 돼!

33 (대부업자는 모두에게 흰 돌을 보여 준다.

34 친구들과 아버지는 축하하기 시 작한다.)

35 친구들: 그녀는 검은 돌을 집었 어! 그들은 자유야!

36 해설자: 현명한 생각이 아버지 와 딸을 구했습니다!

※ 다음 문장을 우리말로 쓰시오.

1 The Two Stones
➡ _____

2 Characters: Father, Daughter, Money Lender, Friends, Narrator
➡ _____

3 Narrator: A long time ago, in a small village in South America, there lived a farmer and his daughter.
➡ _____

4 The farmer was poor, and had to borrow three million pesos from a money lender.
➡ _____

5 But the money lender was not kind, and when the farmer asked for one month to pay back the money, she didn't allow him anymore time.
➡ _____
_____

6 Money Lender: You have no money? That's okay.
➡ _____

7 Your daughter will become my servant instead.
➡ _____

8 Father and Daughter: Oh, no!
➡ _____

9 Daughter: I don't want to be your servant.
➡ _____

10 Father: I don't want that, either! (*to Money Lender*) No, thank you.
➡ _____

11 Money Lender: Do you want to go to prison?
➡ _____

12 Then, let's play a game. I will put two stones in a bag.
➡ _____

13 One is white, and the other is black. Your daughter will pick one.
➡ _____

14 Daughter: What happens if I pick the white one?
➡ _____

15 Money Lender: Then you will be my servant.
➡ _____

16 Friends: Oh, no! She's mean. How terrible!
➡ _____

17 Daughter: What happens if I pick the black one?

➡ _____

18 Money Lender: Then you will be free, and your father doesn't have to pay back my money.

➡ _____

19 Father: What happens if she doesn't play this game with you?

➡ _____

20 *Money Lender: (loudly) Then you will go to prison!*

➡ _____

21 Father, Daughter, and Friends: Oh, no! Prison!

➡ _____

22 *(Money Lender picks up two stones. Daughter looks carefully at her.)*

➡ _____

23 Daughter: (*to herself*) Oh! She has picked up two white stones!

➡ _____

24 She will make me become her servant. What should I do?

➡ _____

25 Narrator: Stop and think. What should she do?

➡ _____

26 She cannot pick a black one.

➡ _____

27 *(Daughter picks a stone from the bag. She drops it right away.)*

➡ _____

28 Daughter: Oh, no! I'm sorry, I've dropped it. (*to Money Lender*) But it's okay.

➡ _____

29 Show us the stone in the bag.

➡ _____

30 Then we will know which one I picked.

➡ _____

31 Money Lender: (*to herself*) I cannot tell them about my trick! Oh, no!

➡ _____

32 *(Money Lender shows everyone the white stone. Friends and Father start celebrating.)*

➡ _____

33 Friends: She picked the black one! They are free!

➡ _____

34 Narrator: Good thinking has saved Father and Daughter!

➡ _____

※ 다음 괄호 안의 단어들을 우리말에 맞도록 바르게 배열하시오.

1 (Two / Stones / The)
➡ _____

2 (Characters: / Daughter, / Father, / Lender, / Money / Narrator / Friends,)
➡ _____

3 (Narrator: / long / a / ago, / time / a / in / village / small / South / in / America, / there / a / lived / farmer / his / and / daughter.)
➡ _____
_____

4 (farmer / the / poor, / was / and / to / had / borrow / million / three / pesos / a / from / lender. / money)
➡ _____
_____

5 (the / but / lender / money / was / kind, / not / and / the / when / farmer / for / asked / one / to / month / back / pay / money, / the / shc / allow / didn't / anymore / time. / him)
➡ _____
_____

6 (Lender: / Money / have / you / money? / no // okay. / that's)
➡ _____

7 (daughter / your / become / will / servant / instead. / my)
➡ _____

8 (Daughter: / and / Father / no! / oh,)
➡ _____

9 (Daughter: / I / want / don't / be / to / servant. / your)
➡ _____

10 (Father: / I / want / don't / either! / that, // *Money* / (*to / Lender*) // thank / no, / you.)
➡ _____

11 (Lender: / Money / you / do / want / go / to / prison? / to)
➡ _____

12 (then, / play / a / let's / game. // will / I / two / put / in / stones / bag. / a)
➡ _____

13 (white, / is / one / and / other / the / black. / is // daughter / your / will / one. / pick)
➡ _____

14 (Daughter: / happens / what / I / if / the / pick / one? / white)
➡ _____

15 (Lender: / Money / you / then / be / will / servant. / my)
➡ _____

16 (Friends: / no! / oh, // mean. / she's // terrible! / how)
➡ _____

17 (Daughter: / happens / what / I / if / pick / one? / black / the)
➡ _____

1 두 개의 돌

2 등장인물: 아버지, 딸, 대부업자, 친구들, 해설자

3 해설자: 오래 전 남아메리카의 작은 마을에 농부와 그의 딸이 살았습니다.

4 농부는 가난했고, 대부업자로부터 3백만 페소를 빌려야 했습니다.

5 하지만 대부업자는 친절하지 않았고, 농부가 돈을 갚을 때까지 한 달을 기다려 달라고 하자, 더 이상의 시간을 허락해 주지 않았습니다.

6 대부업자: 돈이 없다는 거죠? 좋아요

7 대신 당신 딸이 내 하녀가 돼야 겠네요.

8 아버지와 딸: 오, 안 돼!

9 딸: 저는 당신의 하녀가 되고 싶지 않아요.

10 아버지: 나도 그것을 원하지 않아! *(대부업자에게)* 사양하겠습니다.

11 대부업자: 감옥에 가고 싶은가요?

12 그렇다면, 게임을 하나 합시다. 내가 가방에 돌 두 개를 넣겠어요.

13 하나는 흰색이고, 다른 하나는 검은색이죠. 당신 딸이 하나를 집을 거예요.

14 딸: 제가 흰 돌을 집으면 어떻게 되죠?

15 대부업자: 그러면 넌 내 하녀가 될 거야.

16 친구들: 오, 안 돼! 그녀는 야비해. 정말 끔찍해!

17 딸: 제가 검은 돌을 집으면 어떻게 되죠?

18 (Lender: / Money / then / will / you / free, / be / and / father / your / doesn't / to / have / back / pay / money. / my)

➡ _____

19 (Father: / happens / what / she / if / doesn't / this / play / with / you? / game)

➡ _____

20 (Lender: / Money / (loudly) / you / then / go / will / prison! / to)

➡ _____

21 (Daughter, / Father, / Friends: / and / no! / oh, / prison!)

➡ _____

22 ((Lender / Money / up / picks / stones. / two // looks / daughter / at / carefully / her.))

➡ _____

23 (Daughter: / herself) / (to / oh! // has / she / up / picked / white / stones! / two)

➡ _____

24 (will / she / me / make / become / servant. / her // should / what / do? / I)

➡ _____

25 (Narrator: / think. / and / stop // she / what / do? / should)

➡ _____

26 (cannot / she / a / pick / one. / black)

➡ _____

27 ((picks / daughter / stone / a / from / bag. / the // drops / she / right / it / away.))

➡ _____

28 (Daughter: / no! / oh, // sorry, / I'm / dropped / I've / it. // Lender) / Money / (to) // it's / but / okay.)

➡ _____

29 (us / show / stone / the / in / bag. / the)

➡ _____

30 (we / then / know / will / one / which / picked. / I)

➡ _____

31 (Lender: / Money / herself) / (to / cannot / I / them / tell / my / about / trick! // no! / oh,)

➡ _____

32 ((Lender / Money / everyone / shows / the / stone. / white // Father / and / Friends / celebrating. / start))

➡ _____

33 (Friends: / picked / she / black / the / one! / are / free! / they)

➡ _____

34 (Narrator: / thinking / good / saved / has / Daughter! / and / Father)

➡ _____

18 대부업자: 그러면 넌 자유로워질 것이고, 네 아버지는 내 돈을 갚을 필요가 없어.

19 아버지: 내 딸이 당신과 이 게임을 하지 않으면 어떻게 되죠?

20 대부업자: (큰소리로) 그러면 당신은 감옥에 가게 되겠죠!

21 아버지, 딸, 친구들: 오, 안 돼! 감옥이라니!

22 (대부업자는 두 개의 돌을 집는다. 딸은 주의 깊게 그녀를 본다.)

23 딸: (혼잣말로) 오! 그녀는 두 개의 흰 돌을 집었어!

24 그녀는 나를 자신의 하녀로 만들 거야. 어떻게 하면 좋지?

25 해설자: 가만히 생각해 보세요. 그녀는 어떻게 하면 좋을까요?

26 그녀는 검은 돌을 집을 수 없어요.

27 (딸은 가방에서 돌을 하나 집는다. 그녀는 그것을 바로 떨어뜨린다.)

28 딸: 오, 안 돼! 미안해요, 제가 돌을 떨어뜨렸어요. (대부업자에게) 하지만 괜찮아요.

29 가방에 있는 돌을 우리에게 보여주세요.

30 그러면 제가 무엇을 집었는지 우리가 알게 될 테니까요.

31 대부업자: (혼잣말로) 그들에게 내 속임수를 말할 수 없어! 오, 안 돼!

32 (대부업자는 모두에게 흰 돌을 보여 준다. 친구들과 아버지는 축하하기 시작한다.)

33 친구들: 그녀는 검은 돌을 집었어! 그들은 자유야!

34 해설자: 현명한 생각이 아버지와 딸을 구했습니다!

※ 다음 우리말을 영어로 쓰시오.

1 두 개의 돌

➡ _____

2 등장인물: 아버지, 딸, 대부업자, 친구들, 해설자

➡ _____

3 해설자: 오래 전 남아메리카의 작은 마을에 농부와 그의 딸이 살았습니다.

➡ _____

4 농부는 가난했고, 대부업자로부터 3백만 페소를 빌려야 했습니다.

➡ _____

5 하지만 대부업자는 친절하지 않았고, 농부가 돈을 갚을 때까지 한 달을 기다려 달라고 하자, 더 이상의 시간을 허락해 주지 않았습니다.

➡ _____

_____

6 대부업자: 돈이 없다는 거죠? 좋아요

➡ _____

7 대신 당신 딸이 내 하녀가 돼야겠네요.

➡ _____

8 아버지와 딸: 오, 안 돼!

➡ _____

9 딸: 저는 당신의 하녀가 되고 싶지 않아요.

➡ _____

10 아버지: 나도 그것을 원하지 않아! *(대부업자에게)* 사양하겠습니다.

➡ _____

11 대부업자: 감옥에 가고 싶은가요?

➡ _____

12 그렇다면, 게임을 하나 합시다. 내가 가방에 돌 두 개를 넣겠어요.

➡ _____

13 하나는 흰색이고, 다른 하나는 검은색이죠. 당신 딸이 하나를 집을 거예요.

➡ _____

14 딸: 제가 흰 돌을 집으면 어떻게 되죠?

➡ _____

15 대부업자: 그러면 넌 내 하녀가 될 거야.

➡ _____

16 친구들: 오, 안 돼! 그녀는 야비해. 정말 끔찍해!

➡ _____

17 딸: 제가 검은 돌을 집으면 어떻게 되죠?

➡ _____

18 대부업자: 그러면 넌 자유로워질 것이고, 네 아버지는 내 돈을 갚을 필요가 없어.

➡ _____

19 아버지: 내 딸이 당신과 이 게임을 하지 않으면 어떻게 되죠?

➡ _____

20 대부업자: (큰소리로) 그러면 당신은 감옥에 가게 되겠죠!

➡ _____

21 아버지, 딸, 친구들: 오, 안 돼! 감옥이라니!

➡ _____

22 (대부업자는 두 개의 돌을 집는다. 딸은 주의 깊게 그녀를 본다.)

➡ _____

23 딸: (혼잣말로) 오! 그녀는 두 개의 흰 돌을 집었어!

➡ _____

24 그녀는 나를 자신의 하녀로 만들 거야. 어떻게 하면 좋지?

➡ _____

25 해설자: 가만히 생각해 보세요. 그녀는 어떻게 하면 좋을까요?

➡ _____

26 그녀는 검은 돌을 집을 수 없어요.

➡ _____

27 (딸은 가방에서 돌을 하나 집는다. 그녀는 그것을 바로 떨어뜨린다.)

➡ _____

28 딸: 오, 안 돼! 미안해요, 제가 돌을 떨어뜨렸어요. (대부업자에게) 하지만 괜찮아요.

➡ _____

29 가방에 있는 돌을 우리에게 보여주세요.

➡ _____

30 그러면 제가 무엇을 집었는지 우리가 알게 될 테니까요.

➡ _____

31 대부업자: (혼잣말로) 그들에게 내 속임수를 말할 수 없어! 오, 안 돼!

➡ _____

32 (대부업자는 모두에게 흰 돌을 보여 준다. 친구들과 아버지는 축하하기 시작한다.)

➡ _____

33 친구들: 그녀는 검은 돌을 집었어! 그들은 자유야!

➡ _____

34 해설자: 현명한 생각이 아버지와 딸을 구했습니다!

➡ _____

MEMO

2학기 전과정

적중100 plus

영어 기출 문제집

영어 기출 문제집

적중 100 2학기 전과정 plus

2학기

정답 및 해설

천재 | 이재영

중 2

영어 기출 문제집

적중100

2학기

정답 및 해설

천재 | 이재영

중 2

Lesson 5

Understanding Others

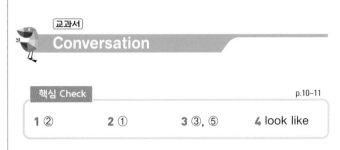

시험대비 실력평가 p.08

01 (o)rdinary 02 announcement 03 ⑤
04 ② 05 ⑤ 06 mind 07 ③
08 ④

01 둘은 반의어 관계다. 친절한 : 불친절한 – 비범한 : 평범한
02 무언가에 대한 새로운 정보를 주며 누군가가 공식적으로 말하는 것
03 whisper는 '속삭이다'는 뜻이다.
04 위험하거나 나쁜 것으로부터 사람이나 사물을 지키다
05 부모가 매주 아이에게 주는 돈: 용돈
06 mind는 동사로 '신경을 쓰다, 언짢아하다'는 뜻이다.
07 사람들은 긴 턱수염을 매우 싫어했다. 그래서 턱수염을 가진 사람을 피했다.
08 '싸워 물리치다'는 의미로 fight off가 적절하고, 두 번째 빈칸은 그들을 공격한 것 때문에 그를 고소했다(accused)가 적절하다.

서술형 시험대비 p.09

01 (1) appearance (2) freedom
02 (1) change (2) train 03 (1) judge (2) mean
04 (1) do well on (2) cared for (3) thanks to
05 (1) face difficulties (2) looked different from
　(3) in prison, protecting

01 (1) 소유격 their 뒤에는 명사형이 적절하므로 appearance를 쓴다. (2) 정관사 the 뒤에 명사형이 적절하므로 freedom을 써야 한다.
02 (1) '어떤 것을 다르게 만들다'라는 동사의 의미와 '비용보다 더 많은 돈을 지불했을 때 돌려받는 돈(거스름 돈)'이라는 명사의 의미를 가지는 change가 적절하다. (2) '사람이나 동물들에게 어떤 일을 하는 방법을 가르치다(훈련하다)'라는 동사의 의미와 '철도 위에 함께 연결된 많은 차량(기차)'이라는 명사의 의미를 가지는 train이 적절하다.
03 (1) 첫 번째 빈칸은 명사 '판사', 두 번째 빈칸은 동사로 '판단하다'라는 의미이므로 judge가 맞다. (2) 첫 번째 빈칸은 '의미하다'라는 동사이고 두 번째는 be동사 뒤에 형용사 '못된'의 의미인 mean이 적절하다.
04 (1) '네가 시험을 잘 보길 바란다.'는 의미로 do well on이 적절하다. (2) '42살의 Joseph Palmer는 평범한 사람이었다. 그는

직업이 있었고 가족을 돌보았다.'는 의미로 과거형 cared for가 적절하다. (3) '그는 아들의 편지 덕분에 석방되었다'는 의미로 thanks to가 적절하다.
05 (1) 어려움에 직면하다는 표현은 face difficulties. (2) 'look+형용사'는 '~처럼 보이다'는 의미로 과거형 looked different from이 적절하다 (3) be in prison: 감옥에 갇히다 / 전치사 for 뒤에 동명사 protecting이 적절하다.

교과서 Conversation

핵심 Check p.10~11

1 ② 2 ① 3 ③, ⑤ 4 look like

교과서 대화문 익히기

Check(√) True or False p.12

1 T 2 F 3 T 4 T

교과서 확인학습 p.14~15

Communicate: Listen-Listen and Answer. Talk
from, ago, worried, shy, good, lucky, friendly, playing, call, I hope

Communicate: Listen-Listen and Answer. Dialog
winning / great / mean / what, look like / has, ponytail / who scored / seventh

Communicate: Listen-Listen More
What / lost / calm down / What, look like / has / wearing / wearing / carrying / look for, announcement, missing / I hope

Communicate: Speak 2-Talk in pairs
have, important / do well on / so

Communicate: Speak 2-Talk in groups
What / What does, like / no / have

Communicate: Speak-Rap Time
I hope, find / do, best / the same / look like / straight / wearing / reading

My Speaking Portfolio
bulletin board, are / made, choice, vote for / mean, promises / choose / seems okay / friendly, talent shows

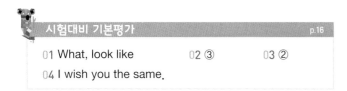

Wrap Up

over there / Which, What does, look / curly, wearing /
sad, wrong / happened / fell off / That's too bad, I
hope, get better

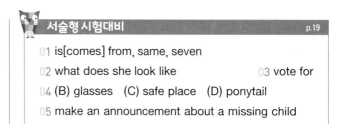

서술형 시험대비　　　　　　　　　　p.19

01 is[comes] from, same, seven
02 what does she look like　　　03 vote for
04 (B) glasses　(C) safe place　(D) ponytail
05 make an announcement about a missing child

01 Gacha는 몽골에서 왔고, Minsol과 같은 반이다. Gacha는 7
　 골을 넣었다.
03 공식적인 서류에 표시를 해서 선거에 출마할 사람을 고르다

시험대비 기본평가　　　　　　　　　　p.16

01 What, look like　　02 ③　　03 ②
04 I wish you the same.

01 사람의 외모를 물어보는 표현으로 'What ~ look like?'를 사
　 용한다.
02 강아지를 잃어버렸다는 말에 이어지는 대답으로 희망이나 바람
　 을 나타내는 'I hope ~.'가 적절하다.
03 내일 중요한 시험이 있으므로 시험을 잘 보길 바란다는 표현이
　 적절하다.
04 '~이기를 바라'라는 표현은 'I wish ~'를 사용한다.

교과서

Grammar

핵심 Check　　　　　　　　　　　　p.20~21

1 (1) expected, to be　(2) (c)aused, to (j)ump
　(3) (f)orced, to sign
2 (1) Before　(2) comes　(3) after

시험대비 실력평가　　　　　　　　　p.17~18

01 ③　　02 who scored the goal just now
03 ⑤　　04 ③　　05 ②
06 That's too bad
07 I hope she'll get better soon.
08 (A) What does he look like?　(B) Can you tell me
more?　　09 ④　　10 ②
11 curly hair, glasses

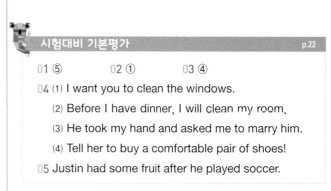

시험대비 기본평가　　　　　　　　　p.22

01 ⑤　　02 ①　　03 ④
04 (1) I want you to clean the windows.
　(2) Before I have dinner, I will clean my room.
　(3) He took my hand and asked me to marry him.
　(4) Tell her to buy a comfortable pair of shoes!
05 Justin had some fruit after he played soccer.

01 상대방의 말을 확인하기 위한 표현으로 '~을 말하니?'의 의미다.
02 명사 the girl을 수식하는 관계대명사절을 만든다.
03 Ben의 'I've heard a lot about her.'라는 말을 통해 Gacha
　 에 관해 알고 있다는 것을 알 수 있다.
04 대화의 내용으로 보아 차기 학생회장 선거라는 것을 알 수 있다.
05 그녀의 외모를 묻는 표현이 오는 것이 적절하다.
06 상대방의 슬픔을 위로하는 표현으로 That's too bad., 또는 I'm
　 sorry to hear that. 등으로 쓸 수 있다.
07 희망이나 바람을 표현하는 말로 'I hope+주어+동사 ~'를 사용
　 한다.
08 (A)는 남동생의 외모를 묻는 표현이 적절하고, (B)는 추가적으
　 로 남동생에 대해 묻는 표현이 적절하다.
09 여자의 남동생이 어디에 있는지는 대화에 언급되어 있지 않아
　 답할 수 없다.
10 '자전거에서 떨어졌어'라는 A의 말에 '그 말을 들으니 기뻐'라는
　 답은 어색하다.
11 주어진 문장은 새로 온 학생에 대한 외모를 묘사하는 글이다.

01 ask의 목적격보어는 to부정사이다.
02 잠자리에 들기 전에 손을 씻었다고 하는 것이 자연스럽다.
03 before와 after는 두 개의 절을 연결해 주는 접속사로 어
　 떤 일이 일어나기 전이나 후의 시간 관계를 나타내며 before
　 는 '~하기 전에', after는 '~한 후에'를 뜻한다. ① Before →
　 After ② Before → After ③ after → before ⑤ After →
　 Before
04 (1), (3), (4) want, ask, tell은 to부정사를 목적격보어로 취하
　 는 동사이다. (2) 시간의 부사절에서는 현재시제를 사용하여 미
　 래를 나타낸다.
05 접속사 after(~한 후에)를 이용하여 영작한다.

시험대비 실력평가　　　　　　　　　p.23~25

01 ⑤　　02 ②　　03 ③　　04 ④
05 (1) to come　(2) to do　(3) expects　(4) to go
(5) after　(6) before　06 ①　　07 ②

3

08 ②   09 ②   10 (1) to tell
(2) to study   (3) (to) push   11 before   12 ③
13 (1) After they played tennis, they went shopping.
    (2) Before Eunji watched the movie, she bought a
        hat.
    (3) The teacher told us to gather at the gym.
    (4) Jiho asked Dohun to clean the window.
14 ⑤   15 ③   16 ①   17 ④   18 ②
19 (1) She asked her brother to help her with her
        homework.
    (2) Jim wanted her to go shopping with him.
    (3) They advised him to leave the place as soon as
        possible.
    (4) Before he rode his bike, Jason put on his
        helmet.
    (5) She will be a good wife when she gets married.

01 want는 목적격보어로 to부정사가 온다.
02 Before는 접속사로 어떤 일이 일어나기 전의 시간 관계를 나타
   낸다.
03 tell은 목적격보어로 동사원형이 아니라 to부정사가 온다. to be
   가 되어야 한다.
04 before: ~하기 전에
05 (1), (2), (4) tell, want, allow는 목적격보어로 to부정사가
   온다. (3) hope는 5형식으로 쓰이지 않는다. (5) 문맥상 after
   가 적절하다. (6) 문맥상 before가 적절하다.
06 빈칸에는 to부정사를 목적격보어로 취할 수 있는 동사가 들어가야
   한다.
07 ② 시간의 부사절에서는 현재시제를 사용하여 미래를 나타낸다.
08 ② 해가 떠오른 시점이 다르므로 두 문장의 의미가 다르다.
09 before 부사절은 after를 사용하여 주절과 부사절을 바꿔 쓸 수
   있다.
10 ask, encourage, help는 to부정사를 목적격보어로 취하는 동
   사이다. help는 동사원형을 쓸 수도 있다.
11 after 부사절은 before를 사용하여 주절과 부사절을 바꿔 쓸 수
   있다.
12 ask는 목적격보어로 to부정사를 쓴다.
13 (1), (2) before와 after는 접속사로 어떤 일의 시간 관계를 나
   타내며 before는 '~하기 전에', after는 '~한 후에'를 뜻한다.
   (3), (4) tell, ask의 목적격보어로 to부정사가 온다.
14 ⑤ make는 사역동사로 동사원형을 목적격보어로 취한다. 나머
   지는 모두 to부정사를 목적격보어로 취하는 동사들로 to do가
   들어가야 한다.
15 ① I read a book before I went to bed last night. ② I
   brushed my teeth before I went to bed. ④ After he
   bought the book, he read it. ⑤ Eric will go swimming
   when Sue arrives.

16 cause, expect, ask, want, tell 모두 목적격보어로 to부정사
   가 와야 한다. ceremony: 식, 의식 / wake ~ up: ~을 깨우다
17 주절은 미래이지만, 빈칸이 이끄는 절은 현재형이므로 빈칸에는
   시간이나 조건의 부사절이 적절하므로 양보절을 이끄는 Even
   if는 적절하지 않다.
18 ask와 tell은 모두 to부정사를 목적격보어로 취하는 동사이므로
   빈칸에는 to부정사가 들어가는 것이 적절하다.
19 (1), (2), (3) ask, want, advise는 모두 목적격보어로 to부정
   사가 와야 한다. (4) 의미상 After를 Before로 고쳐야 한다. (5)
   시간의 부사절에서는 현재시제를 사용하여 미래를 나타낸다.

01 (1) Lucy's dad wants her to be a police officer.
    (2) My mother asked me to buy milk on my way
        home.
    (3) The teacher told the students to bring some
        water.
    (4) She got her two sons to divide a cake exactly
        in half.
    (5) Her family environment forced her not to
        continue her studies.
02 (1) I will let you know my mind as soon as I make
        a decision.
    (2) Nancy wanted her brother to cook ramyeon for
        her.
03 (1) to help (2) to go (3) to stay (4) not to take
    (5) comes (6) have
04 (1) watches, after (2) Before, did
    (3) to call[phone], comes (4) to feed
05 (1) They bought their swimming suit before they
        went to the beach.
    (2) After the students took a bus for one hour, they
        arrived at their destination.
    (3) After they arrived at the museum, they
        appreciated the works in the museum.
06 (1) before she studies math in her room
    (2) after she has lunch with her family 또는 before
        she goes to the movie with James
    (3) after she studies math in her room
07 Laura to study history
08 (1) Before → After (2) after → before
    (3) will come → comes (4) meeting → to meet
09 (1) My parents always tell me to do my best in
        school.
    (2) Good health enabled him to carry out the plan.
    (3) Yuri will put on her uniform after she has
        breakfast.

01 (1) want, (2) ask, (3) tell, (4) get 등의 동사는 목적격보어로 to부정사가 와야 한다. (5) force의 목적격보어로 쓰인 to부정사의 부정형은 'not to 동사원형'으로 쓴다.

02 (1) 시간의 부사절에서는 현재시제로 미래를 표현한다. make a decision: 결정을 내리다 (2) want는 목적격보어로 to부정사가 온다.

03 (1), (2), (3), (4) ask, allow, order, warn의 목적격보어로 to부정사가 적절하다. to부정사의 부정형은 'not to 동사원형'으로 쓴다. (5), (6) 시간의 부사절이므로 주절이 미래시제일지라도 현재시제로 써야 한다.

04 (3), (4) 시간의 부사절에서는 현재시제를 사용하여 미래를 나타내며 ask나 tell은 목적격보어로 to부정사가 온다.

05 before와 after는 접속사로 어떤 일이 일어나기 전이나 후의 시간 관계를 나타내며 before와 after가 이끄는 부사절은 보통 주절의 앞이나 뒤에 올 수 있다. destination: 목적지

06 before(~하기 전에)와 after(~한 후에)가 이끄는 부사절은 보통 주절과 부사절을 바꿔 쓸 수 있으며, before와 after를 서로 바꿔 쓸 수 있다.

07 encourage는 목적격보어로 to부정사를 사용한다.

08 (1), (2) before: ~하기 전에, after: ~한 후에 (3) 시간의 부사절에서는 현재시제를 사용하여 미래를 나타낸다. (4) would like는 목적격보어로 to부정사를 취한다. set: (해 따위가) 지다, 저물다 migrate: 이주하다 migrating bird: 철새

09 (1), (2) tell과 enable은 목적격보어로 to부정사가 온다. (3) 시간의 부사절에서는 미래시제 대신에 현재시제를 사용한다.

교과서
Reading

확인문제   p.28

1 T 2 F 3 T 4 F 5 T 6 F

확인문제   p.29

1 T 2 F 3 T 4 F 5 T 6 F

교과서 확인학습 A   p.30~31

01 Be Different
02 an ordinary person
03 cared for
04 to face difficulties
05 looked different
06 did not like it
07 the man with a beard
08 sit next to him
09 behind his back
10 broke his windows

11 threw stones at
12 stop growing
13 mind
14 to have
15 attacked, threw
16 cut off
17 fight them off
18 accused him of
19 was arrested
20 the victim
21 a man with a beard, went to prison
22 wanted, to know
23 sent, to
24 was in prison, protecting himself
25 became angry, to set, free
26 was freed
27 attitudes toward beards
28 with a beard
29 His name
30 popular, fought for

교과서 확인학습 B   p.32~33

1 The Right To Be Different

2 In many ways, 42-year-old Joseph Palmer was an ordinary person.

3 He had a job and cared for his family.

4 But in 1830, after he moved to a small town in Massachusetts, he began to face difficulties.

5 Joseph looked different from other people: he had a long beard.

6 People did not like it very much.

7 The town's people avoided the man with a beard.

8 They did not want to sit next to him.

9 They even whispered behind his back, "What is he trying to hide?"

10 Some neighbors broke his windows.

11 Others threw stones at him when he walked down the street.

12 They told him to stop growing a beard.

13 Joseph did not mind.

14 He just wanted the freedom to have his beard.

15 One day, four men attacked Joseph and threw him on the ground.

16 "We're going to cut off your beard!" they shouted.

17 Joseph was a big man, and he was able to fight them off.

18 But the men called the police and accused him of attacking them.

19 Poor Joseph was arrested.

20 He said to the judge, "I'm the victim here."

21 Sadly, no one believed a man with a beard, and he went to prison for over a year.

22 Joseph's son, Thomas, wanted people to know the truth.

23 He sent letters to newspapers across the country.

24 People learned that Joseph was in prison just for protecting himself and his beard.

25 Many people became angry about this, so the judge finally decided to set Joseph free.

26 After he was freed, Joseph traveled and told his story to lots of people.

27 Slowly, people's attitudes toward beards changed.

28 Before Joseph died, a man with a beard became the President of the United States.

29 His name was Abraham Lincoln.

30 He made beards popular, but Joseph Palmer fought for the right to have them.

시험대비 실력평가 p.34~37

01 ②, ⑤	02 ③	03 ⑤	04 to stop
05 (A) them (B) Sadly (C) for			06 ③
07 ②	08 ③	09 ①, ④	10 ②, ③

11 appearance   12 students who talk about other people's appearance   13 ④

14 extraordinary → ordinary 15 behind his back

16 ①, ④	17 ③	18 ⑤	19 ④

20 reading   21 (A) differently (B) hungry (C) foolish   22 ②   23 ②   24 ⑤

25 ①

01 ⓐ와 ②, ⑤: ~을 돌보다, ① care about: ~에 마음을 쓰다, ~에 관심을 가지다, ③ look for: ~을 찾다, ④ take off: ~을 벗다, 이륙하다

02 ⓑ different from: ~와 다른, ⓒ the man with a beard: 턱수염을 가진 남자

03 ⑤ 마을 사람들은 Joseph Palmer를 피했고 심지어 그의 등 뒤에서 "그가 무엇을 숨기려는 거지?"라고 속삭였다.

04 tell+목적어+to부정사

05 (A) 'four men'을 가리키므로 them이 적절하다. (B) '슬프게도', 아무도 턱수염을 가진 남자를 믿지 않았다고 해야 하므로 Sadly가 적절하다. Luckily: 운 좋게, (문장이나 동사를 수식하여) 다행히도, (C) 'during+특정 기간을 나타내는 명사', 'for+숫자'이므로 for가 적절하다.

06 ③ 부당한, 불공평한, 자신이 희생자인데 체포되었기 때문에 '부당하다'는 심경을 나타낸다고 하는 것이 적절하다. ① 지루한, ② 무서워하는, 겁먹은, ④ 흥분한, ⑤ 부끄러운

07 위 글은 턱수염을 기를 권리를 위하여 싸웠던 Joseph에 관한 글이므로, 제목으로는 '어렵게 얻은 턱수염을 기를 권리'가 적절하다. hard-won: 어렵게 얻은, ① inform A of B: A에게 B를

알리다, ③ 여론의 압력, ④ notice: ~을 알아차리다

08 ⓐ Joseph's son, ⓑ, ⓒ Joseph, ⓓ, ⓔ Abraham Lincoln을 가리킨다.

09 ① 즉시, ④ 정확히, Ⓐ와 나머지는 '마침내, 결국'

10 Ⓑ와 ①, ④, ⑤는 형용사적 용법, ② 명사적 용법, ③ 부사적 용법(원인)

11 소유격 다음에 명사로 쓰는 것이 적절하다. appearance: 외모

12 추천 독자층은 '다른 사람들의 외모에 관해 이야기하는 학생들'이다.

13 ④ 구입 장소는 알 수 없다. ① The Right to Be Different, ② Joseph Palmer, ③ we should not judge people by their appearance. ⑤ Why did Joseph Palmer want to have a beard?

14 직업이 있고 가족을 돌보았던 Joseph Palmer는 여러 면에서 '평범한' 사람이었지만 1830년에 매사추세츠주의 작은 도시로 이사를 한 후에 어려움에 직면하기 시작했던 것이므로, ordinary로 고쳐야 한다. extraordinary: 보기 드문, 비범한; 대단한

15 behind somebody's back: ~의 등 뒤에서, ~가 없는 곳에서

16 ⓒ와 ②, ③, ⑤는 명사적 용법, ① 형용사적 용법, ④ 부사적 용법(목적)

17 some ~, others ...: 어떤 것[사람]들은 ~, 다른 것[사람]들은 ...

18 ⑤ 모난 돌이 정 맞는다(모난 돌이 석공의 정을 만난다.) 남들과 말이나 행동 등이 달라 미움을 받는다는 속담으로 'A cornered stone meets the mason's chisel.'이라고도 한다. ① 불행한 일은 겹치기 마련이다. (엎친 데 덮친다.) ② 쥐구멍에도 볕 들 날이 있다. ③ 제때의 바늘 한 뜸이 아홉 번의 수고를 던다. ④ 떡줄 사람은 꿈도 안 꾸는데 김칫국부터 마신다.

19 Joseph은 덩치가 큰 사람이어서, 그들을 싸워 물리칠 수 있었다.

20 enjoy는 목적어로 동명사를 취한다.

21 (A) 동사 think를 수식하므로 부사 differently가 적절하다. (B), (C) Stay 다음에 보어를 써야 하므로 형용사 hungry와 foolish가 적절하다.

22 위 글은 '독서기록장'이다. ① (신문·잡지의) 글, 기사, ③ 일기, ④ 수필, ⑤ 전기

23 ②번 다음 문장의 this에 주목한다. 주어진 문장의 'Joseph was in prison just for protecting himself and his beard.'를 받고 있으므로 ②번이 적절하다.

24 Joseph은 석방된 뒤에 순회를 하며 많은 사람들에게 자신의 이야기를 전하면서 턱수염을 기를 권리를 위하여 싸웠기 때문에 '의지가 강한' 성격이라고 하는 것이 적절하다. ② 호기심 많은, ③ 관대한, ④ 창의적인, ⑤ 의지가 강한

25 ⓐ와 ①번은 권리(명사), ② 맞는(형용사), ③ 정확히, 바로(부사), ④ 오른쪽의(형용사), ⑤ 바라던 대로(부사)

01 (A) 42-year-old   (B) different   (C) to sit

02 a long beard

03 (1) 마을 사람들은 그의 기다란 턱수염을 별로 좋아하지
　　 않았다.
　 (2) 마을 사람들은 그 턱수염을 가진 남자를 피했다.
　 (3) 마을 사람들은 그의 곁에 앉고 싶어 하지 않았다.
　 (4) 마을 사람들은 심지어 그의 등 뒤에서 "그가 무엇을
　　 숨기려는 거지?"라고 속삭였다.

04 The four men called the police and accused
　 Joseph of attacking them.

05 he had a beard

06 Joseph's son, Thomas, wanted people to know
　 the truth.   07 ⑤ → for

08 Abraham Lincoln   09 The others → Others

10 growing   11 accused him of attacking them

12 victim   13 (A) over a year   (B) a beard

---

01 (A) 뒤에 나오는 명사를 꾸며주는 형용사의 역할을 할 때는
42-year-old로 쓰는 것이 적절하다. (B) 감각동사 looked의
보어는 형용사를 써야 하므로 different가 적절하다. (C) want
는 목적어로 to부정사를 취하므로 to sit이 적절하다.

02 '기다란 턱수염'을 가리킨다.

03 본문의 difficulties 다음의 내용을 쓰면 된다.

04 네 명의 남자들은 경찰을 불렀고, 자신들을 공격한 것으로
Joseph을 고발했다.

05 아무도 턱수염을 기른 남자를 믿지 않았고 했으므로, '그가 턱
수염을 길렀기' 때문이라고 하는 것이 적절하다.

06 want+목적어+to부정사: 목적어가 ~하기를 원하다, Thomas
의 앞과 뒤에 동격을 나타내는 콤마를 찍는 것이 적절하다.

07 Joseph Palmer는 턱수염을 기를 권리를 '위하여' 싸웠다고 해
야 하기 때문에, for로 고쳐야 한다. fight for: ~을 위해 싸우
다, ~을 얻기 위해 싸우다, fight against: ~에 맞서 싸우다

08 Abraham Lincoln(에이브러햄 링컨)을 가리킨다.

09 '어떤 사람들은 ~, 또 어떤 사람들은 …'의 뜻이 되어야 하므로
The others를 Others로 고쳐야 한다.

10 문맥상 stop 뒤에 동명사가 와야 한다.

11 'of'를 보충한다. accuse A of B: B 때문에 A를 고발하다

12 피해자, 다쳤거나 죽임을 당한 사람

13 Joseph은 그저 자신의 턱수염을 기를 자유를 원했지만 '턱수염'
을 가진 남자에 대한 이웃들의 편견 때문에 '일 년이 넘는 기간'
동안 감옥에 갔다.

---

01 appearance   02 ⑤   03 ④

04 ②   05 like   06 was arrested

---

07 ③   08 ④   09 ②   10 ⑤

11 ①   12 ③   13 ①, ③, ④

14 (1) she saw a giraffe   (2) before   (3) after she saw
a giraffe   15 ②   16 ②

17 (1) we ate ice cream, we watched the movie
　 (2) I untie my hair, I pass the school gate

18 (1) I will take a photo of myself after I get a haircut
　　 tomorrow.
　 (2) Fiona wants Andrew not to come to the party.
　 (3) The situation required me to have strong belief.

19 ①   20 Brush your teeth before you go to
bed.   21 ③   22 beard

23 ②, ③, ⑤   24 ④   25 ①

26 Joseph was in prison just for protecting himself
and his beard.   27 it → them   28 ④

29 ③   30 ⑤

---

01 동사 : 명사의 관계이다.

02 네 명의 남자들이 그를 바닥에 던졌다고 했으므로 ⓐ에는 '공격
하다'가 적절하다. ⓑ는 '수염을 자르다'는 의미로 cut off가 적
절하다.

03 ④번의 judge는 명사로 '판사'다.

04 어떤 일이 일어나도록 하다 / 어떤 일이 발생하는 이유[원인]

05 like는 전치사로 '~와 같은', 동사로 '좋아하다'라는 의미이다.

06 Joseph이 체포가 되었다는 수동의 의미이므로 'be+p.p.' 형태
를 사용한다.

07 '그녀는 어떻게 생겼니?'라고 외모를 묻는 표현이므로 She's
very tall and has a ponytail. 앞에 오는 것이 적절하다.

08 그는 지도를 보고 있다는 말은 사람의 외모를 묻는 말에 대한 답
으로 적절하지 않다.

09 실종된 동생을 빨리 찾기를 바란다는 바람을 나타내는 표현이
적절하다.

10 ⑤번은 대화 속의 남자가 할 일을 묘사한 것이다.

11 빈칸 다음의 대답으로 보아 외모를 물어보는 말이 적절하다.

12 '무슨 일이니?'라는 물음에 (C) 여동생의 팔이 부러졌다는 답이
오고, (A) 무슨 일이 있었는지 묻는다. (B) my sister를 받는
대명사 she로 구체적으로 무슨 일이 있었는지 언급하고, 마지막
으로 (D) 빨리 낫기를 바라는 말이 오는 것이 적절하다.

13 빈칸이 이끄는 절은 현재시제이지만 주절은 미래이므로, 빈칸에
는 시간이나 조건의 부사절이 들어가야 한다.

14 동물을 본 순서에 맞게 after나 before를 이용하여 쓴다.

15 첫 번째 문장은 5형식이고 두 번째 문장은 3형식이다. 3형식과
5형식에 쓰이면서, to부정사를 목적격보어와 목적어로 받을 수
있는 동사는 want이다.

16 ② persuade는 to부정사를 목적격보어로 취하는 동사이다.

17 Before+주어1+동사1 ~, 주어2+동사2 … = After+주어2+
동사2 …, 주어1+동사1 ~

18 (1) 시간의 부사절에서는 미래시제 대신에 현재시제를 사용한다. (2) want는 that절을 목적어로 취하지 않으며 to부정사의 부정형은 'not[never]+to 동사원형'이다. (3) require는 목적격보어로 to부정사를 취한다.

19 warn과 ask는 목적격보어로 to부정사가 오며, to부정사의 부정형은 'not[never]+to 동사원형'이다.

20 brush one's teeth: 양치질하다

21 ⓐ와 ③번은 직면하다, ① 얼굴, ② 표면, 겉면, ④ (시계의) 문자반, ⑤ 체면, lose one's face: 체면을 잃다 crisis: 위기

22 beard: (턱)수염, 사람의 턱과 뺨에 나는 털

23 ⓐ와 ②, ③, ⑤는 형용사적 용법, ① 명사적 용법, ④ 부사적 용법

24 이 글은 '턱수염을 가진 남자에 대한 부당한 행동'에 관한 글이다. ① bully: (약자를) 괴롭히다[왕따시키다], 협박하다, ② 희생자를 수감시킨 판사

25 ① 이웃들이 Joseph의 창문을 언제 깼는지는 대답할 수 없다. ② Joseph's neighbors did. ③ He just wanted the freedom to have his beard. ④ He said to the judge, "I'm the victim here." ⑤ For over a year.

26 'Joseph이 단지 자신과 자신의 턱수염을 지키려다 감옥에 갔다는 것'을 가리킨다.

27 beards를 받는 것이므로 them이 적절하다.

28 ④ 턱수염을 대중적으로 만든 것은 'Abraham Lincoln'이었다.

29 앞에 나오는 내용과 상반되는 내용이 뒤에 이어지므로 However가 가장 적절하다. ① 게다가, ② 그러므로, ④ 예를 들면 ⑤ 게다가, 더욱이

30 위 독서 기록장의 교훈은 'We should not judge people by their appearance.'이므로, 어울리는 속담은 '표지만 보고 책을 판단하지 말라.(뚝배기보다는 장 맛이다.)'가 적절하다. ① 사공이 많으면 배가 산으로 올라간다. ② 기회를 놓치지 마라. ③ 엎질러진 우유를 놓고 울어봐야 소용없다. ④ 남의 떡이 더 커 보인다.

단원별 예상문제
p.46~49

01 unfriendly 02 (A) attack (B) attitude
03 worried, lost   04 ②   05 ③
06 vote for, short hair, friendly, fun and exciting, promises   07 ⑤   08 hopes, class will win, handball   09 ④   10 ①
11 ③, ⑤   12 ③
13 (1) The teacher asked me to close the door.
   (2) Dr. Smith advised her to go to bed early.
   (3) After the soccer match was over, the players lay on the grass.
14 (1) Judy asked him to make sandwiches.
   (2) Tom expected Jane to be thin.
   (3) My advice caused him to stop smoking.
15 looked like → looked   16 Joseph Palmer
17 (A) growing (B) to have (C) was arrested 18 ②
19 ⑤   20 (A) The judge (B) his beard
21 ③   22 ④

01 반의어 관계이다. 유죄의 : 무죄의 = 친절한 : 불친절한

02 (A) 어떤 개가 나를 공격하려고 했을 때, 나의 고양이가 큰 소리로 울었다. (B) 나는 당신의 좋은 태도가 좋아요. 당신은 항상 긍정적으로 생각해요. meow: 야옹하고 울다

04 ⓑ는 남동생의 외모를 물어보는 표현이므로 look for를 look like로 바꾸어야 한다.

05 삼촌과 낚시하러 간다는 말에 네가 꼭 그것을 찾기를 바란다는 말은 어색하다. oval: 달걀 모양의, 타원형의

07 Jiho가 Somin이의 친구인지는 대화에서 언급되어 있지 않다.

08 다음 주 운동회에 대한 Gacha의 바람은 무엇인가?

09 (A) 약간 수줍음을 탔고 한국어를 잘 못했다고 했으므로 무척 걱정이 되었다가 적절하다. (B) 뒤 문장이 '나는 운이 좋은 아이다'로 앞 문장과 대조되므로 '하지만'이 적절하다. (C) 반 친구들이 자신을 '황금 손'이라고 부른다고 했으므로 핸드볼을 잘한다는 것을 알 수 있다.

10 (A)에는 사람의 외모를 묻는 표현이 적절하고, (B)에는 무슨 옷차림을 하고 있는지 묻는 표현이 적절하다.

11 ③ beg는 목적격보어로 to부정사를 취한다. ⑤ 시간의 부사절에서 현재시제로 미래를 나타낸다.

12 ⓑ Would you like me to bring any food to the party? ⓒ Her parents expected her to win the contest. ⓔ She told him to be on time.

13 (1), (2) ask, advise는 목적격보어로 to부정사를 취한다. (3) after: ~한 후에

14 (1) ask (2) expect (3) cause 등의 동사는 목적격보어로 to부정사가 와야 한다.

15 looked+형용사, looked like+명사: ~하게 보이다

16 Joseph Palmer를 가리킨다.

17 (A) '턱수염을 그만 기르라고 말했다'고 해야 하므로 growing이 적절하다. stop+~ing: ~하기를 그만두다, stop+to부정사: ~하기 위해 멈추다, (B) 턱수염을 '기를' 자유라고 해야 하므로 to have가 적절하다. (C) 불쌍한 Joseph은 '체포되었다'고 해야 하므로 수동태인 was arrested가 적절하다.

18 ⓐ와 ②번은 상관하다, 신경 쓰다(동사), ① 기억(력), 마음, 보지 않으면 마음도 멀어진다. ③ 신경, 생각, 관심, ④ (마음을 가진 자로서의) 인간, the greatest mind of the time: 그 시대의 가장 훌륭한 사람, ⑤ 마음, 정신, 건전한 신체에 건전한 정신이 깃든다.

19 ⑤ 판사에게 자기가 '희생자'라고 말했다고 하는 것이 적절하다.

① 공격[폭행]을 한 사람, ② 변호사, ③ 죄수, ④ (약자를) 괴롭히는 사람, ⑤ 피해자[희생자]

20 Joseph이 단지 자신과 '자신의 턱수염'을 지키려다 감옥에 갇혔다는 사실에 대해 많은 사람들이 분개했기 때문에, '판사'는 결국 Joseph을 석방하기로 결정했다.

21 이 글은 Joseph이 자신의 턱수염을 지키려다 감옥에 갇히기까지 했지만, 석방된 뒤에 순회를 하며 많은 사람들에게 자신의 이야기를 전함으로써 사람들의 턱수염에 대한 태도를 서서히 변화시켰다는 내용의 글이다. 따라서 이에 어울리는 속담은 '뜻이 있는 곳에 길이 있다'가 적절하다. ① 무소식이 희소식이다. ② 남의 떡이 더 커 보인다. ④ 뛰기 전에 살펴봐라.(신중하게 행동하라.) ⑤ 연습이 완벽하게 만들어 준다.

22 ④ 몇 사람이 턱수염에 대한 그들의 태도를 바꿨는지는 알 수 없다. ① Because he wanted people to know the truth. ② They learned that Joseph was in prison just for protecting himself and his beard. ③ He traveled and told his story to lots of people. ⑤ Abraham Lincoln did.

서술형 실전문제 　　　　　p.50~51

01 what does she look like?

02 school president / vote / confident / our school a safe place

03 (A) I hope you'll do well on the exam.
(B) I hope so, too.

04 (1) My history teacher told us to hand in the project by tomorrow.
(2) The teacher warned the students to be quiet in class.
(3) Amy's best friend wants her to listen to his songs.
(4) Her manager always forces Melanie to throw away the trash.
(5) The doctor encouraged Jack not to give up doing exercise.

05 (1) Mom told me to walk the dog.
(2) Mark will control Maria's customers until she returns.

06 I set my alarm clock, I went to bed

07 freedom

08 Joseph was a big man, and he was able to fight them off.

09 (A) victim　(B) beard

10 (A) protecting　(B) angry　(C) free

11 Joseph's son, Thomas, sent letters to newspapers across the country

01 외모를 묻는 표현은 'What ~ look like?'를 사용한다.

03 (A) 바람을 나타내는 표현으로 'I hope+주어+동사 ~' 형태를 이용한다. '시험을 잘 보다'는 표현은 'do well on the exam'이다. (B) '또한'의 의미로 문장 끝에 too를 사용한다.

04 (1) tell (2) warn (3) want (4) force 등의 동사는 목적격보어로 to부정사가 와야 한다. (5) to부정사의 부정형은 'never[not] to 동사원형'으로 쓴다.

05 (1) tell은 목적격보어로 to부정사를 취한다. (2) 시간의 부사절에서는 현재시제를 사용하여 미래를 나타낸다.

06 Before+주어1+동사1 ~, 주어2+동사2 … = After+주어2+동사2 …, 주어1+동사1 ~

07 to부정사로 수식받고 있기 때문에 명사 형태로 쓰는 것이 적절하다.

08 목적어가 인칭대명사이므로 fight off them이 아니라, fight them off가 적절하다.

09 Joseph은 따돌림의 '희생자'였지만, 아무도 '턱수염'을 가진 남자를 믿지 않았기 때문에 일년이 넘는 기간 동안 감옥에 갔다. bully: (약자를) 괴롭히다[왕따시키다], 협박하다

10 (A) 자기 자신과 턱수염을 '지키려고'라고 해야 하므로 protecting이 적절하다. prevent: 막다, 예방하다, (B) become 뒤에 형용사가 보어로 와야 하므로 angry가 적절하다. (C) set free 석방하다

11 'Joseph의 아들인 Thomas가 전국에 있는 신문사에 편지를 보냈기' 때문에 알게 되었다.

창의사고력 서술형 문제 　　　　　p.52

|모범답안|

01 [A] (1) A: What does Minsu look like?
　　　　B: He has short hair and is wearing jeans.
　　(2) A: What does Sumi look like?
　　　　B: She is tall and has a ponytail. She is wearing glasses.
　[B] (1) A: I lost my puppy this afternoon.
　　　　B: I hope you'll find it soon.
　　(2) A: I have an important exam tomorrow!
　　　　B: I hope you'll do well on the exam.
　　(3) A: I'm going to my favorite singer's concert tonight.
　　　　B: I hope you have a good time.

02 (1) Dad wants me to come home early.
　(2) My classmates asked me to be quiet in class.
　(3) She told him to fix the computer.
　(4) She didn't allow us to play the piano.
　(5) I advised her to go home early after the concert.
　(6) The teacher forced the students to attend the class.

03 (A) reading   (B) differently   (C) who
   (D) How   (E) Stay hungry.

단원별 모의고사
p.53~56

01 ③	02 difficulty	03 ①	04 ④
05 ⑤	06 ②	07 ③	08 ②
09 ⑤	10 ②	11 ⑤	

12 is she the girl who scored the goal just now?

13 ③	14 ②	15 ①

16 (1) not to drive so fast   (2) to play the piano for her
17 after she had dinner / before she studied history
18 he had a long beard   19 ④   20 ①
21 four men   22 ②   23 People learned that
Joseph was in prison just for protecting himself and
his beard.   24 Abraham Lincoln did.

01 ③번의 attack은 '공격하다'라는 의미로 'to use violence
to hurt or damage someone'을 뜻한다. ③의 설명은
bullying(괴롭히기)에 대한 것이다.

02 반의어 관계이다. 유죄의 : 무죄의 = 쉬움 : 어려움

03 동사로 '바닥으로 떨어지다', 명사로 '여름과 겨울 사이에 있
는 계절'을 뜻하는 fall이 적절하다.

04 What does he look like?는 외모를 묻는 표현으로 ④번은 사
람의 성격이나 성질을 말하는 것이므로 적절하지 않다.

05 (A) 여동생의 팔이 부러졌다고 했으므로 자전거에서 떨어졌다
(fell off)가 적절하다. (B) '곧 회복하기를 바라'라는 바람을 나
타내는 말이 적절하다.

06 (B) 너희 반에 새로운 학생이 왔다는 말을 들었다는 말이 먼저
오고 → (D) 긍정의 답을 하고 저기에 있다는 말 다음에 → (C)
어느 아이인지 묻고 외모를 묻는 말이 온다, → (A) 마지막으로
외모를 설명하는 말이 오는 것이 적절하다.

07 결선 경기에서 최선을 다하길 바란다는 말에 '너도 그러길 바라.'
라는 말이 가장 자연스럽다.

08 잃어버린 남동생에 관한 정보를 제공하고 있는 상황에서 추가적
인 정보를 묻는 것이 가장 적절하다.

10 여학생이 어디서 동생을 잃어버렸는지는 대화에서 알 수 없다.

11 '우리는 훌륭한 핸드볼 선수가 있어.'라는 말에 그 선수가 누구인
지에 대한 정보를 확인하는 말이 오는 것이 적절하다.

12 의문문이므로 be동사로 문장을 시작한다. 그리고 '막 골을 넣은
소녀'는 관계대명사 who를 이용하여 the girl을 수식하는 문장
을 만든다.

13 ① Do you want me to clean your house for you? ②
He told Perry to put on a penguin shirt. ④ The doctor
advised Kathy to stop smoking. ⑤ Ms. Green asked
him to carry the boxes.

14 ② 시간의 부사절에서는 미래시제 대신에 현재시제를 사용한다.

15 첫 번째 문장: expect는 to부정사를 목적격보어로 받는다. 두
번째 문장: 시간의 부사절에서는 현재시제를 사용하여 미래를
나타낸다.

16 tell과 ask는 목적격보어로 to부정사를 쓰고 부정사의 부정은
not[never]을 to부정사 앞에 붙인다.

17 before와 after는 접속사로 어떤 일이 일어나기 전이나 후의 시
간 관계를 나타낸다.

18 Joseph Palmer는 '기다란 턱수염을 기르고 있었기 때문에' 다
른 사람들과 달라 보였다.

19 behind somebody's back: ~의 등 뒤에서

20 ⓐ throw A at B: A를 B에게 던지다, ⓒ accuse A of B: A
를 B 때문에 고발하다

21 '네 명의 남자'를 가리킨다.

22 ⓐ와 ②번은 판사, sentence: …에게 판결을 내리다[형을 선고
하다], ① 판결하다, guilty: 유죄의, ③ 심판하다, ④ 감정가,
감식가, ⑤ 판단하다, 평가하다

23 'for'를 보충하면 된다.

24 did = made beards popular

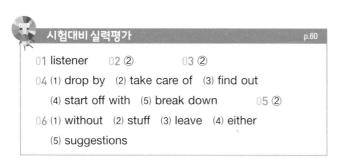

Near and Dear

시험대비 실력평가   p.60

01 listener   02 ②   03 ②

04 (1) drop by   (2) take care of   (3) find out

     (4) start off with   (5) break down   05 ②

06 (1) without   (2) stuff   (3) leave   (4) either

     (5) suggestions

01 주어진 관계는 반의어 관계를 나타낸다. speaker: 화자, listener: 청취자

02 '당신이 너무 많이 지불했거나 또는 당신이 상품을 가게에 돌려주었기 때문에 당신에게 다시 지불되어야 하는 돈의 합계'를 가리키는 말은 refund(환불)이다.

03 exchange: 교환

04 take care of: ~을 처리하다, drop by: ~에 들르다, break down: ~을 부수다, find out: ~을 알아내다, start off with: ~으로 시작하다.

05 주어진 문장에서 text는 '문자 메시지를 보내다'라는 의미로 쓰였으며 이와 같은 의미로 쓰인 것은 ②번이다. 나머지는 모두 '본문, 원문'의 의미로 사용되었다.

06 suggestion: 제안, without: ~ 없이, either; ~도 역시, stuff: 물건, leave: 남기다

서술형 시험대비   p.61

01 remember

02 (1) training   (2) feed   (3) customer service

03 (1) sharing   (2) experience   (3) wall   (4) secret

     (5) text

04 (1) Can you show me the receipt of your order?

     (2) They gave me a full refund of my purchase.

     (3) Jessie promised to keep the news a secret.

05 (1) When you study a new language, you should start off with some vocabulary.

     (2) If you tell a lie to your friends, you can lose them.

     (3) What should I do to break down the wall?

01 주어진 관계는 반의어 관계를 나타낸다. forget: 잊다, remember: 기억하다

02 training: 훈련, feed: 먹이다, customer service: 고객 지원 센터

03 text: 문자 메시지를 보내다, wall: 벽, secret: 비밀, share: 공유하다, experience: 경험

04 receipt: 영수증, refund: 환불, secret: 비밀, promise: 약속하다

교과서
Conversation

핵심 Check   p.62~63

1 (1) happy / wrong   (2) complain / problem

2 (1) Don't forget to   (2) Remember to   (3) sure to

교과서 대화문 익히기

Check(√) True or False   p.64

1 T   2 F   3 T   4 F

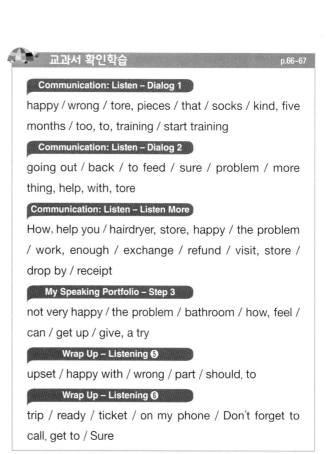

교과서 확인학습   p.66~67

Communication: Listen – Dialog 1

happy / wrong / tore, pieces / that / socks / kind, five months / too, to, training / start training

Communication: Listen – Dialog 2

going out / back / to feed / sure / problem / more thing, help, with, tore

Communication: Listen – Listen More

How, help you / hairdryer, store, happy / the problem / work, enough / exchange / refund / visit, store / drop by / receipt

My Speaking Portfolio – Step 3

not very happy / the problem / bathroom / how, feel / can / get up / give, a try

Wrap Up – Listening ❺

upset / happy with / wrong / part / should, to

Wrap Up – Listening ❻

trip / ready / ticket / on my phone / Don't forget to call, get to / Sure

11

01 ②   02 ⑤

03 (B) → (D) → (C) → (A) → (E)

01 주어진 문장은 헤어드라이어의 문제점을 구체적으로 설명하고 있으므로 (B)가 적절하다.

02 소라는 그녀의 헤어드라이어를 교환이 아닌 환불을 받을 예정이다.

03 (B) 불만 원인 질문 → (D) 불만 설명 → (C) 공감 표현 → (A) 조언 요청 → (E) 해결책 제시

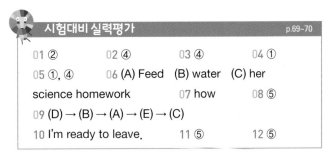

01 ②   02 ④   03 ④   04 ①

05 ①, ④   06 (A) Feed   (B) water   (C) her science homework   07 how   08 ⑤

09 (D) → (B) → (A) → (E) → (C)

10 I'm ready to leave.   11 ⑤   12 ⑤

02 Minsol은 Buster 때문에 기분이 좋지 않음을 알 수 있다. unpleased: 불쾌한, satisfied: 만족스러운

03 Buster는 태어난 지 5개월 되었다.

04 One more thing: 한 가지 더, Conversely: 반대로

05 (a)는 무언가를 상기시키기 위한 표현으로 ①, ④번으로 바꾸어 쓸 수 있다.

07 how you feel: 네가 어떤 기분인지

08 밑줄 친 (B)와 바꾸어 쓸 수 있는 표현은 제안하는 표현이다. ⑤번은 궁금증을 나타낸다.

09 (D) 화나 보인다고 언급 → (B) 불만 표현 → (A) 문제 질문 → (E) 불만의 이유 설명 → (C) 제안

11 수지는 이미 기차표를 전화기에 저장해 놓았다.

12 개를 산책시키러 간다는 A의 말에 숙제를 가져오는 것을 잊지 마라는 대답은 어색하다.

01 He asks her to call him at the train station.

02 She keeps it on her phone.

03 She will come back around 8 o'clock.

04 He should feed and give some water to him.

05 Because Buster tore her homework into pieces.

06 (A) Hairdryer   (B) The air is not hot enough.
    (C) Refund

07 I'm not happy with the school lunch menu.

01 아빠는 수지에게 기차역에 도착하면 그에게 전화할 것을 요청하였다.

02 수지는 표를 전화기에 저장해 놓았다.

03 민수의 엄마는 8시쯤 돌아올 것이다.

04 민수는 Buster를 위해 먹이를 주고 물을 주어야 한다.

05 민수의 엄마는 Buster가 민솔의 숙제를 찢었기 때문에 민수에게 민솔의 숙제를 도와줄 것을 요청하였다.

07 I'm not happy with ~: ~가 마음에 들지 않다

1 (1) do our best   (2) us find his dog
   (3) helped, (to) stand

2 (1) too tired to talk / so tired that he can't talk
   (2) well enough to pick / so well that I can pick

01 (1) to buy → buy   (2) fixed → fix
   (3) to missing → to miss   (4) that → to

02 (1) me go out and play   (2) made me clean
   (3) let me go   (4) too tired to drive
   (5) so busy that

03 (1) She has me do the job instead of her.
   (2) Ms. Jones let Mike drive her car.
   (3) It is too dark to go outside.
   (4) He was so sick that he couldn't go to school.

01 (1), (2) 사역동사의 목적어와 목적격 보어의 관계가 능동인 경우 목적격 보어로 동사원형을 쓰는 것이 적절하다. (3) '너무 ~해서 V할 수 없는'이라는 의미로 쓰이는 'too ~ to V'에는 to부정사를 쓴다. (4) 'too ~ to V'는 'so ~ that 주어 can't 동사원형'과 같다.

02 (1), (2), (3) 사역동사의 목적격 보어는 목적어와 목적격 보어의 관계가 능동인 경우 동사원형 형태를 쓴다. (4), (5) '너무 ~해서 V할 수 없는'이라는 의미로 쓰이는 'too ~ to V'는 'so ~ that 주어 can't 동사원형'과 같다.

03 (1), (2) 사역동사로 쓰인 have와 let은 목적격 보어로 동사원형 형태를 쓴다. (3), (4) '너무 ~해서 V할 수 없는'이라는 의미로 쓰이는 'too ~ to V'는 'so ~ that 주어 can't 동사원형'과 같다.

01 ③   02 ④   03 ⑤

04 You are too young to drive a car.

05 ⑤   06 ②, ④   07 ③

08 This coffee is too hot to drink.

09 ③   10 ④   11 ③

12 Ron got up too late to catch the train.

13 ④   14 ④   15 ②

16 Judy was so fast that she couldn't stop at the finish line.

17 ④   18 ②   19 ①

20 The boy is too young to solve the puzzle.

21 ②, ④   22 ③   23 ⑤

01 have는 사역동사로 쓰여 목적격 보어로 동사원형을 취한다.

02 '너무 초조해서 시험을 잘 볼 수 없었다'는 말이 들어가는 것이 적절하다. '너무 ~해서 …할 수 없는'은 'too ~ to V' 혹은 'so ~ that 주어 can't 동사원형'을 쓰며 시제 일치에 유의한다.

03 모두 목적격 보어로 동사원형을 취할 수 있는 동사이므로 'go'를 쓸 수 있지만 want는 목적격 보어로 to부정사를 받는 동사이므로 'to go'를 쓴다.

04 '너무 ~해서 V할 수 없는'은 'too ~ to V'를 이용하여 나타낼 수 있다.

05 지각동사와 사역동사는 목적격 보어로 동사원형을 쓸 수 있지만, encourage는 to부정사를 목적격 보어로 취하는 동사이다.

06 '너무 약해서 그것을 들 수 없다'고 하였으므로 'too weak to lift it' 혹은 'so weak that he can't lift it'이라고 쓸 수 있다.

07 사역동사의 목적어와 목적격 보어가 능동 관계에 있는 경우 목적격 보어로 동사원형을 쓸 수 있다. '너무 많이 자서 제 때에 그곳에 갈 수 없었다.'는 의미로 too much to go there를 쓰는 것이 적절하다.

08 '이 커피는 너무 뜨거워서 마실 수 없다'는 문장을 쓸 수 있다. 'so ~ that 주어 can't 동사원형'은 'too ~ to V'와 같다.

09 사역동사로 쓰인 make는 목적격 보어로 동사원형을 쓰는 것이 적절하다.

10 'too ~ to V'는 'so ~ that 주어 can't 동사원형'과 같으며, 이때 주절의 시제에 유의하여 couldn't를 쓰는 것이 적절하다.

11 사역동사로 쓰인 have는 목적격 보어로 동사원형 형태를 취한다. 따라서 watch가 적절하다.

12 'too ~ to V'를 활용하여 'Ron은 너무 늦게 일어나서 기차를 탈 수 없었다.'는 문장으로 쓸 수 있다.

13 사역동사 let은 목적격 보어로 동사원형을 쓴다. 따라서 go out으로 쓰는 것이 적절하다.

14 주어진 우리말을 영어로 옮기면 'I was too sleepy to finish my homework.'이다.

15 목적어와 목적격 보어의 관계가 수동이므로 cleaned라고 쓰는 것이 적절하다.

16 '너무 ~해서 V할 수 없는'은 'so ~ that 주어 can't'로 표현할 수 있으며 주절의 시제에 맞게 종속절의 시제를 일치시켜 주는 것에 유의한다.

17 '너무 ~해서 V할 수 없는'이라는 의미로 쓰이는 'too ~ to V'는 'so ~ that 주어 can't 동사원형'과 같다.

18 목적격 보어로 동사원형이 쓰이고 있으므로 사역동사 have를 쓰는 것이 적절하다.

19 이어지는 문장으로 보아 '너무 목이 말라서 더 이상 걸을 수 없었다'는 의미가 적절하다.

20 '너무 ~해서 V할 수 없는'이라는 의미로 쓰이는 'too ~ to V'는 'so ~ that 주어 can't 동사원형'과 같다.

21 내용상 'Amelia는 우리에게 조언을 해 줄 만큼 충분히 현명하다'는 의미가 적절하다. '~할 만큼 충분히 …한'은 '~ enough to V' 혹은 'so ~ that 주어 can 동사원형'을 쓴다.

22 사역동사 let의 목적격 보어로 동사원형을 쓸 수 있으며 '너무 ~해서 V할 수 없는'은 'too ~ to V'이다.

23 '너무 ~해서 V할 수 없는'은 'too ~ to V'로 표현한다.

01 (1) Kevin is too tired to go out.

  (2) Kevin is so tired that he can't go out.

02 blow up the balloon / set by Hippo / eat the nuts / dance

03 Some students were too late to catch the bus.

04 The doctor had me take the medicine every six hours.

05 live alone / to live alone

06 (1) Patrick is tall enough to play the basketball well.

  (2) Patrick is so tall that he can play the basketball well.

07 cry

08 (1) What made you think so?

  (2) Mom let me buy a bike.

  (3) You slept too much to get there on time.

09 old to ride

10 (1) I was too shy to make friends easily.

  (2) I was so shy that I couldn't make friends easily.

11 (1) to watch → watch   (2) left → leave

12 My uncle let me have a piece of cake.

13 A: Did he make you solve this problem?

  B: Yes. But this problem is too difficult to solve.

14 She is kind enough to accept your apology.

01 '너무 ~해서 V할 수 없는'이라는 의미로 쓰인 'too ~ to V'를 활용하여 문장을 쓸 수 있다.

02 사역동사 have는 목적어와 목적격 보어의 관계가 능동인 경우 목적격 보어로 동사원형을 쓰고 수동인 경우 과거분사를 쓴다.

03 '너무 ~해서 V할 수 없는'은 'too ~ to V'로 표현할 수 있다.

04 사역동사로 쓰인 have는 목적격 보어로 동사원형을 쓴다.
every six hours: 여섯 시간마다

05 혼자서 살기엔 너무 어려서 혼자 살게 하지 않겠다는 의미이다. 사역동사 let의 목적격 보어로 동사원형을 쓰며, 'too ~ to V'를 써서 '너무 ~ 해서 V할 수 없는'이라는 의미를 완성한다.

06 'V하기에 충분히 ~한'은 'enough to V' 혹은 'so ~ that 주어 동사 can'으로 쓸 수 있다.

07 make가 사역동사로 쓰이고 있으므로 목적격 보어로 동사원형을 쓴다.

08 사역동사의 목적어와 목적격 보어가 능동 관계에 있으면 목적격 보어로 동사원형을 쓴다. '네가 그렇게 생각하게 만들었다'고 하였으므로 사역동사 make를 써서 make you think so라고 쓰는 것이 적절하다.

09 파파 스머프는 너무 나이가 들어서 롤러코스터를 탈 수 없어서 슬프다.

10 나는 매우 수줍어서 쉽게 친구를 사귈 수 없었다는 의미이다. 따라서 '너무 ~해서 …할 수 없는'이라는 의미로 쓰이는 'too ~ to V' 혹은 'so ~ that 주어 can't 동사원형'을 활용하여 문장을 만든다.

11 사역동사로 쓰인 let과 have는 목적어와 목적격 보어의 관계가 능동인 경우 목적격 보어로 동사원형을 쓴다.

12 사역동사 let은 목적격 보어로 동사원형을 취할 수 있으며 have는 '~을 먹다'라는 의미로 쓸 수 있다.

13 사역동사 make를 사용하여 '그가 너에게 이 문제를 풀게 하다'라는 문장을 쓸 수 있으며, '너무 ~해서 V할 수 없는'은 'too ~ to V'를 이용하여 쓸 수 있다.

14 accept one's apology: ~의 사과를 받아들이다

교과서

Reading

확인문제   p.80

1 T 2 F 3 F 4 T 5 T

확인문제   p.81

1 F 2 T 3 F 4 F 5 F 6 T

교과서 확인학습 A   p.82~83

01 Good evening, This is
02 a special guest   03 Welcome
04 to meet you, for having me
05 want to tell   06 by reading some letters
07 start off with, from   08 Sure
09 from   10 to tell you
11 tries to do
12 without asking, hard to find
13 buys, me study them
14 to say, anymore, let me take care of
15 the same way   16 too young to do
17 get the message   18 do I
19 of two children   20 One, the other
21 too busy to talk   22 get, go back to
23 them, give short answers
24 don't talk much, either 25 to spend more time
26 often, younger
27 them, too old to understand
28 suggestions, Text your idea

교과서 확인학습 B   p.84~85

1 Breeze: Good evening, listeners. This is your DJ, Breeze.

2 Today we have a special guest, Andy Kim.

3 He's a hip-hop artist. Welcome, Andy.

4 Andy: Nice to meet you and thank you for having me.

5 Breeze: Okay. What do our listeners want to tell their family?

6 This evening we will find out by reading some letters from them.

7 Andy, will you start off with the letter from a teenage girl?

8 Andy: Sure.

9 Andy: Hello. I'm a 15-year-old girl from Wonju.

10 I want to tell you about my mom.

11 My mom tries to do everything for me.

12 She cleans my room without asking me, so it's sometimes hard to find my stuff.

13 She also buys books and makes me study them.

14 I want to say to my mom, "I know you love me, but I'm not a baby anymore. Please let me take care of things myself."

15 Breeze: I felt the same way when I was in middle school.

---

16 Andy: Many moms think their kids are too young to do things on their own.

17 I hope the girl's mom will get the message.

18 Breeze: So do I. Andy, will you please read the next letter?

19 Andy: Hi. I'm a father of two children.

20 One is a high school girl, and the other is a middle school boy.

21 They're too busy to talk with me.

22 When I get home from work, they just say hi and go back to their rooms.

23 Sometimes I ask them about their school life, but they only give short answers.

24 We don't talk much at the table, either.

25 I want to say to my kids, "I love you so much, and I want to spend more time with you."

26 Breeze: Andy, did you talk with your parents often when you were younger?

27 Andy: Not really. I loved them very much, but I thought they were too old to understand me.

28 Breeze: I see. Does anyone have suggestions for the "sad" dad? Text your idea to us.

시험대비 실력평가 p.86~89

01 ④　　02 ②　　03 guest　　04 ③
05 ④　　06 She tries to do everything for her.
07 ②　　08 ④　　09 ②
10 Because they are too busy.　　11 ③
12 ③　　13 ③　　14 our listeners
15 She tries to talk about her mom.　　16 ⑤
17 ④　　18 ④　　19 ⑤
20 He has two children.　　21 ③　　22 ④
23 ④　　24 ②
25 He played computer games, rode bikes, and went shopping with his children on weekends.

01 사연을 읽어 주는 사람은 특별 손님인 Andy이다.

02 Andy가 어느 십 대 소녀로부터 온 편지를 읽을 것이다.

03 어떠한 행사에 초대된 사람은 '손님'이다.

04 사연 신청자의 엄마가 방 청소를 얼마나 자주 하는지는 사연을 읽고 답할 수 없다.

05 사연을 신청한 소녀는 자신의 엄마가 자신을 위해 모든 것을 다 해 주려 하는 것이 고민이라고 말하며, 자신이 더 이상 아기가 아니므로 자기 일을 스스로 할 수 있게 해 달라는 말을 하고 있다. 따라서 ④번이 가장 적절하다.

06 소녀의 어머니는 소녀를 위해 모든 것을 다 해 주려고 한다.

07 on one's own은 '혼자 힘으로'라는 의미이다. by oneself와 같다.

08 둘 중 남은 하나를 가리키는 말은 the other이다.

09 빈칸 (B)에는 전치사 from이 들어간다. ① take care of: ~을 돌보다 ② graduate from: ~을 졸업하다 ③ get out of: ~에서 나가다 ④ be full of: ~으로 가득 차다 ⑤ look forward to: ~을 기대하다

10 아이들이 너무 바빠서 아버지와 대화를 하지 않는다고 하였다.

11 'I see'는 '그렇군요.'라는 의미로 상대방의 말을 이해했을 때 쓰는 말이다. 따라서 understand를 대신 쓸 수 있다

12 Andy는 부모님과 많은 대화를 나누지 않았다고 말했다.

13 초대해 주어서 고맙다는 의미의 ②번이 가장 적절하다..

14 청취자들을 가리키는 말이다.

15 편지에서 소녀는 그녀의 엄마에 관하여 말하려고 한다.

16 편지를 보낸 청취자의 이름은 알 수 없다.

17 밑줄 친 (C)와 ④는 강조용법으로 쓰인 재귀대명사이다. ①, ③, ⑤는 주어와 목적어가 같을 경우 목적어로 재귀대명사를 쓰는 재귀적 용법으로 사용되고 있다. ②는 재귀대명사가 관용어구로 쓰이는 경우이다.

18 청취자들이 라디오 프로그램에 사연을 보내는 것이다.

19 Andy의 말처럼, 소녀의 어머니가 메시지를 듣기를 바란다는 말에 동감을 표현하고 있다.

20 아버지에게는 두 명의 자녀가 있다고 하였다.

21 바쁜 자녀들과 대화가 없고, 아이들과 더 많은 시간을 보내고 싶다는 사연이므로 ③번이 가장 적절하다.

22 사연을 신청한 아버지는 편지에서 아이들에게 자신의 사랑과 바람을 전하고 있다.

23 글의 흐름상 don't talk라고 하는 것이 적절하다.

24 (A)에는 '~을 무너뜨리다'는 의미의 break down이 들어간다. break into: ~에 침입하다, break up: 부서지다, 헤어지다, break away: ~에서 달아나다, break off: 분리되다

25 아이들과 대화할 기회를 갖기 위하여 주말마다 함께 시간을 보냈다고 하였다.

서술형 시험대비 p.90~91

01 He is a hip-hop artist.

02 She will find out what listeners want to tell their family by reading some letters from them.

03 special guest , Andy Kim, to read, start off, teenage girl

04 Please let me take care of things myself.

15

05 It is hard to find her stuff.

06 She tries to do everything for her daughter.

07 They are so busy that they can't talk with me.

08 two kids[children], talk with him, spend more time

09 Many of them think that their kids are too young to do things on their own.

10 It's because he thought they were too old to understand him.

11 a wall between us

12 I had more chances to talk with them.

01 Andy Kim은 힙합 아티스트이다.

02 Breeze는 청취자들이 보낸 사연을 읽음으로써 그들이 자신의 가족에게 말하고 싶은 것을 알아보려고 하고 있다..

03 라디오 쇼에서, Breeze는 특별 손님인 Andy Kim을 소개한다. 그녀는 그가 한 십 대 소녀가 보낸 편지를 읽기를 원한다.

04 사역동사 let은 동사원형을 목적격 보어로 취하는 동사이다. 따라서 'let+목적어+동사원형' 형식으로 답을 작성하는 것이 적절하다.

05 어머니가 방을 치우면 자신의 물건을 찾는 것이 힘들다고 하였다.

06 편지에 따르면, 소녀의 어머니는 자신의 딸을 위해 모든 것을 해 주려고 애쓴다고 하였다. try to V: V하려고 애쓰다

07 '너무 ~해서 …할 수 없는'이라는 의미의 'too ~ to V'는 'so ~ that 주어 can't V'와 같다.

08 사연을 보낸 사람은 두 아이의 아버지로, 아이들과 함께 대화할 시간이 없는 것이 고민이다. 그는 자신의 아이들과 함께 더 많은 시간을 보내기를 원한다.

09 많은 엄마들은 자신의 자녀들이 혼자서 무언가를 하기에는 너무 어리다고 생각한다.A

10 Andy는 부모님이 자신을 이해해 주시기에는 너무 나이가 들었다고 생각해서 어렸을 때 부모님과 자주 대화하지 않았다고 말했다.

11 자녀들과 자신 사이에 있는 벽을 가리키는 말이다.

12 '아이들과 이야기할 더 많은 기회'라고 하였으므로 'to talk with them'이 'more chances'를 수식하도록 문장을 만든다.

영역별 핵심문제
p.93~97

01 false   02 ⑤

03 (1) sure   (2) exchange   (3) receipt
   (4) near and dear   (5) wrong   (6) torn

04 ⑤   05 ③

06 (1) She never tells a lie.
   (2) Tom was in trouble because he broke the rule.

---

(3) Jimmy was not a member of the team anymore.

07 ⑤   08 ⓑ → tore   09 ③

10 (E) → (C) → (A) → (D) → (B)

11 ⓒ → to feed   12 feed   13 ②

14 Her brother uses the bathroom for too long in the morning.

15 His suggestion is that Amy can get up earlier and use the bathroom first.

16 ④   17 ③   18 ④   19 ④

20 ③   21 ③   22 ⑤   23 ③

24 too tired to catch

25 The bus driver made me get off the bus.

26 The nurse teacher let me rest in the nurse's office.

27 ③   28 ②   29 ⑤   30 study

31 ②   32 ④   33 ④

34 [B]–[A]–[C]

01 주어진 관계는 반의어 관계를 나타낸다. true: 사실의, false: 거짓의

02 without: ~ 없이

03 be sure to: 반드시 ~하다, exchange: 교환, receipt: 영수증, near and dear: 소중한, wrong: 잘못된, tear: 찢다

04 '누군가에게 무언가를 주고 동시에 그들로부터 같은 유형의 것을 받다'를 가리키는 말은 exchange(교환하다)이다.

05 be in trouble: 곤경에 처하다, trouble: 문제

06 tell a lie: 거짓말하다, be in trouble: 곤경에 처하다, not ~ anymore: 더 이상 ~ 아니다

07 ⑤번은 직업을 묻는 질문이다.

08 tear(찢다)의 과거형은 tore, 과거분사형은 torn이다.

09 위 대화를 통해 Buster가 Minsol의 숙제를 몇 번 찢었는지는 알 수 없다.

10 (E) 헤어드라이어의 문제점 설명→ (C) 사과 및 질문 → (A) 대답 및 환불 요청 → (D) 대답 및 방문 요청 → (B) 대답

11 forget ~ing: ~한 것을 잊다, forget to ~: ~할 것을 잊다

12 '사람이나 동물에게 음식을 주다'를 뜻하는 것은 feed(먹이를 주다)이다.

13 엄마와 아빠는 8시쯤 돌아올 것이다.

14 Amy의 남동생이 아침에 욕실을 너무 오랫동안 사용한다.

15 Brian의 제안은 Amy가 아침에 일찍 일어나서 먼저 욕실을 사용할 수 있다는 것이다.

16 '너무 ~해서 V할 수 없는'은 'too ~ to V'으로 표현한다.

17 make가 사역동사로 쓰이고 있으므로 목적격 보어로 동사원형을 쓰는 것이 적절하다.

18 allow는 to부정사를 목적격 보어로 취하며 '목적어가 V하게 허

락하다'는 의미이다. 따라서 사역동사 'let+목적어+동사원형'과 그 의미가 같다.

19 사역동사로 쓰인 make는 동사원형을 목적격 보어로 취할 수 있으며 'too ~ to V'는 '너무 ~해서 V할 수 없는'이라는 의미이다.

20 '우리가 일기를 쓰게 하다'이므로 '사역동사 have+us+keep a diary'라고 쓰는 것이 적절하다.

21 주어진 우리말을 영어로 쓰면 'The dog was so weak that he couldn't run to the park.'이다.

22 목적격 보어로 to부정사가 쓰이고 있으므로, 사역동사 make는 쓸 수 없다.

23 'too ~ to V'는 'so ~ that 주어 can't 동사원형'과 같다. 따라서 too를 so로 쓰는 것이 적절하다.

24 Azrael은 너무 피곤해서 스머프들을 잡을 수 없다는 말이 들어가는 것이 적절하다.

25 '목적어가 V하게 하다'는 '사역동사+목적어+동사원형'으로 표현할 수 있다.

26 '~가 V하도록 허락하다'는 사역동사 'let+목적어+동사원형'으로 표현할 수 있다.

27 편지를 읽음으로써 청취자들이 자신의 가족들에게 무슨 이야기를 하고자 하는지 알아보자는 의미이다. by Ving: V함으로써

28 자신을 초대해 주어서 고맙다는 의미이다.

29 이 라디오 방송에는 Andy와 Breeze 두 사람이 있다.

30 사역동사 make의 목적격 보어 자리이며 목적어와의 관계가 능동이므로 동사원형을 쓰는 것이 적절하다.

31 엄마가 자신에게 묻지 않고 방을 청소하기 때문에 물건을 찾기가 힘들 때가 있다고 보는 것이 적절하다. with → without

32 밑줄 친 (A)는 진주어로 쓰인 to부정사이다. ①, ② 부사적 용법 중 목적 ③ 형용사적 용법 ④ 진주어 ⑤ 부사적 용법 중 이유

33 소녀는 자신을 아기 취급 하는 엄마 때문에 불행하다.

34 자신과 아이들 사이에 벽이 있음 - [B] 그 벽(it)을 무너뜨리고 싶어서 아이들과 함께 많은 시간을 보내려고 애씀 - [A] 함께 시간을 보내기 위해 한 일들 - [C] 이렇게 해서(in this way) 아이들과 함께 대화할 기회를 더 많이 가짐

단원별 예상문제
p.98~101

01 ④ 02 (C) → (A) → (E) → (D) → (B) 03 ⑤

04 ⑤ 05 The air isn't hot enough.

06 She should bring the hairdryer and the receipt.

07 She is going to drop by tomorrow afternoon.

08 I think you should talk to her. 09 ①

10 (1) Kelly is going to drop by her uncle's house this weekend.

---

(2) She solved the math problem on her own.

(3) Mike wanted to find out the secret of Steve's success

11 ②, ⑤ 12 ⑤ 13 ④ 14 ③

15 that I couldn't play soccer yesterday

16 The painter was too angry to focus on his painting.

17 let us use the science room

18 ④ 19 ④ 20 ③

21 so old that they couldn't

22 They only give him short answers.

23 ③ 24 ④

25 She promises that she will never tell his secrets again.

01 '뜨거운 공기를 머리 위로 불어서 당신의 머리를 건조시키기 위해 사용되는 작은 기계'를 가리키는 말은 hairdryer(헤어드라이어)이다.

02 (C) Minsol의 불만에 대한 반응 → (A) 또 다른 불만 제기 → (E) Buster에게 친절할 것을 부탁 → (D) 불만 및 훈련의 필요성 제기 → (B) 수용 및 훈련을 시작할 것을 제안

03 (A) 잊지 말 것을 상기시키고 있으므로 forget, (B) Be sure to ~: ~을 명심하라, (C) piece: 조각, peace: 평화

04 민수가 집에 약 8시쯤 돌아올 것이라는 설명은 대화의 내용과 일치하지 않는다.

05 소라의 헤어드라이어는 뜨거운 바람이 충분히 나오지 않는다.

06 소라는 환불을 받기 위해 헤어드라이어와 영수증을 가져가야 한다.

07 소라는 내일 오후에 가게를 들릴 것이다.

09 annoyed: 화난, lonely: 외로운, excited: 신이 난, satisfied: 만족한, nervous: 긴장한

10 drop by: ~에 들르다, on one's own: 혼자 힘으로, find out: 알아내다

11 '너무 ~해서 V 할 수 없는'은 'too ~ to V'으로 표현한다. 이는 'so ~ that 주어 can't 동사원형'과 같다.

12 advise는 to부정사를 목적격 보어로 취하는 동사이다. 주어진 문장의 목적격 보어는 동사원형이므로 advised는 답이 될 수 없다.

13 사역동사의 목적격 보어로 동사원형을 쓰는 것이 적절하며, '너무 어려서 생계를 위해 일할 수 없다'는 의미이므로 too ~ to V을 쓰는 것이 좋다.

14 사역동사로 쓰인 have는 목적어와 목적격 보어의 관계가 능동인 경우 목적격 보어로 동사원형을 쓴다.정

15 '너무 아파서 축구를 할 수 없었다'는 말이 들어가는 것이 적절하다. 주절의 시제가 과거이므로 couldn't를 쓰는 것에 유의한다.

16 '너무 ~해서 V할 수 없는'은 'too ~ to V'으로 표현할 수 있다.

17 '목적어가 V하게 하다'는 의미로 쓰이는 사역동사 중 let은 허락의 의미가 강하다.

18 직장에서 집으로 오는 것이고, 자신들의 방으로 들어간다는 의미이다. '~에서'라고 해석되는 from, '~로'라는 의미의 전치사 to를 쓰는 것이 적절하다.

19 부정에 대한 동의는 either를 쓴다.

20 식사 자리에서조차 대화를 많이 하지 않는다고 하였다.

21 '너무 ~해서 …할 수 없는'이라는 의미의 'too ~ to V'는 'so ~ that 주어 can't V'와 같다. 주절의 시제가 과거이므로 couldn't를 쓰는 것에 유의한다.

22 아버지에게 짧막한 대답만을 한다고 하였다.

23 지원이의 이야기로 미루어 보아 sorry가 들어가는 것이 가장 적절하다.

24 지원이 오빠의 비밀이 무엇인지는 위 글을 읽고 알 수 없다.

25 그녀는 다시는 오빠의 비밀을 말하지 않겠다고 약속한다.

서술형 실전문제   p.102~103

01 I'm not happy with Buster.

02 He is five months old.

03 She suggests that Buster (should) need some training.

04 Yesterday they were too busy to start their meeting on time.

05 sleepy to pick

06 My dog is so big that it can't go into the dog house.

07 The man made me push his car.

08 too small to hold

09 (1) She had me play her piano.

   (2) I let them take a walk.

   (3) Did he make you climb the mountain?

10 He will read the letter from a teenage girl first.

11 It's because her mom cleans her room without asking her.

12 study books   13 less → more

14 He wants to share his experience with the "sad" father.

02 Buster는 5개월 되었다.

03 Minsol은 Buster가 훈련이 좀 필요하다고 제안한다.

04 '너무 ~해서 V할 수 없다'는 의미로 쓰이는 것은 'so ~ that 주어 can't 동사원형'이며, 'too ~ to V'과 같다.

05 Lazy는 너무 졸려서 사과를 딸 수 없다는 말이 들어가는 것이

적절하다.

06 'too ~ to V'는 'so ~ that 주어 can't 동사원형'과 같다.

07 '목적어가 V하게 하다' 이므로 '사역동사+목적어+동사원형'을 써서 나타낼 수 있다.

08 강당이 너무 작아서 모든 학생들을 수용할 수 없다는 의미이다.

09 사역동사 make, have, let은 목적격 보어로 동사원형을 취할 수 있는 동사이다.

10 한 십 대 소녀에게서 온 편지를 먼저 읽을 것이라고 하였다.

11 엄마가 묻지도 않고 소녀의 방을 청소하기 때문이다.

12 소녀의 어머니는 소녀의 방을 청소할 뿐만 아니라 자신이 구매한 책을 소녀가 공부하게 한다고 하였다. 사역동사 make의 목적격 보어로 동사원형을 쓴다.

13 아이들과 함께 할 기회를 더 가지면서 아이들에 관하여 더 많이 알게 되었다는 의미가 자연스럽다.

14 편지를 보냄으로써 자신의 경험을 공유하기를 원한다.

창의사고력 서술형 문제   p.104

|모범답안|

01 (A) the air wasn't hot enough   (B) get a refund

   (C) with the dryer and the receipt

02 my mother, I talked back to her in a very rude way, we haven't talked to each other for several days, I will never talk back to you in such a rude way again

01 나는 지난주 가게에서 헤어드라이어를 샀지만 만족스럽지 않았다. 그것은 바람이 충분히 뜨겁지 않은 문제가 있었다. 나는 고객 센터에 전화 를 하였고 이 문제를 설명하였다. 나는 헤어드라이어를 교환하기보다 환불을 받고 싶었다. 환불 받기 위해 나는 가게에 드라이어와 영수증을 갖고 방문할 필요가 있다. 그래서 나는 상점에 내일 오후에 들릴 것이다.

단원별 모의고사   p.105~108

01 ②   02 ①

03 (1) There is not enough food to feed all students.

   (2) Would you pour milk into this bowl?

   (3) Salty food is not good for your health.

04 ②, ④

05 Because Sojin isn't doing her part of the group project.

06 you can get up earlier and use the bathroom first.

24 Breeze는 슬픈 아빠에게 해줄 제안이 있다면 문자로 그 생각을
  보내 줄 것을 요청한다.

07 ⑤   08 ⑤   09 receipt   10 ④
11 He tore my homework into pieces again.
12 ③   13 ④   14 ③, ⑤   15 ②
16 I made Jamie open the window.
17 far away from you to hear   18 ③
19 her mother treated her like a baby   20 ②
21 She wants her mom to let her take care of things
   herself.
22 ④   23 ⑤
24 She asks them to give some suggestions to the
   "sad" father by texting them.

01 주어진 문장에서 work는 '작동하다'라는 의미로 사용되었으며
   이와 같은 의미로 쓰인 것은 ②번이다. 나머지는 모두 '일하다'
   를 의미한다.

02 tell a lie: 거짓말하다, lie: 거짓말하다; 눕다

04 이어지는 대화에서 문제점을 묻고 있으므로 빈칸에 불만을 나타
   내는 표현이 적절하다.

05 Tommy는 Sojin이 모둠 과제에서 맡은 일을 하지 않아 화가
   났다.

08 ⑤번을 제외한 나머지 표현은 모두 불만을 나타낸다.

09 '상품이나 서비스가 지불되었다는 것을 보여주는 종이 조각'을
   나타내는 말은 receipt(영수증)이다.

10 소라는 헤어드라이어를 환불 받기를 원한다.

12 (A)는 이어지는 대화에서 Minsol의 불만이 이어지므로
   happy가 적절하다, (B)는 앞선 아빠의 대화에서 Buster에 대
   해 친절한 태도를 볼 수 있으므로 nice, (C)는 '몇 주 후에'라는
   의미가 이어져야 하므로 a few가 적절하다

13 teach는 목적격 보어로 to부정사를 취하는 동사이다.

14 ③ Wendy woke up too late to hear the news.라고 쓰는
   것이 적절하다. ⑤ 목적어 her는 목적격 보어의 행위 주체가 될
   수 있으므로 go라고 쓰는 것이 적절하다.

15 'too ~ to V'는 'so ~ that 주어 can't 동사원형'과 같다.

16 '목적어가 V하게 하다'는 의미로 쓰이고 있으므로 사역동사
   'make+목적어+동사원형'으로 나타낼 수 있다.

17 나는 너로부터 너무 멀리 떨어져 있어서 네가 하고 있는 말을 듣
   지 못했다는 문장을 쓸 수 있다.

18 on one's own: 스스로

19 Breeze는 중학교 때 엄마가 자신을 아기처럼 대한다고 느꼈다.

20 소녀는 엄마가 자신에게 묻지 않고 방을 청소하는 것에 불만을
   표시하고 있다.

21 소녀는 엄마가 자신의 일을 스스로 할 수 있게 해 주기를 원한다.

22 Andy의 마지막 말에서 소녀의 문제가 흔하다고 생각함을 알
   수 있다.

23 Andy가 부모님과 함께 많은 대화를 나누지 않은 이유는 그들

A Diary from Athens

Reading

확인문제   p.112

1 T 2 F 3 F 4 T

확인문제   p.113

1 T 2 T 3 F 4 T 5 F

교과서 확인학습 A   p.114~115

01 Diary, Athens
02 visiting, aunt, uncle, Athens
03 center   04 gathering
05 were a lot of, busy talking, shopping
06 Assembly
07 Any male citizens, take part in, vote, matters
08 each, freely, matters, vote by showing
09 Counting thousands of, almost
10 again
11 heard, interesting discussion between, named, and
12 questioned, on, meaning
13 too, to, way, discussing
14 best, so far   15 went
16 outdoor, which, hold about, watched, play
17 In addition to traditional, play, interesting
18 far, stage, characters' sadness
19 final, stay
20 must develop, talent, help make, state
21 want to go, a better

교과서 확인학습 B   p.116~117

1 A Diary from Athens
2 1st Day _ I am visiting my aunt and uncle in Athens.

3 Today I went to the Agora in the center of the city
4 It is a gathering place for Athenians.
5 There were a lot of stores, and people were busy talking and shopping.
6 2nd Day _ My uncle went to the Assembly.
7 Any male citizens over the age of 20 can take part in the Assembly and vote on important matters.
8 After they each speak freely about the matters, they vote by showing their hands.
9 My uncle said, "Counting thousands of hands is almost impossible."
10 3rd Day _ I went to the Agora again.
11 I heard a very interesting discussion between a teacher named Socrates and his students.
12 Socrates questioned his students on the meaning of life.
13 I was too young to understand it, but I liked their way of discussing matters.
14 4th Day _ Today was the best day so far.
15 I went to the Theater of Dionysus.
16 At the outdoor theater which can hold about 17,000 people, we watched Antigone, a play by Sophocles.
17 In addition to traditional songs and dances, the play had an interesting story.
18 I sat far from the stage, but I could feel the characters' sadness.
19 5th Day _ Today is the final day of my stay in Athens.
20 My aunt and uncle said to me, "You must develop your talent. You can help make Athens a great state."
21 Now I want to go to school and become a better person.

서술형 실전문제   p.118~120

01 (1) take part in   (2) talent   (3) assembly
   (4) So far   (5) hold   (6) question   (7) discussion
02 (1) citizen   (2) hold   (3) stay   (4) vote
   (5) impossible
03 (1) In addition to   (2) took part in
   (3) was busy enjoying   (4) over the age of
   (5) by doing   (6) between, and
04 (1) They were busy preparing for class.
   (2) A lot of preparation was needed.
   (3) I liked their way of discussing matters.

05 (1) Charlotte is so sick that she can't go to school today.

(2) The box is so heavy that I can't carry it.

(3) The math problems were so easy that we could solve them.

(4) The ribbon was so short that I couldn't tie with it.

06 (1) He spoke too fast for me to understand.

(2) He is so young that he can't drive a car.

(3) Remembering people is important.

07 people were busy talking and shopping

08 assembly

09 voted, important matters by showing

10 I was so young that I couldn't understand it.

11 At the outdoor theater which can hold about 17,000 people

12 The writer went to the Theater of Dionysus.

13 My aunt and uncle told me to develop my talent.

14 (G)oal

15 ②, ④

(1) ② Any male citizens over the age of 20 can take part in the Assembly and vote on important matters.

(2) ④ I was too young to understand the meaning of life.

01 assembly: 집회, 국회, 민회, hold: 담다, 수용하다, so far: 지금까지, discussion: 토론, take part in: ~에 참여하다, talent: 재능, question: 질문하다

02 vote: 투표하다, stay: 체류, 방문, citizen: 시민, hold: 담다, 수용하다, impossible: 불가능한

03 (1) in addition to: ~에 더하여, ~일뿐 아니라 (2) take part in: ~에 참여하다 (3) be busy -ing: ~하느라 바쁘다 (4) over the age of: ~살 이상의 (5) by -ing: ~함으로써 (6) between A and B: A와 B 사이에

04 (1) be busy -ing: ~하느라 바쁘다 (2) a lot of 다음에 단수 명사가 나오므로 단수 동사가 적절하다. (3) 뒤에 목적어가 나오 므로 명사가 아니라 동명사가 나와야 한다.

05 too+형용사[부사]+to+동사원형 = so+형용사[부사]+ that+주어+can't[couldn't]+동사원형, 형용사[부사]+ enough+to부정사 = so+형용사[부사]+that+주어+ can[could]+동사원형, to부정사의 의미상의 주어와 문장의 주어가 다를 경우 의미상의 주어를 써 주어야 한다. to부정사의 목적어가 문장의 주어일 경우 to부정사의 목적어를 쓰지 않았 지만 that절로 바뀔 때 주어가 다른 경우 목적어를 써 주어야 함에 주의한다.

06 (1), (2) too+형용사/부사+to+동사원형: 너무 ~해

서 …할 수 없다 = so+형용사/부사+that+주어+ can't[couldn't]+동사원형 (3) 동명사 주어는 단수 취급한다.

07 '~하느라 바쁘다'는 의미로 'be busy –ing'를 이용한다.

08 assembly: 집회, 민회 / 특히 특정한 목적을 위해 정기적으로 일어나는 많은 사람들의 모임

09 민회에 참석한 남자 시민들은 그들의 손을 들어 중요한 안건에 관해 투표했다.

10 'too+형용사+to부정사'는 'so+형용사+that+주어+can't+동 사원형'으로 바꾸어 쓸 수 있다.

11 부사구 'At the outdoor theater(야외 극장에서)'로 문장을 시 작하고, 주격 관계대명사 which절이 theater를 수식하는 구조 로 배열한다.

12 네 번째 날에 필자는 어디에 갔는가?

13 밑줄 (A)는 직접화법으로 tell을 이용한 간접화법으로 문장을 전환한다. said to는 told로, 인용문의 2인칭 'you'는 문장의 목적어인 1인칭으로 바꾸고, 동사는 to부정사로 바꾸어 준다.

14 숙부와 숙모가 재능을 개발하고 아테네를 위대한 국가로 만드는 데 기여할 수 있다는 말에 학교에 다니고 더 나은 사람이 되고 싶다고 말하고 있으므로 '내 삶의 새로운 목표'가 일기의 제목으 로 자연스럽다.

15 ② 모든 시민들이 민회에 참여하는 것이 아니라 20세 이상의 남 자 시민들이 참여한다. ④ 소크라테스의 학생들이 너무 어려서 삶의 의미를 이해하지 못한 것이 아니라 필자가 너무 어려서 이 해하지 못했다.

단원별 예상문제   p.121~124

01 ④ 02 ⑤ 03 ② 04 ①

05 ③ 06 (1) by (2) take, part (3) far

(4) between 07 ② 08 ③

09 (1) The soup is so hot that we can't eat it.

(2) I was so tired that I couldn't visit you.

(3) Anne is so wise that she can lead them.

10 (1) I saw something called a walking bus.

(2) I was busy taking notes and listening to the teacher.

(3) Consumers are smart enough to know that.

(4) His family was too poor to educate him further.

(5) The bag was so big that it could hold almost 1,000 presents.

(6) But he became so heavy that he couldn't move at all.

(7) This problem is so hard that I can't solve it.

(8) This computer is small enough for me to carry.

11 ⑤ 12 they vote by showing their hands

13 ④ 14 ⑤

15 You can help (to) make Athens a great state.

16 (A) interesting   (B) named   (C) questioned

17 I liked their way of discussing matters

18 the meaning of life   19 ④   20 ②

21 ④   22 talking, shopping, discussion

23 Counting thousands of hands is almost impossible.

01 ① wide: 넓은, narrow: 좁은 ② male: 남자의, 수컷의, female: 여자의, 암컷의 ③ sad: 슬픈, glad: 기쁜 ④ stay: 체류, 방문, visit: 방문 ⑤ impossible: 불가능한, possible: 가능한

02 '밖에서 일어나거나 사용되는; 건물 안에서가 아닌'을 의미하는 것은 outdoor(야외의, 실외의)이다.

03 in addition to ~에 더하여, ~일뿐 아니라, too ~ to ... 너무 ~해서 …하다

04 so far: 지금까지, over the age of ~: ~살 이상의

05 '남자들이나 소년들에게 전형적인 또는 관련된'을 뜻하는 것은 'male(남자의, 수컷의)'이 적절하다.

06 (1) by -ing: ~함으로써, make fun of: ~을 놀리다 (2) take part in: ~에 참여하다 (3) so far: 지금까지 (4) between A and B: A와 B 사이에

07 There are a lot of guys selling things.

08 ① She is too tired to walk. ② My aunt told me that I must develop my talent. ④ The writer decided to go to school. ⑤ I heard a very interesting discussion between a teacher named Socrates and his students.

09 too+형용사[부사]+to+동사원형 = so+형용사[부사]+that+주어+can't[couldn't]+동사원형, 형용사/부사+enough+to부정사 = so+형용사[부사]+that+주어+can[could]+동사원형. to부정사의 목적어가 문장의 주어일 경우 to부정사의 목적어를 쓰지 않지만 that절로 바뀔 때는 써 주어야 함에 주의한다.

10 (1) 부르는 것이 아니라 불리는 것이므로 '수동'의 의미를 갖는 called가 되어야 한다. (2) be busy -ing ~하느라 바쁘다 (3), (5) 형용사[부사]+enough+to부정사 = so+형용사[부사]+that+주어+can[could]+동사원형 (4), (6) too+형용사[부사]+to+동사원형 = so+형용사[부사]+that+주어+can't[couldn't]+동사원형 (7) to부정사의 목적어가 문장의 주어일 경우 to부정사의 목적어를 쓰지 않았지만 that절로 바뀔 때는 써 주어야 한다. (8) to부정사의 의미상의 주어와 문장의 주어가 다를 경우 의미상의 주어로 'for+목적격'을 써 주어야 한다.

11 ⓔ는 동명사 Counting이 주어이므로 단수 동사 is가 맞다.

12 민회에 참석한 남자 시민들은 그들의 손을 들어 중요한 문제에 관해 투표를 한다. 동사 'vote'를 첨가하고, 전치사 by 다음에 동명사 'showing'을 사용한다.

13 필자가 민회에 참석하여 투표를 했다는 내용은 없다.

14 더 나은 사람이 되고 싶다는 말로 미루어 보아 '단단히 결심한'이 적절하다.

15 'help+동사원형/to부정사', 'make+목적어(Athens)+목적보어(a great state)' 형태를 사용한다.

16 (A)는 명사 discussion을 수식하는 형용사 'interesting'이 적절하고, (B)는 Socrates라고 불리는 선생이란 뜻으로 과거분사 'named', (C)는 과거 동사 'questioned'가 적절하다.

17 'way'는 '방식'이라는 뜻이고, 전치사 of 뒤에 동명사 'discussing'이 적절하다.

18 대명사 it은 앞 문장의 '삶의 의미'를 가리키는 말이다.

19 연극 Antigone에 관한 설명으로 전통적인 노래와 춤에 더하여 흥미로운 이야기가 있었다는 의미이므로 첨가의 의미를 가지는 in addition to가 적절하다.

20 ⓐ는 '지금까지'의 의미로 'so far', ⓑ는 '무대에서 먼 곳에'란 의미로 'far'가 적절하다.

21 이 글은 필자가 숙부, 숙모가 계신 아테네를 방문한 내용을 하루하루 기록한 일기 형식의 글이므로 ④가 적절하다.

22 Agora는 아테네 사람들이 모이고 이야기 나누고, 쇼핑하고 토론을 위한 장소이다.

23 동사 'count'를 동명사 'counting'으로 바꾸고 '수천 명의'를 나타내는 'thousands of'를 쓴다.

A Life Full of Fun

시험대비 실력평가
p.128

01 ⑤   02 ⑤   03 ①   04 ④

05 (1) Lastly   (2) spread   (3) plate   (4) is made into

(5) caught my interest   (6) take a look

06 ①

01 pour: 붓다, bake: 굽다, fry: 볶다, cook: 요리하다, publish: 출판하다

02 agree의 명사형은 agreement이다.

03 하나의 언어에서 다른 언어로 바뀌는 것을 가리키는 말은 translate(번역하다)이다.

04 fascinating: 매력적인

05 lastly: 마지막으로, spread: 바르다. plate: 접시 be made into ~로 만들어지다, catch one's interest ~의 관심을 끌다, take a look 살펴보다

06 주어진 문장에서 spread는 '바르다'는 뜻으로 쓰였으며 이와 같은 의미로 쓰인 것은 ①번이다. ②, ③번은 '펼치다', ④, ⑤번은 '번지다, 확산시키다'는 뜻으로 쓰였다.

서술형 시험대비
p.129

01 dead   02 (1) creative   (2) cartoonist

(3) silly   (4) usual   (5) well-known

03 (1) box office   (2) showtime   (3) pay for

04 (1) You should not make fun of your friends.

(2) Lucy is always calm through life's ups and downs.

(3) I take a look at the webtoons of the day.

05 Education, amusement, pollution, suggestion, agreement

01 주어진 문장은 반의어 관계를 나타낸다. dead: 죽은, alive: 살아 있는

02 creative: 창의적인, cartoonist: 만화가, silly: 어리석은, usual: 보통의, well-known: 유명한, 잘 알려진

03 box office: 매표소, showtime: 상영 시간, pay for: ~에 대한 돈을 내다

04 make fun of: ~을 놀리다, ups and downs: 기복, take a look: 살펴보다

05 동물들은 숲속에 놀이공원을 지으려는 도시의 계획을 환영한다.

하지만, 그들은 곧 심각한 오염에 시달린다. 나이 든 코끼리가 한 가지 제안을 한다. 동물들과 도시는 모든 이들을 위한 더 좋은 세상을 만들기 위해 합의에 이른다.

교과서 Conversation

핵심 Check
p.130~131

1 (1) met / haven't, Have / have

(2) Have you ever been / have been / did

2 (1) how to / First, Second / next / Boil

(2) fall asleep easily / First of all, Next, Lastly

교과서 대화문 익히기

Check(√) True or False
p.132

1 F   2 T   3 T   4 F

교과서 확인학습
p.134~135

Communication: Listen – Dialog 1

down / serious, a lot / ups and downs / Have you watched / I haven't . Why / feelings, understand, better / sounds, watch

Communication: Listen – Dialog 2

line / ticket machine, from, machine / how to use the machine / select / watch, what / select, seats / back / Lastly , pay for / simple

Communication: Listen More

Have you ever made / No, I haven't / how to make / First, put, on, spread / help, with / Next, peppers / Add, bake, oven / wait, taste

Communicate: Speak

fried rice / cut, into / next / Put, fry / simple

Wrap Up – Listening ❺

Have, been / have, Actually / you've climbed, haven't you / twice

Wrap Up – Listening ❻

how to draw / First, circle, Next / draw, color, circle, Lastly

01 He needs six circles.   02 ⑤

03 Do you know how to make fried rice?

04 채소를 작은 조각으로 자르고 팬에 기름을 두른 후 채소를 밥과 함께 볶는다.

05 (1) I've never been to Baltimore before.

  (2) Have you ever been to China?

01 Mike는 곰의 얼굴을 그리기 위해 6개의 원이 필요하다.

02 마지막에 입을 만들어야 한다.

05 Have you ever p.p: ~해 본 적이 있니?

01 ②   02 ①

03 Have you watched the animated movie "Shining Days"?   04 ③   05 ④

06 ⓐ put   ⓑ help   ⓒ bake   ⓓ wait

07 ⑤   08 (E) → (C) → (A) → (D) → (B)

09 haven't you?

10 Have you ever been to Sokcho?

11 (1) Have you ever been to Dokdo?

  (2) I have read the Harry Potter series.

01 'Have you ever ~?'의 경험을 묻는 질문에 'Yes, I have.' 또는 'No, I haven't.'로 대답한다.

02 (A)의 'down'은 '우울한'을 의미한다.

04 (A) 기계를 사용하는 방법을 묻고 있으므로 how, (B) select와 병렬 구조로 동사 choose, (C) Lately: 최근에, Lastly: 마지막으로

05 표 매수와 좌석을 고른 후 표 값을 지불한다.

06 bake: 굽다

07 Garcia와 Suji가 피자 소스를 만들기 위해 무슨 재료를 준비해야 하는지 알 수 없다.

08 (E) 볶음밥 만드는 법 질문 → (C) 대답 및 첫 번째 단계 설명 → (A) 두 번째 단계 질문 → (D) 두 번째 단계 및 세 번째 단계 설명 → (B) 반응

09 선행하는 문장의 시제가 현재완료이므로 'haven't you?'가 적절하다

11 Have you ever been to ~?: ~에 가 본 적이 있니?

01 (3) → (4) → (2)

02 He will make nacho pizza.

03 He put nacho chips on a plate.

04 He put pizza sauce, ham, onions. peppers, and cheese.

05 (D) → (E) → (C) → (A) → (B)

06 Yes, he has.

07 Because his uncle lives there.

01 나초 칩을 접시 위에 올려놓고 피자 소스를 바른 후 햄, 양파, 피망을 위에 올린다. 그리고 피자를 올린다.

02 요리사는 나초 피자를 만들 것이다.다.

03 요리사는 첫 번째로 나초 칩을 접시 위에 올려놓았다.

04 나초 칩 위에 피자 소스, 햄, 양파, 피망 그리고 치즈를 올려놓았다.

05 (D) 기계를 사용하는 방법으로 첫 번째 단계 설명 → (E) 상영 시간 선택 → (C) 두 번째 단계 설명→ (A) 앉고 싶은 자리 설명 → (B) 마지막 단계 설명

06 민수는 설악산에 올라가 본 적이 있다.

07 민수는 그의 삼촌이 속초에 살고 계시기 때문에 매년 속초를 방문한다.

Grammar

1 (1) has been   (2) has, left   (3) have called

2 (1) typing   (2) boring   (3) sung

01 (1) hasn't gone → hasn't been

  (2) saw → have seen   (3) did → have done

  (4) have work → have worked

02 (1) living   (2) crying   (3) written   (4) made

  (5) barking

03 (1) I have read 500 books since I was six.

  (2) The boy has already drunk the milk.

  (3) Is this a baked potato?

  (4) Did you find your sleeping bag?

01 (1) 'have gone to ~'는 '~에 가고 없다'는 의미로 결과를 나타내는 현재완료이다. '~에 가 본 적이 없다'는 것은 'have[has] not been to ~'로 표현한다. (2) 지금까지 프로그램을 몇 번 보았다는 의미이므로 현재완료 시제로 표현하는 것이 적절하다. (3) 어제 이래로 아무것도 하지 않았다는 것이므로 과거의 일이 현재까지 이어지는 것이라 볼 수 있다. 따라서 현재완료 시제가 적절하다. (4) 현재완료의 형태는 'have+p.p.'이다.

02 (1) '그 마을에서 살고 있는'이라는 의미이므로 현재분사로 people을 수식한다. (2) 아기가 울고 있는 것이므로 현재분사로 baby를 수식하는 것이 적절하다. (3) 책이 유명한 작가에 의해 '쓰여진' 것이므로 과거분사를 쓴다. (4) '금으로 만들어진 수저'라는 의미이므로 과거분사로 spoon을 수식한다. (5) '짖는 개'라는 의미이므로 현재분사를 쓰는 것이 적절하다.

03 (1) 여섯 살 이후로 계속 책을 읽은 것이므로 현재완료 시제를 써서 나타낸다. (2) 벌써 우유를 마셨다는 완료를 나타내고 있으므로 현재완료 시제를 쓰는 것이 적절하다. (3) 감자는 구워지는 것이므로 과거분사로 potato를 수식한다. (4) 잠자는 용도로 쓰이는 자루를 말하는 것이므로 동명사 sleeping이 적절하다.

01 ④	02 ③	03 ③	04 ③
05 ⑤	06 ④	07 ④, ⑤	

08 Eunji has lived in Busan since she was five years old.

09 ⑤	10 ③	11 ④

12 I have just had a piece of frozen pizza.

13 ⑤	14 ③	15 ④
16 I bought a used car.	17 ③	18 ⑤
19 ④	20 ⑤	

21 The surprising news is not true.   22 ⑤

23 Cold winds blew into the house through the broken window.

24 exciting / excited

01 현재완료 시제와 함께 쓰이면서 특정 시점을 이끌 수 있는 것은 since이다.

02 현재완료의 형태는 'have+p.p.'이다. 따라서 seen이 적절하다.

03 무언가가 '타고 있는' 것이므로 현재분사 burning으로 수식하고, 'Jessica라고 이름 지어진' 것이므로 과거분사로 a girl을 수식하는 것이 적절하다.

04 stop의 과거분사는 stopped이다.

05 주어진 문장은 경험을 나타내는 현재완료이다. 밑줄 친 현재완료의 용법은 각각 ① 결과 ②, ③ 완료 ④ 계속 ⑤ 경험을 나타내고 있다.

06 지금까지 3년 동안 그녀를 만나 왔다는 의미이므로 현재완료 시제를 사용하는 것이 적절하다.

07 목적격 보어로 과거분사를 취할 수 없는 동사는 help와 seem이다.

08 은지는 5살 때부터 부산에서 살기 시작하여 현재도 부산에서 살고 있다고 하였으므로 현재완료 시제를 활용하여 은지는 5살 이래로 부산에서 살고 있다는 문장으로 쓸 수 있다.

09 주어진 문장의 밑줄 친 부분은 현재분사로 쓰인 것이다. '손을 올리고 있는 소녀'라는 의미의 ⑤번이 현재분사로 쓰였으므로

⑤번이 답이다.

10 Has로 묻고 있으므로 has로 답하는 것이 적절하다.

11 ① that smiling girl ② the injured man ③ did you meet ⑤ for three years

12 '막 먹었다'는 완료의 의미는 현재완료 시제를 통하여 나타낼 수 있다.

13 (A) 흥분을 유발하는 게임이라는 의미이므로 현재분사로 game을 수식하는 것이 적절하다. (B) 5살 때부터 기타를 연주해 오고 있다는 의미이므로 현재완료 시제를 쓴다. (C) 과거를 나타내는 어구인 yesterday와 현재완료 시제는 함께 쓸 수 없다.

14 답변으로 미루어 보아 영화를 본 적이 있는지 경험을 묻는 말이 들어가는 것이 적절하다.

15 Paul이 10살 때부터 쭉 Tom이 가르치고 있다는 의미이므로 현재완료 시제가 적절하며, Tom이 Paul을 잘 안다는 것은 현재 상태를 나타내는 것이므로 현재시제를 쓴다.

16 중고차는 used car이다.

17 모두 특정 시점을 이끄는 since가 쓰이지만 ③번에는 기간을 이끄는 전치사 for가 쓰인다.

18 동생이 쇼핑몰에 가서 현재 이곳에 없다는 의미이므로, 현재완료 시제를 사용하여 '동생은 쇼핑몰에 가고 없어.'라는 문장을 쓸 수 있다. 'have gone to'는 '~에 가고 없다'는 의미를 갖는다.

19 그는 오늘 아침 이래로 불타는 태양 아래에서 하루 종일 일해 왔다는 의미이다. 따라서 현재완료 시제를 쓰는 것이 적절하며, '불타는 태양'이므로 현재분사로 sun을 수식하는 것이 적절하다.

20 내가 즐거움을 느끼는 것이므로 과거분사 amused를 쓰는 것이 적절하다.

21 그 소식이 '놀라움을 주는'것이므로 현재분사로 news를 수식한다.

22 주어진 문장을 영어로 옮기면 I have fought with my brother before.이다.

23 blow의 과거형 blew를 쓰고, '부서진 창문'이라고 하였으므로 과거분사로 window를 수식하도록 문장을 쓰는 것이 적절하다.

24 콘서트는 흥분을 유발하는 것이므로 현재분사로. 팬들은 흥분을 느낀 것이므로 과거분사로 쓰는 것이 적절하다.

01 (1) rising   (2) baked, sleeping   (3) dancing
    (4) cheering   (5) sliced

02 Jenny has been friends with Christina since 2010.

03 A: Have you ever cooked fried rice?
    B: Yes, I have cooked it many times.

04 Have you been to other countries before?

05 (1) drove　(2) has been　(3) has rained　(4) lost
　　(5) has read
06 Look at the boy wearing a red cap.
07 My brother has been sick since last night.
08 (1) 현재분사　이유: '수영하는 아기'라는 의미로
　　swimming이 baby를 수식하고 있다.
　　(2) 동명사　이유: 수영하는 용도로 쓰이는 풀'이라는
　　의미로 쓰이고 있다.
09 (1) I have been to Jejudo twice until now.
　　(2) I broke the window yesterday.
　　(3) We haven't seen the movie yet.
10 has lived, 2011, 2011, has learned, for
11 My grandmother has broken her right arm.
12 She made me bring a boiled egg and chopped
　　carrot.
13 has worked
14 (1) boring → bored　(2) making → made
　　(3) excited → exciting　(4) barked → barking

01 분사의 수식을 받는 명사가 행위 주체인 경우에는 현재분사로,
　　그렇지 않은 경우에는 과거분사로 수식한다.
02 현재완료 시제를 이용하여 Jenny는 Christina와 2010년 이래
　　로 쭉 친구라고 쓸 수 있다.
03 경험을 묻고 답하는 말이므로 현재완료 시제를 써서 나타낼 수
　　있다. '볶아진 밥'이라는 말로 '볶음밥'을 표현할 수 있음 에 유의
　　하자.
04 경험을 묻는 말이므로 현재완료 시제를 이용하여 문장을 만들
　　수 있다.
05 과거를 나타내는 어구와 현재완료는 함께 쓸 수 없다. 그러나 과
　　거의 일이 현재까지 영향을 미치는 경우 현재완료 시제를 쓸 수
　　있다.
06 분사가 목적어나 부사구와 함께 쓰일 때는 명사를 뒤에서 수식한
　　다.
07 어젯밤부터 아픈 것이 현재까지 이어지고 있으므로 현재완료시
　　제를 활용하여 표현할 수 있다.
08 현재분사는 명사를 수식하고, 동명사는 '~한 용도로 쓰이는 명
　　사'라고 해석된다.
09 (1) 지금까지의 경험을 나타내고 있으므로 현재완료 시제를 쓰
　　는 것이 적절하다. (2) 어제 일어난 일을 말하고 있으므로 과거
　　시제를 쓴다. (3) 현재완료 시제의 용법 중 '완료'를 사용하여 나
　　타낼 수 있다.
10 캐나다에서 태어난 Jason은 10살이던 2011년에 한국으로 이
　　사를 오자마자 태권도를 배우기 시작했다. 그는 현재 18세이므
　　로 8년간 태권도를 배워 왔다고 말할 수 있다.
11 지난달에 할머니의 오른팔이 부러졌고, 할머니는 여전히 오른팔
　　을 쓰실 수 없으므로 현재완료 시제를 이용하여 오른팔이 부러
　　진 상황이 지속됨을 말할 수 있다.

12 '삶은 달걀'은 삶아진 달걀을 뜻하므로 과거분사 boiled로 egg
　　를 수식해야 하며, '다진 당근' 역시 다져진 당근을 뜻하므로
　　chopped carrot이라고 쓰는 것이 적절하다.
13 현재도 일을 하고 있고, 5년 동안 이 회사에서 일해 오고 있다는
　　의미이므로 현재완료 시제를 쓰는 것이 적절하다.
14 (1) 지루한 감정을 느낀 것이므로 과거분사 (2) 중국에서 만들
　　어진 가방이므로 과거분사 (3) 흥분을 유발하는 모험영화이므로
　　현재분사를 쓰는 것이 적절하다. (4) 짖는 개라는 의미이므로 현
　　재분사로 dog를 수식하는 것이 적절하다.

[교과서]
Reading

확인문제　　　　　　　　　　　　　　　　p.148

1 F　2 T　3 T　4 F　5 F

확인문제　　　　　　　　　　　　　　　　p.149

1 F　2 F　3 F　4 T　5 T　6 F

교과서 확인학습 A　　　　　　　　　p.150~151
01 Land　　　　　　　　02 laugh, saw, above
03 so, successful　　　　04 who make cartoons
05 to catch, make you laugh, creative drawings.
06 have made, for　　　07 many types of cartoons
08 is, a few words　　　09 is, called
10 makes a funny character, laugh, doing, saying
11 Another, is called
12 some parts, are different, bigger than usual
13 on　　　　　　　　　14 Which parts, jump
15 have used, to make fun of
16 several, come together, a comic strip
17 have been, for　　　 18 just amusing stories
19 have also used, for education
20 make, clearer, easier to learn
21 have probably seen
22 have surely seen, animated movies
23 popular among people of all ages
24 are added to, come alive
25 develop fascinating, interesting, through
26 was developed　　　27 is called
28 are published, read them, on
29 popular, them are, into　30 may appear
31 different, exciting than, remain, laugh, relax, learn

1 Boat! Land!

2 Did you laugh when you saw the cartoon above?

3 If so, the cartoonist was successful.

4 Cartoonists are the people who make cartoons.

5 They want to catch your interest, and usually, make you laugh with simple language and creative drawings.

6 People have made cartoons for hundreds of years.

7 There are many types of cartoons, and they play different roles.

8 One form of cartoon is a picture with a few words.

9 It is sometimes called a "gag cartoon."

10 The cartoonist makes a funny character, and the character makes you laugh by doing or saying silly things.

11 Another type of cartoon is called a caricature.

12 In a caricature, some parts of a character are different or bigger than usual.

13 Look at the picture on the right.

14 Which parts of the man's face jump out at you?

15 Artists have used this type of cartoon to make fun of well-known people.

16 When several cartoon pictures come together and tell a story, we have a comic strip.

17 Comic strips have been in newspapers for many years.

18 They are often just amusing stories.

19 People have also used comic strips for education.

20 Comics can make information clearer and easier to learn.

21 You have probably seen comic history or science books.

22 You have surely seen many cartoon movies, or animated movies, too.

23 These are very popular among people of all ages.

24 Movement and sounds are added to pictures, so they come alive.

25 Artists and writers can develop fascinating characters and tell interesting stories through animation.

26 In the 1990s, a new type of cartoon was developed.

27 It is called a webtoon.

28 Webtoons are published online, so you can read them anytime, anywhere on your phone or computer.

29 They are very popular, and some of them are even made into TV dramas or movies.

30 New forms of cartoons may appear in the future.

31 They could be different and even more exciting than now, but one thing will remain the same: they will help us laugh, relax, and learn.

01 ③   02 ⑤

03 It is called a caricature.

04 A cartoonist makes a funny character in a gag cartoon.

05 ②   06 ④   07 They make cartoons.

08 ③   09 ②   10 ③   11 ④

12 It's because they are published online.   13 ④

14 ②, ④   15 ③   16 successful

17 The characters in a gag cartoon make people laugh by doing or saying silly things.

18 ②   19 ④   20 We call it a gag cartoon.   21 ②   22 ③

23 A comic strip is made of several cartoon pictures and tells a story.

24 It's because comics can make information clearer and easier to learn.

25 ③   26 우리가 웃고, 쉬고, 배우도록 돕는 것

01 이어지는 글의 내용을 보면 다양한 종류의 만화는 서로 다른 역할을 한다. 따라서 different라고 쓰는 것이 적절하다.

02 빈칸 (A)에는 by+Ving로 '~함으로써'라는 의미를 완성하는 전치사 by가 들어간다. be interested in: ~에 흥미를 갖 다, give up: ~을 포기하다, turn off: ~을 끄다, be proud of: ~을 자랑스러워하다, one by one: 하나씩

03 두 번째 종류의 만화는 캐리커처라고 하였다.

04 만화가는 개그 만화에서 웃긴 캐릭터를 만든다고 하였다.

05 캐리커처는 유명한 사람들을 풍자하는 것이다.

06 글에는 두 가지 종류의 만화만 제시되어 있다.

07 만화가들은 만화를 만드는 사람들이다.

08 빈칸 (A)에는 기간을 이끄는 전치사 for가 쓰인다. ③번에는 특정 시점을 이끄는 since가 쓰인다.

09 연재만화는 여러 해 동안 신문에 실려 옴 - [B] 연재만화는 종종 단지 재미있는 이야기이고 교육용으로도 쓰임 - [A] 교육용 만화 역사책이나 과학책이 있음. 또한 만화영화도 있는데 - [C] 이는 모든 연령의 사람들에게 인기가 있고 동작이나 소리가 더해져서 그림들이 생생하게 살아남.

10 몇 가지 만화 그림을 모아 연재만화를 만든다고 하였다.

11 (A) 웹툰이라고 불리는 것이므로 수동태, (B) 지칭하는 것이 복수명사 webtoons이므로 복수 대명사, (C) appear는 자동사

이므로 수동태로 쓰일 수 없다.

12 우리가 휴대 전화나 컴퓨터로 언제 어디서나 웹툰을 읽을 수 있는 이유는 웹툰이 온라인으로 출판되기 때문이다.

13 웹툰을 주로 누가 보는지는 알 수 없다.

14 사람을 선행사로 받아주는 주격 관계대명사 who가 쓰이며, who를 대신하여 that을 쓸 수 있다.

15 다양한 종류의 만화가 있다고 하였으므로 만화의 종류가 이어지는 것이 가장 적절하다.

16 바라던 결과를 성취하는 것은 '성공적인(successful)'이다.

17 개그 만화에 등장하는 캐릭터는 우스꽝스러운 행동이나 말을 함으로써 사람들을 웃게 만든다고 하였다.

18 one과 another로 만화의 종류를 소개하고 있으므로 만화의 종류에는 두 가지 이상이 있음을 알 수 있다. another는 남아 있는 것 중 하나를 가리키는 대명사이다.

19 개그 만화에서는 우스꽝스러운 행동이나 말을 함으로써 독자를 웃게 만드는 캐릭터를 볼 수 있다고 하였다.

20 몇 마디 말을 쓴 그림은 '개그 만화'라고 부른다.

21 주어진 문장의 대명사 It은 a new type of cartoon을 지칭하는 것이다.

22 (A) 즐거움을 유발하는 이야기이므로 현재분사로 stories를 수식, (B) 긍정에 대한 동의이므로 too, (C) come alive: 생생하게 살아나다, 활기를 띠다, come live: 생방송하다

23 연재만화는 몇 가지 만화 그림으로 이루어져 있으며 이야기를 들려준다고 하였다.

24 만화는 정보를 더 명료하고 더 배우기 쉽게 만들 수 있기 때문에 사람들은 연재만화를 교육용으로 사용해 오기도 했다.

25 웹툰은 온라인으로 출판되기 때문에 여러분이 휴대 전화나 컴퓨터로 언제 어디서나 볼 수 있다고 하였다.

26 미래에 새로운 형태의 만화가 나타날지라도 우리가 웃고, 쉬고, 배우도록 돕는 것은 여전히 같을 것이라고 하였다.

서술형 시험대비
p.158~159

01 People have made cartoons for hundreds of years.

02 They use simple language and creative drawings.

03 If you laughed when you saw the cartoon above

04 many types of cartoons 05 It makes us laugh.

06 It is a gag cartoon.

07 many words → a few words   wise → silly[foolish]

08 We can use comic strips.

09 movement and sounds are added to pictures

10 They can develop fascinating characters and tell interesting stories through animation.

11 Webtoons were developed in the 1990s.

12 a comic strip / amusing / education

13 will help us laugh, relax, and learn

01 사람들은 수 백 년 전에 만화를 만들었고 현재도 만들고 있다고 하였으므로, 현재완료 시제를 이용하여 '사람들은 수 백 년 동안 만화를 만들어 왔다'는 문장을 쓸 수 있다.

02 만화가들은 사람들을 웃게 하기 위해서 간단한 말과 독창적인 그림을 사용한다고 하였다.

03 If so는 '만약 그렇다면'이라는 뜻으로, '위 만화를 보고 웃었다면'이라는 의미로 쓰였다.

04 많은 종류의 만화를 가리키는 대명사이다.

05 개그 만화는 우리를 웃게 만든다.

06 간단한 말을 쓴 그림이므로 개그 만화이다.

07 만화의 한 형태로 몇 마디 말을 쓴 그림이 있고, 웃긴 캐릭터가 우스꽝스러운 행동을 한다고 하였다.

08 만화는 정보를 더 명료하고 더 배우기 쉽게 만들 수 있다고 하였다. 만약 정보를 좀 더 분명하게 전달하기를 원한다면 연재만화를 사용할 수 있다.

09 동작이나 소리가 그림에 더해져서 그림들이 생생하게 살아난다고 하였다.

10 미술가들과 작가들은 매력적인 캐릭터를 개발하고 만화영화 제작을 통해 재미있는 이야기를 들려준다고 하였다.

11 웹툰이 개발된 시기는 1990년대라고 하였다.

12 만화 그림이 모여 이야기를 들려주면 연재만화가 되고, 연재만화는 재미있는 이야기라고 하였다. 또한 연재만화는 교육용으로 사용된다.

13 해석: 비록 미래에 새로운 형태의 만화가 나타난다 할지라도, 그것은 지금처럼 우리가 웃고, 쉬고, 배우도록 도와줄 것이다.

영역별 핵심문제
p.161~165

01 ①   02 ③

03 (1) Emma poured orange juice into a glass and drank it.
   (2) We have lots of[a lot of] plates to wash.
   (3) I like to fry eggs and lots of vegetables.

04 (1) come together   (2) comic strip   (3) Watch out
   (4) of all ages   (5) jumps out at me

05 ③   06 (B) → (D) → (C) → (A)   07 ⑤

08 (A) a movie   (B) a showtime   (C) choose seats
   (D) pay for the tickets

09 Have you ever made nacho pizza?

10 ⓐ nacho pizza   ⓑ nacho chips

11 ④   12 ⑤

13 (A) down   (B) serious   (C) understand

14 ⑤   15 ⑤   16 ②

17 Do you know the boy jumping on the stage?

18 ④   19 ④   20 ②

21 I have had this problem since last year.

22 ⑤ 　　　　23 ⑤ 　　　　24 stolen, found

25 They have been in the library since noon.

26 ② 　　　27 ③ 　　　28 ④ 　　　　29 usual

30 ③

01 태양에 의해 손상되는 것으로부터 피부를 보호하기 위해 피부에 바르는 로션의 한 유형을 가리키는 말은 sunscreen(자외선 차단제)이다.

02 spread는 '바르다'는 의미로 쓰였다.

03 pour: 붓다, plate: 접시, fry: 볶다

04 of all ages: 모든 연령의, watch out for: ~을 조심하다, comic strip: 신문 연재만화 / jump out at: ~에게 금방 눈에 띄다, come together: 합쳐지다

05 주어진 문장에서 down은 '우울한'을 뜻하며 이와 같은 의미로 쓰인 것은 ③번이다. 나머지는 모두 '아래로, ~ 아래쪽으로'를 뜻한다.

06 (B) 속초 방문한 경험 질문 → (D) 대답 및 이유 설명 → (C) 설악산에 올라가 본 적이 있는지 확인 → (A) 대답 및 올라간 횟수 설명

07 빈칸 (A)에 들어갈 말로 나머지는 모두 제안을 나타내지만 ⑤번은 경험을 묻는 표현이다.

09 'Have you ever ~?' 표현을 사용하여 경험을 물어 볼 수 있다.

11 위 대화에서 피자 소스를 무엇으로 만드는지는 알 수 없다.

12 Anna가 Jinsu가 채소를 작게 자르는 것을 돕는지 대화를 통해 알 수 없다.

13 (A)에서 down은 '우울한'을 가리킨다. (B)에는 대명사를 수식하는 형용사 serious가 적절하다. (C)에는 help 뒤에 원형 부정사 understand가 적절하다.

14 drive의 과거분사형은 driven이다.

15 경험을 나타내는 문장은 현재완료로 표현할 수 있으며, '~에 가본 적이 있다'는 'have been to'를 쓴다.

16 첫 번째 빈칸에는 경험을 나타내어 once, twice, before 등이 들어갈 수 있다. 특정 시점을 이끄는 것은 since, 기간을 이끄는 것은 for를 쓴다.

17 '무대 위에서 뛰고 있는'이 '소년'을 수식하는 구조이므로 the boy jumping on the stage라고 쓰는 것이 적절하다. 분사가 부사구와 함께 쓰이고 있으므로 명사를 뒤에서 수식하도록 문장을 만든다.

18 명백히 과거를 나타내는 어구인 when, ~ ago 등은 현재완료 시제와 함께 쓰일 수 없다. 현재완료의 과거형은 haven't p.p.이다.

19 주소를 잊었고 여전히 기억할 수 없다고 하였으므로 현재완료 시제를 이용하여 주소를 잊은 상황을 말할 수 있다.

20 모두 baking이 들어가지만 ②번에는 baked가 들어간다. ⑤번에 쓰인 baking은 동명사로 '빵을 굽는 용도로 쓰이는 소다'라는 의미를 완성한다.

21 작년부터 지금까지 이 문제를 가지고 있었다고 하였으므로 현재완료 시제로 나타낼 수 있다.

22 주어진 문장의 밑줄 친 부분은 현재완료의 용법 중 '경험'을 나타낸다. 각각 ① 결과 ② 결과 ③ 계속 ④ 계속 ⑤ 경험 용법으로 쓰였다.

23 과거를 나타내는 어구인 the other day가 있으므로 과거시제를 쓰는 것이 적절하다. put은 과거와 과거완료의 형태가 모두 동일한 put–put–put이다.

24 '도난당한 차'이므로 과거분사 stolen으로 car를 수식하고, '발견되었다'고 하였으므로 수동태를 완성하는 과거분사 found를 쓴다.

25 정오에 도서관을 가서 여전히 도서관에 있다고 하였으므로, 현재완료 시제를 이용하여 그들이 정오 이래로 도서관에 계속 있다는 말을 쓸 수 있다.

26 ②번 문장의 주어인 They가 지칭하는 것은 주어진 문장의 Cartoonists이다. 따라서 ②번에 들어가는 것이 가장 적절하다.

27 밑줄 친 (A)는 현재완료의 '계속' 용법으로 쓰였다. ① 경험 ② 결과 ③ 계속 ④ 경험 ⑤ 결과

28 만화가들은 창의적인 그림으로 우리를 웃게 만든다고 하였다.

29 보통의; 아주 자주 발생하는 usual(평소의, 보통의)

30 글의 서두를 만화의 또 다른 종류(Another type of cartoon)라는 말로 이끌고 있으므로, 앞에서 다른 종류의 만화에 대해 언급했음을 알 수 있다.

단원별 예상문제　　　　　　　　p.166~169

01 ⓒ → watched 　　　　　　02 ①

03 They want to buy them from the ticket machine.

04 They will watch it at seven o'clock.

05 She wants to sit in the back.

06 (C) → (A) → (E) → (D) → (B) 　　　　　07 ③

08 They should fry the vegetables with rice.

09 They should prepare vegetables, oil, and rice.

10 ③ 　　　11 ④ 　　　12 ⑤ 　　　13 ⑤

14 ② 　　　15 (1) named (2) broken (3) surprising

16 I will buy the recommended book.

17 Mr. Smith has taught me English since last year.

18 interesting 　　　19 New forms of cartoons

20 ④ 　　　21 ④

22 Movement and sounds make the pictures come alive.

23 ④ 　　　24 ④ 　　　25 ②

26 Because he looks on the bright side of everything and always tries to help others.

01 경험을 묻는 현재완료 시제를 사용하여야 하므로 watched가 적절하다.

02 위 대화를 통해 Kevin이 어떻게 생겼는지는 알 수 없다.

03 Tony와 Emily는 발매기에서 표를 사고 싶어 한다.

04 Tony와 Emily는 영화를 7시에 볼 것이다.

05 Emily는 뒤에 앉고 싶어 한다.

06 (C) 첫 번째 단계 설명 → (A) 도움 제공 → (E) 두 번째 단계 설명 → (D) 다음 단계 질문 → (B) 마지막 단계 설명

07 (A) cut: 자르다, put: 놓다 (B) bake: 굽다, (C) fry: 볶다, spread: 바르다

08 그들은 팬에 기름을 두른 후 채소와 밥을 함께 볶아야 한다.

09 Anna와 Jinsu는 볶음밥을 만들기 위해 채소, 기름, 밥이 필요하다.

10 경험을 묻는 질문에 'Yes, I have.'라고 대답하는 것이 알맞다.

11 모두 '완료'를 나타내지만 ④번은 '계속'을 의미하는 현재완료이다.

12 ① made ② has practiced ③ frozen food ④ The boy walking with his friends가 적절하다.

13 '조리된 닭고기'라는 의미이므로 과거분사로, '소리치는 소년'이라는 의미이므로 현재분사로 명사를 수식하는 것이 적절하다.

14 모두 과거를 나타내는 어구와 함께 쓰여 과거동사가 들어가야 하지만, ②번은 현재완료 시제가 쓰인다. ① found ② has read ③ went ④ took ⑤ raised 혹은 had가 쓰일 수 있다.

15 'Chris라고 이름 지어진 소년'이므로 과거분사로, (2) '고장 난 냉장고'이므로 과거분사로, (3) '놀라움을 유발하는 뉴스'이므로 현재분사로 수식하는 것이 적절하다.

16 '추천된 책'이라고 하였으므로 과거분사로 book을 수식하는 것이 적절하다.

17 Mr. Smith has taught English to me since last year.라고 써도 좋다..

18 흥미를 유발하는 이야기들이므로 현재분사로 stories를 수식하는 것이 적절하다.

19 새로운 형태의 만화를 가리키는 대명사이다.

20 ③는 형용사를 수식하는 부사로 쓰인 to부정사이다. ① 명사적 용법 중 목적격 보어 ② 명사적 용법 중 진주어 ③ 부사적 용법 중 목적 ④ 부사적 용법 중 형용사 수식 ⑤ 형용사적 용법으로 something을 수식

21 온라인에서 볼 수 있는 것은 웹툰이다.

22 동작이나 소리가 그림들이 생생하게 살아나게 한다.

23 만화영화는 모든 연령대의 사람들에게 매우 인기가 많다고 하였다.

24 만화를 제작하는 데 얼마만큼의 시간이 소요되는지는 위 글을 읽고 알 수 없다.

25 글쓴이가 좋아하는 캐릭터는 유머 있고 친절하지만 똑똑하지 않고 가끔 문제를 일으킨다는 연결이 자연스럽다. 따라서 However가 적절하다.

26 글쓴이가 '기영'을 좋아하는 이유는 모든 것의 긍정적인 측면을 바라보고 항상 남을 도우려 애쓰기 때문이라고 하였다.

01 No, he hasn't.

02 It's an animated movie about a teenager's feelings.

03 It can help him understand his feelings better.

04 (1)번 문장은 Amelia가 캐나다에 가 본 적이 있다는 경험을 나타내고, (2)번 문장은 Amelia가 캐나다로 가고 없다는 결과를 나타낸다.

05 I have lost my favorite book.

06 The crying boy ate five boiled eggs.

07 have had, have not had   08 a shaking voice

09 It is from *Black Rubber Shoes*.

10 He is humorous and kind. However, he is not very smart and sometimes causes trouble.

11 Artists have used this type of cartoon to make fun of well-known people.

12 Various types of cartoons and their roles

13 a gag cartoon, makes you laugh, a caricature, a comic strip, amusing

14 They have drawn a caricature to make fun of well-known people.

01 Kevin은 "Shining Days"를 보지 않았다.

02 "Shining Days"는 십대의 감정에 관한 것이다.

03 "Shining Days"는 Kevin이 자기의 감정들을 더욱 잘 이해할 수 있게 도와줄 수 있다.

04 현재완료 시제에서 '~에 가 본 적이 있다'는 have been to로 나타내고 '~에 가고 없다'는 'have gone to'로 나타내 는 것에 유의한다.

05 내가 가장 좋아하는 책을 잃어버리고 여전히 가지고 있지 않다고 하였으므로 현재완료 시제를 이용하여 책을 잃어버린 상황이 지속되고 있음을 말할 수 있다.

06 '울고 있는 소년'이므로 crying이 boy를 수식하고, 삶은 달걀은 '삶아진 달걀'인 boiled egg로 써서 문장을 만들 수 있다.

07 had를 대신하여 eaten을 써도 좋다.

08 '떨리는 목소리'라고 하였으므로 현재분사로 voice를 수식하는 것이 적절하다.

09 '검정고무신' 만화의 캐릭터이다.

10 캐릭터는 유머 있고 친절하지만 별로 똑똑하지 않고 가끔씩 말썽을 일으킨다고 하였다.

11 미술가들은 과거부터 지금까지 유명한 사람들을 풍자하기 위해 이런 종류의 만화를 그려왔다는 것이므로 현재완료 시제를 이용하여 하나의 문장으로 쓸 수 있다.

12 '다양한 종류의 만화와 그것들의 역할'이 글의 제목이 될 수 있다.

13 위 글에서 만화의 종류는 세 가지가 제시되어 있으며 그 종류는 개그 만화, 캐리커처, 그리고 연재만화이다.

14 미술가들은 유명한 사람들을 풍자하기 위해서 캐리커처를 그려 왔다.

|모범답안|

01 (A) down   (B) ups and downs
    (C) watching the animated movie "Shining Days"
    (D) a teenager's feelings

02 Iron Man, Tales of Suspense, a genius scientist, owns a weapon company, invented a suit of armor to save his life, Iron Man, he is very rich and is the leader of the superhero team, the Avengers

01 오늘 나는 별일 없이 우울했다. 요즘, 내 감정이 많이 바뀌었다. 그 때 Jane이 내게 다가왔고 많은 십대들이 기분에 기복을 갖는다고 이야기하며 내 기분을 이해해 주었다. 내 감정을 더욱 잘 이해하기 위해, 그녀는 만화 영화 "Shining Days"를 볼 것을 제안하였다. 그녀는 이 영화가 십대의 기분에 관한 것이라고 설명해 주었다. 이 영화는 괜찮은 것 같았고, 그래서 나는 이 영화를 곧 보기로 결정했다.

01 ④

02 (1) Jake played the role of Santa Clause in the play.
    (2) I feel angry when people make fun of me.
    (3) Cut the vegetables into small pieces.

03 (1) The soccer team members have a common goal.
    (2) It is fun to learn English with animated movies.
    (3) There are ups and downs in life.

04 (1) amusing   (2) probably   (3) movement
    (4) publish   05 ①   06 ④

07 nacho chips / spread / some ham, onions, and peppers / cheese, about 12 minutes

08 ups and downs   09 ⑤   10 ②

11 Do you know how to use the machine?

12 ⑤   13 ④   14 ⑤   15 ④

16 These expressions are often used in spoken English.

17 ⑤   18 (A) laugh   (B) saying   (C) are

19 They have made them for hundreds of years.

20 ⑤   21 ⑤   22 ②

01 가르치고 배우는 과정을 가리키는 말은 education(교육)이다.

02 play the role: 역할을 하다, make fun of: ~을 놀리다, cut A into pieces ~A를 조각으로 자르다

03 common: 공통의, animated movie: 만화영화, ups and downs: 기복

04 movement: 움직임, amusing: 재미있는, 즐거운, publish: 출판하다, probably: 아마도

05 (A)는 도와주겠다는 표현으로 이와 바꾸어 쓸 수 있는 표현은 ① 번이다. 나머지는 모두 도움을 요청하는 표현이다.

06 can't wait to ~: ~가 기대되다 = look forward to

09 주어진 문장은 "Shining Days"에 관해 설명하는 문장으로 ⓔ 번이 적절하다.

10 Kevin의 Nothing serious.라는 말을 통해 심각한 문제가 아니라는 것을 알 수 있다.

12 ⑤ Emily와 Tony는 좌석을 선택한 후 표 값을 지불해야 한다.

13 현재완료 시제에서 부정어와 함께 쓰여 '아직'이라는 의미를 나타내는 것은 yet이다.

14 주어진 문장의 밑줄 친 부분은 '재활용을 위한 쓰레기통'이라는 의미로 쓰이는 동명사이다. 모두 현재분사이지만, ⑤번은 '잠자는 용도로 쓰이는 가방', 즉 '침낭'이라는 의미로 쓰이는 동명사이다.

15 danger는 '예상되지 않은' 것이므로 과거분사 unexpected로 수식하는 것이 적절하다.

16 구어체 언어란 일상 대화에서 쓰이는 말투를 의미한다. 따라서 과거분사 spoken으로 English를 수식하여 문장을 완성하는 것이 적절하다.

17 만화는 정보를 더 분명하고 학습하기 쉽게 만들어 준다는 것이 자연스럽다. more difficult → easier

18 (A) 사역동사의 목적격 보어로 동사원형이 쓰인다. (B) 캐릭터는 우스꽝스러운 행동이나 말을 함으로써 사람들을 웃게 만드는 것이므로 doing과 병렬로 연결되는 것이 자연스럽다. (C) 수의 일치의 대상이 some parts이므로 복수 동사를 쓰는 것이 적절하다.

19 사람들은 수 백 년 동안 만화를 만들어왔다고 하였다.

20 만화는 정보를 더 분명하게 만들어 준다고 하였으므로 ⑤번이 글의 내용과 일치한다.

21 글쓴이는 미래에 새로운 형태의 만화가 나타날지도 모른다고 하였다.

22 온라인에서 출판되는 특성상 언제 어디서든 웹툰을 읽을 수 있다는 강점이 있다.

Lesson 8

Viva, South America!

시험대비 실력평가
p.180

01 wide　　02 ④　　03 (1) waterfall　(2) area
(3) patience　04 ①　　05 (1) probably
(2) across　(3) wide　(4) similar　(5) unique　06 ①

01 주어진 관계는 반의어 관계를 나타낸다. wide: 넓은, narrow: 좁은

02 ④번 문장에서 wonder는 '경이, 놀라움'이란 뜻으로 쓰였다.

03 waterfall: 폭포, area: 지역, patience: 참을성

04 화내지 않고 침착함을 유지하는 능력을 가리키는 말은 patience(인내심)이다.

05 similar: 비슷한, unique: 독특한, probably: 아마도, wide: 넓은, across: 건너서

06 contain: 포함하다, ~이 들어 있다

서술형 시험대비
p.181

01 tourist

02 (1) outer space　(2) waterfall　(3) contain

03 (1) all year round　(2) went away　(3) by myself
(4) social studies　(5) is full of　(6) throw a party

04 (1) The price of the potatoes is 250 won per 100 grams.
(2) The climate of the Sahara Desert is very hot and dry.
(3) You can find koalas and kangaroos on this continent.

05 (1) This region is humid all year round.
(2) There is a big mountain range on the eastern side of Korea.
(3) The stadium was full of excited soccer fans.
(4) By the way, do you know who directed the movie?

01 주어진 관계는 동사와 그 동사의 동작을 행하는 사람의 관계이다. tour: 여행하다, tourist: 관광객

02 outer space: 우주 공간, waterfall: 폭포, contain: 포함하다

03 go away 없어지다, all year round 일 년 내내, 연중, be full of ~으로 가득하다, by oneself 혼자서, 홀로, social studies 사회(과목), throw a party: 파티를 열다

04 per: ~당, climate: 기후, continent: 대륙

 [교과서]
Conversation

핵심 Check
p.182~183

1 (1) Do you know / throw
(2) how old this building
2 (1) You know what / surprising
(2) heard / can't

교과서 대화문 익히기

 Check(√) True or False
p.184

1 F　2 T　3 T　4 F

교과서 확인학습
p.186~187

Communication: Listen – Dialog 1
tomato soup / happy / By the way, where, grown / somewhere / South America / How / social studies

Communication: Listen – Dialog 2
took / traveled, by herself / surprise / especially, pyramids / Are there / above sea level / can't believe it

Communication: Listen More
How was / fantastic / closed, riding / To be honest, scared / how fast, is / no idea / as fast as / surprising / ride / sign, after / maybe

Communicate: Speak
what the capital of Peru is / no idea / know

Wrap Up – Listening ❺
puppy / Where / heard, uncle

Wrap Up – Listening ❻
won first prize / quiet, shy / joined, has changed / join, too

시험대비 기본평가
p.188

01 ②, ④
02 I was told that he got the puppy from his uncle.
03 I can't believe it.　　04 ⑤

01 (A)는 알고 있음을 묻고 있으므로 이와 같은 의도를 나타내는 것은 ②, ④번이다.

04 위 대화를 통해 연극 동아리가 바뀌었는지는 알 수 없다.

시험대비 실력평가   p.189~190

01 do you know where the tomato was first grown?

02 ②, ④   03 ⑤   04 ⑤

05 ⑤   06 ③

07 Do you know how fast this roller coaster is?

08 ④   09 (D) → (B) → (C) → (A)

02 이어지는 대답으로 보아 빈칸에는 이렇게 일세 뇌였는지를 묻는 질문이 알맞다.

03 이탈리아에서 무엇이 처음에 재배되었는지는 알 수 없다.

04 (A)와 나머지 표현은 모두 놀라움을 표현하지만 ⑤번은 안도감을 표현한다.

05 Brian은 해발 3,800미터 정도에 위치한 몇몇 피라미드가 있다는 것을 믿지 않았다는 설명은 대화의 내용과 일치하지 않는다.

06 (A) while ~ing: ~하는 동안, (B) scared: 무서워하는, 겁먹은, (C) That's surprising.: 정말 놀랍다.

07 간접의문문의 어순으로 '의문사+주어+동사' 순서가 되어야 한다.

08 알고 있음을 대답할 때 'Yes, I do.'로 대답한다.

09 (D) 인상 깊었던 사진 설명 → (B) 피라미드에 대한 질문 → (C) 대답 및 구체적 설명 → (A) 놀라움 표현

서술형 시험대비   p.191

01 herself

02 They are talking about the pictures that[which] Ms. Song took in South America.

03 He got a puppy.

04 She wants to get a puppy.

05 (A) Sumin   (B) quiet and shy

    (C) joining the drama club

06 (C) → (B) → (D) → (A) → (E)

01 by oneself: 혼자서, 홀로

02 Jenny와 Brian은 송 선생님이 남아메리카에서 찍은 사진들에 대해 이야기하고 있다.

03 Junha는 그의 삼촌으로부터 강아지를 얻었다.

04 민지는 강아지를 갖고 싶어 한다.

05 오늘 나는 말하기 대회 우승자가 수민이라는 것을 들었다. 나는 많이 놀랐다. 그녀는 작년의 그녀가 아니었다. 작년에, 그녀는 매우 조용하고 수줍음이 많았었다. 그러나 그녀는 올해 연극 동아리에 가입한 후 많이 변하였다. 나는 수민이처럼 좀 더 적극적

이고 자신감 있는 사람이 되고 싶다.

06 (C) 알고 있는지 질문 → (B) 추측 → (D) 정확한 설명 → (A) 어떻게 알았는지 질문 → (E) 대답

교과서
Grammar

핵심 Check   p.192~193

1 (1) the funniest boy   (2) the highest mountain

2 (1) whether   (2) when he left   (3) how tall he is

시험대비 기본평가   p.194

01 (1) what is she → what she is

    (2) how did she break → how she broke

    (3) the famousest → the most famous

    (4) busiest → the busiest

02 (1) the cheapest   (2) the most interesting

    (3) the biggest   (4) the most difficult

    (5) the heaviest

03 (1) Tell me why he came late.

    (2) Can you tell me where she is going?

    (3) Do you remember when the boy went out?

    (4) June doesn't know who built the house.

    (5) Do you know who came in?

01 (1), (2) 간접의문문의 어순은 '의문사+주어+동사'이다. (3) famous는 -ous로 끝나는 2음절 단어이므로 the most를 써서 최상급을 만든다. (4) 형용사의 최상급은 정관사 the와 함께 쓰이는 것이 일반적이다.

02 cheap, big, heavy는 -est를 써서 최상급을 만들고, 3음절 이상의 형용사인 interesting, difficult는 the most를 써서 최상급을 만든다.

03 (1), (2), (3) 간접의문문의 어순인 '의문사+주어+동사'의 어순임을 기억하자. (4), (5) 의문사가 주어 역할을 하는 의문대명사인 경우 '의문사+동사' 어순이 가능하므로 이에 유의한다.

시험대비 실력평가   p.195~197

01 ④   02 ④   03 ③

04 Branda tried to guess if they needed her help.

05 ④

06 That is not the easiest job in the world.

07 ⑤   08 bigger / big / the biggest

09 ⑤　　　10 ⑤　　　11 ③　　　12 ④

13 (that) health is the most important thing

14 more diligent　　　15 ③

16 David is the best student in our school.

17 ③　　　18 ②　　　19 the laziest animal

20 where he works　　　21 ⑤　　　22 ⑤

23 I wonder who made the decision.

24 How do you think we can get to the park?

01 모두 most로 최상급을 만들지만 simple의 최상급은 simplest 이다.

02 remember의 목적어 역할을 하는 간접의문문이 오는 것이 적절하다. 간접의문문의 어순은 '의문사+주어+동사'이다.

03 최상급과 같은 표현은 '부정 주어+so[as] 원급 as'이다. '어떠한 소녀도 Jessica만큼 영리하지 않다.'는 뜻이다.

04 의문사가 없는 의문문의 간접의문문은 if나 whether를 써서 나타낼 수 있다. 따라서 if를 대신하여 whether를 써도 무방하다. try to V: ~하려고 애쓰다

05 간접의문문의 어순은 '의문사+주어+동사'이다. 따라서 ④번이 적절하다.

06 easy의 최상급은 easiest이다.

07 간접의문문을 만들 수 없는 것은 that이다.

08 비교급과 원급을 이용하여 최상급을 나타내는 문장은 '비교급+than any other 단수 명사', '부정 주어+as[so] 원급 as'이다.

09 주어진 문장의 if는 '~인지 아닌지'라고 해석되는 명사절 접속사로 쓰인 if로 의문사가 없는 문장의 간접의문문을 이끈다. 따라서 ⑤번이 옳다. 나머지는 모두 부사절 접속사의 if로 '~라면'이라고 해석된다.

10 believe는 간접의문문의 의문사를 문두로 보내는 동사이므로 Who do you believe made the cookies yesterday?가 적절하다.

11 주어진 문장을 영어로 쓰면 Who is the funniest character in the movie?이다.

12 모두 최상급의 의미를 갖지만 ④번은 '그녀의 목소리는 우리 반에 있는 다른 모든 목소리만큼 아름답다.'라는 의미의 동등비교이다.

13 important는 3음절 이상의 형용사이므로 최상급을 만들 때 the most를 사용한다.

14 '부정 주어+비교급+than'을 이용하여 최상급을 나타낸다.

15 간접의문문에서 의문대명사가 쓰인 경우 '의문사+동사'의 어순이 가능하다. '내가 지금껏 방문해 본 호텔 중에서 가장 편안하다'는 의미가 적절하므로 최상급을 쓴다.

16 good의 최상급은 best이다

17 pretty의 최상급은 prettiest이다.

18 최상급의 의미를 갖는 것은 '부정 주어+비교급 than'이다.

19 lazy의 최상급은 laziest이다.

20 대답으로 미루어 보아 그가 어디에서 일하는지 알고 싶다고 말했음을 알 수 있다.

21 의문사가 없는 문장의 간접의문문은 if 혹은 whether를 써서 만든다.

22 clean의 최상급은 cleanest이다.

23 who는 의문사이자 주어 역할을 동시에 하는 의문대명사이다.

24 think는 간접의문문의 의문사를 문두로 보낸다.

서술형 시험대비
p.198~199

01 the longest, longer

02 (1) Can I ask if[whether] you are mad at me?

(2) Do you know where Tom lives?

(3) Can you tell me who she is?

(4) I wonder what happened to you.

(5) Please tell me why he broke the promise..

(6) When do you think the book will be published?

(7) Let me know if[whether] she is going to tell him the truth.

03 the bravest boy

04 (1) the worst　(2) the best　(3) worse

05 where he is going

06 February is the shortest month of the year.

07 the most popular

08 Let me introduce the most famous places in Korea.

09 who thinks him a thief

10 the most creative person　　11 how old he is

12 Where is the coldest city on earth?

13 is more important than education / is as[so] important as education / more important than any other thing / more important than all the other things

14 Who do you think she is?

15 where Emily is going, if[whether] Emily is going there to see a movie

01 비교급을 이용하여 최상급을 나타내는 문장은 '비교급+than any other 단수 명사'이다.

02 의문사가 있는 의문문의 간접의문문은 '의문사+주어+동사'의 어순이며, 의문사가 없는 경우 if나 whether를 써서 간접의문문을 만들 수 있다. think, believe, guess와 같은 동사는 간접의문문의 의문사를 문두로 배치한다.

03 brave의 최상급은 bravest이다.

04 네 개의 식당 중 식당 B가 가장 좋은 평점을 받았으며, 식당 C가 가장 낮은 평점을 기록하고 있다. good-better-best, bad-worse-worst를 활용하여 문장을 완성한다.

05 그가 어디로 가고 있는지는 모르지만 나중에 말해 줄 것이라고

34 정답 및 해설

생각한다는 대답이 적절하다, 대답은 간접의문문의 어순인 '의문사+주어+동사'에 맞게 완성한다.

06 short의 최상급은 shortest이다.

07 popular의 최상급은 the most를 사용한다.

08 famous의 최상급은 the most를 사용하여 만든다.

09 '누가 그를 도둑이라고 생각하는지 궁금하다.'는 의미이다. 여기서 who는 의문대명사이므로 '의문사+동사' 어순임에 유의한다.

10 '창의적인'이란 의미의 creative는 the most를 사용하여 최상급을 만든다.

11 대답으로 미루어 보아 그가 몇 살인지 아는지 묻는 것이 적절하다.

12 cold의 최상급은 the coldest이다.

13 비교급으로 최상급의 의미를 갖는 것은 '비교급 than any other 단수 명사', 혹은 '비교급 than all the other 복수 명사', '부정 주어 비교급 than'이다. 원급을 이용하여 최상급의 의미를 나타낼 때에는, '부정 주어 as[so] 원급 as'로 쓸 수 있다.

14 think가 있는 문장에서는 간접의문문의 의문사를 문두에 배치한다.

15 의문사가 있는 문장의 간접의문문은 '의문사+주어+동사'의 어순이며 의문사가 없는 경우 'if' 혹은 'whether'를 이용하여 간접의문문을 만들 수 있다.

교과서
Reading

확인문제 p.200

1 T 2 F 3 F 4 F 5 F

확인문제 p.201

1 T 2 F 3 F 4 T 5 T 6 F

교과서 확인학습 A p.202~203

01 where the driest desert
02 the highest
03 they are both
04 is full of, that
05 the driest desert
06 it gets, at all
07 is so dry that
08 what scientists do
09 similar to, they prepare for trips
10 one of the best places
11 see the world's highest
12 It, high
13 cover, patience, luck
14 named after, who, flew
15 still get to, by
16 runs across, through
17 travels from, flows into
18 is interesting
19 no bridges
20 because it usually runs through
21 see the other side
22 swim in
23 home, that
24 the world's longest, range
25 how long the mountain range
26 about, long
27 contains, mountains
28 a third of the people
29 unique animals

교과서 확인학습 B p.204~205

1 Do you know where the driest desert on Earth is?

2 How about the highest waterfall?

3 Yes, they are both in South America.

4 This continent is full of natural wonders that will surprise you.

5 The Atacama is the driest desert on Earth.

6 In some parts, it gets almost no rain at all — only 1-3 millimeters per year!

7 The ground in some areas is so dry that no plants can grow.

8 Do you know what scientists do in such a dry place?

9 The soil in this desert is very similar to the soil on Mars, so they prepare for trips to outer space.

10 The Atacama is also one of the best places on Earth to watch stars.

11 If you go to Venezuela, you can see the world's highest waterfall.

12 It is 979 meters high.

13 Clouds often cover the top, so you need patience and a little luck to get a good view.

14 Actually, the waterfall is named after Jimmie Angel, a pilot from the United States who first flew over the waterfall in 1933.

15 You can still get to the top of the beautiful waterfall only by plane.

16 The Amazon runs across the continent through seven countries.

17 It travels from Peru in the west and flows into the Atlantic Ocean.

18 The Amazon River is interesting in many ways.

19 For the most part, it has no bridges.

20 That is because it usually runs through rainforests and wet areas, not cities or towns.

21 Also, in many places the river is very wide, so you cannot see the other side!

22 You probably do not want to swim in this river.

23 It is home to some very big snakes and fish that eat meat.

24 The Andes are the world's longest mountain range.

25 Do you know how long the mountain range is?

26 It is about 7,000 kilometers long!

27 It also contains the highest mountains outside of Asia.

28 About a third of the people in South America live in the Andes.

29 Many unique animals also live there.

시험대비 실력평가
p.206~209

01 ④　　　　02 continent　　03 ⑤　　　　04 ⑤

05 It is in South America.　　　　06 ⑤

07 He first flew over the waterfall in 1933.　08 ④

09 interesting　　　　10 ③　　　　11 ③

12 It starts from Peru.　　13 ①　　　　14 ①

15 ③　　　　16 ⑤

17 It's because the ground in some areas is so dry.

18 ③　　　　19 ③

20 He was a pilot from the United States who first flew over the waterfall in 1933.　　21 ④

22 Because it is home to some very big snakes and fish that eat meat.

23 Do you know how long the mountain range is?

24 ①　　　　25 ⑤

01 원인과 결과를 이끄는 'so ~ that' 구문이다.

02 '바다에 의해 둘러싸인 큰 땅 덩어리'는 '대륙(continent)'이다.

03 아타카마 사막의 토양은 화성의 토양과 아주 비슷해서, 과학자들은 이곳에서 우주로의 여행을 준비한다고 하였다.

04 'one of the 최상급+복수 명사'이다.

05 아타카마 사막은 남아메리카에 있다고 하였다.

06 빈칸 (A)에는 전치사 after가 들어간다. ① turn off: ~을 끄다 ② be busy with: ~하느라 바쁘다 ③ be full of: ~으로 가득 차다 ④ be good at: ~을 잘하다 ⑤ look after: ~을 돌보다

07 그는 1933년에 처음으로 폭포 너머 비행을 하였다.

08 구름 꼭대기 부분을 구름이 자주 에워싸기 때문에 멋진 경치를 보려면 인내심과 약간의 운이 필요하다고 하였다.

09 흥미를 유발하는 것이므로 현재분사를 쓰는 것이 적절하다.

10 unique는 '독특한'이란 의미이다. 따라서 ③번이 적절하다.

---

11 강이 너무 넓어서 그 건너편을 볼 수조차 없는 곳이 있다고 하였다.

12 서쪽의 페루에서 시작한다고 하였다.

13 산맥의 길이는 7천 킬로미터라고 하였다.

14 사물을 선행사로 취하는 주격 관계대명사가 쓰이는 것이 적절하다.

15 ③번 다음 문장의 they는 주어진 문장의 scientists를 가리키는 말이다.

16 별을 관찰하기에 최고의 장소라고 나와 있을 뿐, 얼마나 많은 별을 관찰할 수 있는지는 나와 있지 않다.

17 토양이 너무 건조해서 식물이 자랄 수 없다고 하였다.

18 (A)는 '경치, 전망'이라는 의미로 쓰였다. ③ 경치, 전망 ①, ②, ④, ⑤ 견해

19 구름이 꼭대기 부분을 자주 에워싸기 때문에 원할 때 언제든 폭포의 멋진 경치를 보는 것은 불가능하다.

20 그는 미국의 비행사로, 1933년에 처음으로 폭포 너머 비행을 한 사람이다.

21 (A) run across: ~을 가로질러 흐르다 (B) 뒤 문장이 앞 문장에 대한 원인을 이끌고 있으므로 That's because (C) 강의 반대편을 볼 수 없다는 의미이므로 나머지 하나를 가리키는 the other를 쓴다. another는 여러 개 중 하나를 가리킬 때 쓴다.

22 아마존강은 몇몇 아주 큰 뱀과 고기를 먹는 물고기들의 서식지이므로 이곳에서 헤엄치는 것은 위험하다.

23 how가 long을 수식하는 것이므로 붙여 써야 한다.

24 (B)는 '대략'이란 의미로 쓰였다. 따라서 Roughly가 가장 적절하다.

25 글쓴이가 폭포에 어떻게 갔는지는 글을 읽고 알 수 없다.

서술형 시험대비
p.210~211

01 dry

02 Because it gets almost no rain at all – only 1–3 millimeters per year.

03 is drier than

04 the driest, similar to, Mars, to watch stars

05 We can see the driest desert on Earth and the highest waterfall in South America.

06 It got its name after Jimmie Angel, a pilot from the United States who first flew over the waterfall in 1933.

07 It's because clouds often cover the top.

08 highest, pilot, plane　　09 It is 979 meters high.

10 [C]–[B]–[A]

11 what the longest mountain range / longer than

12 Do you know how long the mountain range is?

13 how wide the Amazon River is / wide, see
14 It flows into the Atlantic Ocean.

01 너무 건조해서 식물들이 자랄 수 없다는 의미이다. driest의 원급인 dry를 쓸 수 있다.

02 연간 강수량이 1~3mm밖에 안될 정도로 비가 내리지 않기 때문이다.

03 부정 주어와 비교급을 이용하여 최상급을 나타내는 문장을 만들 수 있다.

04 아타카마 사막은 지구상에서 가장 건조한 사막이고, 그것의 토양은 화성의 토양과 매우 유사하다. 또한 그곳은 별을 관찰하기에 최고의 장소 중 하나이다.

05 지구에서 가장 건조한 사막과 가장 높은 폭포를 남아메리카에서 볼 수 있다.

06 폭포의 이름은 1933년에 처음으로 폭포 너머 비행을 한 미국의 비행사 Jimmie Angel에게서 이름을 따온 것이다.

07 구름이 꼭대기 부분을 자주 에워싸기 때문에 멋진 경치를 보려면 인내심과 약간의 운이 필요하다고 하였다.

08 앙헬 폭포는 지구에서 가장 높은 폭포이고 어느 미국인 비행사의 이름을 땄다. 오직 비행기로만 정상에 닿을 수 있다.

09 앙헬 폭포는 높이가 979m라고 하였다.

10 [C]에서 It이 지칭하는 것은 아마존강이며, 일곱 개의 나라를 거쳐 대륙을 가로지를 때 가장 먼저 서쪽 페루에서 시작한다는 것이다. [B] 아마존강에는 다리가 없는데 그 이유를 말하는 문장이 [A]에서 이어지고 있다.

11 대답으로 미루어 보아 세상에서 가장 긴 산맥이 무엇인지 아느냐는 질문을 완성하는 것이 적절하다. 비교급을 이용하여 최상급의 의미를 나타낼 수 있다.

12 간접의문문을 이용하여 문장을 만들 수 있다. 간접의문문의 어순은 '의문사+주어+동사' 어순임에 유의하자.

13 아마존강이 얼마나 넓은지 묻는 말에 '너무 넓어서 건너편을 볼 수 없을 정도'라고 답할 수 있다. too ~ to V: 너무 ~해서 V할 수 없는

14 아마존강은 대서양으로 흘러간다고 하였다.

영역별 핵심문제
p.213~217

01 impatient 02 ② 03 ④ 04 ④
05 ② 06 (1) named after
(2) throw[give, have, hold], party (3) To be honest
07 (A) the tomato soup
　　(C) the tomato came from South America
08 do you know where the tomato was first grown?
09 ⑤ 10 It goes as fast as 140 km per hour.

11 (A) 140 km per hour (B) 8 p.m 12 ④
13 (A) by (B) What (C) can't
14 (A) pictures of beautiful places in South America
　　(B) the pictures of pyramids
　　(C) some pyramids are about 3,800 meters
　　　above sea level
15 ③ 16 ③ 17 ④, ⑤ 18 ⑤
19 Do you remember the happiest moment of your
　 life?
20 ② 21 ④ 22 ④
23 in the town is as[so] wise as
24 if[whether] Paul is free
25 I wonder if[whether] you found what you were
　 looking for.
26 Thursday was the worst day of the week for me.
27 Do you know where the driest desert on Earth is?
28 ⑤ 29 ① 30 ④ 31 ②
32 ④ 33 It is in Bolivia.

01 주어진 관계는 반의어 관계를 나타낸다. patient: 인내심 있는, impatient: 인내심 없는

02 특히 직업으로 항공기 조종 장치를 작동하는 사람을 가리키는 말은 pilot(조종사)이다. crew: 승무원, steward: 스튜어드

03 scared; 겁먹은, 무서워하는

04 주어진 문장과 나머지는 모두 '흐르다'는 의미를 나타내지만 ④번은 '분출'을 나타낸다.

05 ride: 타다

06 name after ~을 따라 이름 짓다, throw[give, have, hold] a party 파티를 열다, to be honest 솔직히 말하면

08 간접의문문으로 '의문사+주어+동사'의 순서가 알맞다.

12 종하는 처음에는 무서웠지만 나중에는 신나했으므로 scared(무서운)에서 pleased(기쁜)가 적절하다. disappointed: 실망한, fearful: 무서운

13 (A) by oneself: 혼자서, (B) What a surprise!: 그것 참 놀랍구나! (C) I can't believe it.: 정말 놀랍다.

14 나는 송 선생님께서 지난여름에 혼자 남아메리카로 여행을 다녀오셨다는 것이 인상 깊었다. 나는 그녀가 정말로 용감했다고 생각했다. 선생님은 남아메리카의 아름다운 장소들의 사진들을 보여주셨다. 나는 피라미드 사진이 정말 좋았다. 선생님께서 몇몇 피라미드는 해발 3,800미터 정도에 위치하고 있다고 설명하셨다. 이것은 매우 흥미로웠으며 나는 언젠가 그곳을 방문하기로 결심했다.

15 주어진 단어를 영어로 쓰면 'He is the most boring person that I have ever met.'이다.

16 주어진 문장의 밑줄 친 부분은 간접의문문을 이끌며 '누구'라고 해석되는 의문대명사이다. 따라서 ③번이 답이다. 나머지는 모

17 주어진 문장은 '정직보다 더 귀중한 것은 없다'는 의미이다. 최상급의 의미를 갖는 문장으로, '비교급 than any other 단수 명사'와 같다.

18 '누가 너를 파티에 초대했는지'라고 하였으므로 의문대명사 who를 사용하여 간접의문문을 만든다.

19 happy의 최상급은 the happiest이다.

20 형용사의 최상급은 정관사 the와 함께 쓰인다.

21 주어진 문장은 부정 주어와 원급을 이용하여 최상급을 나타내고 있다. 따라서 최상급 혹은 '비교급 than all the other 복수 명사'가 빈칸에 들어갈 수 있다.

22 delicious의 최상급은 the most delicious이다.

23 부정 주어와 원급을 이용하여 최상급을 나타내는 문장이다.

24 if를 대신하여 whether를 써도 좋다.

25 의문사가 없는 문장의 간접의문문은 if나 whether를 이용하여 만든다.

26 bad의 최상급은 worst이다.

27 간접의문문의 어순은 '의문사+주어+동사'이다.

28 과학자들이 아타카마 사막에서 연구하는 이유는 그곳의 토양이 화성의 토양과 비슷하기 때문이다. different from → similar to

29 아타카마 사막은 너무 건조해서 식물이 자랄 수 없다고 하였다.

30 많은 관광객들이 사진을 찍기 위해서 우유니를 방문하고, 당신이 찍는 모든 사진이 아름다운 예술 작품이 될 것이라고 하였으므로 ④번이 옳다.

31 (A)는 '일년 내내'라는 의미이다. ① 돌고 돌아 ② 일 년 내내 ③ 모든 너의 노력 ④ 여러 번 되풀이 하여 ⑤ 자주, 매번

32 (B)는 '~하기 위해서'라고 해석되며 to부정사의 부사적 용법 중 목적으로 쓰였다. ① 명사적 용법 중 목적어 ② 진주어 ③ 형용사적 용법 ④ 부사적 용법 중 목적 ⑤ 부사적 용법 중 감정의 원인

33 세계에서 가장 큰 소금 평원은 볼리비아에 있다.

단원별 예상문제
p.218~221

01 ②　　　02 ⑤　　　03 To be honest
04 ②　　　05 ⑤　　　06 By the way
07 It came from South America.
08 Ms. Song, her social studies teacher, taught it to her.
09 Which country do you want to visit?
10 ④　　　11 ④　　　12 ④　　　13 ⑤
14 What do you think she is doing?　　　15 ①

---

16 Please tell me if[whether] she told you her number.　　　17 ④
18 the Atacama　　　19 ⑤　　　20 ③
21 the driest desert, prepare space trips, watch stars
22 ②　　　23 patience　　　24 ③
25 It runs through seven countries.

---

01 이어지는 대화에서 특히 피라미드 사진이 마음에 들었다고 설명하고 있으므로 주어진 문장은 (B)에 들어가는 것이 적절하다.

02 위 대화를 통해 Ms. Song이 남아메리카에서 얼마나 오랫동안 머물렀는지는 알 수 없다.

04 몰랐던 사실에 대해 놀라움을 나타내는 ②번이 적절하다.

05 하나와 종하는 저녁 8시 이후에 탈수 없기 때문에 다음에 타기로 했다.

07 토마토는 남아메리카에서 왔다.

08 송 선생님께서 수진에게 토마토의 산지에 대해 가르쳐 주셨다.

10 Brian은 브라질이 남아메리카에서 가장 큰 국가라는 사실에 깜짝 놀랐다.

11 모두 'est'를 붙여서 최상급을 만들 수 있지만, helpful은 most를 붙여서 최상급을 만든다.

12 의문사가 없는 문장의 간접의문문이므로 if 혹은 whether를 사용하여 간접의문문을 만들 수 있다.

13 모두 최상급의 의미를 갖지만 ⑤번은 '너의 조언은 다른 어떤 조언보다 더 도움이 되지는 않는다.'는 의미이다.

14 동사 think는 간접의문문의 의문사를 문두로 보낸다.

15 'one of the 최상급+복수 명사'를 써서 '가장 ~한 것 중 하나'를 나타낸다.

16 의문사가 없는 의문문의 간접의문문은 if나 whether를 써서 만든다.

17 최상급의 의미를 갖는 '비교급 than any other 단수 명사'이다.

18 아타카마 사막을 의미한다.

19 밑줄 친 (B)는 places를 수식하는 형용사적 용법으로 쓰인 to부정사이다. ① 명사적 용법 중 목적어 ② 진주어 ③ 부사적 용법 중 목적 ④ 감정의 원인 ⑤ 형용사적 용법

20 과학자들은 아타카마 사막에서 우주로의 여행을 준비하고 있다고 하였다. 과학자들이 아타카마 사막으로 여행을 가는 것은 아니다.

21 지구에서 가장 건조한 사막인 아타카마 사막은 우주여행을 준비하고 별을 관찰하기에 좋은 장소이다.

22 앞 문장의 결과를 이끄는 문장이므로 so가 적절하다.

23 화를 내지 않고 차분함을 유지하는 능력은 '인내심'이다.

24 구름 때문에 앙헬 폭포의 정상에서 좋은 경관을 보기 힘들 수 있다고 하였다.

25 아마존강은 일곱 개의 나라를 거쳐 흐른다고 하였다.

01 Sumin won the contest.

02 She was very quiet and shy (last year).

03 She joined the drama club this year.

04 how much water you drink

05 (1) I'd like to know if[whether] you are comfortable.

   (2) I wonder when you came home.

06 (1) the smartest   (2) the noisiest

07 (1) Playing tennis is the most exciting sport

   (2) No other sport is as[so] exciting as playing
     tennis

08 the driest desert on Earth, the highest waterfall

09 (A) They prepare for trips to outer space.

   (B) the soil in the Atacama is very similar to the
     soil on Mars

10 수천 년 전에 있던 물이 모두 말라서 생겼다.

11 It's because the salt flat makes any tourist a
   great photographer.

12 (1) under sea level → above sea level

   (2) during a certain period → all year round

   (3) the most visited natural wonder → one of the
     most visited natural wonders

01 수민이가 말하기 대회에서 우승했다.

02 수민이는 작년에 매우 조용하고 수줍음이 많았다.

03 수민이는 올해 연극 동아리에 가입했다.

04 대답으로 미루어 보아 하루에 물을 얼마나 마시는지가 궁금하다
   는 말이 들어가는 것이 적절하다. 간접의문문의 어순에 유의하
   여 'how much water you drink'라고 쓴다.

05 의문사가 없는 의문문의 간접의문문은 if나 whether를 써서 만
   든다. 의문사가 있는 경우 '의문사+주어+동사' 어순임에 유의한
   다.

06 smart와 noisy의 최상급은 각각 the smartest, the noisiest
   이다.

07 부정 주어와 원급을 이용하여 최상급의 의미를 나타낼 수 있다.

08 지구에서 가장 건조한 사막과 가장 높은 폭포를 가리키는 대명
   사이다.

09 과학자들은 화성의 토양과 비슷한 아타카마 사막에서 우주로의
   여행을 준비한다고 하였다.

10 우유니는 소금 평원으로, 수천 년 전에 있던 물이 모두 말라서
   생긴 것이다.

11 사실, 그 솔트 플랫은 어떤 방문객도 훌륭한 사진작가로 만들기
   때문에 우유니에서 찍은 모든 사진이 아름다운 예술 작품이 될
   것이라고 하였다.

12 (1) 우유니 소금 평원은 해저가 아닌 해발 약 3,656 미터에 위

치해 있다. (2) 이곳은 일 년 내내 방문할 수 있다. (3) 남아메리
카에서 가장 방문이 많은 곳 중 하나이고 유일한 곳은 아니다.

|모범답안|

01 (A) social studies   (B) where

   (C) Italy or somewhere in Europe

   (D) the tomato came from South America

02 Gwanak Mountain, my family, 632 meters high,
   the south of Seoul, the bridges over the Han
   River, all my stress went away

01 나는 아빠의 토마토 수프를 맛보았을 때 매우 행복했다. 그것은
   매우 맛있었다. 나는 수프를 맛보았을 때, 나의 사회 선생님이신
   송 선생님에게서 배운 것이 기억났다. 그녀는 내게 토마토가 어
   디에서 처음 재배되었는지 알려주셨다. 나는 아빠에게 그가 이것
   을 알고 있는지 모르는지 물어보았다. 처음에 아빠는 토마토가
   이탈리아나 유럽 어딘가에서 왔다고 추측했다. 나는 아빠에게 토
   마토가 남아메리카에서 왔다고 말했다. 나는 내가 선생님에게서
   배운 것을 아빠와 공유했을 때 내 스스로가 자랑스러웠다.

01 ②

02 (1) sunrise   (2) view   (3) Mars   (4) scared

   (5) wonders   03 ①

04 (1) A number of works of art were stolen.

   (2) Amsterdam is 4 meters below sea level.

05 (C) → (B) → (D) → (A)   06 ⓓ → ⓐ → ⓒ → ⓔ → ⓑ

07 ②   08 ⑤

09 (A) By   (B) How   (C) learned   10 ③

11 (1) The mountain range is home to many unique
     plants and animals.

   (2) At first, I couldn't understand him at all.

   (3) To be honest, I want to stay (at) home and
     watch TV.

12 (1) Whales   (2) natural   (3) contain   13 ④

14 ③, ④   15 ⑤

16 Singapore is one of the most interesting places
   that I've ever visited.

17 (1) Do you know why she is upset?

   (2) I wonder if[whether] he sings well.

18 ③   19 [B] - [A] - [C]   20 ①, ④

21 We can get there only by plane.   22 ⑤

23 ⑤   24 Because it usually runs through
   rainforests and wet areas, not cities or towns.

25 seven countries, bridges, snakes, fish

01 예를 들어 절벽이나 바위와 같은 높은 장소로부터 냇물 또는 강이 떨어지는 장소를 가리키는 말은 waterfall(폭포)이다.

02 wonder: 경이, 놀라움, sunrise: 일출, scared: 겁먹은, Mars: 화성, view: 전망

03 주어진 문장에서 wonder는 '경이, 놀라움'을 나타내며 이와 같은 의미를 나타내는 것은 ①번이다. 나머지 문장에서는 모두 '궁금해 하다'를 나타낸다.

05 (C) 알고 있는지 여부 질문 → (B) 대답 및 추가 질문 → (D) 대답 → (A) 반응

06 ⓓ 롤러코스터의 속도 설명 → ⓐ 놀라움 표현 → ⓒ 한 번 더 탈 것을 권유 → ⓔ 표지판 내용 설명 → ⓑ 반응

07 ① 일반적으로 말해서, ② 솔직히 말해서, ③ 엄밀히 말해서, ④ 대체로, ⑤ 개인적으로 말하면

08 롤러코스터는 8시까지 운영한다는 설명은 대화의 내용과 일치한다.

09 (A) By the way: 그런데, (B) 이어지는 대답으로 보아 어떻게 알았는지 질문해야 하므로 'How', (C) 알게 된 것을 설명하므로 learned가 적절하다.

10 수진은 송선생님에게서 사회를 배우고 있다는 설명이 대화의 내용과 일치한다.

11 unique: 독특한, at first: 처음에는, to be honest: 솔직히 말하면

12 whale: 고래, natural: 자연의, 천연의, contain: 포함하다

13 모두 '~인지 아닌지'라고 해석되는 명사절 접속사로 간접의문문을 이끈다. 하지만, ④번은 '~라면'이라고 해석되는 부사절 접속사이다.

14 이구아수 폭포는 세계에서 가장 넓은 폭포라는 의미이다. 최상급과 '비교급 than all the other 복수 명사'로 바꿔 쓸 수 있다.

15 who found your book이라고 쓰는 것이 적절하다.

16 one of the 최상급+복수 명사: ~ 중 가장 ~한 것들 중 하나

17 간접의문문의 어순은 '의문사+주어+동사'이며, 의문사가 없는 경우 'if(또는 whether)+주어+동사'의 어순으로 간접의문문을 만든다. (2) if를 대신하여 whether를 써도 좋다.

18 부정 주어와 비교급을 이용하여 최상급의 의미를 나타낼 수 있다.

19 가장 건조한 사막인 이유는 [B] 비가 1-3mm만 내리는 지역이 있을 정도로 비가 거의 오지 않기 때문이고 [A] 토양이 건조해서 어떤 식물도 자랄 수가 없지만 과학자들이 이곳에서 무슨 일을 하고 있다. [C] 그들이 하는 일은 우주로의 여행을 준비하는 것이다.

20 폭포의 높이와 이름의 기원이 언급되어 있다.

21 비행기를 이용해서만 폭포의 정상에 갈 수 있다고 하였다.

22 Jimmie Angel이 폭포 너머를 비행할 때 몇 살이었는지는 위 글을 읽고 답할 수 없다.

23 사람들은 사진을 찍기 위해서 우유니를 방문하는데, 이곳에서 사진을 찍는 어떤 방문객도 훌륭한 사진작가가 될 수 있는 이유가 ⑤번이 이끄는 문장에서 제시되고 있다.

24 아마존강은 대개 도시나 마을이 아닌 열대우림과 습지를 지나 흐르기 때문에 강의 대부분에 다리가 없다고 하였다.

25 아마존강은 남아메리카의 일곱 개 나라를 거쳐 흐르고 강 위에 다리가 없는 경우가 대부분이며 아주 큰 뱀과 고기를 먹는 물고기가 그 강에 살고 있다.

Lesson
Special

The Two Stones

교과서
Reading

확인문제   p.232

1 ㄷ   2 T   3 F   4 l

확인문제   p.233

1 F   2 T   3 T   4 F

교과서 확인학습 A   p.234~235

01 Two Stones
02 Characters, Money Lender, Narrator
03 ago, village, there lived
04 had to borrow, million, from
05 the money lender, asked for, to pay back, allow, anymore
06 no
07 servant instead
09 to be, servant
10 either, thank you
11 prison
12 let's play, put
13 One, the other, pick
14 happens if
15 Then, servant
16 mean, How terrible
17 if, pick
18 free, doesn't have to
19 doesn't play, with
20 *loudly*, Then, prison
21 Prison
22 *picks up, looks carefully at*
23 *to herself*, picked up
24 make, become, should
25 Stop and think
26 cannot pick
27 drops, right away
28 dropped
29 okay
30 Show us the stone
31 which one
32 *to herself*, cannot tell, trick
33 *shows everyone the white stone*
34 *celebrating*
35 picked, free
36 Good thinking, saved

교과서 확인학습 B   p.236~237

1 The Two Stones
2 Characters: Father, Daughter, Money Lender, Friends, Narrator
3 Narrator: A long time ago, in a small village in South America, there lived a farmer and his daughter.
4 The farmer was poor, and had to borrow three million pesos from a money lender.
5 But the money lender was not kind, and when the farmer asked for one month to pay back the money, she didn't allow him anymore time.
6 Money Lender: You have no money? That's okay.
7 Your daughter will become my servant instead.
8 Father and Daughter: Oh, no!
9 Daughter: I don't want to be your servant.
10 Father: I don't want that, either! *(to Money Lender)* No, thank you.
11 Money Lender: Do you want to go to prison?
12 Then, let's play a game. I will put two stones in a bag.
13 One is white, and the other is black. Your daughter will pick one.
14 Daughter: What happens if I pick the white one?
15 Money Lender: Then you will be my servant.
16 Friends: Oh, no! She's mean. How terrible!
17 Daughter: What happens if I pick the black one?
18 Money Lender: Then you will be free, and your father doesn't have to pay back my money..
19 Father: What happens if she doesn't play this game with you?
20 Money Lender: *(loudly)* Then you will go to prison!
21 Now I want to go to school and become a better person.
21 Father, Daughter, and Friends: Oh, no! Prison!
22 *(Money Lender picks up two stones. Daughter looks carefully at her.)*
23 Daughter: *(to herself)* Oh! She has picked up two white stones!
24 She will make me become her servant. What should I do?
25 Narrator: Stop and think. What should she do?
26 She cannot pick a black one.
27 *(Daughter picks a stone from the bag. She drops it right away.)*
28 Daughter: Oh, no! I'm sorry, I've dropped it. *(to Money Lender)* But it's okay.
29 Show us the stone in the bag.
30 Then we will know which one I picked.

41

31 Money Lender: *(to herself)* I cannot tell them about my trick! Oh, no!

32 *(Money Lender shows everyone the white stone. Friends and Father start celebrating.)*

33 Friends: She picked the black one! They are free!

34 Narrator: Good thinking has saved Father and Daughter!

서술형 실전문제   p.238~240

01 (1) servants   (2) pay back   (3) pick   (4) right away
    (5) instead   (6) borrow   (7) mean

02 (1) trick   (2) mean   (3) save   (4) borrow

03 (1) One, the other   (2) one   (3) me do
    (4) which one   (5) has saved

04 (1) He has served this school for twenty years.
    (2) He has two balls. One is white and the other is red.

05 (1) I don't know what Sarah wanted me to do.
    (2) Will you tell me if[whether] you want to go shopping with me?
    (3) What do you think he wants?
    (4) Let me know if[whether] you will go there.

06 there lived a farmer and his daughter.

07 servant

08 is in a small village in South America

09 want, to be your servant

10 One is white, and the other is black.

11 How terrible it is!

12 your father doesn't have to pay back my money.

13 She will make me become her servant.

14 Show the stone in the bag to us.

15 ①, ④
    (1) ① If the farmer's daughter doesn't play the game with money lender, the farmer will go to prison.
    (2) ④ Actually the farmer's daughter picked a white stone.

01 instead: 대신에, borrow: 빌리다, right away: 즉시, 바로, mean: 사악한, 못된, servant: 하인, pick: 고르다, pay back: (돈을) 갚다

02 save: (목숨을) 구하다, borrow: 빌리다, mean: 사악한, 못된, trick: 속임수

03 (1) 가리키는 대상이 두 개일 때, 하나는 one, 다른 하나는 the other로 지칭한다. (2) one은 앞 문장에 사용된 것을 가리키는 부정대명사이다. (3) 사역동사 'make'의 목적어와 목적격보어

로 동사원형이 적절하다. (4) which one you want to have는 간접의문문으로 동사 Tell의 목적어 역할을 한다. (5) So far(지금까지)로 보아 현재완료 시제가 적절하다.

04 (1) 현재완료에서 'for+기간 명사', 'since+시간 명사' (2) one ~ the other ...: (둘 중에서) 하나는 ~, 다른 하나는

05 간접의문문의 어순은 '의문사+주어+동사'이다. 의문사가 없을 경우에는 의문사 대신에 if나 whether를 쓴다. 또한 의문사가 주어일 경우에는 '의문사+동사'의 어순이 되는 것에 주의한다. 주절에 think 동사가 있는 경우 의문사가 문장의 맨 앞으로 나간다는 것에도 주의한다.

06 there lived+주어: ~가 살았다

07 servant: 하인 / 직업이 다른 사람의 집안일을 하는 것이고, 종종 그 집에서 사는 사람

08 이야기의 배경은 어디인가? 이야기의 배경은 남아메리카의 작은 마을이다.

09 (A)의 대명사 'that'은 '자신의 딸이 대부업자의 하인이 되는 것'을 가리킨다.

10 가리키는 대상이 두 개일 때, 하나는 one, 다른 하나는 the other로 지칭한다.

11 형용사 'terrible'을 이용한 감탄문은 'How+형용사+주어+동사!' 어순을 취한다. 문장에서 주어는 앞에 언급된 상황을 가리키는 it을 사용하고 be동사는 is를 쓴다.

12 '~할 필요가 없다'는 'don't[doesn't] have to'를 사용하고, '(돈을) 갚다'는 'pay back'을 사용한다.

13 '사역동사(make)+목적어(me)+동사원형(become)' 형태를 사용한다.

14 '수여동사(show)+직접목적어+전치사(to)+간접목적어'인 3형식으로 문장을 전환할 수 있다.

15 ① 농부의 딸이 대부업자와 게임을 하지 않으면 농부가 감옥에 가게 된다. ④ 대부업자가 두 개의 흰 돌을 가방에 넣었기 때문에 실제로 농부의 딸은 흰 돌을 집은 것이다.

단원별 예상문제   p.241~244

01 ④   02 ⑤   03 ②

04 (1) carefully   (2) borrow   05 (c)elebrate

06 ③   07 ①   08 ③

09 (1) You can choose one or the other of the two rooms.
    (2) I'm not sure if[whether] he will come or not.

10 Characters   11 ②   12 ②

13 ⑤   14 ④   15 ③

16 She should pick the black stone.

17 ②   18 ④   19 black

20 dropped, picked, right away   21 ⑤

01 character는 '등장인물'이라는 뜻으로 나머지는 모두 연극의 배역과 관련된 표현들이다. ① lead role: 주연 ② villain: 악역 ③ cameo: 카메오(유명인이 잠시 출연하는 역할) ⑤ bit part: 단역

02 '누군가가 무언가를 했을 때 그것을 해도 좋고 어떤 문제도 없는 것'은 허락되는 것이다.

03 anymore (부) (부정문·의문문에서) 지금은, 이제는 (더 이상) (= any longer)

04 (1) carefully: 주의 깊게 (2) borrow: 빌리다

05 '특별한 행사나 누군가의 성공을 기념하기 위해 즐거운 것을 하다'를 뜻하는 것은 'celebrate(축하하다)'가 적절하다.

06 ① 저도 역시 Jack을 좋아하지 않아요. ② 크게 말하지 않으면 들리지 않는다. ③ trick: 속임수, 그것은 단지 그녀의 속임수입니다. ④ 경찰은 그를 투옥했다. ⑤ 그 사람은 비열하고 조심성이 없으며 어리석습니다.

07 부정문이므로 either가 적절하다.

08 ① She picked the[a] black one. ② Why do you think she left the party so early? ④ I have two sisters. One is older than me and the other is younger than me. ⑤ How nice the old lady is!

09 (1) one ~ the other ...: (둘 중에서) 하나는 ~, 다른 하나는 … (2) 의문사가 없는 간접의문문은 의문사 대신에 if나 whether를 쓴다. 이 문장에서 that을 쓰면 그 의미가 어색하며 뒤에 나오는 or not과도 어울리지 않는다.

10 영화, 연극 또는 이야기에서 그려지는[묘사되는] 사람

11 '~해야 한다'는 의미로 'have to+동사원형'을 사용한다.

12 보기 ②번의 'lend'는 '(돈을) 빌려주다'는 의미로 본문의 내용과 일치하지 않는다.

13 빈칸은 농부 친구들의 대사로 빈칸 뒤에 'How terrible!'이라고 말하고 있으므로 빈칸에는 '대부업자'에 대한 부정적인 의미인 '못된, 비열한'이 적절하다.

14 제시문은 '두 개의 돌을 가방에 넣을 것이다'라는 뜻으로 (④)번 뒤에 'one ~, the other ~'가 나오므로 (④)가 적절하다.

15 본문은 농부가 돈을 갚지 못하자 대부업자가 게임을 제안하며 농부의 딸을 자신의 하인으로 삼고자 하는 갈등 부분이다.

16 질문: 대부업자의 하인이 되지 않으려면 농부의 딸은 어떤 색깔의 돌을 뽑아야 하는가?

17 제시문은 '대부업자가 두 개의 돌을 집는다. 딸이 주의 깊게 그녀를 본다.'는 의미로 (②) 뒤의 딸의 대사에서 '그녀가 두 개의 흰 돌을 집었어!'라는 내용이 나오므로 (②)가 적절하다.

18 딸이 아버지에게 하는 말이 아니라 대부업자에게 하는 말이므로 ④번에 들어갈 지시문은 'to Money Lender'가 적절하다.

19 빈칸은 친구들의 대사이기 때문에, 가방에 흰 돌이 남아 있는 것을 보고 친구들은 농부의 딸이 검은 돌을 집었다고 생각하는 것이 적절하다.

20 농부의 딸이 대부업자의 가방에 두 개의 흰색 돌이 있다는 것을 알았을 때 무엇을 했는가? / that she picked from the bag은 목적격 관계대명사절로 선행사인 the stone을 수식하는 역할을 한다.

21 본문 내용은 대부업자가 게임을 제시하고 흰 돌 두 개를 가방에 넣는 절정(Climax) 부분에서 갈등이 해결되는 결말 부분(Solution)이다.

22 ⓓ의 대사에 'She's mean.'이라고 3인칭을 사용하고 있으므로 대부업자와 이야기를 직접 나누고 있는 '아버지와 딸'이 아닌 친구들이라는 것을 알 수 있다.

23 돈이 없다면 대신에 당신 딸은 내 하인이 될 것이라는 대안을 제시하는 instead가 적절하다.

24 밑줄 (B)는 '그녀는 야비해'라는 정보로 보아 게임을 자신에게 유리하게 바꿀 수 있다고 추측할 수 있다.

교과서 파헤치기

Lesson 5

01 태도, 자세   02 고발하다, 비난하다
03 던지다   04 ~ 뒤에   05 공약, 약속
06 보호하다   07 피하다   08 약자 괴롭히기
09 어려움   10 석방하다   11 외모
12 등장인물, 캐릭터   13 유죄의   14 걱정하는
15 판사; 판단하다   16 부끄러움을 많이 타는, 수줍어하는
17 감옥   18 턱수염   19 실종된, 행방불명된
20 공격하다   21 이웃   22 자유
23 자신감 있는   24 회장   25 받다
26 권리   27 용돈   28 진실
29 체포하다   30 희생자   31 평범한
32 다정한, 친절한   33 속삭이다   34 인기 있는, 대중적인
35 ~을 돌보다   36 ~을 두려워하다   37 진정하다
38 ~을 석방하다   39 B 때문에 A를 고발하다
40 ~ 덕분에   41 ~을 지지하다, ~을 찬성하다
42 ~을 싸워 물리치다
43 ~을 뽑다, ~에게 투표하다

01 back   02 pass   03 activity
04 carry   05 shout   06 victim
07 vote   08 choice   09 enter
10 hide   11 whisper   12 friendly
13 appearance   14 arrest   15 lucky
16 face   17 mind   18 guilty
19 choose   20 curly   21 ordinary
22 popular   23 anytime   24 promise
25 monthly   26 score   27 freedom
28 protect   29 confident   30 allowance
31 neighbor   32 accuse   33 missing
34 prison   35 so far   36 be afraid of
37 accuse A of B   38 cut off ~   39 be good at ~
40 thanks to ~   41 vote for ~
42 agree with+사람   43 care for ~

1 cause, 야기하다   2 neighbor, 이웃   3 avoid, 피하다
4 score, 득점하다   5 attitude, 태도   6 confidence, 자신감
7 character, 등장인물   8 whisper, 속삭이다
9 attack, 공격하다   10 bullying, 괴롭히기

---

11 choose, 선택하다, 고르다   12 protect, 보호하다
13 change, 잔돈   14 victim, 피해자, 희생자
15 allowance, 용돈   16 arrest, 체포하다

Communicate: Listen-Listen and Answer. Talk

from, ago, worried, shy, good, lucky, friendly, playing, call, will be, I hope, will win

Communicate: Listen-Listen and Answer. Dialog

Is, winning / course, great handball player / mean the girl from / her name / what, look like / very tall, has, ponytail / who scored, just now / her seventh goal / really great

Communicate: Listen-Listen More

What can I do / lost, younger brother / calm down, brother's / five years old / What, look like / has / is, wearing / wearing, green shirt / tell me more / carrying a red backpack / look for, make an announcement, missing / I hope, find

Communicate: Speak 2-Talk in pairs

have an important exam / I hope, do well on / hope so, too

Communicate: Speak 2-Talk in groups

What, your character's name / His name / What does, look like / has no hair / have big eyes / does

Communicate: Speak-Rap Time

(1) lost, this afternoon / I hope, find
(2) do your best / I wish, the same
(3) What does, look like / has long straight hair
(4) Is, wearing / reading a map

My Speaking Portfolio

Look at, bulletin board, are, school president / already made, already made, choice, vote for / mean, with glasses, looks smart, promises / who will, choose / wants to make, a safe place / always has, right / seems okay / looks friendly, talent shows

Wrap Up

1 there is / from, over there / Which, What does, look / curly, wearing glasses
2 look sad, wrong / broke her arm / happened / fell off / That's too bad, I hope, get better

Communicate: Listen-Listen and Answer. Talk

G: Hi, I'm Gacha. I'm from Mongolia. When I first came to Songji Middle School two months ago, I was so worried. I was a little shy, and I wasn't good at Korean. However, I'm a lucky girl. All my classmates are nice and friendly. I enjoy playing handball with them in P.E. class. I'm a good player. They call me "Golden Hand." There will be a sports day next week. I hope my class will win in the handball event.

Communicate: Listen-Listen and Answer. Dialog

B: Hi, Minsol. Is your class winning?

G: Of course. We have a great handball player.

B: You mean the girl from Mongolia?

G: Yes, her name is Gacha.

B: I've heard a lot about her. But what does she look like?

G: She's very tall and has a ponytail.

B: Oh, is she the girl who scored the goal just now?

G: Yes, that's her seventh goal.

B: Wow, she's really great.

Communicate: Listen-Listen More

M: What can I do for you?

G: I lost my younger brother.

M: Okay, calm down. What's your brother's name?

G: His name is Wally Brown. He's five years old.

M: What does he look like?

G: He has brown hair and brown eyes.

M: What is he wearing?

G: He is wearing a green shirt and black pants.

M: Can you tell me more?

G: Oh, he is carrying a red backpack.

M: All right. We'll go out and look for him. Also, we'll make an announcement about a missing child.

G: Thank you so much. I hope I'll find him soon.

Communicate: Speak 2-Talk in pairs

A: I have an important exam tomorrow!

B: I hope you'll do well on the exam.

A: I hope so, too. Thanks.

Communicate: Speak 2-Talk in groups

A: What is your character's name?

B: His name is Buster.

A: What does he look like?

B: He has no hair.

A: Does he have big eyes?

B: Yes, he does.

Communicate: Speak-Rap Time

(1) A: I lost my puppy this afternoon.

B: I hope you'll find him soon.

(2) A: I hope you'll do your best in the final game.

B: Thanks. I wish you the same.

(3) A: What does your sister look like, Claire?

B: She's tall and has long straight hair.

(4) A: Is your father wearing a blue cap?

B: Yeah. Now, he's reading a map.

My Speaking Portfolio

G: Look at the bulletin board. There are posters for the next school president.

B: Yeah, I've already made my choice. I'll vote for Jang Jimin.

G: You mean the boy with glasses? He looks smart, but I don't like his promises.

B: Then who will you choose?

G: Well, I am for number 1, Han Siwon. She wants to make our school a safe place.

B: She always has a ponytail, right?

G: Yes, and Hong Jiho seems okay.

B: She looks friendly, but I don't like talent shows.

Wrap Up

1 B: I hear there is a new student in your class.

G: Yes. She's from Jejudo. Oh, she's over there!

B: Which one? What does she look like?

G: She has curly hair and is wearing glasses.

2 G: You look sad. What's wrong, Jongmin?

B: My sister broke her arm this morning.

G: What happened?

B: She fell off her bike.

G: That's too bad. I hope she'll get better soon.

본문 TEST Step 1   p.09~10

01 Right, Different

02 ways, ordinary person

03 had, cared for

04 after, moved, face difficulties

05 looked different, other   06 did, like

07 avoided, with, beard   08 did, sit, to,

09 whispered, behind, trying   10 some, broke

11 threw, at, down   12 told, stop growing

13 did, mind   14 just, to have

15 One, attacked, threw   16 cut off, shouted

17 able, fight, off   18 called, accused, of

19 was arrested   20 judge, victim

21 believed, with, prison, over

22 wanted, know, truth   23 sent, to, across

24 in prison, protecting himself

25 became angry, set, free   26 freed, traveled, lots

27 attitudes toward, changed   28 Before, died, beard

29 His name

30 made, popular, fought, right

01 Right To Be Different

02 In many ways, an ordinary person

03 had a job, cared for

04 after, moved to, to face difficulties

05 looked different from   06 did not like it

07 avoided the man with a beard

08 to sit next to him

09 behind his back, trying to hide

10 Some, broke his windows

11 Others threw stones at, walked down

12 told, to stop growing

13 did not mind   14 freedom to have

15 attacked, threw him on the ground

16 cut off, shouted

17 was able to fight them off

18 accused him of attacking   19 was arrested

20 the judge, the victim

21 a man with a beard, went to prison

22 wanted, to know

23 sent, to, across the country

24 was in prison, protecting himself

25 became angry, decided to set, free

26 was freed, lots of

27 attitudes toward beards changed

28 Before, died, with a beard   29 His name

30 made beards popular, fought for, right to have

---

15 어느 날, 네 명의 남자가 Joseph을 공격했고 그를 바닥에 던졌다.

16 "우리가 당신의 턱수염을 잘라 버리겠어!"라고 그들은 소리쳤다.

17 Joseph은 덩치가 큰 사람이었고, 그는 그들을 싸워 물리칠 수 있었다.

18 하지만 그 남자들은 경찰을 불렀고, 자신들을 공격한 것으로 그를 고발했다.

19 불쌍한 Joseph은 체포되었다.

20 그는 "저는 여기서 희생자입니다."라고 판사에게 말했다.

21 슬프게도, 아무도 턱수염을 가진 남자를 믿지 않았고, 그는 일 년이 넘는 기간 동안 감옥에 갔다.

22 Joseph의 아들인 Thomas는 사람들이 진실을 알기를 원했다.

23 그는 전국에 있는 신문사에 편지를 보냈다.

24 사람들은 Joseph이 단지 자신과 자신의 턱수염을 지키려다 감옥에 갇혔다는 것을 알게 되었다.

25 많은 사람들은 이에 대해 분개했고, 그래서 판사는 결국 Joseph을 석방하기로 결정했다.

26 Joseph은 석방된 뒤에 순회를 하며 많은 사람들에게 자신의 이야기를 전했다.

27 사람들의 턱수염에 대한 태도는 서서히 변해갔다.

28 Joseph이 죽기 전에, 턱수염을 가진 남자가 미국의 대통령이 되었다.

29 그의 이름은 Abraham Lincoln(에이브러햄 링컨)이었다.

30 그는 턱수염을 대중적으로 만들었지만, Joseph Palmer는 그것을 기를 권리를 위하여 싸웠다.

---

1 다를 권리

2 여러 면에서 42살의 Joseph Palmer는 평범한 사람이었다.

3 그는 직업이 있었고 가족을 돌보았다.

4 하지만 1830년에 매사추세츠에 있는 작은 도시로 이사를 한 후에 그는 어려움에 직면하기 시작했다.

5 Joseph은 다른 사람들과 달라 보였다. 그는 기다란 턱수염을 기르고 있었다.

6 사람들은 그것을 별로 좋아하지 않았다.

7 마을 사람들은 턱수염을 가진 그 남자를 피했다.

8 그들은 그의 곁에 앉고 싶어 하지 않았다.

9 그들은 심지어 그의 등 뒤에서 "그가 무엇을 숨기려는 거지?"라고 속삭였다.

10 어떤 이웃들은 그의 창문을 깼다.

11 다른 사람들은 그가 길을 걸어 내려갈 때 그에게 돌을 던졌다.

12 그들은 그에게 턱수염을 그만 기르라고 말했다.

13 Joseph은 신경 쓰지 않았다.

14 그는 그저 자신의 턱수염을 기를 자유를 원했다.

---

1 The Right To Be Different

2 In many ways, 42-year-old Joseph Palmer was an ordinary person.

3 He had a job and cared for his family.

4 But in 1830, after he moved to a small town in Massachusetts, he began to face difficulties.

5 Joseph looked different from other people: he had a long beard.

6 People did not like it very much.

7 The town's people avoided the man with a beard.

8 They did not want to sit next to him.

9 They even whispered behind his back, "What is he trying to hide?"

10 Some neighbors broke his windows.

11 Others threw stones at him when he walked down the street.

12 They told him to stop growing a beard.

13 Joseph did not mind.

14 He just wanted the freedom to have his beard.

15 One day, four men attacked Joseph and threw him on the ground.

16 "We're going to cut off your beard!" they shouted.

17 Joseph was a big man, and he was able to fight them off.

18 But the men called the police and accused him of attacking them.

19 Poor Joseph was arrested.

20 He said to the judge, "I'm the victim here."

21 Sadly, no one believed a man with a beard, and he went to prison for over a year.

22 Joseph's son, Thomas, wanted people to know the truth.

23 He sent letters to newspapers across the country.

24 People learned that Joseph was in prison just for protecting himself and his beard.

25 Many people became angry about this, so the judge finally decided to set Joseph free.

26 After he was freed, Joseph traveled and told his story to lots of people.

27 Slowly, people's attitudes toward beards changed.

28 Before Joseph died, a man with a beard became the President of the United States.

29 His name was Abraham Lincoln.

30 He made beards popular, but Joseph Palmer fought for the right to have them.

구석구석지문 TEST Step 1   p.19

My Speaking Portfolio

1. will vote
2. looks confident, smart
3. thinks, should be
4. agree with
5. such as, bullying
6. hope, becomes
7. to be a safer place

My Writing Portfolio: My Book Report

1. Right to Be
2. About
3. about, last week
4. really enjoyed
5. learned from, that, appearance
6. who talk, must
7. However, have a question
8. Why, to have a beard

Words in Action

1. Welcome to, Admission, free
2. have in mind
3. If, to visit, look around
4. get hungry, a light snack

구석구석지문 TEST Step 2   p.20

My Speaking Portfolio

1. I will vote for Han Siwon.
2. She looks confident and smart.
3. She thinks school should be a safe place.
4. I agree with her.
5. I like her promises such as no more bullying.
6. I hope Han Siwon becomes the next school president.
7. I really want my school to be a safer place.

My Writing Portfolio: My Book Report

1. The Right to Be Different
2. A Story About Joseph Palmer
3. I read the story about Joseph Palmer last week.
4. I really enjoyed it.
5. I learned from the story that we should not judge people by their appearance.
6. Students who talk about other people's appearance must read the story.
7. However, I have a question about it.
8. Why did Joseph Palmer want to have a beard?

Words in Action

1. Welcome to the travel fair. Admission is free.
2. What countries do you have in mind?
3. If you want to visit South America, you can look around the booths on the left.
4. If you get hungry, you can have drinks and a light snack.

10 feed, 먹이를 주다   11 refund, 환불   12 wall, 벽

13 experience, 경험   14 exchange, 교환하다

15 guest, 손님   16 promise, 약속하다

단어 TEST Step 1 — p.21

01 쓰레기	02 흔한, 보통의	03 쏟다, 붓다
04 전통적인	05 토론	06 공유하다
07 경험	08 먹이다	09 진실, 사실
10 잘못된	11 손님	12 겁먹은
13 환불, 환불금	14 훈련, 훈육	15 짠
16 교환; 교환하다	17 물건	18 화난
19 (기계가) 작동하다, 일하다		20 ~ 없이
21 전갈, 메시지	22 십 대의	23 고치다
24 제안, 의견	25 영수증	26 슬픔
27 찢다	28 이해하다	29 비밀
30 사발, 그릇	31 약속하다	32 청취자
33 문자 메시지를 보내다		
34 (부정문에서) ~도 역시		
35 ~을 돌보다, ~을 처리하다		36 거짓말하다
37 ~에 들르다	38 곤경에 처하다	39 한번 해 보다
40 부수다	41 혼자 힘으로	42 더 이상 ~ 아니다
43 반드시 ~하다	44 발견하다, 알아내다	

단어 TEST Step 2 — p.22

01 puppy	02 suggestion	03 training
04 promise	05 wrong	06 secret
07 trash	08 exchange	09 bowl
10 stuff	11 without	12 traditional
13 experience	14 repair	15 scared
16 common	17 feed	18 guest
19 receipt	20 upset	21 truth
22 work	23 pour	24 salty
25 lie	26 discussion	27 either
28 teenage	29 share	30 listener
31 refund	32 message	33 sadness
34 tear	35 not ~ anymore	36 break down
37 drop by	38 start off with	39 be sure to
40 on one's own	41 be in trouble	42 take care of
43 tell a lie	44 find out	

단어 TEST Step 3 — p.23

1 teenage, 십 대의   2 listener, 청취자   3 puppy, 강아지

4 text, 문자 메시지를 보내다   5 suggestion, 제안

6 repair, 고치다   7 secret, 비밀

8 hairdryer, 헤어드라이어   9 receipt, 영수증

대화문 TEST Step 1 — p.24~25

Communication: Listen – Dialog 1

happy with / wrong / tore, into pieces / often, that / Sometimes, socks / kind, five months / too, to, training / start training, a few

Communication: Listen – Dialog 2

going out with / be back / Around, to feed / Be sure, too / problem / more thing, help, with, tore

Communication: Listen – Listen More

How, help you / bought, hairdryer, store, happy with / the problem / work, enough / want to exchange / get a refund / visit, store / drop by / Don't forget, receipt

My Speaking Portfolio – Step 3

not very happy with / the problem / bathroom for too long / how, feel / can / get up earlier, use / give, a try

Wrap Up – Listening ❺

look upset / not happy with / wrong with / doing her part / think, should talk to

Wrap Up – Listening ❻

Are, ready for, trip / ready to leave / your ticket with / on my phone / Don't forget to call, get to / Sure

대화문 TEST Step 2 — p.26~27

Communication: Listen – Dialog 1

Minsol: I'm not happy with Buster.

Dad: What's wrong?

Minsol: He tore my homework into pieces again.

Dad: Puppies often do that.

Minsol: This is not the first time. Sometimes I find my socks in the dog house.

Dad: Please be kind to him. He's just five months old.

Minsol: You're too nice to him! He needs some training.

Dad: Okay. Let's start training in a few weeks.

Communication: Listen – Dialog 2

Mom: Minsu, I'm going out with your dad for a movie.

Minsu: When will you be back, Mom?

Mom: Around 8 o'clock. Don't forget to feed Buster.

Minsu: Okay.

Mom: Be sure to give him some water, too.

Minsu: No problem.

Mom: One more thing. Can you help Minsol with her science homework? Buster tore her homework into pieces.

Minsu: Hmm .... Okay. I'll do that.

Communication: Listen – Listen More

Mike: Customer Service. How can I help you?

Sora: I bought a hairdryer at your store last week. I'm not happy with it.

Mike: What is the problem?

Sora: It doesn't work well. I mean the air isn't hot enough.

Mike: I'm sorry. Do you want to exchange it?

Sora: Well, can I get a refund?

Mike: Sure. Will you please visit our store with the dryer?

Sora: Yes, I'll drop by tomorrow afternoon.

Mike: Don't forget to bring the receipt.

Sora: Okay. Thanks.

My Speaking Portfolio – Step 3

A: I'm not very happy with my brother.

B: What's the problem?

A: He uses the bathroom for too long in the morning.

B: I know how you feel.

A: What can I do?

B: Well, you can get up earlier and use the bathroom first.

A: Okay, I'll give it a try.

Wrap Up – Listening ❺

G: You look upset, Tommy.

B: I'm not happy with Sojin.

G: What's wrong with her?

B: She isn't doing her part of the group project.

G: I think you should talk to her.

Wrap Up – Listening ❻

M: Are you ready for your trip, Suji?

G: Yes, I am, Dad. I'm ready to leave.

M: Do you have your ticket with you?

G: Yeah, I have it on my phone.

M: Good. Don't forget to call me when you get to the train station.

G: Sure.

본문 TEST Step 1 p.28~29

01 listeners, This, your
02 a special guest
03 hip-hop artist, Welcome

04 to, for having
05 listeners, tell, family
06 out by reading, letters
07 start off with, from
08 Andy, Sure
09 a, girl from
10 to tell, about
11 tries to do
12 without asking, hard to
13 buys, me study them
14 say, anymore, let, take
15 felt, same way
16 too, to, things, own
17 hope, get, message
18 So do, read
19 father, of, children
20 One, the other
21 too busy to talk
22 get, work, go back
23 ask, life, give, answers
24 don't talk much, either
25 say, spend more time
26 with, often, younger
27 too old to understand
28 suggestions, Text, idea

본문 TEST Step 2 p.30~31

01 Good evening, This is
02 a special guest
03 hip-hop artist, Welcome
04 to meet you, thank you for having me
05 want to tell
06 find out by reading some letters
07 start off with, from, teenage girl
08 Sure
09 15-year-old, from
10 to tell you
11 tries to do
12 without asking, hard to find my stuff
13 buys, me study them
14 to say, anymore, let me take care of, myself
15 the same way when
16 too young to do, on their own
17 get the message
18 do I
19 of two children
20 One, the other
21 too busy to talk
22 get, from work, go back to
23 them, school life, give short answers
24 don't talk much, either
25 to spend more time
26 often when you were younger
27 them, thought, too old to understand
28 suggestions, Text your idea

49

1 Breeze: 안녕하세요, 청취자 여러분. 저는 여러분의 디제이, Breeze입니다.

2 오늘은 특별한 손님, Andy Kim 씨를 모셨습니다.

3 그는 힙합 아티스트이시죠. 환영합니다, Andy.

4 Andy: 반갑습니다, 그리고 초대해 주셔서 고맙습니다.

5 Breeze: 네. 우리 청취자분들은 가족에게 무슨 말을 하고 싶어 하실까요?

6 오늘 저녁에 우리는 청취자분들로부터 온 몇몇 편지들을 읽으며 알아보려 합니다.

7 Andy, 십 대 소녀에게서 온 편지로 시작해 주시겠어요?

8 Andy: 알겠습니다.

9 Andy: 안녕하세요. 저는 원주에 사는 15세 소녀입니다.

10 저는 저의 엄마에 관해 이야기하고 싶습니다.

11 엄마는 저를 위해 모든 것을 해 주려고 하십니다.

12 엄마는 제게 물어보지도 않고 방을 청소해 주시고, 그래서 가끔은 제 물건을 찾기가 힘들 때도 있습니다.

13 또 엄마는 책을 사 와서는 저에게 그것들을 공부하라고 시키세요.

14 저는 엄마께 "엄마가 저를 사랑하는 것은 알지만 전 더 이상 아기가 아니에요. 제 일을 스스로 할 수 있게 해 주세요." 라고 말씀드리고 싶습니다.

15 Breeze: 저도 중학교 때 똑같은 기분을 느꼈습니다.

16 Andy: 많은 어머님들이 자녀들이 혼자 힘으로 무언가를 하기에는 너무 어리다고 생각합니다.

17 소녀의 어머님께서 메시지를 들으시길 바랍니다.

18 Breeze: 동감입니다. Andy, 다음 편지를 읽어 주시겠어요?

19 Andy: 안녕하세요. 저는 두 아이의 아버지입니다.

20 한 명은 고등학생인 여자아이이고, 나머지 한 명은 중학생인 남자아이입니다.

21 아이들은 저와 대화를 하기에는 너무 바쁩니다.

22 제가 일을 하고 집에 돌아오면, 아이들은 그저 인사만 하고 자신의 방으로 돌아갑니다.

23 가끔씩 저는 아이들에게 학교생활에 관해 묻기도 하지만, 아이들은 그냥 짤막한 대답만 합니다.

24 우리는 식사 자리에서조차 대화를 많이 하지 않습니다.

25 저는 아이들에게 "너희들을 무척 사랑한단다. 그리고 너희들과 더 많은 시간을 보내고 싶단다."라고 말하고 싶습니다.

26 Breeze: Andy, 어렸을 때 부모님과 자주 대화를 했나요?

27 Andy: 사실 그렇지는 않습니다. 저는 부모님을 무척 사랑하지만, 부모님이 저를 이해해 주시기에는 너무 나이가 들었다고 생각했습니다.

28 Breeze: 그렇군요. '슬픈' 아빠에게 해 드릴 제안이 있으신 분 계신가요? 여러분의 생각을 저희에게 문자로 보내 주세요.

1 Breeze: Good evening, listeners. This is your DJ, Breeze.

2 Today we have a special guest, Andy Kim.

3 He's a hip-hop artist. Welcome, Andy.

4 Andy: Nice to meet you and thank you for having me.

5 Breeze: Okay. What do our listeners want to tell their family?

6 This evening we will find out by reading some letters from them.

7 Andy, will you start off with the letter from a teenage girl?

8 Andy: Sure.

9 Andy: Hello. I'm a 15-year-old girl from Wonju.

10 I want to tell you about my mom.

11 My mom tries to do everything for me.

12 She cleans my room without asking me, so it's sometimes hard to find my stuff.

13 She also buys books and makes me study them.

14 I want to say to my mom, "I know you love me, but I'm not a baby anymore. Please let me take care of things myself."

15 Breeze: I felt the same way when I was in middle school.

16 Andy: Many moms think their kids are too young to do things on their own.

17 I hope the girl's mom will get the message.

18 Breeze: So do I. Andy, will you please read the next letter?

19 Andy: Hi. I'm a father of two children.

20 One is a high school girl, and the other is a middle school boy.

21 They're too busy to talk with me.

22 When I get home from work, they just say hi and go back to their rooms.

23 Sometimes I ask them about their school life, but they only give short answers.

24 We don't talk much at the table, either.

25 I want to say to my kids, "I love you so much, and I want to spend more time with you."

26 Breeze: Andy, did you talk with your parents often when you were younger?

27 Andy: Not really. I loved them very much, but I thought they were too old to understand me.

28 Breeze: I see. Does anyone have suggestions for the "sad" dad? Text your idea to us.

My Writing Portfolio

1. 15-year-old girl from
2. want to say
3. told, his secret
4. got, angry, was in trouble
5. too, to, at that time
6. promise, never tell, secrets

Have Fun Together

1. nothing to do
2. is, place
3. richer than, not happy with
4. made us leave
5. smells good

Wrap Up – Reading Read and answer 3

1. from, who, to share, with
2. did not talk
3. between, break, down
4. tried to spend, on weekends
5. rode bikes, went shopping
6. chances to talk with
7. came to know

5. We played computer games, rode bikes, and went shopping together.
6. In this way, I had more chances to talk with them.
7. I came to know more about them.

My Writing Portfolio

1. Hello, I am a 15-year-old girl from Busan.
2. I want to say to my brother Jaeho, "Sorry."
3. I told Mom his secret last Friday.
4. Mom got so angry, so he was in trouble.
5. I was too scared to say sorry to him at that time.
6. I promise I will never tell his secrets again.

Have Fun Together

1. I have nothing to do. I have no friends.
2. Everything is too small. I don't like this place very much.
3. Heungbu is richer than me now. I'm not happy with it.
4. Mom made us leave home. We're not happy with it.
5. This soup smells good, but I can't eat it.

Wrap Up – Reading Read and answer 3

1. This is a letter from a father who wants to share his experience with the "sad" father.
2. My kids and I did not talk much.
3. There was a wall between us. I wanted to break it down .
4. I tried to spend more time with my children on weekends .

단어 TEST Step 1　　　　　　　　　p.40

01 일기	02 일, 문제, 안건	03 국가
04 집회, 국회, 민회	05 방식	06 전통적인
07 투표하다	08 아테네	09 등장인물
10 남자의, 수컷의	11 야외의, 실외의	12 사람, 인간, 인물
13 개발하다, 발달시키다		14 마지막의, 최종의
15 담다, 수용하다	16 수를 세다	
17 모으다, 모이다, 집결하다		18 불가능한
19 토론	20 의미	21 체류, 방문
22 약, 대략	23 거의	24 시민
25 아테네 사람	26 질문하다	27 슬픔
28 재능	29 모이는 장소	30 ~에 참여하다
31 수천의	32 많은	33 ~하느라 바쁘다
34 ~함으로써	35 지금까지	36 A와 B 사이에
37 너무 ~해서 …하다		38 20살 이상의
39 ~에 더하여, ~일뿐 아니라		

단어 TEST Step 2　　　　　　　　　p.41

01 meaning	02 Athens	03 traditional
04 count	05 male	06 gather
07 stay	08 talent	09 discussion
10 diary	11 matter	12 final
13 hold	14 assembly	15 impossible
16 almost	17 question	18 citizen
19 outdoor	20 about	21 person
22 vote	23 way	24 develop
25 sadness	26 Athenian	27 character
28 state	29 gathering place	
30 so far	31 a lot of	32 thousands of
33 by -ing	34 take part in	35 be busy -ing
36 between A and B		
37 over the age of 20		38 too ~ to …
39 in addition to		

단어 TEST Step 3　　　　　　　　　p.42

1 count, 수를 세다　　2 impossible, 불가능한

3 state, 국가　4 hold, 담다, 수용하다　5 talent, 재능

6 question, 질문하다　7 stay, 체류, 방문

8 vote, 투표하다　9 outdoor, 야외의, 실외의

10 citizen, 시민　11 male, 남자의, 수컷의

12 assembly, 집회, 국회, 민회

본문 TEST Step 1　　　　　　　　　p.43~44

01 Diary, Athens

02 visiting, aunt, uncle, Athens

03 went, center, city

04 gathering place, Athenians

05 lot, busy talking, shopping

06 went to, Assembly

07 male, part, vote, matters

08 each, freely, matters, showing

09 Counting thousands, almost

10 went, again

11 heard, between, named, and

12 questioned, on, meaning

13 too, to, way, discussing

14 best, so far　　　　15 went to, of

16 outdoor, hold, watched, play

17 addition, traditional, play, interesting

18 far, stage, characters' sadness

19 final, stay in

20 develop, talent, make, state

21 want, go, become, better

본문 TEST Step 2　　　　　　　　　p.45~46

01 Diary, Athens

02 visiting, aunt, uncle, Athens

03 went to, center　　　04 gathering place

05 were a lot of, busy talking, shopping

06 went to, Assembly

07 Any male citizens, take part in, vote, matters

08 each, freely, matters, vote by showing

09 Counting thousands of, almost, impossible

10 went to, again

11 heard, interesting discussion between, named, and

12 questioned, on, meaning of life

13 too, to, way of discussing matters

14 best, so far　　　　15 went to

16 outdoor, which, hold about, watched, play

17 In addition to traditional, play, interesting

18 sat far, stage, could feel, characters' sadness

19 final day, stay in

20 must develop, talent, help make, state

21 want to go, become a better

1 아테네에서 쓴 일기

2 첫째 날: 나는 아테네에 있는 숙부와 숙모 댁을 방문 중이다.

3 오늘은 도시 중심에 있는 아고라에 갔다.

4 아고라는 아테네 사람들이 모이는 장소이다.

5 많은 상점들이 있었고, 사람들은 이야기하고 쇼핑하느라 분주했다.

6 둘째 날: 숙부는 민회로 가셨다.

7 20살 이상의 모든 남자 시민은 민회에 참여하여 중요한 안건에 관해 투표할 수 있다.

8 그들은 각자 안건에 관해 자유롭게 의견을 말한 후, 손을 들어 투표한다.

9 숙부는 "수천 명의 손을 세는 것은 거의 불가능해."라고 말씀하셨다.

10 셋째 날: 나는 또 아고라에 갔다.

11 소크라테스라고 불리는 선생님과 그의 제자들이 나누고 있는 매우 재미있는 토론을 경청했다.

12 소크라테스는 제자들에게 인생의 의미에 관해 질문하였다.

13 나는 그것을 이해하기에 너무 어렸지만, 나는 그들의 토론 방식이 마음에 들었다.

14 넷째 날: 오늘은 지금까지의 날 중 최고의 날이었다.

15 나는 디오니소스 극장에 갔다.

16 약 17,000명을 수용할 수 있는 야외 극장에서 소포클레스의 연극 '안티고네'를 관람하였다.

17 전통적으로 있던 노래와 춤에 더하여, '안티고네'에는 흥미로운 이야기가 있었다.

18 나는 무대에서 먼 곳에 앉아 있었지만, 등장인물들의 슬픔을 느낄 수 있었다.

19 다섯째 날: 오늘은 아테네에서 머무는 마지막 날이다.

20 숙부와 숙모는 "네 재능을 개발해야 된다. 너는 아테네를 위대한 국가로 만드는 데에 기여할 수 있어." 라고 말씀하셨다.

21 이제 나는 학교에 다니며 더 나은 사람이 되고 싶다.

1 A Diary from Athens

2 1st Day _ I am visiting my aunt and uncle in Athens.

3 Today I went to the Agora in the center of the city.

4 It is a gathering place for Athenians.

5 There were a lot of stores, and people were busy talking and shopping.

6 2nd Day _ My uncle went to the Assembly.

7 Any male citizens over the age of 20 can take part in the Assembly and vote on important matters.

8 After they each speak freely about the matters, they vote by showing their hands.

9 My uncle said, "Counting thousands of hands is almost impossible."

10 3rd Day _ I went to the Agora again.

11 I heard a very interesting discussion between a teacher named Socrates and his students.

12 Socrates questioned his students on the meaning of life.

13 I was too young to understand it, but I liked their way of discussing matters.

14 4th Day _ Today was the best day so far.

15 I went to the Theater of Dionysus.

16 At the outdoor theater which can hold about 17,000 people, we watched *Antigone*, a play by Sophocles.

17 In addition to traditional songs and dances, the play had an interesting story.

18 I sat far from the stage, but I could feel the characters' sadness.

19 5th Day _ Today is the final day of my stay in Athens.

20 My aunt and uncle said to me, "You must develop your talent. You can help make Athens a great state."

21 Now I want to go to school and become a better person.

단어 TEST Step 1 p.53

01 요리사	02 오염시키다	03 끓이다, 끓다
04 상영 시간	05 아마도	06 매력적인
07 나타나다, 등장하다		08 기계
09 교육	10 붓다	11 선택하다, 고르다
12 마지막으로	13 창의적인, 독창적인	
14 움직임	15 공통의	16 살아 있는
17 재미있는, 즐거운	18 접시	19 맛보다, 먹다
20 개발하다, 만들다	21 간단한, 단순한	22 출판하다
23 평소의, 보통의	24 조리법, 비법	25 ~ 중에
26 계속 ~이다	27 어리석은	28 유명한, 잘 알려진
29 자외선 차단제	30 번역하다	31 고르다, 선택하다
32 캐리커쳐, (풍자) 만화		33 만화영화
34 만화가	35 ~에 대한 돈을 내다	
36 ~에게 금방 눈에 띄다, ~에게 분명히 보이다		
37 ~을 놀리다	38 ~가 기대되다	39 기복
40 조심하다	41 A를 조각으로 자르다	
42 역힐을 하다	43 합쳐지다	

단어 TEST Step 2 p.54

01 appear	02 chef	03 pollute
04 translate	05 creative	06 develop
07 cartoonist	08 dirty	09 alive
10 education	11 publish	12 fry
13 lastly	14 usual	15 pour
16 among	17 sunscreen	18 machine
19 showtime	20 silly	21 boil
22 simple	23 box office	24 common
25 animated movie		26 choose
27 recipe	28 pepper	29 plate
30 taste	31 well-known	32 probably
33 fascinating	34 movement	35 watch out
36 play a role	37 be made into	38 take a look
39 can't wait to	40 ups and downs	
41 make fun of	42 pay for	43 of all ages

단어 TEST Step 3 p.55

1 movement, 움직임   2 usual, 평소의, 보통의
3 showtime, 상영 시간   4 amusing, 재미있는, 즐거운
5 education, 교육   6 appear, 나타나다   7 silly, 어리석은
8 develop, 개발하다, 만들다   9 fascinating, 매력적인

10 translate, 번역하다   11 fry, 볶다, 튀기다
12 remain, 계속 ~이다   13 caricature, 풍자문화
14 publish, 출판하다   15 sunscreen, 자외선 차단제
16 chef, 요리사

대화문 TEST Step 1 p.56~57

Communication: Listen – Dialog 1

look down / serious, Sometimes, a lot / teens, ups and downs / really / Have you watched, animated movie / I haven't, Why, ask / teenager's feelings, will help, understand, better / sounds, watch

Communication: Listen – Dialog 2

look at, line / ticket machine, Let's buy, from, machine / how to use the machine / select, showtime / watch, what / select, choose, seats / sit in the back / problem, Lastly, pay for / simple

Communication: Listen More

Have you ever made / No, I haven't / how to make / Sounds / First, put, on, plate, spread / help, with / Next, peppers / Add, bake for about, oven / can't wait to taste

Communicate: Speak

how to, fried rice / cut, into / next / Put, fry, with rice / simple

Wrap Up – Listening ❺

Have, been to / have, Actually, every year / you've climbed, haven't you / twice

Wrap Up – Listening ❻

how to draw, First, circle, Next, `draw, color, draw, circle, Lastly, make

대화문 TEST Step 2 p.58~59

Communication: Listen – Dialog 1

Jane: Kevin, you look down.

Kevin: Nothing serious. Sometimes my feelings change a lot.

Jane: I understand. Many teens have ups and downs in their feelings.

Kevin: Oh, really?

Jane: Have you watched the animated movie "Shining Days"?

Kevin: No, I haven't. Why do you ask?

Jane: It is about a teenager's feelings. It will help you understand your feelings better.

Kevin: That sounds good! I'll watch it.

Communication: Listen – Dialog 2

Emily: Oh, look at the long line at the box office.

Tony: Yeah, there's a ticket machine over there. Let's buy the tickets from the machine.

Emily: All right. Do you know how to use the machine?

Tony: Sure. It's easy. First, select a movie and a showtime.

Emily: Okay. We can watch the seven o'clock show. Then what?

Tony: Well, select the number of tickets and choose our seats.

Emily: Okay. Two tickets, and I want to sit in the back.

Tony: No problem. Lastly, pay for the tickets.

Emily: It's very simple.

Communication: Listen More

Suji: Good morning, Chef Garcia!

Garcia: Hello, Suji. Have you ever made nacho pizza?

Suji: Nacho pizza? No, I haven't.

Garcia: Kids will love it, and I'll tell you how to make it.

Suji: Sounds good!

Garcia: It's easy to make. First, put nacho chips on a plate and spread pizza sauce on them.

Suji: Okay. Let me help you with the pizza sauce.

Garcia: Thanks. Next, put some ham, onions, and peppers on top.

Suji: Okay. Then?

Garcia: Add cheese and bake for about 12 minutes in the oven.

Suji: I can't wait to taste it!

Communicate: Speak

Anna: Do you know how to make fried rice?

Jinsu: Sure. It's easy. First, cut the vegetables into small pieces.

Anna: Okay. What do you do next?

Jinsu: Put some oil in the pan. Then, fry the vegetables with rice.

Anna: Wow, it's really simple.

Wrap Up – Listening ❺

Judy: Have you ever been to Sokcho?

Minsu: Yes, I have. Actually my uncle lives there, so I visit him every year.

Judy: Really? Then, you've climbed Mt. Seorak, haven't you?

Minsu: Yes, I've climbed to the top of the mountain twice.

Wrap Up – Listening ❻

Mike: Today, I'll tell you how to draw a bear's face.

First, draw a big circle for the face. Next, make two circles on top of the face. After that, draw two circles for its eyes and color them black. Then, draw a small circle for the nose. Lastly, make a mouth.

본문 TEST Step 1   p.60~61

01 Both, Land
02 laugh, saw, above
03 so, successful
04 who make cartoons
05 catch, make, laugh, creative
06 have made, for hundreds
07 types, cartoons different roles
08 One, is, a few
09 is, called
10 makes, character, laugh, saying
11 Another, is called
12 parts, different, bigger, usual
13 at, on, right
14 Which parts, jump out
15 have used, make fun
16 several, come together, strip
17 have been, for, years
18 just amusing stories
19 have also used, education
20 make, clearer, easier, learn
21 have probably seen
22 have surely seen, animated
23 popular among, all ages
24 added to, come alive
25 develop fascinating, interesting, through
26 type, was developed
27 is called
28 are published, read, on
29 popular, them, even, into
30 forms, may appear
31 different, exciting, remain, relax

본문 TEST Step 2   p.62~63

01 Land
02 laugh when, saw, above
03 so, cartoonist, successful
04 who make cartoons
05 to catch, make you laugh, creative drawings
06 have made, for hundreds of years
07 many types of cartoons, different roles
08 One form, is, a few words
09 is sometimes called
10 makes a funny character, makes, laugh, doing, saying

11 Another, is called

12 some parts, are different, bigger than usual

13 Look at, on   14 Which parts, jump out

15 have used, to make fun of well-known people

16 several, come together, a comic strip

17 have been, for many years

18 just amusing stories

19 have also used, for education

20 make, clearer, easier to learn

21 have probably seen

22 have surely seen, animated movies, too

23 popular among people of all ages

24 Movement, are added to, come alive

25 develop fascinating characters, interesting, through

26 type of, was developed

27 is called

28 are published, read them, on

29 popular, them are, made into

30 forms, may appear

31 different, exciting than, remain, laugh, relax, learn

20 만화는 정보를 더 명료하고 더 배우기 쉽게 만들 수 있다.

21 여러분은 아마 만화 역사책이나 과학책을 본 적이 있을 것이다.

22 여러분은 많은 만화영화도 당연히 봤을 것이다.

23 이것들은 모든 연령대의 사람들에게 매우 인기가 많다.

24 동작이나 소리가 그림에 더해져서 그림들이 생생하게 살아난다.

25 미술가들과 작가들은 매력적인 캐릭터를 개발하고 만화영화 제작을 통해 재미있는 이야기를 들려준다.

26 1990년대에 새로운 형식의 만화가 개발되었다.

27 그건 웹툰이라고 불린다.

28 웹툰은 온라인으로 출판되기 때문에 여러분이 휴대 전화나 컴퓨터로 언제 어디서나 볼 수 있다.

29 그것은 매우 인기가 있고, 그들 가운데 일부는 심지어 텔레비전 드라마나 영화로 만들어지기도 한다.

30 미래에는 새로운 형태의 만화가 나타날지도 모른다.

31 그것은 지금과는 다르고 한층 더 재미있겠지만, 한 가지는 같을 것이다. 그것은 우리가 웃고, 쉬고, 배우도록 도와줄 것이다.

1 배다! 육지다!

2 위의 만화를 보고 웃었는가?

3 그랬다면 그 만화가는 성공했다.

4 만화가들은 만화를 만드는 사람들이다.

5 그들은 여러분의 관심을 끌고, 대개는 간단한 말과 독창적인 그림으로 여러분을 웃게 하고 싶어 한다.

6 사람들은 수백 년 동안 만화를 만들어 왔다.

7 만화에는 많은 종류가 있으며, 그것들은 다양한 역할을 한다.

8 만화의 한 형태로 몇 마디 말을 쓴 그림이 있다.

9 간혹 그것은 '개그 만화'라고 불린다.

10 만화가는 웃긴 캐릭터를 만들고, 그 캐릭터는 우스꽝스러운 행동이나 말을 함으로써 여러분을 웃게 만든다.

11 다른 종류의 만화는 캐리커처라고 불린다.

12 캐리커처에서 캐릭터의 어떤 부분은 평소와 다르거나 더 크다.

13 오른쪽의 그림을 보아라.

14 남자 얼굴의 어떤 부분이 여러분에게 분명히 보이는가?

15 미술가들은 유명한 사람들을 풍자하기 위해 이런 종류의 만화를 그려 왔다.

16 몇 가지 만화 그림이 모여서 이야기를 들려주게 되면, 그것이 연재만화가 된다.

17 연재만화는 여러 해 동안 신문에 실려 왔다.

18 그것들은 종종 그저 재미있는 이야기이다.

19 사람들은 연재만화를 교육용으로 사용해 오기도 했다.

1 Boat! Land!

2 Did you laugh when you saw the cartoon above?

3 If so, the cartoonist was successful.

4 Cartoonists are the people who make cartoons.

5 They want to catch your interest, and usually, make you laugh with simple language and creative drawings.

6 People have made cartoons for hundreds of years.

7 There are many types of cartoons, and they play different roles.

8 One form of cartoon is a picture with a few words.

9 It is sometimes called a "gag cartoon."

10 The cartoonist makes a funny character, and the character makes you laugh by doing or saying silly things.

11 Another type of cartoon is called a caricature.

12 In a caricature, some parts of a character are different or bigger than usual.

13 Look at the picture on the right.

14 Which parts of the man's face jump out at you?

15 Artists have used this type of cartoon to make fun of well-known people.

16 When several cartoon pictures come together and tell a story, we have a comic strip.

17 Comic strips have been in newspapers for many years.

18 They are often just amusing stories.

19 People have also used comic strips for education.

20 Comics can make information clearer and easier to learn.

21 You have probably seen comic history or science books.

22 You have surely seen many cartoon movies, or animated movies, too.

23 These are very popular among people of all ages.

24 Movement and sounds are added to pictures, so they come alive.

25 Artists and writers can develop fascinating characters and tell interesting stories through animation.

26 In the 1990s, a new type of cartoon was developed.

27 It is called a webtoon.

28 Webtoons are published online, so you can read them anytime, anywhere on your phone or computer.

29 They are very popular, and some of them are even made into TV dramas or movies.

30 New forms of cartoons may appear in the future.

31 They could be different and even more exciting than now, but one thing will remain the same: they will help us laugh, relax, and learn.

구석구석지문 TEST Step 1 p.70

My Speaking Portfolio – Step 3

1. Here, useful tip
2. washed, many times
3. warm, washing powder
4. Then, leave, for seven minutes
5. Lastly, out of, them
6. look like

My Writing Portfolio

1. Cartoon Character
2. favorite cartoon character
3. elementary school, humorous, kind
4. However, causes trouble
5. because, bright side, tries to, others

Words in Action B

1. Animated Movie
2. to build, in the forest
3. soon suffer from, pollution
4. makes a suggestion
5. reach an agreement to create

구석구석지문 TEST Step 2 p.71

My Speaking Portfolio – Step 3

1. Here is a useful tip for you.
2. I've washed my sneakers this way many times.
3. First, put the sneakers, warm water, and washing powder in a plastic bag.
4. Then close the bag and leave it for seven minutes.
5. Lastly, take the sneakers out of the bag and wash them.
6. They'll look like new sneakers.

My Writing Portfolio

1. Giyeong, My Favorite Cartoon Character
2. My favorite cartoon character is Giyeong of *Black Rubber Shoes*.
3. He is an elementary school student. He is humorous and kind.
4. However, he is not very smart and sometimes causes trouble.
5. I like him because he looks on the bright side of everything and always tries to help others.

Words in Action B

1. The Best Animated Movie for Children's Education
2. Animals welcome the city's plan to build an amusement park in the forest.
3. However, they soon suffer from serious pollution.
4. An old elephant makes a suggestion.
5. The animals and the city reach an agreement to create a better world for everyone.

15 waterfall, 폭포   16 bridge, 다리

단어 TEST Step 1   p.72

01 조종사	02 해돋이, 일출	03 이익, 혜택
04 준비하다	05 다리	06 지역
07 ~당, ~마다	08 자연의, 천연의	09 아마도
10 수도	11 전망	12 대륙
13 겁먹은, 무서워하는		14 비슷한, 유사한
15 환상적인, 엄청난	16 흐르다	17 수줍은, 부끄럼 타는
18 자외선 차단제	19 산맥	20 독특한
21 폭포	22 흙, 토양	23 대양
24 경이, 놀라움	25 인내심	26 예술품, 미술품
27 우주, 외계	28 특히	29 기원, 원산
30 열대 우림	31 포함하다	32 해수면
33 ~을 통하여	34 넓은	35 없어지다
36 ~와 비슷하다	37 솔직히 말하면	38 일 년 내내, 연중
39 ~으로 가득하다	40 ~을 따라 이름 짓다	
41 혼자서, 홀로	42 파티를 열다	43 그건 그렇고

단어 TEST Step 2   p.73

01 prepare	02 benefit	03 view
04 wide	05 capital	06 wonder
07 bridge	08 origin	09 patience
10 waterfall	11 especially	12 sunrise
13 tourist	14 sunscreen	15 fantastic
16 unique	17 flow	18 Mars
19 shy	20 mountain range	
21 similar	22 through	23 soil
24 continent	25 per	26 area
27 sea level	28 scared	29 natural
30 contain	31 probably	32 rainforest
33 ocean	34 across	35 name after
36 by the way	37 go away	38 all year round
39 be full of	40 be similar to	41 to be honest
42 throw a party	43 by oneself	

단어 TEST Step 3   p.74

1 prepare, 준비하다   2 benefit, 이익   3 area, 지역

4 rainforest, 열대 우림   5 continent, 대륙

6 across, 건너서, 가로질러   7 wonder, 경이, 놀라움

8 patience, 인내심   9 soil, 토양, 흙

10 natural, 천연의, 자연의   11 desert, 사막

12 wide, 넓은   13 origin, 기원   14 pilot, 조종사

대화문 TEST Step 1   p.75~76

Communication: Listen – Dialog 1

tomato soup / happy, like / By the way, where, was first grown / somewhere in Europe / came from South America / How / social studies

Communication: Listen – Dialog 2

Did, see, took / What / traveled around, by herself / surprise / showed us pictures, especially, pyramids / Are there, South America / about, above sea level / can't believe it

Communication: Listen More

How was / fantastic, really enjoyed / closed, while riding / To be honest, scared at first / how fast, is / no idea / as fast as / surprising / Let's ride / sign, after / maybe next time

Communicate: Speak

what the capital of Peru is / no idea / didn't know

Wrap Up – Listening ❺

got a puppy / Where, pet shop / heard, uncle / want, too

Wrap Up – Listening ❻

won first prize / quiet, shy / joined, has changed a lot / want to join, too

대화문 TEST Step 2   p.77~78

Communication: Listen – Dialog 1

Sujin: Dad, I like this tomato soup.

Dad: I'm happy you like it.

Sujin: By the way, do you know where the tomato was first grown?

Dad: Italy or somewhere in Europe?

Sujin: No, the tomato came from South America.

Dad: Really? How did you know that?

Sujin: I learned it from Ms. Song, my social studies teacher.

Dad: That's good.

Communication: Listen – Dialog 2

Jenny: Did you see the pictures Ms. Song took?

Brian: What pictures?

Jenny: She traveled around South America by herself last summer.

Brian: Really? What a surprise!

Jenny: She showed us pictures of beautiful places. I especially liked the pictures of pyramids.

Brian: Are there pyramids in South America?

Jenny: Yes. She said some pyramids are about 3,800 meters above sea level.

Brian: I can't believe it.

Communication: Listen More

Hana: How was the roller coaster ride, Jongha?

Jongha: It was fantastic. I really enjoyed it.

Hana: Ha ha. You closed your eyes while riding.

Jongha: Did you see? To be honest, I was really scared at first.

Hana: Do you know how fast this roller coaster is?

Jongha: I have no idea.

Hana: It goes as fast as 140 km per hour.

Jongha: Wow! That's surprising!

Hana: Let's ride it one more time!

Jongha: Look at the sign. We can't ride it after 8 p.m.

Hana: Oh, maybe next time.

Communicate: Speak

Amy: Do you know what the capital of Peru is?

Jinsu: I have no idea. What is it?

Amy: It's Lima.

Jinsu: I didn't know that.

Wrap Up – Listening ❺

Jack: Do you know Junha got a puppy?

Minji: No. Where did he get it? From a pet shop?

Jack: No. I heard he got the puppy from his uncle.

Minji: I want one, too.

Wrap Up – Listening ❻

Mike: Do you know Sumin won first prize at the speech contest?

Sue: I can't believe it. She was very quiet and shy last year.

Mike: Yeah. She joined the drama club this year, and she has changed a lot.

Sue: I see. I want to join the club, too.

본문 TEST Step 1   p.79~80

01 where, driest desert   02 about the highest

03 they, both, South

04 full, wonders that, surprise

05 the driest desert   06 parts, gets, all, per

07 areas, so, that, grow

08 what scientists, such, dry

09 similar, so, prepare, outer

10 one, best places, watch

11 If, to, world's highest   12 meters high

13 cover, patience, luck, view

14 named after, flew over   15 get to, top, by

16 runs across, through   17 travels from, flows into

18 interesting in, ways   19 most, no bridges

20 because, runs through, wet

21 places, wide, other side

22 probably, swim in

23 home, that, meat

24 the world's longest, range

25 how long, mountain range

26 about, long

27 contains, mountains outside

28 About, third, people   29 unique, also live

본문 TEST Step 2   p.81~82

01 where the driest desert

02 about the highest waterfall

03 they are both

04 is full of, that will surprise

05 the driest desert   06 it gets, at all, per year

07 is so dry that, can grow

08 what scientists do, such a dry place

09 similar to, they prepare for trips, outer space

10 one of the best places, to watch stars

11 see the world's highest waterfall

12 It, meters high

13 cover, patience, luck, good view

14 named after, who, flew

15 still get to, only by plane

16 runs across, through

17 travels from, flows into, Atlantic Ocean

18 is interesting, many ways

19 no bridges

20 because it usually runs through, wet areas

21 see the other side   22 probably, swim in

23 home, that

24 the world's longest mountain range

25 how long the mountain range

26 about, long

27 contains, mountains outside

28 a third of the people, live in

29 unique animals, live there

1 여러분은 지구에서 가장 건조한 사막이 어디인지 알고 있나요?

2 가장 높은 폭포는 어떠한가요?

3 그렇습니다, 그것들은 둘 다 남아메리카에 있습니다.

4 이 대륙은 여러분을 놀라게 할 자연 경관으로 가득하답니다.

5 아타카마 사막은 지구에서 가장 건조한 사막입니다.

6 몇몇 지역은 비가 전혀 오지 않아서, 연간 강수량이 1~3mm에 그칩니다!

7 어떤 지역의 토양은 너무 건조해서 어떤 식물도 자랄 수가 없습니다.

8 이처럼 건조한 곳에서 과학자들이 무슨 일을 하는지 알고 있나요?

9 이 사막의 토양은 화성의 토양과 아주 비슷해서, 그들은 우주로의 여행을 준비합니다.

10 또한 아타카마 사막은 지구에서 별을 관측하기에 가장 좋은 장소 가운데 하나이기도 합니다.

11 여러분이 베네수엘라에 간다면, 세계에서 가장 높은 폭포를 볼 수 있을 것입니다.

12 그것은 높이가 979m입니다.

13 구름이 꼭대기 부분을 자주 에워싸기 때문에, 멋진 경치를 보려면 인내심과 약간의 운이 필요합니다.

14 사실 그 폭포는 1933년에 처음으로 폭포 너머 비행을 한 미국의 비행사 Jimmie Angel에게서 이름을 따왔습니다.

15 여전히 비행기로만 그 아름다운 폭포의 꼭대기에 갈 수 있습니다.

16 아마존강은 일곱 개의 나라를 거쳐 대륙을 가로질러 흐릅니다.

17 그것은 서쪽의 페루에서 시작하여 대서양으로 흘러갑니다.

18 아마존강은 많은 점에서 흥미롭습니다.

19 강의 대부분에는 다리가 없습니다.

20 그것은 강이 대개 도시나 마을이 아닌, 열대 우림과 습지를 지나 흐르기 때문입니다.

21 또한 많은 곳에서 강이 너무 넓어서 그 건너편을 볼 수조차 없습니다!

22 여러분은 아마도 이 강에서 헤엄치고 싶지 않을 것입니다.

23 이곳은 몇몇 아주 큰 뱀과 고기를 먹는 물고기들의 서식지입니다.

24 안데스 산맥은 세계에서 가장 긴 산맥입니다.

25 여러분은 그 산맥의 길이가 얼마인지 아시나요?

26 그것은 약 7,000km입니다.

27 또한 그곳에는 아시아 외의 지역에서 가장 높은 산이 있습니다.

28 남아메리카 인구의 3분의 1 정도가 안데스 산맥에 살고 있습니다.

29 그리고 독특한 동물들이 많이 서식하고 있기도 합니다.

1 Do you know where the driest desert on Earth is?

2 How about the highest waterfall?

3 Yes, they are both in South America.

4 This continent is full of natural wonders that will surprise you.

5 The Atacama is the driest desert on Earth.

6 In some parts, it gets almost no rain at all — only 1–3 millimeters per year!

7 The ground in some areas is so dry that no plants can grow.

8 Do you know what scientists do in such a dry place?

9 The soil in this desert is very similar to the soil on Mars, so they prepare for trips to outer space.

10 The Atacama is also one of the best places on Earth to watch stars.

11 If you go to Venezuela, you can see the world's highest waterfall.

12 It is 979 meters high.

13 Clouds often cover the top, so you need patience and a little luck to get a good view.

14 Actually, the waterfall is named after Jimmle Angel, a pilot from the United States who first flew over the waterfall in 1933.

15 You can still get to the top of the beautiful waterfall only by plane.

16 The Amazon runs across the continent through seven countries.

17 It travels from Peru in the west and flows into the Atlantic Ocean.

18 The Amazon River is interesting in many ways.

19 For the most part, it has no bridges.

20 That is because it usually runs through rainforests and wet areas, not cities or towns.

21 Also, in many places the river is very wide, so you cannot see the other side!

22 You probably do not want to swim in this river.

23 It is home to some very big snakes and fish that eat meat.

24 The Andes are the world's longest mountain range.

25 Do you know how long the mountain range is?

26 It is about 7,000 kilometers long!

27 It also contains the highest mountains outside of Asia.

28 About a third of the people in South America live in the Andes.

29 Many unique animals also live there.

구석구석지문 TEST Step 1   p.89

My Speaking Portfolio

1. Which country, to visit
2. where Brazil is
3. in South America, the biggest country
4. What a surprise, the first thing
5. to see, from

My Writing Portfolio

1. Day, Nature
2. went to, with
3. sits in, meters high
4. was surprised at
5. brown rocks, green trees
6. My trip to, made me feel
7. felt like, went away

Wrap Up - Reading

1. the world's largest
2. Thousands of year, all dried up
3. is left about, above sea level
4. one of the most visited natural wonders
5. All year round, unique natural beauty
6. In fact, makes, tourist
7. Every picture, take, beautiful work of art

Wrap Up - Reading

1. Salar de Uyuni in Bolivia is the world's largest salt flat.
2. Thousands of years ago, there was water, but it all dried up.
3. Now, a large salt desert is left about 3,656 meters above sea level.
4. Salar de Uyuni is one of the most visited natural wonders of South America, too.
5. All year round a lot of people visit this place to take pictures of its unique natural beauty.
6. In fact, the salt flat makes any tourist a great photographer.
7. Every picture you take in Salar de Uyuni will be a beautiful work of art!

구석구석지문 TEST Step 2   p.90

My Speaking Portfolio

1. A: Which country do you want to visit?
2. B: Brazil. Do you know where Brazil is?
3. A: Yes, I do. It's in South America. Do you know that Brazil is the biggest country in South America?
4. B: What a surprise! I didn't know that. So, what's the first thing you want to see in Brazil?
5. A: I want to see Iguazu Falls from the sky.

My Writing Portfolio

1. A Day in Nature
2. I went to Kaieteur Falls with my family.
3. The waterfall sits in the Amazon Rainforest in Guyana, and it is 226 meters high.
4. I was surprised at the size of the waterfall.
5. I could see the brown rocks and green trees there.
6. My trip to Kaieteur Falls made me feel good.
7. I felt like all my stress went away.

단어 TEST Step 1   p.91

01 고르다   02 축하하다
03 (부정문에서) 역시, 또한
04 일어나다, 생기다, 발생하다   05 속임수
06 비열한, 못된   07 빌리다   08 주의 깊게
09 백만   10 지금은, 이제는 (더 이상)
11 하인   12 해설자, 내레이터   13 가난한
14 대신에   15 큰소리로   16 감옥
17 (목숨을) 구하다   18 허락하다, 허가하다
19 끔찍한   20 등장인물   21 떨어뜨리다
22 ~할 필요가 없다   23 대부업자   24 (돈을) 갚다
25 즉시, 바로   26 중얼거리다   27 혼잣말로

단어 TEST Step 2   p.92

01 poor   02 borrow   03 drop
04 million   05 carefully   06 save
07 trick   08 narrator   09 terrible
10 happen   11 allow   12 instead
13 pick   14 loudly   15 character
16 mean   17 anymore   18 prison
19 servant   20 either   21 celebrate
22 right away   23 say to oneself 24 money lender
25 pay back   26 to oneself
27 don't[doesn't] have to

단어 TEST Step 3   p.93

1 instead, 대신에   2 trick, 속임수   3 pick, 고르다
4 mean, 비열한, 못된   5 borrow, 빌리다
6 character, 등장인물   7 happen, 발생하다, 일어나다
8 narrator, 해설자, 내레이터   9 prison, 감옥
10 save, (목숨을) 구하다   11 celebrate, 축하하다
12 servant, 하인

본문 TEST Step 1   p.94~95

01 Two Stones
02 Characters, Money Lender, Narrator
03 ago, village, there lived
04 had, borrow, million, from
05 for, pay, allow, anymore

06 have no
07 become, servant instead
08 Daughter, no   09 to be, servant
10 want, either, thank   11 to go, prison
12 let's play, put   13 One, the other, pick
14 happens if, one   15 Then, be, servant
16 mean, How terrible   17 What, if, pick
18 free, have, pay back 19 happens, doesn't, with
20 *loudly*, Then, prison
21 Daughter, Friends, Prison
22 *picks up, carefully at*
23 *to herself*, picked up 24 make, become, should
25 Stop, think, should   26 cannot pick, one
27 *from, drops, right away* 28 sorry, dropped
29 But, okay   30 Show us, stone
31 which one, picked
32 *to herself*, cannot, trick
33 *shows everyone, stone*
34 *start celebrating*   35 picked, one, free
36 Good thinking, saved

본문 TEST Step 2   p.96~97

01 Two Stones
02 Characters, Money Lender, Narrator
03 long time ago, village, there lived
04 had to borrow, million, from, money lender
05 the money lender, asked for, to pay back, allow,
   anymore   06 have no
07 will become, servant instead
08 no   09 to be, servant
10 either, thank you   11 go to prison
12 let's play, put
13 One, the other, pick one
14 happens if, pick   15 Then, will be, servant
16 mean, How terrible   17 if, pick
18 free, doesn't have to pay back
19 happens, doesn't play, with
20 *loudly*, Then, prison   21 Prison
22 *picks up, looks carefully at*
23 *to herself*, picked up, white stones
24 make, become, What should
25 Stop and think   26 cannot pick
27 drops, right away   28 dropped
29 okay   30 Show us the stone
31 which one I picked
32 *to herself*, cannot tell, trick

33 *shows everyone the white stone*

34 *start celebrating*   35 picked, free

36 Good thinking, saved

32 (대부업자는 모두에게 흰 돌을 보여 준다. 친구들과 아버지는
축하하기 시작한다.)

33 친구들: 그녀는 검은 돌을 집었어! 그들은 자유야!

34 해설자: 현명한 생각이 아버지와 딸을 구했습니다!

1 두 개의 돌

2 등장인물: 아버지, 딸, 대부업자, 친구들, 해설자

3 해설자: 오래 전 남아메리카의 작은 마을에 농부와 그의 딸이
살았습니다.

4 농부는 가난했고, 대부업자로부터 3백만 페소를 빌려야
했습니다.

5 하지만 대부업자는 친절하지 않았고, 농부가 돈을 갚을 때까지
한 달을 기다려 달라고 하자, 더 이상의 시간을 허락 해 주지
않았습니다.

6 대부업자: 돈이 없다는 거죠? 좋아요

7 대신 당신 딸이 내 하녀가 돼야겠네요.

8 아버지와 딸: 오, 안 돼!

9 딸: 저는 당신의 하녀가 되고 싶지 않아요.

10 아버지: 나도 그것을 원하지 않아! *(대부업자에게)* 사양하겠습니다.

11 대부업자: 감옥에 가고 싶은가요?

12 그렇다면, 게임을 하나 합시다. 내가 가방에 돌 두 개를
넣겠어요.

13 하나는 흰색이고, 다른 하나는 검은색이죠. 당신 딸이
하나를 집을 거예요.

14 딸: 제가 흰 돌을 집으면 어떻게 되죠?

15 대부업자: 그러면 넌 내 하녀가 될 거야.

16 친구들: 오, 안 돼! 그녀는 야비해. 정말 끔찍해!

17 딸: 제가 검은 돌을 집으면 어떻게 되죠?

18 대부업자: 그러면 넌 자유로워질 것이고, 네 아버지는 내 돈을
갚을 필요가 없어.

19 아버지: 내 딸이 당신과 이 게임을 하지 않으면 어떻게 되죠?

20 대부업자: *(큰소리로)* 그러면 당신은 감옥에 가게 되겠죠!

21 아버지, 딸, 친구들: 오, 안 돼! 감옥이라니!

22 *(대부업자는 두 개의 돌을 집는다. 딸은 주의 깊게 그녀를 본다.)*

23 딸: *(혼잣말로)* 오! 그녀는 두 개의 흰 돌을 집었어!

24 그녀는 나를 자신의 하녀로 만들 거야. 어떻게 하면 좋지?

25 해설자: 가만히 생각해 보세요. 그녀는 어떻게 하면 좋을까요?

26 그녀는 검은 돌을 집을 수 없어요.

27 *(딸은 가방에서 돌을 하나 집는다. 그녀는 그것을 바로
떨어뜨린다.)*

28 딸: 오, 안 돼! 미안해요, 제가 돌을 떨어뜨렸어요. *(대부업자에게)*
하지만 괜찮아요.

29 가방에 있는 돌을 우리에게 보여주세요.

30 그러면 제가 무엇을 집었는지 우리가 알게 될 테니까요.

31 대부업자: *(혼잣말로)* 그들에게 내 속임수를 말할 수 없어! 오,
안 돼!

1 The Two Stones

2 Characters: Father, Daughter, Money Lender,
Friends, Narrator

3 Narrator: A long time ago, in a small village in
South America, there lived a farmer and his
daughter.

4 The farmer was poor, and had to borrow three
million pesos from a money lender.

5 But the money lender was not kind, and when the
farmer asked for one month to pay back the
money, she didn't allow him anymore time.

6 Money Lender: You have no money? That's okay.

7 Your daughter will become my servant instead.

8 Father and Daughter: Oh, no!

9 Daughter: I don't want to be your servant.

10 Father: I don't want that, either! *(to Money Lender)*
No, thank you.

11 Money Lender: Do you want to go to prison?

12 Then, let's play a game. I will put two stones in a
bag.

13 One is white, and the other is black. Your
daughter will pick one.

14 Daughter: What happens if I pick the white one?

15 Money Lender: Then you will be my servant.

16 Friends: Oh, no! She's mean. How terrible!

17 Daughter: What happens if I pick the black one?

18 Money Lender: Then you will be free, and your
father doesn't have to pay back my money.

19 Father: What happens if she doesn't play this
game with you?

20 Money Lender: *(loudly)* Then you will go to prison!

21 Father, Daughter, and Friends: Oh, no! Prison!

22 *(Money Lender picks up two stones. Daughter
looks carefully at her.)*

23 Daughter: *(to herself)* Oh! She has picked up two
white stones!

24 She will make me become her servant. What
should I do?

25 Narrator: Stop and think. What should she do?

26 She cannot pick a black one.

27 *(Daughter picks a stone from the bag. She drops it right away.)*

28 Daughter: Oh, no! I'm sorry, I've dropped it. *(to Money Lender)* But it's okay.

29 Show us the stone in the bag.

30 Then we will know which one I picked.

31 Money Lender: *(to herself)* I cannot tell them about my trick! Oh, no!

32 *(Money Lender shows everyone the white stone. Friends and Father start celebrating.)*

33 Friends: She picked the black one! They are free!

34 Narrator: Good thinking has saved Father and Daughter!

적중 100 plus

2학기 전과정

영어 기출 문제집

정답 및 해설

천재 | 이재영

적중 **1◎◎** + 특별부록

Plan B

우리학교 최신기출

천재 · 이재영 교과서를 배우는

학교 시험문제 분석 · 모음 · 해설집

전국단위 학교 시험문제 수집 및 분석

출세 빈도가 높은 문제 위주로 선별

문제 풀이에 필요한 상세한 해설

중2-2
영어

천재 · 이재영

반		점수	
이름			

문항수 : 선택형(26문항) 서술형(3문항)　　20 ． ． ．

◎ 선택형 문항의 답안은 컴퓨터용 수정 싸인펜을 사용하여 OMR 답안지에 바르게 표기하시오.
◎ 서술형 문제는 답을 답안지에 반드시 검정 볼펜으로 쓰시오.
◎ 총 29문항 100점 만점입니다. 문항별 배점은 각 문항에 표시되어 있습니다.

[경북 ○○중]

01 다음 중 단어의 영영 풀이가 적절하지 <u>않은</u> 것은?　(3점)

① mind: to be bothered by something
② face: to deal with a difficult situation
③ ordinary: average or special in any way
④ attitude: opinions and feelings about someone or something
⑤ confident: having a strong belief in your abilities

[대구 ○○중]

02 ①~⑤의 밑줄 친 ⓐ~ⓔ가 다음 글 속에서 사용된 의미와 서로 같은 것은?　(4점)

> Welcome to the travel ⓐfair. Admission is ⓑfree. What countries do you have in ⓒmind? If you want to visit South America, you can look around the booths on the ⓓleft. If you get hungry, you can have drinks and a ⓔlight snack.

① My parents took me to the book ⓐfair.
② What do you like to do in your ⓑfree time?
③ Do you ⓒmind if I open the window?
④ I ⓓleft my cellphone in my mother's car.
⑤ Do you know that bright ⓔlight can cause pollution?

[경기 ○○중]

[3~4] 다음 대화를 읽고 물음에 답하시오.

> Man: What can I do for you?
> Jina: I lost my younger brother.
> Man: Okay, calm down. What's your brother's name?
> Jina: His name is Wally Brown. He's five years old.
> Man: (A)_____
> Jina: He has brown hair and brown eyes.
> Man: What is he wearing?
> Jina: He is wearing a green shirt and black pants.
> Man: All right. We'll go out and look for him. Also, we'll make an announcement about a missing child.
> Jina: Thank you so much. I hope I'll find him soon.

03 위 대화의 빈칸 (A)에 들어갈 말로 알맞은 것은?　(3점)

① What does he do?
② What does he look like?
③ What's wrong with him?
④ What kind of music does he like?
⑤ What do you want to tell your brother?

04 위 대화에서 Jina의 현재 심정으로 가장 알맞은 것은?　(4점)

① bored　　② worried　　③ excited
④ fantastic　　⑤ interested

[전북 ○○중]

05 다음 빈칸에 들어갈 말로 가장 알맞은 것은?　(3점)

> A: I have an important exam tomorrow.
> B: I hope _____.
> A: I hope so, too.

① you'll have a good time
② I have an exam
③ I won't get up early
④ you'll do well on the exam
⑤ you'll find that soon

06 다음 대화 중 자연스럽지 않은 것은? (3점)

① B: Hi, Minsol. Is your class winning?
　G: Of course. We have a great handball player.
② B: You mean the girl from Mongolia?
　G: Yes, her name is Gacha.
③ B: What does Gacha look like?
　G: She comes from Mongolia.
④ B: What's the problem?
　G: I'm not happy with school lunch.
⑤ B: What's the character's name of the story?
　G: His name is Joseph Palmer.

07 다음 대화를 읽고 내용이 일치하는 것들로 묶인 것은? (4점)

B: Hi, Minsol. Is your class winning?
G: Of course, Junhong. We have a great handball player.
B: You mean the girl from Mongolia?
G: Yes, her name is Gacha.
B: I've heard a lot about her. But how does she look?
G: She's very tall and has a ponytail.
B: Oh, is she the girl who scored the goal just now?
G: Yes, that's her seventh goal.
B: Wow, she's really great.

ⓐ Minsol's class is winning in the handball event.
ⓑ Junhong has heard a lot about Gacha.
ⓒ Gacha is good at playing handball.
ⓓ Minsol is tall and has a ponytail.
ⓔ Minsol's class scored seven goals.

① ⓐ, ⓓ　　　　② ⓐ, ⓔ
③ ⓐ, ⓑ, ⓒ　　④ ⓐ, ⓑ, ⓓ
⑤ ⓐ, ⓑ, ⓒ, ⓓ

08 다음 빈칸에 들어갈 말로 알맞은 것은? (3점)

M: What can I do for you?
G: I lost my younger brother.
M: Okay, calm down. What's his name?
G: It's Wally Brown. He's five years old.
M: What does he look like?
G: He has brown hair and brown eyes.
M: What is he wearing?
G: He is wearing a green shirt and black pants.
M: _____
G: Oh, he is carrying a red backpack.
M: All right. We'll go out and look for him.

① Do you know him?
② Is he going to school?
③ What is he doing now?
④ Can you tell me more?
⑤ What color does he like?

09 다음 중 어법상 옳은 것은? (4점)

① I didn't want him use my cell phone.
② The old lady advised the men worked hard.
③ I asked her to show me her report.
④ She wants her son is healthy.
⑤ He told them to not run in the room.

10 다음 두 문장의 빈칸에 공통으로 들어갈 수 있는 것은? (3점)

• Hippo will _____ Squirrel eat the nuts.
• Owl will _____ Rabbit to play the guitar faster.

① let　　　② help　　　③ want
④ allow　　⑤ make

11 다음 대화를 읽고 답할 수 <u>없는</u> 질문은? (4점)

Alex:　Hi, Minsol. Is your class winning?

Minsol: Of course. We have a great handball player.

Alex:　You mean the girl from Mongolia?

Minsol: Yes, her name is Gacha.

Alex:　I've heard a lot about her. But what does she look like?

Minsol: She's very tall and has a ponytail.

Alex:　Oh, is she the girl who scored the goal just now?

Minsol: Yes, that's her seventh goal.

Alex:　Wow, she's really great.

① Whose class is winning?

② What does Minsol look like?

③ Who's ever heard of the girl from Mongolia?

④ What is the name of the girl from Mongolia?

⑤ What did the girl from Mongolia do just now?

12 다음 대화를 읽고 알 수 <u>없는</u> 것은? (3점)

A: What can I do for you?

B: I lost my younger brother.

A: Okay, calm down. What's your brother's name?

B: His name is Wally Brown. He's five years old.

A: What does he look like?

B: He has brown hair and brown eyes.

A: Can you tell me more about your brother?

B: He is wearing a green shirt and black pants. Oh, he is also carrying a red backpack.

A: All right. We'll go out and look for him. We'll make an announcement about a missing child as well.

B: Thank you so much.

① 남동생의 이름

② 남동생의 나이

③ 남동생이 입은 옷

④ 남동생의 머리색

⑤ 남동생을 잃어버린 장소

13 그림을 보고 다음 〈조건〉에 맞게 문장을 완성하시오. (3점)

조건

• 2~3 단어로 쓸 것.

• after/before를 활용할 것.

• 완전한 문장이 되도록 할 것.

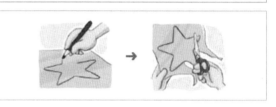

→ _____ a star, cut it out with scissors.

14 다음 〈보기〉에서 어법상 옳은 것의 개수는? (4점)

보기

ⓐ My mother asks me to take out the trash.

ⓑ We played hide-and-seek after we have lunch.

ⓒ Yesterday she allowed her son go to a ball park.

ⓓ My parents always tell me do my best in school.

ⓔ Nancy expected her brother to cook ramyeon for her.

ⓕ Susie was so angrily that she couldn't say anything.

ⓖ The homeroom teacher had me finish the project by 5.

① 1개　② 2개　③ 3개　④ 4개　⑤ 5개

[15~17] 다음 글을 읽고 물음에 답하시오.

In many ways, 42-year-old Joseph Palmer was an ordinary person. He had a job and cared for his family. But in 1830, after he moved to a small town in Massachusetts, he began to face difficulties. Joseph looked different from other people: he had a long beard. People did not like it very much.

The town's people avoided the man with a beard. They did not want to sit next to him. They even whispered behind his back, "What is he trying to hide?"

Some neighbors broke his windows. Others threw stones at him when he walked down the street. (A) 그들은 그에게 수염을 그만 기르라고 말했다. Joseph did not mind. He just wanted the freedom to have his beard.

15 위 글의 Joseph Palmer에 대한 설명으로 옳은 것은? (3점)

① 직업이 없었지만 가족을 돌봤다.

② 단지 수염을 가질 자유를 원했다.

③ 이웃들은 그의 턱수염을 좋아했다.

④ 집에 있을 때 이웃들에게 돌을 맞았다.

⑤ 1830년에 Massachusetts에서 태어났다.

16 위 글의 밑줄 친 표현과 해석이 일치하는 것은? (3점)

① ordinary person - 특별한 사람

② face difficulties - 곤란한 얼굴

③ looked different - 다른 것을 보았다

④ behind his back - 그가 돌아온 뒤에

⑤ did not mind - 신경 쓰지 않았다

17 위 글의 (A)의 뜻에 맞는 문장을 〈보기〉의 단어를 배열하여 완성하시오. (3점)

> 보기
>
> him / stop / told / to

→ They _____ _____ _____ _____ growing a beard.

[18~19] 다음 글을 읽고 물음에 답하시오.

Joseph's son, Thomas, wanted people to know the truth. He sent letters to newspapers across the country. People learned that Joseph was in prison just for protecting himself and his beard. Many people became angry about this, so (A)(decided, free, to, Joseph, the, set, judge).

18 위 글의 제목으로 가장 알맞은 것은? (3점)

① The efforts of Thomas to make his father free

② Joseph's letter which was sent to the judge

③ The bad attitude of people toward Joseph

④ The appearance of Joseph's son

⑤ The difficulty of living in a prison

19 위 글의 (A)의 단어들을 문맥에 맞게 바르게 배열하시오. (4점)

→ _____

20 다음 글의 밑줄 친 ⓐ~ⓔ 중 어법상 맞는 것은? (4점)

One day, four men attacked Joseph and threw him on the ground. "We're going to cut off your beard!" they shouted. ⓐJoseph was a big man, and he was able to fight off them. ⓑBut the men called the police and accused him of attacking them. ⓒPoor Joseph arrested. ⓓHe said the judge, "I'm the victim here." ⓔSad, no one believed a man with a beard, and he went to prison for over a year.

① ⓐ   ② ⓑ   ③ ⓒ   ④ ⓓ   ⑤ ⓔ

[21~23] 다음 글을 읽고 물음에 답하시오.

In many ways, (A)[42-year-old / 42-years-old] Joseph Palmer was an ordinary person. He had a job and cared for his family. But in 1830, after he moved to a small town in Massachusetts, he began to face difficulties. Joseph looked ⓐ_____ other people: he had a long beard. People did not like it very much.

The town's people ⓑ_____ the man with a beard. They did not want to sit next to him. They even whispered behind his back, "What is he trying to hide?" Some neighbors broke his windows. Others threw stones at him when he walked down the street. They told him to stop (B)[to grow / growing] a bread. Joseph did not mind. He just wanted the freedom to have his beard.

One day, four men attacked Joseph and threw him on the ground. "We're going to cut off your bread!" they shouted. Joseph was a big man, and he was able to fight them off. But the men called the police and accused him of (C)[attack / attacking] them. Poor Joseph was arrested. He said to the judge, "I'm the victim here." Sadly, no one believed a man with a beard, and he went to prison for over a year.

21 위 글의 괄호 (A)~(C)에 들어갈 표현으로 옳은 것끼리 짝지어 진 것은? (4점)

	(A)	(B)	(C)
①	42-year-old	– to grow	– attack
②	42-year-old	– growing	– attacking
③	42-years-old	– growing	– attack
④	42-years-old	– growing	– attacking
⑤	42-years-old	– to grow	– attack

22 위 글의 ⓐ와 ⓑ에 들어갈 말로 가장 알맞은 것끼리 짝지어진 것은? (3점)

	ⓐ	ⓑ
①	similar to	avoided
②	similar to	admired
③	happy with	avoided
④	different from	admired
⑤	different from	avoided

23 위 글을 읽고 답할 수 <u>없는</u> 질문은? (5점)

① How long was Joseph Palmer in prison?

② When did Joseph Palmer move to Massachusetts?

③ How many people threw stones at Joseph Palmer?

④ Why did the town's people whisper behind Joseph Palmer?

⑤ What was unusual about Joseph Palmer's appearance?

24 다음 글이 자연스러운 흐름이 되도록 (A)~(E)를 순서대로 바르게 배열한 것은? (3점)

Long ago, penguins lived on an island.
(A) He had a different shape, size, and color.
(B) One day a new bird, Perry, came to the island.
(C) Perry got upset and answered, "I look different, but I can be a good friend."
(D) For many years, they wore the same clothes and lived in the same houses.
(E) The head penguin said, "Hey, you don't look like us. Put on a penguin shirt."

① (A)-(B)-(C)-(D)-(E) ② (D)-(A)-(E)-(B)-(C)

③ (D)-(A)-(E)-(C)-(B) ④ (B)-(A)-(C)-(E)-(D)

⑤ (D)-(B)-(A)-(E)-(C)

In many ways, 42-year-old Joseph Palmer was an ⓐ_____ person. He had a job and cared for his family. But in 1830, after he moved to a small town in Massachusetts, he began to ⓑ_____ difficulties. Joseph looked different from other people: he had a long beard. People did not like it very much.
Some neighbors broke his windows. (A) Others threw stones at him when he walked down the street. (B) They told him (가)[stop / to stop] growing a beard. Joseph did not mind. He just wanted the freedom (나)[have / to have] his beard. (C)
One day, four men attacked Joseph and threw him on the ground. (D) "We're going to cut off your beard!" they shouted. Joseph was a big man, and he was able to fight them off. (E) Poor Joseph (다)[arrested / was arrested]. He said to the judge, "I'm the ⓒ_____ here." Sadly, no one believed a man with a beard, and he went to prison for over a year.

25 위 글의 내용과 일치하지 않는 것은? (4점)

① Joseph Palmer moved to a small town in Massachusetts.
② The four men who attacked Joseph called the police.
③ Joseph Palmer had spent over a year in prison before he was arrested.
④ The town's people did not like Joseph.
⑤ People didn't believe Joseph because he had a beard.

26 위 글의 흐름으로 보아, 주어진 문장이 들어가기에 가장 적절한 곳은? (3점)

But the men called the police and accused him of attacking them.

① (A)   ② (B)   ③ (C)   ④ (D)   ⑤ (E)

27 위 글의 빈칸 ⓐ~ⓒ에 들어갈 말을 순서대로 알맞게 짝지은 것은? (3점)

	ⓐ	ⓑ	ⓒ
①	ordinary	face	voter
②	ordinary	face	victim
③	ordinary	make	victim
④	special	face	judge
⑤	special	make	victim

28 위 글의 괄호 (가)~(다)에 들어갈 말로 어법상 적절한 것을 순서대로 알맞게 짝지은 것은? (4점)

	(가)	(나)	(다)
①	stop	have	arrested
②	stop	to have	was arrested
③	to stop	to have	was arrested
④	to stop	to have	arrested
⑤	to stop	have	arrested

29 다음 글의 Gacha의 심정의 변화로 알맞은 것은? (3점)

Hi, I'm Gacha. I'm from Mongolia. When I first came to Songji Middle School two months ago, I was so worried. I was a little shy, and I wasn't good at Korean. However, I'm a lucky girl. All my classmates are nice and friendly. I enjoy playing handball with them in P.E. class. I'm a good player. They call me "Golden Hand." There will be a sports day next week. I hope my class will win in the handball event.

① excited → unhappy
② upset → sad
③ worried → happy
④ nervous → unhappy
⑤ shy → angry

◎ 선택형 문항의 답안은 컴퓨터용 수정 싸인펜을 사용하여 OMR 답안지에 바르게 표기하시오.

◎ 서술형 문제는 답을 답안시에 반드시 검정 볼펜으로 쓰시오.

◎ 총 30문항 100점 만점입니다. 문항별 배점은 각 문항에 표시되어 있습니다.

[서울 강동구 ○○중]

01 다음 중 밑줄 친 단어가 어색한 것은? (3점)

① My mom is afraid of spiders, so she avoids them.

② She often whispers in my ear, "This is a secret."

③ I like your good attitude: you always look on the bright side.

④ I decided my report card from my homeroom teacher yesterday.

⑤ When a dog tried to attack me, my cat meowed loudly.

[부산 ○○중]

02 다음은 박람회를 안내하는 글이다. 한글 풀이가 잘못된 것을 고르면? (2점)

Welcome to the ⓐtravel fair(여행 박람회). ⓑAdmission(입장료) is free. What countries do you ⓒhave in mind(마음에 두다)? If you want to visit South America, you can ⓓlook around(~를 돌보다) the booths on the left. If you get hungry, you can have drinks and a ⓔlight snack(간단한 간식).

① ⓐ   ② ⓑ   ③ ⓒ   ④ ⓓ   ⑤ ⓔ

[경북 ○○중]

[3~5] 다음 대화를 읽고 물음에 답하시오.

M: What can I do for you?
G: I lost my younger brother.
M: Okay, calm down. What's your brother's name?

G: His name is Wally Brown. He's five years old.
M: What does he look (A)_____?
G: He has short curly hair and brown eyes.
M: What is he wearing?
G: He is wearing a green shirt and blue jeans.
M: Can you tell me more?
G: Oh, he is carrying a red backpack.
M: All right. We'll go out and look (B)_____ him. Also, we'll make an announcement about a missing child.
G: Thank you so much. ⓐ_____

03 위 대화의 (A), (B)에 들어갈 말로 바르게 짝지어진 것은? (3점)

	(A)	(B)
①	like	for
②	for	for
③	like	after
④	for	after
⑤	at	up

04 위 대화의 빈칸 ⓐ에 들어갈 말로 가장 자연스러운 것은? (3점)

① I hope I will find him soon.

② I hope he will lose his way.

③ I hope he will tell me more.

④ I hope I will get better soon.

⑤ I hope I will make an announcement.

05 위 대화의 내용과 다음의 Wally Brown을 찾는 안내방송문이 일치하지 않는 것은? (3점)

이름	Wally Brown
나이	① 5세
눈	② 갈색
머리 모양	③ 짧은 갈색머리
옷차림	④ 초록색 셔츠, 청바지
특이 사항	⑤ 빨간색 배낭을 메고 있음

06 다음 대화의 내용과 일치하는 것은? (4점)

Tom: What can I do for you?
Sue: I lost my younger brother.
Tom: Okay, calm down. What's your brother's name?
Sue: His name is Wally Brown. He's five years old.
Tom: Can you tell me about your brother?
Sue: He has brown hair and brown eyes.
Tom: What is he wearing?
Sue: He is wearing a green shirt and black pants.
Tom: Can you tell me more?
Sue: Oh, he is carrying a red backpack.
Tom: All right. We'll go out and look for him. Also, we'll make an announcement about a missing child.
Sue: Thank you so much. I hope I'll find him soon.

① Tom will go out and look for Sue.
② Wally Brown is five years younger than Sue.
③ Tom asks Sue to describe her younger brother.
④ Sue can't remember what Wally Brown is wearing.
⑤ Sue asks Tom to make an announcement about Wally Brown.

07 다음 대화를 읽고 Sori가 ⓐ라고 말한 이유로 가장 적절한 것은? (2점)

Sori: You look sad. What's wrong, Jongmin?
Jongmin: My sister broke her leg yesterday.
Sori: What happened?
Jongmin: She fell off her bike.
Sori: That's too bad. ⓐI hope she'll get better soon.

① 설득하기 위해　② 사과하기 위해
③ 비난하기 위해　④ 바람을 나타내기 위해
⑤ 불만을 표현하기 위해

08 다음 대화의 내용과 가장 일치하는 것은? (4점)

Sunhee: Look at the bulletin board. There are posters for the next school president.
Taemin: Yeah, I've already made my choice. I'll vote for Jang Jimin.
Sunhee: You mean the boy with glasses? He looks smart, but I don't like his promises.
Taemin: Then who will you choose?
Sunhee: Well, I am for number 1, Han Siwon. She wants to make our school a safe place.
Taemin: She always has a ponytail, right?
Sunhee: Yes, and Hong Jiho seems okay.
Taemin: She looks friendly, but I don't like talent shows.

① Sunhee likes Jang Jimin's promises.
② Han Siwon often has long straight hair.
③ Sunhee agrees that her school should be a safe place.
④ Taemin wants Sunhee to look at the bulletin board.
⑤ Taemin will vote for Jang Jimin for the next class president.

09 다음 대화의 빈칸에 들어갈 말로 적절하지 않은 것은? (3점)

A: What does she look like?
B: _____

① She has big eyes.
② She has a round face.
③ She has a ponytail.
④ She has long brown hair.
⑤ She likes watching TV dramas.

10 다음 대화의 순서에 맞도록 〈보기〉의 말들을 바르게 배열한 것은? (4점)

> B: Hi, Minsol. Is your class winning?
> G: Of course. We have a great handball player.
> B: (A)_____
> G: (B)_____
> B: (C)_____
> G: (D)_____
> B: Oh, is she the girl who scored the goal just now?
> G: Yes, that's her seventh goal.
> B: Wow, she's really great.

> **보기**
> ⓐ I've heard a lot about her. But what does she look like?
> ⓑ Yes, her name is Gacha.
> ⓒ You mean the girl from Mongolia?
> ⓓ She's very tall and has a ponytail.

	(A)	(B)	(C)	(D)
①	ⓐ	ⓑ	ⓓ	ⓒ
②	ⓑ	ⓒ	ⓓ	ⓐ
③	ⓒ	ⓑ	ⓐ	ⓓ
④	ⓓ	ⓒ	ⓐ	ⓑ
⑤	ⓓ	ⓒ	ⓑ	ⓐ

11 다음 대화 중 가장 어색한 것은? (3점)

① A: Is your class winning?
　 B: Sure. We have a great tennis player.

② A: What can I do for you?
　 B: I lost my younger sister.

③ A: There is a new student in your class.
　 B: I'm ready to leave.

④ A: Have you ever made potato pizza?
　 B: Yes, I have.

⑤ A: What's wrong?
　 B: He tore my homework into pieces again.

12 다음 문장의 빈칸에 들어갈 수 없는 것은? (3점)

> • My older brother always _____ me walk the dog.

① has 　　② lets 　　③ tells
④ helps 　　⑤ makes

13 다음 주어진 〈조건〉을 보고 두 문장 내용의 전후 관계를 살펴 before 혹은 after을 사용하여 한 문장으로 완성하시오. (3점)

> **조건**
> 1. 두 문장을 활용하여 4 단어로 작성하시오.
> 2. 사건의 구체적인 시간은 언급하지 마시오.
> 3. 반복되는 명사는 적절한 대명사를 활용하여 작성하시오.

> • Students will ride bikes at 10.
> • Students will have lunch at 12.

→ The students will ride bikes _____.

14 다음 중 어법이 바른 문장의 개수는? (5점)

> • She hoped her to tell the truth.
> • Chris asked Jane to marry him.
> • Yuri told me to learning Chinese.
> • Sally wanted her dad to fix her bike.
> • The dentist said him to stop eating sweets.
> • My parents made me to break my bad habit.
> • My teacher had she turn off her cell phone.
> • My boss talked me to be on time for the meeting.

① 1 　　② 2 　　③ 3 　　④ 4 　　⑤ 5

[15~17] 다음 글을 읽고 물음에 답하시오.

In many ways, 42-year-old Joseph Palmer was an ordinary person. ⓐHe had a job and cared his family. But after he moved to a small town in Massachusetts in 1830, he began to face difficulties. ⓑJoseph looked differently from other people: he had a long beard. People did not like it very much. The town's people avoided the man with a beard. They did not sit next to him. ⓒThey even whispered behind his back, "What is he trying to hide?" Some neighbors broke his windows. Others threw stones at him when he walked down the street. ⓓThey said him to stop growing a beard. Joseph did not mind. He just wanted the freedom (A)to have his beard.

One day, four men attacked Joseph and threw him on the ground. "We're going to cut off your beard!" they shouted. ⓔJoseph was a big man, and he was able to fight off them. But the men called the police and Joseph Palmer was accused of attacking them. Poor Joseph was arrested. He said to the judge, "I'm the victim here." Sadly, no one believed a man with a beard, and he went to prison for over a year.

15 위 글의 밑줄 친 ⓐ~ⓔ 중 어법이 바른 것은? (3점)

① ⓐ ② ⓑ ③ ⓒ ④ ⓓ ⑤ ⓔ

16 위 글을 읽고 답할 수 없는 질문은? (4점)

① What did Joseph Palmer accuse the men of?

② How long did Joseph Palmer stay in prison?

③ Why did Joseph Palmer's neighbors pick on him?

④ When did Joseph Palmer move to the small town?

⑤ What kinds of difficulties did Joseph Palmer have in the town?

17 위 글의 (A)to have와 쓰임이 같은 것은? (3점)

① My parents told me to be honest.

② They expected me to have the job.

③ What are you trying to achieve in your life?

④ He asked us to fight for the right to be different.

⑤ Nancy wanted her brother to cook ramyeon for her.

18 다음 글은 Joseph Palmer에 관한 이야기를 읽고 쓴 독서 기록 장이다. 빈칸 (A)에 들어갈 가장 알맞은 것은? (4점)

A Story About Joseph Palmer

I read the story about Joseph Palmer last week. I really enjoyed it. I learned from the story that we should not judge people by their appearance. Students who talk about other people's appearance must read the story. However, I have a question about it. Why did Joseph Palmer want to have a beard?

• 주인공: Joseph Palmer

• 교훈: We should not judge people by their appearance.

• 추천 독자층: (A)_____

• 궁금한 점: Why did Joseph Palmer want to have a beard?

① Students who have a beard

② Students who want to be judges

③ Students who talk about others' looks

④ Students who talk about books they read

⑤ Students who want to change their appearance

[19~24] 다음 글을 읽고 물음에 답하시오.

In many ways, 42-year-old Joseph Palmer was an ordinary person. He had a job and cared for his family. But in 1830, Ⓐ_____ he moved to a small town in Massachusetts, he began to face difficulties. Joseph ⓐlooked different from other people: he had a long beard. People did not like it very much.

The town's people avoided the man with a beard. They did not want to sit next to him. They even whispered behind his back, "What is he trying to hide?"

(A) He said to the judge, "I'm the victim here." Ⓑ_____, no one believed a man with a beard, and he ⓑwent to prison for over a year.

(B) One day, four men attacked Joseph and threw him on the ground. "We're going to cut off your beard!" they shouted. Joseph was a big man, and he ⓒwas able to fight them off. But the men called the police and accused him of attacking them. Poor Joseph ⓓarrested.

(C) Some neighbors broke his windows. Others threw stones at him when he walked down the street. [가](그들은 그에게 턱수염을 그만 기르라고 말했다.) Joseph did not mind. He just wanted the freedom ⓔto have his beard.

19 문맥상 (A)~(C)를 가장 바르게 배열한 것은? (3점)

① (C) - (B) - (A)　　② (B) - (A) - (C)

③ (C) - (A) - (B)　　④ (B) - (C) - (A)

⑤ (A) - (C) - (B)

20 위 글의 Ⓐ, Ⓑ에 들어갈 말로 맞게 짝지어진 것은? (4점)

	Ⓐ	Ⓑ
①	after	Sadly
②	before	Happily
③	before	Sadly
④	after	Luckily
⑤	before	Luckily

21 밑줄 친 ⓐ~ⓔ 중 어법상 옳지 않은 것은? (3점)

① ⓐ　② ⓑ　③ ⓒ　④ ⓓ　⑤ ⓔ

22 위 글의 내용과 일치하는 것은? (4점)

① Joseph was very small and weak.

② Nobody believed that Joseph was just a victim.

③ Joseph wanted to have a right to cut his beard.

④ The town's people hated Joseph because he was a big man.

⑤ The town's people kindly advised Joseph to cut off his beard.

23 위 글을 읽고 알 수 없는 것은? (5점)

① Joseph moved to a small town in 1830.

② The men called the police to accuse Joseph.

③ Joseph's beard was cut off by the attackers.

④ Joseph had to be in prison for over a year.

⑤ The town's people thought Joseph was trying to hide something.

24 위 글 [가]의 우리말을 주어진 단어를 모두 이용하여 영어로 쓰시오. (필요시 어형을 바꾸시오.) (4점)

> **보기**
>
> him / tell / stop / to / grow

• They _____ _____ _____ _____ _____ his beard. (그들은 그에게 턱수염을 그만 기르라고 말했다.)

[25~26] 다음 글을 읽고 물음에 답하시오.

Joseph's son, Thomas, wanted people to know the truth. He sent letters to newspapers across the country. People learned that Joseph was in prison just for protecting himself and his beard. Many people became angry about this, so the judge finally decided to set Joseph free.
(A) After he was freed, Joseph traveled and told his story to lots of people. (B) Slowly, people's attitudes toward beards changed. (C) His name was Abraham Lincoln. (D) He made beards popular, but Joseph Palmer fought for the right to have them. (E)

25 위 글의 (A)~(E) 중 다음 문장이 들어갈 가장 알맞은 곳은?
(3점)

> Before Joseph died, a man with a beard became the President of the United States.

① (A)　② (B)　③ (C)　④ (D)　⑤ (E)

26 위 글의 내용과 일치하는 것은?　(3점)

① Joseph은 턱수염을 가질 권리를 위해 싸웠다.
② Joseph은 자신의 억울함을 신문에 호소하였다.
③ Joseph은 아들을 보호하려 했다는 이유로 구속되었다.
④ Joseph은 죽기 전에 미국 대통령 링컨을 만날 수 있었다.
⑤ 링컨은 턱수염을 기를 권리를 위해 Joseph과 함께 싸웠다.

[27~30] 다음 글을 읽고 물음에 답하시오.

In many ways, Joseph Palmer was an ordinary person. (A) He had a job and cared for his family. (B) But in 1830, after he moved to a small town in Massachusetts, he began ⓐto face difficulties. (C) People did not like it very much. (D)

The town's people avoided the man with a beard. They did not ⓑwant to sit next to him. (E) They even whispered behind his back. "What is he ⓒtrying to hide?"
Some neighbors broke his windows. Others threw stones at him when he walked down the street. They told him ⓓstop growing a beard. Joseph did not mind. He just wanted the freedom ⓔto have his beard.

27 위 글의 흐름상 (A)~(E) 중 주어진 문장이 들어가기에 가장 적절한 곳은?　(3점)

> He looked different from other people: he had a long beard.

① (A)　② (B)　③ (C)　④ (D)　⑤ (E)

28 위 글에서 알 수 있는 Joseph의 성품으로 가장 적절한 것은?
(3점)

① He is kind to others.
② He is active and sociable.
③ He is emotionally unstable.
④ He does what he wants to do.
⑤ His belief in volunteer work is very strong.

29 Joseph에 관한 내용과 일치하지 <u>않는</u> 것은?　(4점)

① 가족을 돌보는 평범한 사람이었다.
② 메사추세츠로 이사를 한 후에 어려움에 직면했다.
③ Joseph은 마을 사람들을 무서워하며 피했다.
④ 그가 길을 걸어 내려갈 때 이웃들은 그에게 돌을 던졌다.
⑤ 이웃들이 턱수염을 그만 기르라고 말했지만 Joseph은 신경 쓰지 않았다.

30 밑줄 친 ⓐ~ⓔ 중 어법상 <u>어색한</u> 것은?　(2점)

① ⓐ　② ⓑ　③ ⓒ　④ ⓓ　⑤ ⓔ

◎ 선택형 문항의 답안은 컴퓨터용 수정 싸인펜을 사용하여 OMR 답안지에 바르게 표기하시오.
◎ 서술형 문제는 답을 답인지에 반드시 검정 볼펜으로 쓰시오.
◎ 총 28문항 100점 만점입니다. 문항별 배짐은 각 문항에 표시되어 있습니다.

[서울 강동구 ○○중]

01 다음 문장의 빈칸에 들어갈 수 <u>없는</u> 단어는? (4점)

• Can I _____ this shirt for a blue one?
• I don't know what to wear. Do you have any _____?
• When you buy something, don't forget to get the _____.
• Please call me or _____ me.

① text ② receipt ③ know
④ exchange ⑤ suggestions

[경기 ○○중]

02 다음 대화의 내용과 일치하는 것은? (3점)

(The phone rings.)
Man: Customer Service. How can I help you?
Girl: I bought a hairdryer at your store last week. I'm not happy with it.
Man: What is the problem?
Girl: It doesn't work well. I mean the air isn't hot enough.
Man: I'm sorry. Do you want to exchange it?
Girl: Well, can I get a refund?
Man: Sure. Will you please visit our store with the dryer?
Girl: Yes, I'll drop by tomorrow afternoon.
Man: Don't forget to bring the receipt.
Girl: Okay, Thanks.

① The man called Customer Service.
② The girl wants to complain about a staff of the store.
③ The girl is happy with her hairdryer.
④ The girl wants to exchange her hairdryer.
⑤ The girl will take the hairdryer and the receipt to the store.

[경북 ○○중]

03 다음 빈칸에 들어갈 말로 가장 적절하지 <u>않은</u> 것은? (3점)

A: I'm not happy with this restaurant.
B: What's wrong?
A: _____

① The food is too salty.
② The music is so loud.
③ The service is wonderful.
④ The food came out too late.
⑤ The waiter is not kind to me.

[경북 ○○중]

04 다음을 읽고 대답할 수 있는 질문들을 <u>모두</u> 고른 것은? (4점)

W: Minsu, I'm going out with your dad for a movie.
B: When will you be back, Mom?
W: Around 8 o'clock. Don't forget to feed Buster.
B: Okay.
W: Be sure to give him some water, too.
B: No problem.
W: One more thing. Can you help Minsol with her science homework? Buster tore her homework into pieces.
B: Hmm.... Okay. I'll do that.

ⓐ When will Minsu's mom come back?
ⓑ What did Buster tear?
ⓒ What will Minsu's mom do after the dialog?
ⓓ What can Minsol help Minsu to do?
ⓔ What did Minsu's mom ask Minsu to do?

① ⓐ, ⓓ ② ⓑ, ⓔ ③ ⓐ, ⓑ, ⓒ
④ ⓐ, ⓒ, ⓔ ⑤ ⓐ, ⓑ, ⓒ, ⓔ

[5~6] 다음 대화를 읽고 물음에 답하시오.

(The phone rings.)
Man: Customer Service. How can I help you?
Girl: I bought a hairdryer at your store last week. I'm not happy with it.
Man: What is the problem?
Girl: It doesn't work well. I mean the air isn't hot enough.
Man: I'm sorry. Do you want to exchange it?
Girl: Well, can I get a refund?
Man: Sure. Will you please visit our store with the dryer?
Girl: Yes. I'll drop by tomorrow afternoon.
Man: Don't forget to (A)_____.
Girl: Okay. Thanks.

05 빈칸 (A)에 들어갈 말로 알맞은 것은? (3점)

① get up early
② wear a helmet
③ bring the receipt
④ finish your report
⑤ take water and chocolate

06 위 대화의 내용과 일치하는 것은? (4점)

① The girl called Customer Service.
② The girl wants to fix her hairdryer.
③ The girl is happy with her hairdryer.
④ The girl will visit the store again this afternoon.
⑤ The girl received a hairdryer from her father last week.

07 다음 중 짝지어진 대화가 <u>어색한</u> 것은? (3점)

① A: I'm not happy with the science class.
　 B: Same here. I hope it will get more exciting.
② A: I'm not happy with the coat.
　 B: Why? Is it too small for you?
③ A: I'm not happy with the hair salon.
　 B: What's wrong?
④ A: I'm not happy with this restaurant.
　 B: Me neither. The food is too salty.
⑤ A: I'm not happy with the hospital.
　 B: So true. The doctor is so kind.

08 다음 두 사람의 대화가 자연스럽게 이어지도록 (A)~(D)의 문장을 순서대로 배열한 것은? (4점)

Girl: I'm not happy with Buster.
Man: What's wrong?
Girl: He tore my homework into pieces again.
Man: Puppies often do that.

(A) Please be kind to him. He's just five months old.
(B) This is not the first time. Sometimes I find my socks in the dog house.
(C) Okay. Let's start training in a few weeks.
(D) You're too nice to him! He needs some training.

① (B)-(A)-(D)-(C)　　② (B)-(C)-(A)-(D)
③ (C)-(B)-(A)-(D)　　④ (C)-(B)-(D)-(A)
⑤ (D)-(B)-(A)-(C)

09 다음 문장의 의도로 알맞은 것은? (3점)

• Don't forget to close the window.

① 상기시켜 주기　　② 설명 요청하기
③ 가능성 표현하기　④ 충고하기
⑤ 경고하기

10 다음 대화의 내용과 가장 일치하는 것은? (4점)

> A: Customer Service. How can I help you?
> B: I bought a hairdryer at your store last week. I'm not happy with it.
> A: What is the problem?
> B: It doesn't work well. I mean the air isn't hot enough.
> A: I'm sorry. Do you want to exchange it?
> B: Well, can I get a refund?
> A: Sure. Will you please visit our store with the dryer?
> B: Yes, I'll drop by tomorrow afternoon.
> A: Don't forget to bring the receipt.
> B: Okay. Thanks.

① The customer wants to exchange the goods.

② The customer dropped the dryer at the store.

③ The customer is complaining about the product.

④ The dryer will be repaired in the Customer Service

⑤ The customer couldn't get a refund because he lost his receipt.

11 다음 중 밑줄 친 부분의 쓰임이 나머지와 다른 하나는? (3점)

① They sometimes <u>make</u> him borrow some money.

② I want to <u>make</u> a house for my pet dog.

③ I did not <u>make</u> him buy the cell phone.

④ Did your mom <u>make</u> you do the dishes?

⑤ My dogs always <u>make</u> me feel better.

12 다음 우리말을 괄호 안의 단어를 활용하여 영어로 옮겨 쓰시오. (5점)

(A) 그 문제는 너무 어려워서 풀 수 없다.
(solve, difficult)

→ The problem _____.

(B) 무엇이 네가 그렇게 생각하게 만들었니?
(that, make)

→ What _____?

(C) 어머니는 내가 자전거 사는 것을 허락하셨다. (let, buy)

→ My mother _____.

(D) 선생님은 David에게 그의 휴대 전화를 끄라고 하셨다. (have, turn off)

→ The teacher _____.

(E) 나의 부모님은 내가 매주 토요일에 컴퓨터 게임하는 것을 허락해 주셨다. (let, play)

→ _____ every Saturday.

13 다음 주어진 두 문장을 〈보기〉와 같이 한 문장으로 바꾸시오. (4점)

> I am so sleepy. + I can't finish my homework.
> → <u>I am too sleepy to finish my homework.</u>

(1) Susie is so angry. + She can't say anything.

→ _____

(2) The dog is so weak. + It can't run to the park.

→ _____

[14~16] 다음 글을 읽고 물음에 답하시오.

Hi, I'm a father of two children. One is a high school girl, and (A)_____ is a middle school boy. (B)그들은 나와 말을 하기에는 너무 바쁘다. When I get home from work, they just say hi and go back to their rooms. Sometimes I ask them about their school life, but they only give short answers. We don't talk much at the table, either. I want to say to my kids, "I love you so much, and (C)_____."

14 위 글의 빈칸 (A)에 들어갈 단어로 가장 알맞은 것은? (3점)

① one
② another
③ some
④ others
⑤ the other

15 위 글의 밑줄 친 (B)의 우리말을 주어진 단어를 활용하여 영작할 때 빈칸에 알맞은 단어를 넣어 문장을 완성하시오. (4점)

• 그들은 나와 말을 하기에는 너무 바쁘다. (talk)

→ They are _____ _____ _____ _____ with me.

16 위 글의 빈칸 (C)에 들어갈 말로 가장 알맞은 것은? (3점)

① I want to spend more time with you.
② I want to get more short answers.
③ I want to go back to my hometown.
④ I want to know your grades.
⑤ I want to know only your school life.

[17~18] 다음 글을 읽고 물음에 답하시오.

Hello. I'm a 15-year-old girl from Wonju. I want to tell you about my mom. My mom tries (A)_____ everything for me. She cleans my room without (B)_____ me, so it's sometimes hard (C)_____ my stuff. She also buys books and makes me (D)_____ them. I want to say to my mom, "I know you love me, but I'm not a baby anymore. Please let me (E)_____ care of things myself."

17 위 글의 빈칸 (A)~(E)에 들어갈 말이 <u>모두</u> 옳게 된 것은? (4점)

① (A) doing (B) ask (C) finding
　(D) study (E) takes
② (A) to do (B) asking (C) to find
　(D) study (E) take
③ (A) to do (B) to ask (C) to find
　(D) to study (E) take
④ (A) doing (B) ask (C) find
　(D) to study (E) take
⑤ (A) to do (B) asking (C) find
　(D) study (E) taking

18 What does the girl want her mother to do? (3점)

① The girl isn't happy with her mother who treats her like a baby.
② Her mom wants her daughter to do many things for herself.
③ She wants her mother to let her take care of things herself.
④ Her mom thinks that her daughter is too young to do everything.
⑤ She wants her mother to do all the things for her.

[19~21] 다음 대화를 읽고 물음에 답하시오.

> A: Good evening, listeners. (A) This is your DJ, Breeze. Today we have a special guest, Andy Kim. He's a hip-hop artist. Welcome, Andy. (B)
> B: Nice to meet you and thank you for having me. (C)
> A: Okay. What do our listeners want to tell their family? This evening we will find out by reading some letters from them. (D)
> B: Sure. (E)

19 위 대화에서 다음 문장이 들어갈 위치로 가장 적절한 곳은? (3점)

> Andy, will you start reading the letter from a teenage girl?

① (A)　② (B)　③ (C)　④ (D)　⑤ (E)

20 위 대화의 두 사람이 대화하고 있는 장소로 가장 적절한 것은? (3점)

① theater 　② cafeteria
③ police station 　④ school gym
⑤ radio station

21 위 대화의 내용을 통해 답할 수 <u>없는</u> 질문은? (3점)

① What is Andy's job?
② What is Andy's last name?
③ Who is today's special guest?
④ How many listeners are there?
⑤ Who is the writer of the first letter?

[22~23] 다음 글을 읽고 물음에 답하시오.

> Father: Hi. I'm a father of two children. One is a high school girl, and (A)_____ is a middle school boy. They're too busy to talk with me. When I get home from work, they just say hi and go back to their rooms. Sometimes I ask them about their school life, but they only give short answers. We don't talk much at the table, (B)_____. I want to say to my kids, "I love you so much, and I want to spend more time with you."
> Breeze: Andy, did you talk with your parents often when you were younger?
> Andy: Not really. I loved them very much, but I thought they were too old to understand me.
> Breeze: I see. Does anyone have suggestions for the "sad" dad? Text your idea to us.

22 위 글의 (A), (B)에 들어갈 말을 바르게 짝지은 것은? (4점)

	(A)	(B)
①	others	too
②	others	either
③	the other	either
④	the other	too
⑤	another	too

23 위 글의 내용과 일치하지 <u>않는</u> 것은? (4점)

① 아버지는 중학생과 고등학생 자녀를 두고 있다.
② 아버지는 자녀들과 학교생활에 대한 대화를 길게 한다.
③ 아버지는 아이들과 더 많은 시간을 보내고 싶다.
④ Andy는 어릴 때 그의 부모님과 많은 대화를 나누지 못했다.
⑤ Andy는 부모님이 자신을 이해하기엔 나이가 많다고 생각했다.

[24~25] 다음 글을 읽고 물음에 답하시오.

Hello. I'm a ⓐ5-years-old girl from Wonju. I want to tell you about my mom. My mom tries to do everything for me. She cleans my room ⓑwithout asking me. So ⓒthis is sometimes hard to find my stuff. She also buys books and makes me ⓓto study them. I want to say to my mom, "I know you love me, but I'm not a baby anymore. Please _____."

DJ: I felt the same way when I was in middle school.
Andy: Many moms think their kids are too young to do things ⓔon their own. I hope the girl's mom will get the message.
DJ: ⓕSo am I. Andy, will you please read the next letter?

24 위 글의 밑줄 친 ⓐ~ⓕ 중 어법상 옳은 것만을 고른 것은? (4점)

① ⓐ, ⓓ   ② ⓑ, ⓔ   ③ ⓓ, ⓕ
④ ⓐ, ⓒ, ⓕ   ⑤ ⓑ, ⓒ, ⓔ

25 위 글의 빈칸에 들어갈 말로 가장 적절한 것은? (3점)

① accept my apology
② spend more time with me
③ let me take care of things myself
④ knock before you come into my room
⑤ keep helping me until I can do everything well

26 다음 글의 흐름으로 보아, (A)~(E) 중 다음 문장이 들어가기에 가장 적절한 곳은? (4점)

There was a wall between us.

This is a letter from a father who wants to share his experience with the "sad" father.

My kids and I did not talk much. (A) I wanted to break it down. (B) I tried to spend more time with my children on weekends. (C) We played computer games, rode bikes, and went shopping together. (D) In this way, I had more chances to talk with them. (E) I came to know more about them.

① (A)   ② (B)   ③ (C)   ④ (D)   ⑤ (E)

[27~28] 다음 글을 읽고 물음에 답하시오.

Hi. I'm a father of two children. One is a high school girl, and (A)_____ is a middle school boy. They're (B)_____ busy to talk with me. When I get home from work, they just say hi and go back to their rooms. Sometimes I ask them (C)_____ their school life, but they only give short answers. We don't talk much at the table, (D)_____. I want to say to my kids, "I love you so much, and I want to (가)_____."

27 위 글의 빈칸 (A)~(D)에 차례로 들어갈 말로 알맞은 것은? (4점)

	(A)	(B)	(C)	(D)
①	the other	too	about	either
②	the other	too	with	also
③	the other	much	about	either
④	the others	too	about	also
⑤	the others	too	about	either

28 위 글의 빈칸 (가)에 들어갈 말로 가장 알맞은 것은? (4점)

① keep my room clean
② come home early from work
③ talk more with your friends
④ have some time for myself
⑤ spend more time with you

◎ 선택형 문항의 답안은 컴퓨터용 수정 싸인펜을 사용
하여 OMR 답안지에 바르게 표기하시오.
◎ 서술형 문제는 답을 답안지에 반드시 검정 볼펜으
로 쓰시오.
◎ 총 29분항 100점 만점입니다. 문항별 배점은 각
문항에 표시되어 있습니다.

[경기 ○○중]

01 다음 중 단어의 영영 뜻풀이가 바르게 된 것은? (3점)

① listen: to recall or bring back to mind
② throw: to damage something such as paper by pulling it hard
③ guest: someone who is invited to an event or special occasion
④ forget: something that is kept hidden or that only a few people know
⑤ refund: a piece of paper that proves that you have received goods or money

[인천 ○○중]

02 다음 대화의 내용과 일치하는 것은? (3점)

Tom: Customer Service. How can I help you?
Mina: I bought a hairdryer at your store last week. I am not happy with it.
Tom: What is the problem?
Mina: It doesn't work well. I mean the air isn't hot enough.
Tom: I'm sorry. Do you want to exchange it?
Mina: Well, can I get a refund?
Tom: Sure. Will you please visit our store with the dryer?
Mina: Yes, I'll visit your store tomorrow afternoon.
Tom: Don't forget to bring the receipt.
Mina: Okay. Thanks.

① Mina is a hairdresser.
② Mina is happy with her hairdryer.
③ The hairdryer works very well.
④ Mina will exchange her hairdryer for a new one.
⑤ Mina will visit the store again.

[부산 ○○중]

03 다음 대화를 읽고 답할 수 없는 것은? (3점)

Minsol: I'm not happy with Buster.
Dad: What's wrong?
Minsol: He tore my homework into pieces again.
Dad: Puppies often do that.
Minsol: This is not the first time. Sometimes I find my socks in the dog house.
Dad: Please be kind to him. He's just five months old.
Minsol: You're too nice to him! He needs some training.
Dad: Okay. Let's start training in a few weeks.

① What is Buster?
② How tall is Buster?
③ Why is Minsol angry?
④ What does Minsol suggest?
⑤ What does Minsol think of her dad?

[인천 ○○중]

04 다음 대화가 자연스럽게 이어지도록 (A)~(E)를 순서대로 가장 바르게 배열한 것은? (4점)

A: Are you ready for your trip, Suji?

(A) Yeah, I have it on my phone.
(B) Yes, Dad. I'm ready to leave.
(C) Good. Don't forget to call me when you get to the station.
(D) Do you have your ticket with you?
(E) Sure.

① (B)-(D)-(A)-(C)-(E) ② (B)-(E)-(A)-(C)-(D)
③ (C)-(E)-(D)-(B)-(A) ④ (E)-(A)-(D)-(B)-(C)
⑤ (E)-(A)-(C)-(D)-(B)

05 다음 중 짝지어진 대화가 바른 것은? (2점)

① A: What's wrong?

B: My cat tore my homework into pieces again.

② A: When will you be back, Mom?

B: My mom always works every Saturday.

③ A: Don't forget to bring a lot of water.

B: Yes. I am happy with the big water park.

④ A: You're too nice to him! He needs some training.

B: Okay. Let's go to his house by train.

⑤ A: I have a complaint. I find my socks in the dog house.

B: Dogs often do that. So dogs are better than cats.

06 다음 대화의 내용과 일치하지 <u>않는</u> 것은? (3점)

Jane: I'm not happy with Buster.

Mom: What's wrong?

Jane: He tore my homework into pieces again.

Mom: Puppies often do that.

Jane: This is not the first time. Sometimes I find my socks in the dog house.

Mom: Please be kind to him. He's just five months old.

Jane: You're too nice to him! He needs some training.

Mom: Okay. Let's start training in a few weeks.

① Buster is her puppy.

② Buster is a male.

③ Buster is a five-month-old puppy.

④ Buster is kind.

⑤ Buster took Jane's socks into his house.

07 다음 빈칸에 들어갈 말로 가장 적절한 것은? (4점)

A: I'm not happy with school uniforms.

B: What's the problem?

A: _____

B: You are right. Also they are not comfortable.

A: You can say that again.

① They come into my room too often.

② They take away freedom of expression.

③ They help students focus on their studies.

④ They allow parents to save time and money on buying clothes.

⑤ They help students spend less time and energy choosing what to wear daily.

08 다음 대화가 자연스러운 대화가 되도록 ⓐ~ⓓ를 바르게 배열할 때 알맞은 것은? (4점)

A: What is the problem?

B: I bought a hairdryer at your store last week. I'm not happy with it. It doesn't work well. I mean the air isn't hot enough.

ⓐ Sure. I'll drop by tomorrow afternoon.

ⓑ I'm sorry. Do you want to exchange it?

ⓒ I see. Will you please visit our store with the dryer? And don't forget to bring the receipt.

ⓓ Well, can I get a refund?

① ⓑ-ⓐ-ⓒ-ⓓ   ② ⓑ-ⓓ-ⓒ-ⓐ

③ ⓒ-ⓐ-ⓓ-ⓑ   ④ ⓒ-ⓓ-ⓑ-ⓐ

⑤ ⓓ-ⓐ-ⓒ-ⓑ

[9~10] 다음 대화를 읽고 물음에 답하시오.

(*The phone rings.*)
A: Customer Service. How can I help you?
B: I bought a hairdryer at your store last week. (A) 나는 그것이 마음에 들지 않습니다.
A: What is the problem?
B: It doesn't work well. I mean the air isn't hot enough.
A: I'm sorry. Do you want to exchange it?
B: Well, can I get a refund?
A: Sure. Will you please visit our store with the dryer and the receipt?
B: Yes, I'll drop by tomorrow afternoon.

09 위 대화의 내용과 일치하는 것은? (3점)

① A는 헤어드라이어를 고칠 것이냐고 물었다.
② B는 내일 헤어드라이어를 가게로 보낼 것이다.
③ B는 헤어드라이어를 교환하는 것을 원한다.
④ B는 내일 영수증을 가져갈 것이다.
⑤ 헤어드라이어의 공기가 너무 뜨거운 것이 문제이다.

10 위 대화의 밑줄 친 (A)의 우리말을 주어진 단어를 활용하여 다음 〈조건〉에 맞게 영작하시오. (4점)

happy

조건
1. 다섯 단어 또는 여섯 단어의 문장으로 쓸 것.
2. 문장 전체를 쓸 것.
3. 대 · 소문자 구분 있음.

→ _____

11 다음 해석과 의미가 통하는 문장을 주어진 단어들을 재배열하여 작성하시오. (4점)

• 나의 오빠는 나에게 설거지를 하게 하였다.
(made / the dishes / my brother / me / do)

조건
• 주어진 단어를 변형, 추가, 축약, 삭제하지 마시오.

→ _____

12 다음 글에서 (A)~(C)에 들어갈 가장 알맞은 표현은? (대 · 소문자 무시) (4점)

(A)	• _____ the truth. • Don't _____ a lie to your friend.
(B)	• _____ no when you don't like it. • _____ hi when you meet your friend in the morning.
(C)	• She can _____ four languages. • Can you _____ French?

	(A)	(B)	(C)
①	say	tell	speak
②	tell	say	speak
③	tell	speak	say
④	speak	say	tell
⑤	speak	tell	say

13 다음 주어진 우리말과 같은 뜻이 되도록 조건에 맞게 문장을 완성하시오. (5점)

• _____
(누가 너에게 그 과제를 혼자 하게 시켰니?)

조건
• 과거시제를 사용할 것.
• the project, make, by oneself를 사용할 것.
(필요시 형태 변형 가능)

→ _____

[14~17] 다음 글을 읽고 물음에 답하시오.

(A) Hi, I'm a father of two children. One is a high school girl, and the other is a middle school boy. ⓐThey're too busy, so we don't talk much. ⓑ When I get home from work, they just say hi and go back to their rooms. ⓒSometimes I ask them about their school life, but they only give short answers. ⓓWe have enough conversations at the table. ⓔI want to say to my kids, "I love you so much, and I want to spend more time with you."

(B) My kids and I did not talk much. There was a wall between us. I wanted to break it down, so I did the following activities on weekends. We played computer games, rode bikes, and went shopping together. In this way, I had more chances to talk with them. I came to know more about them.

14 위 글의 ⓐ~ⓔ 중 전체 흐름과 관계없는 문장은? (3점)

① ⓐ　　② ⓑ　　③ ⓒ　　④ ⓓ　　⑤ ⓔ

15 위 글의 (A) 문단을 한 문장으로 요약하고자 한다. 빈칸에 들어갈 말로 가장 적절한 영어 표현을 본문에서 찾아 쓰시오.(빈칸 하나에 한 단어씩 쓰시오.) (4점)

A father wants to _____ _____ _____ with his children, but they are too busy.

→ _____ _____ _____

16 위 글의 (B)를 읽고 다음 질문에 대한 응답을 우리말로 쓰시오. (4점)

Question: What did the father do on weekends to break down the wall with his children?

→ _____, _____, _____

17 위 글의 (A)와 (B) 문단의 관계로 알맞게 짝지어진 것은? (3점)

① 칭찬—감사　② 고민—조언　③ 충고—감사
④ 제안—수락　⑤ 요청—거절

[18~19] 다음 대화를 읽고 물음에 답하시오.

A: Good evening, listeners. This is your DJ, Breeze. Today we ⓐhave a special guest, Andy Kim. He's a hip-hop artist. Welcome, Andy.
B: Nice to meet you and thank you for ⓑhaving me.
A: Okay. What do our listeners want ⓒto tell their family? This evening we will find out by ⓓ read some letters from them. Andy, will you ⓔ start off with the letter from a teenage girl?

18 위 대화의 밑줄 친 ⓐ~ⓔ 중 어법상 어색한 것은? (3점)

① ⓐ　　② ⓑ　　③ ⓒ　　④ ⓓ　　⑤ ⓔ

19 위 대화의 두 사람(A와 B)의 관계로 가장 알맞은 것은? (3점)

① 라디오 PD와 청취자
② 라디오 PD와 초대 손님
③ 라디오 진행자와 청취자
④ 라디오 PD와 라디오 진행자
⑤ 라디오 진행자와 초대 손님

[20~22] 다음 글을 읽고 물음에 답하시오.

Hello. I'm a 15-year-old girl from Wonju. I want to tell you about my mom. My mom tries to do everything for me. ⓐShe cleans my room without ask me, so it's sometimes hard to find my stuff. ⓑShe also buys books and makes me studying them. I want to talk to my mom, "I know you love me, but I'm not a baby anymore. Please let me take care of things myself."

DJ Breeze: ⓒI felt the same way when I was in middle school.
Andy Kim: ⓓMany moms think their kids are too young to do things of her own. I hope the girl's mom will get the message.
DJ Breeze: ⓔSo will I.

20 위 글의 밑줄 친 ⓐ~ⓔ 중 어법상 올바른 문장은? (3점)

① ⓐ   ② ⓑ   ③ ⓒ   ④ ⓓ   ⑤ ⓔ

21 위 사연의 주인공의 심경으로 가장 알맞은 것은? (4점)

① scared   ② relaxed   ③ confident
④ unpleased   ⑤ threatened

22 위 글의 내용으로 알 수 없는 것은? (4점)

① What problem does the girl have?
② Whose letter will Andy Kim read next?
③ How did the DJ feel about her mother?
④ What does Andy Kim say about mothers?
⑤ What does the girl want her mother to do?

23 다음 글의 빈칸 (A), (B)에 들어갈 말로 알맞은 것은? (3점)

Hello. I am a middle school girl from Osan. I want to tell my brother Jaeho, "Sorry." I told Mom his secret last Friday. Mom got very (A)_____, so he was in trouble. I was too (B)_____ to say sorry to him at that time. I promise I will never tell his secrets again.

　　(A)　　　　(B)
① angry　　　sad
② upset　　　scared
③ pleased　　surprised
④ shocked　　bored
⑤ satisfied　　interested

24 다음 글을 쓴 사람이 이야기하려는 내용은? (4점)

My kids and I did not talk much. There was a wall between us. I wanted to break it down. I tried to spend more time with my children on weekends. We played computer games, rode bikes, and went shopping together. In this way, I had more chances to talk with them. I came to know more about them.

① If you get along with your children, you should not do your best.
② If you want to get closer to your kids, try to spend more time with them.
③ If your children want to play with you, you can buy them good presents.
④ If you want to be a good father, you don't have to talk a lot with your children.
⑤ Being a good father is not easy, so you have to understand why your kids are busy.

[25~26] 다음 글을 읽고 물음에 답하시오. [부산 ○○중]

Hi. I'm a father of two children, One is a high school girl, and ⓐ<u>another</u> is a middle school boy. They're too busy ⓑ<u>talk</u> with me. When I get home from work, they just say hi and ⓒ<u>goes</u> back to their rooms. Sometimes I ask them about their school life, but _____.
We don't talk much at the table, ⓓ<u>too</u>. I want to say to my kids, "I love you so ⓔ<u>many</u> and I want to spend more time with you."

25 위 글의 밑줄 친 ⓐ~ⓔ를 어법상 바르게 고친 것을 <u>두 개</u> 고르면? (3점)

① ⓐ another → others
② ⓑ talk → talking
③ ⓒ goes → went
④ ⓓ too → either
⑤ ⓔ many → much

26 위 글의 빈칸에 들어갈 말로 가장 알맞은 것은? (4점)

① they only give short answers
② they ask me lots of problems
③ they talk about their school life
④ they want to know about my wish
⑤ they always ask for my suggestion

27 다음 글을 읽고 빈칸에 들어갈 단어의 연결이 어색한 것은? [부산 ○○중]
(3점)

 You're not a baby anymore.
It's ①_____ to fly.

I don't know ②_____ to fly.
Do you have some ③_____?
No. Just do it ④_____ asking me.
Now I can fly ⑤_____.

① time   ② where   ③ suggestions
④ without   ⑤ on my own

[28~29] 다음 글을 읽고 물음에 답하시오. [경북 ○○중]

Will you start off with the letter from a teenage girl?

Hello. I'm a 15-year-old girl from Wonju. I want to tell you about my mom. My mom tries to do everything for me. She cleans my room without asking me, so it's sometimes hard to find my stuff. She also buys books and makes me (A)<u>studying</u> them. I want to say to my mom, "I know you love me, but I'm not a baby anymore. Please let me (B)<u>to take care of</u> things myself."

28 위 글의 밑줄 친 (A)와 (B)의 형태로 바르게 연결한 것은? (4점)

	(A)	(B)
①	study	to taking care of
②	study	take care of
③	to study	taking care of
④	to study	take care of
⑤	to study	to taking care of

29 위 글을 읽고 알 수 <u>없는</u> 것은? (2점)

① 소녀의 나이   ② 소녀의 불만
③ 소녀가 사는 곳   ④ 소녀의 학교생활
⑤ 소녀가 편지에서 언급한 사람

2학년 영어 2학기 기말고사(7과) 1회

문항수 : 선택형(28문항) 서술형(1문항)   20 . . .

◎ 선택형 문항의 답안은 컴퓨터용 수정 싸인펜을 사용
하여 OMR 답안지에 바르게 표기하시오.
◎ 서술형 문제는 답을 답안지에 반드시 검정 볼펜으
로 쓰시오.
◎ 총 29문항 100점 만점입니다. 문항별 배점은 각
문항에 표시되어 있습니다.

01 다음은 음식의 소리법이다. 빈칸에 들어갈 단어가 아닌 것은?
(3점)

<kimchi pancake>
1. _____ the flour with kimchi and water.
2. Heat some oil in the pan.
3. _____ the mixture into the pan and spread it evenly.
4. Cook it for about three minutes and turn it over.
5. Cook the other side for another three minutes.

<pizza toast>
1. Spread pizza sauce on the bread.
2. Put sausages, peppers, and tomatoes on the bread.
3. _____ cheese on top.
4. _____ it in the oven for about five minutes.

① fry   ② bake   ③ add
④ mix   ⑤ pour

02 다음 단어 중에서 –ment를 붙여 명사로 만들 수 있는 단어는 몇 개인가?
(3점)

move / educate / agree / develop / pollute / suggest / translate / amuse / treat / manage

① 4개   ② 5개   ③ 6개   ④ 7개   ⑤ 8개

03 다음 대화의 내용과 일치하지 않는 것은?
(4점)

Suji: Good morning, Chef Tom!
Tom: Hello, Suji. Have you ever made nacho pizza?
Suji: Nacho pizza? No, I haven't made it.
Tom: Kids will love it, and I'll tell you how to make it.
Suji: Sounds good!
Tom: It's easy to make. First, put nacho chips on a plate and spread pizza sauce on them.
Suji: Okay. Let me help you with the pizza sauce.
Tom: Thanks. Next, put some ham, onions, and peppers on top.
Suji: Okay. Then?
Tom: Add cheese and bake for about 12 minutes in the oven.
Suji: I can't wait to taste it!

① Suji has never made nacho pizza before.
② Tom thinks kids will like nacho pizza.
③ Tom teaches Suji how to make nacho pizza.
④ Suji spreads pizza sauce on nacho chips.
⑤ Tom adds cheese after baking nacho pizza in the oven.

04 다음 대화 중 자연스럽지 않은 것은?
(3점)

① A: What do you think about the news?
   B: I heard the shocking news from my friend.
② A: What are you looking at?
   B: I am looking at the fallen leaves.
③ A: How was Tom's birthday party?
   B: It was really exciting.
④ A: What did you eat for lunch?
   B: I ate baked potatoes for lunch.
⑤ A: Do you know the boy dancing on the stage?
   B: Yes. He is my little brother.

05 (A)~(D)에 들어갈 단어가 순서대로 바르게 배열된 것은? (4점)

> W: Good morning, Chef Garcia!
> M: Hello, Suji. Today I'll tell you how to make nacho pizza.
> W: Sounds good!
> M: It's easy to make. First, __(A)__ nacho chips on a plate and __(B)__ pizza sauce on them.
> W: Okay. Let me help you with the pizza sauce.
> M: Thanks. Next, put some ham, onions, and peppers on top.
> W: Okay. Then?
> M: __(C)__ cheese and __(D)__ for about 12 minutes in the oven.
> W: I can't wait to taste it!

	(A)	(B)	(C)	(D)
①	add	boil	Put	fry
②	put	spread	Add	bake
③	fry	pour	Add	bake
④	add	pour	Bake	fry
⑤	put	spread	Cut	boil

[6~7] 다음 대화를 읽고 물음에 답하시오.

> A: Oh, look at the long line at the box office.
> B: Yeah, there's a ticket machine over there. Let's buy the tickets from the machine.
> A: All right. _____
> B: Sure. It's easy. First, select a movie and a showtime.
> A: Okay. We can watch the seven o'clock show. Then what?
> B: Well, select the number of tickets and choose our seats.
> A: Okay. Two tickets, and I want to sit in the back.
> B: No problem. Lastly, pay for the tickets.
> A: It's very simple.

06 위 대화의 빈칸에 들어갈 말로 가장 적절한 것은? (3점)

① Do you often watch movies?
② Do you like watching movies?
③ Why don't we watch a movie tonight?
④ Do you know how to use the machine?
⑤ Can I tell you how to use the machine?

07 위 대화의 내용과 가장 일치하는 내용은? (3점)

① 매표소에는 사람들이 짧게 줄을 서 있다.
② A와 B는 둘은 8시 영화를 볼 것이다.
③ A는 표 판매기를 이용하자고 제안한다.
④ A와 B는 뒷자리에 앉아서 영화를 볼 것이다.
⑤ A는 표 판매기를 이용하는 법을 잘 안다.

08 다음 밑줄 친 부분이 바른 것들로 묶인 것은? (3점)

> W: Kevin, ⓐyou look like down.
> B: ⓑNothing serious. Sometimes my feelings change a lot.
> W: I understand. Many teens have ups and downs in their feelings.
> B: Oh, really?
> W: Have you watched the animated movie "Shining Days?"
> B: ⓒNo, I have. Why do you ask?
> W: It is about a teenager's feelings. ⓓIt will help you to understand your feelings better.
> B: ⓔThat sound good! I'll watch it.

① ⓐ, ⓓ 　　　　② ⓑ, ⓓ
③ ⓐ, ⓑ, ⓒ 　　④ ⓐ, ⓑ, ⓓ
⑤ ⓑ, ⓓ, ⓔ

09 다음 (A)~(D)를 자연스러운 대화가 되도록 순서대로 바르게 배열한 것은? (3점)

> M: I'll tell you how to make nacho pizza.
> W: Sounds good!
>
> (A) Next, put some ham, onions, and peppers on top.
> (B) First, put nacho chips on a plate and spread pizza sauce on them.
> (C) Okay. Then?
> (D) Lastly, add cheese and bake for about 12 minutes in the oven.
>
> W: I can't wait to taste it!

① (B)-(A)-(C)-(D)
② (B)-(C)-(D)-(A)
③ (C)-(A)-(B)-(D)
④ (C)-(B)-(A)-(D)
⑤ (D)-(B)-(C)-(A)

10 다음 짝지어진 대화 중 어색한 것은? (3점)

① A: Do you know who wrote the book?
  B: Yes, I do. It was written by a famous cook, Mr. Cook.
② A: Did you hear that Jason won first prize?
  B: Really? That's surprising!
③ A: Do you know Sumin won first prize at the speech contest?
  B: I can't believe it.
④ A: I'm going to throw a surprise party for him.
  B: Why don't we have a party?
⑤ A: Do you know where Fred put the bread?
  B: Yes. I do. He put it under his bed.

11 다음 중 밑줄 친 부분이 어법상 자연스러운 문장은? (4점)

① It has been really hot yesterday.
② He has made pizza for lunch last Sunday.
③ Our family members live in Pohang since 2007.
④ I have been to Korea to learn taekwondo three years ago.
⑤ She has been interested in Korean culture for a long time.

12 다음 밑줄 친 단어의 쓰임이 다른 것은? (3점)

① The running boy is my classmate.
② The dog is running after a crying baby.
③ He worked all day under the burning sun.
④ There were some exciting rides near the beach.
⑤ Swimming alone in the river is very dangerous.

13 조건에 맞게 다음 우리말과 같도록 문장을 완성하시오. (5점)

> 조건
> • '현재완료(have[has]+과거분사)'를 사용할 것.

(1) A: When did you start living in Seoul?
  B: I _____ _____ _____ _____ _____ _____. (나는 1995년부터 서울에서 살고 있어.)
(2) A: Jihun looks so stressed. Does he have a problem?
  B: Jihun _____ _____ _____ _____ _____ _____. (지훈이는 아직 숙제를 끝내지 못했어.)

[14~16] 다음 글을 읽고 물음에 답하시오.

When several cartoon pictures come together and tell a story, we have a comic strip. Comic strips (A)have been in newspapers for many years. They are often just amusing stories. People have also used comic strips for education. Comics can make information clearer and easier to learn. You have probably seen comic history or science books. You have surely seen many cartoon movies, or animated movies, too. These are very popular among people of all ages. Movement and sounds are added to pictures, so they come alive. Artists and writers can develop fascinating characters and tell interesting stories through animation. ⓐIn the 1990s, a new type of cartoon were developed. We call it a webtoon. ⓑWebtoons are publishing online, so you can read them anytime, anywhere on your phone or computer. They are very popular, and ⓒsome of them are even made TV dramas or movies. New forms of cartoons may appear in the future. ⓓThey could be different and even most exciting than now, but ⓔone thing will remain the same: they will help us to laugh, relax, and learn.

14 위 글의 밑줄 친 (A)have been과 쓰임이 같은 것은? (3점)

① I have just sent the email to him.
② I have ever been to New Zealand.
③ I have taught English since last year.
④ I have not finished my homework yet.
⑤ I have made great works of art several times.

15 위 글의 밑줄 친 ⓐ~ⓔ 중 어법상 옳은 것은? (3점)

① ⓐ   ② ⓑ   ③ ⓒ   ④ ⓓ   ⑤ ⓔ

16 위 글에 대한 설명으로 가장 적절한 것은? (4점)

① Webtoons were developed in 1990.
② The main purpose of comics is education.
③ Comic strips are several cartoon pictures with a story.
④ Some of webtoons are more popular than TV dramas or movies.
⑤ Animated movies are made by adding pictures to movement and sounds.

[17~18] 다음을 읽고 물음에 답하시오.

One form of cartoon is a picture with a few words. It is sometimes called a "gag cartoon." The cartoonist makes a funny character, and the character makes you laugh ⓐ_____ doing or saying silly things. Another type of cartoon is called a caricature. In a caricature, some parts of a character are different or bigger than usual. Look at the picture on the right. Which parts of the man's face ⓑ_____ out at you? Artists have used this type of cartoon to ⓒ_____ fun of famous people.

17 위 글을 크게 두 단락으로 나눌 때, 두 번째 단락의 첫 단어는 무엇인가? (3점)

① It   ② Another   ③ Look
④ Which   ⑤ Artists

18 위 글의 ⓐ, ⓑ, ⓒ에 들어갈 말로 바르게 짝지어진 것은? (4점)

① ⓐ by   ⓑ jump   ⓒ make
② ⓐ at   ⓑ run   ⓒ take
③ ⓐ by   ⓑ think   ⓒ take
④ ⓐ at   ⓑ jump   ⓒ get
⑤ ⓐ to   ⓑ run   ⓒ get

[19~21] 다음 글을 읽고 물음에 답하시오.

People have ⓐ<u>made</u> cartoons for hundreds of years. There are many types of cartoons, and they play different roles. One form of cartoon is a picture with a few words. It is sometimes called a "gag cartoon." The cartoonist ⓑ<u>makes</u> a funny character, and the character ⓒ<u>makes</u> you laugh by doing or saying silly things.

Another type of cartoon is called a caricature. In a caricature, some parts of a character are different or bigger than usual. Look at the picture on the right. Which parts of the man's face jump out at you? Artists have used this type of cartoon to ⓓ<u>make</u> fun of well-known people.

19 위 글의 ⓐ~ⓓ 중 다음 문장의 밑줄 친 단어와 쓰임이 같은 것은? (3점)

- I <u>made</u> my brother do his homework.

① ⓐ   ② ⓑ   ③ ⓒ   ④ ⓓ   ⑤ 없음

20 위 글에서 Caricature의 목적으로 언급된 것은? (4점)

① 풍자   ② 교육   ③ 보고   ④ 반성   ⑤ 기록

21 위 글의 내용과 일치하는 것은? (4점)

① There is only one type of cartoon.

② In a caricature, characters are usually jumping.

③ The point of a gag cartoon is to make you laugh.

④ In a gag cartoon, characters do or say serious things.

⑤ In a caricature, the cartoonist should draw a person exactly the same.

[22~23] 다음 글을 읽고 물음에 답하시오.

Giyeong, My Favorite Cartoon Character

My favorite cartoon character is *Giyeong of Black Rubber Shoes*. He is an elementary school student. He is humorous and kind. _____, he is not very smart and sometimes causes trouble. I like him _____ he <u>looks on the bright side</u> of everything and always tries to help others.

22 위 글의 빈칸에 들어갈 단어가 순서대로 연결된 것은? (4점)

① However – because   ② But – so

③ For example – if   ④ Finally – for

⑤ In the end – that

23 위 글의 밑줄 친 부분의 의미로 가장 적절한 것은? (3점)

① 장난치는 것을 좋아한다

② 생각이 깊다

③ 시력이 좋다

④ 긍정적이다

⑤ 똑똑하다

24 다음 글에서 밑줄 친 ⓐ~ⓔ 중 어법상 <u>어색한</u> 것은? (3점)

You have surely ⓐ<u>seen</u> many cartoon movies, or animated movies, too. These are very popular among people of all ages. Movement and sounds ⓑ<u>added</u> to pictures, so they come ⓒ<u>alive</u>. Artists and writers can develop ⓓ<u>fascinating</u> characters and tell ⓔ<u>interesting</u> stories through animation.

① ⓐ   ② ⓑ   ③ ⓒ   ④ ⓓ   ⑤ ⓔ

[25~28] 다음 글을 읽고 물음에 답하시오.

People ⓐhave made cartoons for hundreds of years. There are many types of cartoons, and they play different roles. One form of cartoon is a picture with ⓐa few words. People sometimes call it a "gag cartoon."

When several cartoon pictures come together and tell a story, we have a comic strip. Comic strips ⓒ have been in newspapers for many years. They are often just (가)amusing stories. People ⓒhave also used comic strips for education. Comics can make information clearer and easier ⓑto learn. You ⓔ have seen comic history or science books before.

You ⓜhave seen many cartoon movies, or ⓒ animated movies, too. These are very popular among people of all ages. Movement and sounds ⓓare added to pictures, so they come alive. Artists and writers can develop fascinating characters and ⓔtelling stories through animation.

In the 1990s, a new type of cartoon was developed. It is called a webtoon. Webtoons are published online, so you can read them anytime, anywhere on your phone or computer. They are very popular, and some of them are even made into TV dramas or movies.

25 위 글의 ㉠~㉤ 중 현재완료의 용법이 같은 것끼리 묶인 것은? (4점)

① ㉠, ㉡, ㉢   ② ㉠, ㉢, ㉣
③ ㉡, ㉢, ㉣   ④ ㉡, ㉣, ㉤
⑤ ㉢, ㉣, ㉤

26 위 글의 ⓐ~ⓔ 중 어법상 어색한 것은? (3점)

① ⓐ   ② ⓑ   ③ ⓒ   ④ ⓓ   ⑤ ⓔ

27 위 글의 (가)amusing과 용법이 다른 것은? (4점)

① The boring movie made everyone sleepy.
② She told me in a shaking voice, "Get out."
③ Who is that dancing man? - He is my uncle.
④ I heard the shocking news from him yesterday.
⑤ Their favorite activity is riding bikes with his father.

28 위 글의 내용과 같은 것은? (4점)

① Cartoon movies are made into movies.
② People can read webtoons on the phones.
③ Gag cartoons are loved by all age groups.
④ Comic strips began to appear in the 1990s.
⑤ Gag cartoons tell a story through a series of pictures.

29 다음 글이 설명하는 캐리커처의 특징으로 알맞은 것은? (3점)

Another type of cartoon is called a caricature. In a caricature, some parts of a character are different or bigger than usual. Look at the picture on the right. Which parts of the man's face jump out at you? Artists have used this type of cartoon to make fun of well-known people.

① 인물의 일부분이 평소보다 작다.
② 인물의 얼굴은 평소와 다르게 그리지 않는다.
③ 캐리커처는 사진을 그대로 그리는 방식이다.
④ 인물의 오른쪽이 캐리커처의 대상이 된다.
⑤ 만화작가들이 유명한 사람을 놀릴 때 사용한다.

2학년 영어 2학기 기말고사(7과) 2회

문항수 : 선택형(24문항) 서술형(1문항)   20 .   .   .

◎ 선택형 문항의 답안은 컴퓨터용 수정 싸인펜을 사용하여 OMR 답안지에 바르게 표기하시오.
◎ 서술형 문제는 답을 답안지에 반드시 검정 볼펜으로 쓰시오.
◎ 총 25문항 100점 만점입니다. 문항별 배점은 각 문항에 표시되어 있습니다.

[부산 ○○중]

01 다음 중 밑줄 친 단어의 쓰임이 적절하지 않은 것은? (3점)

① Water boils at 100℃.

② P.E. stands for physical education.

③ Next, spend some butter on a piece of bread.

④ He did not understand the question and made a silly mistake.

⑤ Walt Disney was a famous cartoonist who created "Mickey Mouse."

[서울 관악구 ○○중]

02 다음 중 영영풀이가 틀린 것은? (4점)

① fascinating: very interesting and attractive

② remain: to stay in the different place or condition

③ select: to choose by making careful decisions

④ patience: the ability to stay calm in a difficult situation

⑤ successful: achieving results wanted or hoped for

[경북 ○○중]

03 다음 대화를 잘못 이해한 학생은? (4점)

W: Good morning, Chef Garcia!
M: Hello, Suji. Have you ever made nacho pizza?
W: Nacho pizza? No, I haven't made it.
M: Kids will love it, and I'll tell you how to make it.
W: Sounds good!
M: It's easy to make. First, put nacho chips on a plate and spread pizza sauce on them.
W: Okay. Let me help you with the pizza sauce.
M: Thanks. Next, put some ham, onions, and peppers on top.
W: Okay. Then?
M: Add cheese and bake for about 12 minutes in the oven.
W: I can't wait to taste it!

① Tom: Chef Garcia는 나초 피자를 만드는 방법을 알려 주고 있어.

② Sue: 나초 피자를 만들 때 치즈를 올리고 나서 피자 소스를 발라야 해.

③ Judy: 나초 피자를 만들기 위한 재료로 나초 칩, 햄, 양파, 피망, 치즈, 피자 소스가 필요해.

④ Tomas: 나초 피자는 약 12분 동안 오븐에서 구워야 해.

⑤ Ann: Suji는 나초 피자를 빨리 맛보고 싶어 해.

[경기 ○○중]

04 다음 중 두 사람의 대화가 어색한 것은? (3점)

① A: Have you ever touched a snake?
   B: No, I haven't.

② A: You know what? Dogs can smile.
   B: Really? That's surprising.

③ A: Do you know how to make fried rice?
   B: Sure, it's easy. I'll let you know.

④ A: Do you know what the capital of Peru is?
   B: I have no idea. What is it?

⑤ A: A camel can go without water for a long time.
   B: Why don't you drink some water?

[5~6] 다음 대화를 읽고 물음에 답하시오.

Girl: Good morning, Chef Garcia!
Man: Hello, Suji. Have you ever made nacho pizza?
Girl: Nacho pizza? No, I haven't.
Man: Kids will love it, and I'll tell you how to make it.
Girl: Sounds good!
Man: It's easy to make. First, put nacho chips on a plate and spread pizza sauce on them.
Girl: Okay. Let me help you with the pizza sauce.
Man: Thanks. Next, put some ham, onions, and peppers on top.
Girl: Okay. Then?
Man: Add cheese and bake for about 12 minutes in the oven.
Girl: I can't wait to taste it!

05 위 대화가 이루어지고 있는 곳으로 가장 적절한 것은? (3점)

① a box office
② a post office
③ a school gym
④ a cooking class
⑤ a train station

06 위 대화의 내용과 일치하는 것은? (4점)

① The girl has made nacho pizza before.
② The onions should be put after the cheese.
③ The cheese should be added at the beginning.
④ The pizza sauce goes on top of the nacho chips.
⑤ The pizza needs to be baked for at least half an hour.

[7~8] 다음 대화를 읽고 물음에 답하시오.

W: Oh, look at the long line at the box office.
B: Yeah, there's a ticket machine over there. Let's buy the tickets from the machine.
_____
B: No problem. Lastly, pay for the tickets.
W: It's very simple.

07 위 대화의 빈칸에 들어갈 대화의 순서로 가장 자연스러운 것은? (4점)

(A) Sure. It's easy. First, select a movie and a showtime.
(B) Okay. We can watch the seven o'clock show. Then what?
(C) All right. Do you know how to use the machine?
(D) Well, select the number of tickets and choose our seats.
(E) Okay. Two tickets, and I want to sit in the back.

① (A) - (B) - (C) - (D) - (E)
② (B) - (D) - (E) - (A) - (C)
③ (C) - (A) - (B) - (D) - (E)
④ (C) - (A) - (D) - (B) - (E)
⑤ (D) - (B) - (C) - (A) - (E)

08 위 대화의 주제로 가장 적절한 것은? (4점)

① how to use the movie ticket machine
② where to get information of new movies
③ how to buy movie tickets using Internet
④ how to handle many buyers at the ticket box
⑤ how to reserve the movie ticket using the phone

09 A의 마지막 말에 대한 B의 응답으로 가장 적절한 것은? (4점)

> A: Kevin, you look down.
> B: Nothing serious. Sometimes my feelings change a lot.
> A: I understand. Many teens have ups and downs in their feelings.
> B: Oh, really?
> A: Have you watched the animated movie "Shining Days"?
> B: No, I haven't. Why do you ask?
> A: It is about a teenager's feelings. It will help you understand your feelings better.
> B: _____

① That sounds good! I'll watch it.
② It was really good this morning.
③ I feel bad at the cafeteria today.
④ It isn't as interesting as yours.
⑤ I'm looking forward to seeing you.

10 대화의 밑줄 친 ⓐ~ⓔ 중 어법상 알맞은 것은? (3점)

> A: Good morning. Chef Garcia!
> B: Hello, Suji. ⓐHave you ever make nacho pizza?
> A: Nocho pizza? No, I haven't.
> B: Kids will love it, and ⓑI'll tell you how to made it.
> A: Sounds good!
> B: It's easy to make. ⓒFirst, put nacho chips on a plate and spreading pizza sauce on them.
> A: Okay. ⓓLet me to help you with the pizza sauce.
> B: Thanks. Next, put some ham, onions, and peppers on top.
> A: Okay. Then?
> B: ⓔAdd cheese and bake for about 12 minutes in the oven.
> A: I can't wait to taste it!

① ⓐ   ② ⓑ   ③ ⓒ   ④ ⓓ   ⑤ ⓔ

11 다음 〈보기〉에 대한 대답으로 적절한 것을 모두 고르면? (2개) (4점)

> 보기
> Have you ever been to Europe?

① Yes, I have.
② Yes, I haven't been there before.
③ Yes, I have gone to.
④ No. I have never been to Europe.
⑤ No. I have ever not been to Europe.

12 주어진 우리말을 〈조건〉에 맞게 영어로 쓰시오. (5점)

> • 우리는 점심으로 구운 감자들을 먹었다.

> 조건
> • potatoes, for lunch를 포함하여 6단어로 쓸 것.
> • 과거형의 어법에 맞는 완전한 한 문장으로 쓸 것.

→ _____

13 다음 중 어법상 옳지 않은 것은? (4점)

① It was really fun yesterday.
② I have watched the movie twice.
③ I have lived in Seoul since 1995.
④ She has read the book many times.
⑤ She has made chicken salad last Sunday.

14 밑줄 친 부분이 어법상 어색한 것은? (3점)

① I got a letter writing in English.
② We had fried chicken for lunch.
③ My dad fixed the broken window.
④ The crying girl over there is my sister.
⑤ Look at the fallen leaves on the street.

[15~16] 다음 글을 읽고 물음에 답하시오.

Did you laugh when you saw the cartoon above? If so, the cartoonist was successful. Cartoonists are the people who make cartoons. They want to catch your interest, and usually, make you laugh with simple language and creative drawings. People have made cartoons for hundreds of years. There are many types of cartoons, and they play different roles. One form of cartoon is a picture with a few words. It is sometimes called a "gag cartoon." ⓐThe cartoonist makes a funny character, and the character makes you laugh by doing or saying silly things. ⓑAnother type of cartoon is called a caricature. ⓒIn a caricature, some parts of a character are different or bigger than usual. Look at the picture on the right. ⓓWhich parts of the man's face jump at you? ⓔArtists have used this type of cartoon to make fun of well-known people.

15 위 글의 밑줄 친 ⓐ~ⓔ 중 글의 흐름상 어색한 것은? (4점)

① ⓐ ② ⓑ ③ ⓒ ④ ⓓ ⑤ ⓔ

16 위 글을 읽고 답할 수 없는 질문은? (4점)

① How long have people made cartoons?

② What makes artists draw a caricature?

③ How do cartoonists make people laugh?

④ What is a picture with a few words called?

⑤ What parts of a character are often different or bigger than usual in a caricature?

[17~18] 다음 글을 읽고 물음에 답하시오.

When several cartoon pictures come together and tell a story, we have a comic strip. Comic strips (A)[have been / has been] in newspapers for many years. They are often just amusing stories. People have also used comic strips for education. Comics can make information clearer and easier to learn. You (B)[have saw / have seen] comic history or science books.

You have surely seen many cartoon movies, or animated movies, too. These are very popular among people of all ages. Movement and sounds (C)[add / are added] to pictures, so they come alive. Artists and writers can develop fascinating characters and tell interesting stories through animation.

17 위 글의 (A)~(C)에 들어갈 말을 바르게 짝지은 것은? (4점)

	(A)	(B)	(C)
①	have been	have seen	add
②	have been	have seen	are added
③	have been	have saw	add
④	has been	have saw	are added
⑤	has been	have seen	add

18 위 글의 내용과 일치하는 것은? (5점)

① A comic strip is made of only one cartoon picture.

② People can't see comic strips in newspapers.

③ Comic strips aren't used for education.

④ Animated movies are loved only by teens.

⑤ In animated movies, movement and sounds make the pictures come alive.

[19~21] 다음 글을 읽고 물음에 답하시오.

Cartoonists are the people who make cartoons. They want to catch your interest, and usually, make you laugh with simple language and ⓐ creative drawings.

People have made cartoons for hundreds of years. There are many types of cartoons, and they play different roles. One form of cartoon is a picture with a few words. It is sometimes called a "gag cartoon." The cartoonist makes a funny character, and the character makes you laugh by doing or saying ⓑsilly things.

Another type of cartoon is called a caricature. In a caricature, some parts of a character are different or bigger than usual. It makes us feel funny. Artists have used this type of cartoon to make fun of well-known people.

You have surely seen many cartoon movies, or animated movies, too. These are very popular among people of all ages. Movement and sounds are added to pictures, so they come alive. Cartoonists and writers can develop ⓒfascinating characters and tell interesting stories through animation.

In the 1990s, a new type of cartoon was developed. It is called a webtoon. Webtoons are ⓓ published online, so you can read them anytime, anywhere on your phone or computer. They are very popular, and some of them are even made into TV dramas or movies.

New forms of cartoons may appear in the future. They could be different and even more exciting than now, but one thing will ⓔremain the same: they will help us laugh, relax, and learn.

19 위 글의 밑줄 친 ⓐ~ⓔ의 영영 풀이로 바른 것은? (4점)

① ⓐ thinking in an available way

② ⓑ showing much thought

③ ⓒ very little interesting and attractive

④ ⓓ information made by people in a book

⑤ ⓔ to stay in the same place or condition

20 위 글의 내용(content)을 표로 정리한 것이다. 〈보기〉 중 빈칸 (A), (B), (C)에 들어갈 말이 바르게 연결된 것은? (5점)

The World of Cartoons	
The type of cartoon	Content
gag cartoon	(A)
animated movie	(B)
webtoon	(C)

보기

ⓐ It is a picture using a pencil or pen without words

ⓑ Pictures come alive with movement and sounds.

ⓒ It is made of several pictures with a story.

ⓓ It first appeared in the 1990s and caught people's interest.

ⓔ It can make information clearer and easier to learn.

ⓕ Cartoonists publish it online, so people can read it on their computers.

ⓖ It is a picture with a few words and funny characters make us laugh by saying silly words.

	(A)	(B)	(C)
①	ⓐ	ⓑ, ⓔ	ⓑ, ⓒ
②	ⓖ	ⓑ	ⓓ, ⓕ
③	ⓐ, ⓖ	ⓒ, ⓓ	ⓑ, ⓓ
④	ⓒ, ⓖ	ⓑ, ⓓ, ⓔ	ⓓ, ⓕ
⑤	ⓖ	ⓔ	ⓕ, ⓖ

21
위 글을 근거로 Minsu와 Sumi가 아래 그림을 보고 나눈 대화 내용 중 바르지 <u>않은</u> 것은? (4점)

Caricature: *Albert Einstein*

Minsu: Look at this drawing. He looks like Einstein.

Sumi: Right. It is Einstein's caricature.

Minsu: Caricature? What is it?

Sumi: ⓐIt is a funny drawing of somebody. ⓑWe call this type of cartoon a caricature.

Minsu: ⓒHis nose jumps out at me.

Sumi: Right. The artist drew his nose differently. ⓓHis nose is bigger than usual.

Minsu: He looks so funny.

Sumi: ⓔYes. The caricature make us laugh at someone known by few people.

① ⓐ   ② ⓑ   ③ ⓒ   ④ ⓓ   ⑤ ⓔ

[충북 ○○중]

[22~23] 다음 글을 읽고 물음에 답하시오.

(A) When several cartoon pictures come together and tell a story, we have a comic strip. Comic strips have been in newspapers for many years. (B) People have also used comic strips for education. (C) Comics can make information clearer and easier to learn. You have probably seen comic history or science books.

(D) You have surely seen many cartoon movies, or animated movies, too. These are very popular among people of all ages. Movement and sounds are (가)[adding / added] to pictures, so they come alive. (E) Artists and writers can develop (나)[fascinating / fascinated] characters and tell (다)[interesting / interested] stories through animation.

22
위 글의 (A)~(E) 중 주어진 문장이 들어가기에 가장 적절한 곳은? (4점)

> They are often just amusing stories.

① (A)   ② (B)   ③ (C)   ④ (D)   ⑤ (E)

23
위 글의 괄호 (가), (나), (다) 안에서 어법에 맞는 표현으로 가장 적절한 것은? (5점)

	(가)	(나)	(다)
①	added	fascinated	interested
②	added	fascinating	interesting
③	adding	fascinating	interested
④	adding	fascinated	interested
⑤	adding	fascinating	interesting

[경기 ○○중]

24
다음 글에서 곰의 얼굴을 그리는 데 필요한 동그라미의 개수는? (5점)

> Today, I'll tell you how to draw a bear's face. First, draw a big circle for the face. Next, make two circles on top of the face. After that, draw two circles for its eyes and color them black. Then, draw a small circle for the nose. Lastly, Make a mouth with a curve.

① 4개   ② 5개   ③ 6개   ④ 7개   ⑤ 8개

[경북 ○○중]

25
다음 빈칸에 들어갈 적절한 말은? (4점)

> A: Do you know how to make fried rice?
> B: Sure, it's easy.
> First, cut the vegetables into pieces.
> Next, heat some oil in a pan and fry the vegetables. _____, put some boiled rice and a little salt.
> Finally, mix and fry them together.

① Then   ② Lastly   ③ Once

④ Second   ⑤ Or

2학년 영어 2학기 기말고사(8과) 1회

문항수 : 선택형(22문항) 서술형(6문항) | 20 . . .

◎ 선택형 문항의 답안은 컴퓨터용 수정 싸인펜을 사용하여 OMR 답안지에 바르게 표기하시오.
◎ 서술형 문제는 답을 답안지에 반드시 검정 볼펜으로 쓰시오.
◎ 총 28문항 100점 만점입니다. 문항별 배점은 각 문항에 표시되어 있습니다.

[부산 ㅇㅇ중]
01 다음 중 단어에 대한 설명으로 적절한 것은? (3점)

① scary: to move in a smooth, continuous way

② similar: existing in nature and not made by people

③ natural: being almost the same

④ contain: to have or hold something inside

⑤ ocean: a sandy or rocky area which receives little rain

[인천 ㅇㅇ중]
02 다음 대화의 내용과 일치하는 것은? (3점)

Sumi: How was the roller coaster ride, Jongha?
Jongha: It was fantastic. I really enjoyed it.
Sumi: Ha ha. You closed your eyes while you were riding.
Jongha: Did you see? To be honest, I was really scared at first.
Sumi: Do you know how fast this roller coaster is?
Jongha: I have no idea.
Sumi: It goes as fast as 140 km per hour.
Jongha: Wow! That's surprising!
Sumi: Let's ride it one more time!
Jongha: Look at the sign. We can't ride it after 8 p.m.
Sumi: Oh, maybe next time.

① Jongha는 롤러코스터를 무서워서 못 탔다.

② Jongha는 롤러코스터의 속도를 알고 있었다.

③ 롤러코스터는 시간당 140km 속도를 낸다.

④ 롤러코스터는 8시 이후에도 탑승 가능하다.

⑤ Sumi와 Jongha는 지금 롤러코스터를 또 탈 것이다.

[전북 ㅇㅇ중]
03 다음 대화를 읽고 문맥에 맞게 빈칸을 채워 세 단어의 영어 문장으로 쓰시오. (4점)

A: She traveled around South America by herself last summer.
B: Really? _____ _____ surprise!

• 전체 문장을 쓸 것.
• 대 · 소문자 구분 있음.

→ _____

[충북 ㅇㅇ중]
04 다음 자연스러운 대화가 되도록 (A)~(E)를 바르게 배열한 것은? (4점)

G: Dad, I like this tomato soup.
M: I'm happy you like it.

(A) Italy or somewhere in Europe?
(B) By the way, do you know where the tomato was first grown?
(C) Really? How did you know that?
(D) No, the tomato came from South America.

G: I learned it from Ms. Song, my social studies teacher.
M: That's good.

① (A)-(B)-(C)-(D) ② (A)-(C)-(D)-(B)

③ (B)-(A)-(D)-(C) ④ (B)-(D)-(A)-(C)

⑤ (C)-(B)-(D)-(A)

[5~6] 다음 대화를 읽고 물음에 답하시오.

M: How was the roller coaster ride, Jongha?

J: It was fantastic. I really enjoyed it.

M: Ha ha. You closed your eyes while riding.

J: Did you see? To be honest, I was really scared at first.

M: (A)너는 이 롤러코스터가 얼마나 빠른지 알고 있니?

J: I have no idea.

M: It goes as fast as 140 km per hour.

J: Wow! That's surprising!

M: Let's ride it one more time!

J: Look at the sign. We can't ride it after 8 p.m.

M: Oh, maybe next time.

(J: Jongha, M: Minsol)

05 위 대화의 내용과 일치하는 것은? (4점)

① 롤러코스터는 분속 140km로 달린다.

② 그들은 롤러코스터를 한 번 더 탈 것이다.

③ 표지판에는 롤러코스터 운영 시간이 적혀 있다.

④ Jongha는 롤러코스터를 타는 동안에 눈을 뜨고 있었다.

⑤ Jongha는 처음부터 롤러코스터 타는 것을 무서워하지 않았다.

06 위 대화의 밑줄 친 (A)를 영어로 바르게 옮긴 것은? (3점)

① Do you know how fast this roller coaster is?

② Do you know how fast is this roller coaster?

③ Do you know how fast this is roller coaster?

④ Did you know how fast this roller coaster is?

⑤ Did you know how fast is this roller coaster?

[7~8] 다음 대화를 읽고 물음에 답하시오.

G: Did you see the pictures Ms. Song took?

B: What pictures?

G: She traveled around South America by herself last summer.

B: Really? _____ (A) _____

G: She showed us pictures of beautiful places. I especially liked the pictures of pyramids.

B: Are there pyramids in South America?

G: Yes. She said some pyramids are about 3,800 meters above sea level.

B: I can't believe it.

07 위 대화의 내용과 일치하는 것은? (3점)

① There are no pyramids in South America.

② Ms. Song traveled around South America alone.

③ Ms. Song went to South America last winter.

④ Some pyramids are about 380 meters above sea level.

⑤ Ms. Song didn't show her students the pictures of beautiful places.

08 위 대화의 빈칸 (A)에 들어갈 말로 옳은 것은? (2점)

① What is it?   ② I have no idea.

③ Nothing serious.   ④ You know what?

⑤ What a surprise!

09 다음 중 빈칸에 들어갈 말로 적절한 것은? (3점)

A: Do you know _____?
B: No, I don't.

① what does Mr. Han want

② when will Mina return home

③ how high is Mt. Everest

④ why was Tom late for the meeting

⑤ what language is spoken in the Netherlands

10 다음 짝지어진 대화가 자연스럽지 <u>않은</u> 것은? (2점)

① A: Don't forget to feed your dog.

B: How can I help you?

② A: What's the problem, sir?

B: This chicken soup is too salty.

③ A: When will you be back, Mom?

B: Around 8 o'clock.

④ A: Be sure to give him some water.

B: No problem.

⑤ A: I'm not happy with my dog.

B: What's wrong? Did it give you some trouble?

11 다음 중 밑줄 친 부분의 어법이 <u>어색한</u> 것은? (3점)

① I wonder <u>what does it mean</u>.

② Please tell me <u>where the restroom is</u>.

③ I want to know <u>when the bus leaves</u>.

④ Do you know <u>how old the building is</u>?

⑤ Can you tell me <u>what we will eat for lunch</u>?

12 다음 중 어법상 <u>어색한</u> 문장은? (5점)

① Namsu is the noisiest boy in the class.

② Thursday is the worst day of the week for me.

③ Yaehee is the most hard-working girl of the four.

④ University of Bologna is one of the oldest universities in the world.

⑤ He is the best teacher, even though he has the less experience.

13 다음 글을 읽고, 괄호 안의 말을 이용하여 빈칸에 알맞은 말을 쓰시오. (5점)

> 조건
> • 아래 나온 3가지 스포츠 중 어느 것이 가장 인기가 있는지 빈칸에 완전한 문장으로 쓸 것.

> In Suho's class, baseball is more popular than basketball. Basketball is more popular than badminton.

→ In Suho's class, _____. (popular)

14 다음 세 사람의 신체검사 결과에 대한 설명으로 옳지 <u>않은</u> 것은? (4점)

이름	키(cm)	몸무게(kg)
Jinho	177	64
Sangmin	175	70
Minseong	172	70

① Sangmin is heavier than Jinho.

② Jinho is the tallest of the three.

③ Minseong is taller than Sangmin.

④ Sangmin is as heavy as Minseong.

⑤ Minseong is the shortest among them.

15 다음 중 어법상 <u>틀린</u> 것의 개수는? (4점)

> • The school festival was excitingest school event.
> • My father wakes up the earliest in my family.
> • Monday is the badest day of the week.
> • Dave is the hard-workingest boy in the class.
> • August is the hottest month of the year.

① 1개 ② 2개 ③ 3개 ④ 4개 ⑤ 5개

[16~17] 다음 글을 읽고 물음에 답하시오.

There is the driest desert in South America. ⓐThis continent is full of natural wonders that will surprise you.

Atacama Desert
The Atacama is the driest desert on Earth. ⓑIn some parts, it gets almost rain at all – only 1-3 millimeters per year! ⓒThe ground in some areas is so dry that no plants can grow. ⓓDo you know what scientists do in such a dry place? The soil in this desert is almost the same as that on Mars, so they prepare for trips to outer space. ⓔThe Atacama is also one of the best place on Earth to watch stars.

16 위 글의 ⓐ~ⓔ 중 어법상이나 문맥상 어색한 문장끼리 묶인 것은? (3점)

① ⓐ, ⓑ   ② ⓐ, ⓔ
③ ⓒ, ⓓ, ⓔ   ④ ⓑ, ⓔ
⑤ ⓐ, ⓒ, ⓓ

17 위 글의 내용과 일치하지 않는 것은? (4점)

① Atacama Desert's soil is similar to that of Mars.
② Atacama Desert is a good place to watch stars.
③ Scientists will travel to outer space to avoid the driest desert.
④ There is only a little rain per year in the Atacama Desert.
⑤ People in Atacama Desert can see the natural wonders.

[18~19] 다음 글을 읽고 물음에 답하시오.

Salar de Uyuni is a salt flat located in Bolivia, South America. For most of the year, it is as dry as a desert. But for a few months every year, the region transforms into the world's biggest mirror.
A salt flat is a field of land that was a lake or a pond a long time ago. The water evaporated over time and left the land dry. When that happened, it left a crust of salt and other minerals to cover the ground. (A) Among all the salt flats in the world, the Uyuni salt flat is the largest. It measures about 10,600 square meters. Its white surface is exceptionally flat and devoid of any other objects. (B) From December to March, something truly magical happens at the Uyuni salt flat. (C) For several weeks at a time, the region receives rain. (D) Due to the white surface and the waters, the Uyuni salt flat looks like a giant, endless mirror. (E) Thousands of visitors come to the salt flat during this time. They get to experience the magical feeling of walking on water while being surrounded completely by the sky.

18 위 글의 문맥상 다음 문장이 들어갈 가장 알맞은 곳은? (3점)

> Then, the entire surface of the salt flat becomes slightly flooded.

① (A)   ② (B)   ③ (C)   ④ (D)   ⑤ (E)

19 Which one CANNOT be answered according to the passage? (4점)

① Which country has Salar de Uyuni?
② What was a salt flat a long time ago?
③ How big is the Uyuni salt flat?
④ How much salt is produced in the Uyuni salt flat per year?
⑤ When do many visitors come to the Uyuni salt flat?

[20~21] 다음 글을 읽고 물음에 답하시오.

Do you know where the driest desert on Earth is? How about the highest waterfall? Yes, they are both in South America. This continent is full of natural wonders that will surprise you. First of all, the Atacama is the direst desert on Earth. In some parts, it gets almost no rain at all – only 1~3 millimeters per year! (A)The ground in some areas is too dry for plants to grow. Do you know what scientists do in such a dry place? The soil in this desert is very similar to the soil on Mars, so they prepare for trips to outer space. The Atacama is also (B)one of the best places on Earth to watch stars. In addition, if you go to Venezuela, you can see the world's highest waterfall. Actually, (C)the waterfall, which is called Angel Falls, named after Jimmie Angel, a pilot from the United States who first flew over the waterfall in 1933. The waterfall is 979 meters high. Clouds often cover the top, so you need patience and a little luck to get a good view. You can still get to the top of the beautiful waterfall only by plane. Another natural wonder is the Amazon, which runs across the continent through seven countries. (D)It travels from Peru in the west and flow into the Atlantic Ocean. The Amazon River is interesting in many ways. For the most part, it has no bridges. That is because it usually runs through rainforests and wet areas, not cities or towns. Also, in many places the river is very wide, so you cannot see the other side! Lastly, the Andes are the world's longest mountain range. Do you know (E)how long is the mountain range? It is about 7,000 kilometers long! It also contains the highest mountains outside of Asia. About a third of the people in South America live in the Andes. Many unique animals also live there.

20 위 글을 읽고, 답을 찾을 수 없는 것은? (4점)

① Why do scientists prepare for space trips in the Atacama?
② How high is the Angel Falls?
③ How can people get to the top of the Angel Falls?
④ How many countries does the Amazon run through?
⑤ How many people live in the Andes?

21 위 글의 밑줄 친 (A)~(E) 중, 어법상 틀린 것을 3개 찾아 바르게 고치시오. (5점)

(기호)	틀린 부분	→	바르게 고친 것
( )		→	
( )		→	
( )		→	

22 다음 글의 밑줄 친 문장의 이유로 가장 적절한 것은? (4점)

Salar de Uyuni in Bolivia is the world's largest salt flat. Thousands of years ago, there was water, but it all dried up. Now, a large salt desert is left about 3,656 meters above sea level. Salar de Uyuni is one of the most visited natural wonders of South America, too. All year around a lot of people visit this place to take pictures of its unique natural beauty. In fact, the salt flat makes any tourist a great photographer.

① Salar de Uyuni is on high ground.
② A lot of tourists have visited the salt flat.
③ Beautiful views attracted some photographers.
④ Pictures taken in Salar de Uyuni are like a work of art.
⑤ Salar de Uyuni was a lake, but all the water dried up.

*attract ~의 마음을 끌다

[23~25] 다음 글을 읽고 물음에 답하시오.

<The Amazon>
The Amazon ⓐruns across the continent through seven countries. It ⓑtravels from Peru in the west and ⓒflows into the Atlantic Ocean. The Amazon River is interesting in many ways. For the most part, it has no bridges. That is because it usually ⓓruns through rainforests and wet areas, not cities or towns. Also, in many places the river is very wide, so you cannot see the other side! You probably do not want to ⓔswim in this river. It is home to some very big snakes and fish that eat meat.

<The Andes>
The Andes are the world's longest mountain range. Do you know how long the mountain range is? It is about 7,000 kilometers long! It also contains the highest mountains outside of Asia. About ((a)) of the people in South America live in the Andes. Many unique animals also live there.

23 다음 중 위 글에서 알 수 <u>없는</u> 것은? (3점)

① 아마존강이 흐르는 7개 나라들의 이름
② 아마존강과 만나는 바다의 이름
③ 아마존강에 다리가 없는 이유
④ 아마존강 건너편을 볼 수 없는 이유
⑤ 안데스 산맥의 길이

24 위 글의 밑줄 친 ⓐ~ⓔ 중 문맥상 의미하는 것이 <u>다른</u> 하나는? (2점)

① ⓐ ② ⓑ ③ ⓒ ④ ⓓ ⑤ ⓔ

25 위 글의 빈칸 (a)에 들어갈 말로 '1/3'이라는 의미를 가진 것은? (4점)

① a three ② a third
③ three one ④ third one
⑤ one point three

[26~28] 다음 글을 읽고 물음에 답하시오.

ⓐThe Atacama is the drier desert on Earth. In some parts, it gets almost no rain at all — only 1-3 millimeters per year! The ground in some areas is so dry that no plants can grow. ⓑDo you know (scientists / a dry place / do / what / in / such)? The soil in this desert is very similar to the soil on Mars, so they prepare for trips to outer space. The Atacama is also one of the best places on Earth to watch stars.

26 위 글의 밑줄 친 문장 ⓐ에서 잘못 쓰인 부분을 바르게 고쳐 문장을 다시 쓰시오. (4점)

→ _____

27 위 글의 밑줄 친 ⓑ의 문장이 다음과 같은 의미가 되도록 괄호 안의 어구를 바르게 배열하시오. (4점)

• Do you know _____?
(과학자들이 그렇게 건조한 곳에서 무엇을 하는지 여러분은 아시나요?)

28 위 글에서 과학자들이 아타카마 사막에서 우주여행을 준비하는 이유가 되는 문장을 찾아 쓰시오. (4점)

Q: Why do the scientists prepare for trips to outer space in the Atacama?
A: Because _____.

◎ 선택형 문항의 답안은 컴퓨터용 수정 싸인펜을 사용하여 OMR 답안지에 바르게 표기하시오.

◎ 서술형 문제는 답을 답안지에 반드시 검정 볼펜으로 쓰시오.

◎ 총 30문항 100점 만점입니다. 문항별 배점은 각 문항에 표시되어 있습니다.

[인천 ○○중]

01 다음 중 밑줄 친 단어의 쓰임이 <u>어색한</u> 것은?   (3점)

① Niagara Falls is a large <u>continent</u> in North America.

② The Alps are the highest <u>mountain range</u> in Europe.

③ There are more than 25,000 islands in the Pacific <u>Ocean</u>.

④ The Sahara is a <u>desert</u> that covers most of northern Africa.

⑤ The Amazon <u>rainforest</u> is home to many kinds of animals and plants.

[대구 ○○중]

02 다음 대화의 ⓐ~ⓔ 중 해당 표현의 한글 뜻이 올바르지 <u>않은</u> 것은?   (3점)

G: How was ⓐthe roller coaster ride, Jongha?

B: It was fantastic. I really enjoyed it.

G: Ha ha. You closed your eyes while riding.

B: Did you see? ⓑTo be honest, I was really scared at first.

G: Do you know how fast this roller coaster is?

B: ⓒI have no idea.

G: It goes as fast as 140 km ⓓper hour.

B: Wow! ⓔThat's surprising!

① ⓐ: 롤러코스터 타는 것

② ⓑ: 비유하자면

③ ⓒ: 난 모르겠어.

④ ⓓ: 시간당

⑤ ⓔ: 그거 참 놀라운 걸!

[경기 ○○중]

03 다음 대화의 빈칸에 알맞지 <u>않은</u> 것은?   (3점)

A: Do you know that Brazil is the biggest country in South America?

B: _____ I didn't know that. So, what's the first thing you want to see in Brazil?

A: I want to see Iguazu Falls from the sky.

① That's amazing.

② That is not true.

③ What a surprise!

④ Are you kidding?

⑤ I can't believe it.

[인천 ○○중]

04 다음 대화의 내용과 일치하지 <u>않는</u> 것은?   (4점)

Chris: Did you see the pictures Ms. Song took?

Jack: What pictures?

Chris: She traveled around South America by herself last summer.

Jack: Really? What a surprise!

Chris: She showed us pictures of beautiful places. I especially liked the pictures of pyramids.

Jack: Are there pyramids in South America?

Chris: Yes. She said some pyramids are about 3,800 meters above sea level.

Jack: I can't believe it.

① Chris and Jack are talking about Ms. Song's pictures.

② Ms. Song went to South America last summer with friends.

③ Ms. Song visited pyramids and other beautiful places.

④ There are pyramids in South America.

⑤ Some pyramids are about 3,800 meters above sea level.

05 다음 중 짝지어진 대화가 옳은 것은? (3점)

① A: Do you know where the tomato was first grown?

B: How did you know that?

② A: Did you see the pictures Ms. Song took?

B: She traveled around South America by herself three months ago.

③ A: I really liked the pictures of pyramids in Peru.

B: Are there pyramids in South America?

④ A: I went to South America in 2018.

B: Really? I'm sorry to hear that.

⑤ A: What did Ms. Song probably say in class?

B: I learned it from Ms. Song, my math teacher.

[6~7] 다음 대화를 읽고 물음에 답하시오.

G: How was the roller coaster ride, Jongha?

B: It was fantastic. I really enjoyed it.

G: Ha ha. You closed your eyes while riding.

B: Did you see? ⓐTo be honest, I was really scared at first.

G: Do you know (A)_____?

B: ⓑI have no idea.

G: It goes ⓒas fast as 140 km per hour.

B: Wow! That's surprising!

G: Let's ⓓride it one more time!

B: Look at the sign. We can't ride ⓔit after 8 p.m.

G: Oh maybe next time.

06 위 대화의 밑줄 친 ⓐ~ⓔ에 대한 설명으로 바르지 <u>않은</u> 것은? (4점)

① ⓐ는 'To speak honestly'로 바꿔 쓸 수 있다.

② ⓑ는 'I don't know.'의 의미이다.

③ ⓒ는 '~만큼 빠르게'의 의미이다.

④ ⓓ는 rides로 고쳐야 한다.

⑤ ⓔ는 the roller coaster를 의미한다.

07 위 대화의 빈칸 (A)에 들어갈 알맞은 말은? (3점)

① how fast this roller coaster is

② who built this roller coaster

③ how tall the roller coaster is

④ how old the roller coaster is

⑤ how many times you can ride this roller coaster

08 다음 대화의 (A)~(E) 중 다음 문장이 들어가야 할 곳은? (4점)

> I especially liked the pictures of pyramids.

G: Did you see the pictures Ms. Song took?

B: What pictures? (A)

G: She traveled around South America by herself last summer.

B: Really? What a surprise! (B)

G: She showed us pictures of beautiful places. (C)

B: Are there pyramids in South America? (D)

G: Yes. She said some pyramids are about 3,800 meters above sea level.

B: I can't believe it. (E)

① (A) ② (B) ③ (C) ④ (D) ⑤ (E)

09 다음 문장의 빈칸에 들어갈 수 <u>없는</u> 말은? (3점)

> • Can you tell me _____?

① what he likes

② why she is angry

③ who gave you the book

④ where the nearest bank is

⑤ how did you pass the exam

[10~11] 다음 대화를 읽고 물음에 답하시오.

Sora:	How was the roller coaster ride, Jongha?
Jongha:	It was fantastic. I really enjoyed it.
Sora:	Ha ha. <u>You closed your eyes while riding.</u>
Jongha:	Did you see? To be honest, I was really scared at first.
Sora:	Do you know how fast this roller coaster is?
Jongha:	I have no idea.
Sora:	It goes as fast as 140 km per hour.
Jongha:	Wow! That's surprising!
Sora:	Let's ride it one more time!
Jongha:	Look at the sign. We can't ride it after 8 p.m.
Sora:	Oh, maybe next time.

10 위 대화의 밑줄 친 문장의 이유로 가장 적절한 것은? (3점)

① Because Jongha was tired.

② Because Jongha wanted to prevent his eyes from getting dry.

③ Because the wind was so strong.

④ Because Jongha was scared.

⑤ Because Jongha hurt his eyes.

11 다음 Jongha의 일기에서 위 대화의 내용과 일치하지 <u>않는</u> 것은? (3점)

<Jongha의 일기>
①I rode a roller coaster. ②At first, it was really scaring but fantastic. I heard that ③the roller coaster goes as fast as 140 km per hour. ④Sora wanted to ride it one more time, but she couldn't. Because ⑤she had to wait until 8 p.m. to ride it.

12 다음 중 어법상 알맞은 문장은? (3점)

① It is the most big ocean in the world.

② It is the most long river in Asia.

③ It is the most highest mountain in Africa.

④ It is the most funniest movie of the year.

⑤ It is the most popular song in Korea.

13 어법상 맞는 문장은 <u>모두</u> 몇 개인가? (4점)

- Do you know who wrote the book?
- Can you tell me how old she is?
- Let me know how much is this book.
- I want to know where does your grandma live.
- I wonder when your new movie will come out.

① 1개 ② 2개 ③ 3개 ④ 4개 ⑤ 5개

14 다음 그림을 보고, 여행객이 되어 안내원에게 질문해 보았다. 주어진 우리말의 내용과 같이 간접의문문을 사용하여 문장을 완성하시오. (5점)

※ 왼쪽 남자부터 오른쪽 방향 순서임.

(1) 여행객 1: Do you know <u>건물이 얼마나 오래 되었는지</u>?

여행객 2: Can you tell me what we will eat for lunch?

(2) 여행객 3: I want to know <u>버스가 언제 떠나는지 (현재시제)</u>?

(3) 여행객 4: Please tell me <u>화장실이 어디에 있는지</u>.

여행객 5: I wonder what that means.

[15~18] 다음 글을 읽고 물음에 답하시오.

The Amazon runs _____ the continent through seven countries. It travels from Peru in the west and flows _____ the Atlantic Ocean. The Amazon River is interesting in many ways. _____ the most part, it has no bridges. That is _____ it usually runs through rainforests and wet areas, not cities or towns. Also, in many places the river is very wide, _____ you cannot see the other side! ⓐYou probably do not want to swim in this river. ⓑ이곳은 몇몇 아주 큰 뱀과 고기를 먹는 물고기들의 서식지입니다.

15 위 글을 읽고 알 수 <u>없는</u> 것은? (2점)

① 아마존강이 시작되는 나라
② 아마존강이 지나는 나라의 개수
③ 아마존강에 있는 다리의 개수
④ 아마존강의 건너편을 볼 수 없는 이유
⑤ 아마존강에서 수영을 하면 안 되는 이유

16 위 글의 빈칸에 들어갈 수 <u>없는</u> 말은? (대·소문자 무시) (3점)

① so   ② for   ③ cross
④ into   ⑤ because

17 위 글의 밑줄 친 ⓐ의 의도를 다음과 같이 쓸 때 빈칸에 들어갈 가장 알맞은 말은? (3점)

> · It is _____ to swim in this river.

① fun   ② safe   ③ wide
④ deep   ⑤ dangerous

18 주어진 단어를 모두 사용하여 위 글의 우리말 ⓑ를 영작할 때 뒤에서 3번째 오는 단어는? (3점)

> It is home to _____.
> (big / snakes / meat / and / that / fish / some / very / eat)

① eat   ② that   ③ fish
④ big   ⑤ snakes

[19~20] 다음 글을 읽고 물음에 답하시오.

<The Andes>
The Andes are the world's longest mountain range. Do you know how long the mountain range is? It is <u>about</u> 7,000 kilometers long! It also contains the highest mountains outside of Asia. About a third of the people in South America live in the Andes. Many unique animals also live there.

19 위 글의 밑줄 친 <u>about</u>과 같은 의미로 쓰인 것은? (2점)

① He is <u>about</u> 190 cm tall.
② What are you so angry <u>about</u>?
③ I don't know what you're talking <u>about</u>.
④ I'm not happy <u>about</u> the lunch menus.
⑤ Do you know what this book is <u>about</u>?

20 위 글의 안데스산맥에 관한 설명과 일치하지 <u>않는</u> 것은? (4점)

① 세계에서 가장 긴 산맥이다.
② 길이가 7,000km에 달한다.
③ 아시아 이외의 지역에서 가장 높은 산들이 있다.
④ 남아메리카 인구의 절반 정도가 거주한다.
⑤ 독특한 동물들이 다수 서식한다.

[21~25] 다음 글을 읽고 물음에 답하시오.

@Do you know where is the driest desert on Earth? How about the highest waterfall? Yes, they are both in South America. ⓑThis continent   full of natural wonders that will surprise you.

Atacama Desert

(가) ⓒThe Atacama is the driest desert on Earth. (나) In some parts, it gets almost no rain at all – only 1~3 millimeters (A)_____ year! ⓓThe ground in some areas   are so dry that no plants can grow. (다) The soil in this desert is very similar to the soil on Mars, so they prepare for trips to outer space. (라) ⓔThe Atacama is also one of the best place on Earth to watch stars. (마)

Angel Falls

If you go to Venezuela, you can see the world's highest waterfall. ⓕIt is 979 meter high. Clouds often cover the top, so you need patience and a little luck to get a good view. Actually, the waterfall is named (B)_____ Jimmie Angel, a pilot from the United States ㉠who first flew over the waterfall in 1933. You can still get to the top of the beautiful waterfall only (C)_____ plane.

21 위 글의 (A)~(C)에 들어갈 말이 올바르게 짝지어진 것은?
(4점)

	(A)	(B)	(C)
①	per	from	by
②	per	after	by
③	per	of	on
④	a	of	by
⑤	per	after	on

22 위 글의 (가)~(마) 중, 주어진 문장이 들어가기에 가장 적절한 곳은?
(3점)

> Do you know what scientists do in such a dry place?

① (가)　　　② (나)　　　③ (다)
④ (라)　　　⑤ (마)

23 위 글의 밑줄 친 @~ⓕ 중에서 글의 흐름으로 보아 어법이 올바른 문장의 개수는?
(4점)

① 1개　② 2개　③ 3개　④ 4개　⑤ 5개

24 위 글의 밑줄 친 ㉠과 쓰임이 다른 것은?
(3점)

① He likes the girl who gave you the book.
② The woman who looks young is my aunt.
③ The man who loves her is my English teacher.
④ I want to know who the winner of the contest is.
⑤ The boy who danced at the party had a good voice.

25 위 글을 읽고 답할 수 없는 질문은?
(4점)

① How high is Angel Falls?
② What is the driest desert on Earth?
③ How did the waterfall get its name?
④ What time is the best to get a good view?
⑤ In which continent can you find the highest waterfall?

[26~28] 다음 글을 읽고 물음에 답하시오.

Do you know where the driest desert on Earth is? How about the highest waterfall? Yes, they are both in South America. This continent is full of _____(가)_____ that will surprise you.

Atacama Desert
The Atacama is ⓐdriest desert on Earth. In some parts, it gets almost no rain at all — only 1-3 millimeters per year! The ground in some areas is so dry that no plants can grow. Do you know ⓑwhat scientists do in such a dry place? The soil in this desert is very similar to the soil on Mars, so they prepare for trips to outer space. The Atacama is also ⓒone of the best place on Earth to watch stars.

Angel Falls
If you go to Venezuela, you can see ⓓthe world's highest waterfall. It is 979 meters high. Clouds often cover the top, so you need patience and a little luck to get a good view. Actually, the waterfall is named after Jimmie Angel, a pilot from the United States who first ⓔfly over the waterfall in 1933. You can still get to the top of the beautiful waterfall only by plane.

26 위 글의 내용과 일치하는 것은? (3점)

① 앙헬폭포는 영국 비행사의 이름을 딴 것이다.
② 비행기로만 앙헬폭포의 꼭대기에 갈 수 있다.
③ 아타카마사막의 토양은 금성의 토양과 아주 비슷하다.
④ 북아메리카에는 지구에서 가장 높은 폭포가 있다.
⑤ 아타카마사막의 모든 지역에서 식물이 자랄 수 있다.

27 위 글의 (가)에 들어갈 말로 알맞은 것은? (3점)

① delicious foods
② beautiful plants
③ natural wonders
④ amazing animals
⑤ wonderful countries

28 위 글의 ⓐ~ⓔ 중 어법상 옳은 것을 고르면? (답 2개) (4점)

① ⓐ   ② ⓑ   ③ ⓒ   ④ ⓓ   ⑤ ⓔ

[29~30] 다음 글을 읽고 물음에 답하시오.

The Andes
The Andes are the world's longest mountain range. (A)여러분은 그 산맥의 길이가 얼마인 줄 아시나요? It is about 7,000 kilometers long! It also contains the highest mountains outside of Asia. About a third of the people in South America live in the Andes. Many unique animals also live there.

29 위 글을 읽고 Andes에 관해 알 수 있는 것은? (4점)

① 산의 높이
② 산맥이 포함된 나라
③ 거주하는 사람들의 문화
④ 거주하는 남아메리카 인구의 비율
⑤ 서식하는 동물의 종류

30 밑줄 친 (A)의 우리말에 맞도록 주어진 단어를 배열할 때 5번째에 올 단어는? (3점)

know / long / do / is / the / range / you / how / mountain

① is   ② how   ③ long
④ know   ⑤ mountain

정답 및 해설

Lesson 5 (중간) 〔1회〕

01 ③	02 ①	03 ②	04 ②	05 ④	06 ③	07 ③	08 ④
09 ③	10 ②	11 ②	12 ⑤				
13 After drawing / After you draw		14 ③	15 ②	16 ⑤
17 told him to stop	18 ①			
19 the judge decided to set Joseph free		20 ②	21 ②
22 ⑤	23 ③	24 ⑤	25 ③	26 ⑤	27 ②	28 ③	29 ③

01 ordinary: average or not special in any way

02 본문과 보기문에서 ⓐ의 fair는 '박람회'를 의미한다. 본문과 보기문 속의 각각 의미는 ⓑ '무료의', '자유로운' ⓒ '마음', '꺼리다' ⓓ '왼쪽', '~을 두고 오다' ⓔ '가벼운[간단한]', '빛'이다.

03 'He has brown hair and brown eyes.'라고 답했으므로 외모를 묻는 'What ~ look like?'가 적절하다.

04 동생을 잃어버렸으므로 'worried'가 적절하다.

05 'I hope' 다음에 희망하거나 바라는 것을 쓴다.

06 'What ~ look like?'로 외모를 물었는데 출신을 답하고 있다.

07 ⓐ 'Is your class winning?'에 'Of course'라고 했다. ⓑ 'I've heard a lot about her.', ⓒ 'We have a great handball player.'라고 했다.

08 'Oh, he is carrying a red backpack.'이라고 추가로 언급하고 있으므로 추가적인 정보를 요구하는 ④번이 적절하다.

09 ① use → to use
② worked → to work
④ is → to be
⑤ to not → not to

10 help는 목적격보어로 동사원형과 to부정사를 취할 수 있다.

11 Minsol이 어떻게 생겼는지는 알 수 없다.

12 '남동생을 잃어버린 장소'에 대한 언급은 없다.

13 별을 그린 후에 잘라내는 것이므로 after를 전치사(+구)나 접속사(+절)로 써서 나타낸다.

14 ⓐ, ⓔ, ⓖ 맞음
ⓑ have → had ⓒ go → to go ⓓ do → to do
ⓕ angrily → angry

15 'He just wanted the freedom to have his beard.'라고 했다.

16 ① 평범한 사람
② 어려움에 직면하다
③ 다르게 보이다
④ 그의 뒤에서

17 told의 목적격보어로 to stop을 쓴다.

18 Thomas의 노력으로 그의 아버지가 석방되었다는 글이다.

19 decided의 목적어로 'to set'을 쓴다.

20 ⓐ off them → them off
ⓒ arrested → was arrested
ⓓ said → said to
ⓔ Sad → Sadly

21 (A) year가 명사가 아니라 형용사처럼 쓰여 뒤에 있는 명사를 수식하므로 42-year-old (B) stop의 목적어로 동명사 growing (C) of의 목적어로 동명사 attacking이 적절하다.

22 ⓐ 이어지는 내용으로 보아 턱수염을 길러 달라 보였다는 것이 적절하다. ⓑ 뒤에서 'They did not want to sit next to him.'이라는 것으로 보아 avoided가 적절하다.

23 Joseph에게 얼마나 많은 사람이 들을 던졌는지는 알 수 없다.

24 펭귄들이 섬에서 살았다는 글에 이어 (D) 오랫동안 같은 집에서 같은 옷을 입었는데 (B) 새로운 새인 Perry가 섬에 왔고 (A) Perry의 모습은 달랐다는 내용이 이어진 후 (E) 대장 펭귄이 Perry에게 펭귄 셔츠를 입으라고 하자 (C) Perry가 '다르지만 좋은 친구가 될 수 있다'고 답하는 순서가 자연스럽다.

25 체포된 후에 일 년이 넘게 감옥에서 보냈다.

26 주어진 문장의 But으로 (E)의 앞 내용과 상반되므로 (E)가 적절하다.

27 ⓐ 'He had a job and cared for his family.'로 보아 ordinary ⓑ 뒤에서 여러 어려움이 나오므로 face ⓒ Joseph이 희생자이므로 victim이 적절하다.

28 (가) told의 목적격보어로 to stop (나) freedom을 수식하는 to have (다) 체포된 것이므로 수동태가 적절하다.

29 처음에는 걱정이 되었지만 지금은 친구들과 잘 지내고 있다.

Lesson 5 (중간) 〔2회〕

01 ④	02 ④	03 ①	04 ①	05 ③	06 ③	07 ④	08 ③
09 ⑤	10 ③	11 ③	12 ③	13 before they have lunch			
14 ②	15 ③	16 ①	17 ④	18 ③	19 ①	20 ①	21 ④
22 ②	23 ③	24 told him to stop growing		25 ③	26 ①
27 ③	28 ④	29 ③	30 ④				

01 ④번은 received 정도가 적절하다.

02 look around: 둘러보다

03 (A) look like: ~처럼 보이나 (B) look for: ~을 찾다

04 방송을 하고 아이를 찾으러 나가겠다는 말에 고맙다고 하며 '동생을 빨리 찾길 바라요.'라고 하는 것이 적절하다.

05 'He has short curly hair'라고 했다.

06 Tom은 Sue에게 동생의 이름, 옷차림 등 여러 가지를 묻고 있다.

07 I hope (that) ~.로 희망이나 바람을 나타낸다.

08 'She wants to make our school a safe place.'라고 했다.

09 그녀는 TV 드라마 보는 것을 좋아한다는 말은 외모를 묻는 말에 대한 대답으로 적절하지 않다.

10 훌륭한 핸드볼 선수가 있다는 말에 이어 ⓒ 몽골에서 온 여자아이 말하는 것인지 묻고 ⓑ 그렇다며 이름이 Gacha라고 하자 ⓐ 그녀에 대해 많이 들었다며 어떻게 생겼는지 묻자 ⓓ 키가 크고 말총머리를 하고 있다고 설명하는 순서이다.

11 새로운 학생이 있다는 말에 떠날 준비가 됐다는 응답은 어색하다.

12 목적격보어로 동사원형이 나왔으므로 tells는 쓸 수 없다.

13 자전거를 10시에 타고 12시에 점심을 먹을 것이므로 점심 먹기 '전'에 자전거를 탈 것이다.

14 순서대로 • her to tell → that she would tell • 맞음
• learning → learn • 맞음 • said → told
• to break → break • she → her • talked → told

15 ⓐ cared → cared for
ⓑ differently → different
ⓓ said → told
ⓔ fight off them → fight them off

16 Joseph이 그 남자들을 무슨 혐의로 고발했는지는 알 수 없다.
pick on: 괴롭히다, 비난하다

17 (A), ④: 형용사적 용법 ①, ②, ③, ⑤: 명사적 용법

18 'Students who talk about other people's appearance must read the story.'라고 했다.

19 이웃들이 괴롭혔지만 신경 쓰지 않았다는 (C)에 이어, 네 명의 남자가 Joseph을 공격했고 그들을 싸워 물리칠 수 있었지만 체포됐었다는 (B)가 오고, 일 년이 넘게 감옥에 갔다는 (A)가 나오는 순서이다.

20 Ⓐ 이사한 후에 어려움에 직면했다. Ⓑ 아무도 그를 믿지 않았으므로 Sadly가 적절하다.

21 ⓓ는 체포된 것이므로 수동태가 되어야 한다.

22 'no one believed a man with a beard'라고 했다.

23 공격한 사람들에 의해 Joseph의 턱수염이 잘렸는지는 알 수 없다.

24 told의 목적격보어로 to stop을 쓰고 stop의 목적어로 growing을 쓴다.

25 (C) 다음의 His가 주어진 문장의 a man을 가리키므로 (C)가 적절하다.

26 'Joseph Palmer fought for the right to have them.'이라고 했다.

27 (C) 다음 문장의 it이 주어진 문장의 a long beard를 가리키므로 (C)가 적절하다.

28 'Joseph did not mind. He just wanted the freedom to have his beard.'라고 했다.

29 'The town's people avoided the man with a beard.'라고 했다.

30 ⓓ told의 목적격보어로 to stop이 되어야 한다.

Lesson 6 (중간) 1회

01 ③ **02** ⑤ **03** ③ **04** ⑤ **05** ③ **06** ① **07** ⑤ **08** ①
09 ① **10** ③ **11** ②
12 (A) The problem is too difficult to solve.
(B) What made you think that?
(C) My mother let me buy a bicycle[bike].
(D) The teacher had David turn off his cell phone.
(E) My parents let me play computer games every Saturday.
13 (1) Susie is too angry to say anything.
(2) The dog is too weak to run to the park.
14 ⑤ **15** too busy to talk **16** ① **17** ② **18** ③ **19** ④
20 ⑤ **21** ④ **22** ③ **23** ② **24** ② **25** ③ **26** ① **27** ①
28 ⑤

01 순서대로 • exchange • suggestions • receipt • text가 들어간다.

02 헤어드라이어를 갖고 오라고 하면서 영수증 갖고 올 것을 잊지 말라고 했다.

03 무엇이 문제인지 물었는데 '서비스가 좋다'는 것은 어색하다.

04 Minsu에게 Minsol을 도와주라고 했다.

05 hairdryer를 샀다가 환불을 요청하는 것이므로 ③번이 적절하다.

06 전화를 걸어 hairdryer의 환불을 요청하고 있다.

07 'not happy with'로 불만을 나타내고 있는데 '맞다며 의사가 친절하다'고 하는 것은 어색하다.

08 강아지들이 종종 그렇다는 말에 이어 (B) 추가로 불만을 언급하고 (A) 잘해 주라고 하자 (D) 너무 다정하다며 훈련이 좀 필요하다고 하자 (C) 몇 주 뒤에 훈련을 시작하자고 하는 순서가 자연스럽다.

09 'Don't forget to ~'는 잊지 말라고 상기시켜 주는 말이다.

10 'I'm not happy with it.'이라고 했다.

11 ②번은 일반동사로 쓰였지만 나머지는 사역동사로 쓰였다.

12 (A) too+형용사/부사+to부정사: 너무 …해서 ~할 수 없다
(B)~(E) 사역동사 make, let, have의 목적격보어로 동사원형을 쓴다.

13 (1) too+형용사/부사+to부정사 = so+형용사/부사+that+주어+can't
(2) too+형용사/부사+to부정사 = so+형용사/부사+that+주어

+can't

14 둘 중의 하나는 one, 나머지 하나는 the other로 나타낸다.

15 too+형용사/부사+to부정사: 너무 …해서 ~할 수 없다, …하기에는 너무 ~하다

16 'Sometimes I ask them about their school life, but they only give short answers. We don't talk much at the table, either.'라고 했으므로 '더 많은 시간을 보내고 싶다'가 적절하다.

17 (A) tries의 목적어로 to do
(B) without의 목적어로 asking
(C) 진주어로 to find
(D) makes의 목적격보어로 study
(E) let의 목적격보어로 take가 적절하다.

18 'Please let me take care of things myself.'라고 했다.

19 (D) 다음에서 'Sure.'로 답하고 있으므로 (D)가 적절하다.

20 'Good evening, listeners.'로 보아 ⑤번이 적절하다.

21 청취자가 얼마나 많은지는 알 수 없다.

22 (A) 둘 중의 하나는 one, 나머지 하나는 the other로 나타낸다.
(B) 부정어 don't가 있으므로 either가 적절하다.

23 'Sometimes I ask them about their school life, but they only give short answers.'라고 했다.

24 ⓐ 5-years-old → 5-year-old
ⓒ this → it
ⓓ to study → study
ⓕ am → do

25 'I'm not a baby anymore.'라고 했으므로 'let me take care of things myself'가 적절하다.

26 (A) 다음의 it이 주어진 문장의 a wall이므로 (A)가 적절하다.

27 (A) 둘 중의 하나는 one, 나머지 하나는 the other로 나타낸다.
(B) too+형용사/부사+to부정사: 너무 …해서 ~할 수 없다, …하기에는 너무 ~하다
(C) about: ~에 관해서
(D) 부정어 don't가 있으므로 either가 적절하다.

28 'Sometimes I ask them about their school life, but they only give short answers. We don't talk much at the table, either.'라고 했으므로 '더 많은 시간을 보내고 싶다'가 적절하다.

Lesson 6 (중간)

 2회

01 ③ **02** ⑤ **03** ② **04** ① **05** ① **06** ④ **07** ② **08** ②				

09 ④ **10** I am not happy with it.
11 My brother made me do the dishes. **12** ②
13 Who made you do the project by yourself?
14 ④ **15** spend more time
16 컴퓨터 게임하기, 자전거 타기, 쇼핑가기 **17** ② **18** ④
19 ⑤ **20** ③ **21** ④ **22** ② **23** ② **24** ② **25** ④, ⑤
26 ① **27** ② **28** ② **29** ④

01 각각 ① remember ② tear ④ secret ⑤ receipt의 영영풀이이다.

02 'I'll visit your store tomorrow afternoon.'이라고 했다.

03 Buster가 얼마나 큰지는 알 수 없다.

04 여행 준비가 되었는지 묻는 말에 이어 (B) 떠날 준비가 되었다고 답하고 (D) 티켓을 챙겼는지 묻자 (A) 전화기에 갖고 있다고 답하고 (C) 역에 도착하면 잊지 말고 전화하라고 하자 (E) 그러겠다고 답하는 순서가 적절하다.

05 ①번은 무엇이 문제인지 묻고 그 문제에 대해 제대로 답하고 있다.

06 Buster가 친절한 것이 아니라 엄마가 Jane에게 'Please be kind to him.'이라고 했다.

07 교복에 대해 불만을 나타내자 'What's the problem?'이라고 무엇이 문제인지를 묻고 그 답에 대해 맞다고 하며 'Also they are not comfortable.'이라고 했으므로 ②번이 적절하다. ③, ④, ⑤번은 좋은 점을 말하고 있으므로 답이 될 수 없다.

08 헤어드라이어에 불만을 나타내는 글에 이어 ⓑ 미안하다며 교환을 원하는지 묻자 ⓓ 환불이 가능한지 묻고 ⓒ 알았다며 드라이어를 갖고 방문해 달라며 영수증도 잊지 말라고 하자 ⓐ 내일 오후에 들르겠다고 하는 순서가 적절하다.

09 A가 'Will you please visit our store with the dryer and the receipt?'라고 하자 B가 'Yes'라고 했다.

10 'be not happy with ~'를 이용해 불만을 나타낼 수 있다.

11 made의 목적격보어로 동사원형 do를 쓰는 것에 주의한다.

12 (A) tell the truth: 진실을 말하다 tell a lie: 거짓말하다
(B) say no: 아니라고 말하다 say hi: 인사하다
(C) speak a language: 언어로 말하다 speak French: 프랑스어를 하다

13 made의 목적격보어로 동사원형 do를 쓴다.
by oneself: 혼자서

14 'I want to spend more time with you.'라고 한 것으로 보아 ⓓ는 'We don't have enough conversations at the table.' 정도로 고쳐야 한다.

15 아버지는 아이들이 대화를 하기에는 너무 바쁘고, 일하고 집에 돌

아와도 인사만 하고 자신의 방으로 돌아가며, 가끔 학교생활에 관해 물어도 짤막한 대답만 하고, 식사 자리에서조차 대화를 많이 하지 않아서, 아이들과 더 많은 시간을 보내고 싶다고 했다.

16 'We played computer games, rode bikes, and went shopping together.'라고 했다.

17 (A)에서 고민을 언급하자 (B)에서 본인이 해결한 방법을 알려주고 있다.

18 ⓓ는 by의 목적어로 동명사 reading이 되어야 한다.

19 'This is your DJ, Breeze. Today we have a special guest, Andy Kim.'이라고 했다.

20 ⓐ ask → asking
ⓑ studying → study
ⓓ of → on, her → their
ⓔ will → do

21 엄마가 모든 것을 해주는 데 대해 불만을 나타내며 자기 일을 스스로 할 수 있게 해 달라는 것으로 보아 'unpleased'가 적절하다.

22 Andy Kim이 다음에 누구의 편지를 읽을지는 알 수 없다.

23 (A) 필자는 엄마에게 오빠의 비밀을 말했고 엄마가 화가 나서 (upset) 오빠가 곤경에 처했고 (B) 필자는 너무 무서워서 (scared) 오빠에게 미안하다는 말도 못했다.

24 아이들과 주말에 더 많은 시간을 보내면서 아이들과 더 많이 이야기할 기회를 갖게 됐고 더 많이 알게 됐다는 글이다.

25 ⓐ another → the other ⓑ talk → to talk ⓒ goes → go

26 일을 마치고 집에 와도 그냥 인사만 하고 방으로 들어가고 식사 자리에서조차 대화를 많이 하지 않는다고 했으므로 ①번이 적절하다.

27 각각 ① time ② how ③ suggestions ④ without ⑤ on my own이 들어간다.

28 사역동사의 목적격보어로 동사원형을 쓴다.

29 '소녀의 학교생활'에 대한 언급은 없다.

Lesson 7 (기말) `1회`

01 ①	**02** ③	**03** ⑤	**04** ①	**05** ②	**06** ④	**07** ④	**08** ②
09 ①	**10** ④	**11** ⑤	**12** ⑤				

13 (1) have lived in Seoul since 1995
(2) has not finished his homework yet

14 ③	**15** ⑤	**16** ③	**17** ②	**18** ①	**19** ③	**20** ①	**21** ③
22 ①	**23** ④	**24** ②	**25** ①	**26** ⑤	**27** ⑤	**28** ②	**29** ⑤

01 각각 <kimchi pancake> 1. Mix 3. Pour <pizza toast> 3. Add 4. Bake가 들어간다.

02 movement, agreement, development, amusement, treatment, management, education, pollution, suggestion, translation

03 'Add cheese and bake for about 12 minutes in the oven.' 이라고 했다.

04 의견을 묻는 질문에 충격적인 소식을 들었다고 답하는 것은 자연스럽지 않다.

05 (A) put A on B: A를 B 위에 놓다
(B) spread: (얇게 펴서) 바르다
(C) add: 더하다, 넣다
(D) bake: 굽다

06 다음에 'Sure. It's easy.'라고 답하면서 작동하는 방법을 설명하고 있으므로 작동하는 방법을 묻는 ④번이 적절하다.

07 A의 'I want to sit in the back.'에 B가 'No problem.'이라고 했다.

08 ⓐ look like → look
ⓒ have → haven't
ⓔ sound → sounds

09 (B)에서 First로 시작하여 (A)에서 Next로 다음 단계를 설명하고 (C)에서 'Then?'이라고 묻고 (D)에서 Lastly로 마지막 단계를 설명하는 순서가 자연스럽다.

10 '그를 위해 깜짝 파티를 열려고 한다'는 말에 '파티를 여는 것이 어떠냐?'고 묻는 것은 어색하다.

11 ① has been → was
② has made → made
③ live → have lived
④ have been → went

12 ⑤번은 동명사로 주어로 쓰였지만 나머지는 모두 현재분사로 명사를 수식하고 있다.

13 (1) 1995년부터 지금까지 살고 있는 것이므로 'since 1995'로 나타낸다. (2) 현재완료의 부정은 'have[has]+not[never]+과거분사'로 나타낸다.

14 (A)와 ③: 계속 ①, ④ 완료 ②, ⑤ 경험

15 ⓐ were → was
ⓑ publishing → published
ⓒ made → made into
ⓓ most → more

16 'When several cartoon pictures come together and tell a story, we have a comic strip.'이라고 했다.

17 'One ~'으로 하나의 단락을 시작하고 'Another ~'로 다음 단락을 시작한다.

18 ⓐ by ~ing: ~함에 의해, ~함으로써
ⓑ jump out at: ~에게 금방 눈에 띄다
ⓒ make fun of: ~을 놀리다

19 주어진 문장의 made와 ⓒ는 사역동사로 쓰였고 나머지는 일반동사로 쓰였다.

20 'Artists have used this type of cartoon to make fun of well-known people.'이라고 했다.

21 'The cartoonist makes a funny character, and the character makes you laugh by doing or saying silly things.'라고 했다.

22 앞의 내용과 상반되는 내용이 나오므로 However, 이유를 나타내는 말을 이끌고 있으므로 because가 적절하다.

23 look on the bright side: 긍정적[낙관적]으로 보다

24 ⓑ 동작과 소리가 그림에 더해지는 수동태이므로 are added가 되어야 한다.

25 ㉠, ㉡, ㉢: 계속 ㉣, ㉤: 경험

26 ⓔ develop과 병렬로 can에 이어지는 tell이 적절하다.

27 ⑤번은 is의 보어로 쓰인 동명사이고 나머지는 모두 현재분사이다.

28 'Webtoons are published online.'이라고 했으므로 ②번이 적절하다.

29 'Artists have used this type of cartoon to make fun of well-known people.'이라고 했다.

Lesson 7 (기말)

```
01 ③  02 ②  03 ②  04 ⑤  05 ④  06 ④  07 ③  08 ①
09 ①  10 ⑤  11 ①, ④
12 We ate baked potatoes for lunch.  13 ⑤  14 ①  15 ④
16 ⑤  17 ②  18 ⑤  19 ⑤  20 ②  21 ⑤  22 ②  23 ②
24 ③  25 ①
```

01 spread: 엷게 바르다, 퍼뜨리다

02 different → the same

03 피자 소스를 먼저 바르고 치즈는 굽기 바로 전에 올린다.

04 낙타가 물 없이도 오랫동안 갈 수 있다는 말에 상대방에게 물을 좀 마시라고 하는 것은 어색하다.

05 나초 피자를 만드는 법을 배우고 있으므로 ④번이 적절하다.

06 'First, put nacho chips on a plate and spread pizza sauce on them.'이라고 했다.

07 발매기에서 표를 사자는 말에 이어 (C) 발매기 사용법을 아는지 묻고 (A) 쉽다면서 먼저 영화와 상영 시간을 고른다고 하자 (B) 7시 영화를 고르고 그 다음을 묻자 (D) 표 매수를 선택하고 좌석을 고른다고 답하고 (E) 표 두 장에 뒷자리를 원한다고 하자 문제없다는 말로 이어진다.

08 발매기 사용법에 대한 대화이다.

09 감정을 더 잘 이해하도록 도와준다고 했으므로 ①번이 적절하다.

10 ⓐ make → made

ⓑ made → make

ⓒ spreading → spread

ⓓ to help → help

11 현재완료의 대답으로 'have.'나 'have not[never]'를 쓴다.

12 감자가 구워지는 것이므로 baked potatoes로 쓴다.

13 'last Sunday'가 있으므로 과거 시제로 써야 한다.

14 편지가 쓰여진 것이므로 과거분사 written이 적절하다.

15 ④는 jump at(~에 선뜻 달려들다, ~을 덥석 잡다)이 아니라 jump out at(~에게 금방 눈에 띄다, ~에게 분명히 보이다)이 되어야 한다.

16 캐리커처에서 캐릭터의 어떤 부분이 평소와 다르거나 더 큰지는 알 수 없다.

17 (A) Comic strips가 주어이므로 have been (B) 현재완료는 'have+과거분사' (C) 동작과 소리가 그림에 더해지는 것이므로 수동태 'are added'가 적절하다.

18 'Movement and sounds are added to pictures, so they come alive.'라고 했다.

19 ⓐ having the ability to invent and develop original ideas, especially in the arts

ⓑ foolish, childish, or ridiculous

ⓒ extremely interesting and attractive

ⓓ to prepare and produce a book or magazine for sale

20 (A) One form of cartoon is a picture with a few words. It is sometimes called a "gag cartoon." The cartoonist makes a funny character, and the character makes you laugh by doing or saying silly things.

(B) Movement and sounds are added to pictures, so they come alive.

(C) In the 1990s, a new type of cartoon was developed. It is called a webtoon. Webtoons are published online, so you can read them anytime, anywhere on your phone or computer.

21 ⓔ의 few를 many 정도로 고쳐야 한다.

22 주어진 문장의 They가 (B) 앞 문장의 Comic strips를 가리키므로 (B)가 적절하다.

23 (가) 동작과 소리가 그림에 더해지는 것이므로 수동태 (나) 캐릭터가 매력적인 것이므로 현재분사 (다) 이야기가 재미있는 것이므로 현재분사가 적절하다.

24 a big circle for the face + two circles on top of the face + two circles for its eyes + a small circle for the nose = 6

25 '그런 다음'을 뜻하는 then이 적절하다. lastly는 뒤에 Finally가 나오므로 적절하지 않으며 다른 선택지들도 어울리지 않는다.

Lesson 8 (기말)

01 ④	02 ③	03 What a surprise!	04 ③	05 ③	06 ①
07 ②	08 ⑤	09 ⑤	10 ①	11 ①	12 ⑤

13 baseball is the most popular sport 14 ③ 15 ③ 16 ④

17 ③ 18 ④ 19 ④ 20 ⑤

21 (C) named after → is named after
　(D) flow → flows
　(E) is the mountain range → the mountain range is

22 ④ 23 ① 24 ⑤ 25 ②

26 The Atacama is the driest desert on Earth.

27 what scientists do in such a dry place

28 the soil in this desert is very similar to the soil on Mars

01 각각 ① flow ② natural ③ similar ⑤ desert의 영영 풀이이다.

02 'It goes as fast as 140 km per hour.'라고 했다.

03 "What a surprise!", "That's surprising.", "I can't believe it." 등으로 놀라움을 나타낼 수 있다.

04 '네가 좋아하니 기쁘구나.'라는 말에 이어 (B)에서 'By the way'로 화제를 바꾸며 '토마토가 처음에 어디에서 재배되었는지 아는지' 묻고 (A) '이탈리아나 유럽 어딘가가 아닐까?'라고 답하자 (D) 아니라며 '토마토는 남아메리카에서 왔다'고 하고 (C) 그걸 어떻게 알았는지 묻자, 사회 선생님이신 송 선생님께 배웠다고 답하는 순서가 자연스럽다.

05 'Look at the sign. We can't ride it after 8 p.m.'이라고 했다.

06 동사 know의 목적어로 간접의문문이 되어야 하며 간접의문문은 '의문사+주어+동사'의 순서로 써야 한다.

07 'She traveled around South America by herself last summer.'라고 했다.

08 "What a surprise!"로 놀라움을 나타낼 수 있다.

09 간접의문문의 어순은 '의문사+주어+동사'이다.

10 개에게 먹이를 주는 것을 잊지 말라는 말에 무엇을 도와줄지 묻는 것은 어색하다.

11 간접의문문의 어순은 '의문사+주어+동사'이다.

12 the less를 the least로 고쳐야 한다.

13 야구가 가장 인기 있으므로 popular의 최상급 most popular를 이용하여 'baseball is the most popular sport'로 쓴다.

14 Sangmin이가 Minseong이보다 더 크다.

15 순서대로 • excitingest → the most exciting • 맞음
　• badest → worst • hard-workingest → most hard-working • 맞음

16 ⓑ almost는 부사로 명사를 직접 수식하지 않으므로 almost rain을 almost no rain으로 고쳐야 어법 및 문맥상 적절하다. ⓔ

'one of ~'는 '~ 중의 하나'라는 뜻으로 뒤에 복수 명사가 나와야 하므로 place를 places로 고쳐야 한다.

17 'The soil in this desert is almost the same as that on Mars, so they prepare for trips to outer space.'라고 했을 뿐이다.

18 주어진 문장의 Then으로 (D) 앞의 내용에 대한 결과가 이어지고 있으므로 (D)가 적절하다.

19 매년 우유니 소금 평원에서 얼마나 많은 소금이 생산되는지는 알 수 없다.

20 안데스 산맥에 얼마나 많은 사람들이 사는지는 알 수 없다.

21 (C) 이름이 붙여지는 것이므로 수동태가 적절하다.
　(D) It이 주어이므로 travels와 병렬로 flows가 적절하다.
　(E) 간접의문문의 어순은 '의문사+주어+동사'이다.

22 'All year around a lot of people visit this place to take pictures of its unique natural beauty.'라고 했으므로 ④번이 가장 적절하다.

23 아마존강이 일곱 개의 나라를 거쳐 대륙을 가로질러 흐른다고만 했지 그 나라들의 이름은 나와 있지 않다.

24 ⓔ는 '수영하다'를 의미하지만 나머지는 모두 '흐르다'를 의미한다.

25 1/3은 'a third'로 쓴다.

26 형용사의 최상급 앞에 the를 붙이므로 the drier를 the driest로 고쳐야 한다.

27 동사 know의 목적어를 간접의문문으로 써야 한다. 간접의문문은 '의문사+주어+동사'의 순서로 쓴다.

28 'The soil in this desert is very similar to the soil on Mars, so they prepare for trips to outer space.'라고 했다. so는 '결과'를 이끌므로 앞과 뒤의 내용을 바꿔 so 대신 because로 쓸 수 있다.

Lesson 8 (기말)

01 ①	02 ②	03 ②	04 ②	05 ③	06 ④	07 ①	08 ③
09 ⑤	10 ④	11 ⑤	12 ⑤	13 ③			

14 (1) how old the building is (2) when the bus leaves (3) where the bathroom is

15 ③	16 ③	17 ⑤	18 ②	19 ①	20 ④	21 ②	22 ③
23 ①	24 ④	25 ④	26 ②	27 ③	28 ②, ④		29 ④
30 ③							

01 continent는 '대륙'이라는 뜻으로 ①번은 waterfall이 적절하다.

02 to be honest: 솔직히 말하면

03 모두 놀라움을 나타내는 말로 쓰일 수 있지만 ②번은 '사실이 아니

다'라는 말로 쓰임이 다르다.

04 'She traveled around South America by herself last summer.'라고 했다.

05 페루에 있는 피라미드의 사진이 좋았다고 하자 남아메리카에 피라미드가 있는지 묻고 있는 자연스러운 대화이다.

06 Let's 다음에는 동사원형을 쓰는 것이 적절하다.

07 질문에 '모른다'고 하자 시속 140km라고 말해 주고 있으므로 얼마나 빠른지를 묻는 ①번이 적절하다.

08 (C) 앞에서 사진을 보여주었다고 한 후, 특히 피라미드 사진이 좋았다고 하는 것이 자연스러우므로 (C)가 적절하다.

09 간접의문문은 '의문사+주어+동사'의 순서로 쓴다.

10 뒤에서 'I was really scared at first.'라고 했다.

11 'We can't ride it after 8 p.m.'이라고 했다.

12 ① most big → biggest

② most long → longest

③ most highest → highest

④ most funniest → funniest

13 순서대로 • 맞음 • 맞음 • is this book → this book is • does your grandma live → your grandma lives • 맞음

14 간접의문문은 '의문사+주어+동사'의 순서로 쓴다.

15 'For the most part, it has no bridges.'라고만 했다.

16 순서대로 across, into, For, because, so가 들어간다.

17 뒤에서 '이곳은 몇몇 아주 큰 뱀과 고기를 먹는 물고기들의 서식기입니다.'라고 했으므로 ⓐ인 dangerous가 적절하다.

18 문장을 만들면 'some very big snakes and fish that eat meat'이다.

19 밑줄 친 about과 ①번은 '약, 대략'이라는 뜻이지만 나머지는 모두 '~에 대하여'라는 뜻이다.

20 'About a third of the people in South America live in the Andes.'라고 했다.

21 (A) per: ~당, ~마다

(B) name after ~을 따라 이름 짓다

(C) by+교통수단

22 주어진 문장의 such a dry place가 (다) 앞의 문장의 장소를 말하므로 (다)가 적절하다.

23 ⓐ is the driest desert on Earth → the driest desert on Earth is

ⓑ full → is full

ⓓ are → is

ⓔ place → places

ⓕ meter → meters

24 ④번은 의문사이지만 ㉠과 나머지는 모두 관계대명사이다.

25 멋진 경치를 보려면 몇 시가 가장 좋은지는 알 수 없다.

26 'You can still get to the top of the beautiful waterfall only by plane.'이라고 했다.

27 이이지는 아타카마사막이나 앙헬폭포의 내용으로 보아 'natural wonders'가 적절하다.

28 ⓐ driest → the driest

ⓒ place → places

ⓔ fly → flew

29 'About a third of the people in South America live in the Andes.'라고 했다.

30 알맞게 배열하면 'Do you know how long the mountain range is?'이다.

MEMO

적중 100 + 특별부록

Plan B

우리학교
최신기출

천재 · 이재영 교과서를 배우는

학교 시험문제 분석 · 모음 · 해설집

전국단위 학교 시험문제 수집 및 분석
출제 빈도가 높은 문제 위주로 선별
문제 풀이에 필요한 상세한 해설

중2-2
영어

천재 · 이재영